HINDSIGHT

True Love & Mischief in the Golden Age of Porn

by **Howie Gordon**
aka **Richard Pacheco**

BearManor Media
2013

Hindsight: True Love & Mischief in the Golden Age of Porn

© 2013 Howie Gordon

All rights reserved.

For information, address:

BearManor Media
P. O. Box 71426
Albany, GA 31708

bearmanormedia.com

Typesetting and layout by John Teehan and Matt Stenberg

Published in the USA by BearManor Media

Front cover painting *Pygmalion and Galatea* (1890)
by Jean-Leon Gerome (1824–1904).

Title page photo courtesy of Vincent Fronczek/Gordon Archive.

Back cover courtesy of Polly Stenberg/Gordon Archive.

ISBN — 1-59393-xxx-x
978-1-59393-xxx-x

- *Gordon Archive.*

for Michael

Table of Contents

Foreword 1

The Prelewd 3

Part One 15

Part Two 87

Part Three 175

Part Four 221

Part Five 407

Part Six 575

Part Seven 621

Part Eight 663

Acknowledgements 668

Endorsements 675

> It's time to rise and corroborate God's well meaning errors

— *Gordon Archive*

Foreword

I have lived across the street from Howie for about twenty-five years. We have been friends for even longer. He told me he was hesitant about asking me to write a foreword because he wasn't sure that I was comfortable having people know that we are friends. Now, I found out early on who Howie was and told him that I had his Playgirl centerfold on my wall for a long time before I met him, and told him that both my mom and I were fans of that picture—I did have a hard time looking Mr. November in the eye, but I got over that. I was there when the kids were born; he was there when I became a grandmother early. He's been through my breakups and hookups. He has been part of my family way before anyone cared about Whoopi Goldberg.

When I was in Berkeley, both he and his wife Carly became my family, and when my mom and my brother Clyde moved to Berkeley, the same thing happened. His family became their family too. And in terms of my mom, their friendship ended with her death whose loss they felt as deeply as my brother and me.

… which brings me back to the idea that he was trying to protect me from the public knowing our family bond. I'm proud that we are connected. (He's taken out ninety-nine percent of any reference to me in this book so don't bother looking … I already looked.)

Truth is, I don't think I knew Richard Pacheco the way I know Howie Gordon. There was no reason really, and I don't want to freak you out, reader, wondering if I had ever seen any of his films. The answer is, yes, I have. And I've been to the Adult Awards ceremonies too.

We as a nation pay a lot of money to see what we profess to find dirty. Think of it like this, if everyone really felt like that, who's keeping the adult industry alive and well? Someone is buying. I know a lot of folk feel that it's destructive to young women and all the other things people speak about, and it may be true, but as you read this book, remember, it was a different time. It was the time of storytelling with an X Rating, and there's no one better to tell this story than my friend Howie Gordon.

– Gordon Archive

Howie and Whoopi at the X-rated "Oscars" (1984).

So, sit back and prepare to laugh and gasp, and if you get moved to say, make yourself even happier, well go for it.

– Whoopi Goldberg,
New York City

– Gordon Archive

The Prelewd

Desperate Cupcakes

It was late in my sleep, the last of the darkness before the dawn. My dream tapes had all been concluded and consciousness was busily rewinding and putting its seatback and tray table into the upright position in preparation for the coming waking up.

She appeared suddenly and without much fanfare. She looked to be a harried clerk like one might find in any Department of Motor Vehicles. "Muse" was the name written on the nameplate at her desk, "Harriet Muse."

Wasting no time, she grabbed my attention with a pointed question: "Tell me, sir, why do you persist on putting word to page to tell a story that most people of the world will think of as a crude braggadocio or else a hideous groan of underachievement?"

Whoa, I was stunned. I mean, slap my balls and send me back to Pittsburgh for a redo. She was talking about my attempt to see my X-rated memoirs into print.

Caught off guard, I burbled some stuff that pretty much doesn't even bear repeating here.

"You know," she said, "once we edit out all the parts that scream 'I am not a stereotype and I didn't really waste my life,' you've got some fairly interesting reading here, but it's a tough sell. You see, you must not be so eager to volunteer your indiscretions." She said it as if she were dispensing the most rudimentary kind of knowledge. "The world wants to rip off the covers and discover these kinds of things for itself.

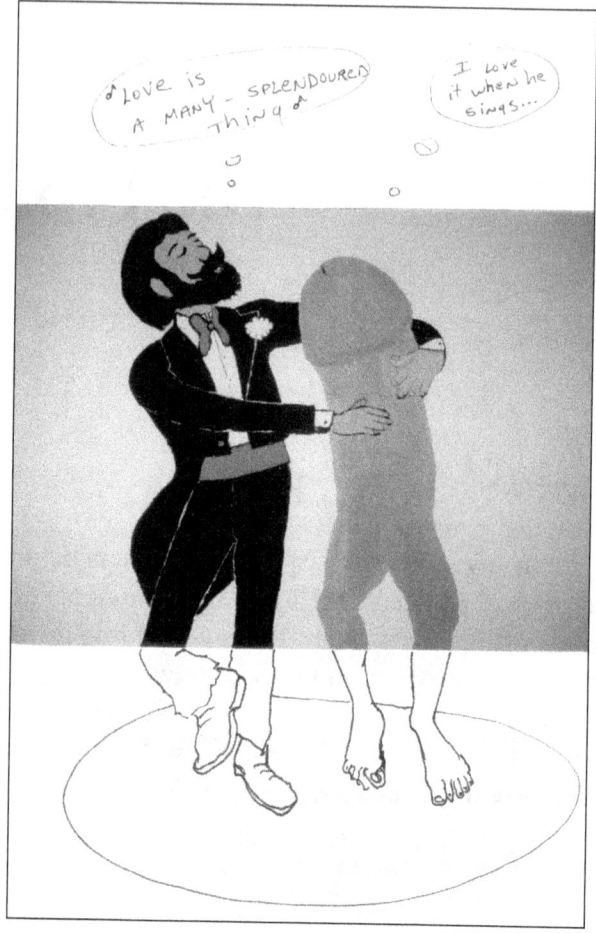

– Gordon Archive

In short, you must learn to hide better if you seek to be found. Next!"

Am I a defender of porn? Well, that's a tough question. Sure I am, but sometimes the domination of male rage in the industry just gets to me. It comes off as so nasty and mean-spirited that it's like sex without humanity. Who but a werewolf could defend that? Yes, men are entitled to their anger and so are women too, for that matter, but sex is so much bigger than that narrow band of human experience. We deserve better than just the forbidden fruit of the dark side.

There is more to sex than conquest and vengeance. I want to see that portrayed too. We are in there. We are having all those experiences, from the awkward, mundane and embarrassing to the frightening, ecstatic and sublime. Sex provides some of the best stuff offered to us as human beings. And in the end, it is spectacularly, the smiling, cunning ruse of Nature to pay us with pleasure for the biological act of reproducing ourselves.

Amazing.

Am I a defender of pornography? Sure I am. To say that sex is not worthy of the public discussion, or is not worthy of artistic interpretation is a madness, a stupidity, and often a hypocrisy of the highest order.

And if I've learned anything of import at all while walking on this path, it's this: When sex is accepted and celebrated for the goody that it is and can be in this life, it takes on a much less obsessive place than when it is denied, vilified, or repressed.

- Gordon Archive

Scandal's Messiah?

"Pornography," wrote film critic James Wolcott, "won't tap into our deepest feelings (rage, jealousy, obsessive desire) until it's made by artists, but until then it can splash happily in the shallows."

The article, titled "Deep Thought On Porno," appeared in the October, 1980, issue of *Esquire* magazine, where Wolcott had some good things to say about the film *Talk Dirty to Me*, the movie that literally made my name in the business:

"… Porno may be crude and misogynistic; it may be filled with gynecological close-ups and with dialogue as monotonously coarse as the chattering of a parrot taught to swear; but it doesn't have to be. Pornography needs an emotional rescue, and a recent film entitled *Talk Dirty to Me* suggests new paths, new possibilities.…"

Anthony Spinelli directed *Talk Dirty to Me*, and no one but Anthony Spinelli would have dared to conceive of a porno film wherein a lonely, almost retarded, young man gets to have the first sexual experience of his life. I got to play that guy. And I got to play a whole bunch of other guys while working for Spinelli—or Sam, as he was known to his intimates in the business. The films of Anthony Spinelli, or Sam Weston, became the backbone of my career. Working alongside actor John Leslie, they made us some of the earlier stars of the industry.

As a filmmaker, Sam Weston was a storyteller first. An actor turned director, he became a pornographer only as a means of last resort to feed his family while trying to make it in the cinematic jungles of Hollywood. The "new paths" or "new possibilities" alluded to by the film critic Wolcott were largely the efforts of Sam and a few other adult directors to "scoop" the Hollywood studios by making "real" movies that just happened to have full-bodied sex in them.

The X-rated industry of that era—the seventies and early-eighties—is now being touted as "The Golden Age of Pornography" mostly for that very reason. Of course, this all happened at what seemed to have been the very climax of the sexual revolution before the plague of AIDS had people of common sense everywhere zipping it all back up and running for cover.

To borrow from baseball, we were like the Negro Leagues of show business. We labored with certainly no less passion—and even occasionally no less skill—making movies at a tiny fraction of what our uptown, mega-financed, Hollywood counterparts had to spend, but we were doomed to wear the scarlet letter.

Despite the mainstream doors that have closed in my face, I still count myself as one of the lucky ones who have been involved with pornography. To begin with, I got out with my life.

Beyond that, the word "pornography" itself, now used to embrace virtually all sexual media, is derogatory. I think it reflects our own sexual self-hatred, our great spiritual and psychological difficulty of trying to cope with our bodies' capacity for giving and receiving pleasure.

In other times, in other places, I might have been burned at the stake, pilloried, or made to rot in a dungeon. Like I said, I count myself lucky. I have a wife and children and am able to walk God's green earth freely. Though I may have had to muzzle myself at a PTA meeting, I have never felt the handcuffs or been dragged into the jails and courts as so many others have. We owe those folks a debt of gratitude.

It's funny how the world works. Few have ever become "sex workers" for any reason vaguely resembling something noble, though that term itself is newish and bespeaks a certain political activism and sophistication. The old saw is that men got involved in "the business" for the sex, and the women for the money. My experience confirmed that to be largely true.

Scratch any centerfold and more often than not you'll hear a tale of too fat, too thin, too short, too tall, my tits were on backward, or the devil made me do it. You dig into the background of strippers and sex stars, especially the ones willing to reveal themselves, so to speak, in public, and you may hear stories of dysfunctional families, drugs, child abuse, alcohol, poverty, low self-esteem, sexual repression, parental neglect, or religious madness.

That out of this gallery of the broken, the curious, the rogues, and the desperate may be born defenders of freedom and sexual pioneers is truly the unfathomable sense of humor of our Creator at work. But on occasion, lust, chaos, and greed have alchemically mingled to produce both beauty and nobility, in addition to all the stereotypical and wretched excesses that one would also expect.

The fact that I can string together two coherent sentences, or that I could act a part without overly embarrassing myself, has led many an interviewer to ask, "What were you doing in porn?" The real question of significance in my mind was:

– *Gordon Archive*

"Why weren't you there with me?" I foolishly expected the heirs to the sixties sexual revolution to be there en masse: they weren't. And it remained sadly unconscionable that the sexual media for the entire culture of that time was largely relegated to an underclass of amateurs and criminals who mostly created a pornographic world of sexual looting and moral midgetry. I thought sex far too important for such an ignominious fate.

Scandal's Messiah? Hardly, but I've got a story and I'm gonna tell it. I don't purport to have all of the answers, but I did ask a few of the questions, a few of the questions that many others of my generation, those heirs to the sexual revolution, perhaps wanted to ask, but when the time came, well, they just didn't raise their hands.

There are, of course, reasons for how a guy like me could end up in the sex industry and I think their revelation pertinent, but please, do me the favor of not taking my "reasons" as "excuses." I've read way too many books where reformed sinners or "born agains" cast blame, make excuses, and try to squirm their way into some kind of new-found respectability while simultaneously cashing in on their scandalous past. No thanks.

You see, when we slime balls account for ourselves publicly, the world seems to want, to require those good ol' excuses like we are filling out an application for a license to have sinned.

Well, fuck all that. I never thought it was sinning to begin with, and frankly, I was there for the pussy. That makes me sound tougher than I am, but it's essentially true.

The money was good too. I was breaking up concrete for five bucks an hour when I got my first movie offer of $200 for getting a blow job. And I had far more compelling personal reasons that I'll get into, but the point is: I make no apologies for my dancing with the devil. I was where I wanted to be. I got into pornography with my eyes relatively open.

Could be that I'll get to the Pearly Gates one day and St. Peter will say, "Yo, Doofus, what were you thinking?" But I don't think so.

The American icon Will Rogers once mused that, "Everyone is ignorant —only on different subjects." As far as sex is concerned, we are right to respect its power, but we do not need to fear it so. Quality information and education remain critical in the unending struggle of our pleasure versus its denial as championed by the twisted forces of ignorance and superstition, especially when they come boisterously down the road belching the word of God and masquerading as religion.

It was this controversial nature of a career in adult films that led me to believe I would one day be held accountable for my actions, if not in a court of law then certainly within my own conscience or before my maker. As a result, far from indulging in the pornographic, the baser of my human emotions, I sought to be a mensch in the X-rated business. I sought to be informed, entertaining, and decent on the public stages of the erotic. And many could argue that put me in the running for what the Sufi's would call "being the wisest man in the kingdom of the fools."

In any case, here comes my tale, told to amuse. If it instructs, if it inflames, if it engorges, take from it what you will. This is a history, and yet, this is personal. This is philosophy, this is psychology, and this is a victory for perseverance and the mystery of common sense. This is my order, made of my chaos, with all the enormously mixed feelings I have had about the world of pornography and my immersion in it.

For while this is a story of struggle and success-against-the-odds, it is also a chronicle of underachievement, irony, and the ultimate surrender to the world as it is.

"If you're going to read only one book about pornography in your whole life, this one should be it!"

– US $100 Bill

– Benjamin Franklin,
Electrician and Founding Father.

An Interview

Q. What's the difference between a porn star and a whore?
A. A camera

Q. That's getting a little harsh, isn't it?
A. Yeah, well, that's all part of it too."

Q. Does the world need another book about pornography?
A. Probably not.

Q. So how did you get to be Richard Pacheco?
A. I put together the conscience of Dr. Jekyll and the lust of Mr. Hyde and we had a go at it. It was the best of me and the beast of me."

Q. Yes, but why? Why did you do it?
A. Because for years I spent more time thinking about my dick than I did thinking about almost anything else. I don't know if I'm abnormal in that I did that or only in that I'm just willing to talk about it.

Q. Are you interviewing yourself?
A. Yes, I am.

Q. Why?
A. Because I ask the best questions.

Q. Do I need to write this book?
A. Yes, I do because I'm turning in my homework.

> "It is no measure of health to be well adjusted to a profoundly sick society."
>
> – Jiddu Krishnamurti,
> *Author, Philosopher*

"There you go again!"
"What? Marty? Is that you?" Marty Kaufman was a literary agent who was trying to help me get published.

"What do you want to go and be quoting Krishnamurti for? Nobody's ever fucking heard of Krishnamurti. People are gonna think you're weird."

"I am weird."

"Yeah, well, lose the quote. Stop trying to prove that you're not an idiot by quoting esoteric famous people."

– Photo by Carly

"Here world, I pass thee like an orange to a child. I can with thee no more. Do what you will."

– Edgar Lee Masters,
Spoon River Anthology

− *Gordon Archive*

Richard Pacheco & Nina Hartley lecture at USC.

"If there be any great pleasure in life without a woman at it, let others look to it."

– Desiderius Erasmus,
In Praise of Folly

Part One

– Gordon Archive

"History is written by the victors, and when we write our own histories, we do so just as the conquerors of nations do: to justify our actions and make us look and feel good about ourselves and what we did or what we failed to do. If mistakes were made, memory helps us remember that they were made by someone else. If we were there, we were just innocent bystanders."

– Carol Tavris & Eliot Aronson,
*Mistakes Were Made (but not by **me**)*

Chapter One

We were headed across Kansas in my yellow Rambler convertible. The top was down, in more ways than one.

The year was 1971. I was a young man of twenty-three. It was summer. It was hot. I had my shirt off. I glanced over at my new lover, Melody. She was older than me and she was taking off her shirt too. There was no undershirt, no bikini top, not even a bra. Her breasts were bouncing in the breeze.

We were not on the back roads of Kansas. We were on Interstate 70. Truckers going by pulled wildly on their horns and yahooed out their windows. I had a shopping bag filled with marijuana in the backseat.

"Melody, what are you doing?" I asked.

"Well, it's hot," came the reply, "I figured I'd take off my shirt too."

"Melody, are you crazy?"

It was the wrong question at the wrong time. In her eyes, I instantly changed from being this fabulously precocious, young, and sensitive man into LBJ napalming babies. I received my first real lecture on women's liberation. And I received it all the way from the middle of Kansas, through Colorado, Wyoming, Utah, and Nevada, right on up to the doorsteps of the commune in Berkeley, California.

I had left my girlfriend of five years and quit a big paying job in Washington, D.C., to be with this woman. I had been thrown out of my parents' house after sleeping with her there. And now I was about to move into her space to live with her and her twelve-year-old daughter in this Berkeley commune.

Oops!

Chapter Two

"So what was the attraction to this woman?" Marty, my agent, asked. "She sounds like a loon to me," he said.

"Well, she was beautiful. She could also be very magical," I told him. "And when it came to sex, she had less shame and guilt than any other woman I ever met. If there was an Original Sin, it wasn't hers. She was unabashedly noisy when we made love and that was very exciting. She was also the first woman I ever met who asked me to fuck her in the ass and that was incredible. She loved that."

"Whoa, whoa, whoa, whoa," Marty said putting up both hands. "You're not planning on putting that in the book, are you?"

"Sure, why not?"

"Why not? It's way too much information! We don't want to know that about you. It's not important."

"Not important? Are you crazy? I left my girlfriend, quit my job, and moved 3,000 miles across the whole country just to fuck this woman in the ass and you're trying to tell me it's not important!?! She was spectacular!"

"This isn't real, is it," Marty asked. "You're just teasing me." Marty said that he believed in me. "If you were a horse, I'd bet on you," he used to say, "but you're too raw. You need editing, refinement, and you've got to stop writing about this shit."

"Okay, Marty, relax it's not real. It's only fiction. It's all just fiction."

"Good," he said, "then we still have a chance. Cause like I told you before, a guy like you is only believable in fiction."

Chapter Three

"In hindsight," my dad said, "it all gets on you pretty fast." He lived to be ninety-two. "One minute," he said, "I was twelve years old playing basketball and the next thing I knew, I was an old man with white hair."

"Hello?" I said, picking up the phone.

"I don't know if I have the right number," the caller said.

"Well, who do you want to talk to?" I asked.

"Is there a Howie Gordon there?"

"Speaking," I told him, "This is Howie Gordon."

"Is this the Howie Gordon that was a *Playgirl* centerfold?"

This guy was going back a lot of years, a whole lot of years. "Yes, it is, I told him without bothering to think too much about it, what can I do for you?"

"You're really good looking," he said. It made me laugh. I knew right away where this phone call was going. I'd had a few of them in my day, but not in a very long time. Usually, they had a story. They were discovering me. They were offering me a part in a big-budget feature. They were going to take me to Belize, the Azores, somewhere exotic for a high fashion photo shoot. They were going to make me a star.

And then it would come. All I would have to do is meet them in their hotel room around midnight.

"Yes, I was good looking," I said, "but that was thirty years ago, pal."

"I bet you're still good looking," he said.

"Well, you'd lose that bet. How old are you?" I asked him.

"Forty-seven," he answered.

"Well, I'm in my sixties now. My centerfold days are over. How did you get my phone number?"

"The Internet."

"The Internet? I had no idea you could get phone numbers off of the Internet."

"You can get anything off of the Internet," he confided, "but don't worry, I'm not a stalker or anything. I just thought you were really handsome."

"Well, lookit, those pictures were taken over thirty years ago. I've had three kids since then. Childbirth has completely destroyed my uterus!"

He laughed. They always laugh at that. It's a line I've used before. It was time to let this guy down easy and get off of the phone. One just hopes that it will end there. Still, despite all the warning bells, after all these years, I was actually tickled to be getting another one of these phone calls.

Chapter Four

"You still bragging about your sex life?" It was God. He and I talk from time to time, not too often, mind you, but every now and then, we talk.

"Well, I guess so," I answered, "if that's what you think I'm doing."

"I thought by now you'd be done over-compensating for having a small dick." What could I say? I was speechless. "And even though I let you be a porn star;" God said, "your sex life wasn't all that great y'know. Midgets actually get a lot more pussy than you ever did."

"They don't call them midgets anymore," I told him. "They're called 'little people.'"

"Blow me," he said.

"What do you mean my sex life 'wasn't' so great?" I asked him." It ain't over yet, is it? I mean, is there something you're not telling me?"

"No, but you're over sixty years old. I think it's a fair assumption to suggest that you're on the downhill side of things."

"Moses lived to be what? 120?"

"Yeah, but I knew Moses and you're not him."

Chapter Five

In the house where I grew up, the hamburgers were made round, about the size of baseballs. My mother made them six or nine at a time in a special black baking pan.

As the Age of McDonald's began unfolding in the early sixties, I took it upon myself to educate my mommy.

"This is America," I told her one night as she was serving me one of those big old round hamburgers. "In America, they make the hamburgers flat." My mother took her heavy spatula and smashed the hamburger on my plate.

"Now, it's flat," she said, "eat!"

Chapter Six

"In the beauty of the lilies Christ was born across the sea,
With a glory in His bosom that transfigures you and me:
As He died to make men holy, let us die to make men free,
While God is marching on.

Glory! Glory! Hallelujah—

Wait a minute. Time out. "Stop the music!" I had a problem. I needed to know what the hell Jesus was doing with a bosom?

Having been born into a family of Orthodox Jews, I was largely unschooled in the matters of Jesus, but up until that moment of singing the fifth and final stanza of the stirring and patriotic "Battle Hymn of the Republic" in Miss Stewart's fourth grade public school music class (take a breath), I had been under the distinct impression that Jesus Christ was a man.

So, tell me now, it's important: What exactly was Jesus Christ doing with a bosom?

Chapter Seven

(Cue the violins.)

I didn't start out in life as the sex star. I looked like the late Larry Mondello, the chubby best friend from TV's *Leave It to Beaver*. Actually, I didn't look like Larry Mondello at all except to say that we were both "husky." And husky, of course, is what you called fat little boys when you were trying kindly to spare their feelings.

Fourth grade, fifth grade, six grade, those were not real happy times. I was "husky." It only got worse when puberty came around to the young men in my crowd. I found myself pretty much standing at the very end of the line.

Y'know, when I was growing up, every man was wondering if he'd ever get to fuck Betty Boop. We all wanted the best that life had to offer. We all wanted to be Joe DiMaggio and marry Marilyn Monroe. We all wanted to be the one who solved the great mysteries and tasted the best fruits. Early on, however, things were not exactly working out that way for me.

Dennis Leibovitz had the super schlong. He should have been the porn star. Dennis was also the first to sprout the wiry pubic hairs around his cock that signaled the arrival of puberty. In time, Melvin, Davy, Lloyd and Louie, Huey and Spud, Barney, Baron, Goose and Stromberg, Stichweh, Shehady, Ronnie the Umbrella, and Wayne, *everybody*, even the pudgy-like-me Ellis had all sprouted their pubic hairs before I did.

We all belonged to a grade club that eventually would be called the MARQUIS and we played a lot of sports together. The Boys' locker room became a nightmare for me. When I took off my clothes, my "friends" would check out my development.

To begin with, I had bigger tits than most of the girls we knew. They jiggled. Yep, it seemed that me and Jesus both had bosoms! And being so overweight, the fat bulged out around my hairless dick and made it look even smaller and lonelier than it was. Surprise, surprise, the fellas, my MARQUIS brothers, they would tease me. We had a wrestler in town nicknamed "Skull" Murphy because he had a shaved head. My friends used to call my dick Skull Murphy.

There was little saving face. I couldn't fight everybody. Besides, one was always vulnerable to the truth. The young herd wreaked its havoc upon me.

I'm sure I sought my revenge where I could get it. And at the risk of spoiling all the remaining high drama for you, one might just guess that this period of my life had a lot to do with me later doing about four million push-ups and eight million sit-ups as I sculpted my body into the stuff of centerfolds. Sniff.

Chapter Eight

In the house where I grew up, I came to share my mother's love for the underdog, chicken schmaltz, Judy Garland, and Mahalia Jackson. Despite her sentimental side, my mother was tough, Pittsburgh tough. She ruled the roost. She was also the unquestioned matriarch of her outside larger family, which included her five brothers. My mother contributed nothing but confusion to the popular notion that women were the weaker sex. I've often thought that she might have been far better served in this life had she been born a man.

On the other hand, my father was a non-aggressive, gentle soul, who complemented my mother well. He should have been born a woman. He was a hard-working man who was just happy to have gotten out of World War II alive. From him, I inherited a commitment to fair play and a tendency to keep all emotions deeply bottled up inside.

I had one sibling, a brother who was almost six years older than me who busted his ass in school. I don't think he ever even saw a "B." It was always all "A's" in everything. We were not very close in those days. I did not share his enthusiasm for learning.

The early family predictions were that he was going to be a nuclear physicist and I was going to be a gym teacher. I loved sports. The fat kid was the catcher in baseball and played the line in football. Basketball wasn't even an option. In band, they gave me the tuba. Oom-pa-pah, motherfucker.

Uncle Izzy also lived with us. He was one of my mother's younger brothers. Uncle Izzy was mentally retarded, they said, and he came to live with us when my grandmother died back in '52. I was four years old.

At first, he was like having another older brother. After a while, it felt like we were the same age. After that, I got older and he just stayed the same. At one point he had undergone some psychological testing and was diagnosed as functioning at the level of an eight-year-old. He was some eight-year-old! Izzy was a source of both astounding joy and mind-numbing exasperation in our family. In the bonding we did around caring for him, our family reached its greatest triumphs. The rewards for our efforts seemed to come back doubled and tripled.

From Izzy, I inherited a precious appreciation for the robust silliness of just about everything in life:

"Hey, How! Guess what?" Izzy would ask.

"What, Iz?" I would reply.

"I can't say, 'Perry,'" he would tell me.

"What?"

"I can't say, 'Perry.'"

"You just said it!"

"No! You don't understand!"

"Then explain it to me, Iz."

"It's haaarrrrrd!" he'd say, drawing out the word for emphasis. It was almost singing. "I watch *Harry Mason* and *Harry Como* on TV. I can't say, 'Perry.'" We easily had that same conversation over a thousand times. It was like our family's version of Abbott and Costello's "Who's on First?"

At our dinner table, it was like if you couldn't say something in about ten seconds, well, just forget about it because Izzy would say something and then we'd all be laughing. As you might well imagine, this severely hampered our abilities to resolve U.S. foreign policy problems or discuss the finer points of Shakespeare.

Uncle Izzy was the center of attention in the daily life of our family. He was the star of the show and my mom was his best straight man. Next came my brother and then my father and I brought up the rear. I learned to be a supporting player in this family dynamic and took my shots where I could.

There were no other American families like ours on TV. *Father Knows Best? Leave It to Beaver? Ozzie and Harriet? Donna Reed?* They were the popular TV shows of the day and no, they were definitely not like us.

My mom spent a good portion of her daily life taking care of Uncle Izzy. She fed him, shaved him, trimmed his nails, dressed him, and just generally tried her best to get him to pass for "normal" to the whole world at large. "You don't understand," if I may borrow a phrase from Izzy himself, but it was like gluing feathers on a cat and calling it a chicken.

From Izzy, we all learned of the total commitment to family. I did say that I loved my family, didn't I? I did, each and every one. Still do.

Chapter Nine

The door to puberty opened when Susie Goldstein walked through it wearing only her bra and panties.

I was sleeping over at Melvin's house that night. We were eleven or twelve. When the phone rang, we happened to be standing near it in this upstairs hallway. Melvin answered it. It was for his older sister, Susie. He called her to the phone.

She came out of her bedroom not knowing I was there. If this were a movie, she'd be moving in slow motion. Maybe a high-school senior, Susie was very much the fully developed woman. She was all jiggle and bounce as she made her way down the hallway to the phone. Full frontal. Dark hair. Flesh and panties and bra. It was voluptuous, even before I knew there was such a word, Rubenesque, as they say. I saw the dark patch right there through her panties.

God in Heaven, something so inside me woke right up. Susie Goldstein came out to answer the phone and there was Puberty!

She caught sight of me then, me and her little brother Melvin. He was smiling diabolically like only a little brother can. Melvin knew exactly what he had done. Susie gasped. Her arms and hands flailed and failed to cover all that was mesmerizing me as she shrieked, turned, and bounced her buttocks back into her bedroom all in one dazzling moment that has lasted in my mind for over half a century. I can still see the crack of her ass through her panties as the bedroom door closes. Her bottom cheeks jiggled.

Oh, my God!

Chapter Ten

I learned about masturbation at summer camp. Chuckie Pearl was a year older when he took some of us younger guys into the bathroom and showed us how to jerk-off. He called it "creaming himself" and he did just that in a toilet stall while we all watched in amazement. Oi, on the one hand, it was completely disgusting. But, on the other, well, who could resist such knowledge? I don't know what the other boys did, but I refrained from trying out this new activity until I got home from camp and found myself some privacy.

Whoa, as some of you may know, Chuckie was really on to something! I soon began dating myself in earnest—often two or three times a day.

"If you rub it, it will come!" the voice would call. And if I'm not mistaken, other boys may have heard this voice too. The voice called, and called, and called, like a telephone ringing. I pretty much answered it every time. I mean, who didn't? Please take a moment, as Mike Meyers might tell you, and feel free to discuss this amongst yourselves.

Personally, I worried back then that a man only had so many orgasms in him. I worried that perhaps I was squandering my share foolishly, but I could not convince my dick of this. The only time my penis ever wanted me to stop was when I became raw from the friction of overuse. The cure, which I stumbled upon all by myself because I was far too embarrassed to ever broach the subject with another living human being, was to pack myself in Vaseline and just wait it out. I discovered that in a couple of days, I could start all over again. What a resilient little organ!

Chapter Eleven

I wanted a girlfriend. It seemed like I had always wanted a girlfriend. Masturbation was all well and good, well, actually, it was both frightening and ecstatic, but I really wanted to be in love. Who knows where that comes from?

As far back as kindergarten, I had always picked out a girl in the

– Gordon Archive.

Seventh-grade Howie.

class and imagined that she and I were in love. Sometimes, I actually told them of my feelings or let them know through a friend. Once, I even gave a girl a giant Valentine on Valentine's Day. Oops, she wasn't interested, none of 'em were.

"Hit your hand on a stone," they say, "and expect it to hurt!" I learned to keep my longings secret. It was the handsome boys, the athletic boys, the slender boys what got the girls. Chubby, pudgy, husky, you can roll your own euphemism here, but the fat guys like me generally rode the bench when it came to true love.

By the time I became a teen-ager, all these early influences worked in combination to make me the kind of kid who overate until he was about to explode. On the outside, I was the fat kid, either being jolly or trying to act tough. On the inside, I was wondering what the hell I was doing with tits. I was alienated and frightened, ashamed and desperately romantic.

Chapter Twelve

"I know what you're trying to do here," Marty the agent said. "You're trying to get people to feel sorry for you with all this 'Davy the Fat Boy' crap."

"Didn't Randy Newman write that song?" I asked him.

"Yeah, I think he did," Marty said. "But it ain't gonna work. It ain't never gonna get you on Oprah."

"I'm just telling my story, Marty. It seems like people should know something about me before I get to the part where I talk about my career in the business."

"The porn business!" he said.

"Yeah, the porn business," I answered. "You remember, 'Richard Pacheco, the smallest cock to ever hit the big time?'"

"I always liked that line," he said. "It's funny."

"Thank you."

"You're welcome, but the bottom line is I'll never be able to get you published."

"So you've said."

"I don't make the rules! Nobody gives a fuck about the porn business. It's dirty. It stinks. And it's not worth anybody's attention."

"Worldwide, it now makes more than $10 billion every year."

"Yeah, well, you may have a point there, but that's got nothing to do with getting you a book deal that's gonna make either one of us any money. Look, I've told you this before. In America, a porn star is—a porn star is a cultural villain. Get it? They're the bad guys! They're up there with wife beaters and child molesters. They're all cunts and whores and Mafia lowlife!"

"But I was the senior class president."

"You! You precious little fuck! You want to be a hero and you want to be funny and poignant and fuck all the girls. You fuckin' think that you can be a porn star in a white hat, but I'm telling you, schmendrick[1], that no such animal exists. Period. It's all fucking trafe[2]! Ferstaysh[3]? Stop wasting my time! In fact, stop wasting your time! You're a good writer! Write about something else! Anything else! Now, get outta here. Let me make some money."

Chapter Thirteen

"So what do you think about that, God? Is Marty right?"

"Marty's got a lot on his mind," God said. "You should maybe cut him some slack."

"He's a gatekeeper! You know I can't sell this book by myself. I don't have a huckster bone in my body."

"I don't know," God said, "You been huckin' me pretty good."

"Well, what am I supposed to do?"

"You? You're supposed to write the damn book already. You're

For Vic, Marina, and Dan, my beloved goyishe children-in-law:

1. Schmendrick: a doofus, a moron, a sad sack, or a dimwit
2. Trafe: not kosher, taboo, unacceptable
3. Ferstaysh? Do you understand?

over sixty years old for Christ's sake. You think you're gonna live forever? Just write the damn book."

"Whatever you say, God."

Chapter Fourteen
When Howie Met Sally

The hottest sex I ever had was in the ninth grade.

The fifties had become the sixties. The aging World War II General Eisenhower had yielded the White House to the young and dashing Senator from Massachusetts. John F. Kennedy was now the president and the "New Frontier" had begun. Years later, they would call it "Camelot."

Among the First Ladies, the young and stunning Jackie Kennedy replaced the doddering Mamie Eisenhower. Things were looking up for America and closer to home; I had somehow found a young woman willing to explore the Garden of Eden with me.

Sally, my sweet Sally! Had I only known that my first hands-on sexual experiences were going to be carved and burned into my erotic psyche for the rest of my sperm-bearing years, I would have done things differently.

I would have insisted that she let me take off her shirt and her bra. I would have begged—even harder than I did—for her to let me touch those breasts. I would have demanded that she let me suck her nipples. They had to have been epic.

Don't get me wrong here; I'm not talking about rape. We were young. We did a lot of wrestling. I just would have wrestled a whole lot better is what I'm trying to say. The roles were very clear back then. The male was responsible for initiating all the sex acts. The female was responsible for putting on the brakes when things got to be too much. It was a negotiation of bumbling lust versus paranoid fear.

Sweet Sally let me take her panties down. She did! She let me finger her vagina. She even sucked my penis—but she would never let me touch her breasts! She wouldn't even let me see them. She always kept on her shirt and her bra. And when the weather was hot, she also wore pads under her arms too.

"Shields," they were called. We were part of a social group that was uptight about letting under-arm perspiration come through and dampen your shirt.

It was a mid-twentieth century curse invented by corporate America to sell antiperspirants. This poor young woman was driven to wearing shields, but, God bless her, she was the first female to ever pull down her panties for me. I never got over it. I don't think I can.

Truth be told, I have spent a lifetime revisiting the memories of my intimate discoveries with Sally. What delicious wetness there was!

It was the great Greek writer Nikos Kazantzakis who once suggested that there really was only one woman in life, one woman with many faces. In much the same vein, in hindsight, those first sexual experiences with Sally were the most powerful of my whole life. All of the rest have been echoes. I'm not talking about romantic love here, but just the sheer power of sexual desire.

What makes it all the more extraordinary was that we never did have any penis-vagina sex. There was no penetration. It was all just petting, but those memories became immortal. Perhaps it was because of the firstness of everything. Those memories have had enormous erotic power. Like personal French postcards frozen in amber, they have returned to me thousands of times and aroused me again and again while I've made love to my wife and all the others.

The passing years can fall off in a blink. I'm back in her game room. I can hear The Kingston Trio singing. It was always The Kingston Trio singing. To this day, if I hear The Kingston Trio singing, I get a hard-on. And if I concentrate real hard, even the smells of Sally's young body remain fresh in my mind forever.

The strange part is that I actually had another girlfriend at the time. Sally and I were "cheating." I was supposed to really be in love with Sharyn, pretty much the only Orthodox Jewish girl in our crowd. Sharyn was the one I took to all the parties. Sharyn was the kind of girl who when we first started kissing — well, neither one of us knew anything about opening up our mouths. We were pre-French, but we'd kiss real hard anyway because that's the way we saw them do it in the movies. We were trying to be passionate … and it was just like in the old Bill Cosby routine, our teeth would cut up the backs of our lips and we'd have to stop the make-out sessions for several days at a time just to heal. The wounded lips and resultant swellings would contribute to short periods of a speech defect that came to be known as the Elmer Fudd Syndrome.

"I wuv you."

"I wuv you too."

I did "love" Sharyn. Her whole family was great. We were good friends. But Sharyn wasn't ready for any heavy petting—and Sally was. Sally opened her mouth. Oh, my God, did Sally open her mouth!

So, Sally and I met secretly in her game room.

"Hang down your head, Tom Dooley,
Hang down your head and cry...."

Forget Viagra, Cialis, and Levitra, The Kingston Trio still works for me.

It all began on a Continental bus ride to Washington, D.C. Our civics class was on a field trip to the nation's capital. Sharyn just wasn't in our class. And in the dark of that nighttime bus ride, as the miles rolled by, Sally and I shared two rickety seats next to each other and couldn't keep our young hands out of each other's laps. We began discovering the shivering ecstasies that were going to change our lives forever.

I've often wondered why Sally chose a chubby like me for our mutual initiation into the erotic world of fun and games. Perhaps it was because her daddy was a big man too—a really big man.

I don't know why she picked me, but I'm glad that she did. Sally never did become a "girlfriend" girlfriend. I didn't take her to any parties and we never went out on a date or anything like that. All we did was just to share the hottest sex that this universe has to offer.

My daddy worked across the street from her daddy. We shared a lot of the same classes and hung out at school with many of the same friends. But after that initial springtime trip to Washington, there followed an entire summer of hot, sultry nights in her game room where The Kingston Trio was playing "They Call the Wind Mariah," and we drove each other nuts with massively titillated and restrained passion.

I used to pedal over there on my bicycle. I'd have a hard-on the whole way.

"A way out here, they've got a name
For wind and rain and fire
The rain is Tess, the fire is Joe
And they call the wind, Mariah."

And don't for a minute think that I haven't checked out Sally since those days. When I saw her at our tenth high school reunion, I confessed how wonderful my memories of our sexual discovery were. There was no missing the invitation I was extending to renew our lustful acquaintance.

She stiffened her back and said to me in a chill voice, "My husband takes care of all of my sexual needs!"

Oh, my God, did she ever miss the point! My wife took care of all my sexual needs too, but so what!?! Sally and I had something special! We had eternal youth and this unique volcanic fire of first lust to remember and share forever, but Sally, my dear sweet Sally, just wasn't there. I sighed and shrugged and sadly deflated.

Well, Goddamn it, I was mad at her. If she was going to dismiss me, then, hell, I was going to dismiss her too. For a while, I tried not to think of her when those old pictures cropped up on my erotic screen during lovemaking or masturbation. I pridefully tried to shut them off and switch to another channel, but the Sally of memory just wouldn't go away. She refused to be dismissed.

In time, I got over her later rejecting me and once again delighted in our steamy, creamy memories. After all, she couldn't take away the memories.

At the twentieth reunion, I had the feeling that she was toying with me. It was like she knew of the lust I was feeling whenever she glanced at me. Was she enjoying being the object of desire without ever having to mention it? The casual glance I gave her as she walked by on the arm of her husband just dripped with my desire, but nothing came of it.

Did I scare her off with my blunt predation? Did her husband even know? Did she ever tell him? I doubt it. At the time, I didn't know any of those answers, but I had hope that by the time we got to our fiftieth reunion, she'd be able to sneak off to a hotel with me. We'd put our false teeth into one of those sterilized drinking glasses and gum ourselves into an insane frenzy. I wondered if she'd even let me touch her breasts?

Sally had large breasts. They were the object of much desire and envy in our adolescent circle of friends. I think it drove her quite mad in those early years. All the small-breasted women dreamed of being big-busted like her. In those days, of course, women could not just save up their money and buy themselves a larger cup size. There were the blessed and the unblessed and that was that.

In moments of heated passion, I would occasionally try to unfasten her bra before Sally was aware what I was doing. Forget about it. That bra was a true engineering marvel. Miles of wire and steel cable went into the noble effort to keep those melons perched high on the vine. This was not a bra to be taken lightly. It refused to be casually undone. It required leverage, blueprints, and the deft hand of a surgeon to unlock the treasures.

Whenever she would discover me trying to get at her lovelies, she'd always threaten to send me home if I didn't stop. I'd stop, for a few minutes, and then we'd reprise the whole scenario once again.

Through her, I'd seen the wisdom in the old axiom, "The grass is always greener on the other side." My voluptuous lover often regretted nature's gift to her of that bountiful bosom. It made her an object that she was ill equipped to deal with in those days. For her part, she simply wished that they had been given to somebody else. She liked to pretend that they just were not there.

I recall vividly and frequently that we petted ourselves to ecstasy on any number of occasions. As I said, we never had actual intercourse where my bare penis entered her bare vagina. We would probably have both spontaneously combusted and burned to death had we allowed that moment to happen. We came awfully close, though. She'd let me take out my penis and press it into the folds of her vagina through her divinely white cotton panties.

They'd be dripping wet. I'd be trying to burst through those panties with all the pressure I could stand to mount on my muzzled member. God, it was hot. It was overwhelming. We were begging for an accident, but the material never gave way. Fruit of the Loom saved our virginity!

We never did get to the point where we could actually just "do it." We both had a morality that pretty seriously said fucking meant marrying and we were only fourteen years old. What we had happened upon quite accidentally was a tryst of sexual discovery. Each of us was well lubricated for a sexual partner, but the words, "I love you," were never spoken. Maybe it was me cheating on Sharyn, maybe it was just the sexual guilt, but, Sally, sweet Sally, let me right the wrong. Let me speak those words now, I love you. And oh, how I wanted you! Amen.

Strangely enough, had our affair continued on a bit longer, I'm pretty sure that she would have let me enter her long before she would have been able to take off her blouse and shown me her breasts. And in memory, it seems like I was gearing myself up to pulling those panties to one side and plunging myself into her heavenly forbidden zone when our affair vanished as rapidly as it began.

We scared each other. We scared each other with our diminishing ability to hold back Nature and keep it all in the pre-penetration stages.

Y'see, one of those times when I was implanted into her vagina about a half-an-inch deep with the panties still in place and straining not to give way, I had an orgasm. It was an Annie Oakley bull's-eye.

She jumped up with her jeans all around her ankles and a startled look on her face. She was sure that I had just impregnated her. She was trying to stick her head between her legs and look at herself. Ha, you're laughing. It's real funny now. It sure wasn't then.

"It's all so wet!" she yelped. She was so genuinely frightened that it frightened me too. Of all the juices, she said, "I can't tell what's mine and what's yours! I don't know if any of your sperm got in me or not!" We were both convinced that she was absolutely, totally and undeniably pregnant. And boy, did we ever get religion!

In the days and weeks that followed, I didn't even masturbate. I was cutting deals with God. If I would refrain from touching myself, would He please let her not be pregnant? Since I was in the habit of "touching myself" two or three times a day, I thought this was a hell of a good offer.

When the time for her period came and her period did not, my fear became anger. I was furious with God. How could He create something as irresistible, as wonderful as sex, and then tie it to the horrors and melodrama of an unwanted pregnancy. This was Hawthorne's Scarlet Letter all over again. I could not comprehend His divine stupidity. I could not forgive myself mine.

As a young man of integrity, I was preparing to do the "right thing" and offer to marry Sally when she finally gave the word that her menstrual flow had begun again. Allah be praised. All thoughts of marriage faded like hookah smoke. The very next weekend, we put The Kingston Trio back on the record player and reclined again in our private paradise of petting. Once more, I wrestled unsuccessfully with her bra and once more, we teased ourselves into liquid explosions. I was, however, very careful never to explode too near her "bull's eye" ever again.

Then, like I said, we just sort of stopped seeing each other. Yeah, like hell, I've been seeing her for over forty years, in living Technicolor and with smell-o-vision during some of the most intimate moments of my life. My dick might have been in Marilyn Chambers, Annette Haven or Seka, but often, I was still thinking about Sally.

She used to call my penis, "Charley." I used to call her vagina, "Ethel."

"Does Charley want to come out and play?" she would singsong coyly.

"Only if he gets to see Ethel," I would answer in turn. It was fairly sick. The Charley-Ethel part finally convinced me. I mean, what kind of names are those to give your genitals?

And if I had only known that I was to have had more sex petting with Sally in the ninth grade than I was gonna get for the entire rest of high school, I would never have let her go!

"Scotch and soda,
Mud in your eye,
Baby, do I feel high!
Oh, me, oh, my —"

When Sally's blue jeans came down that first time and she took my hand and placed it between her legs, I thought the heat in my head would set my hair on fire. She was damp—and hot. She melted into my hand and breathed a hot breath on my neck that made me tingle with an aliveness that I had never before known. This was a new place for me. This was an irresistible place! I had no idea that life could even offer such a thing. It made me wonder what else I didn't know about yet—

"All I need is,
One of your smiles,
Sunshine of your eyes,
Oh, me, oh, my,
Do I feel high!
Give me lovin,
Baby, I'm your guy!"

Chapter Fifteen

Well, we're in the game, but we're still fat. You don't mind if I include you in here, do you? Being a writer can get awfully lonely.

And you know, when I was working as an actor, going to all those auditions, I used to think that I knew something about rejection. Forget about it! A writer doesn't even get out of the house!

You can spend forever writing something and then you finally finish it and send it off to an agent, a magazine, maybe a publisher. You wait forever. Before you know it, it's a month, three months. It's six months later and you haven't heard a Goddamn word!

You've waited long enough. You call them up. Lord only knows how many calls you have to make before you actually get to talk to someone who is supposed to know something about something, and they say, "Nope, never got that. Never saw it. You want to try resubmitting that?"

And fuckin' A, you do!

Chapter Sixteen

"You got a potty mouth!" the Voice said to me.

"Oh, God! I didn't know it was you!" I told Him. "Do you really care about that kind of stuff?"

"Nah, not at all," He said, "just fuckin' with ya."

Chapter Seventeen

Fat. Fat. Fat. I couldn't kick it. All through the eighth and ninth grade and on into the tenth, just couldn't kick it. The waistline was thirty-two, thirty-four inches, and going up. By the age of seventeen, I was knocking at the door of a forty-inch waist. Pretty tough to buy off the rack.

My mother, who was also fighting the battle of the bulge, had taken me to the doctor and had me try a couple of different things. I remember taking thyroid pills for a while. Didn't do nothing. Then there were cans of Metrecal. It was supposed to be this new wonder drink that you'd substitute periodically for meals. It had zero effect, but at least it was chocolate.

It seemed like I was never going to be able to lose any weight. I longed to discover a zipper hidden in my neck that I would one day

– Gordon Archive

The body of my dreams.

pull down and be able to step out of that fat body like a person removing a heavy winter coat.

It was around that time that the dream came.

I was alone and crying. A man approached me. He was very well built, abs like a washboard. I guess he was naked or near to it. He kissed me on the cheek. It wasn't erotic, but it was electric. It sent sparks and shivers through me. I knew I was sleeping and I knew I was dreaming, but something very special was happening, something very real.

It seemed like we used to say such things happened only in *The Twilight Zone*. Or more recently, perhaps, someone might refer to such an incident as an *X-File*. No doubt, earthbound psychologists could and would find an entirely different rendering for these events, but I'm not always completely opposed to magical thinking.

The man told me not to be frightened. He said that he was me in the future. There you have it! Cat's out of the bag! He's crazy. I'm crazy. You're crazy for reading this! But that's what happened, in my dream.

He dried my tears and then posed for me. It was me fourteen years into my own future. I was the 143 1/2 pounds that I would be when I posed to become a *Playgirl* centerfold in November of 1978. I would be at the absolute peak of my physical powers. I'd have the body of a Greek sculpture.

"Just look at who you get to be," he said to me. He was fucking beautiful, almost everything that I could have ever wished for. He told me that I should just take it easy, calm down, and that everything would work itself out. Then, he disappeared.

When I awoke in the morning, I was as fat as ever, but with a new feeling of inner calm. I told no one about my dream. Probably shouldn't even have told you!

Chapter Eighteen

"You're damn right," Agent Marty said, "This is crazy!! Where's all the porn you were talkin' about anyway? Porn's better than crazy! I knew porn would be a tough sell, but crazy, crazy would be fucking impossible! Tell me, is this an acid flashback or something?"

"Relax, Marty," I told him, "it's all just fiction."

Chapter Nineteen

I peaked as a fatty mid-way through my junior year of high school. I stood about five foot seven and weighed in at over 200 pounds. I wore "Husky" clothes. Husky was the last designation possible before the department store said, "Sorry, pal, you're just too fat to shop here."

After the Christmas vacation, in the new year of 1965, there were two major concerns in my life. One had become getting into college and the other, of course, was still to lose weight.

Regarding college, it had begun to dawn on me that my brother's being smart really wasn't going to do too much to get me into college. Though I was still being included in the advanced classes, my academic career to that point had been decidedly mediocre, mediocre and less.

I had always taken it for granted that I was smart because my brother was, but school had been his arena to excel, especially in math and science. I just turned off to all that stuff, barely earning myself passing grades.

Y'see, I was gonna carve out my own path and it wasn't gonna be in doin' no schoolwork! It was gonna be baseball. I was shooting for the Big Leagues! I was gonna play for the Pittsburgh Pirates! And along the way, I'd make it to college alright, but it would be on an atha-letic scholarship. That was the plan, anyway. Yeah, that was the plan.

Chapter Twenty
Continuing Sex Education

It was a school night and I was in the tenth grade. We had high school fraternities in our community. This was the rush season and the fraternities were after their next round of pledges.

The older boys, the seniors, were taking us out for the night. They drove. They had cars. They took us to the Casino Burlesque in downtown Pittsburgh. We were gonna see naked women.

Irma the Body was the headliner. She was a little long in the tooth, but what did that matter to us! We were greener than the hills in May and she was gonna get naked. Besides, Mae West was still considered sexy and she was about 110.

It was a mob scene in the theater that night. Young men were everywhere. They had definitely turned a blind eye to age requirements at the front door. All that mattered was the color of your money. "Move along, son, move along. Show's gonna start in about ten minutes."

Irma the Body did not disappoint. She was voluptuous and creamy and got as naked as the State of Pennsylvania would allow back in 1963. At the end of her act, she took a rose, a long stemmed rose. One could only assume that it had been shorn of its thorns. She placed that rose between her legs and made a wriggling delightful show of squeezing it hard with her thighs. When she withdrew the blossom, it was still intact. She languidly raised it to her nostrils and inhaled the fragrance deeply.

"Hmmmmm," she said with a sleepy smile, "does anyone want to smell my rose?"

Around 300 very teen-age boys lost their minds!

Chapter Twenty-One

I don't know why the weight came off when it did or why it hadn't all those other times before. Didn't seem to be any magic to it. It was all just diet and exercise.

My parents allowed me to largely stay home for most of January and February of that junior year in 1965. I studied hard for the college boards and I exercised. I restricted my diet to meat and salad and began a running program. I took practice test after practice test of the SATs and just about memorized *Thirty Days to a Better Vocabulary*. I studied "specious, rococo, to weltschmerz," like it was Tinkers to Evers to Chance.

I raised my verbal score almost 150 points. I raised my math total by about a hundred. And in just under three months, I lost fifty pounds!

Chapter Twenty-Two

The new me. It was like being reborn. When I went back to school in March, I got my first taste of being a "sex star." Walking down the halls, I got lots of smiles and stares. People were astonished at my transformation, but none more so than me. Before the end of that Junior year of high school, I got myself elected to be the President of our Senior Class.

I gave the bandleader back his fekukteh tuba. No more tuba, I was done with the tuba. Kiss my ass, tuba!

I went from playing center to halfback in football. In baseball, well, I just stayed at catcher. I liked playing catcher. I was pretty good at it. Losing weight only made me better, but I still stunk in basketball.

On the stage, however, I went from being cast as the fat, funny sidekick to contending with all the pretty boys for the romantic leads. That was fun!

And de womens? De womens, dey began to notice me! Girls who had ignored me for years were now sniffing around. My parents were kind of amused by all the girls suddenly come a-calling, but my mother drew the line at lying for me on the phone when I sought her help in juggling some of these new ladies.

My parents were a lot more pleased that I had begun to take my academic life seriously. I had applied to and was accepted by Northwestern University's National High School Institute for a summer program in Journalism. I fancied myself becoming a writer.

My success that summer against top-flight competition from all over the country gave me a huge boost in confidence. I finished second in the class of 150 "Cherubs," as we were called.

Early in the program, one of the teachers took to the blackboard and simply wrote: "A writer writes."

I began keeping a diary on August 4, 1965. Vol. #149 began on May 19, 2013. It remains a work in progress.

By the way, I had a great senior year!

Chapter Twenty-Three

"The book could end right there, y'know," Marty said. "You could flesh out some more chapters about all that painful crap, the rejections, the loneliness, and then, **BOOM!**" I think he scared himself with the noise he made.

"BOOM!" He said more gently, like a stage whisper. "It's like a fairy tale! The Princess kisses the frog and Boom—"

"Enough already with the booms," I told him.

"—and he becomes a Prince! Did you have a girlfriend back then?"

"I did."

"Well, there you go! You're a fuckin' fairy tale!"

Chapter Twenty-Four

"Whatsa matter?" God asked. "What happened?"

"I'm stuck," I told Him.

"So? Get unstuck," He said.

"In the end," I told Him, "it all just sounds like, 'ain't I great? ain't I special? I don't want to write that anymore!"

"You're not at the end," He said. "You're barely past the beginning. You know what, you've just discovered, 'Vanity of vanities; all is vanity,' and now you're depressed. That's happened to a lot of people."

"Didn't Shakespeare write that?"

"No, it was *Ecclesiastes*, a long time ago." We were quiet for a while. "You know what I like about you?" God asked.

"No, what?"

"On your desk," He said, "You took this little, toy dog, it was a plastic Pluto doll from Disneyland. It was made with its tongue sticking out like it was licking something. You took that Pluto doll and you made a real-looking cock and balls for it! Yeah! You put a small screw right into the dog's missing genital area, and then you used some plastic clay to sculpt his brand new cock and balls right over that screw. I watched you do it! That was fucking genius! I mean, I was doing stuff like that in Genesis!"

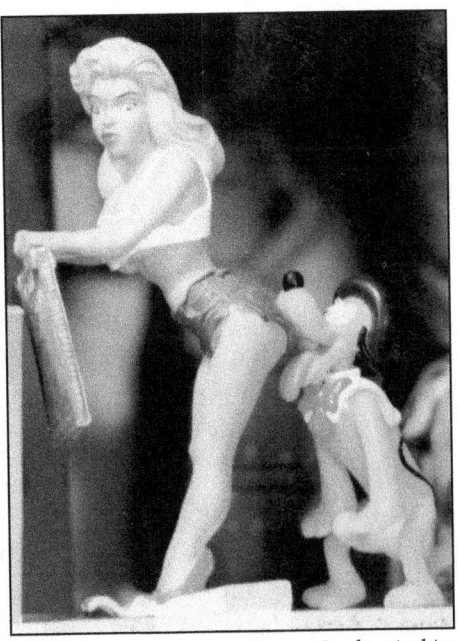

- Gordon Archive

God liked my sculpture.

"And then, you put that dog with his little, erect penis and his tongue sticking out, you put it right behind a small sculpture of a buxom, trashy, hillbilly-type woman wearing extremely short, cut-off jeans. She's bending over with her ass sticking out. You put the Pluto doll right behind her so that it looks like Pluto is licking her ass, and she's got this completely stunned look on her face, y'know? Like there's a cold, wet dog nose right up her ass! Now, that's funny!"

"And that's why you like me?"

"Son, the Lord moves in mysterious ways. Lookee here, " He said. God clearly had fallen into this whole country-western thing. Who was I to stop Him? "This here job you're doing—your job is just to entertain the troops. Stop taking yourself so damn serious!"

"Sex is one of the best things I done. I liked it so much I gave it to all the plants and all the animals. It's only you people that are having so much trouble with it, I just want you to tell your story, son. Y'know? It just might help somebody out."

"Okay," I said, "okay."

Chapter Twenty –Five

I lost my virginity three times.

Number one was with Sally back in the ninth grade. Remember? I was in her an inch deep—actually, on more than one occasion. Her panties used to wrap around me like a cotton condom. That's gotta count for something!

My penis is almost six inches long when it's hard. So, at least one-sixth of me lost his virginity 'round 1963. It wasn't until I was in college three years later that the other five inches got invited to the party.

All through high school, I pretty much thought that if I had penis-vagina sex with a girl, I'd be obligated to marry her. Nah, no thanks. I waited. And then when some of my buddies graduated to paying the whores in Pittsburgh's Hill District, I passed on that too. It grossed me out. I was waiting for true love,

I ended up going to Antioch College in Yellow Springs, Ohio. It's fallen on hard times in recent years, but way back in the 1960s, it was a happening place!

Antioch long had enjoyed a reputation for its experimental programs and its innovative educational philosophies. It was a haven for social activism, Utopian communities, and humanist politics. Antioch's motto came from its founder, the great nineteenth-century educator, Horace Mann, who proclaimed, "Be ashamed to die until you have won some great victory for humanity."

In June of 1966 when I was finishing up high school, none of that meant bupkis to me.

I chose Antioch because I didn't get into Harvard. I chose Antioch because I was afraid that Northwestern would prove too expensive for my family. I chose Antioch because it was a work/study school. You spent half the year studying on campus and the other half earning real money at a real job somewhere that they would provide.

My going there was all my brother's idea. Our parents didn't have a lot of spare change for sending either one of us to college. My brother had gone to Antioch before me and had just graduated. He convinced me that I should go there too, because it would be much less of a financial burden on our parents than any of the other schools I had chosen. Done. I became an Antiochian.

Oi.

In June of 1966, when I graduated from high school, I was a well-adjusted senior class president wearing saddle shoes. I was a good boy. Five-sixth of me was still a virgin. I didn't get in fights. Didn't steal shit. Never was arrested. Never had been expelled. Didn't hang out in pool halls. Didn't drink no beer and the only drugs I took were aspirin and Pepto-Bismol.

After two months at Antioch in the fall, I was an alienated, pot-smoking, socialist, communist, Darwinist, humanist who was going on protest marches and had developed problems with the Draft Board.

There really wasn't anything else to do at Antioch. In place of sororities and fraternities, we had organizations like SDS (Students for a Democratic Society), the Black Panthers, the Young Maoists, the Young Trotskyites, C.O.R.E. (Congress of Racial Equality), S.N.C.C. (Student Non-Violent Coordinating Committee), the A.C.L.U. (American Civil Liberties Union), the S.C.L.C. (Southern Christian Leadership Conference), the Mobilization Against the War in Vietnam, the (Draft) Resistance, and LSD (Lysergic Acid Diethylamide). That last one was a joke. LSD wasn't an organization. It was an exploration, an entertainment. It was twelve hours on a roller coaster where you would surrender your sanity and just hope that it would be returned to you at the end of the ride.

I was so out of my league. I played a lot of touch football. I grew my hair long and dressed like a hippie. In time, I discovered that I liked psychedelic drugs and I definitely signed myself up for the sexual revolution. That much I could relate to.

Soon, the ideas of people like Wilhelm Reich (*The Function of the Orgasm*), and those of Alan Watts (*Nature, Man, and Woman*), helped me to melt whatever barriers I had left from embracing a greater sexual freedom.

In other words, hell with waiting for marriage to have sex. Let's go!

I lost what was left of my virginity when I came back home for Thanksgiving of that freshmen year. Her name was Donna. She was one of the three wonderful women I had been dating during my senior year of high school.

I remember that the first time I ever placed Donna's hand on my bare penis, she just broke out in a scary fit of laughing. Uh-oh, this was not good for my self-esteem. You want to talk about an event that can scar a young man for life? This was definitely one of the top five nominees. It seemed like forever until she calmed down enough to explain that she sometimes laughed hysterically when she got very nervous.

She said that I had surprised her when I placed her hand on my dick. Having never touched one before, it occurred to her that she had no idea what to do with it. And that thought all of a sudden seemed like the funniest thing in the world to her. By then, thank the Lord, it seemed pretty funny to me too. Poor girl was a wreck, laughing, crying, mucous coming out of her nose. Well, we calmed each other down. After that, I made a few suggestions of what she might do with a handful of dick. And we progressed from there.

Then came that fateful night during my first Thanksgiving vacation home from college. My parents had gone out for the evening. Donna's father had dropped her off at our house. He would come back later and pick her up.

Donna and I had enjoyed some heavy petting before I had gone off to college. When I inevitably had pressed the point, she had always insisted upon me keeping my point to myself. Even still, we had come very close to "doing it" several times.

Tonight was gonna be the night. I had a condom and a new philosophy. I was ready. There was preliminary debate. Kissing soon replaced the words. I could tell her resistance was weakening, but who remembers how long all that took? I guess we just lost track of the time.

We were petting and wrestling on my parents' big double bed. Finally, we put a rubber on my penis that I'd been carrying around since the tenth grade. She went on top. She held my cock in place and slowly and carefully impaled herself upon me. We were still. I was all the way in. No doubt about it. This was the actual it. She reported no pain. I began to move slowly. It was great.

Then, there was a loud knocking downstairs at the front door. Uh-oh.

Fuck this shit! I thought. *Whoever it was, they could wait!* It was clear that it was the little head that was doing all of the thinking. I jammed into high gear and tried to come.

The knocking turned into shouting, "DONNA? DONNA? ARE YOU THERE?" It was the maiden's father! He was early. We were late. What did it matter? He was at the front door! I was squirting into the condom as she flew off of me and raced into her clothes. I raced into mine. We both bumbled downstairs. I was still wearing the wet rubber underneath when I waved good-bye.

I refuse to think of this as the night I lost my virginity.

In the great romance novel of my life, I prefer to think that I lost my virginity to Lucy.

I hooked up with Lucy at the very end of high school. She would soon replace all three of the women that I was seeing. We would be a couple for the next five years.

Though a year younger, Lucy had become sexually active way before me. She was the teacher. I was the student. She was smart. And she was a straight-haired blonde looker along the lines of Mary Travers from Peter, Paul & Mary with legs that went from here to Heaven. I counted myself lucky to be with her.

I've forgotten most of the how or why, but I think the first time we ever had sex was on a mattress, on a floor, in a New York City apartment. She wore bikini bottom, leopard print panties, no shy maiden in white cotton, she.

Unhurriedly, thank the Lord, she was the one sitting in the back of the canoe guiding us through all the steps down the river until we went over the falls. I did, anyway. In those days, I was never too sure about women's orgasms. They didn't always say. I couldn't always tell. And I didn't always ask. I just knew that it was gonna be awhile before I could go again. So. I would usually hope that whatever had just happened had been enough for her too.

Lucy's first words to me afterward, apropos of being the teacher, were, "Do you feel guilty?"

"No," I answered. At the time, it was as close to the truth as I could get.

I think from that point on, and for many years to come, my penis pretty much just took over my life and used the rest of me as a disguise.

Chapter Twenty-Six

Lucy and I, and a lot of other young couples in the 1960s, were stuck trying to be Romeo and Juliet and do Free Love at the same time.

Good luck wid dat!

We were fine whenever we'd be together, but both school and work often conspired to put us in different cities for periods of time.

And when that happened, we were the revolution. It was "When you can't be with the one you love, honey, love the one you're with." When we were apart, we were both fucking everything that moved. I'll have one of those and one of those and one of those. We were both dining freely at the lover's buffet of life. Monogamy was so yesterday.

And then when Lucy and I would get back together again, well, we didn't always know exactly how to handle it. To be kind, let's just say that the truth often took a beating. And jealousy, they don't call it "the green-eyed monster" for nothing. Jealousy was formidable and merciless.

But we thought jealousy was like racism and imperialism! We thought it just another outmoded idea to be discredited and disregarded. We were supposed to do better than jealousy! In the Age of Aquarius, we thought we were all supposed to be able to have sex with whoever we wanted to have sex and everybody else was just supposed to be groovy with it.

Seemed like we beat that dead horse for years!

Chapter Twenty-Seven

I made my first "skin flick" when I was a senior in college. Gloria had asked Lucy and me if she could film us having sex.

Gloria was a freshman at Antioch who was as much a novice at filmmaking as she was about sex. She figured she'd kill two birds with one stone and learn a lot about each in the process.

I was instantly all for it. After having been that fat kid, the world was now inviting me to become a movie star! It was like winning an award for having done 900,000 sit-ups. The fact that it was to be a film about sex only made it more exciting.

Lucy, however, had her doubts. She had the curiosity and chutzpah to get naked for a film, but she suspected the young Gloria of having a crush on me, which she found less than amusing. In the end, though, Lucy agreed to make the film.

There was no script. The planning only went as far as picking out a date and a place. When that date arrived, Gloria arrived at our apartment; stage lit our bedroom, and then hid behind her camera waiting for something to happen. I heard Woody Allen worked like that sometimes.

It was awkward. Lucy and I didn't know what to do and there was Gloria hiding behind her camera. When she pushed the "on" button, we fell into some kissing and began taking off our clothes. There was no passion. We felt stupid.

On a whim, I picked Lucy up in my arms and swung her around the room. We laughed. It broke the ice.

I asked Gloria if she minded if we played around a little bit first. Gloria said that we should do whatever we wanted to do. She was more nervous than we were. In her own recollection, she wrote:

> *"I'd never even seen an X-rated film, much less made one. How do you get two people to fuck for the camera? What am I supposed to say? I don't know how to get this started in a movie any more than I do in real life. How do I get this rolling? I need help. I want you guys to show me."*

There was a six-foot cardboard tube in the room with red and white barber stripes around it. I put one end of it over my cock while Lucy put the other end between her legs six feet away. We posed. There was a toy gun. We did some schtick with that too. There was a lot of jumping up and down like humans sometimes do at the zoo when they're trying to get a rise out of the monkeys.

And that was foreplay.

When we began the sex in earnest, Gloria wrote:

> *"Okay, more serious stuff. Howie and Lucy silhouetted*

against the light, bodies close, kissing, touching. Looks like lovers in front of the moon, romantic, tender. Pull back, Howie moves her in front of the camera, pushes her down on the bed, spreads her legs, buries his face in her crotch. Lucy eases back, letting him have her, closing her eyes against the bright glare of the lights. I move back and forth behind him, watching her face, listening, feeling like an intruder with permission, like a voyeur. He moves up, kissing her belly, breasts, neck. Her round hoop earrings catch and reflect the lights. The room heats up quickly from the quartz lights, but they just keep going."

What I remember was that there was an endless scene of Lucy sucking my cock followed by an equally endless scene of me sucking her.

After that, we fucked for about six-and-a-half days.

Gloria shot and shot and shot. She only stopped for reloading. She said nothing. We ignored her.

The truth that Lucy and I shared about our having had sex for the camera that day was that it was not all that much fun. Our private sex was much more exciting. Neither one of us turned out to be much of an exhibitionist. We weren't getting off by being watched. The lights were hot and they just kept getting hotter. The sex became a chore.

In the end, neither one of us reached orgasm. We just stopped. We'd had enough. Of the three of us, Gloria probably got the biggest kick. Her eyes were big like a baby giraffe's as she gathered up her equipment and left. She later wrote:

"When Howie finally rolled off her, they just lay there spooned together. They touched and kissed and whispered to each other so low that I could not hear it at the foot of the bed. When he finally turned to look at me, it was almost as if he was surprised to see me still standing there. He smiled to the camera, spread his legs wide and shook his balls at me, thumbed his nose, and jumped off the bed. Lucy headed for her clothes. Cut. Wrap.

I thanked them, genuflected a few times, grabbed my

equipment and split. Oh, wow, I know I got some good stuff. That was great! Wow, what amazing people. Oh, wow, I can't wait to see it. I wonder if Kodak will process it if I just drop it off at the Pharmacy. Oh, wow, this was so great. So, that's how it's done! Shit, I could never do that. I wonder if Lucy really felt okay about this, I wonder if Howie really had to talk her into it."

And when Gloria was gone, gone and gone, Lucy and I mercifully finished up that sex scene in the quiet darkness of our own love.

Several weeks later, we saw the film. It had no title. It had no credits. And it had no sound. It was amateurish and innocent and really quite cute—right up to the parts where we saw ourselves exhausted, sweating profusely, and trying to extricate ourselves from the situation. But on the whole, we were glad we had done it.

Chapter Twenty-Eight

I graduated Antioch College in 1970 with a degree in both History and Urban Affairs.

You ask, "Did most people who worked as actors in the X-rated industry have college degrees?" And I say that's a very good question to which I don't have the answer. Let's just say, it wasn't required. For the men, the ability to become aroused and have an orgasm in front of the prying eyes of many other men, women, and machines had to be at the top of your résumé, but we're getting ahead of ourselves here.

Lucy and I were playing house in Washington, D.C. While I worked at a firm that served as consultants to what remained of the Federal Poverty Programs, Lucy was finishing her senior year of college.

My job was like being a traveling salesman for social reform. We'd fly all around the country on contracts from the Department of Labor administering "technical assistance" to the programs in need. They were all in need. It was like putting band-aids on cancer.

The Republican Nixon had begun gutting the programs when he took office in 1968. What was left were the mere remnants of what had once been the noble effort of a national War on Poverty initiated by the Democrat John Kennedy and later expanded into The Great Society of

Lyndon Johnson, his successor in the early 1960s.

Anyway, it was so over by 1970. Kennedy and his brother had been murdered. So had civil rights leaders Medgar Evers, Martin Luther King Jr., and Malcolm X. The Vietnam War was still ravaging the nation. We didn't exactly know it yet, but the great "revolution" of the sixties was over. The bad guys had won.

Still, the great liberals on our staff argued that if we helped one person, then it was all worth our pay. And by the way, our pay was good! There was very good money in poverty if you were on the right side of the equation. I made a nice salary cast in the role of the long-haired disenchanted youth trying to work within the system.

Each Monday morning, I'd be part of a crew getting on an airplane bound for one of the nation's ghettoes. We'd spend the week there working and then return to D.C. on Friday for our staff meetings. The locals in the cities where we had been sent usually didn't trust us. They protected their turf, their funding, and worked the Feds for whatever they could get. We'd study their programs, make suggestions, and write reports.

I had worked over three years in this job. From true believer in the earlier days before Nixon, I had become a disappointed cynic. My tolerance for the necessary games of bureaucracy had disappeared.

Toward the end, what I pretty much did was try to fuck as many women as I could in the cities where we went, before returning home each Friday to play house with Lucy. Mostly, I had the good sense not to hit on the women in the actual programs we were working. That was a no-no. But after work, I'd find the hippie part of town and see what I could find. I was twenty-two years old back then. When the wind would blow, I would get a hard-on. I was baffled by people who could sit around in an office all day long and not fuck. It made me crazy.

Chapter Twenty-Nine
Go West Young Man

I'd already been to California a few times. My company had sent me on various trips to both Los Angeles and San Francisco where I had worked on a number of the poverty programs out there, but this trip was different.

For one thing, Lucy and I were just hanging on by a thread. Not surprisingly, too many other lovers had finally combined with too many strange scenes, too many half-truths, and too many outright lies. We couldn't find each other anymore. Our ability to go on loving and supporting each other had been absolutely mangled.

We had a wonderful little apartment behind the Biograph Theatre in Georgetown, but it had grown cold and tense in there. We were living in limbo with too many painful memories as lovers and roommates.

When I got this particular reassignment to San Francisco, I was offered the whole weekend there so that I could show up fresh for work at 9:00 a.m. on Monday. As usual, I was going to stay at a hotel.

Turned out, a friend of mine named Bonnie, a woman who I'd recently had a fling with, was also going to be traveling to California. We made plans to travel together. Bonnie was going to move into a commune in Berkeley called Dragon's Eye. She said they'd probably have room for me to spend the weekend there if I wanted. I wanted. It sounded great. In all the time spent on that job, there had already been far too many hotel rooms.

We took the redeye out of D.C. on Thursday night. It was still morning on Friday, when we pulled up to the front door of that Berkeley commune. There was a flutter of activity. The inhabitants were all busy loading up four cars with food, dogs, sleeping bags, and themselves. They were going camping for the weekend, to a friend's property near Yosemite. Did I want to tag along?

Yes.

Three or four hours later, the sun was high and hot when we arrived at a farmhouse up in the mountains. It seemed like everyone just jumped out of the cars and took off all of their clothes. Whoa!

Chapter Thirty

That night, in the California mountains, Melody first invited me to her bed. I thought she was ten years older than me. Turned out, it was only three or four, but she had a twelve-year-old daughter and was far more experienced than any other woman I had ever touched. I guess that's the point here. She was a woman. It seemed like the rest had all been girls.

By morning, I was completely in love.

Chapter Thirty-One

When I got back to D.C., Lucy and I said our good-byes. I quit my job. I was moving to California, to join Melody, and to join the commune.

Melody flew back East to ride across the country with me. We stopped off to visit my folks in Pittsburgh. I've had better ideas. My mother ended up throwing us out of the house the next day. She was not happy that Melody was older. "What's she want with a schtonk like you?" my mother asked.

She also didn't like it that Melody had a child and she was slightly less than thrilled that my new lover wasn't Jewish. She thought I was stupid to quit my job and to move to California. My parents heard the word "commune" and thought I was joining the Manson Family.

When Melody and I openly slept together that night in my old bedroom, my Mom sent my Dad in the next morning to tell us we had to go.

We went.

Chapter Thirty-Two

Now, you remember what happened with Melody and me on that highway driving through Kansas.

It was a hot summer day. We were riding in my convertible. I took off my shirt to beat the heat and catch some rays. Melody took hers off too. No bra, nothing, I squirmed. Her tits were splendid, especially for a woman who had nursed a baby, but I thought baring them on the Interstate in Kansas wasn't exactly clever. And I said so.

I told her that we were still out here in America and not back in Berkeley. Bad idea, it ended the honeymoon right then and there. She lit into me like I was the Ku Klux Klan. It was my first lecture from her on sexism. And it was not to be the last.

As the miles accumulated, so did my regrets. I was in way over my head with this woman and I could still smell the bridges burning behind me. All across Colorado and on to the great Golden Gate, Melody was on my case for things that I wouldn't learn about for another five or six years.

It was a mismatch that would last a stormy six months.

Chapter Thirty-Three

In the summer of 1971, Berkeley seemed to be filled with beautiful, angry women who had a tomahawk poised for anything moving with a penis. Women's liberation had come into vogue and Berkeley was perhaps its West Coast Mecca.

The Dragon's Eye Commune I was moving into had about eleven women and only three or four men. All of the women were into women's liberation and all of the men were into coping.

Personally speaking, I welcomed the discussion. I had a matching chord for angry women. I was an angry man. I wasn't any more comfortable with society's sex roles than they were. I refused to play the oppressor. If they'd had fathers who had given them some grief, I'd had a mother who provided me with more than a few things to think about. Short of physical abuse or actual sexual misconduct, I felt as much a victim as they did.

It should be said that the feminism of the era did not necessarily equate to being a lesbian. All kinds of different females were bonding together in support of each other to help find new roles and definitions of womanhood.

Unfortunately, there was no comparable movement for the men. It seemed like the only men's groups being organized in town were all about being gay. It was too big a leap for the average heterosexual man. He was pretty much left to fend for himself.

Bottom line was that the women I ended up being interested in were all attracted to the ideas of women's liberation. I wanted to learn what I had to learn in order to still get laid. For that, the commune in Berkeley turned out to be the perfect place at the perfect time.

Chapter Thirty-Four

I knew Carly was my wife within twenty-four hours of meeting her.

Chapter Thirty-Five

Looking back, Melody and I had a great summertime fling. We should have stopped it right there. We never should have tried to play house.

We had our warm, loving moments that could feature red-hot connection, but there were also far too many volatile issues between us that could easily devastate and freeze the entire landscape. It would go from spectacular, steamy sex to a dreary nuclear winter and it would get there fast. Arguing with Melody proved to be an exhausting, brutal experience. She was a fierce warrior.

It didn't take us long to tire of such a roller coaster. I was soon looking for a way out.

Around Thanksgiving, there was to be a big convention in Santa Fe, New Mexico. Turned out that our commune, along with about five others from around the country, all had been sharing some Federal grant funds to study "the uses of drugs in the counterculture." The grant period was officially coming to a close and there was to be this big party to celebrate and to help coordinate reporting all the findings.

Lucy, my ex, had herself joined a commune in D.C. They also had a piece of this grant. When I learned that she was going to be there in Santa Fe, I thought that, maybe, just maybe, she and I might try to put things back together.

Carly was a member of the host Santa Fe commune. When our Berkeley delegation arrived, Lucy wasn't there yet. That night, about twenty-five of us unrolled our sleeping bags on the living and dining room floors. Before lights out, I saw Carly tongue-kissing a very large, naked woman. If someone had told me that Carly was about to become my wife, I would have been skeptical.

In the morning, I grew very nervous and fidgety while awaiting Lucy's arrival. I had to do something. Everyone was getting ready for the journey to the convention site up in the hills outside of the city. I turned to the first Santa Fe person who crossed my path and asked if I could be of some help. It was Carly. She said, "Sure."

She was going to the grocery store for more supplies and I was welcome to come along. There was fresh snow on the ground as we stepped outside. You could hear the crunch. We got into her Volkswagen bus. It was blue and white. When we were seated inside with the doors closed, we just happened to look at each other. My single days were over. I wonder if we had buckled our seat belts?

I'm not going to tell you what it was because, even after all these years, I really don't know what it was. But I am going to try and tell you what it was like.

It was like, as we looked into each other's eyes, it was like God, you remember Her, it was like God just turned down the lights and pressed the "play" button.

Our story was being told to us. Again. She was my wife. I was her husband. It was idiot simple. We'd been married for at least 4,000 years. We were both alive and on the planet at the same time again.

How exactly did this information get communicated? I don't know. I just knew.

I looked at her and hallucinated. She was a dog. She was a horse. She was a tree. She was an Eskimo. She was a woman. She was a man. It was intense. It was bizarre, but it was not scary. She was a game show contestant and the secret word was being flashed over her head.

It said, "WIFE! WIFE! WIFE!!" Just so there would be no mistake.

It was ten o'clock in the morning. There were no drugs involved.

It was the most religious thing I'd ever experienced and it had nothing to do with religion. It also had nothing to do with arousal or sex either. Neither of us could look away.

How long did it last? I don't know. Was she feeling the same things I was? You'd have to ask her.

And then, then the lights just came back on. It was morning. It wasn't "like" morning, it was actually morning and we were both sitting in the front seats of her Volkswagen bus.

One of us asked, "Does this kind of thing happen to you often?"

And the other answered, "No, does it happen to you?"

"Howie?" she said. "Your name is Howie?"

And that's what it was like. It was like "the burning bush!"

Chapter Thirty-Six

"You are so over the top!" Marty the agent said. "I'm embarrassed for you. I am. I'm embarrassed for you! You want to be taken seriously as a writer, as a person, and then you come out with all this Zippity-doo-dah razza-ma-tazz? This chapter is nuts!"

"You're telling me! I used to think it was romantic, but now I think it's insane, a collective delusion that Carly and I must have shared from eating a bad banana or breathing in a toxic fart. I know it sounds crazy! How do you think it makes me feel to tell that story to my own kids?

It stops sounding so romantic, y'know? Could be that it sets the bar a little high when it comes time for them to choose their own mates, don't you think? Like if they don't get a cosmic light show from God like their Mommy and Daddy had, how are they supposed to know if it's for real?"

"I didn't even think of that," Marty said

"But y'know what, Marty?"

"What?"

"That's what happened when I met Carly!"

Chapter Thirty-Seven

The convention became some kind of blur that went on around us. When Lucy arrived, I didn't know what to do with her. I didn't know what to say to her. I knew I had just met my wife.

I don't think Lucy had come with any thoughts of reconciling with me, but still, it seemed hard for her to see me in this awkward situation. We all did our best.

For the most part, Carly and I avoided the larger group and huddled together in a small, mud hut called The Hobbit Hole. Nestled safely within the ageless beauty of snow and mountain, we courted, we wooed, and we traded life stories. We made love, slowly, like we had found each other, again. Didn't want to make any mistakes. We called it "the awesome all rightness."

On the other hand, neither of us was really prepared to have a relationship. She had just broken loose from her first marriage and wanted to taste the wind for a while. She said she wasn't interested in getting involved. Although she denies it to this day, I remember her saying, "Don't get hung up on me. I burn through things fast."

I knew I was breaking up with Melody. I too was looking forward to the freedom of being out of a relationship. I claimed I wanted to fuck around without all the jealousy wars.

Who was kidding who? God, the Universe, or Random Chance, had just presented us with the most precious gift either of us ever dreamed of receiving, and we were wondering whether we should give it back? Uh-uh. Despite our doubts and fears, that wasn't gonna happen.

The real question seemed to be who was going to pack up and move into whose house, or if we should just get a new house somewhere else altogether.

By the end of the convention, we didn't resolve it. We left it as a work in progress. For the moment, I would return to Berkeley as planned. Carly would come visit there soon.

Chapter Thirty-Eight
The Great Curveball

When we got back to Berkeley, it was the first week in December. The holiday season was upon us when I told Melody that I had just met my mate. I was braced for anything, but she was surprisingly gracious and said that she knew it would happen one day. Said she understood that we were never meant to be mates. It struck up a kindness in her like she was mentoring me. I thought it tender. I thought it sweet. It was as if she were walking the groom down the aisle and giving him away.

'Twas then that she dished up this big, sweeping curve ball and I swung full at it and missed by a mile.

She said that if Carly understood anything about women's liberation, she wouldn't expect Melody and me to break up until after the holidays.

This may take a little explaining. Back in the sixties, during the civil rights struggles and all the racial turmoil, one would frequently encounter this argument between a black and a white person. It would usually go like this: The white person would lay claim to understanding some aspect of something to which the black person would contradict by saying, "Unless your skin is black, you will never understand that." And it generally served very effectively to shut the white person up.

Point being here is when Melody said, "if Carly understood anything about women's liberation, she wouldn't expect Melody and me to break up until after the holidays," I took it as something about women's liberation that I just did not understand. Like a secret code, I just took it at face value. Besides, it didn't really matter whether Carly came to be with me in one week or three. We were gonna have the rest of our lives together, I thought.

So, when I called Carly, I said, "Melody says, 'Women's liberation! Don't come until after the holidays.'" Forgive me, Dear Lord, I thought I was making sense. Carly just said,

"Okay."

Chapter Thirty-Nine

Melody and I did not make it to Christmas. We entered a spell where we seemed to fight over everything including where to put the butter dish.

Our relationship ended during one argument that got so intense she plunged her fist through the pane of a glass door. There was a bad gash in her hand. It didn't slow down her arguing one bit. She continued proving her point, gesticulating wildly, sending blood everywhere. I knew we had to get to an emergency room.

I grabbed her and just held her tightly until she calmed down enough to understand that we had to get her to the hospital.

Soon after, I moved next door to another room of the commune that had just opened up.

Chapter Forty

When I called Carly, they said she went to Mexico with some guy. They didn't expect her to come back.

"What?"

They said that she went to Mexico with some guy. They didn't expect her to come back.

Chapter Forty-One

I felt like someone had put a bullet in my head. I went numb. January came and there was still no Carly. I got sick. It looked like the flu, but I knew it was heartbreak. I was sick all of January, all of February, and into March. It was a long time.

There was no word from Carly. Her people in Santa Fe got tired of me calling. It was like, "Get a life, man, she's not here. Snap out of it, dude, she don't wanta hear from you!"

There were other women interested in me at the commune in Berkeley, but I had Carly branded on my brain. I went through the motions a few times, but I didn't know what I was doing with another woman. I would tell them about Carly. These were some bad movies.

I thought about suicide, thought that I could, understand, suicide, if a person had to keep on feeling like this. I just didn't know how to turn the corner. I had met my life, I had met my wife, and somehow let them slip away. I cried a lot. It was a winter of despair.

I think it was ultimately the Spring that brought me back to life. The heat, the plants, the sun, it's just what Spring does. I had rejected suicide as an option because I refused to put my parents through that kind of agony. Period. Once that decision got made, it all became a matter of just trying to feel better, one step at a time.

It helped to reduce the drama by thinking of Carly as just another woman. There had already been a few in my life. I'd known rejection. I sought to put it all behind me as just another inglorious episode and move on.

I found myself in bed one night with one of the few women in the commune I hadn't had sex with yet. We were having one of those wrestling matches. Y'know, she said that she wanted to sleep with me, but she didn't want to have sex. Yeah, yeah, yeah, so we were wrestling about it. It was late at night. And there was a knock upon my door.

There stood Carly. She was by herself. She came to be with me.

The woman I was wrestling with quietly gathered up her things and left my room. She knew all about Carly. The whole commune did. I had been able to speak of little else for a long time.

I was happy to see her.

I was furious that she had run off for so long without any word.

Carly explained that when I had given her Melody's message about "women's liberation" and not coming until January, she thought it was my way of just getting rid of her.

I asked if she was in love with this other guy she had run off to Mexico with. She said that she didn't know what they had, but that she just had to see me again.

I was grateful.

I told her that I didn't mind sharing her love as long as there would be time for us to have what was ours.

With that, we began our life together.

Chapter Forty-Two

When I journeyed back to Santa Fe to be with Carly, I met the other guy. I kind of liked him. We weren't soul mates or anything, but he was all right. It made sense to me. I wouldn't have expected Carly to be hanging out with some dork.

That first night, the three of us went to bed together. I thought we were going to be a three-way marriage. I knew she was my wife and I was willing to find out who he was gonna be.

By the way, The Gomez Road Show, which was the name of this commune where Carly lived, had a revolutionary approach to bedrooms. Nobody "owned" one. All bedrooms were communal property. At bedtime, you just walked in and staked out your claim with whatever partner or partners you had in mind, and then you worked it out with whoever or whatever was to follow.

Wow! It sure served to stir the pot of the group's intimate relationships.

We had nothing like that going on in Berkeley. There was even a song that one of the Gomez Road Show guitar players wrote:

> *"All around the world,*
> *All the boys and girls*
> *Are playin', they're playin'.*
> *All around the world,*
> *All the girls and boys,*
> *They're sayin', they're sayin' …*
> *"Do what you want to do,*
> *Today …*
> *Go ahead …*
> *And play …*
> *With who …*
> *And when …*
> *You want to."*

Chapter Forty-Three

Looking back from these 500 years later, it's amazing to see what a burning issue we made back then of monogamy versus what we saw as our sexual freedom. For so many of us, it was HUGE.

As historians, we learn that ideas and events always happen within the context of other ideas and events. To a world that has been coping with the life threatening sexual plague of AIDS for several generations now, it may seem bizarre to try and understand the much less inhibited time of sexual revolution that was experienced by so many who came of age during the 1960s and the 1970s.

Back then, 1984 was still a book by George Orwell all about some totalitarian state far off into the distant future.

And back then, monogamy was on the way out. It seemed like an idea whose time had passed. Like colonialism and feudalism, it belonged to the world of yesterday. It may still have been something for our moms and dads, but not us.

People shouldn't own each other. People should be free. We were all about being free. Tie two birds together and neither can fly.

The popular access to birth control pills and the established cures for the previously life threatening diseases of syphilis and gonorrhea had truly rocked the world and gave us a sexual freedom beyond what any people had ever tasted before.

"Sex, drugs, and rock 'n roll."

The great demon of jealousy fed like an overstuffed firestorm on all the helpless chaos we provided it during this time.

And just as I had struggled with Lucy and Melody over these kinds of issues, I now struggled with Carly over the same.

Chapter Forty-Four

That night, the three of us went to bed together. I pushed for it. I wasn't looking for any clusterfuck stuff, I was thinking more like a your turn, my turn kind of thing.

I gave them room to go first, but Carly soon turned her attention to me and he got up and left. I made love to her that night the way a man makes love to his wife.

In the morning, the other guy was gone. It was appropriate. I won a war that I thought I had no intention of fighting. I had been willing to settle for just a share.

Chapter Forty-Five

Carly and I had to figure out how to live together. We agreed that we had to tell the truth to each other. We decided that fidelity in marriage would mean that we'd be faithful to telling the truth.

Monogamy was out. Neither one of us wanted monogamy. We were just in love with each other and we agreed to tell the truth and we would work all the rest out.

Chapter Forty-Six

With the Gomez Road Show deciding to close its doors in Santa Fe and all the members scattering in the wind, Carly and I moved back to Dragon's Eye in Berkeley and took a room together.

Our group was also in the process of falling apart. New waves of spirituality were passing through the great political and social youth movements that had brought so many of us together in the sixties. People were now becoming involved with a whole raft of new and ancient therapies and more personal searches for enlightenment. Berkeley seemed to become a place where you either had "the sickness" or you had "the cure."

No doubt, the "revolution" was over. Only the hardest of hardcore politicos seemed to soldier on. For the rest of us, we had been crushed. We were trying to heal. The "Left" seemed to be splintering and eating itself while the "Right" had just overwhelmingly gotten Richard M. "The Boogieman" Nixon elected to a second term.

The commune days with their endless hours of house meetings had become picky-picky in the extreme and just too depressing. They were passing out of vogue. It was a return to every man for himself or, every woman for herself, as the case may be. People were looking for the next big thing.

We, the people, "who had tuned in, turned on, and dropped out," were now looking for ways to drop back in.

About half of our group in Berkeley had become very disenchanted with life in the city. They argued that it was at odds with trying to live in a more spiritual way. They wanted to move us all up to Humboldt County, a rural area, way North of San Francisco and replant the flag there.

I'd visited up there once. I took some psychedelic drug and tripped on a mountaintop waiting to hear from God. I was not disappointed.

God said that he was surprised to see me up there. "There's a whole lot of rattlesnakes around here," He said. "It's not really much of a "people" place and there's no good pizza anywhere. It's at least a two-hour ride to the nearest movie theater and you're probably gonna have to learn how to raise and slaughter your own animals if you want to keep on eating meat. Why don't you just get your ass back to Berkeley," He said paternally. It wasn't really a question.

Chapter Forty-Seven

Carly got interested in sex therapy.

Beginning with the publication of what became the 1966 bestseller *Human Sexual Response*, William Masters and Virginia Johnson emerged as internationally known authorities on human sexuality. Inheriting the mantel once worn by Albert Kinsey in the 1950s, they pioneered further research into the physiology of sex and developed diagnoses and treatments for sexual disorders.

They used to joke that they had the most popular, least-read bestseller in history. People would buy it expecting there to be "juicy" parts and would become disappointed and stop reading when they discovered that it was really all quite clinical.

Carly became involved with a group of therapists and others who were both studying and applying some of this new information. More specifically, she became a psychology intern at a clinic on the UC Berkeley campus, using women's therapy groups as a way of treating what they referred to as pre-orgasmic women.

Chapter Forty-Eight

In recent years, the great porn legend Nina Hartley and I (as Richard Pacheco) have joined forces to do a number of performances together on college campuses.

The show we do, called *Backstage with the Porn Stars*, was initially organized and produced by my daughter Polly as an AIDS Fundraiser at the University of Southern California. Since then, we have performed it at Stanford, UC Berkeley, and UCLA.

I like to open that show by first giving "a gift" to the audience. As

I tell the audience, it might not mean that much to some of them, but for others, it might just offer the keys to the kingdom.

The Gift

Years ago, when I was still courting the woman who would one day become my wife and the mother of my children, she was studying sex therapy techniques.

One day, she came home and said that she had just learned some interesting sex therapy exercises. She asked, if I would I like to try one.

"Well, sure," I told her, feeling very much like a young man who was about to get laid or some variation thereof.

"The first one," she explained, "is called Sensate Focus." It involved non-genital pleasuring. One partner agreed to do the pleasuring and the other agreed to be done to. The one that was receiving the pleasure was bound to accept only that which really felt good.

Okay, without a lot of fanfare, we decided that she'd get pleasured first and I'd do the pleasuring. I would give her a back rub.

I was touching this woman, a woman that I loved, by the way, for less than thirty seconds, I would say, when I started to feel this anger rising in me. "Fuck this!" I thought. I didn't want to do this! I always did this! It got so intense that I didn't want to fake it. It occurred to me at that moment, that I had been touching women like this for what seemed like all my life, in the hopes that, maybe, just maybe, they would touch me back! I had a ton of anger connected to this. It scared me. And it scared her. We had to stop. We had to back off.

Somehow, the subtlety of it all being an exercise instead of just real life had allowed me to see my own feelings. I think we went to bed without any more touching that night and it was at least the next day before she asked, "Want to try another one?"

This time around, we just switched parts. She'd pleasure me. She skipped the non-genital part and went right to sucking my dick. I think that after the trauma of that first exercise she was just trying to get us reconnected, but it didn't have that effect.

Maybe I was just scared because of what had happened earlier, but I couldn't feel anything. There she was sucking my dick and it all felt very, very far away. This was wrong. This was very wrong. I couldn't feel any pleasure! And that frightened me. What I felt was so much fear that I started trembling. I literally started shaking, and then I just popped! I broke out in tears. And the tears, were very young.

And what I was thinking, what occurred to me at that moment, was that nobody in my life, not my mommy, not my daddy, not any teachers, not any doctors, not any clergy, not nobody in authority, had ever said to me in my whole life, that it was okay to experience sexual pleasure.

I tell those college students that I came of age in a time when having sex meant marrying. And if you were doing sexual things and you weren't married, well, you were stealing, you were sinning, you were cheating, and it wasn't okay. And I never knew I felt all that. I never knew all that was even in there. And I had this cry and it was delicious.

"And the gift that I'm giving to you today," I tell them, "… is that I'm going to count to three … and then I want us all to say …

'It's okay for me to experience sexual pleasure.'"

You can sing along at home if you want to.

"One, two, three …

'IT'S OKAY FOR ME TO EXPERIENCE SEXUAL PLEASURE!'"

Good luck to all of you.

Chapter Forty-Nine

While Carly began learning about therapy, I got involved with theater.

I was playing softball one day. It was a typical Berkeley kind of game. Both men and women played. There was a jug of wine on first base and marijuana on both second and third. If you hit the ball over the fence, you were out. The object of the game was anything but competition. I was playing catcher. When I gathered up some dog poop and put it on home plate to discourage the other team from scoring, the pitcher called me out to the mound.

"You ought to think about auditioning for The Magic Theatre," he said. He explained that he was an actor there and thought I might fit in nicely. What he didn't tell me at the time was that he was queer as a three-dollar bill and when he looked at my ass, he thought he might fit in there nicely.

In any case, acting seemed like a good idea. I'd always had a flair for it, so why the hell not!

There were a lot of people there that day when I went in to audition for The Magic Theatre. As I entered the room, a woman shrieked and shouted out my name. "HOWIE GORDON!" She said. It was loud enough to be all capital letters. That, my friends, was truly amazing! I felt like one of the Beatles!

People looked at me quizzically. I could feel the buzz of them turning to each other, "Who's Howie Gordon?"

"What?"

"Who's he?"" It didn't matter that I was nobody. I was already walking on air.

As it turned out, the young lady who screamed was from my hometown of Pittsburgh. Not only that, she had gone to the same high school as me. When I was the Senior Class President, she was two years younger than me in the tenth grade. She said that she'd had an enormous crush on me and when I walked through that door, she just screamed.

Chapter Fifty

– Gordon Archive

About to go on a gender bender.

"I did that, y'know," God said.

"Well, I would guess so!" I told Him. "It seemed so extraordinarily specific! Who else could even begin to dream up something like that?"

"I wanted to give you a false sense of security."

"It worked!" I told Him. "You know it did. I kicked ass in that audition. I got the part!"

"Yeah," He said. "I know. I wanted to see if you could be any good as a homosexual."

"But my character wasn't gay," I told Him.

"I didn't mean in the play," He said.

Chapter Fifty-One

It was a one-act called, *Auto-Destruct* written by Jeff Wanshell. I was the Fourth Mexican. It was a cartoon cowboy exercise in black humor. Three American bank robbers of the Old West escaped and hid out in Mexico where they were terrorized and humiliated by farcical stereotypes of the local banditos. "We don't need no stinkin' badges!"

I was now in the theater. This began my gay period, or at least bi-sexual if you want to be accurate.

Our play had an all-male cast and was being performed on Friday and Saturday nights at Mid-night. One of our lead actors, the one who played the big macho role of the bandit chief, "El Jefe," was Joel, the gay pitcher who had first suggested I try out for The Magic Theatre. He was a good guy and a very talented actor. He took the time to teach me a lot of things. One of them was how it felt to be fucked in the ass.

Chapter Fifty-Two

"What is it with you and all this ass fucking?" Marty the agent asked. "You fuck Melody in the ass. Joel fucks you in the ass. I don't get it! Look, it's very simple! It's not complicated at all. The ass is an "out" valve. Things are supposed to come out of your ass. Any plumber will tell you that! You got a screw loose, you know that? Besides, you think you're gonna go on *Oprah* and talk about ass fucking like you did at UCLA? You're lucky they didn't expel your son!"

"Shut up, Marty," I told him. "I'm trying to write."

Chapter Fifty-Three

Bi-sexuality was like "the new thing" for a while in the early seventies. At least in the Berkeley world where I lived, it became a weird kind of politically correct.

Alright, it was a *Brave New World* out there to me, but I had some questions. I could get in the game. My first one was about cock sucking.

"I'm leaving," Marty said. "I'm walking out the door."

"G'bye, Marty."

When it came to cock sucking, it was unsettling to me that I could ask a woman to do something that I found so repugnant. I mean, beyond the obvious homophobia, it seemed wrong. How could I do that? These were the days of experimenting, so, I experimented. When the opportunity presented itself, I gave it a shot.

You know what? Feh! And I didn't even get to the swallowing part. The hell with that. Bottom line is having an occasional popsicle is about as far as I wanted to go in that direction.

I just ended up being a lousy queer. I was completely non-orgasmic. My first lover didn't care; though, he just wanted to plow my field and plant his seed.

"Again with the ass-fucking!" Marty said.

"You still here?" I asked him. "I thought you were leaving."

"I'm walkin' out the door."

When Joel was fucking me that first time, well, he was plain just getting carried away with his own passion. Bam! Bam! Bam! And he was not a small man either. It hurt! Pinned to the bed, I was like twisting my head around and saying, "Hey! HEY! There's somebody in here, y'know?? Take it easy, pal! Slow down!"

Men! What are you gonna do with them!

When it was over, that is, after he came, I felt like I understood how a mountain felt after they dug a tunnel in it. Yoi! And I thought that every man should know that feeling, at least once. If he had any kind of common sense at all, it would change forever the way he would touch a woman for the rest of his life.

In fairness to gay lovers everywhere, my sex with men never got beyond the novelty act stage with me. I was never in love with a guy. I was never really trying to please him. It was all more like an exercise in physical mechanics, like I was learning how to drive a stick shift. I was lucky enough to be with some guys who were truly hot for me, but my own arousal would only go so far. It seemed like a guy would be sucking my dick forever and I'd be stuck behind closed eyelids, running through my catalog of naked women, and trying unsuccessfully to make myself come. Double Yoi! It was so frustrating on way too many levels.

What was also telling was that Carly remained completely amused by all of these episodes. We'd already hit a fair share of jealousy bumps when I'd have sex with another woman, but none of these guy things ever fazed her in the least. If anything, she enjoyed the stories I would tell when I came home. It amused her.

Eventually, I just stopped it with the men. Enough already, experiment over. The end results were that It had been like taking my brain and making popcorn out of it. It brought me far more confusion than it was ever worth.

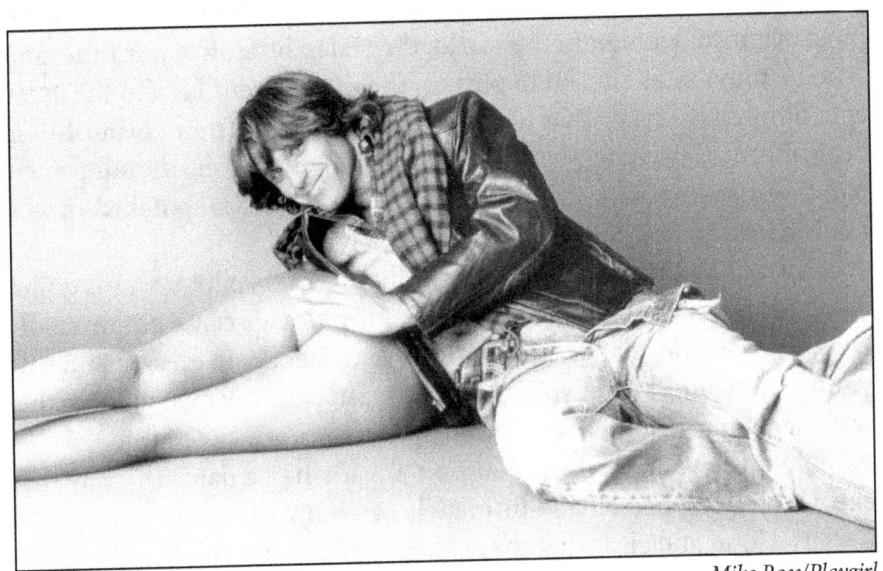

– Mike Ross/Playgirl

I was wired for plump female buttocks.

Chapter Fifty-Four

What made me crazy, what I couldn't understand, what totally discombobulated me, was, that after I'd met the love of my life, and knew unmistakably that she was the love of my life, and after I had moved in with the love of my life, how could I possibly find myself getting distracted, yet again, by some other woman?

How? Tell me how! This wasn't "happily ever after!" This wasn't the way it was supposed to be! After finding Carly, I didn't want to be feeling feelings like this anymore! This was a nightmare in the afternoon.

Carly and I had gone to some hot springs somewhere in the countryside of Santa Fe, or maybe it was in the hills of Santa Cruz. It was a friend's house or a public place, I don't remember that either, but we were in a hot tub. It was a naked place. Another couple joined us there. I don't remember who he was, but she might as well have been Julie Christie. She wasn't, I'm pretty sure, but she was a dead ringer, right down to the blue eyes and the British accent. And she was sitting naked with her blonde pubic hairs right across from me in a hot tub. Oh, Jesus!

This is embarrassing. I hate to even write this. It makes me sound like such a doofus, but, dear friends, I lost my mind.

I was completely in love with Julie Christie. I thought she was the most beautiful woman in the world, the Helen of Troy of our time. She was the movie star chosen to portray the magnificent Lara in the great epic film, *Dr. Zhivago*. No woman had ever looked more beautiful or been more passionate. Probably an entire generation of young men had fallen in love with her, but it fell on me to be sitting naked in this hot tub next to her doppelganger. I was a goner.

It was like I had a number of conflicting auto-pilot systems going off all at once. Number one, all of my male plumage came out immediately. Every smile, glance, and flitting eye contact between me and this young lady said, "I want you." And this wasn't just my dick talking; this was the whole general assembly.

Now, the young lady in question already had a date. The way that she was draping herself and intimately caressing the man she was with declared loud and clear that they were together. As a result, all my flirting had to go into a stealth mode so that she could see it and he could not. That was not an easy thing to do!

And, oh, yeah, I'm sitting there with my new "wife," who I've just been introduced to by God, and with whom I've just taken a vow of complete honesty!

Y'see, I have this one alarm system going off which is trying to hide my feelings from Carly. And on the other hand, I have a new system of trying not to be hiding these things from Carly, even though I am still trying to hide everything from the guy who's with Julie Christie.

See? It's getting complicated. I wonder if they are married? Does it make any difference?

If I was a robot, this was the moment where smoke would've started coming out of my ears and I would've been grinding slowly to a halt. My speech would've become slurred and the lights in my eyes would've started flickering and fading. I was getting stupider, crazier, and dumber by the moment.

Luckily, for me, I was with Carly. She took me by the hand and said, "Let's go." We left that place and didn't look back. I think she saved my life.

Chapter Fifty-Five

Auto-Destruct proved to be a prophetic title. After the run of the play, The Magic Theatre folded in Berkeley. In some kind of political coup, Artistic Director John Lion dismissed the entire rebellious ensemble of actors and moved the theater's operation to San Francisco.

Among the casualties of Lion's move to The City, were John O'Keefe and Bob Ernst. They were two high-powered theater people who had come to the Magic from the University of Iowa to stage John's play, *Jimmy Beam*. It had been the featured show. *Auto-Destruct* was the Midnight companion piece, the clear B-side. The two shows had had the same run. When the theater folded, John and Bob took over the Magic's Berkeley warehouse space and started teaching classes. I spent the next couple of years taking courses from them. Carly took some too. We did a lot of movement work, voice, and focused primarily on experimental theater techniques.

These guys were like the Marines Corps of acting, Navy Seals. They worked hard and they worked their students hard. The time I spent as their student amounted to the only formal training I ever really had as an actor.

It was also during this time that John and Bob joined with their fellow Iowa Theater Lab cofounder David Schein and created the Blake Street Hawkeyes.

Carly and I became Hawkeye groupies and they became family. I did a lot of video work shooting the Hawkeyes. I shot both their group performances and their solo shows. Carly served on their Board of Directors.

In the world of underground theater, the Hawkeyes garnered a large cult following for themselves and became an honored Bay Area institution. A wealth of fine actors and writers came and went with the group that included Cynthia Moore, Whoopi Goldberg, George Coates, Mary Forcade, Deborah Gwynn, Jim Cave, Mark Gordon, Michael O'Brien, Kim Bent, Ellen Sebastion Chang, Jack Carpenter, and Pons Maar.

Chapter Fifty-Six

It was time for me to see if I could earn a living as an actor. I registered with agencies and began going out on auditions.

I landed a part in a supper club in Oakland called 1520 AD. A Brit, who had made his fortune selling washing machines back in merry olde England, was backing the venture. It was cute dinner theater, franchised like a Chucky Cheese. There were already 1520 AD restaurants operating in several American cities.

When you walked in the front door, you entered the great dining hall of King Henry VIII. The show was a Disneyland kind of revue that happened all around you as the actors and waiters performed whilst you were seated and supped upon your choice of a standardized roast beef or a Cornish game hen platter. The food was mediocre, at best, the show was too.

I was cast as the Court Poet. It was my primary job to write and distribute souvenir scrolls for the dinner guests as if they were edicts issued from the King. My history degree stood me in good stead as I was able to ape the flowery language of the day. In addition, I also performed in some of the ensemble routines.

They started me out working for them in Oakland, but within a week, management wanted to promote me to the flagship operation in Hollywood. I got stars in my eyes. I was being discovered. It was all happening pretty fast. I told Carly that I would go down there and get established. And when I had it figured out, she could come on down and move in with me. I made damned sure that she understood that this was not my way of getting rid of her.

I lasted about a week in Hollywood. I couldn't figure out Hollywood at all. I did not speak the language. It was as different from the Berkeley of that era as a place could be. The "Revolution" had just bypassed Hollywood. My flea market clothes didn't cut it. In Berkeley, I was cool. In Hollywood, I was a vagrant. My alienation factor was pretty high. Every day, the fever seemed to go up a couple of notches.

The company had put me in a seedy hotel with cracked walls and spider webs. I didn't know anybody in Southern California and I didn't have a car. Among the actors and actresses at work, I did not make any friends. It seemed like all we did was compete with each other for more lines and center stage. In fact, all of Hollywood seemed like that to me. It was like one giant competition for a toilet paper commercial. It was all wrong for me, the wrong time, and the wrong place.

Fuck it. After a week, I quit the job and returned to Berkeley with my tail between my legs. I forgot all about a career in acting.

Chapter Fifty-Seven

There was a big, heavy, sliding door to the bedroom I shared with Carly in the Green House in Berkeley. When I slid that big, heavy door open one afternoon, there was Carly standing there in the embrace of a tall, handsome man. He had one of his hands down the front of her pants. Oops!

Oh, I did not want to be seeing that. I slid the door closed and went looking for a safe place to be. There really wasn't any. That was my room.

Another time, there was this party to which Carly and I had both been invited. I don't remember what was going on between us, but I somehow had gotten myself into the place where I wanted to try and find some other woman to have sex with me that night, and I told Carly so. Okay, we decided that we'd travel to the party together, but would probably leave with different partners.

We parted ways after arriving and we each went about our own business. Around midway through the evening, Carly found me. She said that her first choice was to go home with me, but if I still wanted to be with someone else, well, she had found a guy and she was ready to leave, now. What did I want to do?

Who knows what I really wanted? I don't remember, but I told her to go ahead. I'd see her tomorrow. We said our goodnights.

Unfortunately for me, I happened to catch a glimpse of Carly as she was leaving the party with her new lover. He was this big, Black guy. Oh, I did not want to be seeing that.

I had sex with three different women that night, in three different scenes, and I enjoyed absolutely none of it. I could not get the picture of Carly leaving the party with that guy out of my brain. I would have joined the Ku Klux Klan that night, that is, if they were taking any Jews as members.

Why did we do things like that to each other? Why did we do things like that to ourselves?

Looking back, I was usually the one who would shut down the intimacy between us and go out seeking another sex partner. And Carly, my beloved, turned out to be very smart about taking care of herself in such moments. She did not choose to sit home alone in victimness and feel sorry for herself. She would take the opportunity to go find another lover of her own and would then match me tit for tat. And as you may already have gotten the hint, I could get pretty lost in the great maw of jealousy myself.

"So why put myself through it?" you ask and that would be a damn good question.

Well, there was all that talk about being part of the free love generation and all, but, y'know what? That stuff all fell off pretty quickly once the bleeding started.

A truer answer might be that if I wanted to fuck around—and Lord knows I did—then I had to be willing to accept the fact that she could fuck around too. It wasn't complicated. Fair was fair. It was to be the price tag I paid for all the extra pussy I wanted. If I wanted a Japanese one, a Chinese one, a Black one, or an acrobat, a singer, or a dancer – and I did – I wanted them all, I didn't want to miss out on anything. If I wanted all the extra cookies in my sex life, then I had to be willing to offer up all the same to her in return. That was the logic and that was the contract, at least in my mind. But me being able to honor it, to live up to it, well, that was proving to be something else entirely. Jealousy was a motherfucker.

All right, I'm not giving away any surprise endings here by telling you that Carly and I are still together. As of this moment, we're in our sixties, and we have somehow managed to live through all of that shit and more. We've been together for forty years. We've raised three extraordinary kids. And we're still trying to figure out exactly what happened and why it all had to unfold the way that it did.

You watch the Discovery Channel. You watch National Geographic. You know that some creatures mate for life, right? Why there's the shingleback skink and there are the whooping cranes. Female gorillas are always monogamous with the silverback of their troupe, but that's only until a younger male takes over. I guess all of God's creatures have to negotiate sometime.

"Don't drag me into it," God said. "I'm just trying to figure out this Facebook thing."

Grey wolves, termites, coyotes, barn owls, beavers, bald eagles, golden eagles, condors, swans, brolga cranes, French angelfish, sandhill cranes, pigeons, prions (sea birds), red tailed hawks, anglerfish, ospreys, prairie voles, and black vultures have all figured out how to be monogamous. Why couldn't I?

The great man was Paul Newman, who said of his wife, "When you have steak at home, why would you go out for hamburger?"

But the great man was also Zorba the Greek, who said, "The only sin in life is when a woman calls a man to her bed and he refuses to go."

I wanted to be both of those guys. I wanted the life of Casanova and the happily-ever-after of married romance at the same time. I tried like Hell to make that work.

Chapter Fifty-Eight

Shortly after Carly and I had taken a room together at what remained of the Berkeley commune, my parents came out to California for a visit. The word "commune" had bothered them. In Pittsburgh, Pennsylvania, the media seemed to always use it to conjure up images of mass murderer Charles Manson, drug addicts, teen-age runaways, and the darker side of hippie life.

Bless 'em, my parents had to see for themselves that their youngest son was all right.

I was all right. It was a good visit. They liked Carly. In fact, they loved Carly. That was the best part. And they saw that we were "safe."

At one point, I got to spend some time alone with my father. I was twenty-four years old. He was fifty-seven.

"Dad," I told him something like, "I feel like I hardly know you at all. I want to know more about you as a person. I want to know more about your life. I want to know how you and Mom have managed to stay married all these years." I was so full of shit. I had no idea what I was talking about.

... 'cuz we started talking, my Dad and I, and before long, he was telling me all about this hooker that he and one of my Mom's older brothers had been seeing together on the side, and my ears stopped working.

It was like his lips were still moving, but I wasn't hearing him anymore. The part of me that was my mother seemed to just go off. "Why, you son of bitch! You piece of shit! You fucking scumbag! How dare you! Who do you think you are?"

Mercifully, these were all just silent love songs playing in the quiet of my own head and not screaming judgments that I was raining down upon my actual father. Apparently, I was not able to extend to him the great benefits of the sexual revolution that I enjoyed for myself.

"Dad, Dad, ya know what?" I stopped him. "This is all wrong. I can't do this. Let's just go back to you're my Dad and I'll always love you, all right? Okay? Okay?"

We never spoke of it again.

And before we jump on the obvious and start blaming my poor daddy for having passed on this promiscuous appetite, it should be pointed out that this same man also sired my older brother, who has proven to be about as monogamous as humanly possible.

Whether it's nature or nurture, the truth seems to be that some men and some women are programmed for monogamy. Carly's parents certainly were. It's near impossible to imagine that either of them had ever had another partner. And Carly grew up knowing that one man and one woman could indeed be enough for each other. I'm not sure what I grew up with, but it definitely wasn't a predilection for monogamy.

I seem to have spent a lifetime wrestling with these issues. I wouldn't badger you with them if they were not so critical in understanding how a guy like me could end up in the X-rated business. You see, for a while there, me being a porn star actually made it a lot easier for Carly and me to be married, but I get ahead of myself.

I've heard two very sane things about jealousy in my life that I think worthy of passing on to you. The first one came from Sherri.

Sherri, along with her husband and kid, all lived with Carly and the others at the Gomez Road Show in Santa Fe. Sherri was gorgeous. To an outsider like me, it seemed like there was always a long line of fellows looking to have a turn with Sherri. Anyway, she did what she did; I didn't really get too deep into her story. She did, however, make one observation that has stayed with me for a lifetime. Sherri is reported to have once said about conquering jealousy,

"You can get yourself to the point where you don't care anymore if your lover wants to be with somebody else, but then, you *don't care anymore!*"

And the other sane observation about jealousy came from Steve Gaskin, a well-known counterculture figure of the 1960s, who co-founded The Farm, a famous spiritual community in Tennessee.

In the early days of their collective, the group practiced a sexual freedom that included open marriages. After a time, however, they reverted back to more traditional unions.

When asked why, Gaskin answered, "Because it (sexual freedom in marriage) makes us crazy faster than we can get sane."

Chapter Fifty-Nine

You live and you learn. Carly and I made lots of changes over the years in order to traumatize each other less and to help give our love a fighting chance. Mostly, they were like a series of little steps, taken one by one.

For instance, the upshot of that sliding door episode where I had stumbled in upon Carly and that guy making out in our bedroom was that we declared our bedroom to be a mutual safety zone. Henceforth, we would only "be" with each other in that room so that neither of us would ever have to endure being surprised like that again. The safety zone was eventually expanded to become the whole house of wherever we were living. That was a good rule.

And Rebecca taught us that there could be no more love affairs.

I first met Rebecca at the Magic Theatre. She was one of three incredible women starring in John O'Keefe's play, Jimmy Beam. John O'Keefe is a man of many extraordinary talents, not the least of which is an ability to hook up with amazing women. For a time, he and Rebecca were an item at the theater. When their affair died of its own natural causes, I flirted with the young diva. Surprisingly, she opened the gates for me. I didn't know what I was getting myself into. I was playing with fire. One thing led to another.

This was not a one-night stand. This was not a casual fling. This was another whole galaxy with another leading lady. It was not the burning bush, but it had a gravitas all its own. I fell in love here.

Carly and I had our cage severely rattled. It was not an easy time. There was a brief period where the only peace of mind I had left was on the Bay Bridge as I traveled between their beds in Berkeley and San Francisco. I thought for a while there that I might have two wives. It got so crazy that Carly said she was willing to give such a thing a try. Rebecca scoffed at the idea.

When the situation finally forced a choice, I chose Carly. At that level, it had been Carly all along.

Carly and I got married on April 9, 1975.

The rule we made was "no more love affairs." There could be a space made for a one-night stand kind of thing, a night out with the boys or girls, as the case may be, but no more regular lovers, no more second, third, or fourth fucks. The experience with Rebecca had taught us to stay away from those kinds of affairs. If we were going to stay married to each other, then those kinds of relationships weren't really going to be fair to anybody.

Chapter Sixty

I wanted to make a big gesture to Carly. Our relationship had just been shaken, but we had survived. I wanted her to feel some sense of the commitment I learned I had to her. Besides that, almost everyone I knew had been married and divorced, including Carly. I wanted the chance to have been married in my life too. I wanted to stand before the world and say, "This is the one." This last love affair had been tough on us. I wanted to relight the candle. When I proposed marriage, Carly accepted.

We were married at dawn on the front lawn of the Berkeley cottage where we lived. We planned an event with a sword dance introduction, followed by a comic monologue, and then a wedding ceremony in three acts.

John O'Keefe was going to do the sword dance, a kind of symbolic slaying of any evil spirits that happened to be lurking about. I was going to do the comic monologue. I thought it would be a Bob Hope kind of thing for our friends. For the wedding ceremony portion, Act I was culled from Adam & Eve in the garden, we would share an apple. In Act II, we would pay homage to our Jewish ancestors by sharing a glass of wine and then breaking the glass in the Hebrew wedding tradition. And the climactic Act III was to be a great leap into imagination and the grand gesture. We would strip ourselves naked and pour a bucket of hot water over our heads.

How did you guess Act III was my idea?

You see, when I get nervous, I mean, really nervous, I've often had this frozen feeling that my energy has somehow left my body and is hovering above my head. I know it sounds whacky, but on the day I was to be married, I knew that I'd be nervous. I wanted some way to feel like I was truly inside of my body. I figured between getting naked in the cold morning, dousing ourselves with hot water, and then with the hug that we'd be giving to each other in such a moment, I was hoping that I would be one hundred percent involved and present in my own body.

Carly didn't even blink. She was all for it.

We didn't sleep at all the night before we were married. Somewhere around three o'clock in the morning we were worrying that no one would be showing up at dawn for this wedding. Could still be married if nobody came? It really just looked like all we legally had to do was fill out the marriage license and mail it in. Bob Ernst was going to be our minister. We just needed our signatures, his, and one witness, I think.

But just to be sure, just in case nobody came, we went outside to our altar in the middle of the night and we married ourselves.

"Do you take—"

"Yeah. And do you?"

"Yeah."

"We now pronounce us, us. We may kiss each other." And we probably did a lot more than that, but it was okay, we were married.

At dawn, all our guests did show up. The yard was full. We even managed to wake up most of the people in the apartment building next door and they joined the wedding party by watching from their windows.

John O'Keefe changed his mind. He didn't want to do the sword dance. Bob Ernst didn't want to do it either. Fine. Cut the sword dance. Howie, do the monologue.

I didn't want to do the monologue. I was a lot more nervous than I ever dreamed I'd be. Facing marriage made me feel very humble all of a sudden. There would be no wise-ass Bob Hope monolog. Fine. Cut the monologue. Let's get 'em married!

Standing there on our homemade altar with Carly, I felt plugged into the spirit of 5,000 years of history. Marriage was a lot more serious than I ever anticipated.

Before we ate the apple, I reached into my pocket and pulled out this little stone. I don't remember where or how, but this little stone had somehow become totally symbolic of our great love. It seemed like we had been passing it back and forth to each other in our most tender moments for years. It just had to show up at our wedding. This time, I passed it to her.

– Tom Linney/Gordon Archive

We were getting married.

Our water bearer had poured very, very hot water thinking that it had to stand in the cold dawn for a long time before we'd get to it in the ceremony. Well, not much went according to plan. We positively flew through the apple and wine parts of the ceremony.

– Tom Linney/Gordon Archive

And in a blink, we were standing there naked.

– *Tom Linney/Gordon Archive*

When we poured the water on ourselves, it was scalding, it was shocking, and that, dear friends, seemed perfectly appropriate!

– *Tom Linney/Gordon Archive*

That hug was something special too!

– *Tom Linney/Gordon Archive*

That's it!

– *Tom Linney/Gordon Archive*

We were married!

Chapter Sixty-One
Our Wedding Night

Having stayed up all night before our dawn ceremony, we were in our bed and sound asleep by 6:00 p.m. of our wedding night. We slept all the way through it until the next day.

Chapter Sixty-Two
The Honeymoon

We sublet the little cottage we inherited from the commune and took off in Carly's VW bus. We had it in mind to spend a year going coast to coast telling loved ones and friends that we had married. We even thought we might cross the big pond to have a look-see at merry olde England.

We got as far as crossing over the San Francisco Bay Bridge and were just short of the airport when the car engine blew up. There was no explosion exactly, but we threw a rod and the engine had to be given last rites. We were ingloriously towed back to Berkeley. Our year-long honeymoon lasted less than two hours.

But Carly's parents, God bless 'em, came to our rescue. They bought us a brand new used engine for a wedding present and we were soon on our way down South to visit them in San Diego. They couldn't have been kinder.

In the great in-law lottery of married life, I truly lucked out. Carly's people are the best. Period.

After San Diego, we headed east. There were a few stops here and there before we landed at my parents' doorstep in Pittsburgh.

Nothing I have ever done in my life has brought more joy to my mom and dad than bringing Carly into their lives. In a word, she's been perfect.

Our wedding ceremony, on the other hand, did not receive such high praise. After viewing the video tape, my mother in particular had been less than amused by the whole hippie-dippy thing.

"If you want to sleep with that woman, in this house, " she said to me when she had me alone, "then you'll get married by a rabbi." She said that our ceremony wasn't "real."

Well, young and stupid as I was, them was fightin' words to me. I was all set to do battle with her, but when I later told Carly all about it, she just cut me off at the pass.

"Let's get married in Jewish," she said, "It'll be fun. It'll make your parents happy and I'd be glad to marry you in all the ways that there are to marry somebody."

Hmmm, I did pick the right woman!

So, we were married again. My mother bought us gold wedding bands. They replaced the genuine zirconium ones we'd gotten at Woolworth's for our first wedding. They'd been turning our fingers green anyway. This time, the ceremony was held in a rabbi's study on August 7 of the same year. It was relatively painless and it did bring great joy to my parents. Izzy was there too. That was great. And for many years to come, my parents were the only people who'd send us an anniversary card every year in August.

We never did make it across the Atlantic to England by the way. We only got as far New England where we stayed a while with our friends Peter and Phyllis and their three kids in Salem, Massachusetts. That was foreign enough.

Peter was the guy who originally had hired me out of college to come work in the poverty programs. He was now running a highly successful employment type non-profit in Boston. He thought he might have a good job to offer me as soon as some funding came through that he was expecting. We hung around. Carly ran a series of workshops in the area for mental health professionals to learn how to run groups for the treatment of "pre-orgasmic women."

Peter and Phyllis had bought one of those old sea captain's houses on Chestnut Street. Greyhound Bus Tours used to drive up and down the street. The house was huge. There was plenty of room for everybody. And it was quite a different life than we were used to in Berkeley, the main event being that we helped them out with their kids. Also, Peter and Phyllis were foodies. They were into fine wines, triple-cream cheeses and gourmet cooking on a daily basis. It was like we were in a training program for "the good life." We became a part of their larger family and were included in their circle of friends. After a lifetime in sunny California, Carly loved the New England winter with its deep snowfalls and nightly fires in the fireplace. And I began a long-time love affair with the YMCA.

It started with racquetball. Peter introduced me to the game.

He was a good ten years older than me, but stayed in excellent shape through a regimen of both running and racquetball.

During the first game we played together, the score was 3-2. That was competitive. He was ahead. Then, the score got to be 13-2. He leapt way ahead because I was tired, out of gas, and staggering. I had to call a time-out. Peter looked at me and laughed, "Welcome to middle age!" he said. "Use it or lose it."

He beat me like a drum that day and for the next six months to come before I won my first game. By then, my game skills were about as good as his and I had worked my body into excellent shape. After a brief spell or parity, I moved ahead and he never beat me again.

By that time, it had become clear that the expected funding that was supposed to provide me with that big job wasn't going to be happening. And after a year or so, Carly and I had grown nostalgic for friends and places and the life that we had left behind. It was time to come home to Berkeley.

Carly went back to her clinic and dove deeper into the therapy world beyond the sex stuff. She decided that she would pursue the credentials necessary to make her living as a therapist. I took a series of odd jobs wherever I could find them.

In the fall of 1977, I took the oddest job I ever had.

Part Two

– Gordon Archive

IN THE KINGDOM OF
THE DIRTY PICTURES

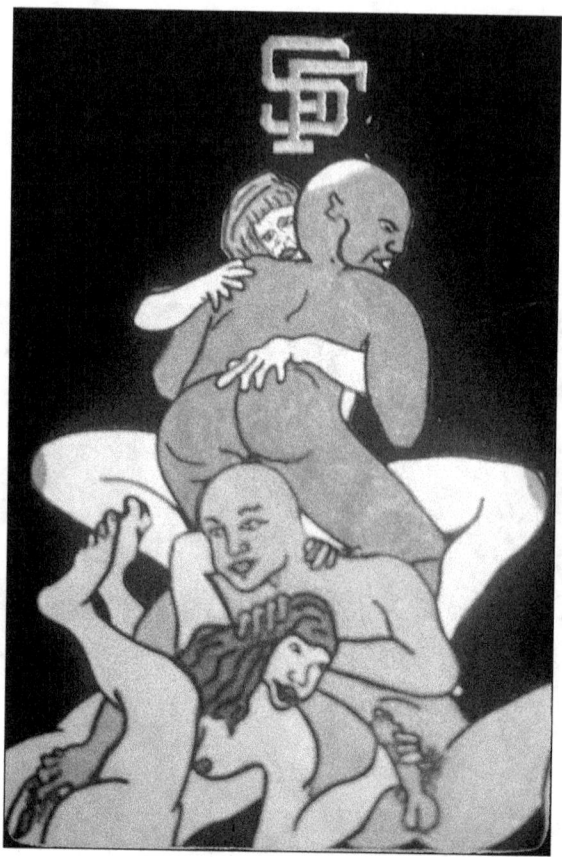

– Gordon Archive

San Francisco.

"I have great respect for San Francisco and for the experience shared by thousands who came there and for what the California experience meant to so many people of my generation. You went there to be free—-so that you could be gay, or you could be an intellectual, or you could be a poet, or you could be a hippie, or you could write pornography. You could do whatever you wanted, and I will always be grateful to San Francisco for giving me its particular kind of tolerance."

– Anne Rice, author
Conversations with Anne Rice
Michael Riley

Chapter One
Beginner's Schmuck

Let me tell you about my first movie.

The call came for my wife. Back when we were acting students with the Blake Street Hawkeyes, we'd met a few agents and gotten ourselves on some casting lists. This here was an agent calling with a feature film. He said that they were looking for women. As I was soon to learn, they were always looking for women.

Carly asked him to describe the film. He said it was "a fun-filled romp through a hospital."

"Is this a porno film?" she asked.

Temporarily disarmed by the complete directness of her question, he phumffed it and said, "Yes, it is."

I learned that agents normally tried not to spill the beans over the telephone. They had a much greater chance at success in casting if they could get the women to come on down to the auditions before they let them know it was going to be X-rated. Back then, it was much more difficult to find women who would act in porn, especially good looking ones. Even prostitutes looked down their noses at porn stars. They valued secrecy in practicing their trade. They didn't want to see their faces ten feet high on a movie screen or being plastered all over the sex magazines.

"I'm not interested," Carly told him, "but I think my husband would be," and she handed me the phone.

"Hello?"

Chapter Two

> *"Well, I try my best*
> *To be just like I am*
> *But everybody wants you*
> *To be just like them*
> *They say sing while you slave and I just get bored*
> *I ain't gonna work on Maggie's farm no more."*
>
> – Bob Dylan,
> "Maggie's Farm"

My fantasy was to meet an X-rated woman. I thought there was such a thing.

It seemed to me that all of my sexual experiences up to that point had been about love. The sex had all come out of love relationships.

"I love you. I love you."

"I love you too. Let's fuck."

As some of you older folks may remember from those looser days before AIDS, all of that sex with all of those lovers begat so much crazy jealousy that it made our heads spin. By now, I was ready for something else. I had my wife and I had all the love I needed. But sexually speaking, I wanted to explore something else.

I wanted to have a sexual experience that had nothing to do with love or relationship. I wanted some sex as "recreation" and I wanted one of those "bad" girls. Y'know, I didn't know any of those "bad" girls. I'd never been with a prostitute and I wanted to be with some kind of "fuck me—fuck me" woman that I thought was really out there, that I thought was real.

Lust, I was talking about lust. I didn't even know it. It was the awakening of the dirty little secret sexual desires that I hadn't even told myself yet. As a young husband, I had no idea how to ask my beloved wife to also be my willing "whore." It just seemed like the kind of madness that a man would rightfully take care of outside of the house and then would come home later with some candy and flowers and a lot of gratitude for his wife's tolerance.

Yeah, I wanted some of that kind of sex, some very, very selfish lust with a sex kitten, a "fuck me-fuck me woman." There'd be corsets and leathers, high-heeled boots laced up to crotchless panties, breasts spilling out of nippleless bras in lush red bordello bedrooms filled up with sex toys like blindfolds and vibrators, handcuffs and paddles. Yeah, there'd be me with a genuine tarted-up, "won't-say-'no,'" woman, all the best drugs and oils in the world, and plenty of time.

And there'd be no "I love you" in any of it. There'd be a thank you and close the door on your way out. Yeah, that's what I thought I wanted. And I had no idea how to tell my wife about any of that. So I didn't.

– Gordon Archive

Miss Martini.

She was right, though, when she handed me the phone for that X-rated audition. I was interested.

My fantasy was to meet an X-rated woman. I thought there was such a thing.

I would meet this X-rated woman at the hotel where they were holding the auditions for *The Candy Stripers*, and I would have sex with her right there in the hotel elevator. I don't know why, but that was the fantasy.

And then I would go home to my wife.

Chapter Three

There were a lot of women to choose from. There was this one, and that one, and another, but none of them jumped out right away as the right one.

The audition was at the Holiday Inn near Fisherman's Wharf. Larry the producer was the man in charge and a lot of people were moving in and out of his hotel suite.

"Fill out these forms," a woman mumbled my way and handed me a clipboard and a pen. "Here's a script," she said. "When it's your turn, you'll go into the bedroom and read for Larry."

                              STELLA
(Raises her skirt and sneaks some fingers into her vagina)
I have to come, George, you get me so hot.

                              GEORGE
Go ahead, baby, let me see you finger yourself.
Stick 'em in deep, baby, fuck yourself!

(GEORGE is furiously pumping his own cock. STELLA turns around and shows GEORGE her ass. She pokes a finger into her asshole.)

                              STELLA
You like when I show you my asshole, honey?

                              GEORGE
I'm gonna come, baby, I'm gonna come.

                              STELLA
Me too, just keep watching my asshole, darling.

    They took individual Polaroid pictures of the men in the living room. We kept our clothes on. The women were then invited to go into the bedroom to have their pictures taken. They would be undressing.
    We waited. When it came my turn to enter the bedroom, there was Eileen. I shook hands with Larry.
    "Eileen," Larry said, "would you mind staying to read with this young man?"
    "Not at all," she smiled kindly.
    "By the way, do we have your picture, honey?" Larry asked.
    "No," she said, "we didn't shoot it yet."
    "Let's get one," Larry said to his camera guy. "You mind stripping down?" he asked Eileen. "In fact, let's take a few."
    "No problem," she said and rose up to meet the task. They didn't ask me to leave. I was surprised and delighted. When she was naked, we all learned that she really was a blonde. Then Eileen made the cam-

eraman wait while she played with her nipples until they stood up hard for the photo. That was fun. She had obviously done this kind of thing before. I was impressed. I liked her. She had a nice smile. She had a great body. She was a natural blonde. Houston, I believe we have lift off! I definitely wanted to fuck her.

"Standing pose," said Larry. Click. "Now," he said, "lie down on the bed and spread 'em." She moved to the bed without a blink. Ooops, her Tampax string was sticking out. She poked it back within the folds of her vagina. Click. "Now, one more thing," Larry added. "Stand up, turn around, bend over, and pull your cheeks apart." Eileen did. "Just checking for hemorrhoids," Larry explained. "They can look as big as testicles on film." Eileen passed her hemorrhoid test.

"Okay, thank you, honey," Larry said. "You can get dressed now."

We played the George and Stella scene. It was awkward at best. Not everyone can talk dirty. And I was a long way from realizing that there is a world of difference between personal sex and professional sex.

"Very good for a first reading," Larry said rising from his chair and extending his hand for me to shake. I stood up and shook it. No mistake, I was being dismissed. "We'll call you in a few days if we're going to use you," he said and turned his attention back to Eileen. There was nothing for me to do but leave.

Standing alone in the hallway, I nonchalantly let about seven or ten elevators come and go while waiting for Eileen to emerge. When she finally did come out and approached the elevator, I acted like I had just gotten there myself. We boarded the next empty car together.

If life were a porno film, Eileen and I would have ripped off our clothes and done a scalding hot sex scene right there in that elevator that would have made both the fictional Stella and George blush. But the Holiday Inn at Fisherman's Wharf only had three floors to begin with and our elevator was already on the second. My fantasy wasn't gonna happen. It was time to move on to Plan B.

"Can I offer you a ride home?" I asked her.

"I have my car here," she said.

"Ding!" rang the bell as we hit the lobby floor. As the door started to open I managed to blurt out,

"You want to go play with me?"

She looked at me and said, "I knew you were gonna ask!"

"Well, yeah, I'm askin'," I said

"Well, all right," she said, "follow me home."

She drove in her car, I drove in my car, and we got to her house. And as soon as we got to her house, she started talking. Well, she was talking, and talking, and talking, and I don't know what happened to "Stella" and "George," but they sure didn't make it back to the apartment with us. They must've made a wrong turn somewhere.

And she was talking. I kept waiting for the "fuck me-fuck me woman" to show up, but she just kept right on talking. And I realized that this was just another person! There was no X-rated woman. It was a delusion. She's got a kid. She's got a life. She was nice enough. I took some pictures with my still camera. She was posing. We touched a little bit. There was zero passion going on between us.

Eventually, the alarm was going off in my wedding ring and I figured it was time to go home for dinner. And I excused myself and went home, a wiser man.

Well, the problem was they called me up two days later and offered me a part in their movie!

Oh!

It was $200 a day for two days work. Day one would be getting a blow job and day two would be taking part in an orgy. Did I want the job?

Chapter Four

"When you come to a fork in the road, take it."
– Yogi Berra

It was the mid-seventies, and all of the dropouts were looking for ways to drop back in. When that phone call for the X-rated audition came along, I was working as a laborer and house painter for a friend's mother out in Walnut Creek. Specifically, I had spent that day in a hot August sun, breaking up a long cement path with a sledgehammer.

Mary used to buy run-down houses, give them an upscale makeover, and then resell them for big bucks. I had become her main foot soldier in the great army of the "half-tusk," the shade of off-white she chose for all of her painting needs.

It had begun a year earlier when Mary had daughter Karen bring out the whole commune for a day's work in the early stages of one of those makeovers. There must have been twenty-three, twenty-four of us hippies running around doing various jobs under her watchful eye. When she paid us at the end of the day, she fired everybody but me. She said they were useless, but that I showed a little talent. I could come back tomorrow if I wanted. It was five bucks an hour and she promised that she'd work my ass off.

Mary and I were a good match. To begin with, I had been struggling financially since I moved to California and I very much welcomed a steady job. She taught me how to paint. And I would get damn near snow blind trying to distinguish between the second and third coats of half-tusk white that she would require on just about everything. Mary taught me the grace of hard work. And I very much took to that. It filled me with a very sane satisfaction to do a job right and make her happy. It gave me a gentle peace to come home from work feeling like I'd earned my tired. And it restored my confidence that I might actually be able to be a grown up and be able to pay my own way in this world.

My salary went from $5 an hour to $7.50 when Mary started lending me out to her friends, but it just wasn't the same after that. That kind of work wasn't particularly special to me. It had been my relationship with Mary. I knew that a significant episode of my life was coming to an end. It was time for me to look to the future and see what was up for next.

I applied to the Episcopal Theological Seminary (ETS) at Harvard. A friend of mine had gone there and shared that it was a great place to study history, which was one of my passions.

Likewise, I applied to the Hebrew Union Seminary, a rabbinical school in Cincinnati for largely the same reason. I could see myself becoming a rabbi, but I didn't really want to have a congregation. I just thought I might want a graduate school opportunity to study some more history.

And then, of course, I got the offer to play the part in a porno movie.

ETS responded first. They rejected me. They said while it was true in the past that they had accepted non-Episcopal students for various postgraduate level studies, this year they were focusing on accepting only applicants who were seriously committed to becoming Episcopal ministers. And thank you very much.

A tough choice remained: rabbi? porn star? handyman?

As it turned out, I soon learned that the first two years of the rabbinical school program would have required me to move to Jerusalem to study Aramaic. Boy, was that ever a wrong number. No thanks.

Then, getting the offer of $200 for a blow job on the same day that I had just been paid $5 an hour for breaking up concrete with a sledgehammer, well, that really helped make my decision.

I'd be trading four days of backbreaking labor for one blow job. And when you threw in another four days hard labor for one orgy, well, it seemed like a good time to move on from being a handyman.

I'm sure there were hundreds of good reasons not to put myself in a porno movie, but ya know what? I couldn't think of any of 'em.

Bring on *The Candy Stripers*! The fat kid is gonna be a sex star!

Chapter Five

> *"Life is trouble, only death is not. To be alive is to unbuckle your belt and to look for trouble!"*
>
> – Nikos Kazantzakis,
> Zorba the Greek

It was two weeks before my first scene in the movie. I was to play Dr. Bishop getting a blow job in a closet from one of the nurses.

Okay. I did my sit-ups. I did my push-ups. My body was spectacular. I had my lines down. But I soon get to thinking:

You can learn your lines. You can do your sit-ups, but there is no way in God's universe you can promise that at 10:00 o'clock on Tuesday morning, you'll be able to get a hard-on!"

There is no Viagra! This is the Dark Ages! It hasn't been invented yet. This is gonna be a trial by ordeal. It's just you, you and her, actually, whoever she turns out to be.

And I'm worried.

I'm worried.

I'm worried. I'm really worried. I'm so worried that one morning I wake up and there are red blotches all over my body! HUGE red blotches! I don't know what's wrong with me. I figure I must have poison oak or something. I call up my friend Michael Rossman, the nature expert.

"How do you get rid of poison oak really quick?" I ask him.

"You don't," he says. And after I describe my symptoms, he says that it doesn't sound like poison oak to him. He advises me to go see a doctor. He's right. I need to know if I'm contagious.

The doctor says, "You're nervous."

"Yeah," I tell him, but I don't tell him why.

"You got hives," he says.

"Hives? I've never had hives before. "

"Well, you got 'em now!" he says. "Go home, take a Valium, and go to bed."

I did. They were gone the next day.

I have to tell you that I secretly really loved this. My favorite author at the time was the great Nikos Kazantzakis. He's probably best known as the author of *Zorba the Greek* but he's written many great books. Kazantzakis was a literary giant. He wrote his own version of *The Odyssey* that began where Homer's ended. It's a thousand pages of poetry. Kazantzakis was always writing about the spirit and the flesh, the conflict between the spirit and the flesh.

He told a story in his autobiography about going to have his very first extra-marital love affair in Europe of the 1920s. He went to Vienna to meet his paramour, his lover. He arrived in town the night before she did, and the next morning when he woke up, his head was like double its normal size! He had turned into some kind of a grotesque gargoyle. It must have been an infection or something, but the doctor who first examined him had no idea what it was. Kazantzakis s head had just spontaneously swollen up to a monstrous size and he was appropriately scared.

Well, as the story goes, he called upon his friend, Sigmund Freud, who happened to be living in Vienna at the time, and asked him for his help. Freud suggested that it might be due to some kind of guilt reaction and advised him to call off his intended affair and go home. Kazantakis took his advice and the swelling soon subsided. It just went away.

All of which I'm telling you because when I got those blotches, I felt just like my hero! I was hoping it would make me a better writer!

Chapter Six

I was practicing getting hard-ons in my car as I drove over the Bay Bridge to the soundstage in San Francisco. And as soon as I would get it up I'd stop because I didn't want to waste it. I just needed the confidence that I could do it. So, I'm riding along and whenever a truck was gonna pass, I'd cover myself up because they could look down into my car and see what I was doing. But, every now and then, I would miss one and they would see me. This made for some insane horn honking and some very amused finger pointing. The guys were laughing at me.

What could I do? I had to rehearse.

Chapter Seven

I believe foreplay consisted of the director saying to me, "You drop your drawers," and then saying to my partner, "You get on your knees and suck his cock. When he gets hard, we'll start shooting."

"What? And give up show business?"

Chapter Eight

Oh, I got hard right away. When she slipped my penis into her mouth, my

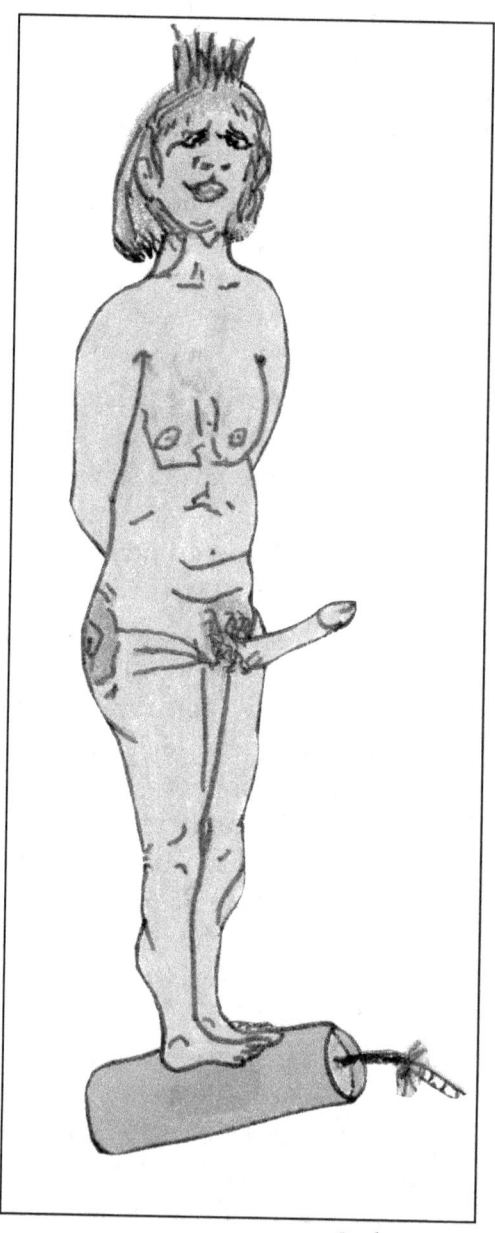

– Gordon Archive

body knew exactly what to do. I just had to stay out of the way. The blood flowed in, I engorged, and it all felt pretty good.

There were like twenty or thirty people on the set that day and I'm looking everyone in the eye. "How ya doin? How ya doin? Welcome to my blow job."

I'm thinking: *Last week, I was busting my ass with a sledgehammer for five bucks an hour and now, I'm gonna get $200 for letting you watch while this woman sucks me.* It was the American dream come true, one of 'em, anyway.

There was no video back then, it was all film. And film was loaded into magazines that contained three, four, five, up to even ten minutes worth of footage before they'd have to stop shooting to reload. When we used up that first magazine, the director called, "Cut." A bell rang, I believe, and the set buzzed into a different kind of action. Crew people popped up from everywhere and started doing their jobs.

Nancy stopped sucking me then. Her stage name was Nancy Hoffman. Mine was Marcus Howard. She stopped sucking me and my erection went away. She's having makeup fix up her hair. Somebody's up on a ladder adjusting a light. People are reloading the camera. Pretty soon, it's time to start up again.

Bob Chinn is the director. He's actually a very kind and gentle soul. Bob directs Nancy back on her knees. She returns my cock to her mouth. God's in His Heaven and all is right with the world. I get hard again. Action! They start shooting again and life is good. Slurp, two, three, four, slurp, two, three, four, and pretty soon, "Cut!" It's another run-out. They have to reload again.

This time Nancy goes to take a pee break. Of course, my penis has deflated again. Eh, that's all right. The crew is discussing last night's game, the Giants or the 49ers. It's all small talk chitchat while they finish reloading the camera. And pretty soon, we're back at it once again. Nancy is sucking me. My cock gets hard. It's a good day at the office, and motion picture history continues to be made.

All right, this starting and stopping business happens maybe five, six, seven, eight, NINE more times, and my dick finally says to me, "HELLO! HELLO! WHAT'S GOING ON HERE? ARE WE GONNA DO THIS? OR WHAT? MAKE UP YOUR FUCKING MIND!" He hardly ever yells at me like that. It was very disconcerting!

I told my dick, "Look, I'm just working here. I don't know!" And

– Gordon Archive

right at that moment Director Bob says, "Okay, we have all the hardcore footage we need, now come!" He said to me, "Now, come!"

I believe that's when it all started to unravel. I looked down at Nancy. She'd been on her knees, on a concrete floor, for forty-five minutes, more or less, diligently sucking my cock. Frankly, at this point, she looked like someone who was ready to take a nap. If this had been a private sexual matter between us, I would have given her a big hug and suggested that we both go out for a slice of pizza or something. And that's when the door opened and I saw for the first time the difference between "personal" and "professional" sex.

We were hired to do a job, and right now, that job was for me to have an orgasm. Her job was to help me have that orgasm. Our personal feelings were supposed to be in the dressing room hanging with our street clothes. Mine weren't. I was stuck thinking that she didn't want to be doing this anymore. And while I'm playing Hamlet and juggling these conflicting thoughts, the director set us back to work.

Nancy revved her engines and started sucking me on fast forward. I wasn't even hard yet and she was trying to make me come. Well, hell, I was trying to make me come too, but, whoa! I wasn't even hard yet! It all started to feel like my dick was in a blender.

No, no, no, no, no, no, no, this was all wrong. This was not gonna work. My erection was nowhere to be found. She was chewing on my limpness and the sperms were all marching the other way in a full retreat. We stopped. We took another break. This one was on me. It was like striking out with bases loaded. I was reeling with the shock.

And when no one was looking, my dick quietly tiptoed off of the set, stole my car keys, and then went home. Gone. Left me standing there alone with a bad grin on my face and dead spaghetti between my legs.

You know what George Burns once said about trying to have sex at age ninety? He said it was like trying to shoot pool with a rope.

They only had this one scene to shoot on this day. They had planned to be done by noon. They were gonna feed us all a fine catered roast beef lunch and then everybody would have the rest of the day off. It was around 11:30 a.m. when my dick went missing. Bob Chinn saw the crazed panic that was engulfing me. "Let's break for lunch," he said. "We'll get the come shot after lunch."

Chapter Nine

They piled their plates high with food and sat down at long tables covered with nice tablecloths. I went into the bathroom and locked the door. It was great to get away from the prying eyes of everybody: people and cameras.

While they dined on their fine roast beef, I continued the search for the lost polar bear in the snow storm. To my mounting fear and humiliation, I could not find him anywhere. Even by myself with the door locked, I could not get my dick to work. I had never met a panic like this before. Ever.

Chapter Ten

When we returned to the set around one o'clock, it was a lot more of the same nothing.

Everybody had resumed their proper positions and Nancy tried once again to get my engines restarted. There was an eerie, hushed silence while she sucked and sucked until her ears touched. Oh, Lord, I died many times that day. The eyes of the people on the set that I had so boldly stared into earlier in the morning were now all boring holes in me. And I had no place to hide. I was free falling in a bottomless pit of shame and humiliation. It was one-thirty. It was two o'clock. They weren't happy and I was scared. Nancy and I stopped and started many more times, all to no avail. It hardly surprised me. If I couldn't get myself going alone in the bathroom, what chance did I have with Nancy in front of an audience of gawkers?

I was thinking: *I'm not a man anymore. I'm not a woman. I don't know what I am. I'm a eunuch. I'm dead. I'm dying. This is Hell.*

It was two-thirty. It was three o'clock. Bob Chinn remained tenacious. He wanted a come shot to end this scene. If they'd been smart about it, they'd have had a stunt cock on standby for just such an occasion. Like a relief pitcher in baseball, he would have stepped in, given them the squirt they needed, and with the magic of movie editing, nobody would have ever known the difference. But for whatever reasons, there was no stunt cock, only me. And Bob needed me to crank one out so that we could all go home. He was willing to give me all the time I needed. Okay, I kept trying to get there. Poor Nancy, she was working awfully hard.

It was three-thirty. It was four. The set was looking like one of those airports where a snowstorm has shut things down and stranded, weary travelers are lying around everywhere just trying to get comfortable. Of the crew, only Bob Chinn remained alert, watching us try every which way we could think of to get me going.

I had started the day with fantasies of becoming the next big porn star and now, I didn't care if they paid me or not. I didn't care if they told me not to come back for that second day at the orgy. Obviously, I stunk at this. And I had no idea of the disassociation that was possible between a man and his penis. For all the good mine was doing me, it might just as well have been yours! Sooner or later, I thought, they would tire of all this and we could all just go home.

It was somewhere around four-thirty or so when I started thinking about the first sexual experience I ever had. Sally. She came out of nowhere and boy, I was glad to see her. You may remember Sally, I told you all about her. Sally was the first girl I ever made out with.

Nancy had actually dozed off and her head was resting on my thigh. Who could blame her? She needed a break. I sat there idly flipping my dick about with my right hand when Sally just showed up in my imagination. Shhhh! I could hear The Kingston Trio....

"Hang down your head, Tom Dooley,
Hang down your head and cry."

Sally! Of course! Where have you been? Back in the ninth grade, I had had the hottest sex in the world with Sally and we didn't even fuck. It was all just petting! Sally! I could still smell her smells.

"Hang down your head, Tom Dooley,
Poor boy, you're bound to die."

We always had The Kingston Trio playing in her game room. She sucked me. She was the first woman ever to suck me! She was the first woman to let me pull down her panties. God, it was still dizzying.

These memories of Sally were like spinach to Popeye. The Phoenix was rising from the ashes.

Bob Chinn was right on it. He poked the cameraman and got him to pay attention. He alerted the soundman and the boom guy too. Nancy still dozed in my lap. Bob motioned for me to extricate myself and stand up. When I did, Nancy's head slid to the floor. Ooops! She looked around, stunned for the moment. The look on her face when she realized where she was came right out of The Three Stooges, but at least she was awake again. My penis, however, had deflated in the excitement. Bob came rushing over. The set had come alive. Everybody in the crew was back in action.

"Whatever you were doing," Bob says to me, "you just do that again." And to Nancy he adds, "You just wait for him."

So, I closed my eyes and went back into that room again. There was Sally. The magic was still there. My dick started to rise. I stroked on. I got myself hard. Then Nancy touched me. Oh, no, BIG mistake!! As soon as she touched me, my dick said, "Hell, No! I'm done with you. You and I are finished! No! No! No! No!" What a temperamental little bastard my dick had turned out to be? One day on an X-rated set and he was already a fucking diva!

It was Director Bob Chinn to the rescue. In one of the more brilliant moves of his long Hall-of-Fame career, he said to Nancy, "Don't touch him!"

And then he said to me, "You jerk off! Just keep going until you come!"

Back to Nancy, he added, "And you sweetheart, don't touch that penis until the first squirt is out! When that first squirt goes out, grab it like you did it!" She certainly earned the right. She had put in the time.

And lo and behold, as he had wished for, it all did happen. I did squirt. She did grab it. They shot the shot. You see this movie, it looks like every other come shot you've ever seen. In all, the scene is divided into two parts that add up to about a minute-and-a-half of screen time. You watch the scene and there's absolutely no indication of all the insane chaos that we had endured to shoot it.

What did I learn? Well, for openers, I discovered yet again that I was not much of an exhibitionist. It did not give me any great buzz to have people watching me have sex. And what completely threw me for a loop was to learn that a sex scene involved a lot more than me getting to make out with an exotic woman. I had to jerk off in front of people! I had to be able to get myself aroused! I had to be able to make myself come! *Whoa, how'd you like them apples?*

I didn't! Not at all!

Somehow, the idea of masturbating in front of other people was unbelievably humiliating to me. I would never have signed up for that! You couldn't have given me enough money to jerk off in front of somebody else! I mean, if it was private and a woman, well, yeah, but if there were men watching too, and an audience of thirty, forty more people and crew, plus the cameras, yoi. My Lord, let me outta here! I had no idea that was gonna be part of the package. The price I paid that day was pretty much all of the dignity I had amassed in my young life. It was horrible to feel that exposed.

And after all of that struggle, when I finally did come—

You remember Rocky, the original Rocky? He didn't win that fight! He just didn't get knocked out! That was his victory! And that's exactly how I felt!

I came! I made it! And when I finally had that orgasm, I heard the cheering of millions! Then a towel came flying in and hit me in the face! Someone said, "Go home, Champ! Sleep it off!"

Chapter Eleven

"Never let the fear of striking out get in your way!"
- Babe Ruth

They invited me back for the orgy and I went.

I know, I know, but I'll tell you why. There was another $200 in it for me. That spoke pretty loud. Besides that, I'd had a few days to recover from the blow job and I didn't think the orgy could possibly get any worse. In fact, I had a hunch it would be a lot easier with other naked people around on the set having sex too.

Chapter Twelve

At first, I was eager to make contact with some of the other men who would be performing in the orgy. I wanted to hear their ideas about the sex. I wanted to ask them how they learned to do it.

Didn't happen. There were no openings. Guys were barely civil to me. Actually, I couldn't get much of a hello out of anybody, male or female, as we all sat around most of the morning waiting for the crew to prepare our set. There were three other actors and about four or five actresses. They were all porn veterans. I was the rookie. They all pretty much ignored me. When you're a nobody in that world, you just are nobody. All the women want to fuck a star. You get a star interested in you, you can drop a name! You got a résumé! You can get some more work! If you fucked a nobody, well, you fucked a nobody. I sat off to the side and bided my time. This was not exactly a confidence building experience for me. Since there was nothing to do but wait, I contented myself with watching them all interact.

Late in the morning, Bob Chinn the director took the men aside and instructed each of us to make a list of the top three actresses we wanted to work with. He explained that he'd go over the lists and then make the assignments. He also told me that I'd be coming up first when we started shooting. "In that way," he explained, "in case you experience any of the 'difficulties' like you did in your earlier scene, we'll just move ahead and then come back and get you later. Okay?"

"Sure," I said. I was more concerned with the fact that I had no women at all to put on my list. Seeing as how I've never been particularly attracted to women who ignored me, it appeared I had a problem. I watched the other fellows for a clue about how to approach the women.

Two of the guys, Don Fernando and Rock Steadie, started strutting their plumage. They literally took out their penises and began approaching some of the women. The girls giggled. It was like an adult version of the second grade. A couple of the women recoiled from their advances. "No pay, no play!" sing-songed another as she also backed away. Seemed like she could have added, "Oooh, cooties!"

Well, I couldn't do it like those guys. That wasn't me. And the only other actor on the set was Paul Thomas. He was a tall, blonde, handsome devil, who seemed to be the alpha male of our bunch. He had let me know pretty early on that he had just performed one of the lead roles in a Bay Area production of *Jesus Christ Superstar*. One had the distinct impression that Mr. Thomas was just "slumming" in pornography. After our little meeting with the director, Paul went back to his newspaper. It was *The Wall Street Journal*. He was checking in on his stocks. Okay, that wasn't me either. The list of my top three choices remained blank.

Chapter Thirteen

Makeup was the best thing that happened to me all morning. I hadn't really paid much attention to it the first time around, on the day of my blow job. I guess I just had too many other things on my mind. But this time, when Sharon the makeup lady finished working on me, she had to leave the room for some reason.

I was left alone looking in the mirror. Wow! I had never ever looked that good! Makeup was awesome! It improves us! I was completely fascinated by that guy in the mirror. Shhh, don't tell this to anybody, but I think I fell in love!

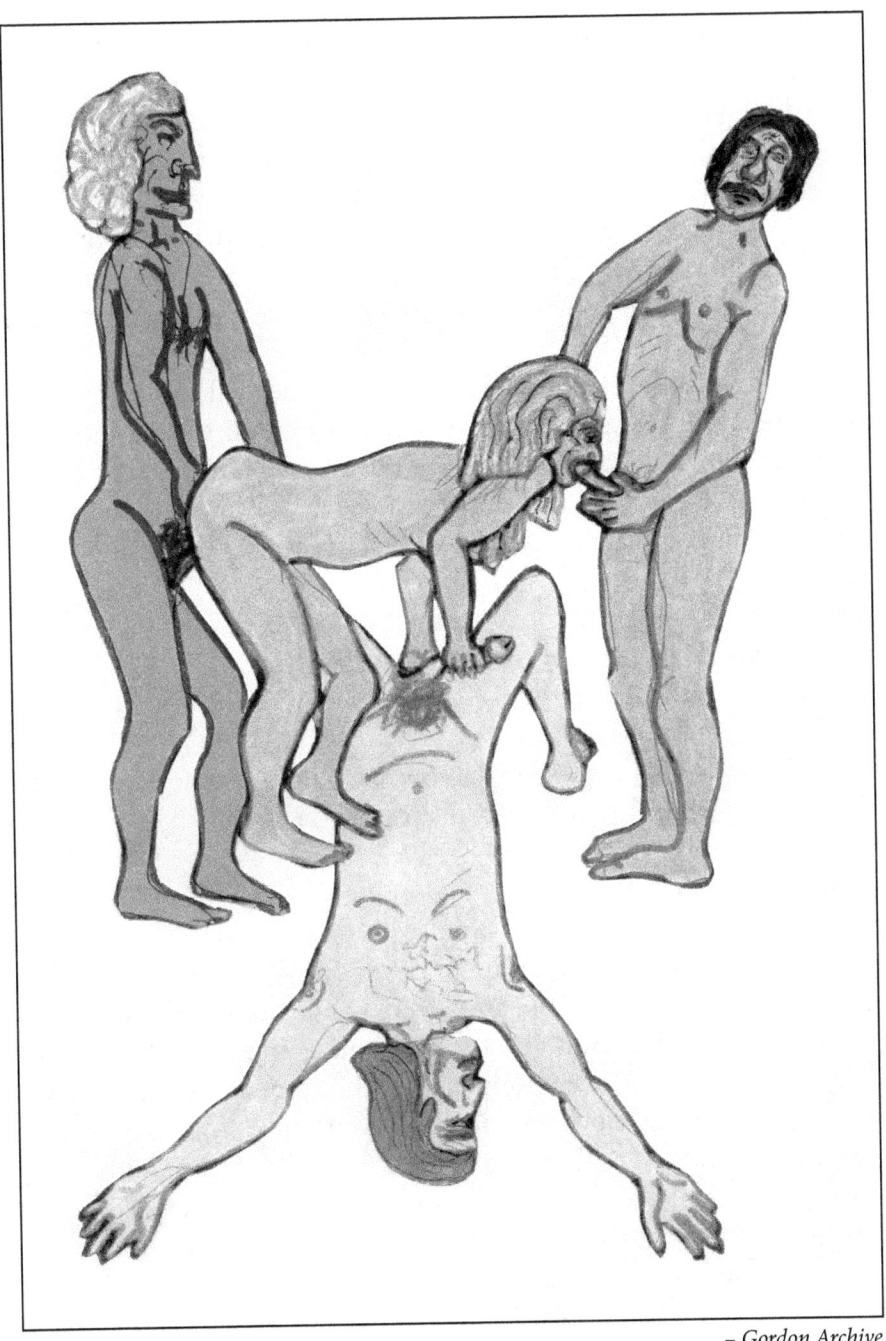

– *Gordon Archive*

Rehearsal!

And when I came out of the makeup room, boy, did I ever land in clover! There in the costume room was a red-headed woman I hadn't seen yet. Phaedra. Phaedra Grant! She was busy "rehearsing" with both Don and Rock. She was bent over blowing one of them while the other pumped into her from behind. It was all pretty as a French postcard.

When our eyes met and she smiled at me, she twinkled. That was all the encouragement I needed. It was a now or never moment and I joined the party. I unzipped myself and she made me very happy with a free hand.

It was exactly the kind of rehearsal you needed in this business to get ready. When one of the guys found himself getting too close to his orgasm, he had to pull himself out and zip himself back up. He had to save "the money shot" for the movie. I took his place until I too reached a similar plateau. When I turned in my list, it read:

1. Phaedra
2. Phaedra
3. Phaedra

When the director assigned us our partners, I had no competition for Phaedra. The other men had all picked other women.

Chapter Fourteen

The set design was really quite clever. Imagine a semi-circle, like the top half of clock. Phaedra and I were in one bed placed at the nine of nine o'clock. There was another grouping going on at the ten, one at eleven, another at twelve and so on. The camera was placed right in the center of the clock and had only to pan slightly to move from one whole scene to another. It saved huge amounts of time and money than if they would have had to break down and move everything from one set to the next. Of course, all this movie stuff was brand new to me. It was easy to become fascinated by it.

As the set readied itself for the first call of "Action," the director gave us all a breakdown of how it was going to go, beginning with Phaedra and me. We were in standby. Out of absolutely nowhere, this angelic male voice comes wafting through the set singing this lilting melody:

"So, let the sideshow begin.
Hurry, hurry, step right on in.
Can't afford to pass it by,
Guaranteed to make you cry ...
Let the sideshow begin.
Hurry, hurry, step right on in.
Can't afford to pass it by,
Guaranteed to make you cry. "

It was a perfect moment. Life doesn't give us very many of those. It was a song called "Sideshow" popularized by the group Blue Magic in 1974. I wish this book could sing those words to you right now. I have no idea what inspired Paul Thomas to just burst out in song like that, but, right then and there, he did, and it was forever engraved in my heart. It was a soaring triumph of voice and heart and the moment. I thank you, Paul. These thirty-some years later, I still thank you. I became your fan for life.

And thank you, Phaedra! Because on "Action" from Bob Chinn, I fell into your warm embrace and a scant 10,000 kisses later mounted the wings that took me to my own soaring triumph of orgasm. I gave the director everything he wanted, no muss, no fuss, no bother. How the hell did that ever happen?

I said to her after I came, "Do you want to come?" because that's what you say at a moment like that if it happens that way, at least that's the way my girlfriends had trained me.

She said to me, and it was to be the first of many times that I would hear this from my movie lovers over the next ten years, "Are you kidding? In front of all these people?"

Boy, was that assbackwards! Generally speaking, the women were being paid two or three times what the men were making because they were the stars of the industry. The paying audience was overwhelmingly male. I understood that, but I was completely amazed that the women didn't have to have real orgasms and I did.

Chapter Fifteen
John and Joey

John Leslie and Joey Silvera. Eyetalian. Very. Coupla big city boys. John was the alpha wolf. Joey was the goofy sidekick. They hated The Beatles. How could anybody hate The Beatles? They did. Think Santino in *The Godfather* telling his brother Michael that he was a fool for joining the Marines to fight for his country.

It was my second movie, *The Legend of Lady Blue*. I was hired for one day to play Hank, a U.S. soldier in a whorehouse in Vietnam. The *Candy Stripers* had been a lark, an adventure. *The Legend of Lady Blue* was an act of getting myself into "the business."

Thirty actors had been brought on the set at 8:00 a.m. They put us in army fatigues and then herded us into a corner of a cold San Francisco warehouse that was serving as a soundstage. The production manager ordered us to, "Stay!" He wanted us on the set, in costume and makeup, and ready when he called. The fact that we sat around useless for a good six hours apparently meant nothing to him. They paid by the day and took complete advantage of that fact. The most exciting thing that happened for hours was when the script girl fell off of her chair and knocked over several cans of paint.

I had two pages of dialogue to do with a guy named Ken. We were to play army buddies in the whorehouse. Ken was a law student who said he made a fair amount of money on the side doing sex films. He explained that he usually made loops, which were sex scenes without any sound. He said that the sex was easy for him, but when he had to do lines, it made him really nervous. I told him that I had it the other way around. He told me that I'd get used to it. It just takes some time. We rehearsed a lot. When we weren't running lines, he was buried in his law books.

The set came alive when Jesse Pierson, the director showed up. Twenty years earlier, he had played Conrad Birdie, the Elvis character, in the big-time Hollywood film of *Bye-Bye Birdie*. It was exciting just to see him. It was like we were all playing minor league ball in Dubuque and a former major leaguer just showed up at the ballpark looking all rich and famous with a sun tan. It completely energized the set.

Actors John Leslie and Joey Silvera soon made their appearance too. It hadn't been all that long since I'd been making out with Carly in the backseat at the X-rated drive-in movie and watching both of them up there on the big screen. They were movie stars too. I wanted to meet them, be their friend, have them like me. I ran up to them like an eager puppy.

It was a big mistake. They had me for lunch. John and Joey just played a game of amusing themselves at the expense of everybody around them. They were assholes. It was their world, you were just visiting. If you weren't in on their joke, you became their joke. I was just another new schmuck on the set and was treated just so. I took enough of their abuse to get the picture and then just tried to stay out of their line of fire. If you would have told me they would one day become good friends, I would have told you that you were out of your mind.

My scene with Ken opened with the two of us wandering around the whorehouse. In real life, I had never been in the army or a whorehouse. It was fun to play. As the story went, Ken's character accidentally stumbled into a backroom where he came face-to-face with Casey, a crazy misfit who had just escaped from the enemy. Casey attacked. He grabbed Ken by the balls with one hand and was threatening them with a knife in the other. I came along, apologized for Ken's intrusion, and got my buddy out of danger.

We got into a long line of soldiers waiting for a turn with the whores. Our line eventually led us into a room where a group of soldiers stood surrounding a bed. On the bed, John and Joey were busy fucking the brains out of a young Chicano woman playing a Vietnamese whore. Ken and I joined the circle of soldiers around the bed who stood watching and masturbating.

That was weird. There was me and Ken and a bunch of short Black men with big dicks. We were all supposed to jerk off.

Halfway through the scene, the director changed the woman playing the whore. Out went the young whore and in came "the Empress of Saigon," the queen of the whorehouse. And she was being played by none other than Phaedra. That's right, *my Phaedra!*

Well, she wasn't "my Phaedra" any more. I had to watch while John and Joey just plowed right into her. The rest of us stood there stroking.

Chapter Sixteen
Things That You Learn the Hard Way #1

Was I jealous? Damn right I was jealous! Phaedra was the fallen angel who had just taken me from the Hell of sexual dysfunction to the Heaven of the successful come shot. But none of that mattered.

In the X-rated world of movie making, you experienced all the same emotional crap that you experienced in your private relationship life, but you weren't really entitled to any of it. It wasn't personal. It was all just a job.

And you had to learn how to take all those pesky little feelings and emotions like desire and love and possession and jealousy and process them all at lightning speeds because, in the morning, you could be doing a tender wedding scene with your one true love, and in the afternoon, she could be taking Jamie Gillis up her ass.

Welcome to Pornoland.

Things That You Learn the Hard Way #2

It took over four hours to shoot that circle-jerk scene. I spent a least two of those hours actively engaged in rubbing my dick without any lubrication. It seemed I was either getting it up or trying to keep it up. The director wanted the jerks in the circle to come. Many of us did. I didn't. My cock was raw. When I left for home that day, my penis felt like it had been sandpapered. I had to pack it in Vaseline for about three days.

I learned. The next time I would use lubrication.

Chapter Seventeen

In 1977, the adult business was calling out to me and I was listening. I was taking notes.

New York and San Francisco were the two major centers of production in the mid-seventies. The New York scene was harder, dirtier, and had a real "Fuck you" kind of gritty to it. You'd expect that from New York. The San Francisco scene was hippie-dippy and outdoorsy. There was a lot more exploited innocence and sunshine.

Almost all of the production companies that shot in San Francisco were based in Los Angeles. They couldn't shoot down there because of political and police pressure. At considerable expense, the LA film companies would have to pack up all their gear, shoot their movies in the Bay Area, and then return to LA for all the post-production. It wasn't exactly legal to be shooting in San Francisco either, but it was a "don't ask – don't tell" kind of situation. If there weren't any complaints, the officials didn't go out of their way looking for illegal productions to shut down. In LA, they did.

Was organized crime involved? Well, rumor had it so, but you'd never really find out much about that by asking any actor. I mean, nobody ever came up to me and said, "Hi, we're with the Tattaglia Family and we've got some great medical and dental benefits if you'd like to sign up with us to make some pornographic movies."

The money that paid our salaries came from production companies. More often than not, we were being paid by check. Deductions were being withheld. Model releases were being signed. Somebody was maintaining books and records. The companies appeared to be perfectly legit.

However, who actually owned those companies and how they got their funding was not exactly information generally made available to the performers.

"The family had a lot of buffers."

- Willie Cicci,
The Godfather: Part II

I actually got to meet "Willie Cicci!" He was played by the actor Joe Spinell and we worked together in a movie. It was my very first job after quitting X-rated films back in 1985. *Tragedy in New York* was an all-Italian gangster movie that had a few shooting days in San Francisco. It was just as formulaic as the X stuff, but instead of a sex scene, they just did a murder every twelve minutes. Nobody in the production spoke any English at all except for the director's wife. She would translate the director's commands to the local actors who had been hired for a couple of days work in this film. Joe Spinell was the star. He played the Mafia Don. I was cast as one of his underlings.

I got his autograph in my diary:

– *Gordon Archive*

Meanwhile, I soon learned that even though a porn actor's salary was a big step up from the wages of manual labor, it wasn't exactly the actors who were getting rich out of the business.

I was told that only three groups of people made real money in the adult films of that era. It was all film back then, by the way, video would not blossom until the mid-eighties. The big money makers were the people who owned the movies, the people who owned the theaters, and the people who owned the distribution networks. Everybody else was a schlub on a salary.

The performers may have been the biggest schlubs of all. There was no union. That meant that there was little or no protection against the rip-offs or the crazies. There was no medical plan. There were no residuals. There were no unemployment or retirement benefits.

Perhaps, worse than all of that, was the fact that the whole adult business was a dead end for the actors. Everybody else from makeup people to directors could get some phenomenal training in X-rated movies and then graduate. They could move on up to join the appropriate union and work their way into the straight world of commercials, films, and TV. An X-rated actor or actress was not going to be invited to join the Screen Actors Guild. And if you were naïve or stupid enough to tell any of the straight Hollywood agents or casting directors that you had worked in porn, they treated you like you had dog shit on your shoes and were getting it on their carpets. There's the door, what's your hurry.

In the beginning of my career, for any number of reasons, I did not want to become known as an X-rated actor. I used a different stage name for each film. There was Marcus Howard, McKinley Howard, and Mack Howard, just to name a few. Eventually, Dewey Alexander became one of my favorites. It was "Dewey" from "Huey, Dewey, and Louie," Donald Duck's nephews and "Alexander" from Alexander the Great, a man who needed no introduction.

On the other hand, on the positive side of performing in adult films, there was one fabulous benefit for some of the women. Many of the actresses also worked as dancers in the strip clubs all across the U.S. and Canada. When they became recognizable from a starring or featured role in an X-rated movie, they could easily double and triple the rates that they would be paid for their dancing. They would become headliners! There was no equivalent experience for the men.

Also on the plus side, there were a lot fewer talented actors and actresses competing for jobs in porn than there were in the straight world. That made it a helluva lot easier to get work. Once there, the starting day rates were usually higher in porn than what actors got at the entry levels of the straight world. With less competition, one had the chance to become the big fish in a small pond.

But mostly, there was the opportunity for sex. Those that came into porn just for the money didn't seem to last very long. In the end, it seemed a lifestyle choice. The people who became the sex stars pretty much wanted to be the sex stars. Some aspect of their personality was being fulfilled by that sexual stardom. Some old score was being settled. The fact that they were being paid for it too, was like a bonus.

In the larger community of actors, the sex stars became like a tide pool of talent that was cut off from the main body of the profession.

With very few exceptions, they became a world and an industry unto themselves. Marilyn Chambers, Linda Lovelace, and Georgina Spelvin were the top porn queens of that era. John Holmes, Harry Reems, and Jamie Gillis were the kings.

Chapter Eighteen

The magazines were the bottom of the barrel in the skin trade. Performers were hired to work in choreographed sex scenes that were shot by still photographers. Many of these same photographers also worked on the motion pictures and their pool of models became a source of actors for the movies. A lot of people started out in the business by first posing for these stills. I did maybe two or three of these magazines. Got like $50-$75 a session. Never saw myself in a finished product.

A short step up from the magazines were the loops. Loops were basically just hardcore sex scenes shot in 8mm or 16mm film. Sometimes there was sound, sometimes there wasn't. Maybe you had costumes and a plot, maybe you didn't.

Video cassettes eventually rendered the entire film loop industry obsolete, but they had been a big business for a long, long time. I think Thomas Edison made some of the first loops with his maid. Maybe not. I made ten of them early in my career. Some actors made hundreds of these. I got like $50 to a $100 per loop and never saw myself in a finished one of these either.

I got some casting advice from a veteran loop producer who once explained to me that the more anonymous I looked, the more work I could get in the industry. "The women are the stars," he said, "and the men are their foils." He instructed me never to bring any attention to myself and away from the female. He suggested that men without tattoos, scars, or any other distinguishing marks would get far more work than those who had them.

I did my first loop for a guy named Daemian Lee. As part of a larger orgy, I had to do a doggie-style penetration of a young well-muscled lesbian named Ronnie. It went well enough. Of course, it would have been a lot easier to do if I'd only had one leg because the other one kept getting in the way of the camera, but we managed. At the appropriate time, Daemian had me pull out and squirt on her bottom. I always hated doing that. Pulling out just made me nuts! It was a crime against,

God, Nature, and common sense, but it was like some kind of Golden Rule in the X-rated Cinema: "Thou shalt make a come shot and thou shalt let the camera see it!"

All right, I was done. On my way out the door though, I happened to walk by a room where I saw Ronnie gently weeping into the arms of her girlfriend. It troubled me. Job or no job, it was hard to see a woman that I'd just been some kind of intimate with, in tears. Was it something I'd done? Had I hurt her? Why didn't she tell me? I had no idea. Was it my fault? Her girlfriend had also been in the orgy having sex with somebody else. Was this some kind of relationship problem between them? Was it none of my business? Should I interrupt them? Should I ask? I didn't know what was my responsibility in that situation, and what wasn't. It troubled me. It still does.

This brings us to feature films. It was a very big step up from the magazines and the loops to the world of feature-length films. Here, you were making movies! They came in two sizes. The cheaper ones were shot in 16mm film. They were made down and dirty and in such a hurry that it made you dizzy. Entire movies were often shot in one day. Appropriately, they were called "one-day wonders." Although by the time I came along, some of these 16mm productions took two or even three days to shoot.

Upon completion of post-production, the final product would be boosted up to 35mm in a lab and prints would be sent out for distribution to all the various X-rated theaters.

The salaries were higher in these films than in the loops or the magazines and some degree of acting went along with all the sex.

The features shot in 35mm film, like *The Candy Stripers* for example, were the very top of the line for performers in the X-rated industry. These were also being made in a hurry, but they were a big step up from the 16mm's. You worked in one of these bigger budget productions and you felt like Joe Hollywood. They were more professional. They were "mo better" all way round. These features paid the highest salaries and usually took five to seven days to shoot. They had scripts, rehearsals, costumes, makeup, the works!

"I coulda been somebody! I coulda been a contender!"

I heard an interview once with the then aged film legend Jimmy Cagney. He was reminiscing about the good old days of Hollywood when they'd shoot an entire movie in just seventeen days. His interviewer was astonished. In over a hundred films in ten years, I was only in one movie that ever took as long as seventeen days to shoot and that one was just a crazy fluke.

Chapter Nineteen

*"There ain't no success like failure
and failure ain't no success at all."*

> - Bob Dylan,
>   from "Love Minus Zero/No Limit"

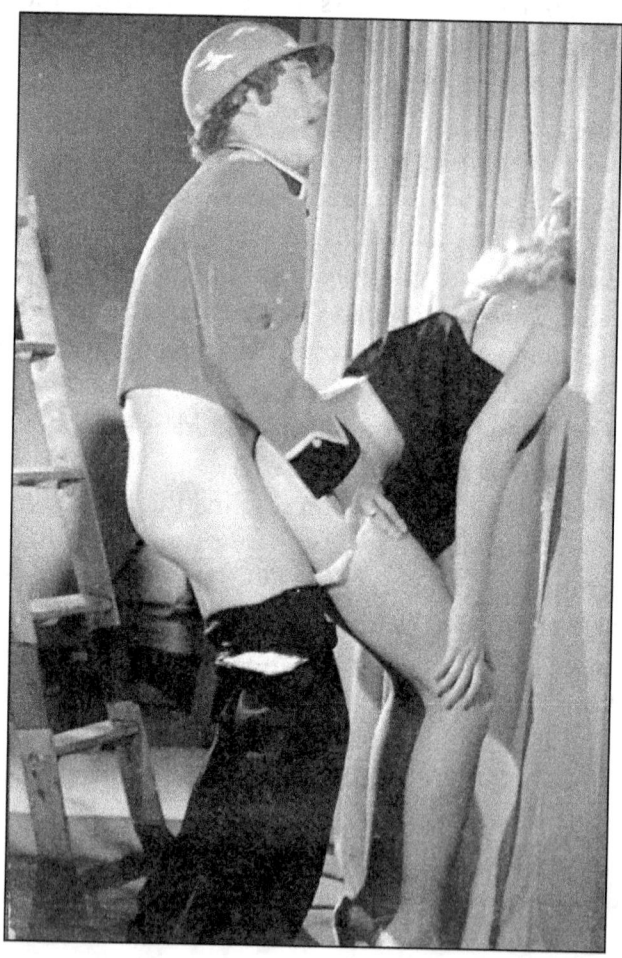

- VCX.com

"Acting" with Carol Connors.

My next four sex scenes produced a total of zero orgasms. I suspect you might understand how this could be a bit of a problem for an aspiring, young porn actor such as myself. Let me put it into the proper perspective for you. Imagine if you will, a hockey player who doesn't know how to ice skate. Yup, that pretty much sums it up.

In *Sensual Encounters of Every Kind*, I was supposed to have sex with Chris Cassidy in the backseat of a Rolls Royce. That sounded like fun didn't it? Well, we started off just great. I was up and in her. I was able to give them lots of hardcore footage at first, bouncing around in that backseat, but then, but then—it's the "but thens" that'll kill ya—I got lost. It was all the stopping and starting over and over again for the camera. It reached a point where my dick just went comatose. Died on the table. Never got it back. Director had me simulate an orgasm inside her.

The only time I ever worked with a fluffer was in *Candy Goes to Hollywood*. The fluffer was supposed to get me hard off-camera and then I was to jump up, run on stage, and stick myself into Carol Connors, the star of the film. Carol was bending over from the waist and waiting for my doggy-style insertion. She may still be waiting.

I had no problem with the fluffer. She repeatedly kept getting me erect. But every time I inserted myself into Carol, my penis wilted like overcooked asparagus. Perhaps we would have had a chance if Carol had merely turned her head and said "hello" to me. But it wasn't to be.

After numerous failures to stay hard in Carol, I got the hook. They took me out of the game. Future Hall-of-Famer Jon Martin was summoned to the set as a stunt cock for me. I had to surrender my costume and stand there in a robe while he stepped up to the plate. Harry Mohney was our director. He told me to watch how a real pro gets the job done.

Five minutes later, Jon Martin was squirting his magic seed on Carol's bottom. I felt about two inches tall.

- Jon Martin

Hall of Famer Jon Martin.

It got even worse in *Telefantasy*. Minutes before we were to go on stage to shoot our sex scene, I was scouring the set in search of Christine, my costar. I found her in a dark corner being fingered by the still photographer. Oops!

Our scene was set in a massage parlor. I played a naked guy on a massage table. Christine played the masseuse. On "Action," she was supposed to suck me until I got hard and then we were supposed to fuck.

When the director did say, "Action," there began some of the most uneasy quiet I ever heard in my whole life. It was the sound of absolutely nothing happening. I was in a full panic mode. She sucked me for what seemed the briefest amount of time and then just spat out my dick and let loose a torrent of nasty, verbal abuse upon me.

– *Gordon Archive*

She was not playing nicely with others!

I was clueless, helpless, and emotionally battered. You could add humiliated to that list too. She was raving. The director had seen enough, thank you. Mercifully, he just decided to scratch the whole sex scene.

– *Gordon Archive*

Chapter Twenty

In my mind, the painted women were all there waiting for me. They were lying on their backs with no panties on. Their legs were spread wide. "C'mon, Howie, what are you waiting for?"

They were on their knees, unzipping me. They were reaching into my pants. They were reaching into my underpants. They were trying to find me.

"C'mon, Howie, we're here for you. C'mon, now."

They were naked. They were naked on their hands and knees and they were swaying their asses at me in hulas of invitation. "What are you waiting for, Howie? What are you waiting for?"

I was waiting for my dick to get hard.

The painted ladies were all right there in front of me, all wanting and waiting. I was masturbating myself, now, trying to get my dick hard. I closed my eyes. I was trying to get my dick hard. The whole production was waiting for me. I was thinking about Carly. I was having sexual fantasies of my wife.

There! Did you hear that? Did you hear that?

It was God laughing!

Chapter Twenty-One
The Man Who Would Be King

During this "Golden Age of Porn," the films and videos overwhelmingly featured male sexual fantasies composed of lust and power.

It was a lovemaking largely devoid of heart, spirit, responsibility, and most intelligence. It was the sexuality of men in groups, the kind that could not show softness, or weakness, or how much a man needed his wife or mommy.

It portrayed an imagined sex life of gangsters, movie stars, business tycoons, and warriors, guys who had the power. These were guys who had the power to easily get who and what and when they wanted.

Women were trophies. Women were comfort stations. Women were good meals at fancy restaurants. Women were use 'em and lose 'em.

Pornography was guys showing off for the guys. It was a meager portion of the sum-total of human sexuality, but it completely dominated an industry whose dollars mostly came from men. These were men, alone, without women, men who wanted to see the unattainable women who had denied them, getting fucked and getting fucked "good."

This skewered sexuality was the backbone of pornography during my era. This is what sold most to guys who were looking to jerk off. And the King of it all at the time was John C. Holmes who stood alone atop a mountain of female conquests with his fourteen inch penis unfurled like the flag of all men everywhere. He was the Achilles of the cock.

The first time I met John Holmes was on the set of *Pizza Girls*. It was my third or fourth movie. For John Holmes, it was number 1,756 or 2,273.

I was scheduled to work that afternoon, but I got an emergency, mid-morning phone call. The crew had inadvertently set fire to the Shakey's Pizza Parlor that had been serving as the location. I was asked to bring my VW van and rush myself to the set immediately to help out the film crew in all the chaos. Eager to please as I was in those early days, I hurried to the set.

When I arrived, firefighters were still hosing down the smoldering Shakey's. Production people were scurrying around them in an irritated frenzy. I recognized superstar John Holmes immediately. There he was schlepping around boxes of equipment like he was some kind of lowly grip. I was impressed.

I had seen John Holmes in dozens of adult films. He looked just like himself. He, with that monster lingam, had already been on top of the X-rated world for well over a decade. I reported to the production manager and soon, I too was schlepping around boxes of equipment like I was some kind of lowly grip. I hoped that someone was taking the time to be impressed by me.

When the vehicles were all loaded, we caravanned to the next location high in the Oakland Hills. It was a private home with a pool and a hot tub. All of my scenes would be shot there.

Pizza Girls was about a heated rivalry between a take-out fried chicken stand and a pizza place. To be kind, it was written in twenty minutes by a brain-damaged chimpanzee. It was very silly.

The movie, of course, starred John Holmes. And it was at once revealing that an actor got top billing in a genre that usually listed only the actresses' names on the marquee. You see, Picasso painted, Sinatra sang, and John Holmes was a porn star, an institution unto himself in the adult film business.

He had the biggest penis I ever saw in my life, on a human being, that is. There were some donkeys out there that could give him a run for his money. Some said his dick measured fourteen-and-a-half inches long when erect. Others argued that it was a mere thirteen-and-a-half. Would-be Holmes biographer, Al Goldstein of *Screw* magazine fame, swore that it was "only" twelve-and-a-half inches long, but Al never paid retail for anything.

By comparison, my own penis measured five-and-three quarter inches at the full height of erection. In the size game, it was like trying to win at poker with a pair of threes.

John Holmes's cock, however, was a marvel to behold. On the set, eyes widened when he lowered his trousers. In another era, Barnum & Bailey might have hired him out for private parties.

Just about every single actress who ever made a name for herself as a sex star in those days had at one time or another been ritually enlarged by his massive organ. It was an awful lot of penis for one mortal man to be carrying around in his pants.

Watching John's cock in action, both on the screen and in person, reminded me of the fat women who often served as models in art classes. In student days, I had been very excited when I learned that our class was to have a live, nude female model. When it turned out to be this gargantuan fat lady, I was very disappointed. After staring at her for a while though, it changed. I started to see all of these different women inside of her. She was so very big that she seemed to contain something from every woman who had ever lived. It was precisely that exaggerated size that revealed the universality of all women.

John Holmes's penis reminded me of that model. His cock was so big that it seemed at times to represent the very essence of maleness taken to the nth degree. And by putting it on the silver screen, that prong poked and spoke for all men and not just for John, the poor schnook who had to live with and care for the beast.

Let's face it, in the battle between the sexes, John Holmes was carrying nuclear weapons between his legs. For good or evil, he could fuck a woman like she had never been fucked before. To his credit and probably his peace of mind, there was a gentle side to Holmes in matters sexual, as well as the standard "fuck the bitch" mentality so characteristic of conventional porn. I've watched many scenes of him delicately and gently offering his enormous cock to frightened women who had to wonder if they could possibly take that huge thing inside of themselves without doing irreparable damage. And I've also seen the other scenes too, where, how shall I put this? Let's just say that "gentleness" was not an issue.

I would suspect that in reality his great cock was at once a gift and a nightmare for the man who had to live with it. A photographer friend of his once boasted to me on John's behalf that more film footage had been shot of Holmes than of any American president. You have to wonder what the man's private life was like. I heard a rumor that an oil-rich sheik had once flown him halfway round the world just to witness that super-sized puppy in action. Goldstein of *Screw* thought he had done the definitive Holmes interview in what turned out to be late in John's career only to discover that much of John's information had been fabricated. It seems that the public John Holmes played pretty fast and loose with "the truth."

Anyway, back on the set of *Pizza Girls*, I was taking some pictures of a young starlet with my own camera when the legendary John C. Holmes called out to me, "Hey, how'd ya like t'have your picture taken with the big fella?"

– Gordon Archive.

John Holmes & Howie.

The picture we took together came out nice. He later obliged me by autographing an enlargement. It made me giddy. I wouldn't have dared to ask. I thought of old high school buddies I would be sending copies to in the mail. It reminded me of when I shook hands with Muhammed Ali.

John's behavior on the set of *Pizza Girls* was extremely mercurial. I saw him take considerable time and effort to educate a raw rookie on some aspect of filmmaking and I saw him reduce an unsuspecting starlet to tears. I was never sure which John Holmes he was going to be at any given moment. I figured to just stay out of his way. He was the star. He was nice to me and I was grateful, but I wouldn't say we had become drinking buddies. It was clear that he was a power on the set with which one had to contend. I did nothing to even vaguely offend.

Holmes was on the set watching when I attempted my sex scene with the young and vivacious Candida Royalle (who later founded her own production company, Femme). Candida, in one of those early scenes in our careers we'd both be only too happy to forget, played a pizza delivery girl on a skateboard. When she knocked on my door with the pizza, I had to deliver the immortal line, "I've got a stovepipe in my pants a-just a-waitin' fer yew!" Fucking Marlon Brando couldn't have done it. One can only hope that the writer was paid enough to afford his necessary medications.

And upon hearing this eloquent declaration of love and devotion, Candida was to fall upon her knees and begin ministering to my manhood. She did so, placing my soft cock in her mouth. The room grew deadly quiet. I closed my eyes and searched for pleasure. It was like trying to find a light switch in the dark. When I did not rapidly become aroused, they cut the camera to wait for me. You want to talk about pressure? People tiptoed about and spoke in hushed tones. Candida dutifully munched on.

I thought I had prepared myself for this moment. A week before we were to shoot this scene, I had called Candida in San Francisco and asked if she would be kind enough to meet with me before we shot this scene. I was hoping that some familiarity, some friendship with each other, might make the task less intimidating for me.

What I really wanted to do was "rehearse" the sex, and I think Candida smelled that all the way across the Bay, but she didn't say no. She was very guarded at first, but, eventually, she agreed to meet with me.

We were on the rooftops in San Francisco. I had brought my camera and was hanging out with Candida and some of her friends. Lailani was one of them. She would be in *Pizza Girls* too.

– *Gordon Archive.*

Lailani.

– *Gordon Archive/Candida Royalle*

Candida.

Candida turned out to be a bold, wild child. I was a married man who had to find a way to get close to her, at least close enough to make one sex scene work, and then find my way back home. We got stoned. And on the rooftops, we did have sex. We were not staring deeply into each other's eyes, but the plumbing all worked and to me, that's what mattered at the time.

And now, we were trying to have sex again on the set of *Pizza Girls*. It was tense, when against the heavy odds, life began cautiously flowing into my dick. Candida was sucking and I was responding. The attentive director whispered,

"Roll sound."

"Sound is rolling," whispered back the audio technician in the storied catechism of moviemaking.

"Roll camera," whispered the director.

"**QUIET ON THE SET!! THIS IS A TAKE!!**" bellowed the production manager at the top of his voice. I jumped a foot. The set exploded in laughter. The director quizzically looked at his production manager as if the poor soul had lost his mind.

"I thought I heard voices upstairs," he said defensively. In the meantime, my timid erection had vanished.

We started over again, but, sadly, my penis had died of fright. Candida applied serious mouth-to-mouth, but it was already too late. I was locked in panic. My cock held the tension of over-cooked spaghetti.

There's an old Indian expression that says, "The bad snake charmer always blames his snake."

"Bad Snake! Bad Snake!"

It was hard to be the little engine that could on the set with John Holmes.

Given my inglorious recent track record, the powers that be had no intention of waiting around for me to revive. They moved ahead to Plan B.

The director had us simulate a wild fuck and told me to be funny. "Ho-ho-ho," I was a laugh a minute. I sang, "She'll be comin' 'round the mountain when she comes," as I feigned intercourse by hiding my soft dick against Candida's bottom and also tried to hide the shame and humiliation that came along with it. They shot this abomination.

Afterwards, I had to surrender my costume to a stand-in so that they could get the necessary hardcore footage they needed. It turned out to be my buddy the production manager. The village idiot would be my stunt cock. They would shoot close-ups of him fucking Candida and then edit them into my scene. The viewers would never know. I had to stand on the sidelines and watch. John Holmes patted me on the head and smiled. There wasn't a rock big enough for me to crawl under. I took great perverse glee when the production manager couldn't get it up either. The scene would remain soft-core.

It was another bad day at the office only this one felt like playing a Little League game in Yankee Stadium. There was something preposterous and overwhelming about trying to fuck somebody in front of John Holmes. You'd just have to say I wasn't up for it.

Holmes went on to make a bunch more movies and, oddly, so did I. Over our careers in the nefarious fraternity of male porn stars, if Holmes was the general, then I probably made lieutenant, maybe captain. I ran into him once at an audition. Afterwards, he invited me to snort some cocaine with him. Sure, why not? It was the early-eighties then. Cocaine was the new marijuana. It was everywhere. The bodies hadn't started piling up on the beaches yet. Within a year or so, the carnage of wrecked lives gave people pause to reconsider this cocaine thing. I was saved by the strength of my wife and our decision to start making babies. I got out of it. I don't know that John Holmes ever made it out.

John and I didn't do too many movies together. Once a year, I'd run into him at the X-rated Awards, which were hosted back then by the Adult Film Association. John Holmes was always an honored guest and a presenter, but he never won any of the prestigious acting awards. Jamie Gillis dominated the field in those years with a bunch of different guys vying for the supporting actor awards. Jamie was Holmes's only real rival to the mythical throne of smut. Indeed, many thought Jamie Gillis to be the true King of Porn with Holmes as a kind of intriguing sideshow.

For one thing, Jamie Gillis was a fine actor. He had that New York sophistication laced with charm and wit. There was an intelligence about him. Skilled at comedy and triumphant in playing characters with darker qualities, Jamie also had that soothing, recognizable voice. Comparatively, Holmes was a country bumpkin.

In his serialized movie autobiography, "The Mad Satyr," published in *Screw*, Jamie Gillis wrote compassionately of John Holmes back in

1975, "Sadly, no one ever considered him (Holmes) as anything but a big dick."

Ah, but that was precisely the point! He did have that big dick! Perhaps he had the biggest dick in the world! Most American men of my generation and older knew the rumor about slain 1930s gangster John Dillinger. It was said that his dick was being saved in some glass jar over at the Smithsonian Institute because it too was so gigantic. John Holmes was the living reincarnation of Dillinger's dick. The kinds of characters he played only added to that association, both on screen and off.

While Jamie Gillis was a big man with a well above average-sized dick, he was still mortal. John Holmes was something else. Like Achilles and Hercules, he rode with the gods.

John Leslie, the top-stud heir to both Holmes and Gillis, once admiringly referred to Holmes as "the Babe Ruth of Porn." If that be so, then Jamie Gillis will forever be Ty Cobb. Talk baseball to me. Sure, Cobb had 4,000 hits, all those batting titles, stole bases and hit .400, but Babe Ruth hit all those titanic home runs. Like Muhammad Ali and Michael Jordan after him, he was bigger than the game he played. Those folks captured the imagination of their generation.

And John Holmes, for whatever acting he could do, still had that huge dick, the Washington Monument of dicks, and it was served up to us in the Ziegfeld Follies of smut.

"So, step right up, Ladies and Gentlemen, under the big top, for your viewing pleasure, believe it or not, the one, the only, Johnny Wadd!"

And we did too. John Holmes was box office, a one-man donkey show. He made a lot of money for somebody. I only hope he made some for himself and whatever family he had.

I used to love to watch the women who were "working" with John Holmes for the first time. You could see the sheer wonder in their faces. They were amazed, as were we in the audience watching them. They could put both hands around his dick when it was hard and still not have him covered. Was that driving a Cadillac or what?

This was going to be the actual moment …

WHEN SHE FOUND OUT IF BIGGER WAS BETTER OR NOT!

There would be no more myth, no more controversy, she would soon know! We would all know. The anticipation was delicious. The energy in those scenes crackled. It was real and electric.

When they'd put their mouths to that dick, it looked like they were eating some kind of German bologna. Then, when they'd try to take him in their wombs, some of those women melted away in a pure religious ecstasy, others seemed to be struggling with what was an erotic trial by ordeal, and, of course, others just had to beg for mercy or scream to stop.

Late in his career, Holmes burst onto the front pages with that drug murder thing in LA. I never did get the details straight. I didn't want to. I didn't want to know anything about it except what I read in the paper.

It was 1982. I was out of the business. We had just had our first baby and I was remodeling the house when the phone call came. It was a guy named Stu from Miracle Films.

"How would you like to do a sex scene with Marilyn Chambers and John Holmes?" Stu asked. He sounded as if he were offering me the keys to the kingdom, like I was supposed to jump up and down and yell, "whoopee!"

Well, I would rather have fallen off a ladder. The very idea of a ménage-a-trois with those two shrunk my gonads. John Holmes had just been in the headlines with three months of squalid tales of drug dealers, betrayals, murders, and police. I thought he was still in jail or protective custody or whatever they were calling it. Stu assured me that the big fella was out and was eager to resume his career.

Oh, goody! I could just see me and my five-and-three quarter inches paired up with John and his fourteen-and-a-half. It would be like going on a see-saw with the offensive line of the Washington Redskins. There would be no balance. My feet would never touch the ground. I just knew that I would never get a hard-on.

Even without John Holmes, Marilyn Chambers was no big thrill for me either. I had worked with her twice and still didn't have a clue who she was. There was absolutely nothing special happening between us. I had a baby. I was retired. I told Stu I was retired.

Stu wouldn't take "no" for an answer. He explained that he was stuck. I had worked with Stu and Marilyn six months earlier on a movie called, *Up and Coming*. The backers were insisting on adding another sex scene before it could be released and for some odd reason my character had to be involved.

"But Stu, I'm fifteen pounds heavier than when we shot last summer."

"I don't care," says Stu, "you can leave some clothes on."

"I don't think so, Stu, I'm way too fragile. I haven't done a sex scene in months and I'm up to my ass in Huggies."

"Come on, pal, it's just like riding a bike."

"Look, Marilyn Chambers and John Holmes are just too much power for me to handle. I won't be able to function sexually."

"Well, hey, you got some power there too!" he said.

If I ever needed proof that he really was stuck, that was it. "You don't even have to have an orgasm," he said. "If it happens, fine . If it doesn't, no big deal. Just be in the scene." Very few producers have ever tried that hard to give me a job. When he finally started throwing more money on top of my already considerable rate, I was unretired. After all, Huggies weren't that cheap.

We shot the scene at the private home of a Marin County proctologist which turned out to be appropriate because John Holmes ended up fucking Marilyn Chambers in the ass.

By the time we shot it, Lilly Marlene and Herschel Savage had been added to the cast. I was grateful. Their addition helped reduce the pressure on me.

We were all on the set early that morning except for John Holmes. He wasn't scheduled to come in until the afternoon. Stu had been right. It was just like riding a bike. Once the cameras started rolling, my squeamishness evaporated. I'd been there before. Y'see, I eventually did learn how to have sex on camera.

Marilyn Chambers was in a buoyant mood. The old boyfriend Chuck Traynor was gone. She had a new one now and she was far less aloof than in our previous encounters. I enjoyed her. There was a lot of kibbitzing on the set with cast and crew and she was just one of the guys. I liked Lilly Marlene a lot too. Lilly was one of the most underrated females of that era. She flat out adored sex. Working with her was always fun, hot, and easy. Rarely did you come across an actress who actually enjoyed the coupling as much as she did.

John Holmes showed up in the middle of the afternoon. He appeared strange and moody. It was just what you'd expect from a guy who'd just been released from months in "protective custody." I didn't really know him well enough except to say, "Hello."

He said, "Hello," back and that was about it. I didn't want to ask about his problems with the cops and the bad guys and he wasn't making any speeches. He kept pretty much to himself that day. I remember that when the sun went down, we all had to bundle up for warmth between takes. Not John. He stayed naked in the cold and appeared comfortable. Somebody whispered the offhand remark, "Well, that's what prison will do for ya."

I was first up in the sex scene department with a double blow-job from Marilyn and Lilly. Piece of cake, it was one of my favorite flavors. All I had to do was kick back while the two willing women traded my lollipop from one mouth to the other. They stayed fresh, I stayed stimulated, and John and Herschel waited in the wings for me to finish. I had no trouble scaling Mt. Come Shot that day, it felt quite good. I was even smug enough to take my time. Eventually, I reached nature's liquid conclusion.

Next, Herschel did an anal scene with Lilly. She was one of the few who actually enjoyed anal sex and no one had heard about AIDS yet. I watched a bit of their tryst from an overhanging balcony and then found the kitchen buffet to nibble at the groceries. I was back there eating when I first heard Marilyn Chambers's screams. They were loud. They were come-and-see-what's-going-on loud.

When I peeked out over the balcony, I saw John Holmes feeding his living monument into Marilyn's ass. She was howling, but she wasn't howling, "Stop." Her face revealed a frenzied confusion of pain and pleasure. She was on-line electric with face ablaze. It mesmerized everybody there to watch as their fury mounted. When Holmes was completely and unbelievably sheathed by her anus, Marilyn went into a yogic breath-of-fire. It was extraordinary. It reminded me of my wife giving birth. Although relatively fresh from my blow-job, my cock hardened again in my shorts. The look on Marilyn's face was like ... I don't even know how to describe it. I had never seen a woman that out of control, that transported during a sex act, cinematically or privately. It was like the sexual equivalent of speaking in tongues.

I don't remember if Holmes came inside of her or gave it the traditional porn pull out and squirt. All I can remember was that look on Marilyn's face. When he withdrew from her ass, you could have parked your car in there. Their scene left me numb. I stumbled through collecting my pay and went home. It was the last time I ever saw John Holmes.

For months afterward, I told people that this was the greatest sex scene ever. I couldn't wait to see the movie. When that day came, I couldn't have been more disappointed. They seemed to have kept the camera locked down on the meat shot. It was a close-up of the cock plunging the asshole ad nauseum. Marilyn's face had been mostly ignored.

In his 1982 film biography, *Exhausted*, Holmes was asked by an interviewer, "If you had it to do all over again, would you do it?"

"I wouldn't change a stroke," Holmes replied.

Well, I bet you he changed his mind. I heard a rumor back then that John Holmes's widow claimed that he contracted the AIDS virus while working on one of his last five videos.

The denial apparatus of the industry kicked in with, "John Holmes was an IV drug user. John Holmes was a bi-sexual. It was an isolated case. It won't happen to me. I won't get AIDS." The industry hardly skipped a beat. Being socially responsible was never its strong suit and John Holmes sadly represented that aspect of the business as well. Since his death, it's been revealed that he continued to work for a time after having contracted the AIDS virus without informing his partners. How else can this be construed as anything but a desperate and despicable act? It is well beyond our reasonable comprehension to excuse. It leaves a sour taste and darkens the entire canvas of what otherwise might have remained a colorful story of an outrageous character.

Be that as it may, somebody had to be the sexual Paul Bunyan and John Holmes, for better and worse, was it. I guess that there have been other colossal schlongs in porn history, I mean, really big dicks. Long Dong Silver and Dick Rambone come to mind. I once heard an old-timer talk about a guy named O.K. Freddy from the Thirties. He said Joan Crawford used to show him off at her parties. But in our generation, it was John Holmes who wore the crown.

Chapter Twenty-Two

Stormy Weather
"Don't know why,
There's no bone between my thighs,
Stormy weather,
Just can't get my poor sperm together.
They're hiding all the time,
All the time."

– Gordon Archive

Stormy Weather.

Q. "What do you call a porn star who can't get a hard-on?
A. An actor.

Pizza Girls made it five in a row. There was no denying my slump. I hadn't been able to have an orgasm in my last five movies.

Ironic, don't you think, that it would be so difficult for me to be successful in an occupation that was held in such low regard and contempt by the mainstream. One would have thought that it should have been a lot easier for me to ruin my life, but I really had to work hard to do it, so to speak.

"Ooo, I wouldn't do that," they'd say. "I wouldn't act in a porn film!" As if they could! As if they'd even been invited to try! As if there were something so easy to do about it that they deserved some kind of special medal for just resisting the temptation to do it.

Well, I was busting my ass trying to do it and the best I could come up with was a .500 batting average. In the porn business, that stunk. If I hadn't come along at a time when the producers were actually hiring actors who could deliver their lines as well as their boners, I would never have lasted in the business. I was only getting work now because I could act a little bit.

Producers didn't really want to risk hiring an actor who was only giving them a fifty-fifty chance of being able to successfully complete a sex scene. There were plenty of guys in the business who seemed to be batting anywhere between .900 and 1.000. That's why you saw those same guys over and over again in porn. They were the reliable ones. It was not anywhere as easy to perform sex as most men would think. Hell, even the great Marlon Brando had dick troubles in the movies:

> *I had one of the more embarrassing experiences of my professional career when we were making this film (Last Tango in Paris) in 1972. I was supposed to play a scene in the Paris apartment where Paul meets Jeanne and be photographed in the nude frontally, but it was such a cold day that my penis shrank to the size of a peanut. It simply withered. Because of the cold, my body went into full retreat, and the tension, embarrassment and stress made it recede even more. I realized I couldn't play the scene this way, so I paced back and forth around the apartment naked, hoping for magic. I've always had a strong belief in the power of mind over matter, so I concentrated on my private parts, trying to will my penis and testicles to grow; I even spoke to them. But my mind failed me. I was humiliated, but not ready to surrender yet. I asked Bernardo (Director Bernardo Bertolucci) to be patient and told the crew that I wasn't giving up. But after an hour I could tell from their faces that they had given up on me. I simply couldn't play the scene that way, so it was cut.*
>
> – Marlon Brando,
> Songs My Mother Taught Me

Speaking of irony, I had already given up on a career in acting several years before I ever did my first professional sex film. Acting and trying to compete as an actor had just freaked me out too much. I could never get over being scared all the time and feeling too vulnerable. Now, trying to make it in the X-rated movies, the sex stuff so traumatized me that "acting" became the place where I could relax. Acting became the place where I could shine. No matter how badly my sex scenes had gone, producers and directors had generally been pleased with my character work.

Then again, in porn … if you showed up …

If you showed up … on time …

If you showed up on time … and were sober …

If you showed up on time and were sober … and had your lines memorized …

Well! If you showed up on time and were sober and had your lines memorized, they treated you like you were Laurence Fucking Olivier. And since there was only a fifty-fifty chance that I would actually be bringing a dick with me to the set, I figured that it was the least I could do.

Chapter Twenty-Three

"If you're normal, I don't want to be."
                    - Adeline Gordon, My Mom

In high school, I thought I had done a pretty good job of trying to fit in. But by college, I sensed the distance between "normal" and me.

The sixties didn't help any. The sixties rewarded iconoclastic behavior. In the great counter-cultural revolution, "out" became the new "in." The avalanche of psychedelic drugs only added fuel to the fire. And, of course, having had the smiling Buddha of my Uncle Izzy around as guru and mentor probably cinched my lifelong commitment to unrepentant foolishness.

I was trying to grow up, but the conventional choices of Doctor-Lawyer-Dentist just weren't going to work for me.

Porn star, on the other hand, well, now, that had some panache.

I took a vote. Even with the troubles, I still wanted it. It was that simple. Porn seemed like the right place for me to be. For whatever the ganglia of mixed motivations that were driving me, I became enamored of the challenge to be able to perform in these films.

I figured I had already taken the best shots that failure and humiliation had to offer and I was still standing. They were still offering me parts. Perhaps I had bottomed out on my sexual nincompoopery. Maybe it was time now for Popeye to pass me the spinach and for me to release my inner boner. Yeah, and for that to happen, I knew I had to get the wreck of my libido into the body shop for some serious repairs. Cue the music! Call Shorty Long and the All-Stars! I had to get myself ready for the "Function at the Junction."

Carly had a good idea. She suggested that when it came time for me to do a sex scene, I should imagine balancing my fear against my desire as if they were the two sides on the Scales of Justice.

If I felt that my fear was outweighing my desire, then it would not be a good idea to start the sex. The odds would be against me achieving and sustaining any kind of arousal. At such a point, my job would be to do whatever I could do to reduce the fear so that my desire would have a fighting chance.

Given the proper stimulation, one's body knew exactly how to experience pleasure. Sometimes, "one" just had to get "one's self" out of the goddamned way. The great baseball sage Yogi Berra once said, "You can't think and hit at the same time!" When it came time to touch, I had to get all those inner voices to shut the fuck up and let my body do what it knew how to do.

Of course, all of this was a lot easier said than done, but just having had this conversation with Carly gave me a framework for beginning to approach the problem with something besides my own shame, rattled machismo and dread. We were gonna get this thing licked!

Looking back, Carly was my first coach. At that stage of our relationship, it was enough for her to know that I wanted a career in the adult business for her to try and help me go out there and get it. And she did!

Wow!

Chapter Twenty-Four
Talk Baseball to Me

"Excellence is never a trivial pursuit, no matter how bizarre the medium for it."

Simon Barnes, Sportswriter, London Times

I began keeping a box score. "In stress, we regress," went the pop psychology slogan and I took it all the way back to Little League.

Just as in the starting days of my baseball career when I worked on my hitting by keeping a detailed record of each at-bat, I looked back on the sex scenes I had played. I broke down each scene into its elements and began keeping my X-rated box score. I was hoping to recognize key factors that would enable me to improve my sexual batting average. Here's what it looked like:

Movie	Partner	Time	Position	Outcome
1. *The Candy Stripers*	Nancy	5-6 hrs	Standing – Oral	Erections - Orgasm
	Phaedra	45 min.	Missionary	Erections – Orgasm
2. *Legend of Lady Blue*	None	4 hrs.	Standing - Masturbation	Erections - Zero
3. Loop	Ronnie	45 min.	Kneeling - Doggy-style	Erections – Orgasm
4. Loop	Marlene	45 min.	Many	Erections – Orgasm
5. *Sensual Encounters of Every Kind*	Chris Cassidy	1 hr.	Many	Erections - Zero
6. *Candy Goes To Hollywood*	Carol Connors	2 hrs.	Standing - Doggy-style w/fluffer	Erections – Zero
	Carrie	6-7 hrs.	Sitting – Oral	Nothing Required
7. *Telefantasy*	Christine	3-5 min.	Reclining – Oral	Zero
8. *Pizza Girls*	Candida Royalle	20 min.	Standing – Oral	Slight Erection - Zero

I was hitting four for nine, a .444 batting average. That's actually worse than I remembered. Still, there were some clues there. I didn't do well when I tried to have sex standing up. That was good to know. Also, though it didn't exactly appear in the box score as a category, I could see by the partner's names that I tended to do poorly if I thought that they didn't want to be with me.

Good luck on that one!

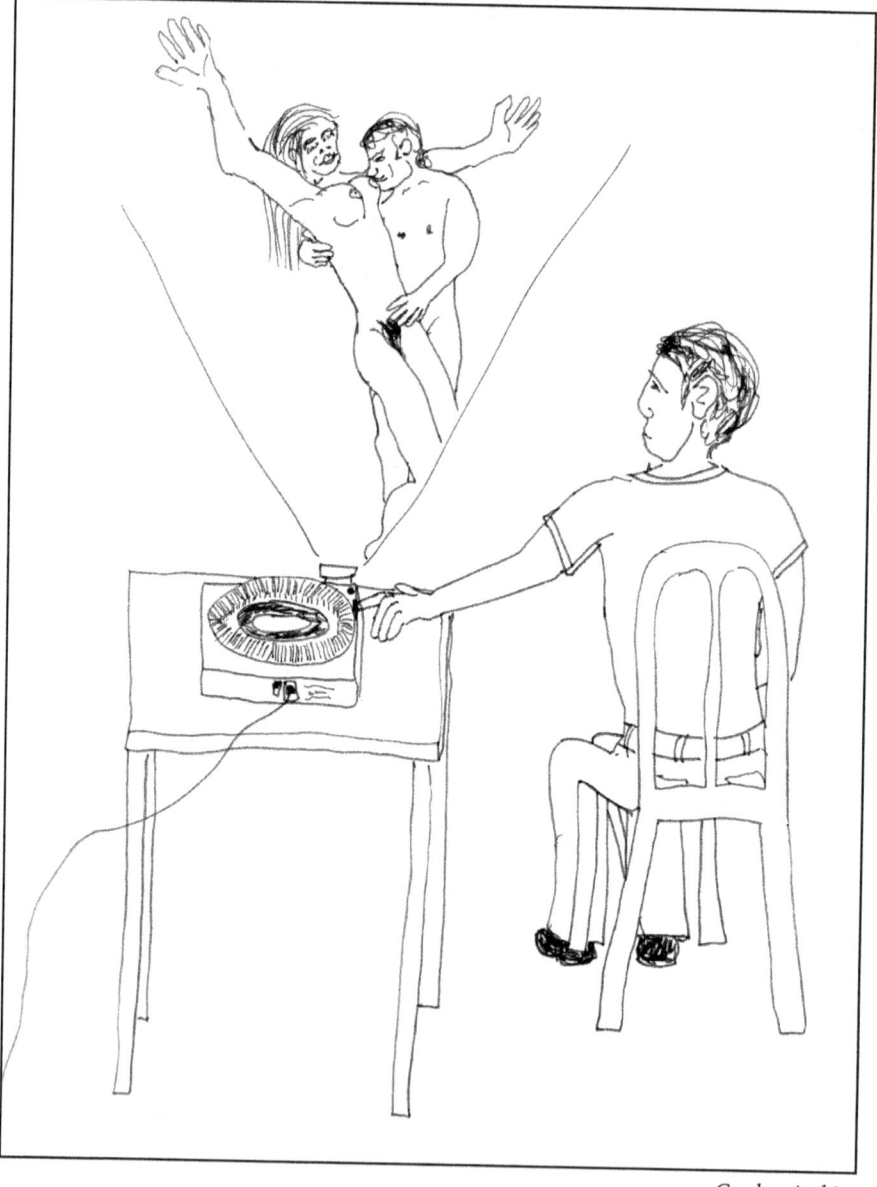

– Gordon Archive

Working on my craft.

Chapter Twenty-Five
Oddly enough, that's his real name.

John Seeman was the first male friend I made in the business. He might actually be a leprechaun. I'm not sure. He isn't two feet tall with a thick Irish brogue, but he's hard to pin down and he does have this otherworldly twinkle to his eye.

Unassuming, you'd have to say, is the word for John Seeman. At first glance on the street, you don't think porn star. You'd think banker, insurance agent, some job where an easy smile and a calm demeanor would go a long, long way in dealing with

– Gordon Archive

John Seeman.

the public. He exuded competence. He looked like he knew what he was doing. He spoke like he knew what he was saying.

When John took off his glasses and got naked, it wasn't exactly Clark Kent to Superman, but he did reveal a taut, compact body that was always in tip-top shape.

John was the first experienced actor I found who would talk to me about the dynamics of performing screen sex. It seemed to be a world of *Live and Let Die* among the other male stars I'd seen. "Why should they help the competition?" was the attitude. John was secure enough in himself that he could offer some words of advice to a struggling newcomer. I will be forever grateful.

As a sexual performer, John was one of the steadiest guys around. Word was that even after he'd finished his own scene as an actor, the producers and directors liked keeping him around the set afterwards just in case another actor fell down on the job.

– Vincent Fronczek

Amusing John Seeman with tales of ejaculatory incompetence.

John Seeman could play the stuntcock. Like the relief pitcher or the closer in baseball, he could come in there and get you a save for your sex scene. The director would come to the mound and take out the failing cocksman. In would step John from the bullpen. Zip-Zip-Zip, he'd get it up. Zip-Zip-Zip, he'd get it off. Hail, John, the conquering hero!

With a wee bit of movie magic in the post-production, they'd edit in a close-up of John's crowing cock to replace whatever limp dick had died on the shores of the female penetration. The audience in the movie theaters would never know the difference. It was said that John could do a come shot during an earthquake.

By the time we met, John was already winding down his performing career and getting more involved behind the camera. I had run into him as the Production Manager (PM) on several shoots. We had fallen into some conversations about this and that and had gradually become friends. Along with photographer Vincent Fronczek, we became a frequent trio together, but we'll get to Vince later.

The role of the Production Manager was a key cog in the X-rated film production of the Bay Area in the seventies and early-eighties. A production company could arrive from Los Angeles and with one phone call could arrange to have their choice of all the available performers, crews, soundstages, equipment rentals, locations, caterers, or whatever else they would need to make their movie. The Production Manager was an extremely important fast lane job. If you wanted to work, you made damn sure they had your phone number.

I don't remember specifically how John got started helping me out with the movie sex, but he did. You know, it's not easy for one guy to admit to another that he's having problems with his dick, but my failures were already a matter of public record within the industry. I was drowning and I wanted to learn how to swim. When John took an interest in me, I was honored to be able to make my confession to him.

We'd been on a few movie sets together and John offered the observation that he thought I was trying to play the game without exercising any of my own personal power. If the director had said to me, "Fuck the starlet doggy style while you're standing on one leg and whistle 'Dixie,'" then that's what I would try to do. John suggested that trying to please everybody but myself might be getting in my own way. He argued that when I came to bat, I had to make things right for me. I had to arrange the scene so that I would be able to sexually function. There came a point, he argued, where it no longer mattered exactly what they wanted.

"Because after all," he said, "if you don't get to your boner, there is no scene anyway."

In time, our conversations about movie making and the arousal process helped me to formulate these concrete measures that I could incorporate into my future attempts at doing a sex scene:

- *Get the director on my side.* I could let the director know that I wasn't confident about a particular scene. It might cost me a job or two, but I would get a lot of support when I did get the job. I could give the director information like if I had to get it up and down too many times—say, over seven or eight—I tended to break down. I would create the director as my ally.

- *Get the actress on my side.* If she didn't like me or I didn't like her, we could go to the director right away and try to arrange for another pairing. Being certain of a willing sex partner would make a world of difference. I would create my sex partner as my ally.

- *Make the set comfortable.* I could tell the director that I didn't want to fuck standing up on a coffee table or underwater in a cold swimming pool. I could make input into the kind of scene they were asking me to do. I had to learn to respect my own limits. I had to learn how to say, "No." I would make the environment an ally.

- *Remove troublemakers from the set.* If a jealous boyfriend or wise-ass crewperson was wrecking my confidence, I could go to the director and let him know. They would be asked to leave the set while I was performing. There was one particular still photographer who used to really enjoy taunting and humiliating me. He would always flirt with the woman I was supposed to work with. That fucker would be gone.

- *Prepare for the scene.* In my case, this meant refraining from orgasm for two or three days prior to a sex scene. This would leave me horny enough to fuck a Volkswagen bus. It also meant staying away from drugs or alcohol on the set, regardless of what anybody else was doing.

Like with Carly earlier, the most valuable aspect of my conversation with John Seeman was the fact that we had the conversation at all. Most of the men of X behaved like roosters looking to dominate the barnyard. There were only so many jobs and one did not reach out to help the competition. Until I met John, "help was not on the way."

As the Catholic Church has known for centuries, confession is good for the soul. The confession of my sexual performance fears to John was made more meaningful because John had successfully navigated the very same waters in which I was floundering. I could never have spent ten years in the business without his help.

Chapter Twenty-Six

Babylove was played by Sharon Kane. I was Beau. It was my first male lead. The film was written and directed by Daemian Lee. I had already done a sex scene earlier for him in one of my first loops.

– *Gordon Archive.*

If John Seeman was a leprechaun, then Daemian Lee must have been a satyr, one of those half-man, half-goat creatures of Greek legend. His long curly hair no doubt hid the short horns and pointed ears, but I was pretty sure that if you took off his shoes, you'd see the hooves. His beard was a well-trimmed goatee and his lechery was a matter of public record.

"I can help you with that," was what Daemian told me when I spoke of the arousal problems I'd been having with screen lust. And he did! In fact, what we ended up doing together was creating an acting class where adult film performers could come and work on whatever they wanted in order to improve their skills.

– Gordon Archive.

The initial class of "the Sex Actor's Film Academy" had a total enrollment of four students and one faculty member. I was there to have a safe place to practice having sex in front of the camera. Sharon Kane got recruited to do some scene study and improvisation. Keith joined us because he was a good friend of Daemian. They had already worked together on a number of projects. Tess completed our ensemble. She was Daemian's biggest fan, all-round assistant, and live-in lover. That was our student body. There were no fees. We were all there on full scholarships.

Daemian, of course, was the teacher. In the back of his mind, he had already arranged financing to direct a small-scale feature film of his own. In addition to helping us with our stated needs, Daemian would use the class to further develop his screenplay and to line up the potential talent for casting what would later become the movie, *Babylove and Beau*.

Our first class met in Daemian and Tess's little apartment. Our next three classes also met in their apartment. We only had four classes and then we went right into the production of *Babylove and Beau*.

During the first class, Daemian placed me on a stool and had me face the video camera. I was naked. My assignment was to masturbate to orgasm.

Y'know, I've often thought during my career that a movie made about what we were really going through offscreen while making some of these porno movies would be far more interesting and entertaining than stuff we were doing onscreen. Backstage in Pornoland was an endlessly fascinating place peopled by extraordinary characters in all kinds of bizarre situations. This particular "rehearsal" in Daemian and Tess's apartment would certainly make for a fine scene in any such production.

My assignment was to face the camera and masturbate to orgasm. In real life, the door got closed and locked whenever I masturbated. I never ever wanted to get "caught" masturbating, and I never did. But this wasn't real life. This was Pornoland. It was a humiliating and embarrassing situation to put myself into, but I was working on my "hitting" and I cranked up the nerve to try.

My classmates were supportive. I had confessed my fears to the entire student body and had asked for their help in using this class to grow stronger as a sexual performer. Daemian had Sharon Kane sit herself underneath the camera lens and face me. She was naked too. She was also masturbating herself. She was generously offering me that view as a stimulation for me to achieve my goal. I went at the task with a determination.

Can you hear the theme song from *Rocky* playing? I'm runnin' through the streets of Philadelphia. I'm doin' a left-right-left on a side of beef.

"I'm workin' here! I'm workin' here!" Would Dustin Hoffman do anything less?

After pumping and sweating and admiring the intimate views of Sharon Kane, my penis gushed forth the precious liquid triumph. I slumped and sighed as my classmates applauded.

Babylove and Beau was the story of a sailor on shore leave in San Francisco.

As Beau, I had four sex scenes to play in the movie. The first one was a three-way with two women playing hookers. One of them was a pornstar-like flashy blonde and the other looked like the young woman you sat next to during a History lecture at college. Nice smile, no heat. Naturally, I was all eager to have sex with the flashy blonde. I thought that the heat would come from her. Dead wrong.

When the cameras started rolling, the blonde was a total disappointment. She was listless and matter-of-fact. Ho-hum, another cock to suck. She appeared bored by it all and blasé just did not do it for me. I think she wanted a paycheck and I think she wanted to do as little as possible in order to get it. Had it been just the two of us, that scene could have been in a whole lot of trouble. As it was, the college girl came through like a champ.

Her name was Roberta. She was actually Sharon Kane's roommate. She was friendly, eager, willing, and wanting. It was a very nice combination for me. She filled all the gaps of desire opened by the blonde's apparent indifference.

Between the two of them, I got it done. I was hard when I was supposed to be hard and I was able to orgasm when the director called for the sacred come shot.

Line drive—base hit! Thank you, Roberta!

My remaining three sex scenes were all with Sharon Kane. I had known Sharon since the orgy scene in *Candy Goes to Hollywood*. She was a big-boned woman in her early twenties with long flowing blonde hair that reached her backside. She looked real. She was warm and friendly with an easy, out-going way and had an innate sense of comedy. She was talented, sincere, and down-to-earth good people. I had gotten to know her better than any other woman I had yet to work with. We had some chemistry going, Sharon and me. I liked Sharon a lot. Beau loved her.

In our first sex scene together, I was fucking her from behind, doggy style, when she suddenly threw her head back and caught me right in the mouth. Boom! I bit my tongue and drew blood. We had to stop filming. When the bleeding finally stopped and we tried to get the sex started up again, my penis was gone. The panic returned. Shit. Daemian didn't waste any time. He had me simulate an orgasm and then I was pulled out of the scene for a stunt cock. Classmate Keith was going to stand in for me.

I got very nervous and crazy when my erection disappeared. Daemian sent me off of the set. Told me I should go out and jog a mile before coming back. It was a strange direction to receive and what was probably even stranger was that I did it.

When I returned, Keith had done the deed and we moved on.

In our second sex scene, we did something a little bit different. We went for the female come shot. Most female orgasms portrayed in the movies were acted. They were not real. It was, no doubt, as difficult for a woman to come on camera as it was for a man. Mostly, directors simply did not want to wait around for something that they couldn't really "see" anyway. A lot of time and money was saved by just having the women "act" their orgasms.

To Daemian and Sharon's credit, we thought that a real female orgasm might play better than a simulation and that became the focus of our second sex scene. In essence, Beau gave Babylove a blow job.

We shot a certain amount of the hardcore oral sex footage and then the camera crew went into stand-by to await the orgasm. I continued to mouth Sharon until she got close and then she cued the camera to roll. We were able to film her having an orgasm.

Somehow, the world remained remarkably unimpressed by this bit of revolutionary cinema.

We shot our last sex scene on a deserted beach near Half Moon Bay. It was a glorious day. We had to pass through a field of ripe artichokes to get to the beach and we all got to pick some to take home for dinner. The film was nearing completion and feelings were running high.

We had shot a lot of montage footage of *Babylove and Beau* rolling around in Golden Gate Park, walking hand-in-hand the streets of San Francisco, and today, they'd make love on a golden California beach.

Babylove and Beau had been on a weeklong ride of falling in love and the sands of time were running out on the romance. Soon, the bubble would pop and Howie and Sharon would have to cope with the return to their normal lives. This lovemaking scene pretty much reflected the climax of the movie, both on screen and off. The scene felt like it was half work and half reward. It was easy sex that day, warm and playful with a double barrel of emotion.

The role of Beau had lasted longer than any I had previously played. Acting 101 — it was hard letting go. I liked being the star and I liked being Beau. An actor worked very hard to become somebody else and then, POOF! It was all over. There was nothing to do but go home and start over. I wrote in my diary:

> Hey, Beau, whatta ya know?
> Everything has got to go!
> Hey, Beau, whatta ya know?
> Everything is gone!

Chapter Twenty-Seven

"You know what I liked best about that Chapter?" Carly asked me.
"No, what?" I said.
"The artichokes. With porn stars, you know it's all so sucky-fucky this and that. It's all so crude. The idea that they go home and eat artichokes for dinner, now, that's just perfect!"

Chapter Twenty-Eight

"Life is what happens to you while you're busy making other plans."
                                              - John Lennon

The phone rang on May 5, 2009. It was my mother-in-law calling on my birthday. I thought I'd be done with this book by then, but I wasn't even close. Maybe I'll be done by May 5 of next year.

In addition to wishing me a "Happy Birthday," Mom was calling to let us know that she had just had a terminal tiff with her assisted living helper who was now being sent packing. Oops.

Mom was in her golden years. She had survived the death of her spouse some four or five years earlier and continued to live on in her own home. She was still sharp as a tack, but now she needed some help physically to keep it all afloat. This last live-in, assisted-living helper had lasted eleven months before this rather sudden and abrupt conclusion.

For a variety of reasons, Mom could not be left alone, and the family decided to send me to Southern California to help her until another caregiver could be hired and placed into service.

When I first married Carly, I thought that the last thing on earth I needed was yet another mother and father. The ones I already had seemed to be just plenty. Well, the long years since have revealed otherwise. I couldn't have been more wrong. I was extremely blessed and lucky in the in-law department and I was more than fine with having the opportunity to be of some service to Carly's mom.

Our brief time together that followed was a treasure. I was able to help with her eye-drop medications, driving to appointments, food preparation, and just generally being a companion and running the house. The one significant thing I wasn't asked to provide was personal care for her in grooming and dressing, but Carly's older sister came around often enough to make that work too. Mostly what I provided was the security and peace of mind that came with not being left alone in a big house

My visit lasted around ten days. Eventually, new assisted-living workers were interviewed and hired and Carly and I chatted in our e mails about my return:

I wrote:

Your mom's taking her nap now. I'm just phumfing around the computer. Thought I'd tell you that I love you.

Ted Clumsily

Carly wrote:

Dear Ted,
Obviously I have not opened my computer for several days.
I just got your love note and I'm wrapping it around my metaphorical shoulders to hold me 'til you get home, when I will be wrapping me around your actual everything until you rinse me off.
I love you more than moon syrup on cloud waffles.

Mini Haha

I wrote:

Good Shabbos, Ms. HaHa!
I have my boarding pass. I am looking to renew my membership in your general everything come the morrow.
Things here appear stable. May they continue on that path.

> *Love,*
> *Shminny Attsairris, the Puerto Rican catcher*

Carly wrote:

Shminny!
I am breathless in wait 4 U.
Please continue from these ideas
toward eventual realization.
You have a boarding pass.
Behind the picture of Dad in the
computer room, I left an unopened
bottle of cherry flavored Maalox.
If you're checking yr. bag, please
bring it home. If not, they
likely won't let you through
security, so leave it there and I'll
plan on some indigestion on my next
trip to SD.
You, my beloved, are the Meow of
the Cat and also its Pajamas.
I adoreth thy general everything.

> *Hunque Hunque Burninlove*

And she picked me up at the airport. As we were heading home, my beloved swore to me after my return from helping to take care of her mother that she would never again get on my case about anything.

I asked, "Would you put that in writing?"

"Don't push it," she replied.

Chapter Twenty-Nine

"So, Marty, you saying you might want to agent this thing after all?"

"Well, that depends. Can you stop writing about your erectile dysfunction?"

"Y'know, when I first dropped out of the business back in 1982, I sat down and wrote 1,000 pages. It was the complete encyclopedia of my career."

"Yeah, I know," he interrupted, "and there's probably about two guys on the whole fucking planet who might like to read something like that, neither of whom, I guarantee you, that you'd want to spend any time with."

"You're killin' me, Marty."

"Yeah, well, I'm tryin'. You know, sometimes you write like you're still getting paid by the word. We're not after volume here. All is way too much. It gets boring. I've had it with all your dick troubles. Enough is enough. Pick and choose. It's time to distill from all that information. Pare and carve. Get it all down to the best of the best and then we'll see what we've got. Okay?"

"Okay."

"Yeah? Really? You said, 'Okay?'"

"Yeah, okay."

"Well, okay then."

Chapter Thirty

After *Babylove and Beau*, I was hitting six for twelve in career orgasms.

Those were not exactly Hall of Fame stats.

My fears and agonies about cinematic sex were all real enough, but there was no way I could escape a certain appreciation for the ridiculousness of my dilemmas. I mean, how many people walking down Main St., U.S.A., were having my kind of troubles at the office?

That year, the next volume of my diary was titled, *What to Do Until Mental Health Comes*. It began with: *The Porno Actor's Prayer*.

A Porno Actor's Prayer

by Marcus Howard

May the good Lord
   Put a doughnut 'round
      my dick...
and give that woman
   a sweet tooth. Amen.

– Gordon Archive.

At this point, pornography continued to be my way of running off to join the circus. The regular nine-to-five just wasn't gonna work for me. And even though I was married, I was nowhere close to being able to make any kind of a commitment that included monogamy. It seemed like I was where I was supposed to be.

My next job came in a loop arranged for me by John Seeman. It was a straight sex scene and I worked in a three-way with a woman named Mandy and a guy named Gene.

I liked Mandy right off the bat. She was a plain, right-nice, down-home Texas girl, about the same age as me. During the preliminaries of makeup and such, she talked a lot about her new boyfriend, Michael Morrison. I talked about my wife. Mandy was real and the touching was easy.

Our partner Gene, on the other hand, was a frenetic young, macho type with a big dick. I didn't have much use for him, but peaceful coexistence was not impossible. If you think that politics makes for strange bedfellows, try working in porn for a while.

When the sex got underway, Gene fucked her first. I kind of just held her while she absorbed his pounding. Gene was being a real man about it. I stroked Mandy's hair and nuzzled her about the neck in trying to defer some of the harshness of his lust. Eventually, Gene squirted his squirt and I took his place. We made a slower, softer love and I made a new friend. Coming was no problem. I was seven for thirteen.

Couple days later, there was another phone call from John Seeman and another loop.

- Vincent Fronczek/Gordon Archive

John Seeman was selling my salami.

This was another threesome, this time with Liza and Flip. It turned out to be a remarkable experience.

From the moment we first touched Liza, she got very LOUD. I mean, VERY LOUD. And the moaning and groaning was extraordinary. This was the intersection of "Hot and Funny."

We were shooting in a residential apartment building. The director and the film crew immediately began shushing her so as not to get the neighbors all bent out of shape. Good luck with that! It was hard to tell if Liza couldn't or wouldn't turn it off. It seemed like some kind of unconscious oral eruption that just came alive with the sex. Wow! I had never met a woman like that before. Liza could get all the dogs in the neighborhood howling for blocks around. Not only could she have brought Lazarus back from the dead but she would have brought him back with a boner.

In most sex scenes, getting the actors and actresses to amplify their real arousal noises was like pulling teeth. Even at orgasm, people were often too shy to let the animal beast get out very far. The director would call for "more" from the "acting" and what was offered up was all too often an embarrassment and an insult to the entire human race. If you've seen even one porno movie, the odds are you know exactly what I'm talking about.

I don't know whether Liza was really turned on and this was just her way, or if she was acting. But either way, she offered up an incredible bit of erotic-comedic genius. Looking back, I wished I'd had the brains to do more work with her. Hers was a remarkable talent!

Flip came within the first two minutes. Liza barely had her motors warmed. I took his place. They had me trying to cover her mouth with my hands while we had sex, but it didn't do much good. She was the wolf woman, lit up. Liza the Moaner! Liza the Moaner was bellowing. She made just about the best sex noises I ever heard and she was making them for everybody! She didn't care who was listening. I doubt that any man within earshot could have possibly avoided getting hard. It was funny and it was hot. I stayed in the saddle as long as I could, but I too seemed to have been swept away by an early orgasm. No matter, Flip was up again and ready to go another round. Ride 'em, fuckin' Liza!

I was eight for fourteen.

Chapter Thirty-One

I shot a magazine for Paul Johnson. He was one of the very best photographers out there. Paul shot sex scenes just like loops, but he used his still cameras and made magazines instead of films. They were called *The Connoisseur Series*. They were very classy. He was very classy. Paul had a knack for putting the right people together and the sensitivity to treat them well. I had a wonderful afternoon working for him in a sex scene with two women. There were no problems at all.

It was a good day at the office. And when a sex scene went really well, you could look and feel like this when you were done:

– Paul Johnson

With Sandy and Teresa in *PRIZE CATCH* (1978).

Chapter Thirty-Two
PLAYGIRL

Back in 1978, Carly and I had a friend who wrote the advice column for *Playgirl* magazine.

"You're in good shape," she said to me one day in a hot tub. It was an understatement. I was almost thirty years old and I was in the best shape of my life. I worked out seven days a week and I was chiseled like a statue. "Why don't you do *Playgirl*?" she asked.

Male centerfolds were still a bit of a novelty item back then. Hollywood mega-star Burt Reynolds had started it all when he did a photo spoof back in 1972 for *Cosmopolitan* magazine. The *Cosmo* piece was called "For the Sexually Active Woman" and it featured a tastefully nude Reynolds—his penis was actually hidden—reclining on an animal skin rug.

The article created a media sensation. Less than a year later, up sprang *Playgirl* magazine in 1973 to cash in on this new phenomenon of male centerfolds.

We shot some nude photographs of me, where my penis was tastefully not hidden, and sent them down to a friend of hers at *Playgirl*. They said they'd get back to us real soon.

– Shirley/Gordon Archive

"Fine with me," I told her. "I'd love to be a centerfold!"

"… and visions of sugar plums danced in his head."

Playgirl. Playgirl was still the skin trade, but *Playgirl* was over the counter. Adult films were under the counter. They were X-rated. *Playgirl* was R-rated. It was out there, in the light of day, right there on the newsrack next to *Time* magazine and *Newsweek* and the *Ladies Home*

Journal. Adult films were hidden in the back rooms or behind curtains, displayed with magazines like *Really Big Bazzooms, Wide Open Beavers,* and *Astonishingly Red Asses.*

I thought that being in *Playgirl* could be a real career move for me. It could represent an astonishing leap from the gutter all the way up to the curb.

I was all for it. *Playgirl* could be the launch pad for me to go back into the straight end of the industry. Hundreds of centerfolds had gone on to successful careers in movies and television, hadn't they? Why not me too?

I hadn't even been picked yet and already I was retiring from the porn business. I wasn't very good at it anyway. Nobody was gonna miss me. I'd had enough of trying to make it all work. The novelty had worn off.

My original thoughts about being in porn as a way of getting extra sexual cookies beyond my married life had proven to be a cruel joke. Overall, the movie sex had been hit or miss. It wasn't fun. It was very hard work. I was completely anxiety ridden and I was bumfuck befuddled when it came down to performing the sex. Enough. Been there. Done that. Who needed to do any more?

Dear Diary, it was fun. I learned a lot. I picked up a few bucks and now, good-bye.

I called John Seeman and told him that I didn't want to do any more sex scenes. He asked if I'd still be interested in doing some straight parts in X-rated films. "Well, sure," I told him, "that would be fine, just no more sex scenes."

I probably slept easier that night than I had in months. I wouldn't have to lie to my parents any more. I was going straight.

To that point, my porn career had been remarkably undistinguished and I figured that I was still flying under the radar. I didn't think the few movies I had done would stand in the way of my renewed attempt at a more conventional actor's life. I was waiting to hear from *Playgirl.*

Chapter Thirty-Three

Exactly two days later, John Seeman called me up and offered me not just one but two different sex scenes, in two different movies, for two different paychecks, all on the same day. After having just declared my "retirement" to John, it was not what I expected. I was flabbergasted, but like the moth to the flame, I found myself interested. I was challenged. Maybe John Seeman knew me better than I knew myself.

No doubt the bank balances were low, because the idea of two paychecks sounded very good, good enough that I could ignore the potential for all the disaster and misery that might be involved in me earning them. I mean, how dare I try to do two come shots in one day?

"Bravery is a man in search of test," the Sufis once wrote. Gotta love them Sufis! Still hadn't heard from *Playgirl* yet. I had already done eleven sex films. I didn't think two more were gonna make much difference!

I unretired, for the first time, and accepted the jobs.

The first job required an audition. The star was a young woman named Tiffany. She only had one sex scene in the movie, and she was actually scheduled to do it with John Seeman. John explained that after they'd met, Tiffany didn't want to work with him. She wanted someone else. She wanted someone more sensitive. John called me. If I wanted the job, I would have to come down to the London Lodge in Oakland where they were all staying and meet this Tiffany.

I did. I drove down to Oakland and I met Tiffany. She told me all about her fears and I told her about mine. It was a fearfest. We had sex in her hotel room and she told the producers afterwards that she would be happy to work with me. I had myself a job.

Tiffany didn't belong in a fuck film. She'd done one previous sex scene in the business and didn't like it. Why she let herself be talked into another attempt was beyond me. Could've been that her bank balances were low too, but I didn't ask. She was young, cute, and adventurous. She was filled with bouncing off the wall energy. She told me that she was in nursing school, but liked flirting around the edges of a career as an actress too. Said she needed some kind of loving contact to feel at ease in doing a sex scene. I could certainly relate to that. We were well-matched for our tryst in Smutland.

Our scene had no dialogue. I never saw the movie and I'm not sure how or why our characters came to be fucking, but they did. And so we did too.

The scene was shot in an office space right at the hotel where they were all staying. We were to make love on top of a desk and then move to the carpeted floor. Foreplay was Tiffany sucking me until I got hard and then we went at the business of fucking for the cameras.

It was odd. She was more nervous than me, and I was nervous. She took great comfort in caring for me. It gave her a focus other than her own fears. I was grateful for the concern. Our scene was mild by contemporary X-rated standards, but as I said, Tiffany was even more out of place than me. She was shaken by directorial cues such as having to open her vaginal lips wider while a crewman shined a bright light into her pubic area and they moved the camera in close, just inches away. It embarrassed her. It grossed her out to have to bend over and spread her ass cheeks for the camera. She wasn't the first. She won't be the last. I helped her get through it as best I could. I, at least, knew the terrain. This was all fairly new to her.

She wanted to make love like we had in the darkness of her hotel room when we met. She wanted to be in love. I don't know what she thought that she was getting into when she took this job. She had already been in one sex film. She should have at least been somewhat familiar with the drill, but she acted like she wasn't.

I had a guess where she was at. I could kind of smell it. She had heard only the good parts. She was going to be "the star" of a movie! There was gonna be a very nice pay check! She would get to pick out the man with whom she'd have the sex. And she had chosen to forget about all of the nasty little things that had freaked her out the first time around. There is a lot of shock and humiliation when you take something as personal and private as the sex act, light it up, and make it a public commodity. It can take some real getting used to.

(A footnote: Shortly after this film wrapped, Tiffany took Carly out for lunch, and confessed she was in love with me. She told Carly that the last man she had been in love with was a married man, who had made her pregnant, and that he and his wife had "forced" her to have an abortion, which she regretted to this day.)

"If I had it to do over," Tiffany told Carly. "I would have kept that baby."

Later, Carly asked me if I was sure this girl had used birth control, and I said I had taken her word for it. Carly said, "PLEASE never put your penis in this woman again."

I didn't.

Meanwhile, when we returned to the set, I got a message to call

Playgirl. It was an art editor telling me that I would be *Mr. November* for 1978!

I'm sure I told anyone who would listen, but there was little time for a lengthy celebration. I was due on the set of my next film. I had to make it from Oakland to San Francisco for my attempt at come shot number two.

I sought out the director in order to get paid. He gave me $200. I told him that he was over-paying me. I had agreed to do the scene for $150. He just gave me his blessing and told me to keep it. *Wow! Hell must have just frozen over*, I thought, and I was on my way to shoot a loop for Bob Gunthner.

John Seeman had told me that Bob Gunthner had been in the business for a long time. He was famous for making one-day wonders, the feature-length films that were shot in just one day. This job, however, was just gonna be a loop, one straight sex scene.

I arrived at a private home in the Richmond District that was serving as our set and there on the couch waiting was my old friend Marlene. I had done my second loop with her, quite successfully I might add, and we were about to have a rematch.

I joined Marlene on the couch. We waited for Bob to get his cameras ready. Marlene was all business. It was actually a welcome change from the coddling that Tiffany and I had done with each other. I wasn't exactly horny, but I wasn't terrified either. I was behaving like a seasoned veteran and I had myself pretty well fooled. I knew I was daring the Fates with this reach for a second orgasm. I tried not to dwell on that.

When Bob was ready, Marlene went to sucking me into arousal. Lo and behold, life stirred anew in my cock. I viewed it as unmistakable proof of the so-called "Coolidge Effect" that Carly had taught me from her days in sex therapy training in reference to male sexual performance. As the story went, the President and Mrs. Coolidge were visiting a farm where Mrs. Coolidge noticed that there was one rooster with six hens.

"Does this one rooster service these six hens?" the First Lady was supposed to have inquired of the farmer.

"Yes, m'am, every day," the farmer said.

"Would you please tell the President that," directed Mrs. Coolidge.

"Mr. President," began the farmer, "your wife asked me to tell you that this one rooster services all six hens every day."

The President surveyed the situation and instructed the farmer, "Would you please tell my wife that those are six different hens."

The sex went well enough with Marlene, who, of course, was my second hen of the day. It just took me a wee bit longer to come, that's all. Other than that, we had no real traumas. I squirted my squirt, got my pay, and went out to dinner with Bob, his crew, and some of the other actors who worked in some of the earlier loops shot that day. We went to the House of Prime Rib on Van Ness. It was serious meat.

Two come shots in one day. I was proud! It occurred to me that my Basic Training was over. I had successfully completed "Beginner's Schmuck" and now had become a "Regular Dick," an experienced foot soldier in porn's great army of slime! "Semper Tumescence!"

On the way home, I noted that my batting average would be going up. I was now ten for sixteen. If I had been bright enough to do the math in my head, I would have known that I was now squirting at a more encouraging .625 clip. And not only was I batting .625 but I was also about to become a *Playgirl* centerfold. Hey, buddy, watch where you put that staple!

Chapter Thirty-Four

– Gordon Archive

Chapter Thirty-Five
Climbing Mt. Narcissus

I wasn't ready to tell my parents that I had acted in some X-rated movies. I just wasn't. And if I didn't tell them, I thought it highly unlikely that they would ever find out. They would certainly not be frequenting any porno houses in Pittsburgh and the consumer videotapes, and the stores that would rent them hadn't yet been invented. Besides, I'd been careful to keep my real name out of all the credits. I worked as McKinley Howard, Mark Howard, Mack Howard, Dewey Alexander, Rafael Sabatini, Dennis Leibovitz, Chang Kai-shek Jr., Barney Dinkin, and Hymie the Magnificent Worm among other stage names.

Being in *Playgirl*, however, was going to be a different story. If I did *Playgirl* I would be using my real name. There'd be a buzz about it in Pittsburgh amongst a lot of the folks who grew up with me. I know because I'd be the one buzzing them about it, "Hey, look at me!"

The whole community would know. My parents would eventually find out. It seemed I should be the one to tell them. Fact is, I felt I had to ask them. I needed to know if me doing *Playgirl* would be all right with them. If they'd have said, "No," then I would've had to let it all go.

"Burt did it!" was my mother's response. "He talks about it all the time on Johnny's show." That would be Burt Reynolds, of course, talking to Johnny Carson about his centerfold posing on *The Tonight Show*. In my mother's worldview, if it was good enough for Johnny's show, it was good enough for America.

I could see that my mother would be no problem. Though my mother would not herself openly approve of a magazine like *Playgirl*—women of her generation and upbringing were not likely to be ogling glossy pictures of naked men—she would nonetheless be secretly proud that her son was treading the same hallowed ground as Burt Reynolds. I didn't tell her, of course, that Burt had posed in *Cosmo*, not *Playgirl*, and that he had discreetly covered up all the good parts that I would be proudly waving.

I was waiting for my father's response. He was also in on this phone call. While my mother went on about how appearing in the magazine had actually helped Burt's career, my father was quiet. His silence was getting loud. His only offering came at the end of that phone call when he warned me to not let the magazine print my real address because there were a lot of crazy whackos in this world. I assured him that I would protect that information.

I could tell that my father was in a bit of shock. When it came to sexual matters he was shy. It was from my mother's side of the bed that I used to steal a copy of *Fanny Hill* for a few moments of frenzied pleasure during my teen years. John Cleland had written an eloquent novel featuring sizzling sex scenes. Thanks, Mom!

By the time my father had geared himself up for what was to be his big father-son sex talk, I was already eighteen and told him that it wasn't really necessary. We were both relieved. Mostly, he just spoke of the need to use protection. There was no AIDS back then. He was worried that I might get a girl pregnant and ruin my life with the consequences. I assured him that I would be careful. We were both awkward and ill at ease. Now, years later with this *Playgirl* thing, not much had changed.

I knew he was wondering what on earth would make me want to do such a thing, but he didn't ask. And though he didn't object either, I knew that he was not thrilled. I had surprised him again. My father was surprised at my ability to surprise him, again. I could see him shaking his head and muttering. "I don't know," he would say. "My son, my son, I don't know." It wasn't exactly a ringing endorsement by any means, but it was good enough. I went ahead full steam with the centerfold project.

I didn't think of my centerfold shoot as a day of work. I thought of it as a ticker-tape parade down Broadway after winning the World Series.

Chapter Thirty-Six

It was July 14, 1978. They had a second-degree smog alert that day in Los Angeles. The thermometer would go up over a hundred degrees. Angelenos were being advised to stay indoors.

There were five of us on the set. Theoretically, Sandy was directing. She was *Playgirl*'s brand new photo editor. I was to be her first centerfold. When I asked her why she chose me, she said that I was literally the first letter across her new desk. She liked that I didn't have any tan lines. She had studied a lot of the previous centerfolds and saw that most of the male models had tanned bodies and white tushies. I was tanned all over. It was different. She liked that.

Sandy had been charged to do three things with *Playgirl*'s centerfold section: upgrade the fashion, upgrade the photography, and present pictures of a man with an erection. She had told me about these things over the phone while I was still in Berkeley. She also babbled a lot about wanting to shoot some pictures of a naked man eating pasta. She claimed that would be an extremely erotic image.

I figured that I could take care of the erection. The rest of it would be in her hands.

Our shoot was being held in the studio home of Mike Ross, the still photographer. He had a plush, penthouse apartment, all chrome and glass. It was stylish in a young, successful, male Hollywood kind of way. Mike was a fashion photographer who seemed to be doing all right for himself. He was dropping a lot of celebrity names and I was suitably impressed. He clearly was playing in a different league than all the photographers I'd met in Pornoland.

Apparently, he was doing a big favor for his old friend Sandy by shooting this first centerfold session for her. For him, I was guessing that shooting for *Playgirl* was like slumming. And I was also guessing that I was about to be his first naked man.

There were two other women on the set that day and a dog. Leslie was our set designer. She was another friend of Sandy's and Leslie was drop-dead gorgeous. She had the kind of beauty that made people do double takes, even in LA. She was stunning.

The other woman on the set was her younger sister, Lisa. Lisa would be the gofer. One could already see that she was going to be just as beautiful as her big sister once the skin cleared up and she stopped being all elbows and knees.

The dog was Bella. While Sandy and I were going over the clothes, Mike was telling us that Bella had just done a shoot with Jaclyn Smith, one of TV's original *Charlie's Angels*. If the numbers Mike was tossing around were accurate, Bella had just made more money than I was going to earn for being a *Playgirl* centerfold. I tried not to take it personally. The dog had an agent. I didn't.

And speaking of clothes, Sandy absolutely hated mine. I'd been instructed to bring a number of outfits, but my wardrobe was one hundred percent Berkeley Flea Market. She doubted that it would constitute the fashion upgrade she had been hired to produce. We had a real problem until Sandy speculated that Mike and I were about the same size. Problem solved. She raided his uptown wardrobe and there I was, a Mr. GQ.

It took a while for Mike to recognize that I was wearing his clothes. Not only did he get himself stuck taking pictures of a man but the goddamned guy was dressed in *his* clothes.

There was a last cup of coffee, some makeup, and we were ready to begin. There would be twenty rolls of film shot that day, twenty rolls with thirty-six pictures each. That was 720 smiles for the camera. My cheeks would be sore by the end of the day.

They put me in a fancy robe to start and had me reclining on some big cushions. Me and my tanned tushy began tossing out those smiles for the cameras.

I was tense. They were businesslike. My smile was forced and nervous. They moved me this way and that. Sandy, Mike, and Leslie were all telling me what to do. I pretty much responded to all voice commands, but I drew the line when the dog ordered me to roll over and play dead.

I didn't know how to use my body as a tease. It was a sexual role reversal I had never attempted before. I bumbled through a striptease somehow, feeling awkwardly feminine. The shoot felt like Disney on Vice. I was Goofy being cast as a female impersonator.

Mike was clicking the cameras and the lights were flashing. About halfway through that first scene, someone noticed that I still had on my wedding ring.

– *Mike Ross/Playgirl*

Ooops, they didn't want any married centerfolds!

Sandy had me remove the ring. Dark makeup had to be applied to the ring of lighter skin now visible around my finger. That done, we started all over again.

Mike pretty much took over directing at this point and shot another ton of pictures. We worked rapidly and I was jaybird naked by the time he stopped shooting. There was a pause. I awaited further direction. Mike tried to get Sandy's attention. She was ignoring him. Ostensibly, Sandy was busy with Leslie arranging costume and set for our next scene, but it was obvious to me, and undoubtedly Mike, that she was definitely avoiding his gaze. Something was up. Mike waited for a bit and then told me to go put on the next outfit.

Okay, so now I'm putting on the new clothes for my second striptease act and I'm wondering if I'm doing something wrong? This is my first shot at high-gloss LA and I do not want to screw it up. Why did Mike start acting weird? Why were the women ignoring him? I had a pretty good guess, but this was their shoot and I didn't want to jump the gun.

They dressed me in a nice casual outfit, a sweater and a sport coat. It was Mike's sweater and sport coat. I'd never dress like that, but I looked pretty good in it anyway.

They gave me a beer and the dog for props. Mike instructed me to undress slowly. He would take pictures all the way through my striptease. A giant fan was turned on and I was faced into the wind. With the breezes blowing through my hair, I was the young Troy Donahue starring in a love movie right

– Mike Ross/Playgirl

out of the 1950s. This part was fun.

– Mike Ross/Playgirl

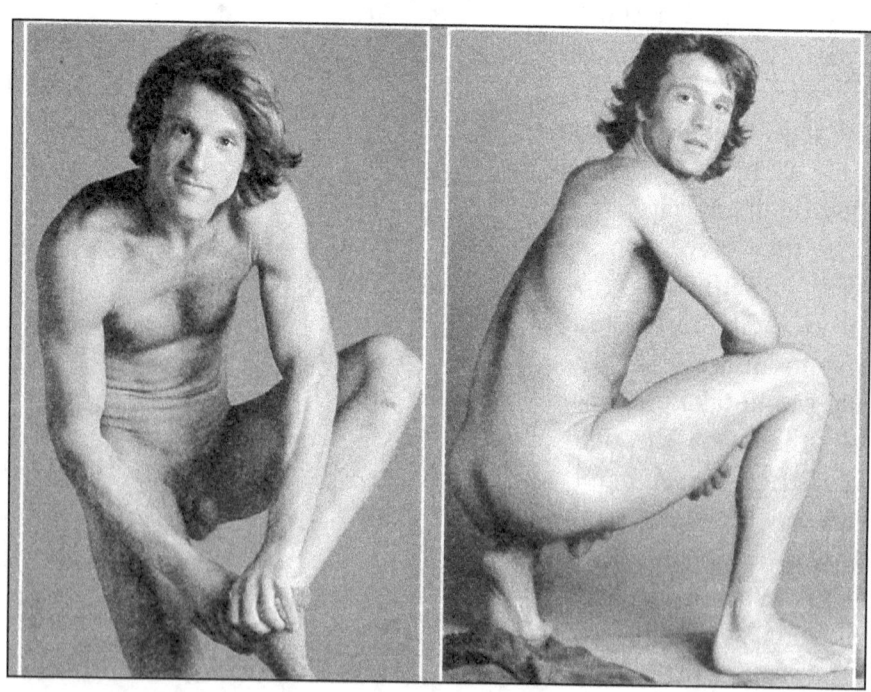

– Mike Ross/Playgirl

– Mike Ross/Playgirl

By the time I was naked and Mike stopped shooting, it had gotten all weird again. Mike had been the only one directing and now he was looking to Sandy who was again pretending not to notice him.

"Is this the part where you want me to get a hard-on?" I asked.

Bingo! Laughter and smiles erupt everywhere! It was like I had just popped the cork on a bottle of champagne and brought out the cocaine.

No one had said a word about erections since I had arrived on the set. It had only been mentioned in that first long distance phone call with Sandy. Clearly, they had all been at a loss to broach the subject in person and were all greatly relieved when I recognized the 500 pound gorilla in the room.

Their awkwardness suggested that they did not know how to proceed with this portion of the program. It didn't appear that any of the women present were going to be offering much in the way of help. No matter, I told them not to worry. I stretched out naked on the floor and closed my eyes. I took matters into my own hands. In the quiet, pretty Leslie started talking dirty:

"You're raising her skirts now to reveal her creamy, milky thighs," Leslie was talking in a stage whisper. It made the other folks laugh. Me too. I told her thanks, but no thanks. She said that she was only trying to help. I told her that there were other ways that she could help, but she did not pick up on it. Too bad, I closed my eyes and returned to the wild kingdom. Wish I could honestly remember what I was thinking.

- Gordon Archive.

– Mike Ross/Playgirl

Whatever it was, it worked. Soon, my penis was hard and I jumped to my feet as Mike went into rapid-fire photography. When my erection began to fade, Mike stopped. I fell to the floor, closed my eyes, and started all over. The magic worked again. I hopped to my feet for round two. We went about four or five rounds before Mike declared that he had all the pictures of me with an erection that he would ever need for the rest of his life.

This portion of our shoot was done. They were elated and euphoric. They hadn't had the slightest idea how they were going to accomplish this part of the session. It gave me the giggles. They were lucky they had me.

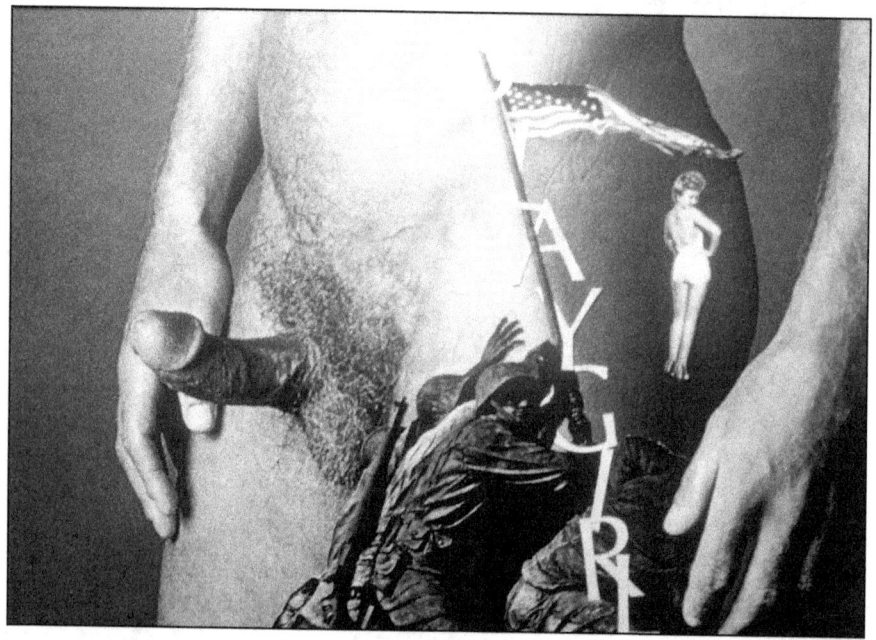

– *Gordon Archive.*

A guy without any sexual performing experience would have probably been more traumatized than they were. For me, it was like a day off. I didn't even have to come!

I had been so bullied and intimidated by their high style LA ways and all the big-time show biz name dropping. This little episode had been a great equalizer. They became much nicer to me and the rest of the photo shoot was all light and airy. They were happy and I was happy that they were happy. Mike began teasing me like a big brother.

Here I was in his house, wearing his clothes and being Mr. Sex Appeal. He joked with Sandy that she should have chosen him and they could have saved some money on the plane fare. Sandy teased back that he never would have been able to get the hard-on.

– Mike Ross/Playgirl

P.S. Y'know, I look at this body and I think, "That's not me! It's just something I made in metal shop."

Chapter Thirty-Seven

"You did it for your father."

"Pardon me?'

"You did it for your father. You lost all that weight and you sculpted that show-off body for your dad."

"Yeah? How do you know?"

"I know."

"And you are?"

"I'm the Ghost of Christmas Past."

"Oh."

"It was dinner time. You're mother had made the mashed potatoes, the kind with the onions fried in schmaltz mixed in."

"Mmmm."

"Yeah, mmmm. They were good. You liked them. You were reaching for your fourth helping when your dad uncharacteristically went ballistic.

"I remember."

"Of course you do."

"No son of mine," he said, his voice rising and his anger sharp, "is gonna be a fat slob!"

It came out of nowhere. It seemed like your father had never said word one to you about your weight. Now, he was exploding. It was like he slapped you across the face.

You were destroyed. You were helpless. You were reduced to rubble. You were ashamed and betrayed and had absolutely nowhere to hide. And worst of all, he made you put back that fourth helping of mashed potatoes under his angry eyes.

Part Three

ONE OF THE GUYS

– *Gordon Archive.*

Officer Pacheco and Father Silvera.

Chapter One

"The mind is its own place, and in itself can make a heaven of hell, a hell of heaven."

John Milton, Paradise Lost

– Gordon Archive/Screw Magazine.

THE TOP TEN LEADING ACTORS:

1. JOHN HOLMES: "Is that a nuclear warhead in your pocket, or are you just glad to see me?" Dead from the neck up, but a monster from the waist down.

2. JERRY BUTLER: Blonde and built, California style. What women mean when they use the word "hunk".

3. JOHN LESLIE: One of the few good actors in smut. Specializes in sleazy, reptilian roles. Can come on cue.

4. BOBBY ASTYR: The funniest man in adult pics. The girls keep on laughing until he drops his pants.

5. JAMIE GILLIS: The professor of porn. Takes his sex seriously: he bones up on it.

6. JACK WRANGLER: A switch-hitter who crossed over from gay films to do straight smut. Doesn't prevent him from exciting the ladies.

7. HARRY REEMS: Has been or never was? Only his agent knows for sure. On the strength of *Deep Throat* and his 10-incher makes the Top Ten.

8. ERIC EDWARDS: The boy next door, naughty and nice.

9. RICHARD PACHECO: The thinking girl's stud. If the role calls for any amount of acting at all, Pacheco should be in it.

10. RON JEREMY: Last and least. Proves there's no such thing as overexposure in the smut biz, because if there was, he'de have retired a long while back.

– Al Goldstein

Where was Paul Thomas? Where was R. Bolla? Why was I on that list? Who knows what goes on in the mind of Al Goldstein? Did he suffer a rare moment of good taste? Tell ya what, I was just grateful for the recognition.

There's a lot of other guys that maybe coulda and shoulda been on that list too. There was Joey Silvera, Mike Ranger, Randy West, Herschel Savage, Billy Dee, Jon Martin, Mike Horner, Bill Margold, John Seeman, and Don Fernando, no doubt, among others. These were some of my friends and colleagues of the era in what amounted to a fairly unique fraternity of the Golden Age players.

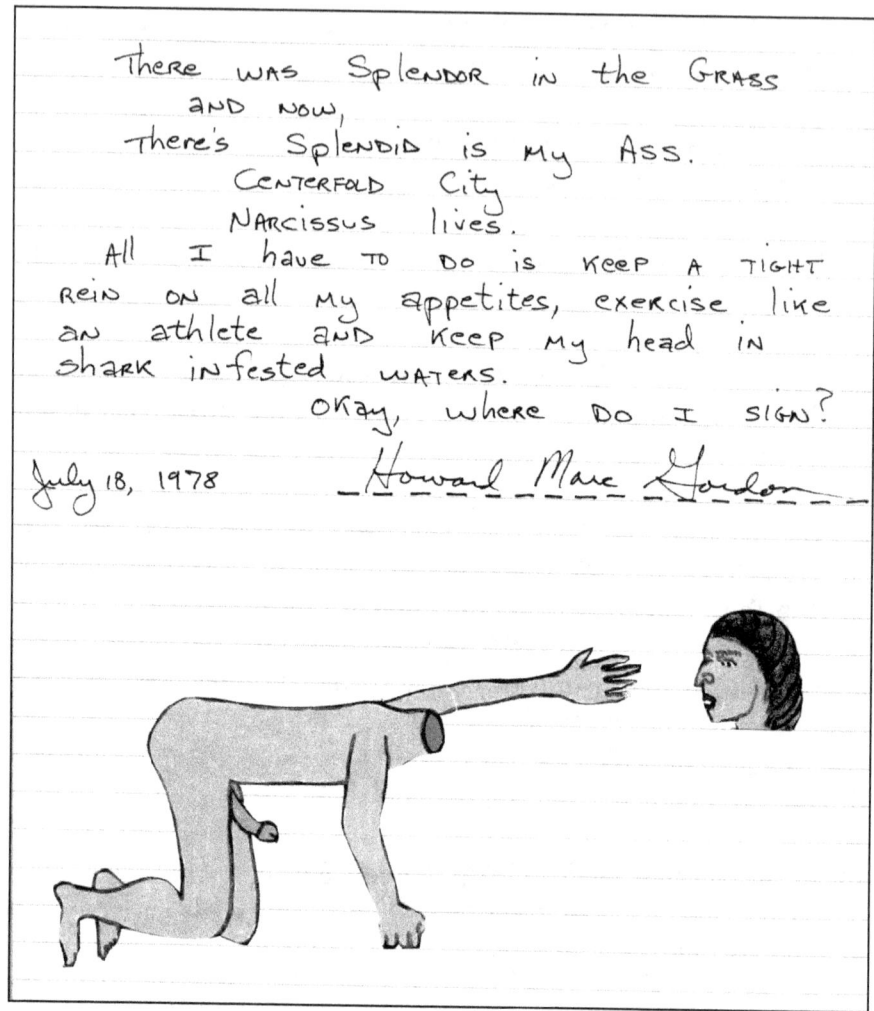

There was Splendor in the Grass
and now,
There's Splendid is My Ass.
Centerfold City
Narcissus lives.
All I have to do is keep a tight rein on all my appetites, exercise like an athlete and keep my head in shark infested waters.
Okay, where do I sign?

July 18, 1978   Howard Marc Gordon

- Gordon Archive

Chapter Two

While the *Playgirl* adventure had rekindled my fantasies of going mainstream, I continued making X Rated movies as a way of financing my trips down South to the straight side of Hollywood. There were flights, hotels, meals. I needed to find an agent. I needed 8 x 10s. Those things cost money.

As far as the adult films were concerned, my basic training was over. I was now considered one of the guys. I was an industry regular getting calls from lots of different producers asking me to come audition whenever they came to San Francisco to shoot. This phase of my career would last a couple of years and carry me through some fifteen to twenty more films and loops.

I met my first pair of breast implants while filming *Tangerine*.

These were the early days of that particular cosmetic surgery and I was not overly impressed. I would not argue that the "new" breasts weren't beautiful to gaze upon. That they were, but it was all downhill from there. The breasts were as hard as baseballs and didn't seem to do too much in the way of arousal for either the toucher or the touchee. And they just didn't move, not even if the owner did jumping jacks or stood on her head. They just stared at you like headlights.

One would hope that the owners of some of those early models have long since upgraded to the newer, improved, and more human-like ones. One would hope.

My leading lady in *Tangerine* was taller than me. When she put on her high heels, it was ridiculous. To compensate, I had to wear platform shoes that made me five inches taller. It was like spending the whole day on stilts. No doubt Boris Karloff wore a similar pair when he played the Frankenstein monster. It was a lot of fun to be taller, but it soon took its toll. After a couple of hours in those shoes, my legs would start to tremble. I would cramp up and get shooting pains. Periodically, I would have to parachute back to earth where I didn't get nosebleeds.

There was a scene in this movie where an actress was supposed to have some kind of sex with a dog. He was a big German shepherd and he was not interested in having sex at all! Poor bastard just sat there whimpering to be saved as the woman stroked his cock in a vain effort to arouse his ardor.

Oh, man, the dog looked toward his master with begging in his eyes to be freed from this indignity, but the owner made him stay. It was a payday.

I'd been where that dog was. He had all of my sympathy. This whole scene belonged in some forbidden cellar in Tijuana. I'm not a big fan of inter-species dating. It was an embarrassment just to be there.

I had to do a sex scene with three young women in *Tangerine*. In the preliminary tangle, when I was moving to this breast or that mouth, one of the young women whispered in my ear, "Do not touch me unless you absolutely have to."

The cameras were rolling. It was a bit of a shock. This was one of those sex scenes that was being completely choreographed by the director. Our moves were not our own. He was telling us whose what went where, whose legs got spread, what should be sucked or fucked, how, and for how long. He did not hear the request that had been whispered in my ear, and with the cameras rolling I hadn't had the opportunity to tell him.

As the scene proceeded, I tried to work around her. At one point, though, the director directly directed that I should now enter and plow the fields of that very maiden who had asked to remain untouched. Came the moment of truth and she allowed my penis into her vagina. She did not seem to object. In fact, once inside my reluctant lover, she soon met my thrusts with some wickedly sweet undulations of her own. I enjoyed the ride.

And I couldn't resist. I whispered in her ear, "Is it okay that I'm touching you now?" She smiled with her eyes closed and shook her head, "Yes."

Chapter Three

It was Agent Marty on the phone. "Uh-oh," he said.

"Marty! How you doin?" I hadn't heard from him in weeks. What do you mean, 'Uh-oh?'"

"'Uh-oh' means that you're back to writing the same book you already wrote in 1985. The writing's a whole lot better, but still, you're just going from one movie to the next and telling the story. It's gonna be slow, repetitive, boring, and way too long. You're gonna have to be more selective.

"I agree."

"I mean, nobody out there is gonna want to read the encyclopedia of your entire career. You were in over a hundred movies, y'know … and some of them were incredible stinkers. Wait a minute, what did you say?"

"I said I agree with you. You're absolutely right."

"Oh," Marty said.

Chapter Four
Things You Learn the Hard Way

Beware adrenalin. It can make you somebody you're not. It can surprise you.

We get excited when we make movies. No surprise there. Especially when it's all pretty new to us. Costumes, makeup, bright lights, people watching, cameras rolling, and we're performing. If you're human, the adrenalin is flowing.

I was making a loop for an old timer named Irv Carsten. I think he began shooting 8 mm porno films sometime during the Truman administration.

It was an outdoor poolside location on a warm sunny day. For the first shot, Irv placed his camera on one side of the pool and wanted me to dive towards him from the other side. When I got across, I was supposed to pop my head out of the water where he'd have me perfectly framed for an extreme close-up. That was the plan. Not too complicated. Did we need a rehearsal? NAH, hell no! Let's just shoot one. Okay.

"... and ACTION!" When I dove across the pool, I was flying. I was so pumped up with nervousness and adrenalin that I went a lot farther than I had planned.

The result was that I banged my head directly into the wall on the other side of the pool. Didn't even see it coming. Pow! Wham! Oi. It hurt.

Poor Irv! When my bloodied face first popped into his extreme close-up, he flew back from his camera like there'd been an electrical shock. That was actually funny. The whole scene, in fact, had some definite Three Stooges qualities going for it. Shame that none of that made it into the movie.

Eventually, I stopped bleeding. With some ice and a frying pan, we got the swelling down to the point where we could continue shooting the scene. Oddly enough, I had no trouble with the sex that day.

"Who did you fuck?' asked the imaginary interviewer.

I haven't got the slightest idea. With what we now know about concussions, that's not surprising at all.

– Gordon Archive

Sam Weston – aka Anthony Spinelli.

Chapter Five
Sam

    Everybody said I had to meet Sam. Everybody said I had to meet Sam. Sam Weston was Anthony Spinelli. Anthony Spinelli was Sam. He was the best director. He hired the best actors and he made the best movies. So, I met him.

    I was still shooting *Tangerine* at the time. I had a day where I was only scheduled to work the morning, so I met Sam in the afternoon.

    We spent the whole time talking about acting and "the business," but Sam didn't fall in love with me until I ordered dinner.

    I had been auditioning for him. It was at the Travel Lodge on Eddy Street in San Francisco.

    He had me read a few pages of script from *Easy*, his upcoming film. After the first time through, he gave me a few notes on my character and then had me read the scene again. It was a dialogue between a man and a woman. He read the woman's part.

    This was already going into more depth than I had ever experienced before at an X-rated audition. Usually, they just took a naked Polaroid of me, asked a few questions about my past sex scenes, and then had me do maybe one cold read out of the script—if there was one.

After the second reading with Sam, he launched into a detailed account of how this scene fit into the larger movie. He got into the inner conflicts of both characters and how they would be resolved. We read it a third time. We read it a fourth time. Sam Weston was in his element. He was having fun. He was directing. He was having his way with me.

The clock lazed through the afternoon. Was my performance improving? I don't know, but it was my first Sam Weston acting class. He put me through my paces. Porn had nothing to do with it. Power, on the other hand, seemed to have a lot to do with it. Sam Weston made it very clear to me from the very beginning that he was the painter and I was the paint.

"Okay, okay," he said scratching his chin and thinking it all over.

Apparently, the audition had concluded. He talked about his shooting dates. It just so happened I was available. When we discussed salaries, I agreed to work for the customary entry level fee of $200 per day as I had done in other feature films. He gave me a script and told me that I should learn the role of "Boy."

Afterwards, Sam offered to buy me dinner at the coffee shop. When I ordered, "Five eggs, sunnyside up, two orders of link sausages, two orders of whole wheat toast, two orders of well-done hash browns, and one large orange juice," Sam put a meaty paw around my shoulders, flashed me a million dollar smile, and became my friend for life.

Chapter Six

I auditioned for a *Dracula* movie. The director liked my reading. He'd had me read for the part of the vampire and I had given him my Bela Lugosi best.

"You know," he said with his thick European accent, "you read that very well, but I think that part belongs to Jamie. I'd like to try you in something else. Let me see."

Jaime. He was talking about Jamie Gillis. I could barely contain my excitement. This film was gonna star Jamie Gillis and Annette Haven, two of the biggest names in the business. It was going to be a big step up for me.

"Would you like to read for the part of Frankenstein?" the director asked. You bet I would, pal, feature films were the place to be. This time

I did a Boris Karloff imitation.

"Very nice," he said to me, "Very nice!" He was pleased. I was giddy. I knew I was going to get the part.

"Yes," he said. "I think I'd like to cast you as the monster."

"Great!"

He went through the details. "We're going to shoot in New York, San Francisco and New Orleans," he said. "The pay will be $200 a day and you should get five or six days of work. We'll pick up all the traveling expenses and you'll also get a per diem when we're on the road.

"That's all fine," I said with delight.

"And one more thing," he added. I was all ears. "About your death scene. When you die at the end of the film, we will have the heroine sit on your face and pee. It will short-circuit your electrodes and you will be electrocuted!" He said it with a childlike glee.

"What?" Oh, I'd heard him all right. I just didn't want to believe what I'd heard. He told me again, only speaking more slowly and deliberately.

"When you die at the end, the heroine pees on your face and you get electrocuted!" He paused. "Do you have a problem with that?"

He wasn't kidding.

Yeah, I had a problem with that. Just between us girls, making sex films was one thing, but getting pissed on was something else. I didn't know what that was, but it wasn't me.

Oh, we went around on it for a while. I tried to convince him to use a stand-in for that part of the death scene, but he wasn't buying it. It got to the point where he said, "Look, take it or leave it."

I heard Bob Dylan singing on the record player:

> "No, no, no, it ain't me, Babe.
> It ain't me you're looking for, Babe."

Chapter Seven

I earned my SAG card by whistling "Hooray for Hollywood" and carrying a camera tripod up and down several flights of stairs in a Bank of America commercial.

Chapter Eight
Hot Legs

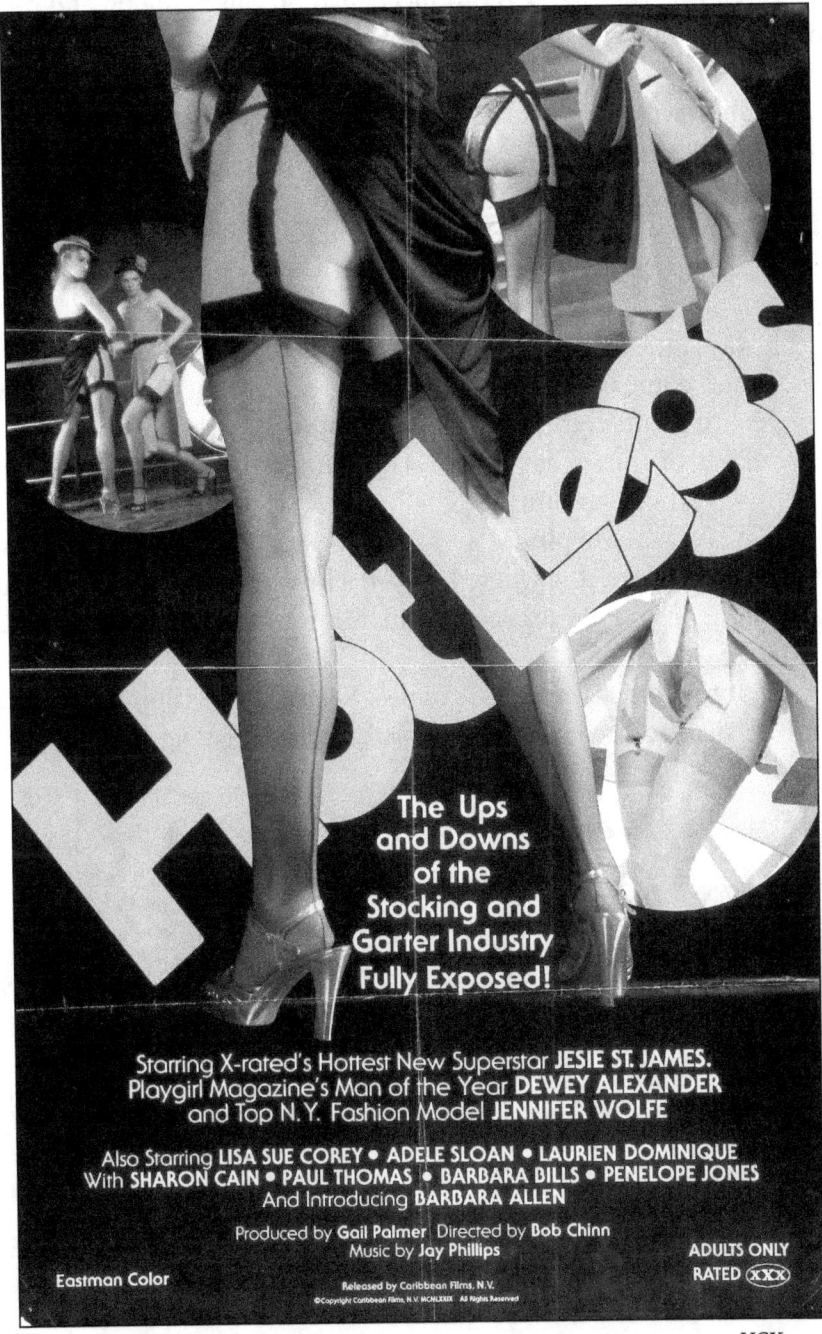

– VCX.com

Notice that they advertised "*Playgirl* Man-of-the-Year - Dewey Alexander." *Playgirl* didn't want me to mention that I'd had anything to do with porn. The *Hot Legs* producers had promised me up and down that they wouldn't mention *Playgirl* at all. When they figured they could make an extra nickel out of the publicity, they betrayed their pledge to me. Sadly, it was often par for the course in the X-rated industry.

"Oh! We didn't know you wanted to keep that secret," they would say when you called to protest. It was like trying to uncrack an egg after the movie came out. Oddly enough, there was no "Dewey Alexander" in *Playgirl* to be found. As I told you I would, I used my real name in the magazine.

It wasn't the first time, neither would it be the last, that an X-rated production company would violate an agreement they made with me. One had to wonder, though, and take pause in seeking redress when these kinds of things happened. After all, one had to consider who exactly would you be suing?

Hot Legs was the pinnacle of the "Dewey Alexander" phase of my career. It was a lead role where I played a lot of scenes beyond the customary one-and-done sex scene which I'd been pretty much doing up until then.

I got to work with Jesie St James, Sharon Kane, Bob Chinn, and Paul Thomas, future Hall of Famers all, and career-long friends.

- Gordon Archive

Dewey Alexander and Laurien Dominique.

And I had a surprisingly successful sex scene with Laurien Dominique that absolutely nobody was expecting. Director Bob Chinn had presided over some of my earlier failures and was expecting no more than a soft-core simulated scene from me. But when Laurien and I got it going, we got it going. Dewey Alexander the Great!

Chapter Nine

Sam Weston had a whiff of the big time early. He produced and acted in a successful "art" film called *One Potato, Two Potato*. It was a controversial interracial love story done just as the 1960s were getting started. It starred Barbara Barrie, Bernie Hamilton, and Richard Mulligan. What, you never heard of them?

Sam's older brother was Jack Weston. You had to have heard of him! For years, he was a wildly successful character actor on stage, in films, and on TV. Sadly, Jack's success never seemed to do too much to help his younger brother Sam get his own footing in the game. I was always curious about that, but it was never really any of my business.

Sam produced a western called *Gun Fever* in those early years too. It starred Mark Stevens, a second tier Hollywood actor, not the later New York porn star of the same name. I don't remember Sam talking about any more straight credits. Like so many before and after him, Sam became a career minor leaguer knocking around Hollywood in search of that one big break. He had a wife and three kids. He had to feed 'em. Had to put a roof over their heads. He had to pay the bills. There were some funky jobs like selling encyclopedias and then one day, porn came along. It became his calling.

By the time we met at the Travel Lodge in San Francisco, he had just won some kind of X-rated Oscar for directing the film *Sex World*.

Chapter Ten
(from my 1979 diary)

Life Among the Extras

It's my first straight picture, Purple Haze. *They're telling us that it's the sequel to* American Graffiti. *It's starring Ronnie Howard and Cindy Williams. I already met both of them!*

It's lunchtime. The stars are in their air-conditioned campers and I am writing this in the back of my Volkswagen bus. From the ambition-crazed mob of hundreds of extras, I was chosen early this morning to be one of the four stand-ins! We were cut from the herd and escorted up to the mountain top.

We lucky four have been anointed "the second team!" Our job is to spell the lead actors while cameras are focused, sound levels are checked, and lights are adjusted in readiness for the next shot. When all preparations have been completed, the "first team" actors are summoned from their trailers and we are shown back down the mountain after having been that close to glory.

We get $50 extra for our efforts. I was selected because I bore a height, weight, and coloring resemblance to the film's costar, Will Seltzer. There is a rumor here that he is Richard Dreyfuss's younger brother.

There are many, many rumors in this crowd of extras. There is also an endless patter of self-promotion and name-dropping. Everyone here has an 8 x 10 glossy at the ready. Blinding desire is mirrored everywhere you look.

Forget pornography, this is naked ambition.

I got an unexpected acting lesson this day from the great Bob Ernst. During the big mob riot scene, a thousand extras are all running this way and that, laughing, playing, and having a good time. They've taken so long shooting this scene and generally treated the horde of extras so badly all day that it appears nobody amongst us really gives a shit anymore that we are still making a movie. Nobody, that is, except Bob Ernst. Running along beside him, I saw that he may have been the only person there who was still concerned with staying in character. I was amazed.

Chapter Eleven
The Sensuous Detective

Serena had the title role and we played an odd sex scene together. I had to overpower her, tie her up, and spank her as foreplay. I was completely out of my league. Serena was a major player. She was living with Jamie Gillis, for God's sakes! When it came to doing any kind of an SM scene with an experienced woman, I was a clueless cub scout. It was like Jerry Lewis driving a Ferrari.

When the director called, "Action," we shot something, but my heart wasn't in it. Tying up a woman, spanking her? I didn't think this was going to go over very well with the feminist crowd in Berkeley! I played a very quick paddy cake on her tushy and got to the sex as soon as possible. I was embarrassed, titillated, and completely humiliated. But. I got hard. I got in. I got off. Job well done.

– Gordon Archive

Serena.

When I was wrapped for the day, paid off, and on my way out the door, Serena asked me for a ride back to her hotel. "Well, sure," I said, anxious to please, and off we went.

Once there, she invited me to come hang out in her room. Well, okay, I thought. She's a big star. Could get me some more work if we became friends. Maybe she wants to mess around some more, y'know, in private. Teach me a little bit about what's what.

What she didn't tell me was that she had just used me to walk off the set after having had a big blowout argument with the director. I was her getaway driver.

Within fifteen minutes, the producer, the director, and the entire cast and crew were all standing below us in the hotel parking lot and beseeching their star to return to the production. It was a full-scale diva snitfit and I was Serena's accomplice in *The Runaway Honey*!

For a while, both sides used me as a go-between since Serena would not meet with them. Serena was trying to reach Jamie Gillis for advice. He was out of town. When they finally did hook up by phone, I quietly excused myself and went home.

Chapter Twelve

> *"Good directors can bring certain things out of you, with their intensity or gentleness or sensitivity or understanding. They can make an actor feel he can do no wrong."*
>
> Robert DeNiro, *Parade Magazine*, 11/8/09

In rehearsing for *Easy*, Sam was every bit as good as advertised. He cared more about the acting than any other director I ever met in the business. Period.

When Sam couldn't find work plying his trade as a director in straight Hollywood, he proceeded to make a name for himself by doing it in porn. The result was, that along with Gerry Damiano and a few others, Anthony Spinelli led the pack in creating the erotic films that now make up the catalog of porn's so-called "Golden Age."

To begin with, we had rehearsals! I'd tell friends I was off to rehearse my next adult film and they'd give me this knowing "Heh-heh-heh" elbow in the ribs like I was off to the orgy.

Hardly. We'd be sitting around the table in the Howard Johnson's Banquet Room in Mill Valley. We'd be running lines. Learning the script. Improvising. Drinking too much coffee. Developing characters. Imagining backstories. Rewriting scenes. Blocking. Smoking too many cigarettes. And then we were running lines again. Did I say we were running lines? Yes, over and over, we'd be running lines. "Let's take it from the top," he would say, and we would. At our own expense, I might add, there was rarely any pay for this rehearsal time. With Sam, you just gave it.

All this preparation would save us hours once we started shooting, and that would be a good thing too, because it was not uncommon for an Anthony Spinelli day to last a very looooonnnnnnnggg time once we finally got on a set. Alone among porn directors, Anthony Spinelli would shoot between ten and twenty takes of a particular shot until he felt he'd gotten what he needed out of it. He could get very meticulous out there and be very demanding of both actors and crew. Producers could often be seen standing off to the side and pulling out their hair as Spinelli emptied their wallets in overtime costs.

I loved this part of working for Sam. The training was invaluable. The process was fun.

The problems I had with Sam were all about sex.

Chapter Thirteen

Long before I ever played in one as an actor, I was a fan of X-rated movies. These, of course, were the days before you could watch sex videos at home and you had to go out to the adult theaters and drive-ins to get in on some of these new, voyeuristic thrills. I was almost always amazed at how bad the movies were. I'm not even talking about the acting or the filmmaking skills at work here, I'm talking about the sex, the quality of the sex.

It used to astonish me! Here you had naked men and naked women apparently eager and willing to have hot wet sex right in front of a camera and yet they still managed to find ways to fuck it all up!

It was the rage that used to get to me, the meanness and the rage.

Okay, okay, one and one are eleven. I'm not stupid here. I can understand how unlikely it would be for a culture as fucked up about sex as ours has been to generate any kind of healthy sexual media, but it was just too much. So many of the sex scenes were hostile and brutal. They were odes to male domination run amok. It would be embarrassing and insulting to watch these movies with a woman who had an IQ higher than a plum.

The sexual revolution of the egalitarian sixties had moved the culture to allow sexual activity to appear up there on our movie screens and what did we get? We got extreme close-ups of Josef Stalin and Attila the Hun squirting their come in women's faces. This was the sexual revolution? Fuck! It killed my buzz. It wasn't what I had signed on for.

When I first read the sex scene that Sam wanted me to do in *Easy*, it was more of that same brutal crap and it depressed the hell out of me.

Chapter Fourteen

"You sure you want to take this on?" Marty the agent asked.

"How can I not?" I answered. "It was one of the central issues of my career."

"I don't know," Marty said. "It's a bog. It's a swamp. It's like getting into a land war in Asia, attacking Russia in winter. You're swimming in some very murky water there. Who are the good guys? Who are the bad guys? And who the fuck are you to say? It's the battle of the sexes, y'know? So much bullshit has been slung in there that it's really hard to say what's good and bad, right and wrong."

"It's not about good or bad, right or wrong," I told him. "It's all just about balance."

Chapter Fifteen
Welcome to the Circus

Porn has long been a bastion of male fantasy.

Men have been the driving economic force behind adult materials since the days of Fred Flintstone and Barney Rubble. From creation to consumption, porn has overwhelmingly been a man's world. The sexual fantasies contained therein were the fantasies where men got to have sex all the ways that men wanted to have sex. The real sexual concerns of actual women were never very much of an issue in the depiction of these male fantasies.

A case in point may be *Deep Throat*, the highest grossing X-rated movie of all time. In that story, a woman discovers that her clitoris is located in her throat. Has this ever happened in real life? Don't think so. It's a male fantasy. Why? In real life, most men don't get their cocks sucked near as much as they want. BUT … if a woman really had her clitoris in her throat, she probably would be sucking a lot more cock. See? It's a joke!

The clitoris in the throat remains a fiction, but don't worry, our scientists are working on it.

"Vengeance Is Mine!"

Actor Bill Margold once described a common male sexual attitude in porn very well. In an interview for a 1991 book called *Porn* by respected UCLA Professor of Psychiatry, Dr. Robert Stoller, the porn veteran spoke about it this way:

> *My whole reason for being in the Industry is to satisfy the desire of the men in the world who basically don't care much for women and want to see the men in my industry getting even with the women they couldn't have when they were growing up. I strongly believe this, and the industry hates me for saying it. But I really believe that even the most satisfied Casanova-Don Juan-satyr has always wanted somebody he couldn't get, and because of that he starts to harbor a revenge. So we come on a woman's face or somewhat brutalize her sexually: we're getting even for their [the men viewers'] lost dreams. I believe this.*
>
> *I've been told this by people in audiences after I've done horrible things on screen to women. I'm not hurting them. It's only an act, but it looks real—because I can scare people—I have a booming voice and I can become very intimidating. That gets the audience excited. I've heard audiences cheer me when I do something foul on screen. When I've strangled a person or sodomized a person, or brutalized a person, the audience is cheering my action, and then when I've fulfilled my warped desire, the audience applauds....*

And so it was too, with Anthony Spinelli. The sex scene he wanted me to perform in *Easy* was of this same brutal style of porn that I'd mostly managed to avoid in my career until now. First it was with Serena in *The Sensuous Detective* and now it was with Spinelli, of all people, the great director, who was asking me to really get into it for *Easy*. I was crestfallen. It wasn't lovemaking. It wasn't even sex. It was revenge. It was mean and hostile and not my cup of tea at all.

"Which side are you on, boy? Which side are you on?"

In matters sexual, I've always been a big fan of reciprocity and fair play.

It gets me hot to see and feel a woman get hot. I like when we can ride over the falls together.

Growing up, sex was always filled with such guilt, repression, and recrimination in my life that I have taken great pains to make sure that my partners were in tune with me. It was the pursuit of the two-way street where "you get yours and I get mine." Not only was that the romantic ideal but it was also good politics, and nothing really more than common sense.

Still, it was an attitude rarely reflected in porn movies where the one-way street of male fantasy thrived. Not only that but it was usually the He-Man Highway where the men involved were oft reduced to their most primitive, intimidating selves.

"Bend over, bitch!" the He-Man would say. "Bend over, bitch, and tell me that you love it." It was the sexuality of the harem, of prostitution, of powerless men imagining unlimited power. Those were the guys with the dollars who were buying this porn. That was the kind of sex they wanted to see. Porn has never been about the sexual search for truth or justice. It's always just been about the business.

Since the rise of adult films in the seventies, it's been a cruel joke on the culture to present these hostile, vindictive male fantasies as if they are the sum total of the human sexual experience. But that's pretty much what's happened in the absence of a broader audience. The cultural sadness is that this one narrow point of view has dominated the whole of our sexual media.

Do angry men have a right to their fantasies? Of course they do. It's not their fault that nobody else making sex movies has figured out how to make any money from showing a different point of view.

Where are all those other voices?

Sam didn't want to get into an argument with me about sexual politics.

"Actors act," he said, "Good guys, bad guys, what's the difference? It doesn't matter."

In the straight world, one might argue that it didn't matter, but porn was being held to a different standard.

I always thought that the preponderance of male domination was like the industry continuously shooting itself in the foot in terms of gaining any large-scale mainstream acceptance. It kept porn mired like a bad joke in the minor leagues. Common sense said that without a more balanced approach to human sexuality that would genuinely appeal to women, there would be no rise into respectability. How could there be? There was so little there to respect.

– VCX.com

Dewey Alexander & Jesie St. James in *Easy*.

Chapter Sixteen

I took the job in *Easy*. I made Sam's movie. I played the fucking scumbag just like the fucking scumbag Sam wanted me to play.

Tell me, if I had played Hannibal Lecter in *The Silence of the Lambs*, would it have been a step up or a step down?

I took the job in *Easy*. I made Sam's movie. One worked for Anthony Spinelli. One paid one's dues. I figured that porn's past may have belonged to the Neanderthals like Margold and Sam, but I thought that the future belonged to the children of the sexual revolution. Porn couldn't do anything but get better. I'd surf that wave as far as it could take me.

Thirty years later, a writer friend of mine named Graham Hill actually sent me a copy this very scene from the movie *Easy*. Of all the scenes I have ever done, it was probably the last scene I ever wanted to see again, but I did watch it. I wrote him this letter:

Dear Graham,

First of all, thanks very much for thinking of me and sending along that snippet of movie.

When I watched it, I marveled at that body I had. My Lord, I was in such good shape.

Also, the acting I did in that scene did not embarrass me. Watching it these many years later, I felt like I had nailed the part. And the sex scene, once it got started, was hot and sizzled. Jesie St. James and I were well matched to become the two-headed beast and it showed up there on the screen.

Where I die a thousand deaths is in the sexual politics of that scene in Easy. *I regret playing that part. Even though it was my introduction to Anthony Spinelli and it paved the way for me to enter the upper echelons of the men in porn, I find it disturbing and unconscionable to have portrayed that kind of male rage in the movies. I won't go into any more detail here. I've actually written at length about it in my memoirs.*

Just between us girls, Graham, the bottom line is that the business didn't need me to add to the avalanche of misogyny that so pervaded the sexual quality of the industry. In hindsight, it is one of the regrets of my career that I ever lent my mind and body to any such effort.

I don't argue that men don't have a right to their anger, I've said they do, but the business was (is?) radically out of balance in its portrayal of human sexuality, to the great detriment of common sense everywhere.

xo,
H.

Chapter Seventeen

I still made the occasional loop. A loop, you may recall, was a short film usually shot in 16 mm that would play in stalls at adult book stores or be sold through a vast system of plain brown envelope mail orders to people who had their own projectors. Loops were heavy on sex and light on acting and salaries.

A buck was still a buck and there were certainly worse things one could do for an hour besides having sex.

Peter and Iris were shooting these particular loops. They would come to town every so often and arrange for two or three days of marathon loop making. It was like a factory. Couples or threesomes or whatever mating groups would be lined up and shot every hour on the hour. I was working again with Mandy on this one. It was like having coffee with an old friend. They were shooting MOS (mit out sound). This meant that we could actually just talk to each other during filming:

"Hi, Mandy, nice to see you! We better get undressed, they're ready to shoot. How've you been? Mind if I finger you while we talk? My wife is fine. Yeah, she's busy with a Master's program in psychology. Would you please suck me now? They want me to have an erection. You and Michael Morrison broke up? God, I'm sorry to hear that. Could you spread your legs a little wider? They want to see your asshole. Nice. No, I hadn't heard that Desiree Cousteau was thinking of dropping out of the business. I have to take off your bra now.

Glod itch hod to tlalk wif a mouf flull. Hmm, that feels good. When are you going back to Texas? Suck a little harder, dear, I'm losing my erection. That's much better. Do your parents know that you've been doing movies? No, I haven't told mine yet either. What? They want you to turn over now. God, these lights are hot. Are they serving lunch? They want doggy style in your ass. Do you mind? I have a small cock. It shouldn't hurt too much. Yeah, I think they pay you $50 extra for this. Oh, my, that feels amazing. Yeah, I'm gonna come soon. Where do they want the come shot? Peter, where do you want the come shot? Okay, okay.

That was nice! I think we're wrapped. Do you want to have

an orgasm?

They need the set. We could go in a backroom or something. I'd be glad to suck you off. It's just after two o'clock. Well, maybe next time then. Mandy, it's been really good to see you. That was terrific!"

Chapter Eighteen
Things You Learn the Hard Way Part II

We were shooting a loop. She was famous, a big-time star and I was still nobody and eager to please. She had a yeast infection, or a bladder infection, or that's where they buried Jimmy Hoffa, but it's too cheap a shot to just make fun of it! No woman wants to smell like that and no man in his right mind wants to have to pretend that he doesn't notice it. Because that's what I did.

It was just me and her and the cameraman. We were in a one room apartment. He was playing with his cameras on one side of the room and we were starting to undress on the other. I suppose I noticed it first. It smelled like a dead gerbil. I thought it was coming from her. Hell, I knew it was coming from her, but I didn't say a word. She was a big star! I was a still a nobody. What could I say?

When the cameraman caught the scent, he picked up his head like an animal in a nature film. A distinctly unpleasant quizzical look came upon his face. He sniffed as his gaze darted about the room. When our eyes met, I nodded toward our leading lady.

"You're kidding!" he mimed back at me, "No!" He was trying not to laugh. I didn't think it was so funny. Maybe now, but not then. I had to try to fuck that woman. He was the director! He was the one who should have done something about the situation. Yeah, what he did was use long lenses and shoot as much as possible from the other side of the room!

I was in the trenches that day. Breathed through my mouth as much as possible, but I did it. We did it. I wonder if she could smell herself? Or if it was a situation like, y'know, where your own farts don't really bother you as much as they do the next person?

In any case, we successfully completed the mechanics of copulation that day though I fear that the footage might be less than inspiring to witness. Then, on the other hand, with knowledge of the backstory, it might prove to be a classic! If I ever see it, I'll let you know.

P.S. Years later, I surprisingly stumbled upon the reason for the bad odor of that day. It had all been her boyfriend's doing. He was a weird one, he was, who for a time while they were dating had forbidden her from "freshening" herself after sex scenes. He actually told me this, himself. He claimed that he enjoyed "the pungent ripeness of that odor." Said it was a turn-on for him.

Cut to a swimming pool sex scene in another movie.

It was March in Marin County, on a sunny and cool day. The water was not heated. The director had rented himself a fancy underwater camera and he wanted to use it. I'm not gonna tell you the director's name. He

– Gordon Archive/VCX.com

Working with Jesie.

turned out to be a real asshole. Alright, his name was Bart Scum.

Me and Jesie St. James were gonna do this pool scene. That was good, I always preferred working with friends. Water was cold, but I actually got it up and got it into her. We were fucking. Director was shooting under water. Got himself some footage.

Oops! Turned blue and got the shakes. Hard-on went bye-bye.

Panic said, "Hi!" Had to take me into the house and warm me up by the fireplace. Got myself back to normal and then returned to the pool for more.

Take two. There was no take two. Panic and I were doing the cha-cha and my erection was nowhere to be found. Soon got the shakes and turned blue again. Back to the fireplace. Take three was a repeat of take two.

That was about it. I was a mess. Director decided to yank me and put in a relief pitcher to complete the scene. In fact, he took the job himself. And—he decided to move the sex scene from the outdoor swimming pool and shoot it inside, in front of a roaring fireplace. The director fucked Jesie St. James. The assistant director shot the scene.

After we were done and paid, Jesie confided to me that this director had been hitting on her all week. She had been turning him down. In the context of the movie, she didn't think that she could say, "no," and still get a paycheck. Jesie explained all this to me so that I would understand that I had been set up to fail.

Chapter Nineteen
Behind the Camera

- Gordon Archive

Michael Morrison.

I didn't know that Milton Ingley was dead. I looked him up in Wikipedia and found out that he was gone. I confess that on some bad days, I've looked myself up in Wikipedia just to make sure I'm still here.

Michael Morrison was his stage name, but we all called him Milton. There was me and John Seeman and Vincent Fronczek and Milton. We formed a sort of male coffee clatch in those early days of our careers. We'd often find work for each other and have little photo sessions and dinner outings. We were all in the business and we were all buddies.

(Y'know, "Aunt Peg" just died a few days ago. Aunt Peg, aka Juliet Anderson, was another luminary from Porn's Golden Age. She was seventy-one and they say that she just passed on in her sleep. God willin' *and the creek don't rise, I'll be going to her memorial at The Center For Sex and Culture in San Francisco. Makes me think I better hurry up with this book already. Nobody gets forever.)*

So back to Milton. I found myself behind a camera back then because Milton Ingley needed my help. He was production managing a low budget masterpiece and his still photographer didn't show up for work.

As I suspect I've already said before, reliability, upon either cast or crew, was often a thorny issue in Pornoland.

Sure, I would help Milton out for the day. I was an amateur photographer and had been for years. I'd never managed to comprehend much of the relationships between light and distance, film speed and f-stops, but I had a Canon AT-1, and when you looked through the viewfinder, if you could put the line through the circle and clicked, you could get yourself some pretty good pictures! It was a simple mechanical manipulation that precluded the need for any real knowledge of photography. I had a good eye for composition and Mr. Kodak, of course, did some very fine darkroom work for me.

On the set, Milton put a light meter around my neck. "I don't know how to use that," I told him.

"Doesn't matter," he said. "It's a prop. Just makes you look like you know what you're doing." He pointed out the German producers to me. "They don't speak any English so don't worry about 'em. Just use your camera the way you normally do. You'll do fine. Smile and wave at 'em." I did.

The day's work would be two sex scenes. I would shoot my stills when the motion pictures cameras weren't running. Not quite up to video yet, everything was still being done in film. Besides that, it would be my job to grab the actresses when they were not having sex and shoot lots of cheesecake photos of them as long as we didn't interfere with the production.

I watched two sex scenes that day that put me through a ton of changes. To begin with, I got a boner early on during the first one and was struck with the realization that there'd be nothing I could do about it until much later when I'd get off, so to speak, from work. My arousal continued all through that day with the constant bombardment of sexual stimulation and there was no release. I was quite bonkers! I never felt like that when I was an actor, but I sure did that first day on the crew.

I developed an entirely new respect for the crew people. How they could just go on hour after hour doing their jobs with all that sexual stimulation going on around them was a mystery to me. I was beside myself with lust. I was spinning schemes and fantasies, one after another, looking for an actress who would slink off into the shadows with me for some sex play. Uh-uh, did not happen, which brought me to the second great enlightenment of the day.

It was amazing to watch the actresses flirt and fondle with the actors, but then totally draw the line with even looking at a member of the crew. Silly me, I'd never even noticed this before. It was separate and unequal, like the airline difference between coach and first class. It was the House of Lords versus the House of Commons.

I wanted to let those actresses know that I'd been an actor before! It was like, *"Hey! I used to be somebody!"*

"Yeah," seemed to come back the attitude which said, "maybe you were, but right now, you're just another jerk-off on the crew, so keep your bloody hands off me!" My overtures were ignored! Boy, was I shocked! How could those guys stand it? Stewing in the indignation of rejection and class warfare, I was exploding with desire.

(It should be noted here for the record that this rejection of crewmen by the actresses did not generally apply to the directors of photography, the head cameramen. They pretty much made out like bandits. All the actresses wanted to have sex with them. They were the guys who were responsible for making the actresses look good on film. It was good to have them on your side.)

John Leslie and Star Woods did the first sex scene. They had fun. I didn't. And it only got worse when Blair Morse worked with Bonnie Holiday in the second.

Bonnie Holiday was exquisite. It took my breath away to watch her sweating and moaning in the heat of her passion. Blair Morse fucked her for what seemed like hours. Every time I sensed he was ready to come, he'd back off and then he'd fuck her some more. He actually was doing that for his own pleasure! It shocked me to see an actor do that.

I had progressed by then to where I could do a competent sex scene, but this was an entirely different galaxy. Blair Morse was a complete revelation to me. It never even dawned on me to take the kind of time he was taking to enjoy the sex like that. He was just having himself a private party and Bonnie Holiday was the entertainment. The director was letting them run with it. Smart fellow.

During the breaks, shooting my stills of Bonnie, I couldn't have flirted with her any harder. She just looked at me with dreamy eyes that seemed to say, "Uh-huh, call me in about a month, I'm doing fine just now." She was too. She was loving Blair and he was loving her. Me and the rest of the crew were climbing the walls.

It was a hot scene. By now, you and I both know that it doesn't always happen that way.

In my second adventure behind the camera, I worked sound.

– *Gordon Archive*

I was Vincent Fronczek's boom man.

– Gordon Archive

In fact, I hit Seka in the head with the boom mic that day. Oh, it was an accident, but she's never let me forget about it.

Vincent Fronczek was probably my best friend in the business. He was a photographer by training and choice, but did a lot of sound work too. I liked to call him, "The Count."

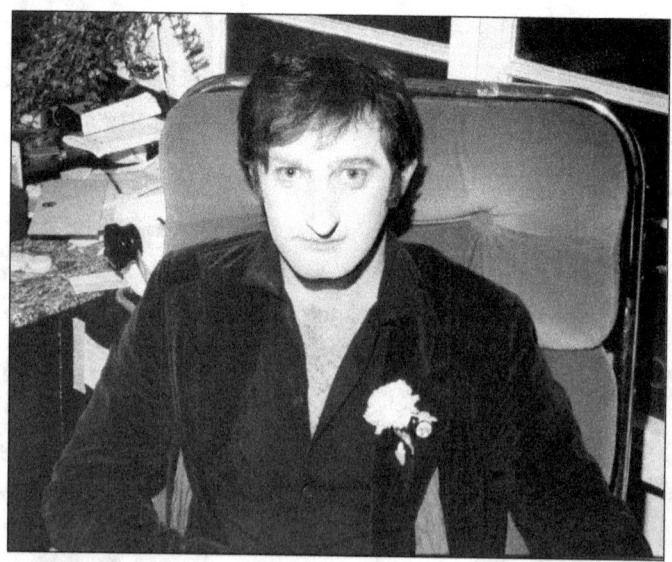

– Gordon Archive

Vincent "The Count" Fronczek.

To people meeting The Count for the first time, it may have appeared that he was a few cards short of a full deck. Vincent liked it that way. He played at being more eccentric than he really was. He was very convincing. He had a slight speech impediment that he made worse when he really didn't want to talk to you and that totally disappeared when he did. In later years, he explained to me that it was one of the ways he used to protect himself.

- Gordon Archive

First and foremost, Vincent Fronczek was an artist. I always thought of him as the Toulouse Lautrec of the X-rated world. From photography to watercolors, design and woodworking to gardening,

Vincent Fronczek had the golden hands. Still does. His social skills never matched his creative ones and unscrupulous employers often took advantage of him. His friends took it upon themselves to look out for him. We still do. Vincent is one of the innocents. He's an angel running around on this planet. He's a natural resource.

Vincent put a star on my locker one day after he'd seen me perform. It's when I knew I had arrived.

Chapter Twenty

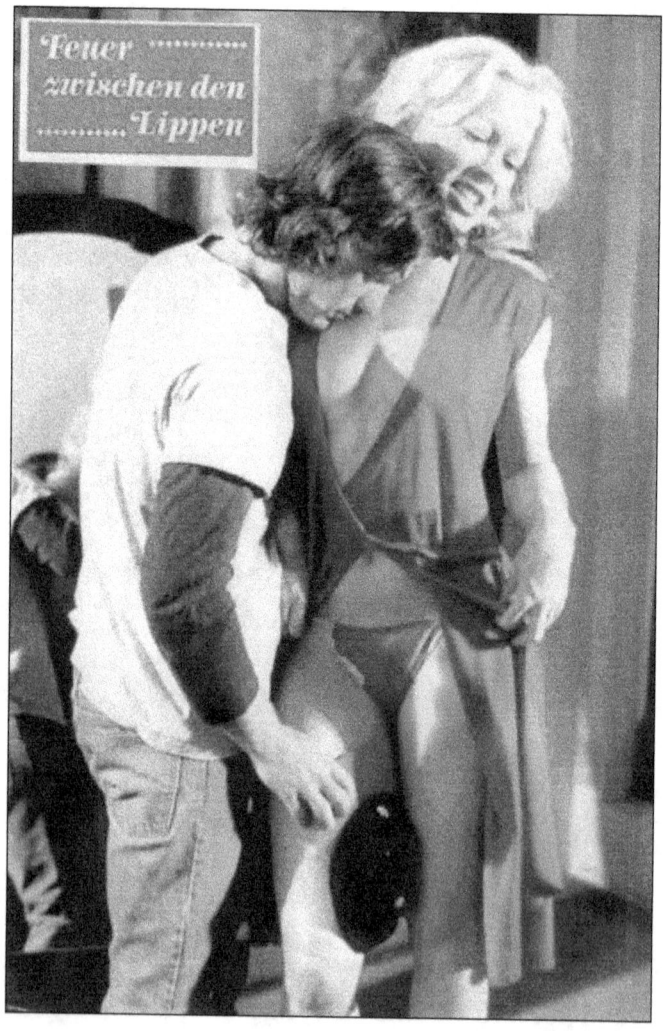

- VCX-com

In Vista Valley, I had another sex scene with Jesie.

– VCX-com

I used to like honey. I wasn't a serious devotee or anything, but I used to like a little in my tea ... when I had tea ... and it was good mixed with butter and peanut butter on toast too. Yeah, I actually used to like honey, but that was all before I shot my second movie with Anthony Spinelli.

It was called *Vista Valley PTA* and was pretty much just a remake of *Easy*, which had scored very well at the box office.

The foreplay featured me squirting honey all over Jesie's vajajay and then licking it off of her en route to the eventual in-and-out.

As I recall, there must have been a lot of dialogue during the honey-licking sequence because Sam had us shoot it over and over again. Take after take, I had to squirt that honey and lick her clean. And take after take, it went on and on and on, maybe all afternoon. We shot that scene over thirty years ago. I haven't ever been able to eat any honey since.

- VCX-com

The sex scene itself was another one of those vengeful, male dominating mambos that have always made porn such a big Mother's Day favorite.

This one was preceded by a long telephone conversation where I had to graphically intimidate Jesie's character with all this threatening, ominous talk about the nasty things that I was going to do to her. Oi.

When we shot it, Jesie sat at a big wooden desk. The camera was in tight on Jesie showing her transform from being initially frightened to being completely aroused by such an experience. I think she ended up masturbating.

For sound purposes, I was an off-camera voice hidden under the desk so that we could record both sides of the conversation.

It was a long scene. In true Spinelli fashion, I'm sure that we shot it a whole bunch of times. I was menacing, menacing, and menacing. Then, I was menacing, menacing, and menacing some more. I fucking hated it. It was not who I wanted to be when I grew up.

If it had been a straight movie, think of the Jack Palance/Robert DeNiro bad guy character in *Cape Fear*. I could've been putting myself in line for an Oscar. But it wasn't a straight movie, it was porn, and I thought that my playing such a character was contributing to the delinquency of a culture. Sex deserved a better fate than more homage to male rage.

At what turned out to be the end of a long day, I had just finished slowly speaking all my nasty, chilling madness yet again and there was all this heavy tension in the room. We were just stewing in it waiting for Sam to call, "Cut."

I blew it up. I made a joke and the room exploded in laughter. Everybody was laughing, everybody but Sam. When our eyes met, he looked sad, like I had just kicked his puppy. He had been working hard to create that mood and my joke had utterly destroyed it. It was an awkward moment for us. I had long passed the point where I gave a rat's ass about that particular scene, but I did care about Sam's feelings.

We got over it. Our relationship survived. Hell, our relationship thrived. The best was yet to come, and he never asked me to play one of those angry, vengeance-driven motherfuckers ever again.

Chapter Twenty-One
Talk Dirty to Me.

"There's no crying in porn!" That's what Sam told me the producers first said when they saw his rough cut. "The kid's fucking crying, Sam! What is this shit?" They were not happy. "There's no fucking crying in porn!"

Talk Dirty to Me was different. It was different from the very beginning. Sam told me he wanted to do a "buddy" picture. Said he wanted me to play in it with John Leslie. "You two will be great together," he said. I told Sam I thought he was fuckin' nuts.

– Gordon Archive

Fuckin' Nuts!

I didn't want any parts of John Leslie. He and his pal Joey Silvera had been mean to me when I'd first met them on the set of *Legend of Lady Blue* and I was not eager for a rematch.

"John and Joey are great together," I told Sam. "John and I got nothin'!" I tried to give the part to Joey. I didn't want to work with John.

"You're so wrong on this, kid," Sam said. "You and John will have great chemistry. Trust me on this," he said, "I know what I'm talking about. You two will make magic." And you know what?

We did.

The crying scene was being shot at sundown, golden hour. We were going to use natural lighting. This put us under the gun. It was a long scene, at least a five-minute take, maybe longer. We'd only get one or possibly two shots at it when the sun would be just right.

We were in a hilltop apartment in San Francisco. I would be at John's side while he played the harmonica. The setting sun and the San Francisco Bay would be our backdrop through a picture window. I would weep while he played and deliver my lines about the loneliness of my life.

"There's no crying in porn!"

I was playing a character based on my Uncle Izzy. He was my mother's younger brother, the mentally retarded uncle I lived with when I was growing up.

I was playing Lenny. He wasn't near as far gone as Izzy, but they had a lot in common. John Leslie was playing Jack. He was the guy taking care of Lenny, kind of like a gruff older brother. Jack & Lenny loved each other. Let's just say it was a stretch for John and Howie to get there, but I think we did.

Talk Dirty was different. It was different from the very beginning.

Sam had once been friends with a young retarded man. His name was Melvin and he lived on the same street as Sam at one point. Melvin was a beloved figure on that street. The whole neighborhood seemed to take care of him. Sam told me that he thought it would be great do a picture about a guy like Melvin. When I showed up in Sam's life, an actor familiar with my own Melvin-like character, the seed soon germinated for Sam and his writer son, Mitch, to write the script.

– Gordon Archive/KBeech.com

Lenny and Jack, it was a buddy picture.

Jack was a confident womanizer with a trail of naked bodies behind him. Women seemed to fall at his feet. He was Joe Namath the quarterback and Mickey Mantle the centerfielder.

- *Gordon Archive/KBeech.com*

Jesie St. James and John Leslie.

He was macho incarnate, smart and tough, and a man of the world. A lot of guys had played this character before in porn. It was nothing new. But none of them had ever had a sidekick like Lenny.

Lenny was neither Melvin nor Izzy. We played him as an immature young man, shy of women, slow of wit, and more of a homeless urchin of the street. When the story is joined, Jack already has become his friend and protector. Jack has taken him in. They live together like brothers. Jack takes care of Lenny. It humanizes his character. It shows us a heart that is rarely revealed in any leading man of

- *Gordon Archive/KBeech.com*

Lenny.

porn. It makes him more than a conquering dick. In addition to whatever else he is, it also makes him likable.

– Gordon Archive/KBeech.com

It was different from the very beginning.

On June 23, 1979, it was a week before shooting was to start. We were in rehearsal. My wife and I had invited some movie people over to our Berkeley cottage for a fancy dinner. There was Sam and his son, Mitch, John Leslie, Annette Haven, Juliet Anderson, Michael Morrison, Vincent Fronczek, and John Seeman.

We really did put on the dog that night: triple cream cheeses and patès, breaded oysters, a cucumber soup, Beef Wellington, and a tasty French dessert called Dacquoise. The champagne flowed. We were showing off for the movie people.

It got to be after midnight. There was laughter and we were all feeling the wine. Annette Haven and John Leslie were putting on quite a show. They were two alpha personalities hurling barbs at each other. It was a duel of wits; it was the battle of the sexes. They were locked in a comical struggle for gender supremacy. Neither gave an inch. They had done this dance before and were comfortable keeping us all laughing.

And then the phone rang. Who was calling this late? I went into another room to answer it. It was my Dad. He was calling from the East coast. It was the middle of the night. My Daddy was crying. Over the phone, I could hear my mother wailing in the background.

My Uncle Izzy had died. They were calling to tell me that Izzy was dead.

I couldn't hear the laughter in the next room anymore. It was a dim echo. Izzy was dead. How could that be? Izzy could get so creative with names. When he couldn't figure out how to pronounce Mrs. Bohonek, he called her Mrs. Mahoney. And when it came to trying to say Billy Kubiak, Izzy called him Billy Half-a-cup. A Volkswagen was a "ranchwagon." Hubcaps were "Hepcats." Hawkeye was "Hucko." Everything cost "about 600." And, of course, he'd look you right in the eye and say, "I can't say Perry."

How could Izzy be dead? He was sixty years old. Doctors said his mind worked like an eight-year-old. That meant that he'd been eight years old for fifty two years!

"Hey, How, when you leavin'?" That's what he'd say to me whenever I came home for a visit. His hello was, "Hey, How, when you leavin'?"

They told me that Izzy died in his sleep with a smile on his face.

– Gordon Archive

Uncle Izzy.

My Dad described the last day of his life to me. I'd had a T-shirt made for Izzy with a picture of his face on it. I had given it to him on his last birthday. My mother didn't like it. He was smiling in the photo and it showed that he only had one upper tooth remaining. My mother said it made him look funny. She didn't want him to wear it and he never had … until this morning. This morning, he came down from his room in the attic wearing it for the first time. My mother said he was very proud of it.

Many neighbors later told my parents that Izzy had stopped by that morning. It was as if he'd walked the neighborhood to say his good-byes.

In the early afternoon, my mother had left him home alone as was their custom. She went out shopping for the evening meal. When she returned, she said that she found him in his room asleep with a "sweet" smile upon his face. When she touched him to awaken him, his body was already cold. "It went through her like a knife," she said, he was gone.

Carly had somehow let our guests know that I had just learned of a death in my family. Sobered by the news, they were packing up and getting ready to leave when I came back. I told Sam it was Uncle Izzy who had died. There was a special hug. We were supposed to start shooting this movie in six days. We both knew there were some real decisions to be made. We would be in touch.

There was no sleep that night. I called my brother overseas in Israel. It was a phone call I didn't want to make and it was a phone call he didn't want to get. My parents had asked me to do it. I did it.

When I tried to book a flight into Pittsburgh, the best I could do was one getting into town late in the afternoon. When I told my parents this, they let me know that the funeral would already be over. The Orthodox Jews put their dead into the ground in a hurry. I would not be able to make it home in time for the funeral. They suggested that I not come. Whoa! I felt wrong in not being there for Izzy's funeral, but I couldn't beat the clock and I wanted to abide by my parents' wishes. I think they were so caught up in their own loss that they didn't want to have to worry about my pain. They were protecting me from death again and they were protecting me from the full face of their own grief.

To play Lenny or not to play Lenny, that was the question. This was a fuck film for God's sake. I was in mourning. Lenny was Izzy. Izzy was Lenny. Could I do this? Should I do this? Fuck show business! The show did not have to go on. I had a choice.

I roiled in these seas without my old family. There had been five of us, mother, father, brother, Uncle Izzy, and me. Now, one of us was gone. The other three were beyond my reach. For the first time in my life, the circle was broken. This was grief. This was sorrow. This was bitter. This was the price of having loved deeply. There were no cures and no short cuts.

There was, however, my wife! We were a "new" family in the making, one with "fuck and death included." I thank God and all her cousins that I had my wife there to help me through this.

Obviously, in the end, I decided to make the movie. Izzy was such a fine and gentle soul. He would make a splendid mentor for my Lenny. In my own way, I chose to honor my Uncle Izzy's memory with this performance.

– Gordon Archive

Talk Dirty was different. It was different from the beginning.

– *Gordon Archive*

Cameraman Jack Remy.

We were going to shoot this crying scene as one long master. There would be no punching in for close-ups. This was it.

When Sam called, "Action," John Leslie launched into a quietly, soulful harmonica. He was a very talented musician. Who knew?

I began sobbing and delivered my long tale of sadness and loneliness.

When we completed the scene, there was applause from the crew. That was rare. Sam was on his feet coming towards us when the applause started. He turned back to the crew, and with one withering look, shut it off like it was water from a tap.

They were breaking the mood. Sam wasn't done yet. He hadn't gotten what he wanted from me. He leaned in close.

"We're gonna go again," he said, "right now." He took my face in his hands. "This time," he said, "I want you to let it out, just let it out," and he went back to his place behind the camera.

A strange thing happened then after, "Action." John played his harmonica. The tears flowed from my eyes. The long speech poured from my lips. The scene was playing itself. It was all happening on automatic pilot. Inside, I was somewhere else. Inside, I was watching my own movie, a different movie. I saw my dead Uncle Izzy stick his head out from behind the clouds. He said,

"It's okay. Go ahead. Use it."

The hair was standing up on my neck. The camera was still running.

The scene was finishing itself. "And cut!" Sam had a smile on his face. He was happy with it. We were done.

It was the only time in my life that I ever felt like I "understood" acting, and I really didn't know if I even approved of it. It reminded me of reading about the barnstorming theater troupes of medieval Europe. They were often persecuted by the Church. They were subject to arrest, being tarred and feathered, and being run out of town by the local clerics. Their sin, to the medieval mind, was that they "played" with life. Some people argued that life should not be played with.

Anyway, that was my own private little world at that moment. Around me, they were offering congratulations and breaking down the set. John Leslie looked at me and smiled. "The actor!" he said, mocking me with love like a real big brother. That was sweet. Sam was right about us. We were good together. This was still just a fuck film. It wasn't *Gone with the Wind* or anything, but we were breaking some new ground together and that was good.

My sex scene with Sharon Kane was up next. Sam was looking after me. "You have to go from being as sad as you've ever been in that last scene," he said, "to as happy as you've ever been in this next one! You hit the peaks with Anthony Spinelli!" he shouted and cracked himself up.

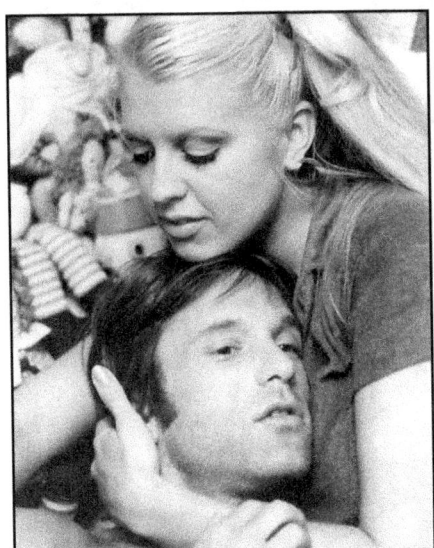

- Gordon Archive/KBeech.com

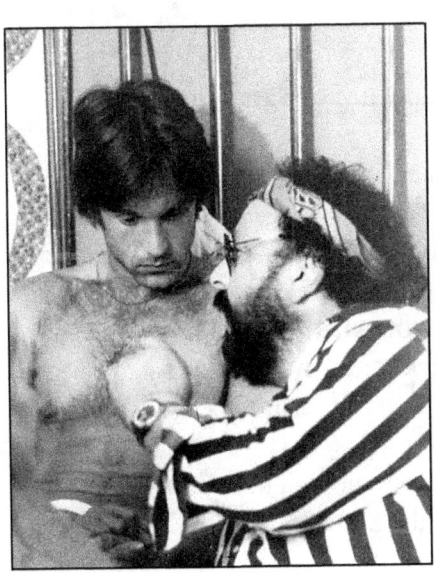

- Gordon Archive

Being directed by Anthony Spinelli.

– *Gordon Archive*

Spinelli with still photographer Mark Focus.

When we were signing our model releases and getting paid after shooting this movie, Sam put a meaty paw around my shoulder and said, "Kid, you did a great job, but I'll tell you what. I don't want any fucking Dewey Alexander's in my movie. Pick a new name," Sam said to me. I turned to his son Mitch who had written the script.

"What's my name?" I asked him.

Mitch looked me up and down and said in a heavy Spanish accent, "Richard Pacheco." He held the "o" for a long time and kept nodding his head.

"How do you spell it?" I asked him. He told me. Then, I signed my new name.

TALK DIRTY TO ME

RUNNING TIME: 80 MINUTES

Marlene	JESIE ST. JAMES
Jack	JOHN LESLIE
Helen	JULIET ANDERSON
Lenny	RICHARD PACHECO
Husband	AARON STUART
Doctor	CHRIS CASSIDY
Rose	SHIRLEY WOODS
Jill	DOROTHY LeMAY
Waitress	HOLLY McCALL
Catering Truck Operator	ANTHONY SPINELLI
Real Estate Agent	CARL REGAL

Jack and Lenny (John Leslie and Richard Pacheco) are two guys whose one aim is to lay as many girls as possible. Jack never fails to score, while poor Lenny always strikes out and ends up watching. Jack meets wealthy and lonely Marlene (Jesie St. James) at the beach. He vows to Lenny he'll bed her within three days, knowing he has what she craves. First, though, he teases her with erotic performances with his other girlfriends. Poor Marlene can only listen to his dirty talk, and fantasize it's her he's talking to. Finally, Jack has Marlene so frustrated she's ripe for his delightfully dirty language. The effect is immediate and total — Marlene explodes into arousal and, oblivious to everything else, drags him to her bedroom for an electrifying display of love-making that exceeds even his wildest hopes!

LENNY, JILL, ROSE AND JACK

HELEN AND JACK

MARLENE AND JACK

DOROTHY LeMAY AS JILL

- Mark Focus/KBeech.com

That's actually Sharon Kane on the bottom right.

Chapter Twenty-Two

Y'know, there's another Richard Pacheco! I went to his website. He's got a shaved head and a beard. Doesn't look a bit like me. Lists himself as an actor, writer, director, and producer. Shit, I don't know, maybe he is me. Could I have been living in Bedford, Massachusetts all these years without even knowing it? Do I have a life I'm keeping secret from myself? Is this The Twilight Zone? Am I an X-File?

I wonder if people who look up Richard Pacheco on the Web and see this guy just figure that's just what I must look like nowadays? Our biographies seem to be bleeding into each other a bit. I saw a filmography of mine that listed a movie "I" made in 2005 and when I looked it up, it was him!

Wow! Sure puts a dent in any feelings of uniqueness and immortality. I wonder how that Richard Pacheco feels about having to share his name with a guy like me? Jesus, sorry, pal.

Chapter Twenty-Three

It turned out that "there was no crying in porn," after all. Over Sam's most strenuous objections, the producers chopped that crying scene right out of the movie. "Tore its guts out!" Sam screamed. Bottom line, it was their movie. They paid for it. They owned it. They had the right.

Fuck it. That and a whole lot of other disagreeable shit had led to a World War III situation between them and Sam. They had a three-picture deal going in with each other. *Talk Dirty to Me* was just supposed to be the first. Now, after all the feuding, capped by cutting out the film's climactic scene, they couldn't even be in the same room.

I called them up and asked if I could have the footage. I just wanted to see it. It was one of the most extraordinary moments of my life. "Sure," they said, "sure." They didn't care at first, but it never happened.

When *Talk Dirty to Me* became this big-time X Rated hit, anyway, everybody immediately started talking sequel. The producers wanted John and me to make *Talk Dirty Part Two* without Sam. Sam asked us not to do it. He wanted us to make our own sequel without them.

It got messy. When I sided with Sam, the producers stopped taking my calls. They never gave me that footage. I never even got to see that crying scene.

Part Four

– Gordon Archive

STAR DREK

The Continuing Discussion of My Career in Pornography: An At-Once Tantalizing, Yet Traumatizing Exploration of Human Love and Erotic Coupling featuring Intimate Variations of the St. Valentine's Day Massacre and other Basic American Love Rituals.

Chapter One

*"Every time I try to make it,
I end up stepping in it."*

– David Schein, Blake Street Hawkeyes

When *Talk Dirty to Me* was released theatrically, it made a lot of waves.

It was not the monster epidemic that swept the country like *Deep Throat* had done almost a decade earlier, but a lot of adult producers sat up and took notice. They smelled the possibility of bigger profits for a better product. They smelled greater legitimacy. They smelled "the crossover film."

For directors like Spinelli, the crossover film became the Holy Grail of adult films. It would be a movie with explicit, hard-core sex that would be so well done that it would cross over into the mainstream markets. It signaled a brief period in the making of adult films that called out for bigger budgets, better scripts, and better performances, better everything. It was the perfect time for a guy like me to be in the business. If I'd had to depend solely on my skills as a "cocksman," I'd have been one and done after *The Candy Stripers*.

Reviews of *Talk Dirty* started turning up in places that usually ignored the adult film industry, like *Esquire* magazine for one.

In the article titled "*Deep Thought* on Porno," reviewer James Wolcott suggested that if porn continued to develop with the kind of emotional content as portrayed in *Talk Dirty to Me*, it might actually be growing up and be able to offer some real cultural value as an art form. And again, as I mentioned earlier, Wolcott concluded by saying that "until porn was made by the artists, it would continue to wallow in the shallows of human experience."

Richard Pacheco got rave reviews for *Talk Dirty to Me*. I never quite understood that. My best work was on the cutting room floor. The character was great, but the finished movie, eh. My guess is that the movie, and all the performances in it, get a whole lot better when you compare them only to the other porn films made that year. In which case, we were *Gone with the Fucking Wind*.

At the 1981 Adult Film Association Awards (AFAA) in Los Angeles, John Leslie won the Best Actor "Erotica" for his performance as Jack. I won Best Supporting Actor for playing Lenny. *Talk Dirty to Me* was named Best Picture of the Year in a tie with *Urban Cowgirls*. The tie was a bit of bullshit, but we didn't let it rain on our parade.

The Awards were *A Night at the Opera* with Groucho, Chico, Harpo, and Scummo! We all got to dress up in ball gowns and tuxedos and play "Oscars." We even got to ride in limousines! By the time we arrived at the Playboy mansion afterwards, I felt like a little kid staying up way past his bedtime. There was the mighty Hugh Hefner in his pajamas shaking our hands and saying hello to everybody. Wow. We swam naked in his palace of pools. It was a magical night of fulfilled dreams.

Later in the year, at the rival New York Critics Adult Film Awards on the East Coast, we won all the awards again.

The phone was now ringing for Richard Pacheco. There were job offers and interviews. It was heady stuff! *Talk Dirty to Me* was a big hit, but not everyone was pleased. I received one scathing phone call from a veteran porn actor and self-proclaimed industry spokesperson named Bill Margold. To be kind, he "argued" most vociferously that we were taking the industry absolutely in the wrong direction. He was not gentle in making his points. Wasn't much of a conversation going on. He was pitching and I was catching. His view was that porn belonged to cultural outlaws who needed to remain cultural outlaws. "Porn should be kept in the gutter where it belongs," he scolded.

By the end of that phone call, I felt like I had spoken with a buzz saw. We did not exactly see eye-to-eye. If Margold's view of sex and the industry were the only one available, I'd have much rather taken a job at Taco Bell. It seemed like I had made a formidable enemy for myself without even trying. Margold was a loud, strident, sensationalist voice who was dedicated and active in many phases of the X-rated business. Fortunately, our paths did not cross all that much while we both worked as actors in the late seventies and early-eighties.

In the end, the industry actually proved large enough to accommodate the both of us.

When Margold and I would meet in later years, it was always civil and with a handshake. By then, we had many industry friends in common. For all of his hard-edged bluster, I came to see in Margold a guy who behaved quite differently behind the scenes than you'd expect from someone with his ultra-abrasive public persona. Like my mentor, Spinelli, Sam, Bill Margold was very protective of the young actresses and actors he met in the fields of porn. He had a well-earned, avuncular reputation for making many life-saving efforts to help the lost, the wild, and the drowning kids who got caught up in drugs and in the torrid life of LA in the fast lanes.

Shhh, don't tell anybody, but Bill Margold is really one of the good guys!

- Adam Film World

Sam Weston as Anthony Spinelli.

The success of *Talk Dirty to Me* made Sam the top director in the industry behind only Gerry Damiano. It elevated John Leslie to a leading man status matched only by the big boys like John Holmes, Jamie Gillis, Harry Reems, and Marc Stevens.

– *Adam Film World*

John Leslie on top!

For me, it was like being called up from Triple A to play in the Majors.

"Richard Pacheco" became my full-time name, and I joined the ranks of a whole slew of second tier talent that would feature guys like the aforementioned Bill Margold, Paul Thomas, Eric Edwards, Joey Silvera, R. Bolla, Bobby Astyr, Herschel Savage, Jon Martin, Ron Jeremy, Mike Ranger, Jerry Butler, Mike Horner, Randy West, Don Fernando, Billy Dee, and, no doubt, some other significant players.

We were the actors of what I would call the second great wave of porn. It was begun after the initial successes of the groundbreaking *Deep Throat* and *Behind the Green Door* generation. Our era transcended the last of the films being made in the mid-to-late-seventies on up to the complete video revolution that revamped the industry by the mid-eighties. That's when the guys like Tommy Byron, Peter North, Sean Michaels, and Robert Bullock started showing up.

Many fans and critics refer to our era as the Golden Age of Porn.

Pericles was doing pop shots and the sexual revolution was at its zenith.

– Gordon Archive

I became a Big Leaguer, one of the SPINELLI ALL-STARS.

Chapter Two

It was 1979. The Pirates won the World Series, the Steelers won the Super Bowl, and I was *Playgirl* Magazine's MAN-OF-THE-YEAR. It was a good year for Pittsburgh.

- Gordon Archive

My son Bobby would call it "A Stilltahn (Steeltown) Trifecta" in this birthday offering he gave me many years later.

If I were a gambler, like my mother and father and all of my uncles and aunts before me—except maybe for my Uncle Izzy—I'd have to say I was riding a nice little hot streak.

And for dessert, the director of *Insatiable* called and offered me a lot of money to get a blow job from Marilyn Chambers, the number-one X-rated female star in the world.

"Gee, I'll have to think about it a minute. Let me get back to you."

– Gordon Archive

"Top of the World, Ma!"

The Ivory Snow Lady

Marilyn Chambers wasn't a regular porn queen like Annette Haven, Seka or Vanessa Del Rio. She wasn't a regular in the industry. She hadn't come up through the ranks. Much like John Holmes was among the men, Marilyn Chambers was in her own special category. Her name recognition and status all came from the great Ivory Snow scandal of 1972.

As the story goes, when filming had been completed on her starring role in the groundbreaking Mitchell Brothers' pornographic film *Behind the Green Door*, newcomer Marilyn let them know that she was "the Ivory Snow Girl." In supermarkets all across the nation, she was being featured on box covers of Ivory Snow soap suds.

Many have written that Marilyn was pictured cuddling a baby under the infamous Madison Avenue tag line of "99 and 44/100% pure."

Now it just so happens that my friend Albert Levy gave me an actual box of the Marilyn Chambers Ivory Snow soap suds (Regular size, 13 ozs. with the original soap still in it) and I have just scanned it my ownself into the computer.

As you can see in the photo below, it is simply not true that Marilyn is posed under the phrase of "99 and 44/100% pure," but then, as we have seen time and time again, History—with a capital H—is often written by only those who can manage to get it published! For the record, then, the phrase "99 and 44/100% pure" appears only on the back of the Ivory Snow box, in the upper right corner in red ink.

– Gordon Archive

Still, The Mitchell Brothers were savvy enough to use that phrase as well as tons of pictures of a tastefully naked Marilyn posing with a box of Ivory Snow in their advertising for *Behind the Green Door*.

Maybe it was one of those slow news days, but the story of Marilyn's "double life" as a soapsuds model and a porn star struck a HUGE chord in the mainstream media. It was everywhere. Marilyn was quoted at the time as having joked that her appearance in *Behind the Green Door* would probably help Proctor & Gamble to sell even more soap!

– Kenjii.

It was Marilyn's "fifteen minutes of fame" even before Andy Warhol got famous for coining the phrase about having "fifteen minutes of fame."

Procter & Gamble kept the story growing when they fired her as their model and pulled all of her boxes off of the store shelves. Marilyn did a world of interviews and hit all the TV talk shows. Ticket sales for *Behind the Green Door* soared. The Mitchell Brothers became notorious. The Ivory Snow boxes became collector's items. In fact, I know where you can get one.

And Marilyn Chambers's fifteen minutes of fame ended up lasting for the rest of her life.

Now, let's talk about that blow job.

Y'know, I could tell lies here. Who's gonna know? Marilyn's long gone now. She passed on to that great come shot in the sky back in 2009. Only fifty-six years old, she was. That was too young.

I could write about how thrilled she was to have had sex with me. How she had whispered in my ear after having a positively torrential orgasm that I was the best lover she ever had. Yeah, I could say that, but, ah, that's not exactly how it happened.

The movie was called *Insatiable*.

"Odd name for a sex film," my wife observed. "Why would anybody want to make a sex film about a woman who can't be satisfied? Sounds like being in Hell to me."

The movie was being made by Miracle Films. They had the best motto in the business: "IF IT'S A GOOD FILM, IT'S A MIRACLE!" It rang true on sooo many levels!

A gaffer named Charlie Stephens picked me up in his ailing sports car for the long ride to the set in the Sacramento Delta. Charlie was good fun. We got stoned and bullshitted the miles away. Always liked Charlie.

– Gordon Archive

(L-R) Charlie Stephens, Michael Lewin, and Harry Lee.

Mostly, guys—and girls—on the X-rated film crews of those days were very energetic and alive people. In fact, I often had the thought that the wrong people were in front of the cameras. They were funny and they had fun. They were knowledgeable, sharp, fast-talking and glib. They absolutely worshipped the movie business. Film crews were hip. Or at least they had me fooled.

Charlie's car coughed and sputtered, but somehow we made it. When we got to the hotel, we hung out in the bar and waited for our people to return from some location work. As Fate would then have a wicked laugh at my expense, an absolutely stunning woman flirted with me and tried to pick me up. Sonuvabitch, wouldn't ya just know it? The last thing on earth I needed the night before shooting a sex scene was a hungry woman! Experience had painfully taught me the need to save my sperms for the battle to come. Sex was definitely not on my agenda that night. Retreating alone to my bed, I rested my loins and memorized my lines.

In the morning, I was driven from the hotel to the set and there was Marilyn. She was in David Clark's makeup chair. Her hair was up in rollers, but there was still no mistaking the fact that she was a real thoroughbred. We were introduced. It was light and easy. I acted like I belonged as I stowed my gear to get ready for the day's events.

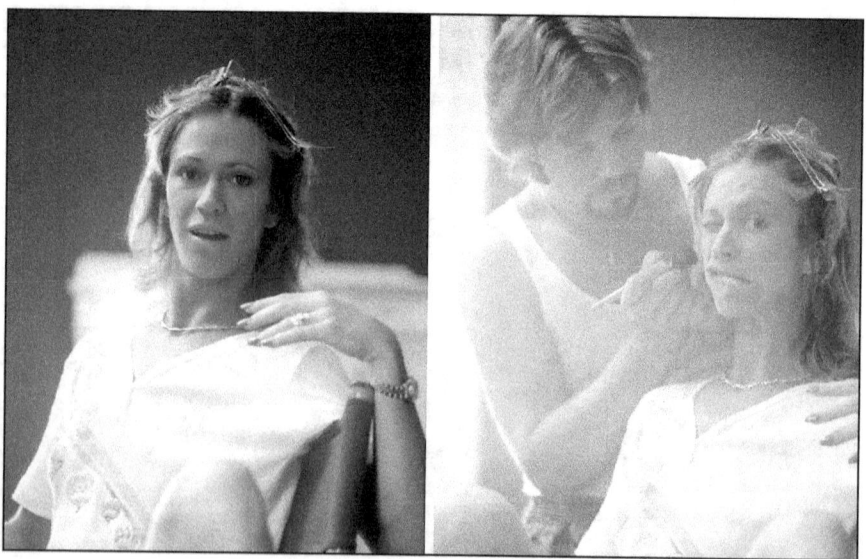

- *Gordon Archive*

Marilyn backstage with David Clark in makeup.

Marilyn had her own hairdresser with her. This was already big doings compared to most of the women I had met in the business. Marilyn made lots of jokes and so did I. Keeping it light was the order of the day. I took out my camera and with her permission, snapped some pictures.

I was hoping that this would be a day I would want to remember. I was hoping that these would be some pictures that I would want to share with all of my Marquis buddies from high school. 'Hey, Goose! Lookahere! Go fuck yourself!"

– *Gordon Archive*

Howie & Marilyn in the Ferrari.

Marilyn and I ran our lines. She knew hers and I knew mine. Good, good, it was all good. She appeared to like me well enough. Our scenes were going to be shot out of sequence. The blow job would come before lunch. It seemed like we were behind schedule before we even got started. They were already trying to speed things up.

Oddly enough, the story we were shooting in the film mirrored our real life situation. She played a famous actress who has sex with a nobody.

I wasn't exactly a nobody, but certainly compared to Marilyn, I was.

Her character was running away from fame in a Ferrari, and my character had run out of gas and was hitchhiking when Marilyn pulled over to render assistance. Before she was about to become overwhelmed with her "insatiable" desire for my nubile body, she handed me a bit of a rubber hose and suggested that I siphon some gasoline from her car into my gas can.

Then, in that special burst of magic that only pornographic movies seem to be able to provide, while I was sucking her hose, she would begin sucking mine. Tee-hee, very funny, let's shoot the shot. "And Action!"

– Gordon Archive

Well, the problem was I had never siphoned gasoline before. I dipped one end of the hose into her tank and began sucking on the other. I should have tried acting. We did some very stupid double entendre dialogue before I was surprisingly rewarded with a mouthful of gasoline …

– *Gordon Archive*

TERRIBLE! REALLY, REALLY. REALLY TERRIBLE!

I couldn't spit it out fast enough! Have you ever tasted gasoline? DON'T!

Eventually, I recovered enough for us to continue shooting the scene, but my penis had to do it without me. There was enough pleasure in her sucking that it was able to get hard, but it was acting, Academy Award acting! I was completely distracted by that god awful taste still in my mouth. I would have killed for a glob full of peanut butter. Blow job? What blow job?

But Marilyn sucked like a pro and they soon had all the hardcore footage they needed except for the come shot, the almighty come shot.

Director asked me if I was ready to come. He just wasn't paying attention. On a one-to-ten scale, I was about a 2. They were all in a hurry to get to lunch. For me to come from her sucking could have used up a goodly portion of her remaining youth. Perhaps I exaggerate. Realistically, it would have taken thirty minutes to an hour, if it would have been even possible for me to come at that point. It has always taken me a long time to come from a blow job, on screen or off - and that's without drinking any gasoline.

So, I did everyone a favor that day. Rather than use up Marilyn for that long, with all the potential for disaster that it included, I took matters into my own right hand. If it was my orgasm that they all awaited and who knew better than me how to turn me on? Everybody loved the idea and I lay down next to the Ferrari and closed my eyes.

In my own private little world, I began to masturbate. Talk about taking one for the team! Ah, the glamour of it all! I don't know what Marilyn did. They were probably touching up her makeup. She was on stand-by, after all, waiting for the call that my squirt was imminent.

I can't be sure, but it seemed like it didn't take me all that long. I can't remember who or what I was thinking about, but whatever and whoever, it worked! When I felt myself getting close, I jumped up and hit my mark like Marlon Brando! Marilyn was there on her knees in a flash.

The director called for action and the rest you can see for yourself in the movie. A lot of people did. *Insatiable* was probably the most popular film that I was ever in.

I was at the beach in San Diego one day and I spotted this insanely erotic-looking woman sitting nearby. When the man she was with saw me staring at her, I looked away.

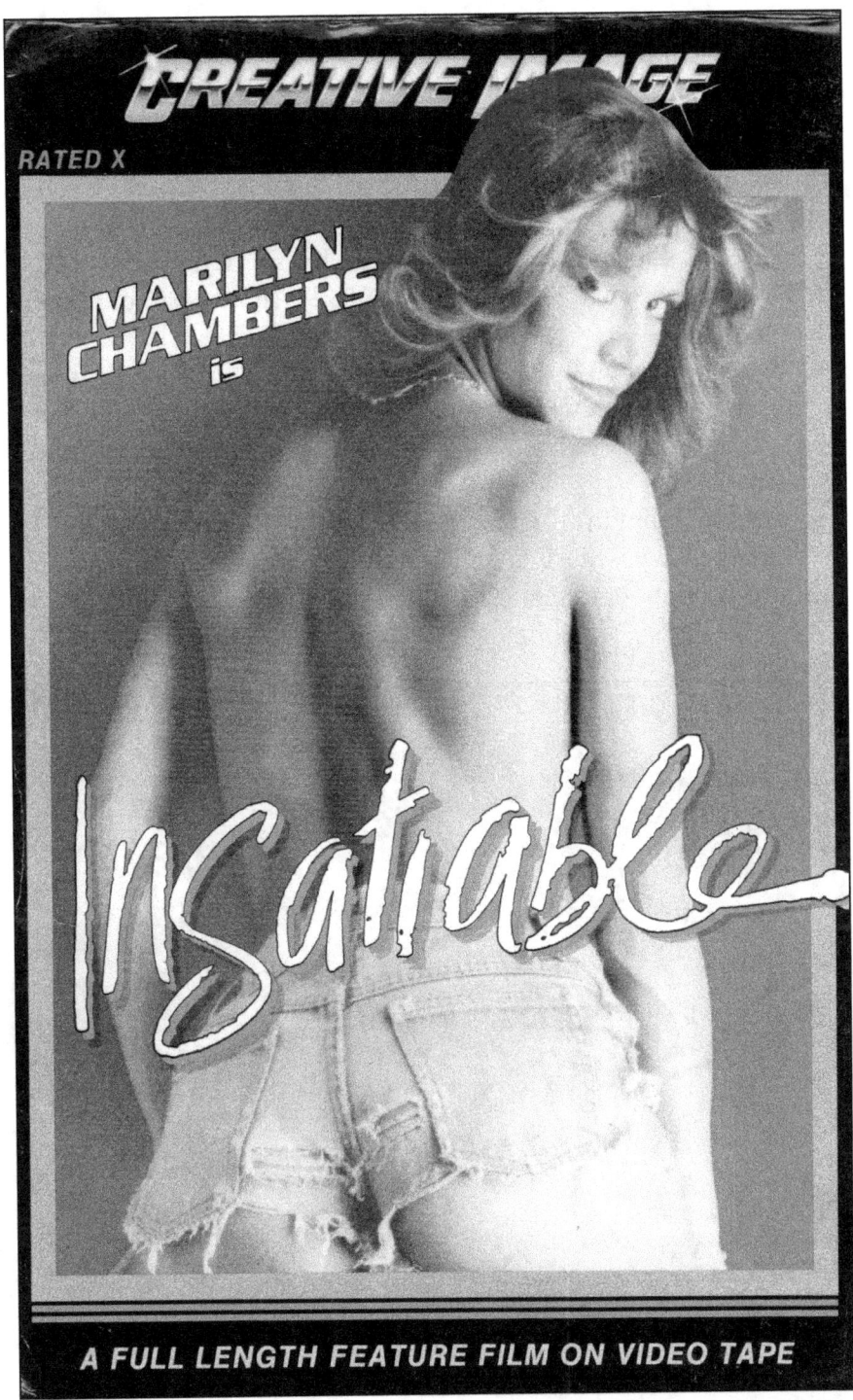

– *Miracle Releasing of Nevada, Inc.*

A few minutes later, he again caught me looking at her. Again, I turned away. When he saw me staring yet again a third time, he rose up and started coming towards me. Oh, shit, he was big. Well, here it comes, I thought. I quietly clenched the fingers of my right hand into a fist.

He got up close to me, leaned down, and said, "Weren't you in *Insatiable*?"

"YES!" I said, way too loudly. "YES! THAT WAS ME!" I said in the joy of relief. "I WAS IN THAT MOVIE!" And we had ourselves a nice little chat.

I can't tell you how many of my old high school and college friends were jealous to learn that I'd gotten a blow job from Marilyn Chambers. She had a huge following. I didn't always tell them the truth about that experience.

Maybe I shouldn't even have told you.

Luckily for us, Marilyn and I were able to meet again in several future sex scenes, ones that left a much better taste in our mouths.

– *Gordon Archive*

For Posterity.

Chapter Three
Schmeckle Movies in California

The telephone was ringing. I was drunk and on the outside of my locked front door. The ringing was going on inside and I was having trouble getting the key into the keyhole. Finally!

I rushed to pick up the phone. "Hello?"

"You're busted!" came a hard, raspy voice over the line.

What? My mind raced into overdrive. It's amazing how fast those two little words can sober you up. I knew that getting busted was one of the occupational hazards of the business I was in. I figured it was just my time.

"Didn't you hear me?" the voice asked, "I said you were busted." Visions of courtrooms and lawyers swirled in my brain. I saw myself in handcuffs. Was I being arrested? What was the charge? I wondered who I should call first. I did not want to hear the heavy, rolling sounds of iron doors closing behind me.

"What are you in for?" the killer would ask.

"Smut," I'd tell him.

Hey, wait a minute, I thought to myself. This ain't right. I heard a familiar sound in that raspy voice.

"Is this Jimmy?" I asked.

"Yeah," he said, "and you're busted!" It was my cousin Jimmy calling from Pittsburgh, Pennsylvania. Now, I was confused. If I was getting busted, why was my cousin Jimmy calling from Pittsburgh to tell me about it? I guess I wasn't as sober as I thought.

"What are you talking about, Jimmy? I asked him. "Tell me what happened?"

"Cousin Burton saw you in a porno film!" he said.

What? I started laughing. Another country heard from — cousin Burton! I was so relieved that nobody was dead and that the KGB wasn't involved that I just started laughing. This wasn't gonna be about cousin Jimmy at all, this was gonna be about cousin Burton!

Okay.

From what I could put together, cousin Burton was a lawyer who worked for Valium in Washington, D.C. Apparently, he skipped out of work one afternoon and took himself down to the Pussycat Theatre to see an X-rated movie. This, of course, was in the prehistoric days before home video.

Just my luck, cousin Burton stumbled into *The Candy Stripers*, my first adult film, and cousin Burton thought he recognized me up there on the screen. He got so excited that he drove all the way home to Maryland, picked up his wife in suburbia, left their kids with some neighbors, and then drove all the way back to the porno house in Washington in order to show her the movie.

"Is that cousin Howard up there?" he asked

"Yes, that's cousin Howard up there."

"You're sure that's cousin Howard?"

"Yes, I'm sure that's cousin Howard," she said.

Well, cousin Burton got so excited that he done lost his mind. He called my parents! He was going to tell on me. I was thirty-two years old. I hadn't lived at home in fourteen years. cousin Burton was thirty-seven.

It turned out that my parents were not at home when he called, so cousin Burton called his own mom, my Aunt Lil. He told her that he had just seen cousin Howard in a porno film!

Well, Aunt Lil made cousin Burton promise not to tell my mother. It seems that Aunt Lil had once taken my mother to see the scandalous movie *Last Tango in Paris*. When Marlon Brando began buttering up Maria Schneider's asshole, my mother dragged my Aunt Lil out of the theater. This, by the way, was all news to me. I guess Aunt Lil felt pretty sure that my mother would not take cousin Burton's news very well. She decided she would protect my mom from this bit of distressing information about her youngest son.

"So, how did you find out about all of this?" I asked cousin Jimmy, who, after all, was telling me all these stories. "Did Aunt Lil tell you?"

"No," Jimmy said, "Aunt Kitty told me. I think she got it from Aunt Rose." Now, this was getting very complicated. If Aunt Kitty and Aunt Rose knew, that meant that Uncle Chink and Uncle Manny knew too, and so would Uncle Leo."

"But don't worry," cousin Jimmy said, "everybody swears they'll all keep it secret from your mother and father."

My heart dropped. I felt the anguish of being an embarrassment to my parents. I imagined the relatives whispering behind their backs at the next Bar Mitzvah. My parents wouldn't even know what was happening. It was no good.

"Why didn't Burton just call me?" I asked Jimmy.

"How the hell should I know?" Jimmy answered. "He's a jag-off!" It didn't really matter. The cat was out of the bag. I knew that it was now time for me to call my parents and tell them about my X-rated film career.

First, I had to de-fuse Jimmy. He was wired. He was acting as my agent, but his attitude was all filled with sin and scandal. I tried to act like this was no big thing.

I tried very hard to believe that myself. I really had no idea how my parents would react. The only thing I had going for me was that I was their son. The apple's not supposed to fall far from the tree, right? Biology seemed to suggest that my actions would not be too farfetched for my own parents to be able to comprehend. But I'll tell ya what, I was not overjoyed that I had to call my parents and tell them that I had been in some porno movies.

– Gordon Archive

"Your Mother Should Know".

The sexual revolution of the 1960s seemed to just completely skip Pittsburgh. In the city of Roberto Clemente and the golden triangle, pornography was still an incredibly seedy thing. The mob-run theaters were in the crappiest parts of town and the vibe was absolute lowlife. It was not the pre-AIDS, upbeat San Francisco scene at all. There were no Mitchell Brothers hobnobbing with the city's artists, intelligentsia and cultural elite.

In Pittsburgh, pornography was still equated with racketeering, mobsters, illegal gambling and prostitution. It was "schtick drek" (a piece of shit)! There was no Sexual Freedom League. There was no socially redeeming value. Pornography was vice, a crime. To the Jewish community there, it was decidedly trafe (not kosher). Sexual liberation, Wilhelm Reich, Esalen Institute, Masters and Johnson's sex therapy, all of that was just California bubbameinz (silly talk). In Pittsburgh, a dirty movie was still just a dirty movie.

By the time I reached the age of thirty-two, all that longhaired generation gap crap of the sixties was over for me. I was now into just getting along with my folks. I had come to appreciate their acquired wisdom based simply on their years of raising a family, staying married, and being alive. I no longer wanted to know their dark secrets or have them be my friend. I had given up on trying to reeducate them or change them with each new wave of therapy I had discovered in the counter-cultural Mecca of Berkeley in the seventies. I had come the full circle back to just loving them and being grateful that they had brought me into this life and nourished me.

I knew I had a real curveball to throw at them! I just hoped that they could handle it.

As I approached that telephone call back home, I prepared myself to become the black sheep of the family. I prepared myself for excommunication. I could see the headlines:

Dateline Pittsburgh - LOCAL JEWBOY DISCOVERED FUCKING SHIKSAS FOR CASH IN CALIFORNIA — news at 11.

Well, for good or bad, I was about to reunite the characters of myself. Richard Pacheco, porn star and wonderful figment of my imagination, I'd like you to meet your real parents, Sam and Adeline Gordon. I picked up the phone and dialed. My wife got on the line with me. I needed her there for moral support.

My mother answered the phone. My dad had gone out to get a

haircut. We did a little small talk. She was having the walls washed and the new carpeting installed. It was keeping her busy. She was getting the house ready for my brother's return. After ten years in Israel, my brother, the doctor, was moving his family back to Pittsburgh. My parents were ecstatic about his return.

"Listen, ma," I always called her "ma," "I have to tell you something."

"Yeah?" she said.

"Yeah," I answered. "I did a couple of X-rated movies awhile back." The truth was I had done thirty features, ten loops, and two magazines by then, but I did not want to open with the sledge hammer ... "HEY, MA, I'M A PORN STAR! I FUCK SHIKSAS FOR A LIVING!" I thought I'd take it a little slower and see how the medicine was going down.

"Yeah, I did a couple of X-rated movies awhile back. I didn't tell you about it before because I didn't think you'd be too crazy to hear about it."

"Ye-ahhh," she said haltingly. My mother was no dummy. She was waiting for all the bombs to fall.

"Yeah, well, cousin Burton stumbled into one of my movies playing in Washington and —"

"He goes to see those movies?" my mother asked me.

"I guess so, ma," I told her. "Anyway, he got himself all excited at seeing me and he called Aunt Lil."

"Aunt Lil?" my mom asked. "Why didn't he call you?"

"Good question, ma."

"Did Lil call you?" she asked.

"No, it was cousin Jimmy," I answered.

"Cousin Jimmy?" she said, "how did he know?"

"I think he heard about it from Aunt Kitty or Aunt Rose, I'm not really sure, ma. Cousin Burton told Aunt Lil, and I think Aunt Lil told Kitty and I think it maybe was Aunt Rose told Jimmy ... Look, Ma, I don't know. Jimmy was kind of excited when he told me all this. The bottom line is that it's all over the family grapevine and I wanted you and Dad to hear about it from me before you got wind of all the gossip that's goin' around." There was a pause.

"What was the movie's name?" she asked.

"The *Candy Stripers* was the one that Burton saw," I answered.

"How much did they pay you?" she wanted to know.

"I got $200 a day for a couple of days work in the film." It was the truth. There was a moment of silence. "I worked with Marilyn Chambers," I added. That was technically a lie. I worked with Marilyn Chambers in another film, but I somehow thought that Marilyn Chamber's fame might somehow help to legitimize the whole thing.

"Who?" my mother asked.

"Marilyn Chambers, ma," I said, "you know …" Jesus, I thought the whole world knew about Marilyn Chambers. "You remember, ma, the Ivory Snow girl, on the box cover, the woman with the baby?"

"You worked with a baby?" she asked.

"No, ma, Marilyn Chambers was on the Ivory Snow package with the baby. Then when they found out she'd worked in *Behind the Green Door*, they fired her. Remember? It was all over the papers."

"Oh," said my mother. Awkward silence. "So, that's your news?"

"That's it," I said.

"You want to know what I think?" she asked.

"Yeah, ma, tell me whatdya think?"

"Plllbbbbbbb!" she said. "That's what I think." My mom gave me the raspberry! I laughed. My wife laughed. My mom laughed. That was basically it! Soon, we all said our good-byes. I hung up the phone, relieved.

I imagined my mom meeting one of her friends at the kosher butcher shop. "So, how are your kids?" the friend would ask.

"Fine," my mother would answer. "My son, the doctor, is coming back home from Israel and my other son, he's making schmeckle movies in California."

Several days later, my old Chevy died. When I called a tow truck to make the funeral arrangements, I was told that I needed to have the car's title. I had to call my Dad and ask him to send it to California.

On the phone, Dad told me, "No problem." Then he said that cousin Jimmy had told him that I had won some kind of award. I had told Jimmy that I had won me a couple of Best Supporting Actor Awards. I had told him and then forgotten all about it. Jimmy told my Dad, and when my Dad mentioned it, I habitually just started to lie. Then, I remembered, I no longer had to.

"Yeah," I said, noticing a little pride creeping into my voice, "I won a Best Supporting Acting Award." There was a brief pause.

"You want to know what I think?" my Dad asked. Uh-oh, here we go, I braced myself for what was to come.

"What?" I answered.

"How's your health?" he asked.

"Fine," I told him, taken back a little.

"How's your wife's health?" he asked.

"She's fine too." I told him.

"You love your wife?" he asked.

"Yeah, Dad, I do."

"Does she love you?"

"Yeah."

"Well, then everything's okay," he said, "and that's what I think!"

Over the phone, I could hear the smile on his face. I don't think in my heart that my Dad could understand at all what I was doing. He was much too shy about such things. Even so, he had found it in himself not to worry about it, not to let it come between us. I wanted to cry then, but held my emotions in check. It would've just made us both uncomfortable. The men in our family held their emotions in check. I think that's why I was drawn to acting. You get to have emotions. You get to express emotions. Hell, you've got to express emotions, but that's another story.

The moment between father and son passed just as it had between mother and son earlier. There was no hellfire and there was no celebration. It just wasn't going to be any big deal between us. I'm sure that volumes exist in what wasn't said, but our bond had managed to survive the fact that their son made some schmeckle movies in California.

I was a lucky man. I wonder sometimes about the conversation that must have taken place between my mom and dad when he came home after getting that haircut when I first gave mom the news. In later years, he claimed that he didn't even remember it.

Cousin Burton became one of my biggest fans for a while. He knew more about X-rated movies than I did. He used to call me long-distance on his company's dime to gossip about his favorite porn stars. He had a big crush on Vanessa del Rio. I used to plot revenge while I humored him. I was gonna ask Vanessa to lure him to a motel, chain him to a bed, and leave him stuck there with a cucumber up his ass.

Eventually though, Burton found the common sense to apologize to me for starting all the wildfire family gossip that led to my confession to my parents. And I forgave him. In the end, he did me a favor. I didn't like having a secret life from my parents. It was good for all of us to get the cards on the table. Besides, I thought, in a couple of months, none of this would matter anymore anyway. I was going straight!

Chapter Four

– *Gordon Archive*

Carly and I were house hunting in LA. We were looking to find a place in Venice Beach. No matter that one-room garages were selling for a million-two because I was *Playgirl's* Man-of-the-Year!

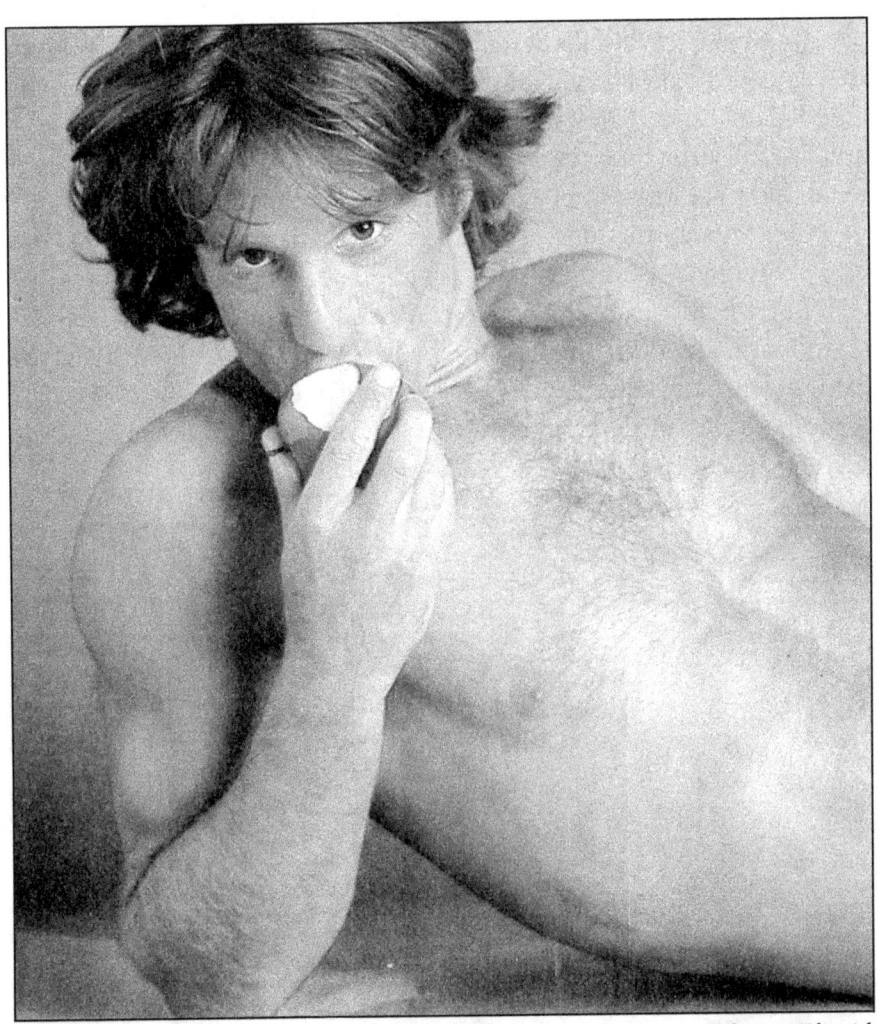

- Mike Ross/Playgirl.

Soon, the doors to movie star success would swing wide open and I'd be working in feature films with the likes of Dustin Hoffman and Whoopi Goldberg. All the Hollywood dreams would come true. I had my lottery tickets punched for fame and fortune and I was ready to win.

Thirty years later, I'm embarrassed now to look through old diaries and observe myself in what was the ambitious dementia of such pedestrian longing, but I think that's only because I failed at it.

What? Did I ruin the ending for you? Did you somehow think I got as famous as Jack Nicholson and you somehow just missed it?

Nah, I died at the Alamo next to Davy Crockett, but he had a better agent. I went over the falls at Reisenbach with Holmes and Moriarty, but they got all the press. I got fat next to Elvis eating bacon, peanut butter, and banana sandwiches, but he's the one who died sitting on the toilet and I'm still struggling at the computer to tell my side of the story. I want to get it right, to pass it on to the children, and them to their kids.

"Are you shittin' me? Grandpa fucked schiksas for a living?"

"Yeah, he did, and he got pretty good at it for a while."

But when it came to that great, mainstream Hollywood, movie star dream, I was just part of the huge legion of the Never Was. We came from everywhere and we all wanted the chance to be the next Rudolph Valentino or Cary Grant. We all wanted a piece of that pie-in-the-sky. Didn't you?

– *Gordon Archive/Playgirl*

AM Los Angeles with Regis.

I don't know why it didn't happen for me. I was the long shot that was supposed to pay off. I had a plan and everything. *Playgirl* was going to give me a half-time job being their centerfold director. I would prep the guys and help them through their shoots. It was perfect. I had resisted moving to LA while I would just be another unemployed actor, but the half-time gig from *Playgirl* took all the desperation out of such a move. I could earn enough money for us to live and still have the time off for the auditions that would make me a star.

Carly could quit her job at the Berkeley clinic and then reestablish herself as a therapist in LA. Lord knows that Los Angeles could certainly use as many mental health professionals as it could get.

We could even move ahead with our plans to make a baby.

Chapter Five

My first assignment for *Playgirl* was to write the following introductory letter:

So, You Want to Be a Centerfold

Congratulations! If you are reading this, chances are *Playgirl* has already selected you as a future centerfold for the magazine.

This is a little note to help you prepare for your upcoming photo session from someone who has been through it. I was MR. NOVEMBER in 1978 and went on to become the MAN-OF-THE-YEAR for 1979.

I think we can safely assume that if you have been chosen as a centerfold, you are in reasonably good shape and are sexually attractive in your own unique way.

What you should know in advance is that as part of depicting you as a sexually attractive male, PLAYGIRL photographers may want to shoot some nudes of you in various stages of arousal, in common parlance — with a hard-on.

This may or may not be a difficult objective for you, but just in case, here are some pointers:

1. PRACTICE being photographed with an erection by your photographer, wife, lover, friend, or whatever — before you get to the actual *Playgirl* session.

2. EXPERIMENT with whatever you think will help you achieve a state of arousal in a pressure situation. Examples: books, pictures, or having a sex partner present who will help you during the session. Remember to have these things present on the *Playgirl* set. I used masturbation. It worked.

3. COMMUNICATE and coordinate with the *Playgirl* director. They may be as bold or as bashful about this aspect of the session as you are. Speak to them in advance about how you feel about this part of the experience. Relate to them as your ally. They will be there to help you.

4. IF AT FIRST YOU DON'T SUCCEED, DON'T PANIC. Arousal comes and goes, especially under pressure. Nobody expects you to be Superman. With the proper stimulation, your body knows what to do automatically. The idea is to get yourself into the right frame of mind to let nature take its course—then, to let the *Playgirl* photographer take a few photographs of you in your full glory.

5. Keep in mind — We're not talking about standing on one leg balancing an egg on your nose for two hours with an erection. This part of your session may only take five-to-ten minutes out of what should be a three-to-six hour modeling experience. If achieving the erection proves difficult, do not become freaky; 99.9 % of males are not experienced with getting hard-ons in public situations.

Take your time and just let it happen. Be prepared to stop, take as many breaks as necessary, and start all over again.

6. My personal advice is to relate to the whole thing as fun. I thought it was an honor to be selected as a centerfold and found it personally gratifying that the *Playgirl* people

thought of my body as sexy.

As I stared at the pages of *Playboy* when I was a young man, I took myself to the promised land while looking at their delicious women.

Now, women will look at pictures of you and dream themselves into ecstasy. Have as much fun with it as you can. Treat it as the delightful adventure which it is and may the Gods of Eros be with you.

Best wishes, Howie Gordon
GOOD LUCK!!!!

Chapter Six

It was the age of Studio 54. Cocaine was now everywhere. It was the new marijuana. If you pulled out a joint, especially in LA, people looked at you like you were some kind of dinosaur.

It was at least a year before all the bodies started piling up on the beach.

I was far too susceptible to this drug. By myself, I could've easily strayed with the lemmings and run right off the edge of the world. It was Carly who eventually saved us from the madness. She said, "Look, I'll be a mother or I'll be a party girl. I won't be both. We have to choose."

We chose.

– Gordon Archive

Chapter Seven

- Gordon Archive/Playgirl

Playgirl's Man-of-the-Year! It was a great title, but it turned out to be one of little substance. The tone was really set for me right off the bat.

The Phoenix Suns were in town. It might even have been the very same day that I'd found out that I'd won the title. See? See what I mean? Just saying it like that sounds like I'd knocked out Mike Tyson or something. Far from it.

The Suns were in the Bay Area to play the Warriors. We're talking NBA basketball here. Through my old pal Gary Graham, I'd made friends with Joe Prosky, who was the trainer for the Phoenix team. Gary and Joe went all the way back to the early sixties when Gary pitched in the Cubs organization.

Whenever Phoenix came to town, I'd often be invited to join them for the game and then a Mexican dinner afterwards. Some of the Suns players would usually come along too. It was as close as I would ever get to the Major Leagues of anything.

So, I'm the Man-of-the-Year now and both Gary and Joe are tickled for me. After the game, Joe invited me into the visiting team's locker room. They'd just kicked the Warrior's ass. Joe introduced me to Gar Heard, one of Phoenix's starting forwards.

"Hey, Gar," he said, "I want you to meet *Playgirl*'s Man-of-the-Year." Wearing only a towel and a smile, the superbly chiseled Gar Heard looked down at me. His smile got bigger and he shook my hand. Gar Heard was six-feet-six inches tall. His nipples were taller than me.

In that instant, I learned everything I needed to know about how seriously to take myself in this Man-of-the-Year thing.

Chapter Eight

In the world of centerfolds, I was once again on the wrong side of sexism.

For openers, *Playboy*'s Playmate-of-the-Year got a Corvette, a movie contract, a modeling contract, some endorsement deals, and a bushel or two of money.

For *Playgirl* …

– *Gordon Archive*

Chapter Nine

Among my duties for *Playgirl* that year was to every now and then make a personal appearance at some kind of minor league road show where I'd sit next to a *Playboy* Bunny or a *Penthouse* Pet and autograph semi-nude pictures of myself for a weekend.

It was one like that in Hartford at the Civic Center VAN-TASY AUTO SHOW, which featured Cycles, Vans, Pickups, 4 X 4s, Off Road Vehicles, and me.

I got to hang out for a couple days with Candace Collins. She was *Playboy's* Miss December. That was kind of fun. We actually hit it off pretty well, but there was no nooky in it for Bonzo because she had her sights set on Charlie Pasarell, the tennis pro who was playing just around the corner in the AETNA World Cup Tennis Tournament. Life in the big city, what're you gonna do! Still, wasn't so bad sitting next to her all day, having people standing in lines waiting to get our autographs. Makes you think you're somebody!

- Gordon Archive

Signing autographs with Candace Collins.

Chapter Ten

And then, of course, there was:

– Gordon Archive

The bus ride to New York

It had been a long weekend, but I was all packed and ready to go. I sat on the bed taping stuff in my diary.

– Gordon Archive

"Appearing Live and In Person - *Playboy's* Miss December — Candace Collins and *Playgirl's* Man-of-the-Year — Howie Gordon at the Hartford Civic Center's VANTASY Auto Show!"

I had carefully cut the ad out of the newspaper. It would be something to show the grandchildren one day, wouldn't it?

"Wow, grampa," they'd say, "was that really you?"

"Sure was, young'uns," I'd tell them. "Your grampa was one hot tamale!"

Next up was a major-league commercial for Martini & Rossi in New York City.

When the limo dropped me off downtown at the Hartford bus station, I stood there curbside with a suitcase in each hand. After three days of lines of women waiting for my autograph, nobody even looked at me twice. I understood how Cinderella felt when her royal coach turned back into a pumpkin. I headed into the bus station to pick up my ticket for New York.

Actually, I was late. I was the last one to board that Greyhound bound for New York City. As soon as I got on, the driver closed the door and began backing out of the station.

I was greeted by what I thought was an odd sight. You know how buses have all the seats in rows of twos? Well, there was one person sitting in every single row. I was the first person who was going to have to take a seat next to someone else. What made the selection odd was that there were all male passengers and only one woman. She had blond hair and was fairly attractive. In a fit of bravado—I was still feeling my oats—I made my way toward the back and sat down right next to the only woman on the bus.

"Hi," she said with a big, warm smile. That was nice.

"Hi," I returned her greeting, "how are you?"

"Fine," she said. "Going to New York?"

"Yeah." We were in seats 33 and 34.

Within ten minutes, I had out my copy of *Playgirl* and she was checking out my centerfold spread. I showed her the clippings in my diary and we chatted and chatted. After a while, she said, "Mind if I ask you a personal question?"

"No, not at all," I answered.

She told me her name was Veronica LeBlond. Could that possibly be her real name? We chatted into the miles and into the dark. Then,

Glory Be, we were making out. Not all the way out, mind you, but from the kissing, she allowed me to unzip her jeans and slide my hand down under. I found Xanadu. We were hiding from everybody. It was a delicious ride to the finish where her thighs squeezed my hand in spasm. What a thing to hold onto!

Then it was my turn. She unzipped me and began the gratitude. We had me covered with a jacket or something. Who knew what those around us were aware of? Nobody said nothin'. I concentrated on the pleasure. There was no hurry.

Y'know, this kind of stuff happened to Jamie Gillis and John Leslie. It did not generally happen to me. When my orgasm was getting close, bright lights suddenly filled the night. I opened my eyes to see that we were in some kind of tunnel. I was too far along to care and she mercifully did not stop her handiwork. When I came, we were just pulling out of the tunnel and into Manhattan. What an entrance! New York never looked that good.

Chapter Eleven
Speaking of Jamie Gillis

Jamie Gillis just died. It's 2010 now. My story pauses here.

- Gordon Archive

Jamie Gillis Passes Away
Posted Feb 19th, 2010 07:26 p.m.
NEW YORK—Adult industry legend Jamie Gillis succumbed Friday to a battle with cancer in his hometown of New York City. He was 66.

A longtime New York acquaintance of Gillis' tells Adult Video News (AVN) the strain of cancer afflicting him was melanoma. The disease was diagnosed a mere four to five months ago, the source said.

Gillis will be cremated at a private ceremony. He requested that in lieu of flowers, contributions be made to the NYC Police Athletic League, an organization that assisted him as a boy and continues to aid New York City children. Donations can be made at www.palnyc.org/800-PAL-4KIDS/donate.aspx.

Veteran adult director Wesley Emerson forwarded the following email from long-time Gillis friends Ashley and April Spicer to AVN Friday evening regarding Gillis' death:

"It is with great sadness that I report the passing of Jamie Gillis. A wonderful and charismatic man and most treasured friend, he will be greatly missed by his partner Zarela, his family, his many friends, and countless fans around the world.

Despite the immense grief we feel for the loss of our friend, we are comforted by a quotation from Albert Camus that Jamie often quoted to us: 'Happiness, too, is inevitable.'

AVN will provide in-depth coverage surrounding this news in the days to come."

– Adult Video News

Remembering Jamie

It started out as a class. It ended up as an event that actually surprised itself. In another era, it would have been called a happening. It was a happening too, the real deal. An experience that could only happen because it was *The Mad Satyr*, Jamie Gillis himself, who had sounded the call to the congregation.

Maybe he was beginning to understand that we'd all come out of the woodwork for him. With Jamie Gillis, it was like Robin Hood calling out to the Merry Men of Sherwood, and the Merry Women too for that matter. Jamie always liked to mix the sexes. On a good day, it always made everyone just a wee bit merrier.

– Gordon Archive

The Master Class.

"Jamie Gillis's 'An All Day X-rated Seminar,'" said the ad, "with guest appearances by porn stars Annette Haven, Kym Wilde, John Leslie, Richard Pacheco, and others."

It was billed: "Learn the ins and outs of making amateur and fetish videos." It was held on July 16, 1994, at the downtown San Francisco Holiday Inn. And the place, dear friends, was packed.

Some of the "others" turned out to be John "Buttman" Stagliano and Ed "Dirty Debutante" Powers. The *Adult Video News* (AVN) sent Mark Kernes and Yoram "Don" Dahan. San Francisco's own Empress Madeline of *EROTICA SF TV* was there. Joe Elliot came to tout his new line of videos. There was Steve & Sindy from Candyman Video, Dr. X from High Society, REDBOARD's Duck Dumont, starlets Taj Mahal,

Valeria, and Sherri Parks, Mistress Vicky Gold, actor J.P. Anthony, and Bay Area Talent Agent Dan Barros.

And we were all hosted by the charismatic Mr. Gillis. He was the grand ringmaster of this dog and pony show. "Step right up, ladies and gentlemen, step right this way."

My lord, did those people ever get their money's worth! After nine hours, nobody wanted to leave. The hotel had to kick us out. Speakers at the end of the day were jammed for time. Nobody expected what happened to happen. Not even Jamie.

Flashback Within a Flashback

It's 1982. We're in Hollywood. We're staying at a remarkably seedy motel in a blighted neighborhood. They serve a weird Chinese breakfast here. Naked women, naked women that you really don't want to see naked, are standing out by the newspaper racks in the late night. They scream and cackle and they talk to themselves. Lots of bottles get broken in this neighborhood. It's like New York City. Jamie feels right at home. That's Jamie Gillis; he's in the next room. Jerry Butler lives across the hall. We are making an X-rated movie (Bad Girls IV). We are working for Svetlana, the wicked witch of the West, Los Angeles by way of Hungary.

They serve us new, young female porn stars for lunch. And we have to memorize lines and work in this second grade production that passes only for adult fare because there is naked sex in it. The movie is being illegally shot on the city streets of LA. There are no permits. They didn't offer them back then in LA. We have an Israeli production manager who watches out for the police. He is the kind of guy who can make Orthodox Jews cheer for the Arabs.

Jamie Gillis got me through that job. Svetlana was a sadist who practiced improvisational sadism on her actors. We just didn't get along. She fired me three times. I quit twice. She got under my skin. She appeared to enjoy it. Some guys pay extra for that, but I never responded well to abuse. Wasn't my thing. It was all Svetlana's turf, though, she was the director.

The witch was paying very well. I wanted to be able to finish that movie. Svetlana just didn't get to him the way she got to me. They had a history. He was a big star and she owed him for past kindnesses. I had no such diplomatic immunity.

She put the itch in bitch and ran me ragged. Never would have made it without Jamie. He got between us and defused things before they boiled over. At night, back at the crazy motel, he'd get me to chill out and we'd laugh at her chaos. Made it through three weeks on that job. Got my big fat paycheck. Earned every fucking penny. Never would have made it without Jamie.

After his seminar was over, Jamie asked me, "Do you think it went alright?" There was me, him, and John Leslie. We were having the post-game show at a North Beach bar. I had video-taped an earlier version of Jamie's class some months before. After that one, we had discussed the strengths and weaknesses in great detail. "So, what did you think of this one?" he asked. "Tell me, what was the downside?"

"The downside? The only downside," I told him, "was that we had to leave! The downside was that the clock strikes midnight and Cinderella's carriage turns back into a pumpkin." I told Jamie that I thought we had just witnessed the birth of an X-rated *Bingo Long and the Traveling All-Stars*.

I counseled the big guy to drop the whole business part of the show, add a few more name stars with stories, a couple of songs and strippers, put in some big screen video clips from adult movies, and let's take the whole show to Broadway!"

I thought he had the makings of an extraordinary Golden Age of Porn Review. We could all hang out with each other and feed for a long time at that trough. We could tour the country. We could go abroad.

Jamie Gillis was the Pied Piper of people pursuing personal pleasure. He was like a viral infection of joy. Where he went, joy seemed to follow. He seemed to have an unparalleled appetite for sexual adventure.

Y'know, folks, nothing is ever as it appears to be.

They tell us that pornography is supposed to be this and that and the other thing. And porn's leading men, guys like John Leslie and Jamie Gillis, they're the men's men that good society purports to dismiss and dishonor as brutes and rulers of an indecent empire.

Well, John Leslie, he of the cobra-green eyes and volcanic alpha-male mentalities is also among the most sensitive of human creatures I have ever met. And Jamie Gillis, the Casanova of our generation, the dark prince who wanders in all those places that most of us only see with our eyes closed, he is a man so bursting with life that others can't help but bloom in his presence.

These are not the bad guys, world. These are supreme sensualists. I'm honored to call them both friends. Their ideas, their lives fascinate me, enrich me. I am bigger for having known them.

At dinner, John tells me a story about Jamie. It's about a time when Jamie was so broke that he couldn't afford to buy the fruits and melons of which he is so fond. "You know what he did?" John asks me. "He used to go to that fruit store, pick up the melons, and just smell them!" It's a story that amazes and touches John.

Later, Jamie, well lubricated by a few glasses of red wine, is recounting a tale of lost love to us. Unexpectedly, tears fill up his eyes and roll down over his smile. He is more surprised and embarrassed by this sudden display of emotion than we are. He apologizes to us. It is so unnecessary. He is our big brother.

This world, my friends, is often an upside-down place. Secretly, scumbags are frequently hidden behind the masks of public virtue while those free spirits we would so quickly condemn and dismiss from polite society are often apt to be the real people of heart and substance that are the worthy.

Chapter Twelve

"Well, that came out of nowhere," Marty the agent said.

"I know, death can be like that," I said.

"No, no, I mean, in your book," he said. "We haven't even really met Jamie as a character in your story yet and you're already writing about him dead. Doesn't that bother you?"

"Did you read the story that Eric Edwards told about him? I saw it on the ladieznight.com website."

"Yes, I heard (he died) last Friday," Eric said. "What a shock. I worked in many a film with him and we were good friends, yet totally opposite in our characters. I can't remember who told me this, but a famous Jamie Gillis line was once when he was eating out a girl, the director said he couldn't see the action and told Jamie to move aside a bit. Jamie's response was, 'If you wanted a smaller nose, you should have

hired Eric Edwards!' I shall miss him."

"What about your book?" Marty asked.
"What about it?'
"Well, you were cruising along talking about becoming a star and all of sudden you just got off the train and it's like you're headed somewhere else."
"Hey! Jamie Gillis just died. We're sitting shivey here, man! He was like one of the founding fathers! There was Abraham, Isaac, Jacob, George Washington, Bob Dylan, Muhammad Ali, and Jamie Gillis!"

I first met Jamie in 1978. It was at the Adult Film Association's Awards Banquet in Hollywood. Jamie was collecting his third straight Best Actor award. I suggested to John Leslie that they should just give up and name the award after him. They should call it "The Jamie." I still think it's a pretty good idea.

Jamie once told me. "We were making *Misty Beethoven* back in the seventies," He told this story a lot. Said he was pretty excited about that movie. Said he thought it was gonna be great.

"I turned to one of the crew guys," Jamie said, "and I told him, 'Y'know, this is probably the best adult film ever made.' You gotta understand," Jamie said, "that these guys usually worked in straight movies. They were just doin' this porn movie on the side for extra money. Well, the crew guy looked at me like I was crazy."

"He said, 'Best adult film?' y'know? 'So what? Big fuckin' deal,' he said. Well, that kind of set the tone for me about my career in the X-rated business."

It kind of set the tone for a lot of us. It seemed that X-rated movies would always be "small potatoes" as far as the outside world was concerned. Still, a lot of us found a home there. Jamie Gillis found an iconoclast's empire.

"Y'know, a lot of people didn't like Jamie Gillis," Marty said. "I know one porn queen who told me, 'He was an asshole, a jaded jerk, and a non-consensual pusher of boundaries.'"

"Yeah, well, life's messy like that," I told him. "Not everybody likes everybody else. Why, impossible as it may seem, there may be some people out there who don't even like me!"

The world sighs an audible, "Gasp!" Cut To:

Chapter Thirteen
And now, back to our story

- *VCX.com*

It was the first day of the shoot and they left without me! Can you believe that? I was like twenty minutes late and they were already gone! The bus was nowhere in sight. I couldn't believe it! I woke up late with a head cold. I was sick. I rushed and got myself together as fast as I could. I thought I was bulletproof with Anthony Spinelli. I thought he would have waited for me. He didn't.

It was a real eye opener. He was letting me know that I wasn't as big a star as I thought I was. He was letting me know that the movie was going to go on without me.

I was just lucky that another couple showed up late and missed the bus too. But unlike me, they at least knew where the location was. I hopped in their car and we made it to the set.

Sam didn't say a word to me about it when we got there. He didn't have to. I don't think I was ever late for another one of his shoots again.

And after looking around, I understood why Sam hadn't waited the bus for me. This was a huge cast with big-time star voltage. There was Jamie Gillis looking positively regal. He was a bigger man than I suspected and had a commanding presence. Like a king he sat there with John Leslie, the heir apparent, at his side. They seemed to like each other. Jamie was the old superstar Joe DiMaggio and John was the young Mickey Mantle, the new kid in town. They were surrounded by a whole bunch of rookie wannabes hanging on their every word and bumping into each other while trying to impress.

Nearby, porn's great beauty Annette Haven was a queen holding her own court. She was giving lecture to a bevy of starlets that included Dorothy Le May, Lisa Thatcher, Brooke West, Misty Regan, and some others. I'd met Annette a time or two before, but like with Jamie, this was my first time on a set with either one of them. They both had the aura of X-rated royalty.

The working title was *Rah-Rah-Rah* and we were a traveling high school football team complete with a full roster of players, coaches, cheerleaders, and teachers.

It was a genuine zoo. And stuck in a bad case of life imitating art, Anthony Spinelli had the unenviable task of trying to control this large and rowdy bunch while shooting exteriors for a film without any permits. For the next three days, he exhorted us to keep a low profile while we traversed the back roads of Sonoma County shooting scene after scene on that school bus.

At one point, we were parked on the side of the road taking a break. Keeping a "low profile," Brooke West was sunbathing topless with her ample breasts on display for all the world to see. Cars going by honked wildly. When Sam came over to see what all the ruckus was about, he scolded Brooke and told her to cover up. When she was slow to respond, he threatened that he would fire her. To which Brooke sassed back with one of the great retorts in all of porn history:

"Big deal!" she said, "so, I won't be a porn star!"

That we didn't get busted and were able to complete the shoot was nothing short of miraculous. Whether it was worth it, is a whole other story.

– Mark Focus/VCX.com

Savage Levene with Dorothy Le May.

High School Memories was one of my least favorite Anthony Spinelli films. Making it just sucked. It was hot, I was sick, and it seemed that Sam was just distracted from the very beginning. Rumor was there were the usual backstage squabbles going on between him and the producers, but this time, it seemed to really make a huge difference.

To begin with, this one had no rehearsal time at all. I can't think of a single other Spinelli film or video that we ever made without rehearsal. And once on the set, when we weren't actually shooting, Sam was completely missing in action. He was nowhere in sight. This was totally out of character for Sam. He lived to be on the set. I think he hated getting stuck trying to control that many loose cannons. He was a film director and did not want to be the head counselor at a summer camp for juvenile delinquents. Sam wasn't having any fun. Lord only knows what else was going on in his life at the time, but this movie, despite a first-rate cast, never quite seemed to have a chance. It just got lost in the chaos.

Chapter Fourteen

Fellow X-rated actor Michael Morrison once invited Carly and me to one of his famous S & M parties in Sausalito. Carly said that she would only go to an M & M party, but promised that she would eat the chocolate until it hurt.

Chapter Fifteen
Lenny Again

- VCX.com

Carly and I went to "The Awards" in July of 1980. It was the 4th Annual Erotic Awards Ceremony put on by the Adult Film Association of America (AFAA). Porn Diva Georgina Spelvin used to refer to these gatherings as "the Company Picnic." Every year it seemed that Jamie Gillis would win a Best Actor and she'd win a Best Supporting Actress. This year was no different. They both won those awards again for *Ecstasy Girls*.

Ted Paramour's *Ecstasy Girls* and Henri Pachard's *Babylon Pink* shared all the awards that year and they both got to make lots of speeches and get their pictures taken.

Producer Sidney Niekerk didn't win anything. We were sitting at his table with Anthony Spinelli, Spinelli's wife, and John Leslie. I wasn't nominated that year. In fact, I was just attending on a ticket purchased by *Playgirl*. It was research. I was writing an article for them called, "The Men of X." Didn't even mention myself in the piece, still figured I was on my way out of the industry.

Years later, Sam would say that the main reason *Nothing to Hide* finally got funded was because of how jealous Sidney Niekerk got that night while watching those other producers come up to the podium and make their speeches. Sidney wanted to do that. He wanted to produce a picture that could win it all for himself. So, Sidney took out his wallet.

Enter Anthony Spinelli. Or should I say, reenter. As a director, Sam had an on-again off-again relationship with Sidney the producer. Sidney even adopted the stage name of "Bernardo Spinelli" as if the two were great brothers.

I remembered them fighting like cats and dogs on the set of *Easy*. While Director Sam was putting me through twenty takes of a horrendous scene, Producer Sidney was putting his arm around me and whispering in my ear not to listen to Sam, "that crazy director." Sidney was telling me that he hired and fired directors all the time. Twenty minutes later, the two of them would be hugging and kissing.

No doubt, they were an extremely odd couple, but they were about to partner up again and make what many still consider to be the best X-rated movie of all time.

Nothing to Hide began with two weeks of rehearsal. That was a real X-rated revolution right there.

— VCX.com

As a true sequel, John Leslie and I were playing Jack & Lenny again. We'd had the whole *Talk Dirty to Me* as a rehearsal. The characters were completely fleshed out. Michael Ellis wrote us a good script and we spent those two rehearsal weeks improving it before we ever went in front of the cameras. Where *Talk Dirty* had been Jack's story with Lenny as the offbeat sidekick, *Nothing to Hide* costarred both characters. It was a story about Lenny falling in love and Jack coping with his jealousy and learning how to let go of his little buddy. It was an attempt to add a real movie to the sex.

– *VCX.com*

Jack and Lenny Polaroid.

Make no mistake, *Nothing to Hide* was still a porn movie. But for a minute there, we hijacked the crap and kicked it all into another direction.

It gave a breath of fresh air to an industry mired in muck. And it gave hope that our sexual media might one day grow up.

John Leslie was fabulous in this movie. Once again, he did all the heavy lifting in the sex department.

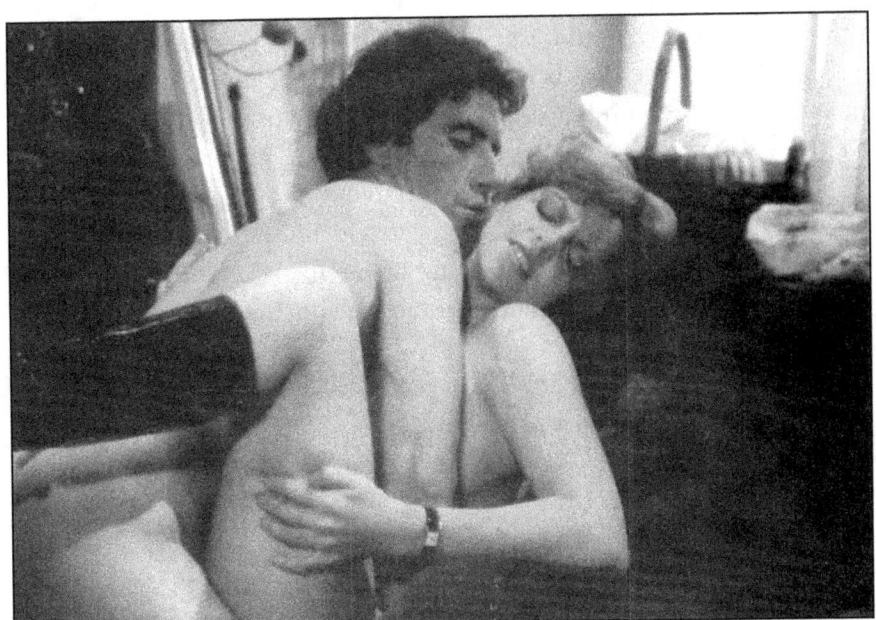

– VCX.com

John Leslie & Holly McCall.

Shown here with the wonderful Holly McCall, John played in four sex scenes with four different women. As Lenny, I only had one, with Karen, my soul-mate and bride-to-be.

Spinelli spent a long time looking for the right Karen. She had to act the mirror of the backward Lenny, who was a pretty strange duck. We began rehearsals without the part being cast. Then one day, Sam just found her.

We spent some time getting acquainted. I learned that Tigr was a drummer into "new wave" music and cul-

– VCX.com

Her name was Tigr. She would use the name Chelsea Manchester in the credits.

ture. She also described herself at the time as a vegetarian, bi-sexual lesbian. Within the first thirty minutes of our relationship, she called me sexist. Oi. I remember suggesting to Tigr that she wait until she had a chance to meet some of the other "gentlemen" in the business before she decided that I was one of the bad guys.

Truth was, I liked Tigr. She was young and bright and just full of piss and vinegar. It was encouraging to me to see this kind of strong, independent young woman attracted to the business. There was nothing "porny" about her.

Off-camera, there would be no blazing, passionate love affair between us. I looked twenty-three and crazy, but I was thirty-three and happily married. I was "old wave." As Karen, though, she was just about the perfect mate for Lenny.

Our sex scene was great. It was played in character with the passion as awkward as we were. It came toward the end of the movie after Karen has accepted Lenny's proposal of marriage. We were young and innocent, inexperienced and scared and that's how Spinelli directed the scene. It was light years away from the "Bend over, bitch," of most porn.

– *VCX.com*

Lenny and Karen get ready to have sex.

When we undressed, we stood looking at each other for a long time in silence and then went into each other's arms.

- VCX.com

Karen and Lenny embrace.

At one point during the lovemaking, I moistened my finger in my mouth and stroked one of her nipples. "What are you doing?" Spinelli said, "Lenny would never do anything like that." Once a sex scene heats up, it's easy to forget all about the movies and characters. Usually, Spinelli would just take a snooze during the sex scenes and leave it all up to his cameraman. Not this time, though, Spinelli was vigilant. He kept us locked into Lenny and Karen.

Many have criticized this scene as being way too personal too real. They squirmed too much with us over the sexual anxiety. Others said that they felt guilty and embarrassed watching people like Lenny and Karen make love. It was hard to even call what they did fucking. I can understand that. It certainly was different. Hardly anybody's idea of whack-off material.

- VCX.com

Putting on the condom.

Oddly enough, it was a complete accident that we used a rubber in that scene. Tigr had shown up without any birth control. We were counting days from her last period and trying to guess if it was safe for me to come inside her. Bullshit, I wasn't about to make a mistake who could knock on my door twenty years later and say, "Hi, Daddy!" We used that rubber for our own protection first. It's always been ironic that people who have praised that scene usually talk about our putting on the rubber. When I came, I came inside of the rubber and inside of her.

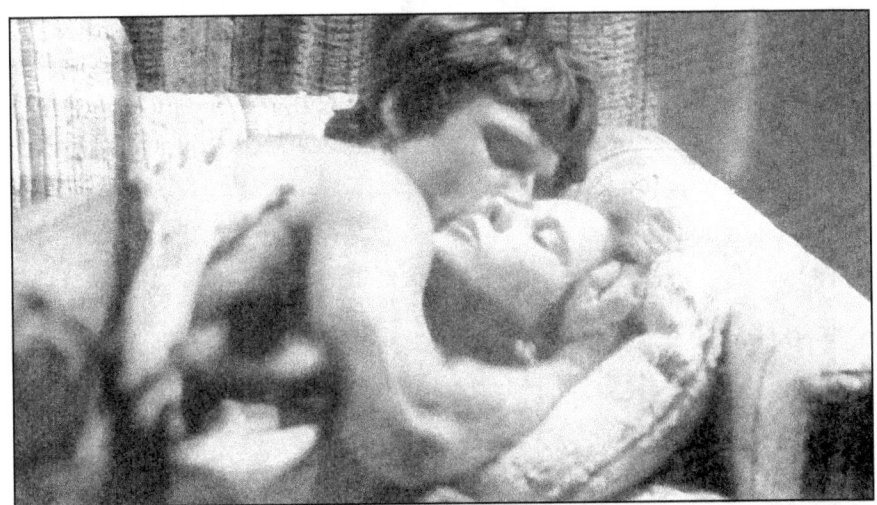

– VCX.com

Lenny and Karen make love.

I was holding her and catching my breath when Tigr began to weep. That was not in the script either, but Sam kept the cameras rolling. It was great. Tigr was great.

– VCX.com

The wedding.

The last scenes filmed were those of our wedding. We shot those in Los Angeles at this crazy little wedding chapel, which I've seen in a whole bunch of movies. The fly in the ointment was that every five minutes, a plane took off from nearby LA International. Made the soundman crazy.

– VCX.com

THE KISS.

When all the scheduled shots were done, Spinelli wanted us to improvise a food fight with wedding cake. None of this footage ever made it into the movie, but I own a scar on my forehead from the incident. Tigr had picked up a whole tier of the wedding cake and was supposed to smash me in the face with it. Hey, it's the movies! As she swung to do it, the cake slid off the tier and I got bashed with the metal serving tray. Saw stars. It was appropriate.

We were just a few miles from Hollywood.

– Kathleen Nuzzo.

– Kathleen Nuzzo

The happy couple.

When *Nothing to Hide* was released, we won everything there was to win. Many considered it to be the crown jewel in Spinelli's long and distinguished career as an adult filmmaker. It made me a star in the industry and it made John Leslie a superstar.

"Warm, wonderful and sexy. An absolute masterpiece."
- Female Forum

"… a highly emotional film, inhabited by real people who have the ability to make you laugh and cry. Highly recommended on every level and thoroughly deserves its rating. 100%"
- Al Goldstein

– Jackie Giroux/Gordon Archive

Sam had made a nice little movie.

"The coming of age of adult films. The Spinelli's big hit, while loaded with the usual quota of sex, deals with genuine human emotions, including love, friendship, and romance. Richard Pacheco and newcomer Chelsea Manchester are a knockout!"
- *Sir* magazine

"... a dramatic and erotic masterpiece, that makes you laugh, cry and generally feel good all over. (FULL)
- *Hustler* magazine

– Gordon Archive

We won everything there was to win. (L-R) Richard Pacheco, Ricky Frazzini, Anthony Spinelli, and John Leslie.

Chapter Sixteen

I was riding high. Finally had a few bucks in my pocket. I decided that I wanted do something nice for my Aunt Kitty and Uncle Manny's upcoming wedding anniversary.

Kitty and Manny were my favorite aunt and uncle. She was the vivacious Ukrainian Catholic who converted and married into a family of Orthodox Jews. On her wedding day, at the reception that night, she gathered all the nieces and nephews around her and said to us, "Manny and I can't have any children of our own, so, you'll all be our kids. And I want you all to know that I'll be Jewish 364 days a year, but on Christmas, yins can all go to hell!" And she let out a cackle of a laugh that lit the room. I thought it was the greatest thing I ever heard.

I called Aunt Kitty and told her that I wanted them to have a night out on me. A limousine would pick them up, take them to their favorite restaurant, and then drive them home.

Aunt Kitty said that was real nice of me, but, "No, thanks."

I protested. I cajoled. I pleaded, "Let me do this for you. You'll have fun. It'll be a kick!" All to no avail, Aunt Kitty just wasn't interested. I couldn't believe it. I continued berating her with my offer of a big night out in Pittsburgh.

Finally, exasperated, she said, "Look, your Uncle Manny's favorite restaurant is Long John Silver's … and I'm not going to Long John Silver's in a limousine!"

― *Gordon Archive*

Aunt Kitty and Uncle Manny.

Chapter Seventeen

I was in LA when we wrapped *Nothing to Hide*. I spent the night at the home of an old high school girlfriend who was trying to make it there herself as a musician and a straight actress. I would fly home in the morning.

It was a bad idea. Carly freaked. We had a crazed long-distance phone call that night.

It's been a long time since we discussed the jealousy wars and the tensions of having other lovers, but that doesn't mean that those battles weren't all part and parcel of the women who came and went during my marriage and career.

The work ones were a lot easier on Carly than the personal ones, that's for sure, but on this particular night, I was furious with her for begrudging me some out-of-town time with an old girlfriend. I always figured geography relaxed the rules. I was in another city.

On the other hand, I heard the voice of my mate, my wife, in fear and distress over the phone and that just wasn't right either.

That there was conflict was "nothing new under the sun." That the boundaries were shifting was always a topic for heated conversation and the prospect of monogamy still brought out my fangs and claws. I just wasn't interested. I couldn't imagine that I ever would be.

I wished that she could accept my old lovers for the two or three nights a year I sought them out without all that trauma. She would roll her eyes at such a comment, implying that I was grossly understating the pain of the situation.

We could each both do both parts of the argument. We'd had it that many times.

I was willing to accept her old lovers if she still wanted them. I knew it could get rough out there in the seas of jealousy. I bled there too, but it appeared to be the price we had to pay to live with the kind of freedom that we wanted. Only, Carly had stopped wanting it. I didn't. Besides that, she told me I was full of shit. She claimed I got pretty insane when I was jealous too. Couldn't really argue with her there, but I was still willing to go through it.

A lot of times, I gave in to her wishes. I was hoping that by so doing, it would buy me a little of that freedom every now and then without all the fireworks, but she didn't see things that way. The X-rated work was one thing, but she wanted all the personal ones to be done and gone. She wanted to ignore the fact that she married a man who still took great pleasure in his old loves. I always figured that if you'd been lucky enough to ever find love with anybody on this planet, why on earth would you ever want to let it slip away?

We had colliding and competing visions of marriage. We weren't alone. A lot of couples were still walking that tightrope. It was like the tippy-tippy end of the sixties. Soon, our children would come along. That would change everything. And not long after that, there'd be AIDS to contend with too. That would change everything else!

Chapter Eighteen

"Wait a minute, now, wait a minute. Back up here. You were going so good. You were movin' to LA. What ever happened to your straight career?"

"Oh, yeah, my straight career. Who wants to know?"

"We're your unborn grandchildren."

"Oh, it's you guys!"

"Yeah! We wanted to know how come you didn't turn out to be Jack Nicholson?"

"Well, the short answer is that Jack Nicholson already had the part. And the almost clever, face-saving, long answer was that I had my hands full just trying to be Howie Gordon. You kids deserve the truth and the sad truth of the matter is that I gave it my best shot."

Every visit to LA impressed me more and more with the fact that I was living in the wrong town. If I ever really wanted to get anywhere in the straight movie biz, LA was gonna be a must. There was no getting around it. The action was there. When I was in town, I'd go make some rounds, get all caught up in some promises and introductions, and then I'd go back home and forget all about them. I just didn't want to live there. Our home was in Berkeley and it seemed like every time I turned around in LA, it was always time to be heading back.

If God wanted me to be a movie star, She was gonna have to figure out how to make it happen with me living in Berkeley.

I got as far as Richard Pacheco and that pretty much was the ceiling. Big-time stardom just wasn't meant to be. I never played catcher for the Pirates either. Or middle linebacker for the Steelers. I never followed Alexander the Great into Persia and I never got to have sex with Julie Christie. I wanted to be a basketball star like my father, but it turned out to be my worst sport. Hours and hours of practice made absolutely no difference. Even today, when I go to throw a balled-up wad of paper into a wastebasket, I generally miss, not always, but most of the time.

Alas, dear grandchildren, the list of my failures is a long one. Oi, you should have seen me in high school chemistry. I was clueless for an entire year.

But I did make a hole-in-one once. In golf. That was pretty cool! It was with a seven iron on #4 at Lake Chabot. Sucker went right into the cup.

And I'm pretty sure, despite all my bitching to the contrary, and with sincere apologies to every other woman that I have ever loved, I may actually have succeeded in having had the best wife that anybody has ever had in the whole long history of wifery.

Chapter Nineteen

Remember that bus ride to New York where I got that handjob from Veronica LeBlond on my way into town?

Yeah, well, I was going there to do this print job for Martini & Rossi. It was probably the highlight of what was my very short career as a commercial male model.

– Martini & Rossi.

Y'see, the woman I was with in those last two photos was sitting on a stool. I was standing next to her. If she would have risen to her feet, my mouth would have come up to her boobies. In that world, the women are tall and the men are supposed to be taller. The photographer told me that I was "perfect," but about five or six inches too short.

The only reason I got this job was because of little Stevey Freedman—himself about six feet four inches—who was a dear sweet friend of mine who just happened to be in charge of shooting this major league ad for his company, Martini & Rossi. They worked around my height that day because Steve asked them to and he was signing the checks. It was to be my only big-time modeling job in New York City ... or anywhere else for that matter. Thanks, Steve. It was fun.

– *Martini & Rossi.*

Chapter Twenty
The Playgirl job falls through.

Go believe we were house hunting in LA again. We started out in Venice and then drifted over to the *Playgirl* offices in Santa Monica. When we got there, they told us there had just been a $2 million accounting error and that the job they were gonna give to me, no longer existed.

Oh. Okay.

It was March 5, 1980. We were trying to get pregnant. It didn't seem like a good time for the two of us to move to LA just to be unemployed. Carly decided to continue on in her job as a therapist in Berkeley. I decided that I would stay with her in Berkeley, work in X for a while longer for the money, and would try commuting to LA to get my straight career going down there.

I found an agent. Actually, it was a whole agency. And we planned that when they had an audition for me, I would just fly down to LA and do it.

The first was for the movie *The Right Stuff*, the one about pilot Chuck Yeager and the astronauts. I was to meet with Casting Director Lynn Stalmaster on a motion picture lot. This was the real thing.

He was alone when they sent me in to meet the great man. I had seen the name of Lynn Stalmaster as the casting director in the closing credits over a thousand times. If you were my age, you had too. In movies and TV shows, he'd had his hand in a jillion of them.

He looked me up and down with a seasoned eye. I was nervous, but he seemed to allow for that. He was used to it. He'd been sizing up horse flesh for a long time. They had me read for the role that eventually went to Dennis Quaid. I was supposed to play it all cowboy. It was *Pizza Girls* all over again.

I was terrible. Nervous and terrible. And all wrong for that part. Lynn Stalmaster knew it and I knew it and after about five minutes, the interview was over.

The only salvation was that I felt I registered somewhere on his radar.

He knew exactly who I was in the game, how raw and all, but he appeared to make the mental note that if the part ever showed up that called for one of me, he would now know exactly who to cast. I may have imagined it, but it let us both have some dignity and humanity in this game of the flesh market. There was a handshake good-bye.

I left there all aflutter. The short-notice plane fare had been a couple of hundred dollars. The car rental was over a hundred too. Carly didn't want me staying with my old girlfriend, so, I think there was a hotel bill, and throw in some money for food too.

Bottom line was that my little commute to LA had cost us over 500 bucks. And that was 500 bucks for five minutes of me being scared.

Hmmmm....

Fuck that shit!

Chapter Twenty-One

Did I tell you I was in love with Annette Haven? I was. It was a long line and I was in it.

She was a proud swan in the sea of cocksucker red lipstick. Oh, she could, and did, suck cock with the best of them, but there was just so much more to the ensemble.

– *Gordon Archive/Annette Haven.*

Annette was already a reigning Queen when I entered the business and she seemed to live the part both on screen and off. John Seeman first introduced me to her. He took me to her San Francisco apartment on Vallejo Street where she would hold court. It was like an inverted barnyard. Annette was the rooster and all the men would sit around clucking like hens and vie for her attention. I remember a day when Annette wore a see-thru blouse and we all tried hard not to drool on the furniture. Sophisticate Raul Lomas, perhaps the classiest director of photography in the X-rated business, once opined that Annette Haven's breasts belonged in The Louvre. I wouldn't have argued with him.

- *VCX.com*

Annette in *The Seven Seductions of Madame Lau.*

Like the suitors for Penelope while Odysseus was away at sea, the men would gather at Annette's apartment in the afternoon and each would dream that he would be the one invited to stay for dinner and to spend the night.

I would always go home. I had a wife. Annette respected matrimony. Annette respected herself. We would never have the hanky-panky on the side, but one day … one day, we would get to work together.

Chapter Twenty-Two

They find you, y'know. They smell your wannabe in the water and they really do come at you like sharks. You wouldn't think that they'd waste their time with nobodies, but, then again, that's who's most vulnerable, now, isn't it?

He gave me a name when he called, but what does it matter? I'm not gonna tell you his name. There's no point. It could easily have been, "Just-Didn't-Take-My-Meds-Today" or "I want to fuck you in the ass," but you don't know any of that right away when you're just picking up the phone.

"Hi. Is this the Howie Gordon," he asked, "the one that's been in *Playgirl*?"

"Yes, it is," I told him. "What can I do for you?"

"It's what I can do for you, pal!" he said. "I'm a film producer and I want to cast you in my movie."

That's all it took. I was hooked. He said it was a $24 million sci-fi movie and that I was the handsome man who would be perfect for the lead part. He'd seen me in *Playgirl*. He'd seen me in *Insatiable*. He was dropping names of famous people left and right, but he wanted me to play his lead actor.

Vanity, vanity, the sin was mine. I was perfectly willing to believe that I was Lana Turner and he was Fame & Fortune discovering me sitting at the mythical Hollywood lunch counter in Schwab's Pharmacy. It was my turn, that was all. I was ready for it. 'Bout fuckin' time too!

"I don't want to cast stars," he said, "I want to make stars!"

Yes, Sir! The first time he said that, it was such magic to my ears. By the fifth or sixth time he said it, I was no longer smiling. I couldn't stop the fire alarms from going off in my head. I did not want to hear them either. I did not want to believe that this guy was crazy as I already knew he was. Besides, so what? There could still be a real job here, couldn't there? I mean, he could be crazy and still be a real Hollywood producer, right? You show me in the manual where it says that all the Hollywood producers have to turn out to be sane?

I gave this guy a lotta time, but the longer he talked, the more painfully it all sank in. My whacko meter was beeping off the charts. The evidence was overwhelming. This guy was a 24 karat loon. When he finally invited me to a secret midnight script reading in his hotel room, I'd had enough. At that point, it seemed that all there really was left to decide, was, who was gonna bring the Vaseline.

Chapter Twenty-Three

The working title for my next film was *Jackie And the Dreams*. It was to be a road picture about a team of barnstorming male strippers playing a small town in backwater USA.

- Vincent Fronczek/VCX.com

John Leslie was Jackie.

Jackie Sail was the manager. Had to be played by John Leslie, just had to be. Jackie was a former dancer himself, as well as an actor, entertainer, and musician. He was now the General in charge of this bumbling, little circle of male buffoonery. Jackie was the hustler who kept the show alive. He organized us, arranged the bookings, and drove the Cadillac that served as our tour bus.

Jackie emceed the show. He introduced the dancing Dreams for all the ladies to enjoy. We were three struttin' roosters, each one more sexy than the next.

– Vincent Fronczek/VCX.com
Randy West kissing Vanessa Del Rio.

Sebastian was "the vain one." Played by Randy West, Sebastian lived for the beauty of his own reflection in mirrors … and in the eyes of all the women that he seduced.

Jonathon was the boy next door, "the sensitive one." I was an actor given to disappearing into books when I wasn't trying to land a role on the New York stage.

– Vincent Fronczek/VCX.com

I was Jonathon and Joey was Joey.

Joey was "the mean one," "the bad boy." Played by Joey Silvera, he was the master put-on artist who drove the womens wild. Lookout, because when he took to the stage anything was possible.

We were ... *The Dancers.*

Spinelli sprung it on me full blown. "We got the script! We got the money! And we even got a whole month to rehearse this thing!" You couldn't help but love Sam when he was like this. He was buoyant! He filled the room with his happy. It was infectious. And when he said, "we" like that, well, Dear Lord, you were ready to hit the beaches at Normandy or go defend the Alamo.

He wanted me to play a dancer. Uh-oh....

"A what?" I asked him.

"You're gonna play a dancer!" he said, "a male stripper."

"Sam, I can't dance!" I told him.

"You'll learn," he said. He didn't even blink.

It was all scar tissue, y'know, a carryover from my days as the fat kid. When my friends were out there doing the jitterbug and the twist, I was standing on the sidelines watching. I was too embarrassed and humiliated to dance. I didn't want to do anything that called attention to my body. I learned to slow dance, but that was about it. Sam had no idea of the ghosts he had just awakened in me.

"We got a choreographer," he boasted. "This guy was one of the originals at Chippendales!"

Chippendales was a famous nightclub in LA. In the late seventies, they were the first to feature male strippers for women. Their idea caught fire. Chippendales rapidly grew to be so successful that they had twenty-six franchised nightclubs up and running at their peak. They were in New York, London, Hamburg, all over the place.

"Sam, I'm just not a dancer!"

"What are you, crazy?" he asked. He had no idea and I didn't particularly want to tell him about it. "Look," he said. It was his quit-fuckin'-around voice. "You're an actor, you'll act. Howie, this is a good part for you! We're not talkin' ballet here! You don't gotta be Gene Kelly. We got a choreographer, he'll teach you a few steps, show you a few of the moves, and you'll do just fine. You gotta trust me on this, Howie. You'll be fine."

I thought I would keep a day-to-day journal on the making of this film, but I was so traumatized by my very first "dance" lesson that I didn't wanna have to face the prospect of any more self-awareness.

Y'see, you have not done it all until you've done a slow strip tease in the Mill Valley Howard Johnson's banquet room for a total audience of one man. His name was Tron and he was our choreographer.

Did I say he was gay? He was gay. And now we've added homophobia to the process of me dancing with my ghosts. Tron's direction as he sat in the back of the room that first day was for me to take my time and to try to turn him on.

Oh, okay.

He put on some music and then he waited.

I did something for him that day, some grotesque burlesque of a man pretending to be a woman. After all, women were the strippers, not men! I tried aping what I remembered them doing, but I didn't feel very sexy. I felt very stupid.

I couldn't exactly look Tron in the eye. If he was the kind of guy who liked watching a cat torture a mouse, or a spider play with a fly, then maybe he was getting himself turned on, but I doubt it. I bumbled this way and that and had a thoroughly humiliating experience in taking off my clothes for him. I was completely lost as I roamed the forests of the gender befuddled.

Tron eventually stopped the music. He apparently wasn't impressed. He had me sit down and then I watched him.

He was fucking great! He moved well, was a strong dancer, and looked seductive! He was personally and erotically alive! It was a no-brainer. The part was his. I would just give it to him.

He didn't want it! "You're shittin' me!" I said. I tried to talk him into it. I would absorb the financial loss, quit the business, and move to Minnesota to raise potatoes. Tron just said, "Let's get back to work."

For three weeks, I stripped for Tron almost every day. He designed a dance routine for me that wasn't overly complicated and we did it over and over and over. Eventually, I began to gain enough confidence to think that this was all gonna be okay.

Of course, my fellow "Dreams," Joey and Randy had to perform their strip routines too. Early on, they both had gotten one whiff of Tron and just disappeared. They both told Sam that they had worked as male strippers in clubs before and that they knew what they were doing. They said that they'd work on their own routines by themselves. Sam let them do it, but assured them that Tron would be available if needed.

I assumed it was Tron's gayness that put them off, but who knows? I thought of Tron as beyond women and even beyond gay. I wondered about his relationship with the pet boa constrictor that he had brought with him from New York, but none of that even mattered to me. I was so frightened of having to dance, having to strip, that I put myself completely in his care, for better or worse.

We spent a lot of hours in that banquet room, alone, together, working on my routine. I certainly appreciated his instruction and I grew to like him too. When I asked Tron to autograph my diary one day, he wrote,

"Only in decent exposure, will you find 'De' cadence."

About a week before we were to film the dancing sequences, Randy and Joey both kind of sheepishly made their way into the banquet room and sought out Tron's help too. We all ended up stripping for Tron in the banquet room.

Chapter Twenty-Four

One of the best parts of working on *The Dancers* was the camaraderie that came alive backstage with the guys. I just loved this time of working with John, Joey, and Randy.

– *Vincent Fronczek/VCX.com*

(L-R) Randy West, John Leslie, Richard Pacheco, and Joey Silvera.

I was staying at the Howard Johnson's in Mill Valley and it was like being on the road with them. We had a blast. Somehow, there were enough lines, enough scenes, enough women, and just enough everything for everybody. What could have been a disastrously competitive nightmare turned out to be one of my all-time favorite cooperative efforts. It just worked out that way during the whole shoot.

John Leslie was playing our boss and we were *The Three Stooges*. It was the right blend at the right time and in the right place. We ended up caring for each other and pulling for each other. It was a pretty rare experience in my X-rated travels.

Joey Silvera was a Kiwi bird with one wing stuck in an electric socket. He was the original, self-proclaimed Art Bombhead. He and John Leslie were both Italian and they went back a long way together. Joey could talk to John in a way that nobody else could. It made John more vulnerable and it made John more likable.

Randy West was the new kid on the block this time, but he was bigger than all of us, handsome, and full of confidence. The pieces fit together beautifully. The movie gave us common ground, a team to play for, and a game to win

The Dancers also featured Spinelli at his finest. He was interested, vital, and at the top of his game. He was happy. And when Sam was happy, the set was happy. The movie thrived.

Oh, he still had his inevitable clashes with his producers, but he did most of that backstage and kept us free of the chaos. Occasionally, it would spill out onto the set. It could get pretty silly. One time, an assistant producer literally interrupted a shot and scolded Sam in front of everybody because a production assistant had bought the expensive kind of potato chips. You think Martin Scorcese has to put up with that crap?

No matter, Sam had years of experience of holding the producers at bay with one hand while continuing to work on the movie with the other. Sam often told me, "Don't worry about it. All producers are pricks! It's just the nature of the job."

The money for this film was German and that promised money was harder to get at than Sam had originally been led to believe. The boss man on the set spoke no English and Sam had to spend hours speaking with him through a translator in order to get the production money he needed, often on a daily basis. Sam said it was like pulling teeth. By the end of the shoot, he was calling them "The Nazis."

December 8, 1980

– Gordon Archive.

You can read the headline there, *'Low budget' film creates some high embarrassment."* Well, that's us! That's *The Dancers.*

The sub-headline read, *"Shooting of porno movie given Richmond's blessing and aid."* The story went like this:

> City officials are red-faced after the discovery that they and some of Richmond's top business executives gave advice and police protection to what turns out to be a porno film crew.
>
> Two weeks ago, a youthful-looking filmmaker appeared before the Richmond City Council to explain that his production company would soon be coming to Point Richmond to film a "low budget" movie about "three guys in a song and dance group and their shrewd manager."
>
> Looking somewhat Hollywood in his pointed-toe suede shoes, Ricky Frazzini, of the Los Angeles based A-B Productions, told the council that Point Richmond was just the quaint little town that his crew had been searching for as a backdrop for their movie.

> *He said he had met with Police Chief Leo Garfield to discuss how traffic in Point Richmond night have to be rerouted slightly during portions of the filming.*
>
> *He also said the local chamber of commerce had been really helpful.*
>
> *The city fathers, apparently flattered that their fair city had been chosen above all others for the production, asked whether Richmond would be mentioned by name in the film. "Oh, no," replied Frazzini.*
>
> *The council is probably quite happy now that Richmond will not be mentioned by name, since a script synopsis obtained by the* Independent & Gazette *shows that the film contains many explicit sex scenes.*
>
> — The North East Bay Independent & Gazette

The article went on to explain that someone recognized Georgina Spelvin while she and I were shooting an outdoor scene in the park. The rest of the piece featured reactions of various townspeople who were either amused or outraged that their city was playing host to a porno film.

We waited for a police bust that never came. In the end, we just went back to work. The city officials and the police department continued to help us. When we weren't actively shooting a scene on location, Sam had us keep to the Winnebago and maintain a low profile in between shots. What happened between our company's higher-ups and the city officials will have to appear in somebody else's book. I just don't know. All I can tell you was that I was happy that I didn't have to go to jail. I'd never been busted on a shoot and I wasn't particularly interested in getting started. At least we had permits. In most of the X-rated filming I'd ever been a part of, the exteriors were almost always "stolen."

On the day of the great dance recital, I found this star taped to my locker at Bob Vosse's sound stage by the Count Vincent Fronczek.

– Gordon Archive.

Thanks Vince, that helped. Inside the locker, I had my dance costume and a bottle of tequila. That also helped. I'm not normally much of a drinker. In fact, the tequila belonged to someone else on the set, but when I noticed it there, I asked if I could borrow it for a while. A sip or two might calm down my very edgy nerves. Can't recall ever having had a drink before performing before, but on this day, it made sense. I was scared.

Bob Vosse's studio had been arranged to look like a nightclub and the set was perfect. It was designed and built by Brian Costales and dressed by Bob Jones. Brian, it should be noted, often worked as Sam's set designer. He was one of "the boys" and always did great work for Sam. Quiet, resourceful, artistic, reliable, and smart, Brian Costales was a gem. Sam was lucky to have him.

The audience was packed with female extras. Half of them were professional strippers who were friends of Tron. The other half were students of a collegiate human sexuality class where I had given a talk a month earlier. They were a loud, raucous, and eager group. Like the set, the audience was perfect too, and Sam had them all revved up to a fever pitch before we even got started.

John Leslie opened with a harmonica act and then introduced Randy who did the first strip of the night. The place was electric. He had ten minutes. We all had ten minutes. Win, lose, or draw, we had ten minutes. I had a sip or two of Tequila. By the time that Randy finished and I was making ready to go on, I wasn't feeling much pain. I might have had a third and a fourth sip of Tequila while I was waiting. I never did tell Spinelli. It wouldn't have loomed large in my acting legend with him.

I had done it a thousand times. The crowd loved it. They were being paid to love it. Who could tell the difference? I was giddy. What the hell had I been so nervous about? This was fun! I especially enjoyed reaching into my jock strap and then showering the audience with handfuls of rose petals.

While I was dancing, there was one lady in the front row who was just burning holes in me with the eyes of pure lust. She seemed so turned on that it turned me on to watch her. I played all my teasing actions to her. It carried me through the first half of my routine and then I was supposed to go out into the audience and collect some tips before we'd cut the shot.

- Vincent Fronczek/VCX.com

I danced. I did my routine.

In the midst of all the screaming female chaos, I went right to her and sat down on her lap. When I moved to kiss her, she avoided my lips and whispered in my ear, "I'm a lesbian and if you don't get off of me right now, I'm gonna break your dick." She was smiling when I pulled back to look at her — and I was smiling too, as I gingerly removed myself from her lap. The cameras were still rolling and I recovered enough to move on to another lady or two. And then, cut. That lady was a helluvan actress!

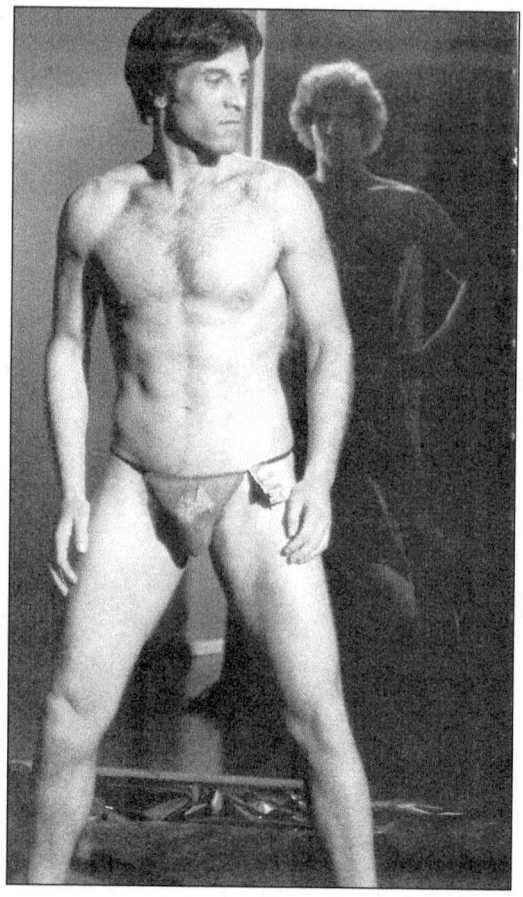

– Vincent Fronczek/VCX.com

The second half of my act was to commence with me talking a shower. The audience would see me in silhouette behind a curtain. They had rigged a working shower for me on the stage! That was pretty cool. It was a very arty shot. To begin the scene, Sam wanted my shadow to have an erection in the shower.

As we prepared for the call of "Action," I took myself in hand to get "up" for the shot. Uh-oh, there was nothing doing. Nobody was home. My dick wasn't interested in my right hand at all. The costume lady caught my eye. We'd been having a bit of an after-hours affair with each other.

"Whattaya say, lady?" I asked quietly. There was no mistaking my plea for her assistance. She blushed and flustered,

"Then everyone will know!!" she shushed at me and quickly disappeared.

"Need some help, luv?" It was the melodious British voice of Miss Kay Parker coming to my rescue. She was John Leslie's love interest in this movie and we were meeting for the first time on this set. She took my penis in her hands and looked at me with eyes that positively sparkled.

I started breathing again.

"We're waiting, Howie," Sam said, "Whenever you're ready."

Kay dropped to her knees then without me even having to ask and took me in her mouth. Not even thirty seconds later, she said, "You're ready." It was the beginning of a lifelong friendship.

I cued Sam. Sam called, "Action!" And the second half was underway.

Me and my erection took our silhouetted shower and then we went dripping wet back out into the audience of screaming, grabbing females armed only with a towel.

- Vincent Fronczek/VCX.com

I kissed this one and that.

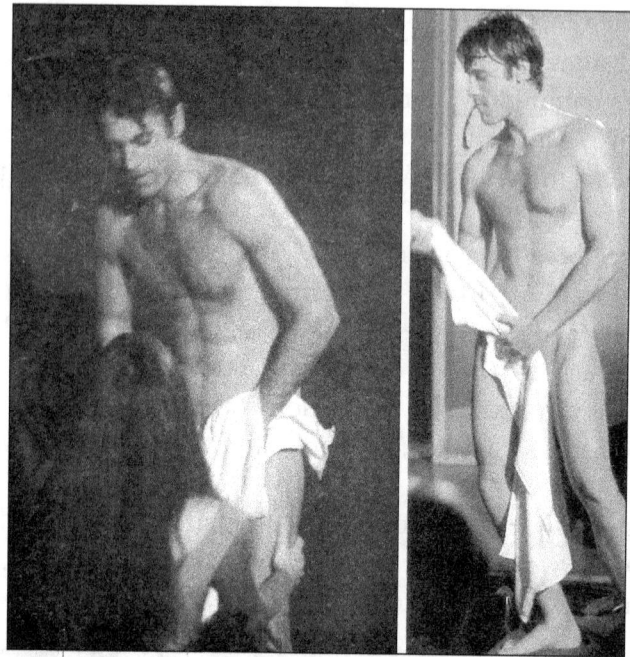

– Vincent Fronczek/VCX.com

More towel wrestling.

I even took the occasional glance at my lesbian friend. She was still smiling and cheering. Lady was a great actress! My ten minutes moved to a close. It had all been one exciting blur. I happily made my exit.

Next up would be Joey. After that, the three of us would take the stage together for the finale.

Joey blew them away. Randy and I got 'em wet and Joey caught the explosion. That's actually the way Tron had designed it and it worked. In fact, it worked a little too well. Joey was "the bad one!" He was Mr. Mean. He was crackin' a whip and driving the crowd into a frenzy.

A couple of women in the audience just lost it. They forgot who they were and what they were doing and just jumped up on Joey in the middle of his routine and were all over him. Sam had to call a cut to insure everyone's safety. It had flipped out of control. The pot had boiled over. It was like the audience had had a premature ejaculation.

An incredible crescendo was being built. It was too bad things got out of hand when they did. After a relative calm had been restored and shooting began again, Joey did fine, but it just wasn't the same. There had been some very special magic at work that couldn't quite be regenerated.

– Vincent Fronczek/VCX.com

JOEY!

Sometimes, when it comes to magic, you don't get a take two. None of this is visible in the movie, but that's the way it unfolded on the day we shot *The Dancers* dancing.

– Vincent Fronczek/Gordon Archive

Happy backstage after the dance.

Oh, yeah, before the finale, Randy, Joey and I were chatting in a corner when John came up to us and loudly plopped himself down on a big, lidded basket.

We just started laughing. We knew, but John didn't, that inside that big, lidded basket was a very large snake! It was Tron's boa constrictor who was going to dance with Randy in the last act. John, smart boy that he is, quickly put two and two together and catapulted himself way off of that basket. Might even have set some kind of record. Wow, never saw the King Salami move that fast, before or since. We pulled back the lid and introduced John to Tron's snake.

I thought *The Dancers* lost a lot in the way the footage of our stage show was ultimately edited. It was sad. In the final version of the film, they cut most of John Leslie's music and his dancing completely out of the film. They chopped up all of our dancing routines and interjected them with other parts of the story. I thought the straight version of our stage show in real time would have been incredible, but the powers that be took it all in another direction.

It was like they had too much movie and they made all of their cuts to meet the demands of your typical hard-core fare. They went for the easy choices and left a lot of another great movie, a different kind of movie, on the cutting-room floor. It was hard to put so much of yourself into a project only to feel defeated by the editors or whoever else ended up calling the shots, but such is the nature of making movies, porn or otherwise.

Georgina. Georgina.

I have saved the best for last. Georgina.

What an honor it was to work with this woman!

Years before I ever entered the business, as a fan, I sat in a darkened Pussycat Theatre and viewed *The Devil in Miss Jones*. It wasn't "porn." There was no "porn" yet, as we've come to know it. This was the very beginning. It was just a regular movie with sex in it, but there was nothing regular about it. It was scary. It was bizarre. It was terrifying.

It was Gerry Damiano giving birth to an industry, and he may have done so by making an initial offering that has yet to be equaled. Georgina Spelvin was his leading lady, and his cook on the set too, but you'll have to read Georgina's book to get all of the details.

Part Four

The Devil Made Me Do It

A Memoir by Georgina Spelvin
Erotic Icon of the Seventies

– Georgina Spelvin.

Gerry, Georgina, and all the rest of that cast and crew, they made a work of art. Don't take my word for it. Go see it. It's out there. It's still a most disturbing movie.

I met Georgina on the set of *Candy Goes to Hollywood*. It was a big movie with a big cast. It all came to a halt when she entered the soundstage and passed through the set saying her "Helloes" and shaking hands. "Call me, George," she said, taking mine. I was nobody. She was George, the modest megastar. We shook hands.

Three years later, Sam had cast her as my love interest for *The Dancers*. As Mel Brooks's 2000 year-old man would say, "I was thrilled and delighted."

Sam would have loved that. It would've made him laugh. I used to love to make Sam laugh. Loud and hearty, his laugh would light the room. I miss Sam. I've missed him now for years.

Once I found out that I would be working with Georgina, the script was suddenly not good enough. I had read our sex scene. It just wasn't good enough. I complained to Sam and asked for the opportunity to do a rewrite.

He told me to take a shot. Said if he liked mine better, maybe we'd use it. Wonder of wonders, Spinelli loved my rewrite! Said we'd do it my way.

When Georgina got to town and checked into her room at the Howard Johnson's in Mill Valley, I handed her the twelve new pages of our scene. It was very different and much longer than the original. She was charming and gracious about receiving a revised script.

When we met for rehearsal, three hours later, She was off book! She had the whole new scene memorized! Knocked my socks off, she did! Did not expect that from "a porn queen." I was impressed. You should be too. Stuff like that didn't happen every day in the world of X-rated films.

All went well the day we shot that scene. Her character of Catherine was in awe of my character Jonathon's acting ability.

In a scene of pillow talk, I told her that anybody could act. To prove the point, I convinced her that even she could "do" Shakespeare. We used the words to "Cupid," the old Sam Cooke pop song and I "showed" her how to deliver them like a soliloquy from Hamlet:

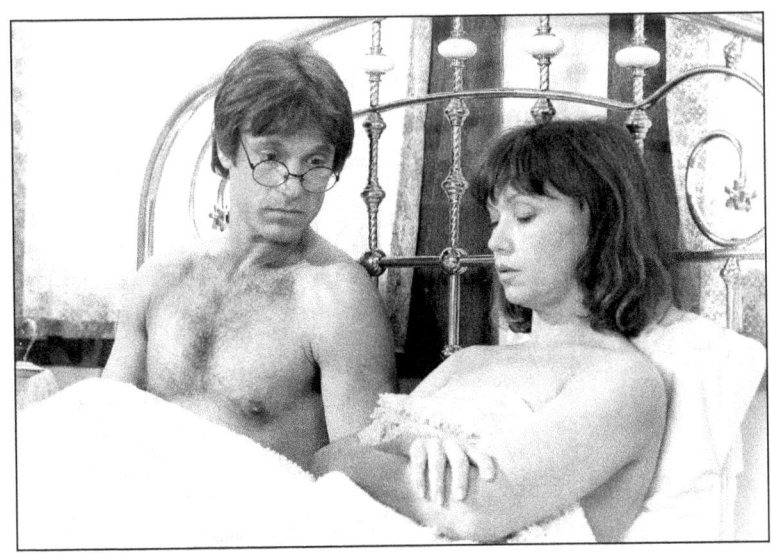

– Vincent Fronczek/VCX.com

Howie & Georgina.

"Cupid, draw back your bow
And let your arrow go
Straight to my lover's heart,
For me, no one, but me."

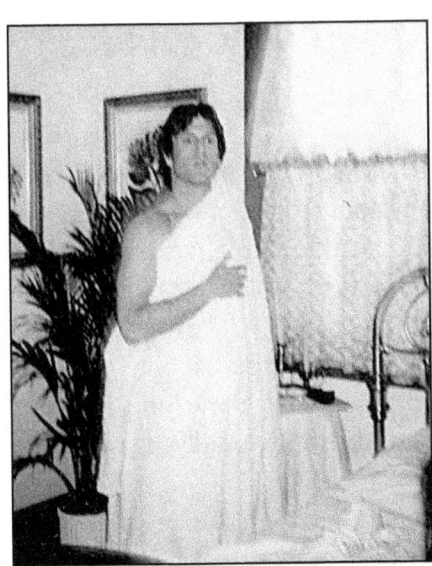

– Vincent Fronczek/VCX.com

We delivered the lines. I was good … she was better!

It was a wonderful little scene, clever, even, if I do say so myself. I don't know if it translates here, you should check it out and decide for yourself. Again, not your everyday porn.

— *Georgina Spelvin*

Timeless Georgina.

When it came to our actual lovemaking in the movie, well, I consider it one of the three great sex scenes of my career. By comparison, a guy like John Leslie, say, may have had three great sex scenes in a month. I only had three in my whole career, so, I sure as hell can remember them.

I don't know exactly what it was, I can only guess, but I couldn't get rid of my boner that day. I was cocky. I could've done jumping jacks or hung a tennis racket from my dick and still it would've stayed hard like a velvet bone.

I was so proud to be bedding this great Lady Guinevere that nothing but my very best would have been acceptable. It was happening on a cellular level. My body rose to the occasion! It wouldn't let anxiety get in the way.

– Vincent Fronczek/VCX.com

It was a great day.

– Vincent Fronczek/VCX.com

I think it was "The Lancelot Effect."

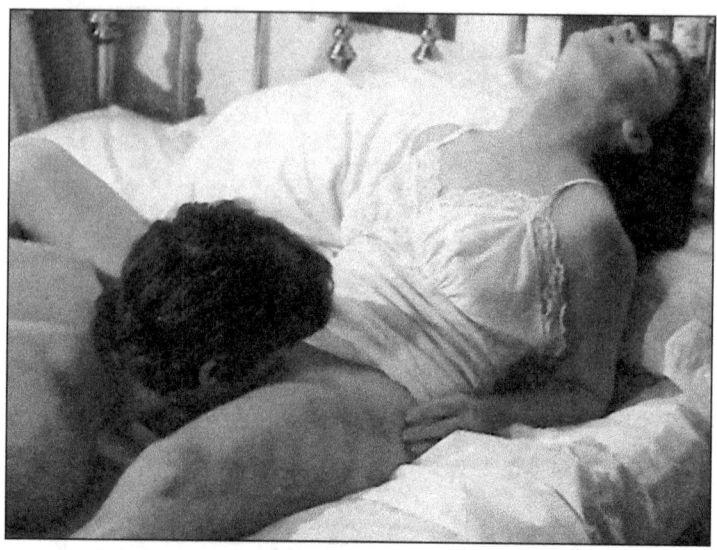

– Vincent Fronczek/VCX.com

We played a tender love scene.

– Vincent Fronczek/VCX.com

There were sweet whispers.

When I came, I came inside of her. There was no pulling out in gross display of the inane and insane come shot.

Anxious to return the favor, I continued to stimulate her. But every time she got herself close, there'd be a cut, or a film run-out, or some other distraction. She finally said that it was starting to make her crazy, so we stopped trying.

That night, back at the HoJo, where I might have offered to "finish" the scene, my wife showed up to pay me a conjugal visit. When Carly was around, I was a married man. We didn't swing and we didn't leave each other hanging. As it turned out, Carly and Georgina hit it off really well and spent several hours talking about books they'd read while I watched a football game.

– Kent Smith/Adam magazine

Georgina and I would later win numerous Best Supporting Acting awards for our roles in *The Dancers*.

P.S. By the end of the film, of course, Sam hated the producers and they hated him. It gave Sam great pleasure to learn that my little Shakespearian improvisation using the words of Sam Cooke's "Cupid" was going to cost the producers an additional $5,000 for the rights to use those words in the movie.

Deemed too critical to be edited out after the movie had been wrapped, they had to pony up the extra money. Sam was overjoyed.

In a similar vein, while the production was winding down, word came from the producers that we would not be allowed to keep our costumes.

It pissed me off. This was being really cheesy. These were Goodwill clothes for God's sake. We'd been living in them for a month. We busted our asses working for them in those clothes. There was real sentimental attachment to them. Nope, all the costumes had to be returned.

We had been on a great ride, but it was all coming to a halt. I gave my clothes back to Barbara, the costume lady, and she checked them in through "Customs." She later stole me back the shirt that I had come to love and gave it to me gift-wrapped for Christmas. Thank you. For everything.

Jackie and the Dreams. We kidded around a bit when the movie was completed about literally taking the live show of *Jackie and the Dreams* out on the road. We were ready. Life was all set to imitate art. We had a great act at a time when male strippers were a very hot item. But, sigh, sigh for what might have been. We all had money in our pockets. It was almost Christmas and what the Hell! We didn't do it. Within two weeks, I'm sure I gained ten pounds and was just grateful that I'd never have to dance like that again.

Every now and then, Spinelli threatened us with a sequel, but it never happened.

And that's the story of *The Dancers* I would tell you solely by plumbing the depths of my memory.

Here's what I would add after jolting myself awake by actually sitting down and watching the whole movie once again, these thirty years later.

The Dancers, which is by far one of the best porn productions I was ever in, was not a good movie. There were some wonderful moments in it, but it was maybe eighty percent of a good movie. And I'm being generous, of course, because I'm in it.

One could argue that it was on its way to becoming a good movie, but it sadly fell short. It fits into that apologetic category of "good for porn." That's a genre where you apply different standards than those used in evaluating mainstream films or TV. In a porn film, if you are not too humiliated by what transpires in between the sex scenes, then you may have yourself a rollicking success on your hands because in the land of the blind, the one-eyed man is king.

In the finished cut of *The Dancers*, there remain whole scenes where either bad performance, poor writing, or grating background music are still left in the movie. As one of the collaborators who wants to take pride in this work, it's embarrassing that an editor could have made those decisions and that a director or producer could have let those "errors" pass.

Even the great "Cupid" scene that I wrote and acted with Georgina wasn't nearly as good as it was in my memory. I could have been a lot better. Georgina's performance still holds up. She far out-classed me in that scene. Again, for porn, I was Laurence Olivier and she was Meryl Streep. But when viewed critically, as a regular movie, I think the scene could have been very much improved.

How odd, that even with these glaring flaws that smell of your basic high school production value, *The Dancers* was still wildly celebrated and honored as an award-winning production. I'm sure you'll understand how it gives me no great pleasure to point out that "the Emperor wore no clothes."

The other great problem I have with *The Dancers* is that at its very heart, it suffers from the same cynical, misogynist poison that haunted so much of porn. As an actor in porn and a husband and father, it confronted me with my own contradiction once again.

The Dancers celebrated the male lifestyle of hunting women for trophy. Either by charm, wit, guile, or deception, men sought to access "the flower" of women and once attained, did not even bother to put those flowers in a vase before running off to the next conquest. It was the ennobling of Casanova and the reduction of women to mere prizes in a continuing game of lust.

As a believer in true love, as a husband and a father of three, in particular, two daughters, I found this a sad, damaged, and juvenile exercise, even while I practiced it.

Chapter Twenty-Five

"Where could you possibly go from there?" Marty the agent wanted to know.

"I have no idea," I told him. "I had no idea that was even coming."

"You're book is getting real," he said, "Mazel Tov."

Chapter Twenty-Six

Fresh from *The Dancers*, I got myself a featured role in a national television commercial. Kawasaki Motorcycles was promising me a big payday. There'd be $500 or $600 paid for the one day of shooting, and then another $5,000-$8,000 more in residuals that would be paid for the run of the ad. Hot damn, and thank you, ma'am!

We shot Kawasaki Saturday Night three days before Christmas.

- Gordon Archive

Kawasaki Saturday Night.

It was a fun and easy night shoot. The set was festive and merry. Why wouldn't it be?

And afterwards, we started spending some of that money. We had a fun holiday that year. Bought a buncha stuff.

Shortly after the new year, I got a letter from the J. Walter Thompson Company who had produced the ad. Paragraph 2 said something like:

> *This is just to advise you pursuant to Paragraph 26 B.1 of the 1979 Commercials Contract pending between us that none of the footage or sound track in which you rendered services on the date(s) specified above will actually be utilized by us in our commercial.*
>
> *Sincerely yours, thank you very much, yours truly, and go fuck yourself,*
>
> *Mr. & Mrs. Kawasaki*

Did they tell us why they killed our commercial?
No, not a peep. Sayonara!

– *Gordon Archive*

Ooops!

Chapter Twenty-Seven

Y' see what was going on here? The straight stuff wasn't exactly panning out. I had another $500 audition where I had to fly down to LA again. Didn't get that job either. It was for a TV pilot called *Ethel and the Elephant*. That show actually made it on to the air. I think it lasted maybe three or four episodes before it got cancelled.

But you know what else got cancelled? It was my desire to go on chasing a straight career!

In a review of *Joan Rivers: A Piece of Work*, a documentary about the show business life of the longtime comedienne, *The San Francisco Chronicle* writer Mick La Salle wrote:

> "She (Rivers) describes the showbiz life as one of constant rejection; and over the course of the film, we see that's true. People who fail in show business get rejected all the time. Successes, like Rivers, get rejected most of the time."

I flirted with it, but I couldn't ignite an LA career while commuting from Berkeley. My wallet couldn't take it, and neither could my ego nor my marriage.

In the straight world, having been *Playgirl*'s Man-of-the-Year, was like winning a beauty pageant in Kansas. It qualified me to move to LA and to start making the rounds.

But no, I didn't want to move to LA. In LA, I was nobody. I didn't want to be another nobody looking in the windows on Rodeo Drive. Berkeley fit me better. In Berkeley, I knew who I was. Child of the Sixties, I liked me. I liked us.

Besides, working out of the Bay Area in the smaller pond of X-rated films, I was already a rising star.

How did the old Robert Frost poem go?

"Two roads diverged in a wood, and I—

I took the one less traveled by,

And that has made all the difference."

I believed in sex. I believed in love. I thought that we were the generation that was gonna make lust respectable.

Yeah, let's see where that takes us.

– Mike Ross/Playgirl

Cover Boy!

Chapter Twenty-Eight

Did I tell you that Carly and I were engaged to get pregnant? We were. And you know what? It wasn't easy. Month after month, we failed!

Holy shit! Made you wonder about all those years of worrying about the birth control. Here we were trying to get pregnant, and it wasn't happening. It just wasn't happening!

"Perseverance furthered," counseled the *I Ching*.

Chapter Twenty-Nine

"There you go again, Mahatma Howie! Why you fucking quoting the *I Ching*?"

"Marty! Marty the agent! It's good to see you! Haven't heard from you in pages! How you doin'?"

"Better than you, asshole, I picked up a penny from the sidewalk this afternoon."

"Marty, that hurts."

"And Robert Frost! Jesus, that's just tacky. Are you ever gonna finish this fucking book?"

"What do you care?"

"Publishing is changing. I think we can sell it on the Internet."

"Oi."

Chapter Thirty

Loni Sanders. As close to Tinkerbell as I ever got. She was such a pixie that I could hold her bottom in one hand. And I have small hands. She made me feel like Shaquille O'Neal.

We were working for The Louis Brothers in *Please Mr. Postman*. The Louis Brothers were an in-group of X-rated crew people who were pooling their own money and doing this production for themselves. One of the brothers was actually a woman. She was the production manager who hired me.

This was not Spinelli porn, pushing the envelope and trying to take the industry to the next level. The Louis Brothers were more like the factory workers of porn. It was down, dirty, and cheap. They were only paying me half my rate, but I took the job anyway because we had plumbing problems at home that couldn't wait until a better-paying job came along. They said that they were "happy to have an actor like me in their film." They said that, "as long as I didn't slow them down or cost them any extra money, I was free to act all I wanted."

– Lonnie Sanders

"Howard," she called me, "Howard. Thanks for all the help. Along with the help, thanks for the good time."

Please Mr. Postman was another high school play with a lot of explicit sex. The only good thing about being in the film—other than paying off our Berkeley plumber, who, by the way, had a PhD. in Philosophy from Princeton—was that I got to meet and work with Lonnie Sanders. She was an absolute delight.

Having only done one or two movies, Lonnie was still new to the business. She was fresh, cute, and vivacious. I liked her. I took a big brotherly interest in her. One could see that Lonnie needed to learn the ABC's of the business. She was doing two sex scenes a day and not getting paid nearly enough for them. She was tossing in the extras like doing trailers for nothing. She had no idea what she was worth in this business.

She told me that she was living in LA and I suggested that she get herself into an acting class down there as soon as possible. Any good-looking woman who could handle the sex and also call herself an actress could double her rate overnight. With just the sex, it took a little longer.

Lonnie said that X-rated actor Mike Ranger was her boyfriend and that he was helping her make her way into the business. I didn't know him very well and I suggested that she meet with Annette Haven who had always been very generous and outstanding at teaching the new women how best to play the game with a minimum of exploitation and a maximum of profit.

When Lonnie and I did our sex scene, it was like eating strawberry shortcake with lots of whipped cream. You get lucky sometimes.

Chapter Thirty-One
The Business of the Business

Producer Harold Lime called to offer work in his upcoming *Centerspread Girls*. He was lavish with his praise of my talent as he told me that he wanted me in his film. He promised to send a script.

Harold Lime was a biggee amongst X-rated producers and I was hot to work for him. When the script came, he indicated that I would be playing W.W. Williams, a bible-thumping hypocrite who publicly preached a Fundamentalist morality and then privately acted the lecher. It was alright. It was double the budget of the Louis Brothers stuff. It had possibilities.

I hated negotiating salaries. I was lousy at it and it always made me crazy. Like Harold Lime, the producers would call, tell me how wonderful I was, and explain how much their movie needed me. Then, they'd ask me what my rate was.

I'd tell them my rate. Then, they'd tell me that I wasn't that wonderful, they didn't need me that badly, and they'd counter with a substantially lower offer. I always thought that a rate was a rate, y'know, like a price in a menu. Period. When it says a steak cost $20, you don't go offering the waitress $15! The producers always treated my rate like it was the first figure in a negotiation process. I'd get angry. They'd get indignant. I'd get alienated. They'd tell me, "Take it or leave it." I'd leave it. They refuse to pay my rate, fuck 'em, I turn the job down. See my lower lip sticking out here? See, I'd show them!

If I would take a job at a lower salary, I'd feel resentful. I'd have to take direction from some turd who had just hammered me into lowering my price. No good. It didn't work.

No sir, this "business" part of "The Business" was never my strong suit. Back in Pittsburgh, it seemed like the family business had always been to not be very good at business. My mother was forever teasing my father about what a schnook he was in such matters.

Oh, there was always food on the table, but the blue collar nature of his business affairs never rose very high up the ladder of the great American Dream. It bothered both of them more than it bothered me.

By the time I came of age in the sixties and "The Revolution" was afoot, "business" or American corporate greed had been identified as one of the great villains of the late twentieth century. Sure, I wanted money and the good life and all of that, but not at the expense of the war in Vietnam or supporting oppressive dictatorships all over the world in the name of Wall Street and American corporate profit. We wanted America to be the good guys.

Did you notice how I slipped out of the "I" and into the "we" there? Joined the revolution, I did. Grew my hair long. We thought we were all part of something pretty big back then. We thought it was a rebirth for America and a reaffirmation of all that good guy stuff in the Declaration of Independence that had once made this country the light of the world.

Business was the bad guy. We were getting fat off the resources of the world. What'd they call it? "The American Century!"

Well, clearly, when it came to this business thing, I had some gaps in my education. Yeah, so, ya know what we did? We made my wife Richard Pacheco's business manager!

Carly was far better at that stuff than I was anyway. She volunteered to handle that aspect of the business and I was happy to go into the next room and turn on the TV while she did all the negotiating.

In the end, she'd just present me with the offer and we'd decide to take it or leave it. I now had a buffer. Like Willie Cicci said in *The Godfather*, "The family had a lot of buffers."

When Harold Lime didn't want to pay my rate, I turned him down. Oh, he could well-afford to have paid me, he just didn't want to. He figured I'd cave in and go to work for less, but I didn't. If Harold Lime wasn't going to pay my rate, then nobody else would either. I turned it down. I had to establish myself. They made *Centerspread Girls* without me. Paul Thomas ended up playing the part they offered me. But ya know what? The next time Harold Lime called to offer me a job, he paid me my full rate with no questions asked.

I never had those kinds of problems working for Anthony Spinelli. Sam would always give me a raise before I even had to ask.

Chapter Thirty-Two
2010, from my diary ...

I was talking to my mother-in-law yesterday. I had read her the "business" chapter as she has been occasionally curious about the progress of this memoir. I deemed it sufficiently innocent and unprovocative enough to be able to share it with her. Unlike my own parents, she and her husband were actually very good at business. They had owned and operated several successful retail businesses over the years. My father-in-law even spent some time teaching business at the college level.

He's gone now, as are my folks, and my mother-in-law is the last remaining parent. We have developed a great relationship over the years, one I think that has delightfully surprised us both. I have shared that the last thing I ever thought I needed was another mother. But over time, I had to admit that I was wrong. My in-laws were both incredible people. I lucked out in that department and have always done my best to show the immense gratitude I feel for all the love and care extended to me and the kids. We have truly been a family.

So, that's what makes what she told me yesterday, after more than thirty years of waiting, all the more poignant. She told me yesterday, after thirty years of keeping it to herself, that when Carly first told her that I was working in the X-rated business, she got sick.

She remembered that we were driving her and her husband to the airport where they were to fly to Western Canada to begin a cross-continental railway adventure. They did fly to Canada, but she said she got so sick trying to absorb our news that she had to cut short the whole vacation and go home.

My heart sank, but I understood it. I had faced all of those same feelings before when I first told my own parents.

She said that she always wanted to think of her family as part of some kind of refined cultural elite. Clearly, my choice of occupations had smashed that aspiration to pieces, but she held her tongue. For thirty years, she held her tongue.

She wasn't actually scolding me now. She was more being wistful, kind of confessing a long ago hurt between two people who had somehow grown to love each other anyway. She was letting me know that I had demanded a lot, but that she had given it, as best she could, even though it ran against her every fiber.

Then she talked about the kids, her grandchildren. She worried about what difficulties I had lain upon their heads by having chosen my path through life. Carly and I have often worried about that too. We worried from what might emerge at an elementary school or on a little league playground to what might one day get said by the parents of a partner that they'd fallen in love with and wanted to marry. We have worried.

Chapter Thirty-Three
Mike

Mike was the coach. Stanford-educated, but could still kick your ass in a hurry if he wanted to. Mike was coaching my son's little league baseball team. The players were all eleven or twelve years old.

It was early in the year. We were at the field getting ready for a game one day when Mike came right to me.

"We might have some trouble today," he said. "One of the mothers on the other team knows who you are!" Surprised me. I hadn't said word one to anyone in the whole league about me being Richard Pacheco.

"Of, course," Mike added, "I knew who you were the minute you walked on the field."

I admit that was gratifying.

"And I just wanna say," Mike continued, "that anybody who's been all up in Nina Hartley's booty, is all right with me. If anything happens today, I'll take care of it," he said. "I'll take care of it."

That was even better.

And as far as I know, nothing did happen, except that Mike and I became buddies. That was good. And then the kids went on to have themselves an outstanding season. That was great!

Chapter Thirty-Four
Damiano

If I had to put four faces on the Mt. Rushmore of Porn, I'd have to choose Gerry Damiano and John Holmes, and then Georgina Spelvin and Marilyn Chambers. Although it wouldn't take too much prodding for me to drop Marilyn and stick Vanessa Del Rio up there. As I said

Damiano.

Vanessa Del Rio.

before, Marilyn just got famous from the Ivory Snow thing. Vanessa Del Rio was a true peoples' champion. Men everywhere loved her.

Fact is, you could talk about substituting in Jamie Gillis, Linda Lovelace, or maybe even Annette Haven or Seka to be up there too. But the one space you wouldn't mess with at all would be the one reserved for Gerard Damiano.

He was the Moses of the industry. He led us out of the desert of eight mm stag films and delivered us to real motion picture theaters with paying customers out there eating popcorn in the audience.

So, when the word passed around that the great Maestro was coming out West to shoot a new movie, we all got in line to kiss the ring

The film was called *Never So Deep*. It was a farce, a silly old baggy-pants piece of fluff. It stunk.

When the Great Recorder comes to discuss the ground-breaking contributions of Gerard Damiano to the world of adult films, it's not likely that this film will ever be mentioned.

It was like hooking up with Babe Ruth at the end of his career when he was playing for the Boston Braves. Forgetaboutit.

Probably the best thing that happened on this whole shoot was having an off-stage rendezvous with Maria Tortuga while we were waiting to go on one afternoon.

- Maria Tortuga

Maria Tortuga and friends.

We snuck off to a broom closet and I gave her a blow job. She gave me this autographed picture as a thank you. In case you can't make out the writing, it reads: "Howie Sweetheart — See ya back in the broom closet, LOVE Maria Tortuga." This was the kind of fringe benefit, of course, that often made being in the adult business a lot of fun.

Damiano gave me two parts to play in the movie. One was that of a Hindu tourist visiting a peep show in North Beach and the other was that of a famous French film director.

 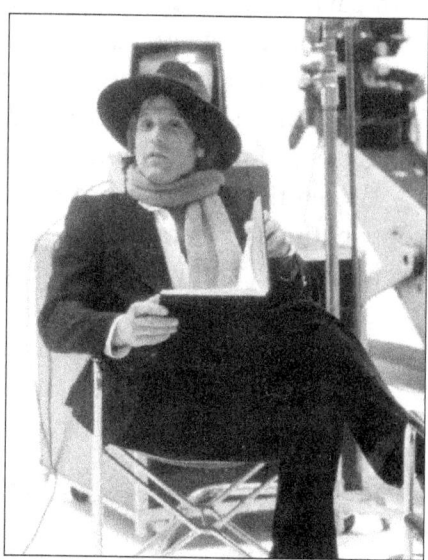

– Gordon Archive

His direction to me consisted of two words, "Be funny." I was funny. At least in that first scene I was. I made him laugh. Don't know what he was doing in the second one, though, because I was too busy trying to get my dick to speak French.

It was Loni Sanders again, but it bore no resemblance to our red-hot first encounter. This time, we were in a three-way with Mike Horner. It was on a desktop in my office. I was the French director in this scene. Loni was on her back on the desk. I was supposed to be fucking her at one end while Mike got head at the other.

With me standing on the floor, I was too short for my penis to reach her vuvuzela. They brought in an apple box for me to stand on and cheat the shot. I may have told you before that I don't like standing up for very long when I'm having sex, especially when it's in the movies. In this scene, I was supposed to take the stand-up sex all the way to orgasm. Additionally, I was supposed to do it all while improvising a steady French-accented, comic monologue. It was a recipe for disaster. It was comical all right, but it wasn't much of a sex scene. Maybe Gerry was laughing at that. If you weren't me, you might have thought it was very funny.

– Gordon Archive/VCX.com

God bless Loni Sanders. She was trying. I actually did get an erection and gave them some of the in-and-out footage they wanted, but it was a struggle all the way. My dick was up and down. It was difficult to stay aroused. And friends, when that penile yo-yo stuff starts, you try being funny in a French accent.

It was Mike Horner to the rescue. He had already had his orgasm from the blow job and was watching me sweat bullets. When it became clear to one and all that it would likely take an act of God for me to have an orgasm, Mike Horner volunteered to take my place. He wanted a second helping of Miss Sanders. It was fine with me and it was fine with her.

In no time at all, he was up and in the saddle. Way taller than me at six feet one inch, he didn't even need to use the apple box. Mike had a big grin on his face as he rode on to glory.

Seemed like Mike always had a big grin on his face. At the time, he was probably one of the most under-rated, under-publicized, and likely under-paid actors in the business. The man had talent. He could act with anybody. And he for sure could fuck like a rabbit.

I invited Mike to share his memories of that scene with me:

- Mike Horner

Mike Horner.

"I vividly remember some parts of this movie, though I was merely a bit player, and not yet very accomplished at acting (that took a few years of acting classes), and I particularly recall your acting. At one point, playing the director, you threw the fake script in the air in a gesture of fake inspiration and it was funny, and drew laughs from the crew. Forty years later, I was playing Bill O'Reilly in "Who's Nailin Pailin" and used the same

gesture in a fake fit of anger by my version of O'Reilly. As my arm went up and scattered the pages, I had an instant remembrance of you performing the same gesture and I gave you some measure of credit for placing that little idea deep in my brain.

I hadn't remembered that the girl was Loni Sanders, who I always admired. Thanks for the memories."

– Mike Horner

I liked Mike—still do. I always enjoyed seeing him on the set. He was a team player who always had a nice word for everybody. Mike Horner was high on my list of actors I would cast as a leading man when I moved up to writing and directing my own movies. I looked forward to that happening one day.

After writing this chapter, I later had some later doubts that maybe I'd been too harsh on Gerry Damiano. I mean, who was I to be so critical of the great master? So, I looked up Never So Deep *in some of the old reviews.*

In Adam Film World's 1984 Film Directory, *they wrote: "Despite his success and reputation, Damiano has had his fair share of turkeys, which out of respect we won't mention."*

And to cap it off, after detailing a synopsis of Never So Deep *in his own* X-rated Videotape Guide, *sex educator and reviewer Robert Rimmer wrote:*

"Please, Gerard, don't make a sequel."

Chapter Thirty-Five
Veronica Hart

There was a knock on my door, at least I thought it was my door. It was Veronica Hart. I'd seen her around. We'd said hello before. She was a New York actress who was coming on like gangbusters in the business.

There were at least three different film companies staying at the Howard Johnson's in Mill Valley that night. I was with Spinelli. She was with somebody else. She was wearing a fur coat.

Turned out, she wasn't knocking at my door at all. She was knocking at the door next door. It was the door of Raul Lomas, the suave cameraman from Brazil. All the pretty girls were knocking on the door of Raul Lomas, the suave cameraman from Brazil. Must have been when we were shooting *The Dancers*. Raul and I had adjoining rooms at the HOJO. She was knocking at his door.

"Go away now, I'm busy," came Raul's voice from inside. Veronica looked at me and I looked at her.

"Want some company?" she asked. I smiled and invited her in. She let her fur coat fall open. She wasn't wearing anything underneath.

It wasn't long before we were cast opposite each other in Anthony Spinelli's *Between the Sheets*. I was eager to work with her on screen. Veronica Hart was in the midst of a meteoric rise to become one of the top performers in the business. She was an actress of the first order and her sex scenes growled! The young maiden was Hall of Fame stuff from the get-go.

– *Adam Film World*

Veronica Hart.

While reviewers didn't think of *Between the Sheets* as one of Spinelli's major efforts, I thought it was a charming idea. It featured a lot of the big-name X-rated talent of the era in what amounted to a series of vignettes all held together by a talking bed.

Somewhat akin to one of my Hollywood favorites, *Tales of Manhattan* (1942), Annette Haven, Seka, John Leslie, Vanessa Del Rio, Eric Edwards, Aracadia Lake, Joey Silvera, Tigr, R.J. Reynolds, Veronica Hart and myself took star turns in being some of the lovers who used the bed in the over 200 years of its amorous history. It started with the first couple during America's Revolutionary War and traveled through time until it got to Veronica and me, who were using it now.

- Adam Film World

Heat!

I actually lobbied Sam to cast us as the 1960s hippie couple, but he had this whole, long kind of existential mishmush of dialogue that he really wanted Veronica and me to play as the present day couple (1981). We did it his way. You didn't win too many arguments with Sam.

I can't remember exactly what it was about. It was heavy. It was dark, something about office politics. She was my boss. Ambition, alienation, might have had something to do with John Lennon's assassination too. That was a big moment that touched Sam deeply. I don't know. It was long, about eight pages long and dense. Veronica and I rehearsed the hell out of that scene before we ever got on the set and it still took us all day to shoot it. It got the full Spinelli treatment. But, six months later when the movie came out, none of that stuff was even in there. They had cut it so all that remained was the sex scene.

– Gordon Archive

Veronica & Howie.

Who those people were and why they were having sex didn't seem to concern the editor very much. Why should I let it bother me? Besides that, the sex scene was pretty good. Pornoland.

Chapter Thirty-Six
Kelly Nichols

It was *The Mistress*. We were shooting *The Mistress*. I met Kelly Nichols for the first time and got all stupid.

- Kelly Nichols

Kelly Nichols.

Sure, there was the glitz and the glamour, the porn and the pose, but once the war paint came off, there was something else underneath.

– *Kelly Nichols*

This wasn't subtle. This wasn't casual.

- Kelly Nichols

This wasn't something to be trifled with....

I wasn't even working with her in this movie. Well, I had a scene with her, but it was all dialogue. There was no sex. I wanted to have sex though. What was going on here? I was married. I think she was married too. Sure, I wanted to be in the business and all, but that had nothing to do with getting myself all stupid. I didn't want to get stupid. I was fighting with myself. Something about Kelly Nichols just made me stupid.

It didn't go anywhere then, we didn't have sex. I worked with another girl in *The Mistress* and we did have sex. In fact, it was the first time I got up close and personal with a bikini-waxed woman. Lord, have mercy, I truly loved that. I absolutely adored it. You could finally see what was going on down there! And when you got right down into it, it was like kissing Mother Nature right on the lips. Did not want to take my face out of there.

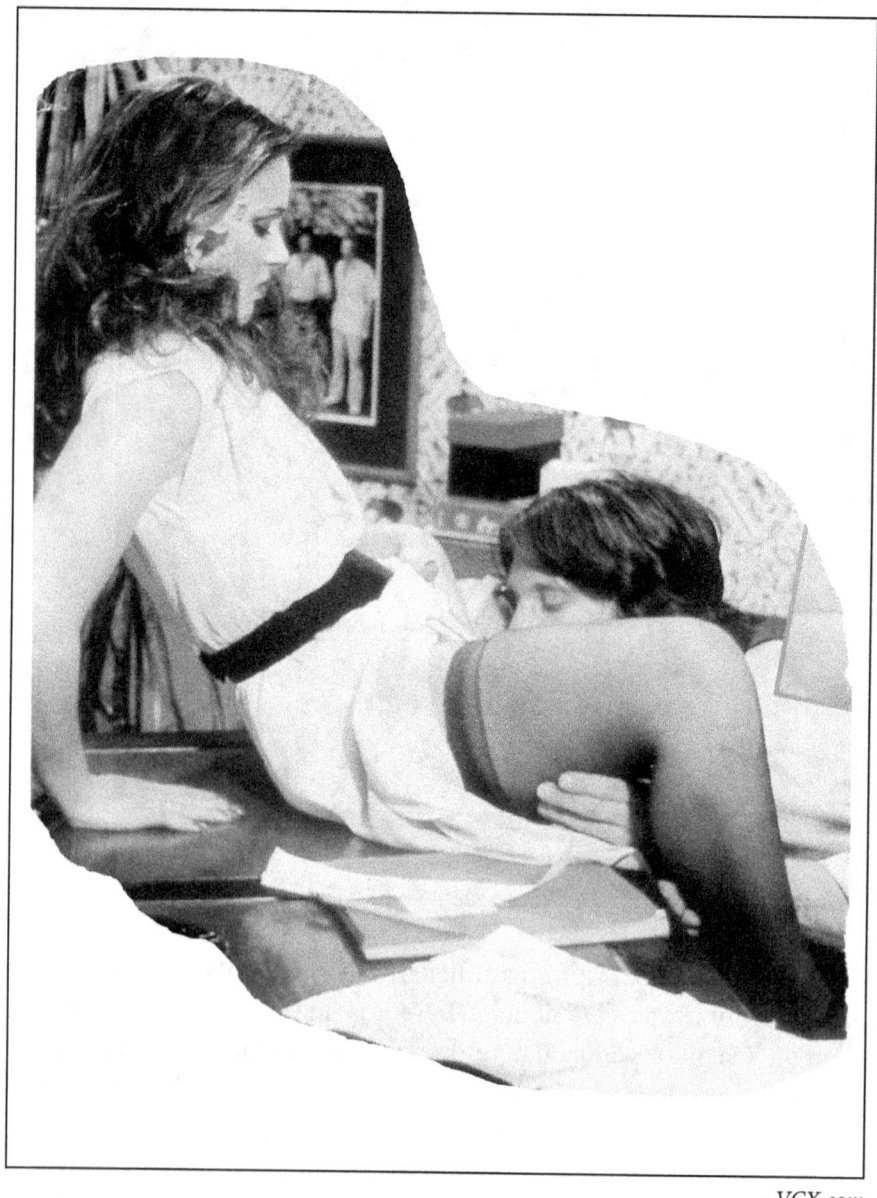

- VCX.com

With Brooke West in *The Mistress*. It was the first time I ever met a shaved woman.

Hair had always been the big problem with oral sex. Sometimes it bothered me and sometimes it didn't. Depended on my mood, the thickness, the odors, lots of factors were at work down there, but nothing could bring things to a halt faster than a stray hair getting caught in your throat. Gagging did not do much to enhance foreplay. It was just a step or two above farting.

This clean-shaven thing, this was a get-out-of-jail-free card! This was smooth sailing. This was soft, sweet, and sacred stuff. It was wet, wild, and free. Vagina pudding. The tongue was on a rampage, let loose in paradise. This was a joyous event. Flicking, licking, nose and tongue, my whole face was rolling around in the wet and wonderful.

Chapter Thirty-Seven
Which Brings Us to Annette Haven Again

To me, she was *Liberty Leading The People.*

– Ferdinand Victor Eugène Delacroix – *La liberté guidant le peuple*

Annette was another special woman, but not just to me. She was special to the whole industry. Not near enough fuss has been made about her in celebration. There was no one else like Annette Haven.

We'd had four years of getting-to-know-you foreplay before we were finally cast as lovers in *Las Vegas Maniacs*, I had her quite idealized by then.

First of all, she was a star of the highest order.

– *Caballero*

Anthony Spinelli often said she was a throwback to an earlier Hollywood, one that had been lit up by the likes of Jean Harlow and Greta Garbo, Bette Davis and Joan Crawford. "Annette didn't just walk into a room," he'd say, "she swooped in." Sam would howl with glee when she'd make such an entrance. "And once inside that room," he observed, "Annette would proceed to own it." Sam admired her style and chutzpah, how she managed seemingly to do it all with a smile, flashing eyes, and a sharp tongue.

In the world of porn, one that was so utterly dominated by men flexing their muscle and their fantasy, Annette Haven made a huge difference.

In the early seventies, when the industry was just getting started, Annette was porn's great beauty when so many of the other women just weren't.

She soon made the X-rated world her personal domain. She had star power and she knew how to use it. Her beauty was a weapon. She quickly understood what it meant to be the box office and she kept that edge throughout her entire career.

If other actresses tried to do some of the things that she did routinely on a set, they'd be fired, gone, and history.

If the producers wouldn't treat her the way that she demanded, she'd be gone. Annette played it as if they needed her more than she needed them. Very few ever called her bluff.

Annette Haven made an enormous contribution to humanizing the men's locker room aspect of making adult films. You just didn't see certain kinds of male behaviors on her sets that you saw on others. What am I talking about?

Well, for one thing, I doubt that Annette Haven ever took a come shot in her face. In a business whose sexuality was dominated by male rage, she kept the beast at bay. I marveled at her spirit. She was Wonder Woman, Batgirl, and Sarah Bernhardt, all living in the body of Venus.

That she was a unique star in her own right was a big enough deal, but what truly made her special was that she was also very protective of all the other women around her. Annette went out of her way to teach the young actresses how to survive in the erotic jungle of Pornoland. She was the Mama Bear. You messed with her cubs at your peril. If she saw a guy being abusive to a woman on a set, she'd get right up in his face. If need be, she'd bring the show to a halt and get the producer to either set the guy straight or get rid of him.

While other women may have had those same impulses, Annette Haven was the one who acted on them. And pretty much alone amongst all of them, Annette Haven had the will and the power to back it all up. If she walked off the set in the middle of a production, it was gonna cost somebody a lot of money. Producers were inclined to keep her happy.

If it's not clear yet, I can just tell you that she was my fuckin' hero.

Sexloose (Las Vegas Maniacs)

I had two days in this film. I played a cat burglar who broke into Annette Haven's house. She was a police detective who caught me red-handed. This being Pornoland, naturally, we would have sex.

I thought I was eager for the embrace, but once begun, I became as tentative and caring as I could be while still working in a movie.

– Hustler Video/LFP Video Group, LLC

I had always perceived Annette as so strong, so tough. When we got eyeball to eyeball and I was poised for the penetration, I was taken aback to suddenly see her as vulnerable. It gave me pause. There was a sadness to it. This knowing seemed far too intimate. In some ways, it just seemed wrong.

— *Hustler Video/LFP Video Group, LLC*

— *Hustler Video/LFP Video Group, LLC*

These feelings were way out of place. We were dancing in the ballroom of public sex. These were personal feelings. They had no business here. They were supposed to be left in the dressing room. We had a job to do. I had a job to do. Hell, I didn't even know what she was thinking. This was all just going on in my head.

Surprisingly, the sex still happened anyway, as if it had a life all its own. A lot seemed to pass between us while the cameras rolled. Eventually, I reached my orgasm and I thought the scene concluded, but no.

That day, Annette insisted on doing her own orgasm for real. She refused to simulate it. She argued that it would look better. She DEMANDED that the director shoot it that way. Wow, if there hadn't been an Annette Haven, we would have had to invent her.

I know I've told you before that most of the actresses I'd ever worked with had confided that they could "never come in front of all of these people!"

It was an aspect of the movie sex that I'd always hated. In the real world, it left me all alone to seek out my arousal while my partners just made a bunch of phony noises. It sucked.

And here now was Annette Haven insisting on doing her own come shot. I thought that was great. It was both my honor and a pleasure to help her get to the ecstasy.

At the very end of that ride, Annette kind of hyperventilated herself into a faint. She went out cold there for a little while. I just held her until she made her way back to the planet. It was very peaceful and never seemed like she was in any danger.

In the finished movie, there appears little trace of what was happening between us as lovers that day. The scene was cut fast and looked like any other ten sex scenes. *Las Vegas Maniacs* was largely a waste except for the fact that it broke a lot of the intimate ice in getting to know Annette, and it served as an excellent foreplay for the epic love scene we would later share in *The Seven Seductions of Madame Lau*.

Chapter Thirty-Eight
The Seven Seductions of Madame Lau

I read the script in my urologist's office. I'd play the famous British explorer, Christopher Hamilton. I had conquered Everest and the North and South Poles, but had grown weary of the external world.

This film would now trace my spiritual search into the meaning of erotic love. My guide in this odyssey would be the mysterious Madame Lau, portrayed by Annette Haven.

Lest one think porn had dared an original thought, this film was just "piggybacking" on the *The Seven Faces of Dr. Lau* (1964). It starred Tony Randall.

In *Madame Lau*, I had arrived in the land of the X-rated leading man. I would be doing seven sex scenes in six days. This was John Leslie territory. For me, it was going to be like cliff-diving in Acapulco. This was obviously a big risk being taken by the producers and Director Charles De Santos. I don't know if I would have hired me, but I took the job when they offered. At this point in my career, I was feeling just cocky enough to give it a shot.

– VCX.com

Howie the male lead.

Speaking of which, I was at the urologist's office to have my sperm analyzed. It was just possible that after all my turbulent early years in the business, some of my sperm were suffering from Post Traumatic Stress Disorder (PTSD). Carly and I had been trying to get pregnant for six months and it just wasn't happening. It was now time to bring in medical science to kick the tires and check the oil and water.

– VCX.com

Annette Haven as Madame Lau.

The doctor had asked me to

not have an orgasm for four days prior to my office visit. I had sperms backed up into my brain.

My urologist looked like Mr. Rogers. First, he had me piss into three different cups. Well, you didn't see that every day in the Wonderful World of Make-Believe. Then, he measured my testicles. That was fun. This should have been the first scene in the movie.

After these preliminaries, he donned the rubber glove and stuck a finger right up my ass. "To check your prostate," he said. No flowers, no candles, no nothin', just stuck his finger right up my ass. Boy, oh, boy, how was *Madame Lau* ever gonna top this?

The grand finale was my own come shot. You know what? I was lucky to have gone through the Basic Training of adult films. A civilian could've easily freaked out in this scene. The doctor gave me two cups. He wanted me to squirt the first blast of orgasm into one cup and then switch cups for the rest. He coulda been directing loops.

No problem, Doc, I'm a professional. Just gimme a little makeup and tell me where the camera's gonna be. Unfortunately, no nurses were being provided as tech support and none volunteered. They put me in a little room alone and I made do with some fond high school memories and my ever-loving right hand. Soon, I was the proud father of two cups of sperm. I gave them to the doctor. The doctor smeared some on a slide and placed it under his microscope.

"They look good," he said. I beamed with pride. "You want to see?"

"Sure, I do." There they were, hundreds of little Howie's looking for an egg. Pretty much told the story of my life, right there.

"You and your wife keep on trying," the doctor said. "You're doing fine. If you don't get pregnant in the next six months, you come on back." And out the door I went. It was like I just had my batteries recharged.

Okay, I was ready for *Madame Lau*. I was ready for anything. I called Director Charles to see about rehearsal and I got Tigr from *Nothing to Hide*.

She was going behind the camera to be the production manager on this one. Tigr suggested that Carly and I stop trying to get pregnant and just adopt her. She also told me that there wasn't going to be any rehearsal, citing too many conflicting commitments and too little time.

Uh-oh, that was definitely not a good sign. It never was. Made me feel bad and mad. This was my first lead in a big-time movie. I wanted to hit a home run. Fucking Pornoland!

Chapter Thirty-Nine

Madame Lau began with producer Aaron Linn flying the director and me up to the Clear Lake location in his own private airplane. Well, that was a nice unexpected touch of class. I already felt like the great international explorer Christopher Hamilton and we hadn't even started shooting yet. The rest of the cast and crew were being driven up from San Francisco.

The day was given over to costume fittings and generally getting ready. There was a lot of partying. I stayed away. I studied my script and hung out by the pool working on my tan. I needed all the rest I could get. I was about to embark on a sexual marathon.

Day One

On the morning of the first day, naturally, we were shooting the very last scene of the movie first.

Briefly, the story of *Madame Lau* was this: Leaving behind Veronica his wife, Christopher Hamilton sought out the infamous Madame Lau as a teacher of erotic love and spiritual union. They engaged in a sequence of metaphysical conversations filled with simplistic, mystical truths, all of which led to scenes of Christopher getting laid, one way or another.

In the conversations, lots of candles were lit, incense was burned, and Tarot cards were read. In the sex scenes,

- VCX.com

Reading the Tarot Cards.

bosoms and booties, cocks and cunts abounded.

> *"Excuse me!"*
> *"Marty! What you doing here? I'm busy."*
> *"I was just wondering. Do you have to say 'cunts' there? Women just hate that word."*
> *"'Bosoms and booties, cocks and cunts,' I like the alliteration. Now, will you get the fuck out of here?"*
> *"And you say 'fuck' too much!"*
> *"Marty, now is not the time."*
> *"I can't wait to get this shit to an editor."*
> *"Good-bye, Marty."*

So. So after Madame Lau has taken Christopher on this whole sexual merry-go-round, he ends up all enlightened and he returns home to his wife. It actually sounds a lot like my career. In a plot twist at the end, though, we discover that Madame Lau really was Christopher's wife all along, in disguise. This gets revealed to the audience, but poor schmendrick Christopher never did figure it out.

– Gordon Archive

With Kay Parker and Director Charles De Santos on sticks.

Kay Parker played my wife. And as I mentioned before, we were beginning by shooting the film's ending first. In the climactic love scene on the beach, Kay and I would be having sex with each other for the first time. We started out hot and eager for each other. When the cameras rolled, as Christopher, I declared my new and profound and undying love for her. We embraced. We kissed.

– *VCX.com*

We began to make love on the beach …

– Gordon Archive

… but we soon had to stop because the mosquitoes were eating us alive!

Tigr was dispatched on an emergency run for bug repellent. When it arrived, we slathered ourselves silly with the toxic potion and then proceeded to have to kiss, suck, and lick it from each other's bodies for the rest of the scene. What? And give up show business?

That wasn't even the worst of it. I had been hired with the contractual agreement that I would only have to perform "one sex scene" per day. This was a business matter. Each sex scene was $1,000. Because the script called for me to do seven sex scenes in six days, it was decided that one of those sex scenes would just have to be "simulated." Problem solved. Hardly.

From an artistic point of view, I have generally preferred that "simulated," or R-rated sex scenes, be shot with the performers actually having real sex and then just hiding the X-rated parts with the appropriate camera angles. In that way, the audience is spared the agony of having to watch the actors "acting" like they're having sex, which is most often an embarrassment of semi-biblical proportion.

But in this case, because of the financial concerns and faced with the prospects of my own physical limitations, my idea for this particular "simulated" sex scene was like no erection, no penetration, no orgasm, no nothing. Because I would have to do a complete-full-bodied sex scene soon afterward, on that same day, I wanted everything in that first sex scene to be acted. They'd just have to settle for the best job we could give them.

The producers and directors didn't see it that way. They wanted the "simulated" sex scene to involve like an hour of real, hardcore action with only the orgasm "acted" at the very end.

I never dreamed that they would ask me to perform all this real sex and stop just short of orgasm. That was crazy. I never would have agreed to that. It was an hour's worth of sex without coming. That sound like any fun to you?

Unfortunately, we didn't discover this little difference of opinion until we were already on the set and up to our short hairs in it.

My solution would have added another shooting day to the schedule and put another $1,000 in my pocket. They made it clear that wasn't going to happen.

Well, you're one person when you're negotiating a business deal and you're quite another when you're on a set taking direction. This was my first day on the film. Hell, this was our very first scene! I let myself get bullied, but I swore it would be the last time.

Kay Parker was an angel about all this, by the way. She just hung in there with me. As the simulated sex progressed, I got so close to coming at one point with Kay that if she would have blinked ... but she didn't. And so I didn't.

- VCX.com

Copulating and coping.

When they got all the footage they needed, we acted the orgasm and got up and walked away.

I was grateful to have worked with Kay Parker that day. And I've since been grateful to have known Kay Parker all my life.

Throughout the afternoon, we did a bunch of dialogue scenes, shot some action footage of the airplane, and I tried hard to uncross my eyes.

At twilight, the magic hour, the second sex scene finally commenced. I was getting a blow job from Phae Burd in the cockpit of the airplane. It had been eight hours since I'd been ready to spill my seed with Kay. By the time that Phae started to suck, I was ready to explode. In what might have been the shortest blow job of my life, I thought I was going to come right through the top of her head. Mercifully, Phae safely and expertly released the pressure, and day one of *Madame Lau* passed into history.

I was granted the luxury of the return flight home in the producer's private plane. That was nice. I was tired. It turned a two or three hour drive into a thirty-minute flight.

Day Two

– VCX.com

Blindfolding Howie.

You think you're catching a break. It says right there in the script that four women are going to pleasure me. That's one, two, three, four women are gonna pleasure me, all at the same time, and then, Annette Haven is going to anoint me with oil and give me a hand job.

That's four women! That's eight tits! That's eight hands! That's four tongues! That's four vajayjays! That's four asses with eight butt cheeks. That's forty fingers and forty toes and sixteen lips! And Annette Haven, well, that's Annette Haven!

What could possibly go wrong with all of that? Funny you should ask.

The room was cold. Even with the stage lights on, the room remained cold. I was blindfolded and naked. I got the shivers. They had to stop shooting when I started shaking and put a blanket on me. Take two. Take Three. Take Four. Take Five.

One of the women had a bad cold. She was hacking and wheezing and coughing up phlegm. In between shots, those were among the sounds I heard while I lay there bound and blindfolded. Then upon "action," a tongue would get shoved down my throat. Made me worry about whose tongue it was.

I kept trying to push it out.

— *VCX.com*

Be careful what you wish for.

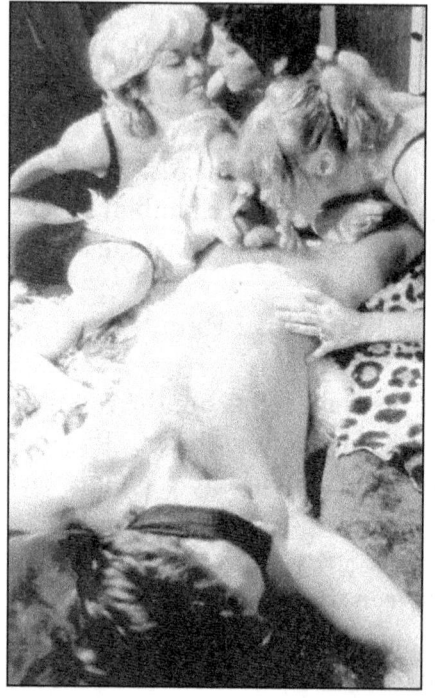

- VCX.com

Check, please!

And another of the women was having some fun with me. Every now and then, there'd be a nip with some teeth or a flick of a finger nail on the head of my penis. I'd flinch. This kind of pain wasn't working for me at all. I told the director to tell whoever it was to cut it out. I expected him to protect me.

Four tongues, eight tits, sadly, none of this was arousing. I have nothing but bad memories and then complete relief when Annette Haven finally made her entrance and shooed all the rest of them away.

We were doing a parody of what was then a very famous sex scene in *Behind the Green Door*. As foreplay, wholesome Marilyn Chambers was being roughly pawed and savaged by a whole group of guys who eventually all gave way to Johnny Keyes, cast as the greatest African stud muffin of all time.

Inter-racial sex was still a screaming taboo back then. This was a raw scene of in-your-face lust.

In our little scenario, we reversed the genders. I had the Marilyn Chambers part and Annette played the Johnny Keyes role.

She was completely done up

- VCX.com

Saved by Annette Haven.

in black makeup with an Afro wig and wearing a necklace made of tiger teeth. Annette was in little-girl-playing-dress-up heaven. She loved playing the part. And I loved her being there. She was the cavalry come to rescue me from the banshees.

She got me up and off quickly and I got into a hot shower and licked my wounds.

By the end of the second day, I knew that *Madame Lau* was in trouble. We were making two different movies at the same time. The parts being directed by Charles De Santos were going after funny slapstick, while the parts being directed by Christie MacDonald, oozed metaphysics and sought deep meaning.

Charles touch could be seen right from the opening blow job scene in the airplane. It featured me getting head while I was trying to land a seaplane. Three times I touched down on the water and three times I shot back up in the air because I was out of control with arousal. Once was almost funny. Three times was the Pornoland sledge hammer. In addition to which, my sex noises sounded like they were being dubbed in by Jerry Lewis.

If that wasn't *Three Stooges* enough, we had Carol Doda in the movie. She was still channeling Mae West. "Is that a pistol in your pocket or are you happy to see me?" She played my secretary Dolly Jean and had a running love affair with Madame Lau's driver Guido. It was pretty silly stuff and the whole movie might have been better served if we had just kept it all going in that direction.

Because on day two, when we moved to San Francisco to shoot the rest of the movie, Christie MacDonald took over directing large chunks of the script. I thought he was just the art director and that he was helping Charles out, but he wasn't doing anything funny.

Specifically, Christie seemed responsible for all of the deeply meaningful mystical chit-chat that would be going on between Madame Lau and Christopher Hamilton for the rest of the movie. And there was a lot of it. In between related sex scenes, it was dark and moody stuff. There was no intentional ha-ha involved. It was come shots and Kierkegaard.

Day Three

It came out of nowhere. On day three came the best sex scene I ever had. It was with Annette Haven.

I know, I know, I said earlier that the best sex scene I ever had was with Georgina Spelvin in The Dancers. *And you know what? It was. And in a couple of chapters from now, I'm gonna tell you that I did the best sex scene I ever had with Samantha Fox in* Irresistible. *And it was too!*

You probably forgot by now, but you're still listening to the man who lost his virginity three times back in 1966.

All three of these sex scenes were great. I was in more than a hundred and these were the only great ones. "Great" is not a term I bandy about loosely. Choosing the best between them is impossible. Near perfect they were, each in their own way. They were just different, that's all. All three deserve to be called the greatest. Like Jack Johnson, Joe Louis, and Muhammad Ali, like Marilyn Monroe, Brigitte Bardot, and Julie Christie, all three were the greatest.

And this one in Madame Lau *was all about Annette Haven.*

– Gordon Archive/Annette Haven

The Main Event.

On day three, it seemed like Annette and I had been doing hours and hours of this long, dry dialogue. Our biggest challenge was just to remember the lines, which were being written and then rewritten as we went along. It wasted time, money and energy that we hadn't done all this in rehearsal, but, aside from Spinelli, that was the X-rated business.

At the end of that very long day, Annette and I got to make love. It was like a reward.

I would not presume to speak for Annette Haven, but after what had been our long courtship, it seemed that Annette and I had developed some genuine passion for each other. Since such a union did not fit into our private lives, we had it to give to the movies. We had experienced foreplay in that getting-to-know-you embrace in *Las Vegas Maniacs* and in the hand job from the day before. This was to be our main event.

We were two young and healthy bodies at the very peak of our physical powers. We were both born lucky enough, and had worked hard enough, to be pretty! In addition, we both took our acting seriously. In our scene work, we were as eager to win the respect of each other, as we were to please our bosses.

– VCX.com

The set that day was a dark, candlelit room. We began the lovemaking with a massage. I was placed face down on a glamorous bed of fur while Annette oiled and massaged my back, bottom and legs.

It was the bridge over the troubled waters. It was not the usual, "You drop your drawers and you suck him until he gets hard" kind of direction. This was something else. This was taking the time to develop the mood and relax the lovers. This was taking the time to get it right.

Annette's massage was lovely. Her strong hands and long strokes eased away all the pre-sex jitters I knew so well. The massage turned me dreamy and cuddly. There were soft lights, fuzzy furs, and Annette Haven was caressing my entire body. I became eager for the sex. Arousal came all by itself. All I had to do was turn over.

– VCX.com

When I did, Annette mounted me and joyously rode for her own pleasure as well as mine. Giddy-up. In a massive understatement, she liked being on top. It was all fine with me. The cameras rolled. There was no need for an "Oh, baby," soundtrack or any of the traditional porn mugging of acting passion. We were genuinely there.

We'd both been through enough movie sex to let them get all the angles and footage that they required without letting their process be in our way. It became one of the few times in my entire career that I was ever more into the sex than I was the filmmaking. They played with their lights and cameras and we played with each other.

When they finished shooting, they quietly shut down their equipment and just left the room. We hardly noticed. We continued until all the wax was melted, for both of us. It was a lovely experience.

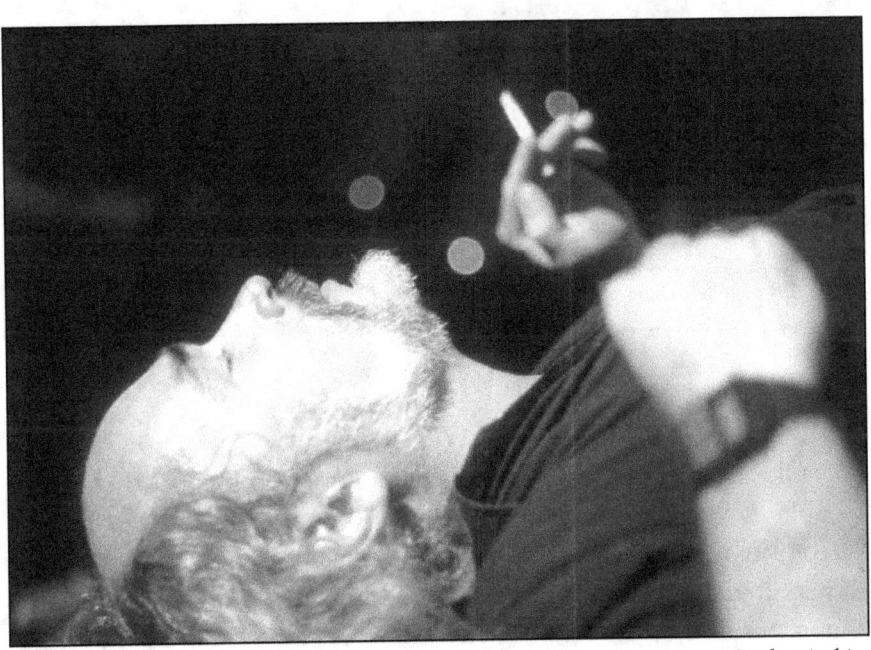

– Gordon Archive

Charles de Santos.

Director Charles is to be applauded for his fine touch in creating this scene, as well as his wisdom in knowing when to leave well enough alone.

When I'm eighty years old and dream back on the days I pretended I was Casanova, this will be a scene that I should like to see again.

Day Four

On the fourth day, I was pretty pooped. They had me do an outdoor scene on a San Francisco rooftop with Georgina. I had to struggle to get it up and keep it up. I felt embarrassed. I was reduced to hanging in there.

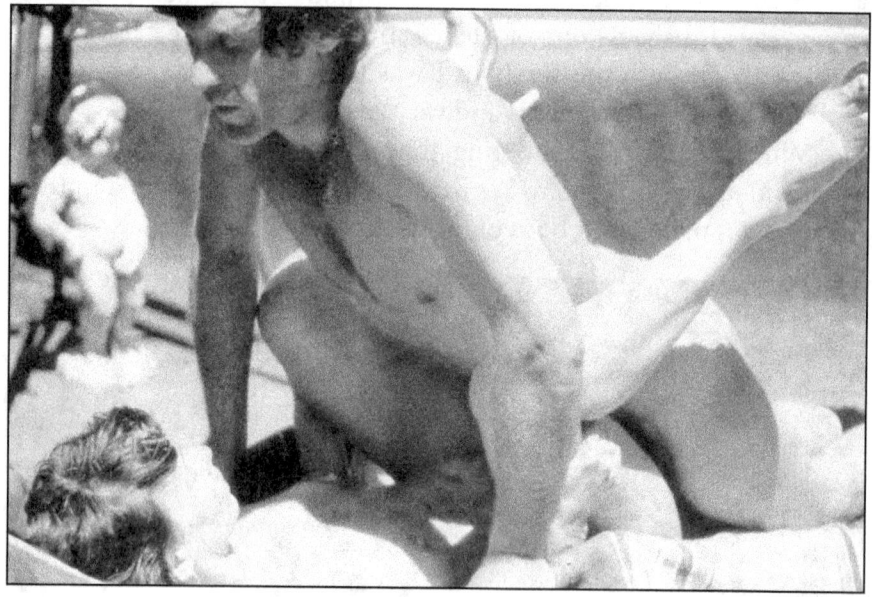

– *VCX.com*

Georgina & Howie on the rooftop.

Like a boxer used to three-round preliminary fights, I was having trouble moving up in class and going at this longer distance. I apologized over and over to Georgina for the delays. No woman really wants to hear that. It's humiliating enough that the guy is having trouble getting aroused. It's just a trying situation all way round. Georgina was sympathetic and patient. For that I was grateful. A man is just so pathetic and vulnerable when his great blade wheezes and sputters.

Nature abhors the vacuum. The young bucks paw the earth and snort. They will attack the old stag and try to kill him. If not, they will just drive him off and take over his females. But these were not the African plains of the Serengeti—this was just a rooftop in San Francisco.

Eventually, we tortured me into an orgasm and I went home to try and get a good night's sleep. I still had two days to go.

– Gordon Archive

Y'know, one must marvel here how the author can expect our sympathy. All he has to do is have sex to earn his daily bread and yet he has the nerve to complain. I suppose that's the whole point. There were no bad days in the dream of being the sex star. Reality proved to be something else. I read somewhere that it was the great English playwright, George Bernard Shaw, who once said, "Hell is when you have to do, what you like to do!"

Day Five

There was a lot more dialogue with Annette and I had to have sex with three different women and come on a mannequin.

The ladies of the day were Phae Burd, a young, uncredited French woman, who barely spoke any English, and Laura Lazare. Both Laura and the mannequin were made up to look like Farrah Fawcett, the femme fatale of the age.

It was a workmanlike day at the ranch. I did my job well. The French girl deserved some note. She was memorable because she began wildly screaming as soon as I entered her. She bounced and bucked and did all the work of the sex at a furious, phony, and unsustainable pace. It was a good show, but it didn't fit the scene at all. We had to calm her down. She was a young, happening ball of fire. Without the benefit of language, it took a while.

And she certainly awakened somebody else's interest besides my own. When she went to dress herself after the scene, she discovered that someone had stolen her both her pants and her panties. She had to leave the set that day with her raincoat buttoned.

Day Six

The last day of the shoot, it was another sex scene with Annette.

– VCX.com

Annette & Howie as teenagers.

We were teenagers making out on a couch. I wanted to deflower her. She didn't want me to do it. Then she did. Then she didn't. Then she did again, and we did it.

When I arrived on the set that day, producer Aaron Linn smiled at me and said, "You look a little tired." I was, but this was the last scene, the home stretch. Nobody was in a hurry and the pressure was off. The scene itself was a real turn-on for me. I'd had a lot of experience wrestling with girlfriends in the backseat. There were a lot of hot memories in that vault.

Annette and I were very comfortable with each other here. It was nostalgic and charming. This was puppy love and it was nice.

- *VCX.com*

Putting on the condom.

We used a condom in the scene, as we would have back when we were both a lot younger. You didn't see many condoms in the porn world of the Golden Age. Birth control pills had rendered them relics and AIDS had yet to become a factor in the need to protect ourselves from disease.

I thought the best part of the scene happened just after I had come. Annette hadn't, but she'd been very close. In a way that only Annette Haven could, she threw everybody off of the set but me and we continued until she got hers too. Then, we invited them back in to finish their movie.

Epilogue

Several months later, Annette and I were summoned to a San Francisco studio to do some voice-overs. We held hands while we watched ourselves making love on the screen and tried to match the movements of our lips with appropriate moans and groans. It was all very awkward and silly. We had no sex in the studio that day though I confess I had hoped we might. It seemed that our time had passed.

Epilogue Part Two

I watched the movie! Twenty-eight years later, I watched the movie. Wow.

The music was good! How often can you say that about a porn film? Tucki Bailey wrote the original score and Kathleen Amorose wrote the lyrics to "The Temptress," *Madame Lau's* theme song. Hey guys, if you're still out there, nice going!

I did the whole movie in a British accent. Occasionally, it wasn't bad! And once in a while, mind you, I actually nailed Richard Burton's voice. Thank you very much.

Then, there was my body. I was in my early thirties then, still in peak physical condition. Wow, what a gift it was that I got to have a body like that even for a little while. My thanks to the great cosmic prop man!

There really were two directors, by the way! In the opening credits, *both* Charles De Santos and Christie MacDonald are listed under Director.

Remember all that time I spent telling you about how I didn't have an orgasm with Kay Parker in that first love scene on the beach? Well, forget that! When you watch the movie, you'll see that I did! Apparently, they shot another couple on the beach at Clear Lake and cut their orgasm footage into my scene with Kay. I could tell because, when I came, all of a sudden my ass was a whole lot hairier than it was in the rest of the scene. It was movie magic!

Speaking of which, they also added more hardcore footage to my scene with Georgina too. I was so caught up in my own sexual meltdown that day that I hadn't noticed how terrific Georgina really was in that scene. She played my boss and my mentor, a kind of Mrs. Robinson figure and her performance was outstanding.

When you see this scene in the movie, it's actually quite good. It's hot. It's got nothing to do at all with my earlier depressing remembrance of torturing myself into arousal. This was one scene that they really did "fix in the post." It was a huge improvement!

But more than all of this, what really jumped out at me from watching the movie after all these years was in seeing how much I was in love with Annette.

Our sex scenes just crackled with it. I had always remembered that first scene as being so special between us, and it was, but it was the second one that completely surprised me, the one where we were the young lovers. I rarely knew passion like that in the movies. When I heard the sounds of my orgasm in that scene, it had nothing to do with acting, and that's as good as it gets.

Chapter Forty

> Q: *How can you tell if an elephant has been in the refrigerator?*
> A: *You can see his footprints in the butter.*
>
> - old elementary school riddle

Yeah, let's talk about that elephant in the room again. I hear this married man going on and on about loving Annette Haven and I wonder what's up with that? I know for a fact that he also loved Kelly Nichols too. And there was Sharon Kane way back at the beginning of his career. And later on, there'll be Shauna Grant and Kay Parker and Nina Hartley.

Is it only men who are foolish enough to think that they can keep people compartmentalized into relationships that don't spill over on to each other? I'll keep this woman over here and that woman over there.

Do women think like that too?

Actors and actresses play with life, both on screen and off. For most, it's all just part of that lifestyle.

Cybill Shepherd wrote well of the practice in her autobiography, *Cybill Disobedience* (2000):

> "It's a nod to the hyper reality of the film business that

everybody in Hollywood knows the maxim: no names on location. Cast and crew conspire in an implicit acceptance and discretion about the phenomenon of musical beds, about who is seen emerging from which star's trailer or which grip's room at the Motel 6. The set is like an office Christmas party, where indiscretions are absolved when the party's over, or like the miniature village around the model trains that I coveted as a child, a bantam community assembled for fun. Everyone has a common purpose, everyone is paid to be creative, and everyone can pretend to be someone else. It's a dreamscape of sorts, basically free of familial and adult responsibilities. I was twenty years old when I entered that world, mischievous and recklessly self-absorbed."

Yeah, it was fun to play pretend. It was fun to be a star. It was fun to make money. But, the greatest gift by far of working in the X-rated industry was the incredible intimacy I got to share with some truly extraordinary women along the way.

Y'know, you can fuck somebody all day long, or even fuck them two, three, four, maybe five or six different times and still never have a whiff of intimacy. The carnal knowledge of having sex does open the door, but it doesn't necessarily get you invited into the house.

Just as in real life, intimacy is different. It's something else. It's special. It only happens when it happens, but getting naked and going through the make-believe of such biblical knowing, certainly creates all kinds of opportunities that most people don't get to have while they're working in an office. Besides, that's not make-believe. That's real life, and the consequences for such behaviors there tend to be much more severe.

Actors and actresses are lucky that way. They get to make trade of feelings and emotions as if these things are somehow controllable commodities. And when they're not, when things get tangled and the shit hits the fan, there is still that safety net. It all comes out in the wash when the film or play is wrapped and the make-believe abruptly comes to an end. Somebody turns off the lights, locks up all the doors, and says,

"Everybody go home."

The industry served us well in the early years of our marriage. I was in no way ready to embrace monogamy then, and being an actor in the X-rated world provided me with a safety valve, a protected zone where I could continue to sort out the confusions and contusions of my lusts and loves without putting too heavy a burden on my primary relationship. We had an arrangement. What happened on a movie set or a location was one thing, what happened at home was another.

All that, by the way, was seriously about to change. On September 15, 1981, Carly phoned from the doctor's office to tell me we were pregnant. The balance of power would never be the same.

Chapter Forty-One

– Gordon Archive.

We called the baby "Junior Mints" right from the start.

I wrote in my diary:

> *A big turn of the wheel.*
> *The egg took the sperm. "Houston, we have lift-off!"*
> *A newt was hard at work yesterday growing its tail in Carly's belly. Sometime in late May or early June, another in a series of biologically reproduced humans will make an entrance on the grand stage of earth-life drama. Carly and I have volunteered and pursued the seeding of this new being and will serve as parents when the egg is hatched.*
> *Nothing will ever be the same. It already isn't. Twelve months of sperm chasing egg has already remodeled our union in a dozen significant ways and from now on, our little family is going to be busy gearing up for the population explosion.*
> *Carly says, "Don't call the baby a newt!"*

"To Horse! To Horse!" There are a trillion-zillion things needing instant change. This is as good as conquering the world, Alexander, and you don't even have to leave home to do it!

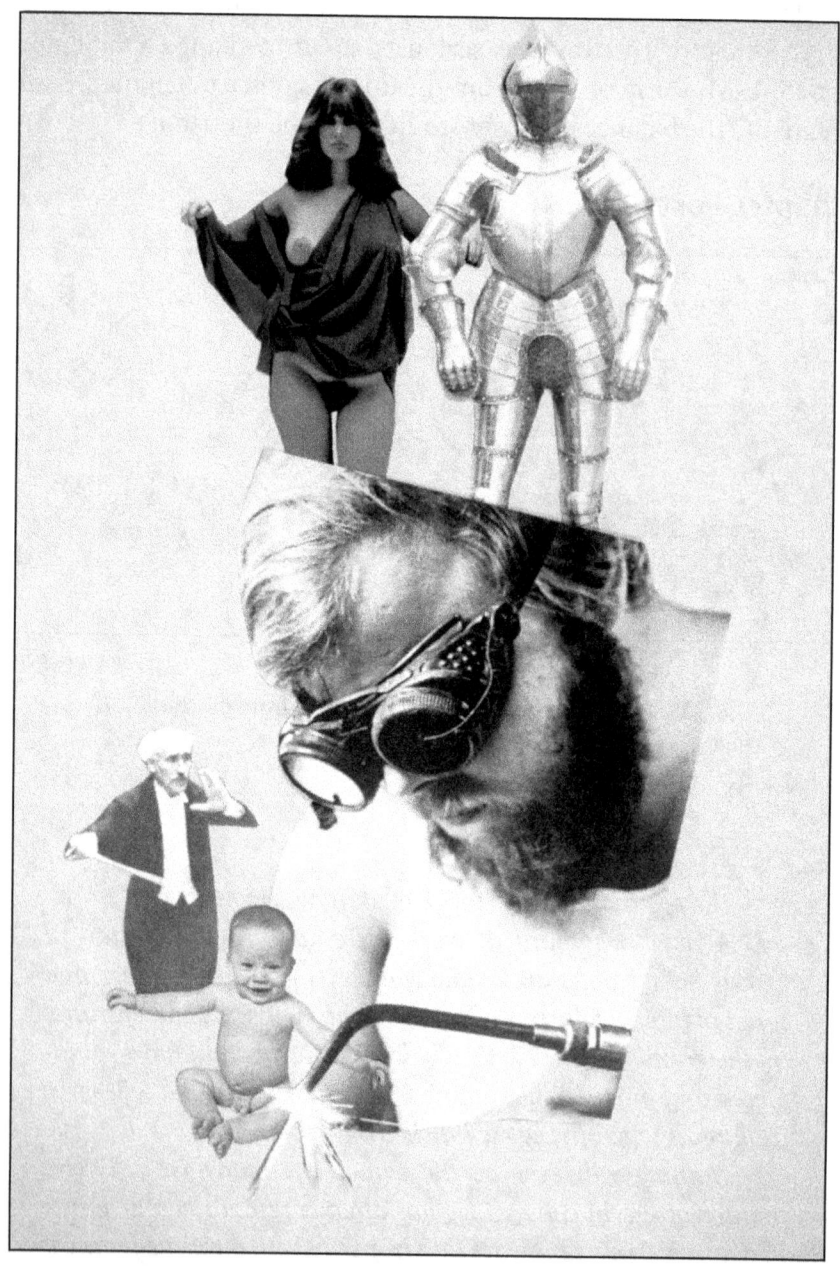

– *Gordon Archive.*

We're makin' a baby here!

Chapter Forty-Two

Weeks passed without any offers of new work. That wasn't cool. It was a most unwelcome time for a dry spell.

Spinelli wanted me to meet his old friend Chris Warfield. They were about to shoot *It's Called Murder, Baby*. It was a big-budget 1940s period piece which would eventually be released as *Dixie Ray*. John Leslie and Lisa De Leeuw were set to star. Hollywood veteran Cameron Mitchell had a role in it. Chris was producing. Sam was directing. Sam just wanted me to meet Chris to see if he might have a part in it for me.

We gathered at the Holiday Inn in San Rafael. I took along my portfolio. I met Chris Warfield. Spinelli praised me to him and him to me. Chris began looking at my book of photographs. He was turning the pages telling me how good I looked. Unfortunately, he was holding my book upside-down. I didn't correct him. Chris Warfield was suffering from glaucoma. He was very close to blind. It was sad. Chris had nothing for me in this film. Spinelli was just trying to be a friend.

On the way home, I stopped by Michael Morrison's in Sausalito to audition for a more typical X-rated film called *The Mansion*. I met Eli the director and read for him. He liked my reading and offered me a part doing a sex scene with Danielle, the film's young star. I had never met her, but recently had heard both John Leslie and Joey Silvera raving about her body.

I told Eli that the part was okay enough, but that I wouldn't work with anyone who had herpes. Now that I was pregnant, it was a whole new ballgame. I wasn't going to fuck it up. It was my understanding that an outbreak of herpes in a delivering woman would eliminate the possibility of a normal vaginal birth and would require a Caesarian section. Eli said he'd respect my wishes and would check everything out in advance. Fine. He then proceeded to offer me exactly half of my daily rate. I politely declined. He was nice about it. So was I. He told me that he wouldn't always be making such low-budget features and he hoped that we'd get to work together in the future. I told him that would be swell and that's how we left it.

Chutzpah

A week later, I'm lying in bed late one morning when the phone rings. If you must know, I had just finished masturbating. Shhh!

It's Eli. They were in the middle of shooting their movie. A guy they had hired to work with Danielle couldn't get it up. Was I willing to rush over and take his place? They would gladly pay my full rate.

It was an hour's ride to the set. It would maybe be another hour before we got to the sex. Would that be enough of a refractory period?

"Sure," I told him. "I'll be right over." I couldn't believe I said that. Never knew I had that kind of chutzpah.

"Bravery is a man in search of a test," once wrote the Sufi's. This was opportunity knocking—about $1,000 worth. I was game to give it a shot. I didn't say a word about my masturbation, but I did ask about herpes. Eli told me that Danielle was fine. "Good," I said, "good."

When this book gets made into a movie, this will be the scene where I'm rushing across the Golden Gate Bridge in my VW bus and we'll be listening to Gordon MacRae singing "My Boy, Bill" from the soundtrack of the Broadway show, *Carousel*.

> *"I got to get ready before she comes!*
> *I got to make certain that she*
> *Won't be brought up in slums*
> *With a lot o' bums like me*
> *She's got to be sheltered*
> *And fed and clothed*
> *In the best that money can buy!*
> *Now, I never knew how to make money,*
> *But, I'll try, By, God, I'll try!*
> *I'll go out and make it or steal it*
> *Or take it or die!"*

The set was a private home in Marin, I met Danielle. She was pretty. She was also young and wild and fairly discombobulated by the time I showed up on the set. We had some plot dialogue to contend with before we had to put up or shut up with the sex. I figured that all worked in my favor. It gave me more time to recover from my earlier orgasm. Director Eli went over my part with me.

I was to play a Mexican gardener whom real estate agent Danielle mistook for a wealthy patrician interested in buying the property. She seduces me thinking it will lead to a sale. It was silly porn by the numbers, par for the course.

This was Danielle's second attempt at the same scene. She was eager to get it done. I wrote in my diary:

I got aroused, but it was weak. I lost my hard-on a few times and mercifully, got it back each time. Much sweat later, I spilled some seed on Danielle's tummy and thought immediately about getting paid. I knew I had dared to skate on thin ice and that I was lucky to have not fallen in.

- Gordon Archive.

This one was all about the money.

Chapter Forty-Three

Around the fifth month of that first pregnancy, Carly and I hit a really big snag. I was in the midst of another dry spell of no movie work and our sex life at home had become a dismal mess.

I asked myself, *"Do you think I should be afraid to write embarrassing things about myself?"* And I answered, *"I don't see how you could write anything else."*

Confessions of a Pregnant Husband

After examining my wife, the good doctor had calmly assured us that our sex life could continue until very late in the pregnancy. "Unless, of course," he said, "you should encounter some discomfort."

Well, I knew he was going to say that. I'd already read it in all the books. I was just stalling for time.

Carly looked over at me apprehensively. I could not meet her gaze. Under a smiling mask, I was a man in a panic trying stubbornly to bluster my way through the confusion.

Well, yes, Doctor, I should have said. *We have encountered some difficulty in our sex life. We don't have one anymore and I think that I'm about to explode!*

But I didn't tell the doctor that and my wife joined me in the conspiracy of silence. Unwilling to play our little psychodrama in public, we made the good show of being the happy couple as we gathered up our things and left his office. He was actually the wrong kind of doctor anyway. Looking back, we didn't need the obstetrician-gynecologist for Carly, we needed a shrink for me.

It was the fifth month of our first pregnancy. The problem was that I had already lost my lover to my child and the kid wasn't even born yet. Welcome to parenthood. It's not what you would imagine either. *I was the one insisting that we not have any sex!!*

Can you believe that? I sure couldn't. It made no sense to me at all. I was so horny I was ready to burst. Oh, we still slept together in the same bed, but we didn't touch anymore. When her foot would drift over and touch mine under the covers, I'd pull mine away. Do you know what my mother would have called that? "Cutting off your nose to spite your face!" Hi, mom!

How did I allow myself to get twisted into such a pretzel of conflicting emotions? I wasn't sure, but I knew it had gotten to the point where I couldn't find my own ass without a seeing-eye dog.

Sex and pregnancy, there was the joker that just about destroyed our marriage. We humans have been making babies since the days of Adam and Eve. You'd think that we'd pretty much have it all figured out by now, right?

It just seems to be our human nature, that each generation must rediscover the wheel for itself. Each couple having that first baby seems doomed to act as if they were the first people on earth to ever give birth. Carly and I were no different.

In the beginning, it was all strawberries and cream. After twelve long months of trying to conceive, we finally got the word that the magic had taken place. We were pregnant and we glowed.

It was one of those events in life that felt like we had at last reached the finish line. For about ten seconds. Holy shit, we were pregnant! Everything was just getting started.

There were wonderful and excited phone calls to parents, relatives and friends. The International-Hand-Me-Down-Baby-Network soon began leaving gifts at our front door. We had to sign up for doctors and classes. The baby's nursery had to be planned. Construction and painting had to happen. We felt like it all had to be done by tomorrow because the baby was on the way. It was a time bursting with creative energy.

This initial euphoria eventually yielded to a more practical approach as we settled down to pace ourselves for the nine-month marathon into parenthood. We wanted the baby. We were going to have the baby. We felt blessed.

Prior to any thoughts of children, Carly and I were basically on a once-a-day sexual program. The old saw went, "A day without wine is like a day without sunshine." Well, we pretty much felt that way about sex. It was the highlight of our day. Orgasm was very important to both of us. Variety was encouraged to be part of this program and we both shared responsibility for orchestrating our fantasies into mating rituals.

As we continued into the pregnancy, however, our sex life began to change. In deference to her changing body, we seemed to have the sex more and more to accommodate her needs. I had the task of remaining passionate without offending her rapidly changing body.

At first, I thought nothing of it. Like most pregnant spouses, I suppose, I had never loved my wife more.

As the weeks passed, though, sex became more and more difficult for us. Instead of increasing her arousal, my touch frequently made her flinch. It was not a pleasant experience for either one of us to encounter. I became hesitant about touching her. Her breasts became so sensitive that a stiff breeze seemed able to make her jump. Her body's need for orgasm totally disappeared. All of our old, well-established sexual rhythms and patterns became useless.

To my shock, guilt and disappointment, the more my wife's belly grew, the less interested I became in having sex with her.

A good therapist might have said, "Because he feels responsible, for having made her pregnant, he is even more sensitive and vulnerable to her feelings of resentment. Whatever goes wrong in the pregnancy will seem to him as though it is his fault."

I would have said, "Bingo!" to that, pal, but we weren't seeing a therapist. And as far as sex was concerned, I had lots of desire, but less and less of it was for my own wife! Oops! Yes, I was having fantasies about other women! Almost all of them! I was mentally undressing them in elevators, at the supermarket, on the street.

What is it with these elevators? That's a recurring theme in here.

Don't bother me now, I'm on a roll. I was daydreaming about the neighbor's breasts. I was imagining Carly's friends without their clothes on. I wasn't acting on any of these impulses, mind you, but my dick was definitely looking everywhere. The guilt was enormous. It seems my timing couldn't have been worse.

As our sexual encounters at home became more and more like another chore that I had to perform, I simply started to withdraw from her. Hell, I had just finished twelve months of incredibly passionless, medically-directed-technical-like sex in order to get pregnant. Now that we were finally there, I just didn't want any more exercises in obligatory sex. The thrill was gone and I was having trouble faking it.

Naturally, being a man, I kept all of this to myself while the frequency of our sexual intercourse dwindled.

All of his loneliness, the good therapist would have observed, and his resentment about being displaced can get turned in on himself. Although he may wish he could be angry or show some outward sign of resenting the intrusion of the pregnancy, he must remind himself of his own responsibility for it.

No one seems to care what a father-to-be is going through. His wife or mate has her hands full with her own adjustment. It seems that her parents and even his parents are more concerned about her. All their friends ask her how she's feeling.

It's a shame I didn't have this therapist as my tennis partner at the time. He could have saved us a world of trouble. Alas, all I had was me and I had painted myself into a corner. I seemed determined just to sit there and wait until the paint dried. I wrote in my diary:

> *Frankly, chums, I'm ready for a long boat ride to the Ukraine.*
> *My salad has been tossed so much lately that it's starting to look like guacamole.*
> *On the darker side of pregnancy, it is awfully hard to be Sir Galadad, the perfect husband, on a 24-hour call. It's been five months and I have ignored every call of the wild that has come my way in the name of decency, true love and the nuclear family, but I'll tell ya what, kids, the gas shortage has come home. I feel like I have three kind words left for my wife and they are, "See you later!"*
> *I'm ready to go to Europe and come back after the baby is born.*
> *This doesn't seem too real to me as a possibility, but not much does these days except service—husbandly service. The biggest surprise of the pregnancy so far is how turned off I've become to having sex with my pregnant wife."*

It was the pattern in our relationship that if one of the partners hit some kind of sullen bump and withdrew their affections, they were allowed about three days to work it out by themselves. It was usually me and at the end of that time Carly would do the confrontation and ask the appropriate questions.

We would try to act like the best friends that we were and create a back room where we could both go to find out what they were doing out there with their lives. It was a concept that had worked well for us in the past, but this time around, the results were not so great.

I met her first attempts at understanding me with stiff-armed rejection. When she continued pressing, I finally confessed that I had absolutely no desire left to have any more sex with a pregnant woman. I said that it just turned me off completely.

Did you ever hear words coming out of your own mouth that you couldn't quite believe yourself? That's where I was stuck. I was like ice fishing on a frozen lake without any hole. I was arguing passionately like I knew what I was talking about and yet, I couldn't quite find the way to get at the real stuff underneath the surface, but I didn't let that stop me. I blustered on.

There's an old phrase in psychology that "in stress, we regress." Well, believe it. I found myself dusting off my old sixties and seventies anti-monogamy speeches. As you might well imagine, Carly turned to utter mush. She was not overly thrilled to hear that I was actually entertaining the idea of having other lovers at this particular point in our relationship.

In an elevator?

Oh, shut up! I felt like a total slime, but I really didn't know what else to do anymore. I was exploding internally. Desperation was talking. I just wanted to keep her at arm's length. I kept my own comfort in my journal:

> This pregnancy has my responsible-mate button turned up to 99.9 and Carly has gotten very used to it. It's only five months down and four to go. Even then, the old ways are over. There's no return to normal. We're going to be having a baby living around here.
>
> It makes me dizzy. I'm just doing a lot of shaking my head and hanging on.
>
> I could use a weekend of oblivion with a couple of Las Vegas hookers and what I get are more natural childbirth classes and books about newborns. My life is one giant should. I've been doing pretty well on all the tests, but, seriously folks, I'm ready for a break.
>
> The problem is that Carly doesn't get any breaks. She can't put her belly on the shelf and say, "I'll be back Monday," so, I'm shamed into sticking with it too.
>
> I don't know what we're going to do about sex. Putting myself into a pregnant woman is one of the most redundant experiences I have ever encountered. I have no taste for it. They say that love can move mountains. Well, it better because unless our sex trip gets a little bit more harmonious, I hate to even think about it.

Obviously distressed, Carly could not long endure my stubborn requests to be left alone sulking, skulking, and spewing poison. When she decided that she wanted to probe my insides, there weren't too many forces in the known universe that I could use to stop her.

One day in the midst of all this, she just announced that she plainly refused to accept my right of privacy in this situation any longer. I responded by putting an ashtray through a double-hung window to keep her at bay. Whoa, Nellie, this was definitely a no-no and "one toke over the line, sweet Jesus." It sure gave me a lot to think about as I cleaned up all the broken glass and had to replace the window. I was fucked up.

There was help out there, I guess. I don't know why I didn't seek it. John Wayne lives, I suppose! A man was supposed to be able to take care of his family. A man was supposed to be able to take care of himself. It seemed like I was failing on both counts and just trying hard to ride out the storm.

The ashtray through the window alarmed us both a lot. It revealed the depth of my chaos and the passion of my frustration. My wife's resolution after much argument, pain and grief was to accept my proposal that we weren't going to have sex again until after the baby was born. This was supposed to be a victory for me. It wasn't. It was dumb. Even I knew that. It made no sense. A murky distance developed between us. It was like back in the old days when we were courting and still had secrets from each other. Our whole relationship seemed to be on trial.

Despite her tears and over her protests, I arranged a time-out for myself to go have a lost weekend with a hooker-type I knew. I thought of it as just calling the plumber to get my pipes cleaned. Carly didn't think of it that way at all. She was crushed. In the past, she would have just gone out, picked up some other guy, and matched me tit for tat. With her swollen belly, it wasn't like she could play the game the way we used to.

When the time came for my date with "the plumber," I ended up canceling. I called my own bluff and came up empty. I got in deep enough to see that I didn't really want to have sex with another woman, I was in enough trouble already with the woman I had. We passed that weekend in some kind of suspended animation, barely talking to each other.

Then one day, not long after, for reasons known only to God and a few of her cousins, the clouds just parted and the sun finally came out. I woke up early one morning to go off and do some job interview and just stared at Carly while she slept. *I missed our love.*

Her breathing was fitful and uneasy. I stroked her hair and she calmed. I tried to imagine what the baby looked like napping in her belly. A warm flood of emotions washed over me. Something that had been badly out-of-whack was falling back into place. I wanted to hug and kiss her all over. It had been far too long. I had loved this woman above all others so much so that I had made her my wife. Now, she was carrying my child. I popped. The tears came, but I had to go. I had to leave. She slept through the whole thing. I left her this note:

"Hey, this was the part where he totally panicked. I love you. I'll see you later."

When I got home that night, I swallowed a lot of pride and confessed all my sins. I was tired of all the constant worrying about the pregnancy. I was incredibly scared about us having a baby. And most importantly, I was frustrated and angry at the way the pregnancy had dealt her such a controlling hand in everything, especially in all of our acts of intimacy.

A powerless man does not many boners make. You can quote me. I explained that I couldn't quite seem to put together my lust with her pregnant body.

The road back began with love. I loved my wife and I loved that we were going to have a baby. I just got a bit lost in the jet stream of such a miraculous comet.

When it came down to the nitty-gritty of our having sex, we had to throw out what almost ten years of being lovers had taught us. It no longer applied. Okay, we had to go back to square one and learn how to touch each other all over again. After all, it was still "us." We could do this. Yes, there were grateful hugs and tears.

That night, Carly put on some trashy negligee and we laughed and squealed like we hadn't done in months. Love had us laughing again. We were ready to go on.

Most people think of the nine months of the pregnancy as the time it takes for the baby to develop, but the lovers need that time too, to begin becoming parents. There is such a wondrous bubble of intimacy that surrounds the creation of a new life between a man and a woman. Old ways are exploded and new ways must be found.

We grew into something way beyond the basic lust that it had taken for us to start our baby's life. Our full energies seemed to get soaked up into making each other feel safe and ready to become parents. It was clear that the nine months provided a growing time for everybody. One marvels at the Creator's plan and rightfully so. We had jumped our five-month's hurdle. We were ready to keep right on going.

When a man learns his wife is pregnant, the good therapist says, "he is likely to feel a flood of differing emotions. One of his first reactions may be a feeling of exclusion. He may even be fearful of losing a kind of closeness with her."

Feelings of being excluded are real ones for a young father-to-be. Not only is his wife likely to withdraw some of her energy and attention from him but she also becomes the center of everyone else's attention. Everyone is concerned with her, her health, and her feelings. They all want to take care of her. He is almost alone. No one asks him how he's doing in this period of adjustment. It can fuck him up!

Yeah, yeah, yeah, now, you tell me. Well, better late than never.

Chapter Forty-Four

At seven months pregnant, *Irresistible* came along. It was a big budget picture being produced by Sandra Wynter and written and directed by her husband, Eddie Brown, and it was right on time.

"Summer" and Eddie were probably the best husband and wife team in the business. I had auditioned for Summer before. At Annette Haven's apartment in San Francisco, she had read me for *1001 Erotic Nights*. Summer offered me a part in that, but she didn't want to pay my rate. I agonized over it. I wanted to work for them. But if I didn't hold out for my rate, no one besides Spinelli was ever gonna pay it. She wouldn't budge. In the end, I bought her some red roses, gave her kiss, and said, "No, thanks."

Now, it was paying off a year later when she cast me in the lead for *Irresistible* at my full daily rate. I liked Summer. She was a dish, a vivacious woman, smart, and with beautiful eyes. I wished that she would play one of my lovers in the movie. Like in *Madame Lau*, there would be a lot of them. This would be another sexual marathon for me but Summer Brown wasn't putting herself on the menu, on screen or off.

Too bad. At our first meeting at Annette's house, Summer had whispered in my ear, "I'm having a party in my mouth. Ya wanna come?"

Whoa! Maybe that was an oldie but a goody, but I had never heard it before. It sure spun my head around, but Summer was just laughing at me, having some fun with the younger man. She didn't mean anything by it at all.

- *TVX*

What? Yeah, I know this is a long way from being seven months pregnant with my one true love and our first baby on the way, but that was the very nature of this business. You left yourself, your wedding ring, and your clothes in the dressing room when you went out there and you had to be one hundred percent sexually available to whatever Fate or the director was gonna throw your way.

> *"Christ, y'know it ain't easy.*
> *You know how hard it can be.*
> *The way things are going,*
> *They're gonna crucify me."*
>
> *- John Lennon,*
> *"THE BALLAD OF JOHN & YOKO"*

Admittedly, it was an odd time to be leaving home, but it was the male lead in a prestigious movie and the bucks were very good. Carly and I decided that I should take the job.

Chapter Forty-Five

The phone rang. Carly answered it. A male caller. He asked if Howie was there. Carly told him, "Yes," and then asked, "who's calling?"

"Bill," he said. I came to the phone.

"Hello?"

"Is your penis big and hairy?" asked Bill.

"Ah, Bill," I said, with all the air completely coming right out of me. "Is that the best you can do?"

"No, I really want to know," he said.

"See a shrink, Bill," I suggested and hung up the phone. Carly said,

"We got to get an unlisted number!"

Chapter Forty-Six

Samantha Fox had won Best Actress at the LA Erotic Awards two years in a row. That made her the reigning Queen of the industry. She was coming in from New York to San Francisco to play my wife in *Irresistible*. I wanted to greet her in style.

– Platinum pictures

Samantha Fox.

I rented a limo and picked her up at the airport with a big bouquet of roses. Summer thought it was such a good idea that she even split the costs with me. That was nice of her. Samantha was properly tickled by the whole circus of it.

Samantha and I were put up at a hotel in San Francisco where we shared adjoining rooms. We had a week to wait before our one and only sex scene in the movie.

Early on, we spent a lot of time together rehearsing our dialogue and doing some getting-to-know-you. I was full of pregnancy stories. She was telling me all about Bobby Astyr, the boyfriend back in New York. He was a big X-rated star in his own right, often referred to as "the clown prince of porn." I had met Bobby once. I remembered his comment that "God was in-between Samantha Fox's legs." I was looking forward to gaining insight into Bobby's views of theology.

Samantha and I wondered if we were supposed to be having offstage sex. Should we practice? Rehearse? Find the lust? See if the plumbing worked? What?

Somehow, it didn't seem like the right thing to do. We decided on just being buddies and saving it all for the cameras.

I was grateful. I had to do six sex scenes in five days. I would need a lot of sleep, but I would still be very much looking forward to meeting Samantha Fox at the end of the rainbow. She was a talented, delicious woman.

Every day on the set with her became foreplay. I enjoyed watching her work. She was clearly a top-of-the-line professional. It was called The Golden Age because a lot more juice went into the performance aspect of the movie. And among the best of us, there was always great pride taken in the acting. A lot of us enjoyed that as much as the sex. And a lot of the others thought it was a complete waste of time. Well, fuck them.

Backstage, Samantha and I spoke a lot about relationships. She was trying to figure out how to get Bobby to propose marriage. I enjoyed the scheming with her. Hell, I was happy just to know her.

When our sex scene finally did come around, it was spectacular. I couldn't have written a better script for it than the way it unfolded.

Late in the afternoon, we were doing some dialogue in bed. There had been no sex yet, just a lot of talk. During a break, Samantha had to leave the set to take a phone call from her Bobby. He was at the New York Adult Film Critic's Awards Show. When she got back in bed with me, she told me that I had just been given their Best Actor and their Best Supporting Actor Awards for that year.

WINNERS: The Adult Film Critics voted "Amanda By Night" Best Picture and its star Veronica Hart Best Actress. Richard Pacheco (left) swept the men's awards, winning both Best Actor (for "Nothing to Hide") and Best Supporting Actor (for "The Dancers"). A Special Achievement Award was given to Georgina Spelvin (left) for her "longtime contributions to the erotic film industry."

– *Johnny Castano/ADAM*

A sweep in New York!

Wow, that was a stunning bit of foreplay! The reigning Queen had just crawled into my bed and told me I'd been chosen King. Her eyes revealed a happiness and a respect. My spirits soared. I felt that I had earned my place to be next to her.

We finished shooting the dialogue and then dressed for the climactic love scene of the movie. Costumed in 1964 wedding finery, we were going to shoot the love scene of our wedding night. We'd been building up to it all week.

When the sex was about to commence, director Eddie Brown made a gesture of genius. He put on some mood music. It was Air

Supply's "Every Woman In the World," a popular love song of the day.

– Vincent Fronczek/TVX

Nose to nose with Samantha.

– Vincent Fronczek/TVX

It was ten pounds of uncut schmaltz. I adored it. They would later edit it out of the film so that they wouldn't have to pay anybody residuals, but Eddie wanted to use it during shooting for the effect it would have on us. It was brilliant! It was a majestic home run right out of the ballpark!

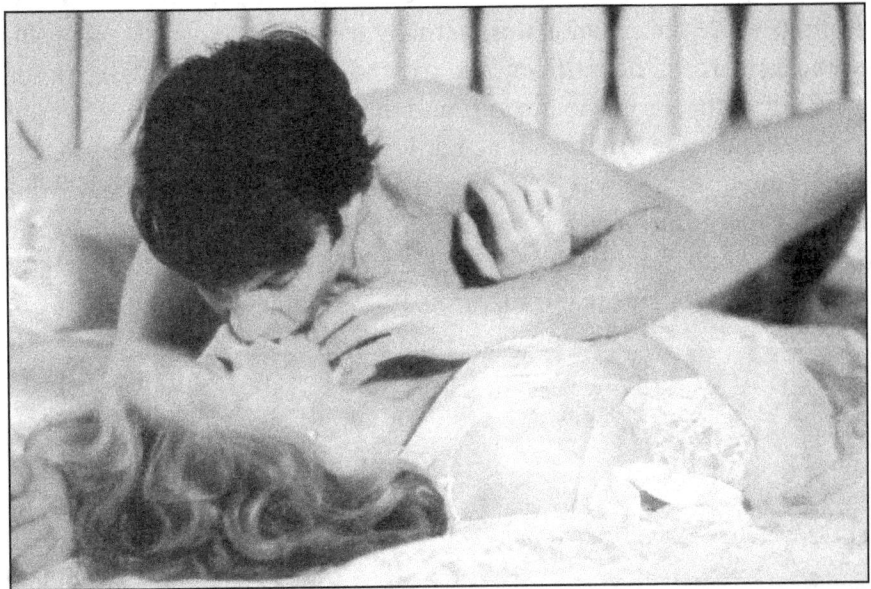

— Vincent Fronczek/TVX

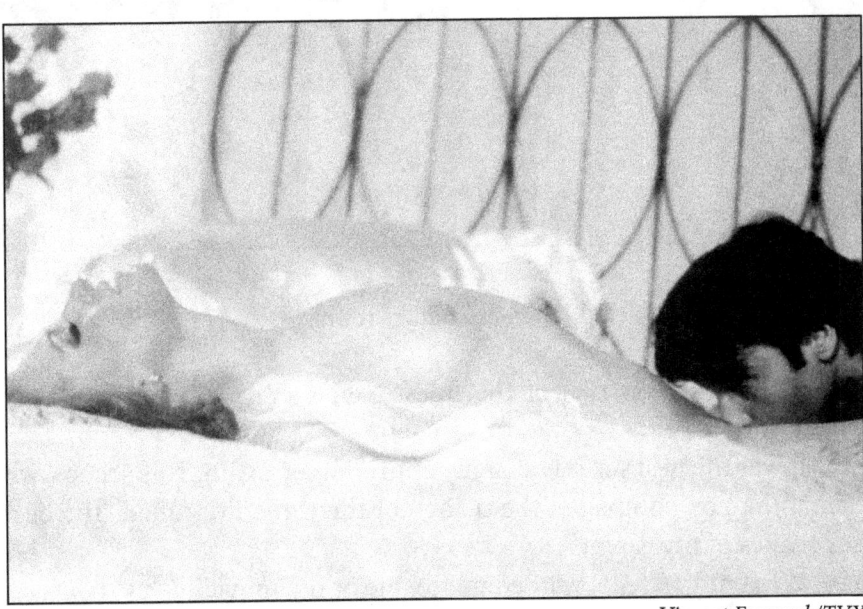

— Vincent Fronczek/TVX

The music elevated the beast. A sex scene became a love scene. Our spirits entwined. We were a husband and wife in the movie who had just rediscovered each other after surviving an intense marital crisis. This was the healing. This was the consummation. This was a romantic joining of love and lust. What a joy it was to be feeling all of those feelings while the cameras were actually rolling. The specialness of this scene came from the intimacy and trust we had earned with each other.

Samantha Fox was strong, and proud, and beautiful. She was creamy and free. I marveled at Eddie's touch and then I marveled at hers. I ate it up. She was every woman in the world to me. She was my Carly. I was her Bobby. For one brief moment, it was all the same stuff. It was transcendent. In that scene, we were two actors at the height of our powers on a free trip to paradise.

– Gordon Archive

Director Eddie Brown.

The music was one of the finest triggers any director had ever pulled for me.

It was the best sex scene of my entire career, again. This scene with Samantha Fox completed the trilogy of the three I've called "the best sex scenes of my career."

When my parents wanted to see one of my movies, *Irresistible* was the one I chose. I showed them the R-rated version, *Simply Irresistible*.

It played on Showtime for a while. What a kick it was to see my name in the TV listings. My dad confessed that he was surprised I actually spoke lines in the movie! "You were good," he said. "My son, the actor!"

And my mother wanted to see me on the *Johnny Carson Show*. Couldn't give her that one. It never happened.

Chapter Forty-Seven

"You're stuck again!"

"God! It's you!" I was surprised to see Him. A visit from God is always something special.

"What's going on?" He asked.

"The Steelers," I said. He just interrupted me.

"Fuck the Steelers!" He said.

"You did! Last night," I told him. "You had New England shit all over them. They couldn't even touch Tom Brady."

"This isn't about the Steelers," He said.

"You're right," I told him.

"I know," He said. "It's funny how it always seems to work out that way." There was a pause. "You haven't written anything in almost two months."

"I know."

"Say his name," He told me.

"Harold," I said.

"Good," He said. "Now, say it again."

"Harold."

"Okay," He said, "Now, get back to work."

Chapter Forty-Eight

My in-laws were driving up from San Diego. It was late March of 1982. They were driving North for the baby shower and bringing us a crib. When the phone rang, I thought it was them. It wasn't. It was Harold's wife.

"Harold flipped out," she said. I didn't know what to say. "All the way out," she continued. "He killed himself. He put a steak knife through his own heart." Jesus.

She gave me whatever details she gave me then, but none of it really registered. There was just the one glaring fact to comprehend. My friend Harold was dead.

Harold was my partner. Harold was my buddy. Harold and I were gonna conquer the world together.

First it was Harold and David and David and Harold. They were like best friends from before kindergarten. By the time they got to high school, David had to straighten up to one day make it into medical school. He began refusing some of Harold's invitations to run off and join the circus. David had to stay home and do his homework. I didn't. That's when Harold and I started having some after school adventures. On a dare one day, we hitchhiked all the way from Pittsburgh to Michigan State. It was a great trip. I became the stand-in best friend.

We had a pretty good run there as Butch and Sundance, but just after college, back in 1971, when Harold first told me that he was the reincarnation of Jesus and I was Peter, well, shit, I knew we were headed into a world of trouble.

There was a lot of talk in those days about the "generation gap," but not too many people were discussing manic depression and schizophrenia.

Look, it's a long story and this is neither the time nor the place. Besides, I've already written that book. It's called *Dear How* and it's sitting on a shelf somewhere. Trust me, it's depressing. For our purposes today, it's now 1982, and my partnership with Harold has just been permanently dissolved. Well, maybe not exactly, but I'm the only one left who is still attending the board meetings.

When the next call came, I stopped crying and answered the phone. It was Carly's parents. They were calling from Highway 5 just this side of Bakersfield. Okay. They'd had a fire in their car! What? It's okay. They were safe. They'd even been able to save the crib they were bringing to us, but their car had been destroyed.

"Can you please come and get us?" they asked.

"Yes! Of course I can. Of course I can." I didn't tell them about Harold. I didn't tell them about Harold. I had to collect myself. I had to collect myself and stop saying everything twice. I had to jump into the Volkswagen bus and get on the road. Carly was at work. I left her a long note.

It was either dark and raining when I started out or else it was just me. Carly was pulling up to the house as I was backing out of the driveway. Thank the Lord. I gave her all the news and she climbed on board the bus. We hit the road together. There was a lot of crying in the dark.

I didn't fly across the country for Harold's funeral. The only person that I would have wanted to see there was already dead.

Rumors reached me of some kind of ooga-booga about whether a suicide was allowed to be buried in certain kinds of Jewish cemeteries, but I didn't keep up with any of that crap. I still don't even know where he's buried.

Harold was so Nutsy Fagin by the end that many of us who loved him were just grateful that he only killed himself then, and that he didn't take ten other people with him on his way out the door.

Gimme strength, Lord. If I live to be a hundred, I'll still be trying to get over it.

Chapter Forty-Nine

Eighth month of pregnancy, we were getting ready for a Gemini baby. We had a budget. We'd been able to set aside enough money so that we could both just take it easy until the baby was born. After that, there was even enough for a few more months just to get ourselves used to being parents.

We had all the basics covered, but there wasn't enough money in the budget for a video camera. Hell, we needed a video camera. How can you start a new family without a video camera?

I was a star now. I was winning awards. I was charging $1,000 a day. If they weren't offering to pay me that, I was just sayin' "No," to the job, but we didn't have a video camera. Hell, we needed a video camera.

There were no "big" pictures on the horizon. There were no $1000-a-day jobs in sight. So, I went slummin'. I took a job at half my rate. I got 4 days in a low-budget number that would buy us that video camera.

Got off on the wrong foot, I did, when I showed up at the hotel for a rehearsal the night before shooting was to start. I landed in the director's room where a starlet was holding court. She was completely drugged out of her mind. Cocaine was my best guess and she couldn't stop talking. There were like seven people sitting around all waiting for her to shut up.

The director was a young cameraman I knew who was moving up to the director's chair for this job. He was helpless. Everyone in the room was waiting for him to tell her to shut up, but it appeared he didn't want to risk offending the porn princess. I was spoiled. Anthony Spinelli would have fired her, or at least got her out of the room and put her to bed until she sobered up. It was the director's job to manage this kind of crap.

I sat there for a while until I couldn't stand it anymore. I gave her both barrels about being completely unprofessional and wasting everybody's time. The starlet was stunned and the director was horrified.

Oddly enough, I was the one that he wanted to leave the room and to calm down. Evidently, my cock would be a lot easier to replace than her pussy. He didn't really care about all my acting awards.

Okay. They didn't fire me, but after that, the starlet and I were never scheduled to be on the set at the same time again. And that was a very good idea.

I had one sex scene to do in this film and it was with an actress who turned out to be having a serious outbreak of genital herpes that day. I'd been told herpes could be very big trouble for a woman giving birth so we had to create a scene to protect me in order to protect my wife.

The foreplay was not a problem. She stroked me. She sucked me. When it came time for me to appear to enter her, we placed a towel inside her thighs that completely shielded us from any skin-on-skin contact. The camera was strategically placed so that the towel would never be seen. When I "entered" her, I fucked the towel. Viewers would never know.

And that's how we got a video camera.

Chapter Fifty

Her name was Marci. It was Anthony Spinelli's *Reel People*. I think it was the most intense orgasm I ever had in the movies.

I watched it twenty-eight years later and was still amazed. I had to replay it four times. I could see on film how it had surprised me. That was rare.

When we shot that scene, I hadn't slept in three days. I'd just gotten back to the set from the hospital where my wife had only hours before given birth to our first baby. It had been Hell and Heaven and Heaven and Hell. Through a difficult birth, I had just born witness to the magic of creation. I was raw.

Anthony Spinelli was way out in front of the adult industry when he conceived and directed *Reel People*. His was the first movie to intentionally feature "amateur" sex in front of the cameras.

– *Ricston/Arrow*

Spinelli's *Reel People*.

Spinelli was on to something big, but his timing was just a little off. To begin with, *Reel People* was shot on film.

Several years later, after video had completely taken over from film, guys like Jamie Gillis and Ed Powers used "amateur porn" to create a huge craze in the industry. The lowered costs of production and the relaxed technical needs of shooting video made it a natural for amateur porn to flourish. It soon became its own genre within the business. But back in 1982, it was Anthony Spinelli who was there first.

In his initial project, Sam interviewed a number of people about their sexual fantasies and then offered some of them the chance to make those dreams come true in his movie.

Reel People featured a "professional" cast of Juliet Anderson, John Leslie, Gayle Sterling, Paul Thomas, Priscilla Shields, and Richard Pacheco. Those amateurs who chose to "star" in their own sexual fantasies were soon partnered up with the "pros" to help make it all happen.

It was a different kind of erotic movie and it had some very hot scenes in it, mine included.

Sam needed investors to make *Reel People*. Money behind porn was no different than money behind anything else. It was conservative. It didn't like to take risks. None of the conventional porn funding sources were interested in backing Sam's oddball idea.

Sam asked me if I wanted to invest any of my money in his film.

Well, sure I did. Sam was making my name in this business. He was my friend, my mentor, my advisor, and my director. Naturally, I wanted to help him out.

I only said, "No," once to Sam in my whole career. I had shown up for work one day and without asking me, he had arranged for me to do a sex scene with an older woman. I was early thirties, she was early sixties. It was beyond anything I could even imagine. Every inch of me said, "No." Sam was taken aback by the rigidity of my response. He thought I'd go for it. I didn't. He thought he could talk me into it. He couldn't. He had to get somebody else to do it. He did.

But that was it. That was the only time I ever said, "No," to Sam and was able to make it stick. "Yeah, I'd like to invest some money in your film," I said, "but first I'm gonna have to talk it over with Carly."

Okay, so Carly and I had saved up a little money to take care of us while we were having the baby. When I told her that I thought we should take about half of that and invest it with Sam, she stuck her foot so far up my ass I could've licked her toes. You don't rock the boat of a pregnant woman.

Alright, so we weren't gonna touch that money, but we still wanted to help out Sam. We decided to go to the Bank of America and took out a personal loan. For $2500 we became ten percent owners of *Reel People*. Wow, we were just like the grown-ups! Carly and I were now associate producers!

Shooting got underway Sunday morning, May 15, at the Circle S Ranch in Lafayette. They often held swing parties there. Place had a giant hot tub. It was a great location.

While Spinelli began conducting his amateur interviews, I was on standby with the other stars of the film waiting for him to match us up.

However, since I also was an associate producer whose personal money was now tied up with the success of this production, I also found myself sweeping floors, schlepping equipment, moving furniture, and even buying, preparing, serving lunch, and cleaning up afterward.

In the early afternoon, we hit a major snag. Spinelli took Ricky Frazzini and me aside and confessed that he was not feeling well. Ricky was like Sam's personal assistant, his right-hand man. He also was another one of the producers of this film.

Sam was shaken and his color was not good. Spinelli was a veteran of open-heart surgery, but he didn't feel the need for us to call 911. His plan was just to go back to his motel room and lie down. He wanted Ricky and me to continue and finish shooting the first day's work. He gave us our marching orders and then quietly left the set. He did not want to alarm anybody else and he fully expected to be back in the saddle bright and early the next day.

Ricky and I were now co-directors. Between us, we had zero directing experience. We were not exactly brimming with confidence. Our first act was to call a production meeting and tell everybody else what had just happened. We didn't think it was such a good idea, or even possible, to keep it all a secret.

Right away some argued that we should just shut the production down. The logic was that we hadn't shot that much film yet and maybe it would just be better to quit right now before we wasted a lot of money. This was Spinelli's movie. No one else really knew what was going on and nobody really knew if Spinelli would really be coming back tomorrow.

On the other hand, Spinelli had given us his orders. We knew what he wanted us to do for the rest of the day. If we didn't get that done, it was guaranteed to push us behind schedule and over-budget even if Spinelli was able to come back and continue shooting tomorrow.

The consensus was to press on. We'd finish the day's work and let tomorrow take care of itself.

Ricky and I began by interviewing Chuck. Our voices would later be edited out and replaced by Spinelli's.

Chuck was an aviator who had the fantasy of having sex with two, beautiful, young women. What a coincidence! We just happened to have Gayle Sterling and Priscilla Shields all ready and waiting for him.

When Chuck dropped his drawers, he stunned us all. Chuck the mild-mannered aviator was hung like a donkey. When aroused, he was so big that he couldn't even get himself into the tiny Priscilla, though she diligently tried every which way to take him in. It was Gayle Sterling who recognized Priscilla may have been in some danger of being stretched beyond her physical capacity, and she made it her business to come to the young maiden's rescue. She redirected the ardor of Sir Chuck's great beast to her own more accommodating sheath, and both Priscilla and the scene were saved from any harm. As the scene progressed, it seemed that Gayle and Chuck were being amply rewarded for their efforts.

It was late in the afternoon as we were putting the lovers through their paces when I was called off the set for a phone call. It was Carly.

"Come home," she said, "labor's started."

I walked in the front door around 11:30 Sunday night. Our friend Karen was standing next to Carly with a clipboard. She was timing the minutes between the contractions.

Karen was a dear friend who had already given birth to two of her own children. Thank God somebody was there who knew what was going on because I turned out to be almost useless. I took all the La Maze classes with Carly, but when the real shit hit the fan, I was stuck doing bad Ricky Ricardo imitations in reruns of *I Love Lucy*.

Karen turned out to be the real labor coach. Thank God.

Y'see, we were gonna do natural childbirth. This was Berkeley. This was the revolution. We were reinventing every wheel there ever was. La Maze, Bradley, Natural Childbirth, whatever it was, bring it on.

For the "birth experience," we had each invited best friends to be there to help us out, to back us up in the Alternative Birthing Center at Alta Bates Hospital. Carly had invited Karen and I had invited Bob Ernst. They were both gonna help us out with the birth. When the moment came, Karen was able to get there and Bob Ernst wasn't. Thank God it worked out that way because Bob Ernst would have probably been as useless as I was in trying to help a woman give birth. Well, maybe not, he grew up on a farm. In any case, I was glad that Karen was there. She helped.

Look, would it be too much of a copout if I just stopped right here and spared us all the little details of me recounting the baby's birth?

Carly labored for over thirty hours, and for most of that time, I was just freaked out, stupid and dumb with anxiety, wanting to be helpful, but running around like a catfish doing the hundred-yard dash on dry land.

I was born in the wrong generation. Like my father before me, I should have been out there in the waiting room, reading endless magazines, and pestering nurses, "Is it time for me to give out the cigars yet? Is it time?"

I had no business being in there with a laboring woman, especially my wife! You know what it was like? I'll tell you what it was like. Every woman who has ever heard me say this just cringes when I say it, but that's all because they're not a man!

If they were a man, they might just agree with me when I say that being with your wife while she's going through a labor pain is like watching God fuck your wife and you don't know whether you're gonna get her back dead or alive when He's done with her. It's fuckin' scary. And if you've just taken six fucking La Maze classes, believe me, there's nothing you can fucking do to stop all the pain! "Pant-Pant-Blow," my ass!

Now, I know that I promised my mother-in-law that I would try to not to say "fucking" too fucking much, but there's nothing I can do about it in this fucking chapter.

And I'll tell you something else. If I could have gotten my hands on that fucking Natural Childbirth teacher when Carly was going through all those labor pains … I would've … I would've … I would've really hurt her feelings.

Back then, those natural childbirth classes were like some kind of political thing. They were adversarial. The doctors were painted as the bad guys. You wanted your new baby to be all healthy and holy, but the doctors were gonna hurt them with their corporate over-drugging birthing techniques.

"The doctors are going to tell you what you have to do," the teacher would say, "but you're gonna tell them, 'NO!'"

Yeah, on the strength of my six fucking touchy-feely role playing sessions at the community center, I'm supposed to dictate medical procedures to the doctors and nurses who work at the hospital.

When the first labor pain hit Carly, all her plans for natural childbirth flew right out the window. She wanted drugs. Now. She wanted help with the pain. I wanted help for her from the doctors. The last thing on this earth I wanted to do was to argue with them. I was furious with our birth class teacher for all the absolute garbage she put into our heads.

It was malpractice. It was criminal negligence. It was sadism.

Carly labored over thirty hours. A lot of shit happens in thirty hours. It was dark. It was light. And then it was dark again.

When it was first time to go to the hospital, we couldn't get Carly out of the Barcalounger. It was the only place in the house she felt at all comfortable laboring in. She wanted us to carry that chair out to the car with her in it and then take them both to the hospital.

First off, Karen and I weren't strong enough. And number two, it wouldn't even come close to fitting into the backseat of a Camaro.

"Can't we please take the chair?" Carly asked.

"No, honey, we can't."

I broke down around the fifteen hour mark.

I wanted to get out of there from the very beginning, but I made myself stay. I was the husband. I was the birth coach. It was my job. I had to stay. Carly couldn't get up and leave, could she? How could I?

So, I stayed, but I was freaking out. I wanted to get out of there. *Shut up!* I was telling myself, for hours. *You're not going anywhere. Help Carly, you asshole! Just do it.*

Hours, man, I wanted to get out of there. I wanted to get out of there. Karen was helping Carly and there were nurses there too. They were busy angels who came and went and you didn't even know their names. I wanted to get out of there. Man, I wanted to get out of there. Hours passed like that.

Why? What was it? Seeing my wife in pain? Seeing my wife in pain and feeling like I was powerless to help her? Seeing my wife in pain and feeling like it was all my fault?

I finally surrendered around the fifteenth hour. *Karen's got this under control*, I heard the voice in my head say. *There are doctors and nurses here. I'm just gonna take a little break. It'll be okay if I take a little break. I'm just gonna take a little break.*

"I'm just gonna take a little break." There, I said that one out loud. I don't remember if anybody even looked up.

I got out of that room. After fifteen hours, I got out of that room, but I took my guilt with me. I let Carly down. I let myself down. I got out of that room and I felt like a spineless creep.

The hospital had a little courtyard. It was a wee patch of outside completely surrounded by the four hospital walls of the inside. There was a tree there and a bench. There was outside air. There was a square of sky. There was a bush. I think there was daylight.

I sat on the bench. I breathed the air. And then the tears came. Oh, man, did the tears come! I had failed everybody. I had failed myself. I fucking wept. It was a cloudburst.

And then I was done. And calm. And restored. And I was ready to get up and go back into that room. I was ready to go help Carly do whatever we had to do to bring our baby into this world.

The doctors didn't want to administer any pain medication until Carly dilated to seven centimeters. The bulk of her labor was spent moving glacially toward that seven-centimeter dilation. It took hours, painful hours.

When they finally did give her some medication, the labor proceeded at an accelerated pace. It was exactly the opposite of what we'd been told. Pain medication was supposed to retard labor. With Carly, it had the exact opposite effect.

When labor exceeded the thirty-hour mark, a decision was made to administer petosin to stimulate contractions. Alarms went off as the baby's heartbeat shot up over 200 and the room jumped into an emergency gear. Carly was rushed into an operating room. I was told they were going to do a C-section.

I thought the baby was dead now and they were trying to save Carly. I was rushed into sterile hospital garb and ushered into the OR.

When they took Carly off the petosin, the baby's heartbeat had returned to normal. They backed off the C-section and were now urging

Carly to just push the baby out. She was fully ten centimeters dilated. The next step was to push the baby out.

Carly pushed for another hour. The baby did not seem to want to come out. The doctor suggested that perhaps Carly might be too weak after all the laboring. A decision was made to let her try to push for only a little while longer before moving along to a C-section.

It was 11:37 p.m. on May 16. I was just behind Carly, holding her and encouraging as she struggled mightily with all the pushing. We were looking into a mirror placed at the foot of the bed for her to see. Came the moment and there was the baby's head beginning to emerge and then crowning. Wow!

The baby's full head was out now. It was shaped like a salami and covered with goop, but it was alive and crying. Juliana was being born. Her shoulders and the rest of her infant body soon followed. Then came all of her luggage and a brand new Honda Civic.

Relief, exaltation, the echo of fading terror, breath, and gratitude, this was a state of grace. There was much busyness and smiling. They cleaned up the baby and stitched up my wife. We were all in a bubble. It was a state of grace.

– Gordon Archive

Me and Junior Mints.

I stayed at the hospital until around two in the morning. Carly and the baby were asleep when I left. I came home and tried to sleep myself, but it wasn't happening, too much adrenaline.

I hung around and enjoyed the haze. I rested. It was dark and then it got light out. It was a new day.

Ricky called me early in the morning. Oh, yeah, Ricky! I was in a movie. Sam's movie! Sam was fine. They had been shooting it for three days now. Today was gonna be their last day. Sam wanted to know if I'd be able to work.

"Yeah, sure, I could do that."

My call was to be there at noon.

For many years to come, Sam Weston would remind me of the smile I had on my face when I drove up to the set that day. He had three kids of his own. He knew exactly what that smile meant.

I gave cigars to everybody.

Spinelli had me scheduled to be in the last scene of the day. I wouldn't get to work until 9:00 or 10:00 that night. In the meantime, he wanted me to help out wherever I could.

First up that day, Spinelli had put together a young, amateur couple who each had shown up separately with the fantasy of becoming a porn star. They both wanted to have sex and real orgasms in front of the camera. They were all smiles and eager when they went out on the set together, but when they came back off, the woman was in a huff and the guy was grumbling. He'd had his orgasm and she didn't get hers. Now, they hated each other.

I took the woman back out on the set and asked Spinelli if he still wanted her to try for an orgasm. He said that he did, but that the guy was a real jerk.

I offered to stand-in. Our leading lady brightened at the prospect and so did Spinelli. I had my first job as a "stunt tongue." With the camera in close on her face, I helped Milady get very, very happy.

It was all in a day's work for an associate producer.

Marci's fantasy was to have sex with fifty men. Spinelli couldn't give her fifty, but I was told that she'd had about eight or ten guys over the last three days and I was to be her grand finale.

We didn't start shooting until around 1:00 in the morning. I was heading into my third straight night without any sleep. I was a different kind of tired, but I still got hard and was happening when we started the sex. That's when we hit about four hours worth of technical problems, chief of which, the batteries for the camera had run out. We had to recharge them. We had to wait until the batteries were recharged.

When we finally did get back to work, I was more worried about staying awake than getting a boner.

"Sit up, Howie!" Spinelli said.

"I am sitting up," I argued.

"No, you're not! You're lying on your back dreaming you're sitting up. Sit up!" He was right.

Marci was a nice enough woman. When we finally got it going, the sex was slow and smoldering for what seemed like a long time. At one point, I imagined my newborn daughter was there watching.

"What are you doing, Daddy?" she asked me.

"I'm fucking this woman, Honey," I told her. "This is how Daddy makes his living." I didn't know it at the time, but I had just taken my first step toward monogamy.

When I got close to orgasm, Marci whispered in my ear, "I want to hear the noise you make when you come."

Good Lord, it triggered this guttural bellow that began in my toe nails and worked its way up and out of my mouth. I never heard a sound like that ever come out of me before. It was extraordinary.

I collapsed in Marci's arms. Sam freeze framed on the happy smile she had on her face.

Spinelli hit problems in the postproduction and needed more money to complete his film for release. He had a new investor interested, but the deal hinged upon Spinelli's being able to buy back the ten percent of *Reel People* that he had sold to me and Carly.

It was not a problem. We weren't exactly "players" looking to make a big killing on this deal. We were just trying to help our friend get his own production company started. Sam paid us double what we had invested and we were delighted. We paid off our initial bank loan and then bought a whole mess of diapers.

"Life is not always all peanut butter and Jelly," my friend Harold used to be fond of saying, and this saga of *Reel People* took a sad and bizarre turn several years later down the road.

We had a friend named Paul who was involved with a lot of sexual swinging communities. He had met Marci in one of those groups and they somehow had discovered that they had me in common. It was one of those "small world" stories Paul told me. He was in and out of our life periodically, but I never did see Marci again.

Sometime later, it was Paul who called me with the news that Marci had taken her own life. He knew her far better than I did. They had become friends and lovers. He told me this and that about her life. It was just sad.

Not too long after that, I was home alone when there was a knock on the front door of our cottage. When I opened it, there was Paul standing there looking very freaked out. His eyes were very large and he was covered with a chalky, white dust.

"I need to take a shower," he said. "Do you mind if I take a shower here?"

After the cremation, it had fallen to Paul to take Marci's ashes and to spread them upon the waters of the San Francisco Bay as had been her request. This, Paul did, but he did not account for the wind.

Part Five

**MY ENTIRE CAREER
WAS LIKE A MAN
STICKING HIS HAND
UP HIS ASS AND
TRYING TO GROW
GERANIUMS**

Chapter One
From a Cad to a Dad
In 106 Easy Lessons

So, we had a baby. The entire universe is telling you that your life will never be the same after that but you don't really know what that means. There's still Monday, Tuesday, and Wednesday and eventually, after all the hoopla, you just go back to doing what you were doing, only now you gotta take care of this baby too.

The nine months of pregnancy and the child's birth had already completely turned us into scrambled eggs. The game was on. Our antes were in there. We were coping. We just had to keep on playing the cards that we got dealt.

Carly's parents and my parents finally got to meet each other when they were all introduced to their new granddaughter. It was a special time for everybody, accounting for many pictures in the great family scrapbook of our lives.

Our first babysitters were the family and then later, friends. Eventually, we got introduced to the wonderful world of professional childcare.

Driving one babysitter home after a night out at the movies, she asked me whether or not our house had ghosts. She thought a ghost had come to check her out after we had left for the movies. If she had asked me that before we left, we never would have made it out the front door.

Another time, with a different sitter, we got home to discover her calmly sniffing lines of cocaine off a mirror. Not only was she unapologetic, she actually started scolding us for going out at all. She said our daughter was too young for childcare.

We had our hits and misses with the babysitting brigade, but eventually, we did find all the help we needed. Carly was able to resume her career as a therapist and I was ready to get myself back into the movies.

Chapter Two

The very best part of the LA Awards that year was that Veronica Hart and I both brought our babies to the afternoon rehearsal. The flower of the porn world cooed and giggled with our newborns. It was a delight.

That night, Richard Bolla and I tied in the Best Supporting Actor category and shared the podium for our thank you speeches. We had never met before. He was mostly East Coast and I was mostly West. Being in competition and all, I didn't expect to like the man, but I did. He was a gracious guy and he had bright eyes with an easy and welcoming smile. We rarely crossed paths, but when we did, I always enjoyed his company.

– Gordon Archive

Chapter Three

I resumed my career with a round two of Marilyn Chambers. I played a prestigious LA disc jockey named Tommy Harper and she

— *Miracle Releasing of Nevada, Inc.*

was the young country western singer Cassie Harland, who was, as the movie's title suggested, *Up 'n Coming*.

In our little scene, Cassie was offering Tommy sexual favors in trade for his promoting her new single on the radio. They used to call that, "payola." It was illegal.

I'd been out of the business for a couple of months. It felt like an eternity. I had put on a few pounds. Pregnancy can be tough on a fella, y'know. She eats, you eat with her. I wasn't exactly fat, but my sculptured Greek god body was gone. Oddly, nobody really seemed to care much but me. In the mainstream porn business, the eyes were all focused on the woman. Still, like the biblical Samson with his hair, that chiseled body I'd made had given me some strength. Now, I'd lost that edge. No more centerfold body, I was just another actor.

And it had been a long time since I had done my last sex scene. There had even been talk between Carly and me about my saying good-bye to the business. I was fragile. I was living in this new bubble of intimacy with my wife and baby. It was a long, long way from the land of lust and come shots.

Besides that, when I had been working regularly, it was the frequency of doing those sex scenes that had helped me to develop some sexual confidence. As I was about to discover in this last phase of my career, with longer periods of time between the sex scenes, each one of them would feel like a comeback. There was too much time for me to worry about things. It was a return to the high anxiety levels about sexual function that had deviled me in the early days. I was a veteran now. I was supposed to know how to handle this pressure. It was a cause for concern. Viagra was still twenty years away.

Well, if I was going to jump back in and restart my career, a Marilyn Chambers movie was a great way to do it. They were always top of the line.

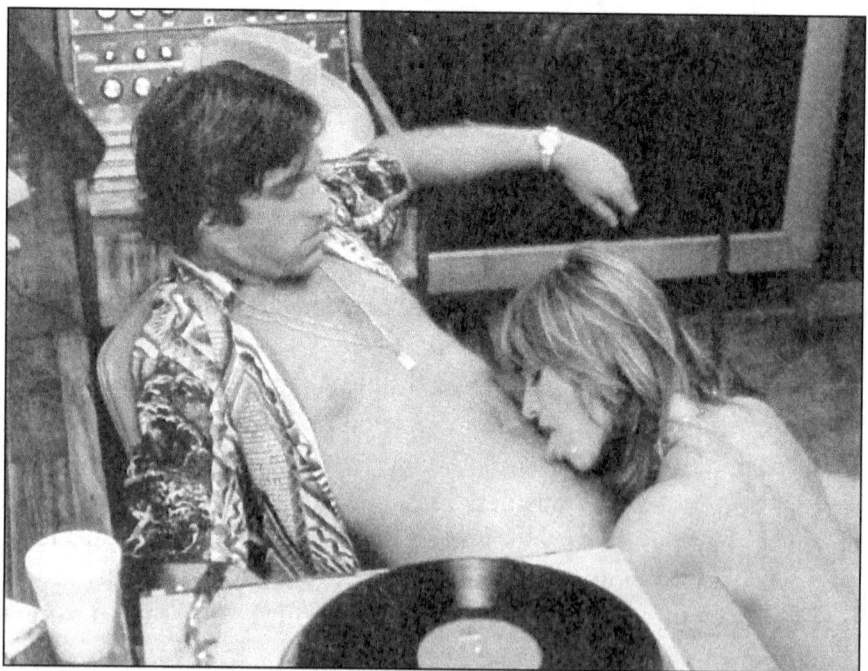

- Miracle Releasing of Nevada, Inc.

Pacheco and Chambers Round Two.

"It's a blow job scene and you won't even have to come!" was the way the producers put it to me. And the money was good too. They were making it easy for me. We'd have diaper money for five months. Deal.

In *Up 'n Coming*, Cassie Harland gave Tommy Harper exactly one half of a blow job. When she was sure that she held his interest, she abruptly stopped sucking and told Tommy that she'll be back to finish it when her new song reached number one on the charts! Slick old girl that Cassie Harland!

Tommy Harper wasn't at all happy about that and neither was I. Tommy couldn't do anything about it because the script said so, but I hung around backstage hoping that I could get Marilyn to finish the job for me privately.

Fat chance. Chuck Traynor immediately had her changing clothes and running lines for the next scene. She did sign an autographed picture for me though.

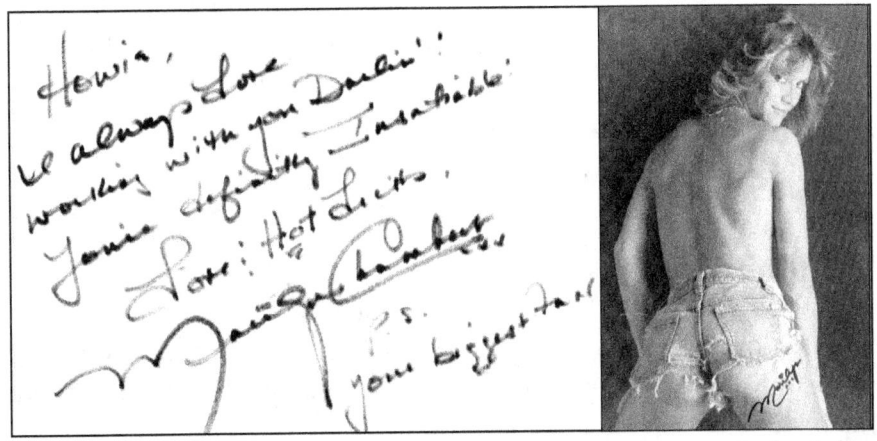

– *Gordon Archive*

Marilyn in my diary.

Wham-bam-thank you, ma'am! I was paid off and sent on my merry way. If there were any sound effects here, you'd hear a wolf howling at the moon. Many years later, Marilyn had these kind words to say in an online interview:

CRAVE MAGAZINE: Who has been your favorite actor to work with?

MARILYN CHAMBERS: A guy named Richard Pacheco, he was really good. He played in *Insatiable*; he was Artie Goldberg, the guy I picked up in the Ferrari. He also played in *Up 'n Coming*, he was a DJ. He was really easy to work with, he's a great guy. I really liked working with him. Working with Robert Klein was really cool. I've been really fortunate, it's not that I've worked with so many famous people, but I have had the opportunity to work with a lot of great actors in my career. I have to tell you too that John Holmes was not the evil person that everyone tried to make him out to be, that was not the whole story. I also have to mention David Cronenburg, working with him in *Rabid*, the horror film that I did for him, that was really fun, I think David Cronenburg is a great director.

> – *Behind Chamber Doors*, Mar/Apr 2005
> An Interview with Marilyn Chambers
> by Robin Steeley

Chapter Four

The bad news was that I didn't work again for the next three months. Fortunately, that was also the good news.

I got to be a full-time daddy with Carly and our new baby. We were in Kitchee-Kitchee-Koo Heaven. Not many other daddies got to do that.

On the other hand, out of work is not good for actors, porn or otherwise. Between the adjustments to parenting and the withdrawal from working, I was nuts.

There was the odd negotiation or two, but nothing quite happened. Cecil Howard became my annual overture from a New York producer. He had a good reputation for making classy films. When he called, he was full of praise and all excited about bringing me to Manhattan for his next project. His zeal quickly evaporated when Carly, now acting as my manager, told him my rates. He stated simply that he couldn't afford us.

As time passed and the bank accounts dwindled, the doubts set in. Will I ever work again? Is this acting thing over? Are my rates just too high? What about graduate school? Is it too late? What subject would I study? What do I want to be when I grow up? Did I want to grow up?

I got in the habit of cutting out grocery coupons. I wondered how was I ever going to pay for my kids' college educations?

Silly me! Little did I know that we were already going to go broke just trying to pay for their elementary schools.

Chapter Five

When I was a little kid—maybe eight, nine, and ten—I used to sit on the sofa with my Mommy. She used to let me tuck my feet under her bottom while we watched TV. It was not unlike a hen sitting on her eggs. I loved that.

Chapter Six

Summer and Eddie Brown came to town and brought an end to my drought when they hired me for *Naughty Girls Need Love, Too*.

Unlike *Irresistible*, the earlier big-time production that I did with them, this one was to be a lower-budget quickie without a lot to brag about. Still, I would have three days work with two sex scenes.

I was just grateful for the job.

For me, it was another "buddy" film, this time with Randy West. Instead of the dim-witted, socially backward Lenny of *Nothing to Hide* and *Talk Dirty*, I would be playing the computer nerd, socially backward Walter of Marina del Rey. Either way, "socially backward" was the operative term.

Once again, as a girl-shy bumbler, I would be engaging an older brother-like figure to help me get the girls.

– Summer Brown

Pacheco and Randy West.

As Skip, Randy West was a sun-worshipping jock, a legendary ladykiller in an upscale LA singles community. He would be my teacher in the ways of love.

Dan Shocket, a reviewer for Al Goldstein's *Screw* magazine wrote:

> "Richard Pacheco portrays a fabulously wealthy young man who can't seem to find women. If you believe that, have I got a set of encyclopedias for you!"

My concession to playing the "shy" Walter was to wear a pair of eyeglasses. Obviously, it wasn't enough.

I always enjoyed Shocket's reviews. He was one of the few regular adult film reviewers who wasn't a shill for the industry. Most reviewers worked for porn magazines that were tied into the films' producers in various ways. This frequently resulted in absolute turds getting five-star reviews. Shocket was a free agent. Al Goldstein let him say what he wanted. And what Dan Shocket wanted was to see good X-rated movies. Of *Naughty Girls Need Love, Too*, he said:

> This film is in reality a series of expertly photographed loops. The scenes range from silly to sizzling, but they are sure to incite surreptitious fondling in theaters throughout the world. The only danger is that you may start to think about it. That would be a mistake.
>
> A single moment, the tiniest instant spent in contemplation can cause the whole film to fall apart. This will lead you to wonder if the monkeys who randomly typed the script were being sadistically tortured or were simply contemptuous of their audience. Every stereotype is presented without any suggestion of originality. Anyone who can't guess what happens at least twenty minutes before it occurs is probably writing the producers next script.
>
> Let's just say this film is a triumph for actors over the absence of a screenplay.

My first sex scene was a blow job from two ladies. I worked with Lyn Francis and Lyn Richards. It was memorable only in that it was my nineteenth successful sex scene in a row. In my next scene, that streak would be broken.

I'm not sure when things went south with Rachel Ashley. Maybe it was because her mother was on the set. She seemed like an agent, a protectress, and an advisor. That didn't exactly thrill me, but it shouldn't have been a problem either. Rachel and I actually started off like gangbusters.

She was sucking me and I was all up and flying. Rachel was young, fresh, and zaftig. You know from zaftig? A busty *Penthouse* Pet, she would have made Reubens drool. If she'd been a member of the Donner Party, there would have been a lot more survivors. Built like Vanessa Del Rio, she had large breasts and a large behind.

Shocket wrote:

> *Rachel Ashley portrays a blowsily attractive woman with great tits. For most of the film, she is dull and silly, which is about what her part calls for. Suddenly, Pacheco gets on top of her and starts being sensitively gentle. Women critics are mother-bear protective of Pacheco and this scene shows why. In response, Rachel becomes warm and hot and natural. Not only are you horny but you're so happy for them.*

Dan Shocket was fooled by movie magic, but I'm not surprised. Recently, someone sent me a copy of that scene that was snipped out of the movie. Between the acting and the editing, it looked red hot, but that's not what happened at all.

Like I said, we started off swell when she was sucking me. I went from cold and anxious to hot, hard, and ready. Then, we reversed the roles. I began to suck and nibble her. And while I did, I was fucking the bed, her ankle, anything with which my erection came into contact.

Rachel made the noises of pleasure, but I felt like something was wrong. I felt like the flower was just not opening. It was nothing concrete, nothing visible, just a feeling. Man, the last thing a male porn actor needs are his feelings!

When they had enough footage of me sucking her, we were directed to move into a penetration shot. We never made it.

I thought I was eager. As I tried to enter her, it just wouldn't work.

Our hips were not fitting together in a way that made access to her vagina easy. Yeah, I don't know what that means either.

She did her best to take me in, but it wasn't happening. My erection started to wilt. I just had the feeling that she didn't want me inside of her.

I was getting one message from her on the surface of things that said all systems are go, but I could not shake "the feeling" that she was really saying, "Stop."

I got confused. You've all been down this road with me before. Those earlier experiences had taught me to avoid these kinds of mental gymnastics, but I was stuck. As I tried hard to push in past the outer gates, I got bent back in half for my efforts. Ouch. I lost my erection.

Uh, anybody seen my erection?

I got it back a couple of times, but every time I tried to penetrate, I lost it again. Worry blossomed into fear and fear was frightening. Shame was just around the corner. Rachel was lying there with her legs spread wide. There shouldn't have been any fucking problem—or any "fucking" problem either—but there was. Eddie gave me some time to try and work it out, but I remained baffled. My penis had lost interest and then Eddie Brown did too. We were wasting his time. He was on a tight schedule.

Eddie came to the bed of my travail like a manager coming out to the pitcher's mound. He was calling for a relief pitcher. I was being sent to the showers. "Shake it off, kid, you'll get 'em next time."

Randy West came in for me and fucked Rachel Ashley silly. Boom! Boom! Boom! They shot all of their hardcore close-ups using Randy's cock as if it were mine. Boom! Boom! Boom! Most people would never notice the change in the color of the pubic hair or the shape of the dick. Boom! Boom! Boom! And he squirted his come on her bottom.

After a brief clean-up, I was sent back in to shoot some matching soft-core simulation. I actually tried to get hard and salvage the scene during these shots just to prove that I could. I couldn't.

Up until that scene, I had gone to bat nineteen straight times without a misstep. My streak was broken. My confidence was shook. I had memories of the old days. It wasn't pleasant to linger on those thoughts because I had a huge job lined up beginning the very next day. I was leaving for Hollywood to do a three-week shoot for David Marsh and Svetlana.

Chapter Seven

TAURUS (*April 20 - May 20*)
Jupiter demands that you lay a seductive ghost to rest

– *Gordon Archive.*

Who am I to argue with Jupiter?
Her name was Colleen.
She was eighteen.
I was thirty-four.
It was a perfect storm.

I Blame It on Hollywood

I do. I was living there for three weeks on location and I blame it all on Hollywood, all of it.

Unlike Homer's hero Odysseus, who remained securely tied to the mast so that he might hear the fabled, irresistible call of the Sirens, *without* falling victim to their curse, *I got loose!*

– *Gordon Archive*

Based on the Herbert James Draper painting of Odysseus and the Sirens (1909).

I came untied from the mast. I heard the Sirens' song and I dove in the water. I swam recklessly ashore and went looking for trouble. Again. I wasn't getting any younger. I was making my move. This was my chance.

It was the whole LA package that dizzied me. Again.

It was the glittering glob of fame and fortune that enraptured me, led by its dazzling muses of sex, drugs, and the three-picture deal.

I was on the loose again in LA. My boner was a divining rod serving my ambition. The soap opera became my life. It was messy.

– Gordon Archive

Colleen. I was thirty-four. She was eighteen.

Veteran porn star Eric Edwards once said to me, "I don't know, Howie, every year I get a year older—and every year, they're still eighteen."

You tell yourself you're only getting close because you have to be able to do a love scene with her, but by the middle of the second week, she's sleeping over in your hotel room.

Oh, I said all the right things. I told her I was married and had a kid. I told her I loved my wife and was going home after the movie. I'd be unavailable for any personal relationship, but we still had almost two more weeks to go in LA.

I played Harry. She played Susie. Our characters were supposed to be falling in love. They got hit by Cupid's arrow and unexpectedly had sex with each other in the back of a shoe store. Afterwards, on the beach at sunset, they were looking deeply into each other's eyes. This was the dialogue:

> Susie: I like what we did, but I'm embarrassed. I'm not usually like that.
>
> Harry: Well, it doesn't happen like that with me either all the time. Y'know, it just happened.
>
> Susie: Harry, do you care about me?
>
> Harry: Susie, I think you're great.
>
> Susie: You're the kinda guy I could fall in love with.
>
> (They kiss. A dog barks. Deep eye staring. Hands on faces, stroking hair.)
>
> Harry: Susie, you are very special.
>
> Susie: What does that mean?
>
> Harry: It means I'm afraid to say words like "love."
>
> (They kiss again.)

I played scenes like this before, but they were usually played in one day, and I'd be on my way back home that night, the next morning at the latest. We still had two more weeks to go in LA.

We had no chance.

Chapter Eight
Why don't you try acting?

"Well, if you thought your mother-in-law, your wife and kids weren't gonna like that last chapter, this one ought to really do the trick!"

"Oh, go fuck yourself!"

"Sounds like I already did."

"Look, I concede that the judgment of history has been, of necessity, very harsh on the era of "The Sexual Revolution." These behaviors that I see myself doing with other women back then, they seem unconscionable today to a world entering its third decade of the AIDS epidemic—especially when one considers that they were done by a husband outside of his marriage.

But the world was a different place then! It was a very different place! Sexual freedom was a meaningful lifestyle choice! It was! It was! It was a great social experiment, and not just some empty-headed slogan for selfish or damaged, addled-brained hedonists.

Or maybe not.

I seem to have a hard time being who I was then ... now.

And trying to write about it, trying to amass some level of sympathy for myself, is not an easy task. Could I tolerate a volume describing the 110 other cocks that Carly fondled, and all the intimacy that went along with them when they were touched? Which of those sexual encounters opened up her nose and made her wet? Which ones made her retch? Which ones touched her heart and got her all the way up to asking the question, "Am I with the right man?"

Jesus, I don't know.

All through my years acting in the business, my years writing about it, and my years of making personal appearances, people have always asked me, "What did your wife think?" What did your wife think? What *did your wife think?*

This was never a question I could answer to anybody's satisfaction ... especially for the women in the group. There was nothing positive I could say that wouldn't seem like so much self-serving bullshit. I needed Carly to speak for herself.

But being a therapist all these years, it was never her wish to take on being the public Mrs. Richard Pacheco. She wanted to keep a low profile. As far as her clients were concerned, she wanted the details of her private life to remain private. Period.

Okay, so I asked her, if she wouldn't do these personal appearances with me, would she at least be willing to go on record in writing. Would she make a statement that I could honestly share with these people who wanted to know what my wife thought about my having had a career in the porn business?

She said she would. And she did. And this is what she had to say:

Q: What was it like to be married to a porn star?

The long answer:

I believe in art, and I believe in art that depicts human sexuality. To me, sex can be the centerpiece of some of life's most ecstatic experiences; ecstatic and nasty and goofy and terrifying and sacred and divine and no big deal. Art that understands and represents our sexuality can be a vital thing, and films need actors.

Still, the truth for me is this: thinking back on the days of Richard's involvement in X-rated films is a little painful and embarrassing. Those feelings are mixed in with my pride in his work and my belief that he really did bring a strong and healthy sensibility to an art form that had been filled with some pretty sad ideas about sex. He was a hard working actor and a crusader for quality films, and he took my chubby little ass swimming naked at the *Playboy* Mansion. Plus, we made some lifelong friends from the industry.

So, why is it uncomfortable for me to remember? Being married to any actor can be emotionally dangerous territory, but especially one who plays love scenes and sex scenes. Where's the line between "acting" and reality? Are we connecting, or are we pretending to connect, or are we lingering here with the connection that we just made? It's that offscreen time, now that could definitely kill ya. I see why Hollywood marriages are so fragile.

Well, either it was truly comfortable for me then, and I've really, really changed, or else I was operating with a huge amount of self-deception. I do experience jealousy, I hate it, and if I never have to feel it again, it would be fine with me. I am not aroused by the sight or the idea of my mate with someone else. At best it's neutral, or awkward. At worst, it's the worst. And a complete turn-off.

I spent the hippie days trying to transcend the base emotions, like jealousy. Hey, jealousy was a bad idea, so we were just going to eliminate it! Well, we stopped the Vietnam war, we smoked a lot of weed, but we didn't get rid of jealousy. I'm sure there must be people somewhere who did, but I'm not one of them.

Sex can come so close to the essence of who we are that we protect ourselves there. I think that's human nature. We defend ourselves where we are most vulnerable.

So, I guess the answer is, "I muddled through." Having kids altered my awareness of how irrevocably vulnerable I am to this man, and my muddling skills melted like snow. Still, I love him, I like him, I'm proud of him and I'm amazed at where we've been together in the last thirty-five years.

The short answer:

I used to be a really good sport.
I'm not a really good sport anymore.

Chapter Nine

Nice Girls Do was the working title. It was later released as *Bad Girls IV*.

This is the film where I bonded with Jamie Gillis. He was the star of this movie. We were working for Svetlana and David Marsh.

Svetlana and David had the worst reputations in the business. Why did I take this job? It was for the money. They were going to pay me for fifteen days work spread out over three weeks. It was *mucho dinero*.

– *Gordon Archive*

Jamie Gillis.

I had worked for them in their original *Bad Girls*, but it was only for one day. I got through it okay. They weren't guilty of anything particularly noxious that day other than bad taste, but that was just a hand in the glove of an X-rated movie. When they offered me a big-paying, costarring role here, I figured I could handle it. I figured I could handle it. I figured I could handle it.

One time, when I'd had a call from a certain New York producer offering me a job, I called Sam Weston to ask if he knew anything about the guy.

Sam said, "Oh, no, no, you don't want to work for him."

"I don't?"

"No, no, you don't," Sam said. "Because when he's not making movies, he's out there breaking legs."

Svetlana and David weren't bad guys like that, not to my knowledge anyway. I don't think they ever killed anybody or caused anybody's limbs to be broken. Still, they managed to qualify as two of the worst people I ever met in the business. They were nasty. Clearly, God must have created them when He was getting ready to take a colonoscopy. All these years later, the stench is still strong.

In the three weeks of this production, they created an atmosphere full of chaos and confusion. Svetlana was the director and she was the worst one I ever had. She was not fit to lead people. She was a sadist who thrived on chaos and directed her players and crew with humiliation and insult. David played the producer and acted as her stooge. They did bad cop-good cop. She would make messes and he would clean them up. When you'd get to trusting him, he'd screw you too. I learned that both of them would just as easily lie to your face, as other people would say, "Good morning."

He was British and she was Hungarian. I thought of them as poster children for Euro trash. They're the only people I ever met who I would have loved to have seen deported.

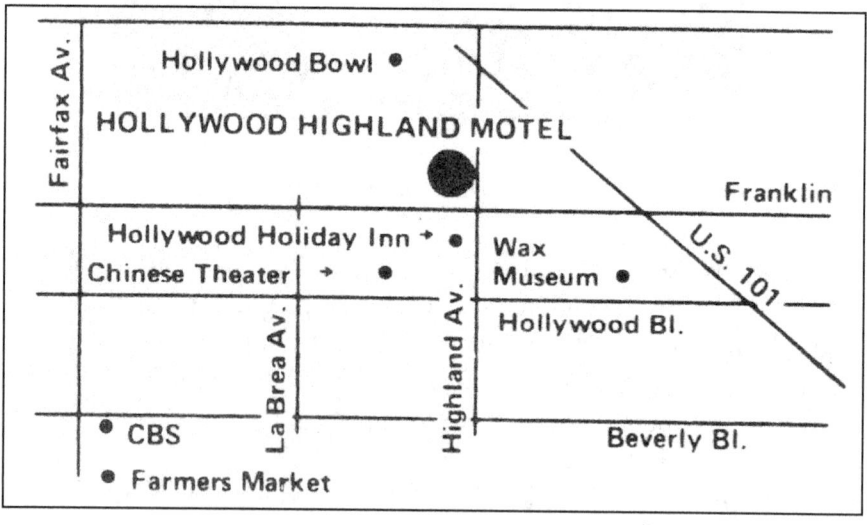

– *Hollywood Highland Motel.*

Jamie Gillis lived in the next room down from me at the Hollywood Highland Motel. They served a free Chinese breakfast there. This was a rat's ass place right next to the Hollywood Bowl where Svetlana and David housed the out-of-town talent and crew. The neighborhood itself was decorated nightly in freshly broken glass and it played host to an array of LA's mentally challenged and prostitutes of every variety and various genders. Jamie said he felt right at home. It reminded him of the old Times Square in New York.

Jerry Butler lived down the hall from us. Jerry and I were Jamie's supporting players. This was a lot of male star power.

- Gordon Archive

Jerry Butler was the new kid in town. He was handsome, well-built, and proved to be a very talented actor.

Brought dumbbells in his suitcase from New York. His muscles had muscles. Said he was after a straight career as an actor. Said he'd already done a few things on Broadway. Maybe did the best Curly Howard I ever heard.

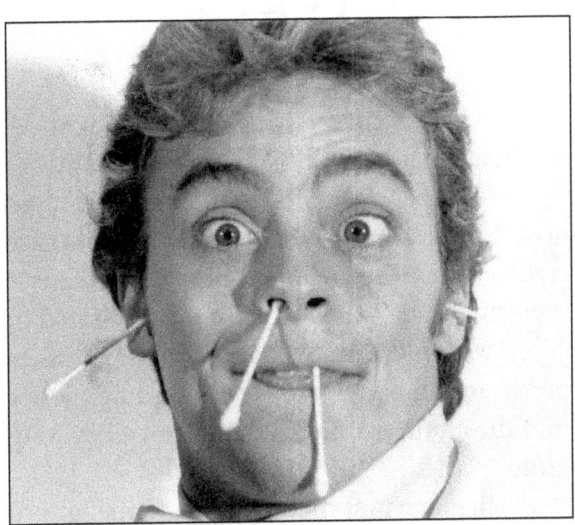

- Gordon Archive

Said that this porn thing was just going to be a brief diversion for him.

"Uh-huh, could ya hum a few bars of that, I think I know that tune."

— *Gordon Archive*

Tina Ross was working opposite Jamie.

— *Monique Gabriel*

Monique Gabriel was Jerry's love interest.

And I, of course, was all set to work with Colleen, who would eventually get her billing as Shauna Grant.

We were three powerful, experienced actors working with three novice actresses. Apparently, all three of these women had just turned eighteen and it seemed like all three were just taking out their titties for their first shake-down cruise in an X-rated movie.

I was told that Svetlana and David liked them new, young, and pretty and that they excelled at finding these girls and launching them into the adult business. It had been a key to the success of their earlier films.

When we first met the girls, Jamie ignored his own costar and sat right down in Colleen's lap and started to woo her. Well, that was a bit of a surprise. We both knew that he was supposed to work with Tina and I was supposed to work with Colleen, but one did not tell the bull goose moose where to put his antlers.

Svetlana wouldn't even introduce me. I was dressed in a long, red bathrobe that made me look like Michael from *Peter Pan*. Svetlana later told me that when she saw me in that robe, she was too embarrassed to introduce me. Well, that was nice of her to share. Seemed like Svetlana never missed an opportunity to spread a little good cheer.

In the meantime, Jamie was getting nowhere with Colleen. One could see that he frightened her. When I took the opportunity to introduce myself, I didn't do much better. Thinking I was being gallant, charming, I kissed her hand. With big eyes, she looked at me like I was from outer space.

Okay, I told her that I'd see her on the set. Jamie told her his room number.

Once outside their room, I "suggested" to Jamie that he fuck her as soon as possible, and get it out of the way, because I was supposed to be in love with her by the end of the week. He said that he'd do his best.

Chapter Ten

Well, Svetlana started me off with a lie.

Oh, it wasn't any great blockbuster of deception, more like just a little evil sprinkled lightly on my french fries. She came to my room and told me that I wouldn't be working today.

"Is that so!"

Earlier that week, when I called from up North to tell her that I'd just been hired to do a computer commercial for the eighteenth. She told me not to take the job because I'd be working for her that day.

So, I cancelled the job. And here I am, bright and early on the eighteenth in sunny LA — and now she tells me I won't be working. Then she added, "Of course, you knew that already, I told you that when you were in San Francisco."

"What?" This is how this woman operated.

I told her that she had said no such thing to me. I reminded her that she told me *not to take that job because I would be working for her today.*

She said, "Oh, no, I told you that you didn't have to be here today. You must not have been listening."

Now, she was pissing me off.

I told her again that she had said no such thing. I could see her smile breaking through under the mask. She was actually going to look me in the eye and keep on doing this. We repeated the dialogue twice more before she laughed and flitted on to another subject like a tangent to a circle making a clean getaway.

That's the way she began with me, full of shit and combative. And I'm wondering, what am I supposed to do? That's who she is and that's the way this shoot is going to go. If this wasn't such a big pay day, I'd be on my way home now. That she cost me $300 for the commercial I gave up makes me mad. That she plays me for a total fool makes me furious. I bite my tongue. It's too early. I've got three weeks to go with her as my director. Oi.

A simple apology was all that was needed. Shooting schedules change all the time in production. But no, that level of simple kindness and taking responsibility was beyond her. Maybe she was afraid I was going to hold her accountable for the lost income. She had to make it out to not be her fault, but the in-my-face lying was just so crude.

We lost each other that day. The chaos had begun.

As I mentioned earlier, I would have never gotten through it without Jamie Gillis. She didn't get to him the way she got to me. They had a history. Jamie had been a big star who had worked for them when they were just starting out. He had done them favors. They owed him. Svetlana kept her beast in check with him.

I had no such luck. Svetlana abused me. She fired me three times and I quit twice. She got under my skin. She seemed to enjoy it. Jamie got between us and defused things when they started getting ugly. And even when they did erupt, he was there afterward to smooth things over. Never would have made it without Jamie.

Chapter Eleven

I'm in the makeup room with Colleen. She's walking around mostly naked with her hair up in rollers. She's being nonchalant and cool while she lets the whole world know that she is a natural blond.

Okay, I'm having a hard time not staring. She's gorgeous. She's the most American looking woman I've ever seen. She looks like fresh cheese off a Midwestern farm.

– *Gordon Archive*

We moved to the set and played some dialogue scenes. If I were her, I would enroll in an acting class like yesterday. She's got world-class good looks, but is completely clueless as an actress. We'll just have to see what we can work out here.

– *Gordon Archive*

Randy West came to the door of our set wearing a very realistic policeman's uniform. It was a dance costume that he uses in strip shows. Randy announced that he was looking for me. Having never met him before, both Jamie and Jerry thought he really was a cop. They let him in.

When I saw Randy, I smiled and stepped toward him with my hand held out to shake. When I got close, he pulled out his revolver and fired two LOUD blasts into my stomach. I thought I was dead.

Blanks. When I realized that I hadn't been shot, I wanted to bash his skull open. I restrained myself. Randy was well over six feet tall and built like an All-American. He was laughing hysterically. He thought it was very funny.

I was just happy that I wasn't dead. The fact that I hadn't shit my pants was a bonus.

Chapter Twelve

By the end of the first week, the news from home wasn't good. One of my wife's colleagues at the therapy institute had been diagnosed with a life-threatening cancer. Carly was shook-up, tired, and alone. We talked a long time on the phone. I told her that if it got too funky, she should just jump on a plane and we'd hold each other up the best way we could.

I told her that working for Svetlana and David was proving to be a difficult experience.

Beyond that, Carly was also not pleased to hear that I'd had a couple of offscreen sexual encounters, one with Monique Gabriel and Jerry Butler, and the other with Laurie Smith.

Laurie started out in this film as an actress but became the makeup artist when

– *Gordon Archive*

Laurie Smith.

Svetlana fired the first one after only a couple of days.

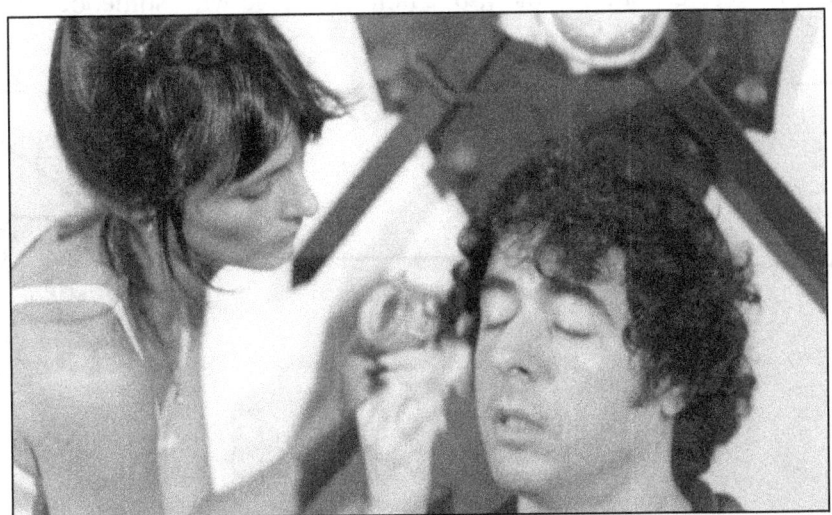

– Gordon Archive.

Laurie making up Jamie.

It's hardly news at this point that backstage sex was part of the lifestyle that went along with being on location in a porn film. If you were not saving up your desire for the next day's sex scene or for some other personal or strategic reason, this casual kind of backstage sex was always going on amongst the cast, and the crew too for that matter, although there definitely was a "caste" system at work about mixing the two.

Not only was this kind of sex pleasurable for its own sake but it was like rehearsal sex. It toughened you up for the business that we were in that often required us to have sex with strangers. Besides that, these two "strangers" that I just had sex with could turn out to be my costars tomorrow. Guys were all different, but I always felt my job was easier to do if my partner and I were not just "meeting" for the first time on screen.

In any case, on this film, and just about every other one I ever worked on, there was usually a lot of tip-toeing in the hotel hallways after midnight. And who was with whom in the coffee shop at breakfast the next morning was always fascinating.

This kind of sex, especially in another city, had never been "verboten" between me and Carly before. In that changing landscape of our "open" relationship, we were up to the part where flings and one-night stands were considered okay, but falling in love with somebody else was taboo.

– *Gordon Archive*

Writing in my diary at the motel.

Carly had never been on my case about backstage sex with porn actresses before, but things were changing. Hell, I thought I deserved some extra credit for not calling up an old high school girlfriend who lived in LA and had been a major source of jealousy squabbles between Carly and me in the past. Dumb. Just bringing up her name was a bad idea.

Carly was making my life harder. I was making her life harder. I slept by myself that night. I pouted.

Chapter Thirteen

My call was for five o'clock in the afternoon. When I showed up on the set, Svetlana told me that they were never going to get to my scenes. They were way behind schedule. She said I could leave. I hung around awhile, playing cards with Jamie, and then I went back to my room and watched TV.

The next day it rained blissfully on Los Angeles. After four days of baking in the heat, it was wonderfully chilly. I was grateful.

I worked in one short scene in mid-afternoon and hung around waiting to do an outdoor shot of walking with Colleen. Colleen, by the way, had warmed considerably. We've enjoyed talking to each other all day.

Over the phone, Carly told me that the baby played with a rattle for the first time today. It made me cry. She also told me that I was allowed to get laid even though she was 400 miles away with a stomach ache because it was written down in the law books that God gave to Moses.

I'm not sure exactly what that meant either, but I was grateful that we were both laughing about it.

Chapter Fourteen

An early morning five-thirty wake-up call. Laurie and Colleen both spent the night in my room. While Laurie slept or pretended to sleep in one bed, Colleen and I made love for the first time in the other. Yeah, I noticed too. I said, "made love."

It was dark and quiet and under the covers. This girl was not a porn queen. In mid-stroke, she asked me to look at her. It was fascinating. The animal came to her beautiful face and she was alive and refreshing. It was a glowing moment and a gift. It gave me pause.

"Look at me...." Photo courtesy of Gordon Archive.

Alright, alright, I can see it now. In hindsight, this was where the lifeguard, the wifeguard, should have blown his whistle and told me to get the hell out of the deep end. This was where he should have said, "What the hell do you think you're doing here, Mr. Husband with a brand new baby?"

But there was no lifeguard there. And this was just Hollywood. This was just work and this was just fun. This was where grown-ups competed to play make-believe like children and got paid for it. On camera, off camera, it got to be hard to tell the difference, especially for a guy sleeping by himself in a crummy motel.

I wasn't thinking of Carly and the baby in Berkeley. I was thinking of me and myself playing the movie game in Hollywood. I wasn't thinking of hurting Carly. I was just wondering, what am I going to do tonight?

I was disconnecting from one life and making up another one. I thought of it as a temporary condition, like riding a roller coaster or taking a drug. I thought of it as rehearsal. I thought of it as free play. I thought of it as a privilege of the profession and an adventure in an alternative universe.

It all seemed very doable.

Chapter Fifteen

The set was a shoe store where my character worked. Svetlana and David were late when we arrived so I curled up on a couch and went to sleep in the stockroom.

I was awakened by Svetlana howling like a banshee. She was screaming at me because the girls had slept in my room. Svetlana had spies everywhere. I told her who slept in my room was none of her goddamned business. She insulted my breath. I backed away. I told her that I couldn't handle any more insults until I had a cup of coffee.

In the makeup room, I learned that she and David had gotten lost on the way to the set. She had arrived in a tornado of a snit-fit and was pissing on everybody.

To pour salt on her wounds, the soundman had been robbed the night before. Several sound tapes had been stolen out of his car. All those scenes were going to have to be reshot.

This was the way the day started and it all went downhill from there.

David and Svetlana both directed that day and spent a good deal of time arguing with each other. This was a common occurrence when they were both on the set. We shot one scene where I had to come running out of the stockroom and do a hook slide on the carpet in front of Colleen. David directed one take. Svetlana directed another. This one was no good for sound. That one was no good for camera. David wanted to try it this way. Svetlana wanted to try it that way.

I slid on that floor, carpet over concrete, twenty times. On the nineteenth try, something in my left knee went "pop."

I told them both that I had just hurt myself. They wanted one more take. I told them it was going to be the last one. We shot it. When I hit the floor, the pain was again sharp in my knee. I ignored it and finished the scene. I didn't want to have to try and do it again. Within half-an-hour, my knee swelled up to the size of a bowling ball.

I was worried. I'd already had a major surgery on my right knee. It was no picnic. I knew what was involved. It took nine months out of my life for the healing and the physical therapy. I was afraid that I was

– Gordon Archive

We had just passed the halfway point.

going to have to go through all of that again.

While we were still in the shoe store, I asked David Marsh if the film had insurance. He said that it did. I told him not to bullshit me because I knew that it could get expensive. He said, "No problem. We'll take care of you."

We wrapped around nine-thirty that night. I limped back to the hotel and put my knee on ice.

Chapter Sixteen
Yom Kippur

It was supposed to be a day off!

The production manager called early to arrange for the three guys to go and get fitted for tuxedoes for a coming scene. I told him that I was going to have a hard time getting the pants pulled up over my knee. It was still swollen to twice its normal size. I could barely stand on it to hobble to the bathroom.

John Leslie called from Philadelphia. He wanted to know if Colleen's ass was really as fine as he had heard. I didn't know what to tell him. Colleen's ass was lying right next to mine in the bed when he called. My first reaction was jealousy.

Colleen had spent the night with me again. Despite some heavy flirtation from Jaime, she had bedded down with me. Jaime was seriously infatuated. He sat at Colleen's feet like a puppy. I made a lot of room for him, but Colleen kept hiding behind me. He was danger. I was safe.

Last night with Colleen had none of the first night's heat. I was hurting. I had been protecting her from Svetlana and Jaime. Now, she was going to take care of me. It didn't really work. Desire had been one thing, but this kind of caring was something else. It felt very awkward to have somebody besides Carly even attempt to care for me when I was hurting. It was like playing house in a comic book. It felt wrong.

Svetlana called. This phone call went South in a hurry. She wanted me to work more days than we had agreed upon in our contract and she wanted me to add them all in for free.

Well, that sucked. I hardly knew what to say to her. I told her that she would have to discuss it with Carly, who was being my business manager.

"No," she said, "I'm not going to do that."

Then, "I'll discuss it with her," I told Svetlana, "and with my fellow actors too. If we can come up something that seems fair, I'll do it."

She called me "unprofessional" again. She said that I was the highest paid actor on the set and that I should do the additional days for free. Further, she said that I was not permitted to discuss my salary with anybody.

I reminded her that we had made no such agreement. I told her that I strongly doubted I was being paid more than Jamie Gillis. I told her that she used the word "unprofessional" every time that she didn't get her way, and I suggested that she had a very, very odd way of asking me to do her a favor.

That's when Svetlana started shouting at me over the phone. She continued to berate me about my salary and I screamed back, *"I CAN'T EVEN WALK, BITCH!! WAKE UP!!!"*

That's when she hung up the phone.

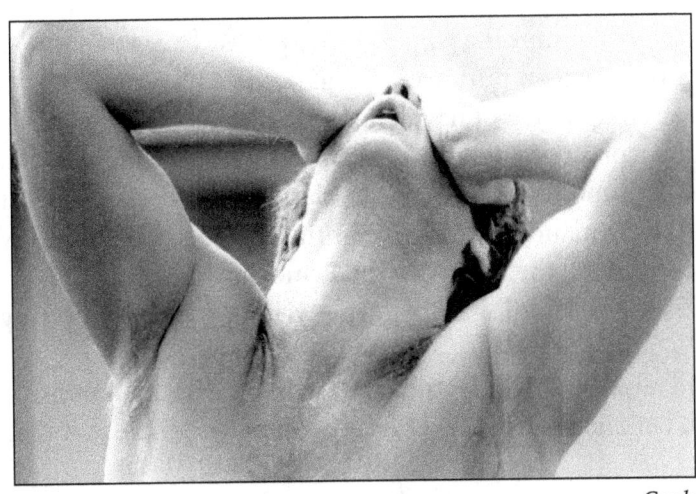

- Gordon Archive

And a Happy Yom Kippur to you too!

I couldn't believe what had just happened. I was shivering. I knocked on Jaime's door. He was gone. I didn't know what to do. I started packing to go home.

Jaime came back soon and I told him my troubled tale. Then, the phone calls started. First came the production manager. Then, David called. And then, Svetlana called again. Another uneasy peace had been restored. It was agreed that Svetlana and I would never discuss business again. All future negotiations would take place between David and Carly.

As a peace offering, David wanted to take Jaime and me out to dinner. Svetlana couldn't even look at me for the first half of the meal. When she finally did perk up, I got it that she was irritated with me because my leg injury meant that she was going to have to change her shooting schedule. I was stupefied, yet again.

In the end, they didn't even need any more days from me than what we had originally contracted. The entire confrontation had proved unnecessary. In the process, Svetlana hadn't even bothered to see if there might have been a peaceful solution before she sent in the bombers. It was just her way, Svetlana against the world.

Behind Svetlana, tagged along the dutiful David. At thirty, he looked like fourteen. He cleaned up well after her. They made a good combination. My sympathy went out to anyone who was unlucky enough to come under their dominion. I would never work for them again.

At the restaurant that night, I mentioned to Svetlana, "Y'know, I didn't hurt my leg on purpose." She gave me a half-smile and then the poor dear complained of having a headache.

Not surprisingly, there were more unpleasant incidents between Svetlana and me. We continued to clash. In hindsight, it all starts to sound like two students caught fighting on the playground who are then forced to tell their story to the Principal.

"It's all her fault!" I seem to be writing over and over again. "I didn't do nothin'!"

And even though I still believe that's largely true, enough is enough. Let's just say we never did get along and leave it at that.

Chapter Seventeen
Overnight Sensation

- Gordon Archive

A star was born that night!

By the third week, it was probably the word-of-mouth buzz started by Jamie Gillis that made Colleen Applegate a star.

Like John Leslie calling from Philadelphia, all of "the guys" wanted to meet Colleen and all of the producers were trying to get her lined up for their next picture.

After shooting one day, Jaime took Colleen and me to a big party that was a special private screening of *Society Affairs.*

When we arrived, Harry Reems was putting his hands and feet in cement in front of the Pussycat Theater. We discovered too late that it was a tuxedo affair. They let us in anyway. Doors opened when you were with Jamie Gillis.

The movie was a dog. It was supposed to be Harry's big comeback movie. The only scene worth mentioning in the entire film involved Kelly Nichols bending over in a wedding dress. When Harry raised her skirts, the view was spectacular. There were audible gasps in the audience, mine among them. Colleen told me to be quiet and Jamie fondled her leg.

Afterward, there was a fancy feed. Colleen was the belle of the ball. She was blossoming in the spotlight. She was the new kid in town and they were all lining up to talk to her.

Producer Ted Paramour asked me for a private word. He told me that he had a new film that he wanted to discuss with me. When I went over to talk to him about it, he spent twenty minutes asking me if I could deliver Colleen.

I waved Colleen over and told Ted to speak to her himself. He was charming.

A star was born that night. It was clear that they all wanted to make Colleen the next Prom Queen of the X-rated business.

Chapter Eighteen

I suppose we need to talk about cocaine.

– Gordon Archive

Laurie and Colleen were coke buddies together. At this stage, they seemed to use it almost daily as a pick-me-up like others would drink a cup of coffee.

When they would offer some to me, I'd decline. I'd gone a few rounds with cocaine and got myself knocked out every time. I couldn't handle it. It was not a casual, social drug to me. It was a dangerous binge drug, which I found way too easy to abuse. With Carly's help, I had learned to say, "No." I said, "No."

Colleen liked her sniff of coke and drank her Bailey's Irish Cream. It was chocolate milk with alcohol and hard drugs.

It didn't really get in the way of this movie, but it would come into play quite seriously later in Colleen's short life.

The shooting in LA was winding to a close. Colleen autographed my diary.

> Howie—
>
> I have really enjoyed working with you and becoming friends. I hope we can keep in touch and hopefully work together again — or just get together on a social basis. I have learned a lot from you — about myself and business. Anyway, I think I've written enough —
>
> Thanx for everything
>
> Love & friendship
> Always
> Colleen Applegate
> "Callie Hollander"
>
> Thank you!
> Love too!
> XXOO

– Gordon Archive

Colleen hadn't chosen a stage name yet and we made sport of finding her one on the set one afternoon. We all decided she should be "Callie Hollander."

Jamie came up with two movie scenarios that he wanted to make with her. One would star Colleen as the daughter of a Nazi Commandant at a concentration camp who would fall in love with him as a Jewish prisoner.

The second would be all about a girl who tried to make it big in sex films. That movie would end with the big, famous, male sex star taking her back home to Indiana and telling her to stay there. He'd tell her she was too sweet for that business. He'd tell her that he didn't want to see her lose that innocence.

Shame we didn't make that last movie.

Chapter Nineteen
The Long Awaited and Much-Anticipated Sex Scene

Oi, fergedaboutit! Not with a bang, but a whimper, it was a natural disaster. It was a "Hall of Lame" scene. It was the anticlimax of my entire career. You can't begin to imagine how unhappy this made Svetlana—and that was just the good news.

Q: Can you have a simultaneous premature ejaculation?
A: Yes, if you both come before the camera gets enough hardcore footage, or any hardcore footage at all, for that matter.

In the foreplay, Svetlana was already displeased. The touching was quiet, frightened, and tender. By now, the last thing that either Colleen or myself wanted was to have sex in front of Svetlana, but it was still our job.

Svetlana wanted more animation from us. Colleen wanted the lights turned out and the covers pulled up. I just wanted to finish the scene and go home. We were up in San Francisco now. The magic between us of LA was gone. It was over. After three weeks, I had slept at home with Carly last night. We didn't have sex. I was saving it up for this scene, but we had reconnected. And I had reconnected with my daughter too. I was home.

And Colleen? Colleen was already halfway into John Leslie's arms and her next picture. She was on her rocket to stardom.

I had forced Svetlana and David to honor their contract with me and shoot this sex scene in San Francisco. In her own typically sweet and diplomatic way, Svetlana had tried several times to bully me into shooting it in LA. It was illegal, risky, and dangerous to shoot sex scenes in LA. All of the reputable companies came North and shot theirs in San Francisco. Only the slimiest and most desperate tried to shoot their sex scenes in LA.

I had held my ground and forced them to come up here.

Not to belabor the obvious, but in hindsight, it was a big mistake.

Doing the right thing turned out to be the wrong thing. I should have risked the arrest because the San Francisco shoot was a colossal flop. But there was no way to predict that, there was no way to see it coming.

At least we didn't get arrested.

Svetlana wanted a scene of raw, animal lust like the one I had given her in the original *Bad Girls* with Tanya. It had been a spirited, energetic coupling. When I played that scene, I was a lean and mean young halfback eager to run hard in Saturday's big game.

In this sex scene with Colleen, I was a limping, battered older man. In the makeup room before we started, Colleen and I were talking about death and friendship and things so totally inappropriate to our coming sex scene that even we took notice of it and had a good laugh.

When Svetlana wanted more animation, we gave her more animation. We acted the passion. It felt phony. It was phony. I'm sure it had to look phony, but they shot it anyway.

When it came time for the actual fucking, Svetlana left the room. That was a sigh of relief for everybody. Eugene, the director of photography, was left in charge. I would cue him when we got it going.

In mere seconds, I was hard and inside of Colleen. It felt wonderful. Too wonderful. Way too wonderful!

Eugene was filming our faces when our arousal just took off. We'd been at it only moments and I was on the verge of coming. Colleen seemed to be right there with me. We were having a terrific time, but I realized that they had absolutely no hardcore footage!

I froze. I tried to stop my orgasm, a difficult, most ungallant task. Colleen moaned her disapproval. I told Eugene to shoot some hardcore stuff, NOW, that I was close to coming. Wrong. Two hesitant strokes later, I came anyway. I came inside of Colleen. Oi. It was all a big mistake.

By the time Eugene got in position to shoot some hardcore footage, all he got was my fading erection ingloriously plopping out of Colleen. I had never come that fast ever. What are you gonna do? Once again, the sex had proven to be an inexact science.

Well, I could now add "premature ejaculation" to the list of honors I had achieved in this life.

At first, I thought, No problem! I'll just wait a little while, get another hard-on, and then give them all the hardcore footage they need.

It never happened. There was something about having tried so hard to shut down the orgasm that got in the way of trying to up and restart the arousal engines. Literally, it was like flooding your carburetor when you try to start your car. If you can't wait long enough for the flood to subside, you'll just keep wasting your battery trying to get the engine going. If you don't wait long enough, you'll just get a dead battery. I've done that. More than once. To both my car … and my dick.

We tried for a long time to get me going, but failure and terror gave way to more failure and terror. Despite the best live efforts of Colleen the lover and me doing an exhaustive masturbatory search throughout my entire sexual memory, we, all of us, could not get another glimmer of life out of my poor, dead dick.

A stunt cock would have been extremely helpful at that point. Jon Martin, Mike Horner, John Seeman, Ron Jeremy, Randy West, you were the guys that had bailed me out before. Where were you now? They were nowhere to be found on this day.

And beyond the shame and confusion of a dead dick, I had to face the wrath of the Dragonlady.

I told Svetlana that I'd try all night if she wanted, but that nothing was happening. She took me at my word and wrapped the set. I felt badly. I was disappointed that I hadn't given her the scene that she wanted. Svetlana was disappointed because she didn't get the scene that she wanted. And the crew was disappointed because they all just wanted to have been home in bed two hours ago. It was lose-lose everywhere you looked and I did not expect Svetlana to go quietly without exacting her pound of flesh.

When the storm came, I accepted her rage. In all fairness, I had earned a fair amount of this abuse and I figured that she was entitled to her say. So, I kept my cool. Maybe that's what put her over the edge. I expected her to be an asshole and she was, but she crossed a line somewhere way beyond my "It's my fault line," and I had no choice but to start defending myself.

I'll spare us all the details. Like I said before, it's two kids who got caught fighting on the playground and then taken before the Principal.

Svetlana and I ended our relationship with people having to come between us that day, to keep us apart. In what may have been the unkindest cut of all, I have to admit that she got in the best blow when she spat out at me. "And if I'd have wanted a sex scene like that, I could have had real actors!"

Bitch sure knew how to hurt a guy.

Y'know, in hindsight, maybe Svetlana and I should have done that sex scene. We certainly had a ton of passion going on between us. Of course, it was homicidal in nature, and not erotic, but maybe we could have worked with that. It suggests an anal penetration scene of absolutely biblical proportion. No doubt, it certainly would have been a bone of contention as to which one of us was going to take it up the ass.

I would have voted for her.

P.S.

When I started seeing doctors about my knee, I called David Marsh's office twice to get the name of the film's insurance company. Both times I was told that he was in a meeting and would get back to me. He never did.

Carly tried calling him at home one night. When he answered the phone and Carly identified herself, he quickly gave the phone to Svetlana. Regarding my knee injury, Carly reported Svetlana said:

"He was already hurt before the movie. He never was really hurt. He had a little bruise. He miraculously recovered. He slipped once, but he's all better now. We're not paying for anything. Good-bye."

What a surprise. Naturally, I was furious. I called a lawyer friend of ours. I wanted to sue them. I wanted them to be held accountable. I spoke to a number of producers of the Adult Film Association. Several volunteered assistance in any action that would legally rebuke David and Svetlana. It seemed that the Marshes had offended lots of people. We were invited to become pawns in other peoples' games of revenge.

Carly talked us out of it. She said "that woman" had just brought out the very worst in me. Carly said that I had come back from LA spewing poison. She said she didn't even want to be around me when I was talking about Svetlana. She pointed out that a lawsuit could be costly and could keep David and Svetlana in our lives for months, if not years to come.

Carly voted that we just try to get back to our lives and forget that David and Svetlana ever existed. At first, I resisted that notion.

I was diagnosed with a partial tear in the meniscus. Surgery wasn't indicated. It was suggested that when the swelling went down, I begin physical therapy. The doctor also recommended some anti-inflammatory drugs.

Anti-inflammation seemed to be the general prescription for just about everything at this point. As John Leslie would have said, it was time to "calm the fuck down." Okay, we decided to just forget David and Svetlana. In fact, we decided that I'd retire from the business.

Chapter Twenty

Dad, you never told me anything about all the girls you kissed before mom. I don't know how old you were when you first had sex or who was the first woman you ever had sex with. Or where you had it? Did you do it in a bed? Was it in a car? What position? Did she suck your dick?

Dad, we shoulda maybe talked about some of that stuff. I was so clueless. I coulda used some help from you with all the preliminaries. You never told me how you even learned anything about sex either. Or did you? And I just forgot. Maybe you told me that your brother Jack taught you. I don't remember now. It seems that you just showed up in my room one day when I was seventeen and told me to use protection.

We did talk about that hooker you and Uncle Leo had been seeing, remember? I was twenty-four then, when you and Mom came out to California and first met Carly. You told me about it when I said we should be friends. I said that we should talk about stuff. It happened when we were alone one day. You told me that you and Uncle Leo were seeing a prostitute on the side.

I got angry then, Dad. The part of me that was my mommy got pissed at you, angry and indignant. How dare you cheat on my mommy?

Sorry, that it freaked me out so much, Dad.

Will my kids handle all this any better?

Chapter Twenty-One

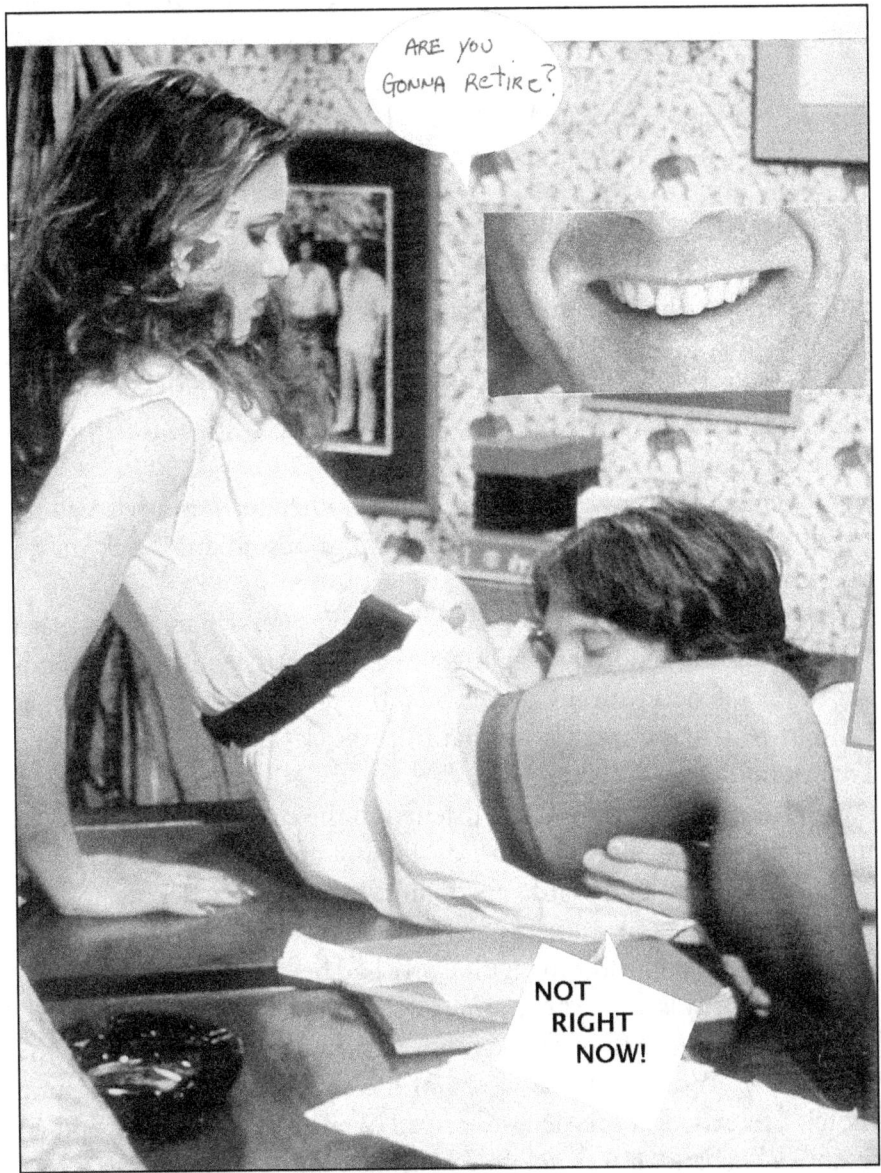

– *Gordon Archive/VCX.com*

Chapter Twenty-Two

The roots of our little family had been shaken. We needed to heal. "Abandonment," was a word that Carly used. Being left alone at home with our baby had felt like abandonment. In some ways, it didn't even matter what I was out there doing. It's just that I wasn't at home with her.

In hindsight, I wanted to be the happily in the happily married family man, but I also wanted to be Casanova, the man with the magic pee-pee.

I wanted my homey bliss with the woman I loved and I also wanted to be paid well to go to exotic locations, play pretend in the movies, and get to have hot sex with every other kind of woman imaginable.

Was that too much to ask out of life?

Apparently, yes, if I wanted to stay married to Carly, it was. If I wanted to have a family with her, it was. And now, she was letting me know all about it.

I remember Carly once asking my mother for her advice about being married. My mother told her without hesitation, "Stick up for your rights."

During my senior year of high school, after I had lost all that weight and was suddenly juggling a few new girlfriends, I was standing in the kitchen with my mom when the phone rang. I told Mom as she was reaching to pick it up that if it was, say, Linda, "Tell her that I'm not home."

"Hello," my mom said. She listened to the caller and then handed me the phone. "It's Linda," she said. "I'm not gonna lie for you."

Thanks, Ma, and thanks for telling my wife to "stick up for her rights."

My actual homecoming with Carly had been romantic and sweet, but that part was very short. There followed a lot of tension in our house. After the pace of Hollywood, Berkeley was like watching the grass grow. And after three weeks of life as a single man living in a motel, I returned to the sleep-deprived ozone of a new father and an attentive husband. It was not an easy transition.

Carly was more fragile than I had ever seen her. The single parenting, the long separation, and her friend's struggle with cancer had all combined to frazzle her. I wasn't in such great shape either.

We thought maybe I should retire from the business. We thought maybe I shouldn't be a porn star anymore.

– Gordon Archive

We fought a lot. We were still in the process of deciding what to do about David and Svetlana. And in those days right after the movie, Colleen was calling a lot.

We were still friends, Colleen and I. She was telling me all about the exciting new things that were happening in her career. She was asking for my advice. It was her ride up. It was volcanic.

Carly didn't like her calling. I tried to tell her it was just business. Carly wasn't buying it. She said that the mere mention of her name revived all the anguish of our separation. She wanted me done with Colleen.

One night, Colleen called way too late and woke us both up. I grabbed the phone and took it into the next room so that Carly could get back to sleep.

Carly followed me with a scowl on her face. She made a thumbs-down gesture and then went back to bed.

On the phone, Colleen prattled on about the latest movie and the latest producer promising stardom. On the surface, at least, it was all business. She talked business details and sought business advice, but I was getting all of the heat and none of the pleasure that went along with having a full-blown love affair. It was like paying a tax for what had already taken place between us earlier. It stunk.

Colleen soon came to the Bay Area to work on a Bob Chinn film. She took a cab over from San Francisco to visit us. She met Carly and she met the baby.

As you might imagine, it was tense and odd. With Carly and Colleen in the same room, I felt like two different expressions were trying to fit on my face at the same time. It was actually physical and it was quite impossible. They were incompatible. I couldn't get both of those faces on me at the same time, and I was a stumbling bumbler coping with that revelation.

For her part, I think that Colleen had to see for herself that there really was a wife and a baby. Nothing spectacular happened. Carly didn't bite her head off or anything. In fact, she was the gracious hostess. Still, Colleen seemed somehow to get the message that I really wasn't available.

I thought that had been made clear all along, but sometimes, men, and I suppose women too, are just plain stupid. Colleen found a different me, at home with Carly and the baby, than the man she had known in LA. The movie really was over and all that went with it.

After this visit, her calls became less frequent and soon stopped altogether.

There were a lot of pros and cons discussed over whether or not I should resume my career. This last movie, as crazy as it had been, had bought us some time, but neither one of us ever wanted to endure another long separation like that. Carly was horrified at the prospect of being a single parent again. She didn't want me off in New York or LA, fumbling with the next Colleen.

When forced to choose, I didn't want it that way either. We had worked hard to make a baby together. I wanted us both to raise that child. I had no doubts of that. Everything else had to line up behind that.

Yeah, so, I did retire from the business. I wasn't gonna be a porn star anymore.

Chapter Twenty-Three

My retirement lasted six weeks. When Stu Segal called with that job in *Up 'n Coming*, we were back in the business. He made us an offer that was too good to refuse. It bought us a lot of Huggies.

Carly was already acting as my salary negotiator. It had become her job to serve as my buffer in the financial dealings when the producers or directors invariably tried to lower my rate during a negotiation.

For me to continue on in the business, we decided that we would have to expand Carly's powers further. The career had to better reflect our partnership. For instance, if a job involved too long a separation between us, she would have the right to veto it.

More importantly, she would also have the right to veto any potential sex partner for me, period. If a woman gave her the heebie-jeebies for any reason whatsoever, we would request another partner or just let go of the job. There were any number of women in the business that Carly had met with whom she didn't mind me working. But if she felt a woman was too needy, or looking to fall in love with me, or likely to start calling our house after Midnight, she now had the power to veto them.

We would just take a pass on any deals that smelled like they were going to upset our family applecart.

- Gordon Archive

Howie and Baby Jo.

Chapter Twenty-Four

January of 1983, we hadn't told Carly's parents yet about my career in porn, but that day was just around the corner.

Phil Donahue's people called me in January and invited Richard Pacheco to be on their show. They hadn't put it together that Richard Pacheco was also Howie Gordon and that I had already been on their show three years earlier as *Playgirl*'s Man-of-the-Year.

Interesting situation. Should I tell them? Would Donahue or anybody from his staff even remember me when I came walking out from backstage?

The other guests invited to be on this Donahue-Does-Porn episode were actresses Veronica Hart and Seka, and Marga Aulbach, who was one of the producers of *The Dancers*.

It was tempting. Donahue was the Oprah of his day, the top-rated afternoon talk show on TV. A lot of people watched that show. And that's why we turned it down. We weren't ready for that kind of big publicity.

To many, it may just seem like splitting pubic hairs, but it was one thing to take the national stage as a *Playgirl* centerfold and quite another as a porn actor. It was the difference between an "R" Rating and an "X." The difference also was that my in-laws didn't know anything about my porn career, and if I'd have done this Donahue show, they probably would've found out.

I took my lead from Carly. We weren't ready to cross this bridge. Carly said that she was afraid that her parents were going to send her to her room for about a million years because she had married a porn star. Later, she accused me of exaggerating. She said that they would only send her to her room for about fifty years.

Chapter Twenty-Five

Carly got a bug up her ass that we should buy a house.

Beyond what we were spending on childcare and diapers, we had about thirty-two cents in the bank, but Carly wanted to buy a house. On a recent visit, her parents had made some comment about being willing to help us out with a down payment. It had gone in one of my ears and out the other. But Carly wanted to buy a house.

Next thing I knew, Carly was dragging me and the baby to open houses every Sunday afternoon. Y'see, football season was over. The NBA wasn't up to their play-offs yet. And baseball was still in spring training. What was a fellow to do? Carly wanted to buy a house.

We saw lots of beautiful homes and some fixer-uppers too. They all cost hundreds of thousands of dollars we didn't have, and it freaked me out. I hated it. I was still defining wealth as having enough peanut butter to get me through the munchies. Having a baby had made me a nervous wreck, but shopping for houses had me ready for a straightjacket. It was a job for a grown-up. I wasn't even remotely qualified.

When it came to the real "adult" world of insurance policies, taxes, property management, stocks & bonds & investments, annuities, gratuities, and how to avoid probate, Carly and I were babes in the woods.

It was a kind of a deaf and dumb by choice. Berkeley, for a lot of people like us, was a Never Never Land where we were all still waiting for Bob Dylan to become Peter Pan and lead us up against the bad guys. It was something like that, but Dylan never did want the part and nobody else came even close. Besides, all the house meetings got to be such a drag. The sixties were long over, but a lot us were still stuck in that time.

Carly had found her way back into the mainstream by becoming a therapist, but when I looked into the mirror, I saw a college graduate who had largely majored in whoopee. I was now an unemployed porn star. Try telling that to your wife's parents!

I liked being a porn star. It had some panache. I was happy with that. And when I had played it just right, Carly was even happy with it too, but it remained a daunting task to think that we could share that information with her folks.

I didn't really know what Carly's parents thought of me. I was just irritated that I had to worry about another set of parents at all. I was doing fine with my own at the time, who needed the aggravation?

Carly and I had been married for seven years. We now had a baby. It was their grandchild too. They had two grandsons already by Carly's older sister, but this was their first granddaughter. They were doting. They were wonderful. They were Carly's parents, for God's sake! Yoi, this was a tough scene to play.

We told them about the odd straight job I would do here and there in local Bay Area commercials, but, so far, had said nothing about my X-rated life. I guessed they thought of me as a guy who just hadn't found himself in the business world yet who was content to live off their daughter, the psychologist. What a can of worms!

I stopped going on the Sunday afternoon house hunts. Carly went alone with the baby. I stayed home with Señor Marijuana.

Chapter Twenty-Six

Irresistible won the Best Picture award from the New York Adult Critics in March. I was nominated Best Actor for that movie and also Best Supporting for Damiano's *Never So Deep*.

I lost twice.

Jamie Gillis got the Supporting award and John Leslie got the Best Actor for, of all things, *Talk Dirty to Me*, Part Two.

I wasn't thrilled for John. I had turned down a role in that movie when I stayed loyal to Spinelli in his feud with the *Talk Dirty* producers. Not only did John break ranks with us and get himself a big payday for that movie but now he was picking up what I thought would be my Best Acting trophy for *Irresistible*. It wasn't my night.

Chapter Twenty-Seven

On May 12, 1983, I was having a tough day at the typewriter. I had writer's cock. As the blank pages stared at me, I had already beat off twice and it was just before three o'clock.

I was frustrated and cranky when the phone rang. I picked it up and said, "I can only stand to hear good news right now. What is it?"

Carly's voice at the other end said, "I'm pregnant!"

Chapter Twenty-Eight

I used to have fantasies about having sex with the women of the X-rated movies. Now, I'm having fantasies of managing a Little League team.

– *Gordon Archive*

Another baby!

Chapter Twenty-Nine

Being introduced to Dave Friedman was like being taken behind the curtain to meet the Wizard of Oz. Dave Friedman was the grandfather of the entire X-rated film industry.

– Adult Film Asssociation of America (AFAA)

Dave Friedman.

And when Dave Friedman invited me to join a Blue Ribbon industry delegation, which he was presenting to *The Sixth World Congress of Sexology* gathering in Washington, D.C., I was honored to be included.

There was no salary, but the Adult Film Association of America, of which Friedman was the long-time president, would be picking up all the expenses for me, Carly, and the baby. Besides the career boost of being included with industry luminaries, it was a free trip to the

East Coast and a chance to let my parents have a visit with their new granddaughter.

WELCOME TO THE 6th WORLD CONGRESS OF SEXOLOGY

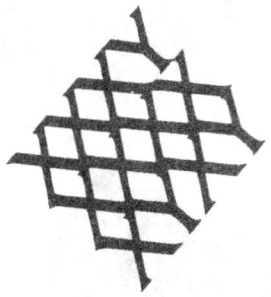

Sponsored By
THE WORLD ASSOCIATION FOR SEXOLOGY
And Organized By
THE UNITED STATES CONSORTIUM FOR SEXOLOGY

Washington, D.C., U.S.A.
May 22-27, 1983

– Gordon Archive

Dave Friedman assembled quite a crew. He began with three queens.

— *Gordon Archive/Annette Haven/Seka/Kay Parker*

(L-R) Annette Haven, Seka, and Kay Parker, three of the top actresses of the day.

He added Director Anthony Spinelli, Producer Marga Ahlbach, Producer Chuck Vincent, First Amendment Attorney John Weston, Jimmy Johnson, president of the Pussycat Theater chain, and yours truly.

— *Gordon Archive/Seka*

Seka makes her point.

It was a big step up for the makers of adult films to be taken seriously by a body of mental health professionals who dealt responsibly with sexual issues. We had on our industry's best face as we talked about the possibilities for the sexual media in American culture.

And we acquitted ourselves well. The mainstream stereotypes of those who participated in the making of pornography were so damning and pervasive that when people discovered you could actually walk and chew gum at the same time, they were often stunned.

Dave Friedman understood this all very well. He'd been fighting for adults to see adult materials most of his life. When we were all done with our days work in DC, I got to have a late night walk with him back at our hotel. I had served him well as an apologist for sex films and he rewarded me with a giant cigar and regaled me with some tales of his past. I felt like one of the boys.

Believe it or not, Friedman was not a fan of the X-rated movies we were making back then. They had become too explicit for his taste. "Left nothing to the imagination," he said. It's ironic how the rebels and pioneers of one generation become the fuddy-duddies of the next. The great Mae West comes to mind.

"You show 'em the sizzle," Friedman was famous for saying, "not the steak."

Dave Friedman was a master pitchman, a flim-flam man schooled in the days and ways of the American carny, the traveling road show. "The secret of my stuff was the old carnival tease," he told the *LA Times* in 2002. "The audiences would think, 'Oh, boy, we didn't see it this week, but next week....'

They never did see it, but they kept coming back!"

Friedman made a bunch of sexploitation films in the fifties and sixties, "nudie cuties" like *Lucky Pierre* that pushed at the obscenity laws everywhere in the nation. Like some kind of glad-handing, folksy rogue,

– *Adult Film Association of America*

"... they kept coming back!"

you got the feeling that Dave Friedman was a likable fellow who was always two steps ahead of the local sheriff.

– *Kay Parker/Gordon Archive*

"You show 'em the sizzle, not the steak."

"Here's Kay Parker tastefully illustrating Dave's point.

Always looking for the next big moneymaker on the fringes of mass culture, in 1963, he moved on from strictly sex films to make *Blood Feast*, a "splatter movie" with blood gushing everywhere. According to his *LA Times* obituary, Friedman said that the film cost $24,500 to make and turned a $6.5 million profit.

"It was crude. The acting was terrible, and the effects were homemade," Friedman was reported to have said of his film. "But it was just something new, something no one had ever dared to do before."

Other splatter movies followed as well as more soft-core comedies like *The Erotic Adventures of Zorro*.

Dave Friedman died on Valentine's Day, 2011. He was eighty-seven years old. His memoir is titled, *A Youth in Babylon: Confessions of a Trash-Film King*. It was published in 1990.

Chapter Thirty
Payback

Before we left the Sexology Conference in Washington, Sam took me aside and told me he was working on a new project with Seka.

Seka was the hottest star in the business at the time and Sam was excited. He told me this was going to be a very big picture and he wanted me to play the male lead in it.

It was welcome news. I hadn't had a paycheck in six months and Sam let me know that this was gonna be a big one. Though it wasn't spoken out loud, I knew this was my payback for remaining loyal to him and turning down the offer to work in the *Talk Dirty* sequel made without him directing. Usually with Sam, John Leslie got the lead role and I was his costar. This time, it would be reversed.

Sam swore me to secrecy. I could tell Carly, but that was it. He said that there were still a lot of ways that this deal could fall apart so he wanted to keep his cards close to the vest. This was late May of 1983. He wanted to start filming in July. The only reason he was telling me now was because he wanted me to head back to the gym and get myself into the best shape of my life. The character I was to play was a gym owner who worked as a personal trainer to the stars. Sam wanted me back in my *Playgirl* Centerfold's body.

All right, I agreed to it. Putting a carrot like that on a stick was about the only way I could get this ass of mine back in the gym. I was getting awfully tired of doing sit-ups. But for a big job like this, I would revisit Narcissus again.

And speaking of heavenly bodies, Seka was in on all of this because she not only was going to star in this movie but she was also going to be one of the film's producers. She wrote this note in my diary:

– Gordon Archive/Seka

Seka, my next leading lady!

Chapter Thirty-One

We went to Pittsburgh after DC and while we were there, Aunt Kitty took us out to her favorite Chinese restaurant.

When we were reading our fortune cookies afterward, my Dad asked, "Where's mine?"

"It's in your cookie," we told him.

"Oh, no!" he said, "I ate it!"

Chapter Thirty-Two

When we got back to Berkeley, we were stunned to see Official

County Notices posted on both our cottage and on the big brown house in front that the entire property was being put up for Public Auction. It was just two weeks away.

Our landlord had defaulted on his loans. He was a contractor who had been buying up run-down properties with the intention of fixing them up and then reselling at a profit. For whatever reasons, his real estate empire had gone kerflooey and the powers that be were now biting his ass. The entire property was being put up for Public Auction in two weeks.

"You said that already."
"I know. It made me nervous."

The very next day, I was in bed reading when I heard Carly suddenly scream outside. The back of the brown house was on fire!!

It was serious. You could hear the fire. Dried cedar shingles were crackling. Windows were exploding. The place was lit up!

Carly rushed into the cottage for the baby. I rushed by her for the garden hose. I got water on the fire just as Carly carried Juliana out toward the street. I was joined a moment later by a stranger visiting next door who had rushed over with their garden hose running. We sent another neighbor into the front of the brown house to make sure all the people were out of there. Someone else called the fire department.

We battled the blaze with our two little garden hoses for a very long five minutes before the big guys showed up with their heavy artillery. We hadn't come close to putting out the fire. but we did slow it down some from spreading. The firemen had it out in about ten minutes. Then they tore into the house with axes to make sure there were no hidden embers.

The fire had centered in an added-on room that had been damaged by the blaze and then totally destroyed by the firemen. The rest of the house was still intact. Firemen said our quick response had probably saved the brown house, our cottage, and the two neighboring buildings on either side. They said we were all very lucky.

This began a series of improbable events that saw Carly and I becoming homeowners within the next few weeks.

What?

This began a series of improbable events that saw Carly and I becoming homeowners within the next few weeks.

First of all, the fire, following on the heels of the Official Public Auction notices, looked awfully suspicious. Everyone pretty much assumed foul play, but it didn't really take fire officials very long to dismiss that notion. They said it was just a coincidence. The fire had apparently been started by an article of clothing left draped over a space heater by one of the tenants.

It actually made sense to us. The guy who lived in that room was a real unconscious Joe. My mother would have described him as the kind of fellow who would lose his feet if they weren't attached. It was easy to imagine him as the cause of such a blaze. He moved out hours after the fire and hasn't been heard from since.

We had a one-year-old baby and we were pregnant with number two. We either had to buy the property, now, or worry about where to move if we didn't fit into the new owner's plans.

The money came from Carly's parents. And so did all the patience, skill, and knowledge about how to play such a hand as negotiating and buying a house.

Carly and I, who knew next to nothing about such things, did our best to say, "Thanks," and tried to follow their orders. They were such grown-ups. We were such pretenders. It wasn't easy for anybody.

Having a baby had cut into our own time to act like children, and now real estate was really threatening to remove whatever foolishness that remained. We were playing with Carly's parents' money. We did not want to make any mistakes. I can't speak for Carly here, but as much as I wanted it, I also found myself resisting the whole thing.

Termite reports, insurance rates, water bills, gas bills, earthquake preparedness, fixed rates, variable rates, low-flow toilets, gas lines, property taxes, square footage, titles, escrow, fire damage, police reports, contractors, plumbers, carpet layers, carpenters, sheet rock guys, cement guys, electricians, Bank loans, second mortgages, liens, spleens, and fucking baked beans, I didn't want any part of any of it. I had a few issues.

I wanted to run away to Never Never Land and hang out with Peter, Pan, and Mary. When I had the money to buy a house, I'd buy a house. This was all bullshit!!! I wasn't ready.

Uh, it was Carly who conducted the negotiations with our landlord. Coached by her parents, that is, Carly conducted the negotiations. She was soon joined by a lawyer friend of ours who her folks recommended we hire to see us through the deal. I was about as useful in this process as I had been at the hospital when Carly was giving birth.

As the purchase unfolded, and I had occasion to speak to a number of our friends who were homeowners, I was surprised to learn that almost all of them had received serious financial backing from their parents when they first bought a house.

Oh.

Okay, that calmed me down some, but there was still one more very large elephant in the room. It was time for Carly's parents to know about my career. They needed to have a clear picture of our finances and it was just time. Not surprisingly, Carly got this job too. They were her parents.

Sometime later, I asked Carly to write the story in my diary.

She wrote:

> *Maybe it was on Saturday, I'm not sure, but one day while my parents were visiting recently, I told them that Howie had made some X-rated films.*
>
> *I picked them up at the hotel where they were staying and after they got in the car I said:*
>
> *"I had a conversation with Sis while she was here that caused me to rethink some things, and I wanted to share it with you. We were talking about Howie, and she was asking questions about him, and his work and our money, and finally I said I was going to tell her a secret, and now I'm going to tell <u>you.</u> The secret is that Howie has made some films that have included some explicitly erotic scenes — some X-rated films. We never said anything to you about it because we felt you might be embarrassed, or <u>we'd</u> be embarrassed, or you'd disapprove — I'm not sure exactly why, but it just felt awkward and we never did. But the point is, he's done it — and made some very good money at it — and we began to realize that he must look like a kind of a bum to you, and that it was unfair to you to go on seeing things without this information. What began as just something we didn't think it was important to share, after a while we realized had become an active deception, which was not what we wanted to be doing at all.*
>
> *"You guys have always been so generous to us, and now*

lending us all the money to buy this house — and just all the things you've given us over the years, we didn't want you to be thinking that Howie didn't even have the willingness to earn any money — he earned as much money last year as I did, as a matter of fact.

"So now you know. I don't know how much you want to know, or how much he wants to say, but you certainly can ask any questions you have."

By this time we had arrived in the driveway of our house. My father began talking about a conversation he'd had with Howie in which he (Dad) had suggested that Howie take a course in accounting so that the business of managing our new property would not seem so scary, and went on to say that he felt pride of ownership was a wonderful change he felt he could see in Howie already.

As we came up the front walk my mother said, "I only have one question. What will your children tell the other kids at school who ask what their daddy does for a living?"

I replied, "They'll say he's an actor." A few paces later, I added, "These films have all been made under a different name. Nobody has to know anything we don't choose to tell them."

My mother turned and gave me a big hug and a kiss and said, "God bless you."

And that was all. (Later she asked his stage name, and I told her.)

On the very next page of my diary, Carly drew a cheery picture in colored felt tip pens. It was a big tree set against the backdrop of a smiling sun and birds flying. Under the tree, the Potato Head Family was waving. There was Mr. Potato Head in a Derby hat, Mrs. Potato Head with a ribbon in her spud, and Baby Potato Head with a teeny ribbon. The baby said, "Hi." It was happy. I could see what a relief it had been for my wife to tell her parents about my career in X. The caption over her picture read,

"So there you have it!"

It was a relief for me too. For the first time in almost seven years, I didn't have to worry anymore about who knew I was in the business.

– Drawing by Carly

Carly told her parents.

Everybody I cared about now knew. Everybody else could just go fart under the covers and enjoy themselves. I counted myself extremely fortunate that our parents were able to accept my "unorthodox" career choice without any major traumas. Not all adult performers shared such a benign fate. Over the years, I'd heard stories of fractured families and bitterness that went as far as suicide. I was one of the lucky ones.

On June 6, 1983, the thirty-ninth anniversary of D-Day, Carly and I signed a contract to buy the property from our struggling landlord. We beat the County Auction by two days.

On July 22, thanks to the incredible generosity of Carly's parents and the perfect lining up of all just the right stars, the title of ownership officially became ours.

Chapter Thirty-Three

Twenty-five years after Carly first told her parents about my career, my mother-in-law finally let me know what really happened. It was on the eve of my son premiering his one-man show, *Debbie Does My Dad* in San Francisco. Family confessions were abounding.

My mother-in-law explained that she and Carly's dad had flown to Canada right after the conversation in which they had received the news of my adult career. They were about to catch their train for their intended cross-country Canadian journey. My mother-in-law swears that she got so sick trying to recover from the shock of Carly's news that they had to cancel their trip and fly back home where she took to her bed.

She was a rabbi's daughter. She had a view of herself and her family as part of a cultural elite. I had ridden through that notion of refinement and community standing like a Cossack with a saber. This was a *Fiddler on the Roof* moment and then some! Like Tevya's struggles to embrace the men his daughters fell in love with, she had to move a long way to find room in her heart for me.

She waited more than twenty-five years to tell me that story, but by then, we were all living in another galaxy. We had found love and devotion for each other and I'm sure glad that we did.

Chapter Thirty-Four

"All's well that ends well, I suppose," Marty the literary agent said. He was quoting Shakespeare. "But that was a pretty tough chapter," he added.

"You're telling me!" I said.

"You sure you want to put that in there? It's not exactly you at your best," Marty said. "You come off like every parent's nightmare. I mean, what would you do if one of your own daughters suddenly showed up at your front door married to a clown like you were in those days?"

"Oi," I said, "Oi."

"Exactly. So, whatta ya think?" Marty asked. "You do remember where the 'delete' button is, don't you? People reading this to find out about the 'Golden Age of Porn' don't need to be tuned in to this level of your personal life."

"Oh, I think that ship sailed a long time ago, Marty. I don't know if this is even about porn anymore. I think that writing your memoirs is a lot like taking an all-expenses paid trip through Purgatory where you have to watch all of your life, the good, the bad, the embarrassing, and even the incomprehensible. You have to watch all of your life up there on the big screen and find a way to write about it."

"Well, nobody's making you write these memoirs!"

"I am," I told him, "I am."

Chapter Thirty-Five

The best part of going to the Adult Film Association Awards that year in LA was taking my friend John O'Keefe.

– Gordon Archive

Always loved "The Awards."

I thought that John O'Keefe was the finest actor in the world, bar none. To begin with, like Richard Burton and Ronald Coleman, he had one of those rich, melodic voices. He had the alchemy to make spoken language into music.

Out of the theatrical incubator of the University of Iowa, O'Keefe was even more keen on being a playwright and a director than he was on promoting his career as an actor. He once told me that it made him crazy to have to take direction from people who were dumber than he was.

As powerful as he was as a performer, he became even more celebrated and honored for his work writing and directing over the years.

John O'Keefe, Bob Ernst, and David Schein were the founding members of Berkeley's Blake St. Hawkeyes, a legendary Bay Area ensemble of the avant-garde. And John and Bob were my first two acting teachers. Carly took their classes too. From our beginning as their students, we developed fertile friendships with them both that have lasted for years.

During the summer of 1983, John was working at the Padua Hills Playwrights Festival near LA, when we invited him to take the night off and join us in town for porn's big awards show.

For me, it was a replay of the New York Awards held earlier that year. John Leslie won Best Actor, Jamie Gillis got Best Supporting, but my picture, *Irresistible*, was once again named Best Picture of the Year.

After the show, we were driving through Beverly Hills in our limousine on the way to the *Playboy* Mansion for the after prom. John O'Keefe and I had shared some pretty lean times together back in Berkeley, and here we were riding in a stretch limo through Beverly Hills. We were going to Huey Hefner's house. Fuckin' A. We stood up in the back of the limo and stuck our heads out through the sunroof. It was a dark night filled with bright stars and warm breezes. All we had to do was look at each other.

Later, back inside, John said, "Oh, shit! I'm out of cigarettes!"

"No problem," I told John. "We'll just stop at a Seven-Eleven and get you some more." Our driver, an English fellow, who had a pretty refined voice of his own, said,

"Sir, there are no Seven-Elevens in Beverly Hills."

It seemed like we laughed for twenty minutes.

Once inside Mr. Hefner's *Playboy* fortress, John O'Keefe simply died and went to Heaven. I owed *Screw* publisher Al Goldstein a huge thank you for his smuggling John onto the guest list. I'd never seen John more tickled. For once, he was undeniably on the inside of the American Dream instead of just hanging around on the outside with his nose pressed against the glass. It made our night joyous.

Carly and I left early. We'd been on this ride before and we wanted to get back to the hotel to be with our baby. John stayed at the Mansion until the sun came up. He'd gotten himself stranded. He somehow had missed connection with the ride that we had arranged for him. Ron Jeremy bailed him out. Ron Jeremy drove him all the way back to the Padua Hills Playwright's Festival. That was really nice of him. Thanks, Ron!

Win, lose, or draw, "The Awards" were always special.

Chapter Thirty-Six

Just before Seka's film got started, I did my first TV talk show appearance as Richard Pacheco. I'd done a fair amount of these TV things, but they had all been as Howie for *Playgirl*.

This show was *Finnerty & Company*, a local TV talk show in Sacramento. I was on an adult film panel with fellow performers Annette Haven, Juliet Anderson, and John Seeman. We did pretty well considering that it was a fairly conservative environment.

My biggest mistake was offering a car ride back to the Bay Area to both Annette and Juliet. In hindsight, I should have picked just one of them, because on this particular occasion, they did not exactly bring out the best in each other. My car radio was broken and I had two hours and 120 miles of just-trying-to-stay-out-of-it.

Though it was chilly outside, every now and then I had to open the window just to let some of the words out.

Chapter Thirty-Seven
The Greatest X-rated Movie Never Made

We spent over $600,000 making this Spinelli epic, which should have been the pinnacle of our X-rated careers. But World War III broke out between all the powers connected to this film and the movie ended up being stashed in a vault somewhere by angry owners who vowed never to release it to the public. So far, they haven't.

The movie had the now ironic title of:

– Gordon Archive

The movie that never was.

There were so many plots, sub-plots, intrigues, betrayals, and private agendas that went along with the making of this movie that this is really a hard story to tell. Frankly, there was a lot of juicy stuff going on here that really was none of my business. An accurate rendition of this story would resemble a treasure map that had been torn into several key parts that would all have to be pieced back together to gain any glimmer of the whole truth.

It will never happen, but I will tell you what I can.

In the middle of a trend toward making lower budget feature films, *Sunny Days* came along like a blockbuster fluke. It started big and it started great. It was top drawer all the way. All the excitement was because of Seka.

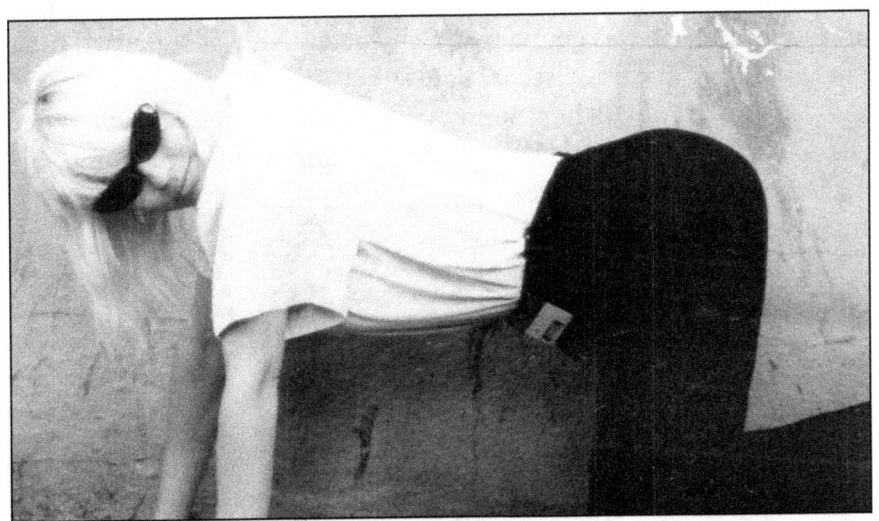

– Gordon Archive/Seka

The way that Spinelli explained it to me was that the producers had come to Seka with their checkbooks open.

She had been out of the business for a while, but spelled out some terms for them under which she might be induced to make another film. Sam said that the numbers were high and the word was that the producers didn't even blink. Seka was back in the business.

Seka had risen from the loops to the top of the adult industry. She was the reigning blond bombshell of the Age. Nobody had confused her early films with great drama, but the sex had always been superb. In this film, Seka wanted to take a big step up as an actress. She arranged for Anthony Spinelli to direct. And not only would Seka star in this film but she would also share in producing it as well.

Spinelli. Sam. He was acknowledged as the most legitimate director and the best acting teacher in the business. He dispatched his writer son, Michael Ellis, to Chicago to hang out with Seka and develop a screenplay based upon her life. Within a couple of months, there was a script. Spinelli hired John Leslie me and for the film, but I would play the lead this time. The money was great.

Rehearsals started in early August. As usual, Spinelli and I butted heads a lot. He'd take what he liked of my ideas and then bend me to his will with the rest.

His son had originally written Seka's "character" as Seka. I thought that was all wrong. Here she was trying to make a dent for herself as an actress and she was gonna play a character that was supposed to be herself? Didn't make any sense to me.

I suggested we call her "Sunny." Seka could look very sunny. When she was smiling, she could light the room. Sam went for it. "Sunny" became her character and *Sunny Days* became the movie.

I also managed to get my old acting teacher Bob Ernst cast in the role of "Sunny's" acting coach in the movie. Bob Ernst was an actor's actor. While Fame and Fortune may have eluded him and been awarded to the fluffier and less deserving, no one who has ever seen him perform has ever walked out of a theater less than amazed by his talent. Sam was happy to have him.

I wasn't so successful with suggestions about my own character. I named him Dugan. That much, Sam allowed. But while I was thinking of a

- Gordon Archive

Bob Ernst of The Blake St. Hawkeyes.

quiet guy with an understated strength, Sam was thinking of a clownish buffoon. I was after Gary Cooper. Sam wanted Lou Costello. Y'know, maybe I was lucky after all that this movie was never released. Lord only knows what kind of performance I gave trying to resolve that conflict. It was not a fun process, but it was becoming a familiar pattern.

Lately, it seemed like whenever I'd come up with a solid handle on how I wanted to play a character, Spinelli would figuratively blindfold me, spin me around seventeen times, rip off the blindfold, and then call, "Action!"

Either he liked my performance when I was off balance and confused or else I was just being punished for trespassing upon what he perceived as his domain. Sometimes it seemed that the only point he was really trying to make was who held the power. He never gave an inch in those arguments, often I felt, to the detriment of the picture.

Sunny Days was a lot more of the same. The only difference was maybe I argued a little harder. This was a big opportunity for me, I wanted to give it my best effort. We'd done a lot of projects together. Maybe I was getting to the stage where I was stretching my own wings a little more. I wanted to try more of my own ideas. Could be I was getting ready to fly out of the nest.

"You act! I direct!" Sam had told both John Leslie and me on many, many, many occasions.

John would argue more vociferously than me and he would pout longer when he didn't get his way. But in the end, he too would bow to the will of Spinelli. We were his odd couple. We were his boys. In both cases, the relationships were personal. They went beyond "the business." There was a lot of love there. Still is.

Seka and Spinelli fought a lot too, but that was a different story. Sam didn't always win those confrontations. And he was not the least bit happy about it either.

Seka had the ear of the producer. I don't know if she was actually going to be credited as an associate producer or an executive producer herself, but whatever she was, she got Sam hired and it appeared she could get him fired too.

As an actress, even the star, her job was to obey the director. She had made the point of wanting Spinelli in the first place. He had accepted the task of eliciting a strong dramatic performance from her. She was to be the paint. He was to be the painter. However, in league with her friend the producer, Seka could also tell Sam where to get off and she frequently did.

I didn't envy Seka trying to wear those two hats at once. And I didn't envy Spinelli either, his position of trying to direct her. The two of them had some nasty go-rounds. I got stuck in the middle a lot working as a bridge. It was a thankless job. They both expected my total allegiance.

On one occasion in Seka's dressing room, the name-calling got so bad that I just excused myself and told them that I'd be in my dressing room when they were finished. I should have done more of that.

Spinelli was pissed at me for getting involved at all. He figured that she might think she had an ally and that would make her stronger. I don't think it ever even dawned on him that I actually agreed with her position, over his, any number of times. Sam was fond of saying, "When you work for me, you take the first bullet." I had always tried to back him up. Sam treasured loyalty.

But this film was a different story. It was muddy. As far as I could see, the conflicts were really all just about power. The cause of an argument over some movie detail would rapidly degenerate into a confrontation of just who was gonna get their way. As an experienced director, Spinelli was a heavyweight champion at this kind of infighting. But Seka, well, she was the knockout with the knockout power. She was new at taking over the management of her professional life and was enjoying using the power of her box office. Their backstage squabbles should have been on Pay-Per-View. Probably was a better movie than the one we were making. Certainly didn't lack for any genuine passion.

I think it was a huge job for Seka to be directed by Spinelli after a whole career where, basically, the sex had been enough. It was a three week shoot. That was a long time for an X-rated movie. I think it just wore her down. I think she got tired of being vulnerable. I think she got tired of taking orders. Every now and then, she just had to assert the power that she knew she had and go against Spinelli. And when that happened, she was not gentle. These were two very tough birds. It was often messy.

The Lioness and the Rabbit

I didn't want to do that first sex scene on the first day. I wanted more time on the set to get used to things again. I wanted more time to get to know Seka. I was overruled.

I hadn't been on a movie set in nine months. That was a long time.

We started shooting that day at one-thirty in the afternoon. It was Friday, August 12. It was a hot, hot day in Bob Vosse's old San Francisco soundstage and things were not going well.

We were just gonna quickly do a couple of dialogue scenes before the sex, but we managed to keep screwing them up. When the actors were good, the cameras were bad. Throw in a mix of sound problems, lighting problems, and Sam just not being happy with a take problems, and people were getting downright cranky. Next thing you know, it was nine o'clock at night and we had to stop farting around, relight the set, and do our big sex scene. *Take a breath.*

I was nervous. I was nervous. I was nervous. These were performance jitters. Did I tell you that I was nervous? I was nervous. Seka was Secretariat. This was the Kentucky Derby. And the sad truth was, I was not ready to ride her in this race.

I *thought* I was prepared. I had trained hard. I knew all my lines. My body was beautiful. I'd even had my fingernails manicured. I'd heard that Seka had this thing about guys with dirty fingernails. Mine were all cleaned, trimmed, and pretty. I hadn't had an orgasm in four days. I should have been able to fuck a Volkswagen. But ya know what?

Lust was a feeling that had first wavered when Carly and I got pregnant and then vanished completely during all the 3 a.m. feedings. And now, we were pregnant again. I hadn't had sex on camera in nine months and the last time had been that disastrous epic with Colleen in Svetlana's movie. I was not eager for the erotic combat. I had no confidence. I felt like Samson after the haircut. I was not ready for another trial by ordeal.

This was like beginning the baseball season with a Game Seven of the World Series. Seka was the American League Champ. I was supposed to be the National League Champ. This was supposed to be a big sex scene in a big movie! They were paying me a lot of money. I was supposed to be a star. I was trying to run here with Jamie Gillis and John Leslie. I was supposed to know how to do this. I was supposed to go up to the plate and get a big clutch hit here with men on base.

I was being asked to have sex with Seka! Good God, she was this amazing lioness! You want to know what the problem was? I'll tell you what the problem was:

It was now Showtime and I rolled the dice. I was hoping to be Studly DoRight or Randy Cowboy or Billy the Bone and what I came up with ... was *Bunny Gardenia!* You ever been *Bunny Gardenia?* He was a fucking rabbit! This sex scene was gonna be *"the lioness and the fucking rabbit!"*

"Woe was me!" I did not know what to do. I was too revved up. Is this too much information? Can you stand to know this about a man?

I needed to calm down. I needed a game changer. Okay, I took a half of Valium.

I should have *talked* to somebody. I should have talked to Seka, or Sam, or even called Carly, but I didn't. I mean, who wanted to hear the cowboy sing a song of fear?

Asshole! Stupid! Fuck! Shit! Piss! The Valium was a *terrible* idea! It didn't relax me at all. It *stunned* me. It was like getting hit in the head with a hammer. I got nauseated and dizzy. It was hot. It was so hot! It was hard for me to walk. I had to lie down. I had to realize that taking the half of Valium had rendered me even less capable than I was before I took it! Dumb! Dumb! Dumb!

I wanted only to lie down and not be hot any more. I didn't want to have to do *anything*. For the moment, forget about how I got here, but the idea that I was waiting to do a sex scene was just plain cruel ... to me ... to Seka ... to Spinelli, and to the whole damn movie. Ladies and gentlemen, I fucked up.

I tried sleeping. Runaway bunny. I couldn't fall asleep, but I tried to rest myself and calm myself down. I tried contacting my penis. "Hello? Anybody home?"

Somebody was there, but they were not answering the front door. They were upstairs and they were groggy. I worried. I had to wake them up. I ate a little. Sugar, I figured, get some quick energy. I had a piece of wretched chocolate cake and some apple juice.

If Viagra, Cialis, and Levitra had been around back then, I would have thrown them all in a blender with some orange juice and a banana and made myself a sexual smoothie. Fear and stupidity can make for dangerous allies. Probably would have ended up in the hospital.

Then the call came to get into makeup.

Put up or shut up. Susan the makeup lady began to work on me. After a while, I told her that I was feeling very, very far away and nauseated. I was too embarrassed to mention the Valium, but I did tell her that I didn't know if I could do the scene.

Susan, very nurse-like, said, "Well, that doesn't sound like you," and she put a cold compress on my neck and shoulders. Seka came by. I told her that I was not in great shape. I was apologetic. Next thing I knew, Spinelli was hovering. I "suggested" that he might want to have a contingency plan ready to shoot something else because I didn't know if I could make it. He told me to let him know as soon as I could tell.

The next thing I knew, Seka and I were in bed.

We were kissing. I was scared. I was listening to a lot of different radio broadcasts going off in my head. I liked Seka, though. I thought she was my buddy.

Y'know, all these years later, it's apparent to me that I was so self-absorbed in my own internal dilemmas at that point, that I had absolutely no idea what Seka was going through when we shot this scene. I'm going to ask her to please tell her side of this story. And if she's willing, I promise that I'll put it in here, right next to mine.

So, we were kissing and I didn't know if they were filming us or not. The scene was supposed to have started with some dialogue, but we never did it. We were just kissing.

Then we touched each other's genitals a bit. Actually, we rubbed our legs over each other's private parts. She was wearing a matching blue bra and panties. I had on my birthday suit, augmented by body makeup.

I started getting aroused. I definitely viewed this as a gift from God and pulled down her underpants for whatever might be happening next. I wanted to finger her. She was so all brand-new to me that I felt like I was wearing big, thick mittens. I wasn't sure where to touch her or how. I was playing with a warped deck.

"Deck," I said, "not dick." But that too actually. For while I fumbled with this new piece of woman flesh, I lost what little arousal that had come to pass.

When my dick shriveled, I had a conversation with myself that began with, *Uh-Oh*, and continued on with me wondering if, and how, my erection was ever going to be coming back. All this happened while I was fumbling to be pleasuring her female parts with my left hand.

Y'know, sometimes, you can't walk and chew gum at the same time. I don't think I looked her in the eye very much.

Somehow, after a bit, I found myself sucking her vulva.

I was a "vulvasucker!" Now, there's a term you don't hear all the time. "Cocksuckers" are everywhere, even on Showtime and HBO. But I don't care how much cable you watch, you're not likely to hear about too many "vulvasuckers," not even on The L Word! "Muffdivers," maybe, but not too many "vulvasuckers." Alas, I digress....

I found myself sucking her vulva. All of it. Anything. I was fishing for her response and looking hard. I was trying not to look or lick too hard, but just be soft, and finding something that I could feel she liked.

I'm workin' here! I'm workin' here!

Man, I was nibbling and nervous. I had no idea what the cameras were doing and it seemed like six months since I had last heard from Spinelli. After maybe twenty minutes more of me sucking her, my dick wasn't hard yet and I didn't know nothin'. I imagined that they were sick of this position, but were either being too shy or too nice to say anything.

When I added my fingers to the pussylicking, I discovered the hard stubble of my beard. It had been twelve hours since my last shave.

"Oh, my God!" I thought, "I've been torturing this poor woman with sandpaper chin and she's been either too shy or too nice to say anything."

I covered the stubble with my hand and tried to use only my tongue. my lips, and my teeth as the oral sex continued.

Seka later told me that she'd had an orgasm during this time. For vanity's sake, I certainly wanted to believe her, but I was all twelve of Santa's reindeer when we shot this scene and I had no idea what was real.

Okay. I knew we had to change positions. Even if nobody was saying anything, I still knew it. So I came up her body and we fell into another kiss. By now, I should have been hard and I should have been fucking her. I wasn't and we weren't. I started fingering her again. One improvises and waits for the gods to decide. I wanted her to touch me back. She did … with kind of a feathery touch. It wasn't enough. I wanted her to squeeze me hard, yank me, pull me. She did me one better. She journeyed down my body and took my cock in her mouth.

Well, Halle-fucking-lujah! I felt a breath come into my body like I hadn't been breathing at all.

Still, I didn't harden right away and I fought the fear of knowing that. I tried to stop panic. Breathe. The warmth was good. I knew that if this sex scene was gonna happen at all, this was gonna be my best shot. I remembered Carly's advice from the early days, "Stick to what feels good." I began to move my hips. There was more breath, deeper breath. I pumped. She sucked.

Trickle. A trickle of pleasure was breaking through the panic. I remembered the word, "yes." Seka, God bless her, she worked me. It was slow going, but she worked me fine. Brick by brick, she dutifully built that boner.

The moment of truth was soon at hand. Would I survive the withdrawal from her mouth and remain hard enough to enter her vagina? It was like a football play, breaking the huddle and then rushing to the line of scrimmage.

"Hike!"

I made it! I was in. Now, pump, you motherfucker, pump for your life! All systems were go! *Houston, we have lift off.* Ride 'em, cowboy! Bunny Geranium was in the saddle! "I'm an old cowhand on the Rio Grande."

Seka was a thoroughbred. It was a sprint. The ride was short and sweet. They got enough footage and that was that. The rest of it was for us. The come shot was gonna be inside. This was a very un-porn like miracle. I always hated pulling out and squirting for the cameras. I thought that it was a crime against Man, Woman, God, and Nature, and good taste. We weren't gonna do that today. The come shot was gonna be inside. I saw the finish line.

The cameras were probably on our faces when I came. I hope we had the good sense not to be acting.

Right afterwards, I whispered in Seka's ear that we should redo this whole scene tomorrow. I was apologetic. I thought the scene was nothing. Chaotic. Bizarre. Out to lunch.

But, no, people were saying, "Fine!" Seka and I were dripping with sweat. They gave us towels.

I didn't know. I couldn't believe it. How could they use that scene? I was astonished. The camera people said they had all kinds of coverage. They got coverage? Where was I? I got nuts! I thought that Seka was surprised at how looney I was.

That was it. Ricky, the production manager, told me it was a wrap. He said I should come back tomorrow to finish the dialogue scene that we didn't get to today. I was going to get an extra day of work out of this! He told me to go home and relax.

I know I promised you a long time ago that I would take you on no more long drawn-out tales of my misadventures with my dick, but, frankly, I don't see how this one could have been avoided.

As filming on this movie progressed, we all had better days, much better days. I even got a second chance at a sex scene with Seka.

Coming down the home stretch, Sam got worried there wasn't gonna be enough sex in the film. He wanted to add one more sex scene and he wanted Seka to be in it. For whatever reasons, her first response was to go ballistic on him. They were off to the races again. Eventually, they resolved it with a compromise. I had nothing to do with it. Seka agreed to do another sex scene—if she could pick her partner and—if she would get to orchestrate the scene. Spinelli agreed.

Seka chose me to be her partner, thank you very much. And she wanted to do the entire sex scene under the covers. Wow!

The other side of exhibitionism is the resentment for the intrusion. And after years of having spotlights and cameras up your ass, the resentment sure can build. A whole sex scene under the covers! This may have been a very childish act, but I was all for it. We had so much fun. I've never seen the scene, but I'll bet it plays real hot. It was such a grand tease.

It was late in the shoot. There were no performance jitters. We'd been on the set daily for more than two weeks. We knew each other. We knew what we were doing. It was kind of like taking a victory lap.

Funny thing, I had a video camera I'd been bringing to the set all through this movie. I actually have about six hours of backstage video from *Sunny Days*. Sometimes, when I was in a scene, I'd get somebody who was just hanging around the set to shoot some footage for me. When this sex scene started, I had Sam's son, Mitch, running my camera. It was on a tripod right next to the big film camera. Together they both shot the dialogue set-ups to the sex and then Mitch thought he turned my camera off. He didn't want to shoot the sex scene, or be in the way, or whatever, so, he turned off the camera, got up, and walked away.

Well, two things happened. First of all, the camera was left still recording. And secondly, when he walked away, he bumped the camera. Now, instead of being focused on the bed, it was focused on a night table, next to the bed, with a lamp on it. As the scene progresses, you hear the noises of our lovemaking and see the lamp begin to move from our gyrations on the bed. A tremor becomes a wiggle and then a shake as this continues throughout the entire sex scene.

It's like a film that was shot by Andy Warhol in 1964. It could win a prize at some Eastern European art festival.

Chapter Thirty-Eight

On August 25, I was hanging out with the movie crowd in Seka's room back at the hotel. I called home to check in with Carly. She told me that she had just received the results from our amniocentesis tests. At five months, we had a healthy female fetus growing nicely in Carly's womb.

Juliana was gonna have a sister. Polly was on the way.

Chapter Thirty-Nine

By the time we wrapped *Sunny Days* after all the filming in San Francisco and Chicago, it had become something that cast and crew were all very proud of and eager to see completed and released.

As you already know, that hasn't happened.

At one point, before everything irrevocably blew up, Seka was invited to be a guest on a talk show hosted by Alan Thicke. He was another late night wannabe who got clobbered in head-to-head competition with Johnny Carson *on The Tonight Show*. But before they cancelled him, Thicke had Seka on his show in a bold attempt to attract some ratings.

I'm glad he did because Seka brought with her a clip from *Sunny Days*. It is the only footage I've ever seen from the movie. I managed to record it off the TV. In it, we were just strolling down the lakefront in Chicago and talking about love. It was very sweet. And it was great to see us on television in that mainstream spot.

We had crazy high expectations for this film. I had crazy high expectations for this film. I expected it to take my career to the next level, whatever that was gonna be, and I expected that soon I would be making a whole lot more money for my young and growing family.

Oopsie!

Sunny Days became a phantom, a ghost of what it might have been that now only haunts itself. Very few people in the industry remember it and most people have never even heard of it, but I contend that it remains ...

- Vincent Fronczek/Gordon Archive/Seka

"Just a little bit of love?"

THE GREATEST X-RATED MOVIE NEVER MADE.
Seka's side of the story

May 30, 2011

I have to tell you what I remember about that whole thing. I knew that I was making some big bucks for doing the movie in the first place and I had pretty much control over most everything. That being said ...

I wanted the people in the movie to be people I really liked and respected. I wanted them to be paid VERY, VERY well and to be treated like actors and not livestock. Now that you know that, you know why Howie was playing the lead male role. I was and still am just crazy about Howie. We were friends then and we are still friends to this day. Howie, I love you my darling, sweet friend.

Now, about that day. I could tell that Howie was very nervous as he was acting a bit strange, but not knowing how he normally acted before a sex scene, I didn't want to say anything to him because as we all know, all a woman has to do is say one wrong word and the dick is going to run away and hide and he AIN'T coming out again 'til he knows the coast is clear. So, I just watched and waited, watched and waited. We all watched and waited for a long time that day and it was not because of Howie. Doing any kind of movie is a lot like being in the army ... hurry up and wait.

Now, it's time and we are in bed kissing, sucking and being sucked. I thought to myself while Howie was down there in the throes of the war that he was going through (that I was unaware of), HOLY CRAP, the boy knows what he's doing! Howie, I don't know if I ever told you, but you eat some good pussy. Back to that, I was getting wet and sweaty when I noticed that he had a twelve-fourteen hour beard. I have to tell you, that is what put it over the top for me. It was very tender and rough at the same time — a very delicate tight rope to walk and Mr. Gordon was the master. That was what made me want to give some of that pleasure back to him — so I slid his manhood into my mouth gently sucking, licking, and tonguing his lovely unit. The next thing I remember he was inside of me and I was in heaven. We were sweating, dripping from almost every orifice. Then, as quickly as it seemed to happen, it was over and we were just there in an orgasmic heap, basking in the afterglow of one hell of a roll in the sheets.

It was not until much later that I knew of the pure HELL that Howie had been going through. You know, looking back on it, Howie is pretty much like that with most things in his life. There are few men in this world that have their big head control what happens with the little head, Howie is one of those men — and the man that I have been with for some ten years now is the same way. So, Howie, you see after all, you were and are the kind of man that I have always looked for. A man that knows how to use his head.

I love you Howie.
Seka

Chapter Forty
Sober Monday

> "I always fall in love while I'm working on a film. It's such an intense thing, being absorbed into the world of a movie. It's like discovering that you have a fatal illness, with only a short time to live.
>
> So you live and love twice as deeply. Then, you slip out of it, like a snakeskin, and you're cold and naked. What worries me is that when these loves die, they hardly leave traces on me. I wonder why I don't suffer."
>
> – Natassia Kinski, actress,
> *Time* magazine, May 2, 1983

I don't know why you didn't suffer either because I was seriously into self-inflicted wounds myself. Since *Sunny Days* ended, I smoked a ton of pot and munchied myself into a good extra ten pounds while trying to make the reentry from the swashbuckling X-rated movie star to the stay-at-home husband, daddy-of-one, and expectant-daddy-of-another.

When I'd been home three weeks, it was arbitrarily time to put away the pot and sober up. Carly was nudging me back toward writing my X-rated memoirs and I was going to try and go with it. It had been my plan all along to have them done by January 1, 1984. Guess I'm running a little late!

It was a friend's cancer that was kicking our asses hard in those days. He was a fellow therapist at the clinic where Carly worked. Carly's pregnancy had all of her emotions on the surface with the shields down and the cancer in our friend was spreading. Nobody was talking about how much longer he had left, but that seemed to be the undercurrent of things, all the words between the lines.

Carly's belly was starting to get out there as we moved through our sixth month at the end of summer. I was eager for the fall. I'd had enough of the hot, sunny weather. It was hard to sit inside and write on such days. I wanted the cool comfort of the fog.

Birth and death are always happening at the same time, all over this earth, aren't they? It's just that we don't often feel it. We did that year.

It was a time to revise, rededicate, and make plans. My tobacco smoking was beginning to scare me. Our friend was a Marlboro man and he was dying of lung cancer.

He died on a Friday afternoon. Shortly before that, he told Carly that he'd had a dream Thursday night in which he'd left his body. When he woke up Friday morning and found himself still in it, he was pissed.

Carly told me that his last hours were peaceful and without pain. When she finally got home late that day, after having been one of the sisters of mercy who attended to him at the end, she was strong and shaken at the same time.

Several days later, I found getting through the memorial service to be scary and tough. I took solace in tuning it all out and writing a letter to be read at my own:

Don't make eulogies for me,
I didn't know shit.

And if the Truth be told,
I don't think you know all that much either.

I long ago made my peace with the fact
that the human mind was just way too puny to comprehend
just about any of the important anythings.

Since I'm already gone,
I'm just delighted to not have to be where you are …
sitting there, fucking grieving, that's the worst.

Go home. Go play some miniature golf.
Death is the great humbler of us all.

Since I'm gone, I suppose now, I know who
killed Kennedy … both Jack and Bobby.

Think of me as a fart that smelled like a rose.
I know I did!

Chapter Forty-One
Sex Play

Producer Ted Paramore flew me down to LA for a day of rehearsal.

Sex Play was going to be shot in Los Angeles. More and more of the adult films, and now, the adult videos, were being shot down there. Evidently, the police heat had been turned way down. I have no idea why. The world was changing. It was cheaper to shoot down there and except for the posh, twisted miracle of *Sunny Days*, cheaper was the magic word for the X-rated industry back at the end of 1983.

X-rated films and their movie houses were dying. The video revolution was deeply cutting into the profits. Perhaps rightly so, for all of the obvious reasons, people preferred to stay at home to watch their

– Photo by Carly

I changed from the remodeling Daddy at home smoking a crayon and carrying around a baba of appa juice …

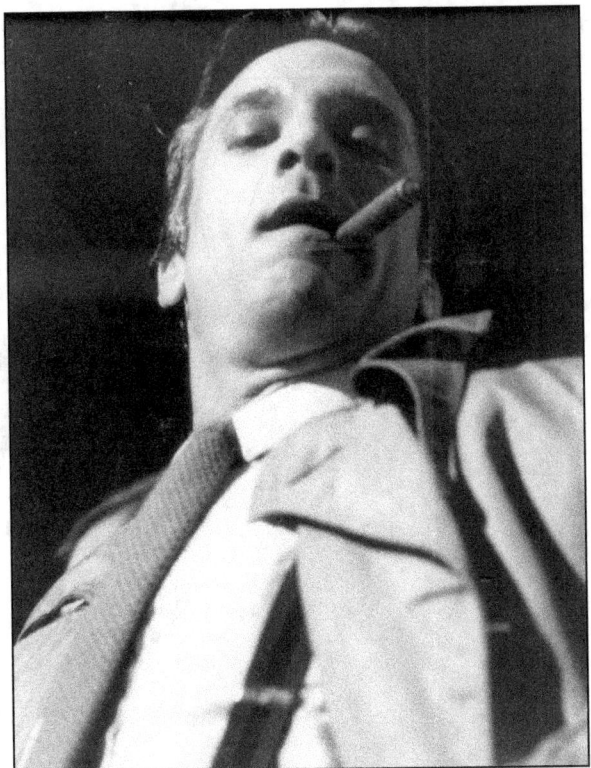

– Hustler Video/LFP Video Group, LLC

… and turned back into Pacheco the actor playing a detective in a movie.

sexy movies. In order to keep their profits up, budgets for making films were going down. *Sex Play* was such a film.

It began life as *The Fan Club*. It was the story of Jeff Justice, porn star. Played by the talented, handsome, adult veteran Eric Edwards, word was that Jeff Justice had become impotent. The plot hinged upon the premise that if this secret information somehow got leaked out to the public, then his studio would lose millions of dollars.

Porn loved to portray itself as if it were bigger than it was, like it was the financial equal of the straight Hollywood. But it was not often the straight corporate Hollywood of today that was depicted; it was usually the one from the days of the Big Studios. A cigar-chomping, X-rated producer like Ted Paramore loved to pretend that he was a Warner Brother or a Louie B. Mayer, only operating in smut.

Ted was an award-winning, successful producer and a charming rogue to boot. He could bounce a check on you every now and then.

– *Gordon Archive*

But eventually, he'd make good on it.

Ted once took me out to lunch to a great deli in the Valley. I think it was called Canter's. My test for a great deli has always been, do they have stuffed kishki in gravy? They had stuffed kishki in gravy.

Ted Paramore and Anthony Spinelli; although they were often fiercely competitive with each other, they both really played for the same team. They were lifetime LA Dreamers. They each worked hard and waited for the call to step up from the minor leagues of porn and take their places behind the camera just like the real Hollywood big boys.

"I'll have the stuffed kishki, please, extra gravy. I don't care what it costs."

This movie had a plot. I read all about it in the script, on the morning I flew down to LA for the rehearsal. Unfortunately, large chunks of that plot would later be expunged when the money ran out.

At the rehearsal that afternoon, I sat in a room where there were three women that I'd already had sex with, three more that I was scheduled to have sex with, and besides all of them, there were two more women that I actually wanted to have sex with. Imagine that.

What was the protocol for this type of moment? I didn't know who to talk to first, or who to touch, or even where to look without slighting somebody. I solved, or rather avoided, the problem by keeping pretty much to myself. Later, I did check in with the three women that I was to work with in the movie. Business before pleasure, I suppose, and I had to ask each of them if they had herpes. Each woman told me that she did not. I decided to believe them. This wasn't exactly being very scientific.

It wouldn't be too much longer before that question would become, "Do you have AIDS?" or "Are you carrying the HIV virus?" And by then, just their word would no longer be good enough either. The world was changing.

I was impressed with the work of director Robert McCallum on that rehearsal day. He was quick to the point with an eye toward being simple and eliminating any confusions.

I worked with Kay Parker in this film too.

– *Gordon Archive/Kay Parker*

Yes, I loved her. Still do. Kay Parker was unique in the business. She had a natural immunity about her, a true heart that made the beast of pornography stand down. She was like the good witch in *The Wizard of Oz*. We worked together three or four times in all and were usually lucky enough to find whatever magic we needed to transcend whatever manure they were throwing at us. We allowed each other dignity and humanity. We had the grace to appreciate each other. We brought the best parts of ourselves to the dance and we never had to apologize to anybody, about anything, ever.

Kay Parker was Hall of Fame stuff and one of the best people that ever happened to the X-rated business.

– Kay Parker

Kay Parker. God save the Queen.

I also was very impressed by Helene, the red-headed production manager. She fell into that special category of one of the two women that I actually wanted to have sex with. She had a ton of chutzpah, two guns, and a fancy sports car. When she told me that she also worked some as a straight Hollywood agent, I told her that I would love to have an agent who had her kind of nerve. She shook hands with me and said if she could get me anything outside of the X, then we'd work out a deal. I gave her some headshots and wished her luck. This was a sex scene begging to happen if I hadn't had to rush off to make the plane ride back home. She drove me to the airport.

Oh, don't worry, I heard it too. It's that same old song again.

You want to know how a guy that gets us all goo-goo eyed over his great love for his pregnant wife and young baby can still get his nose all wide open when a loosey-goosey, red-headed, two-gun Annie Oakley comes zooming around the corner with her top down?

What can I say? It's like a recurring theme with him. You can't really tell if he's bragging or if he's ashamed. It might just depend on who he thinks the audience is at any given moment. He gets like a politician who changes his message to fit the crowd.

Why am I talking about him like he's not even here? Have we given up all pretense of supporting characters and just surrendered to all the voices in his own head? Howie! Are you splitting up with yourself? Get it together, man!

I didn't want to be monogamous in 1983, or 1984, or 1985 ... and maybe my explanation back then would have been to say, "Well, there's breakfast, lunch, and dinner, y'know. Maybe even a midnight snack sometimes. You don't always want to eat the same food, do you?" But even I could see that was too glib, crude even, and unworthy of beings who spoke of true love and dared to imagine the soul.

Then again, I'm not always as sensitive as my press clippings proclaim. I'm like any other man. I don't always see things too clearly when I'm standing there with a boner, allegedly, pointing in the wrong direction.

I didn't want to be monogamous. I knew that. And so what if I couldn't explain it. Are all things rational? It was a feeling. And when I thought of being forced into monogamy, my claws came out. I had an animal self that just didn't want to hear about it.

I wanted my wife and my family ... and I wanted whatever else I wanted too.

> *Do I contradict myself?*
> *Very well then I contradict myself,*
> *(I am large, I contain multitudes.)*
>
> – Walt Whitman, *Song of Myself*

When in doubt, quote somebody famous and then run for cover.
Was I really any different from any other man? Or was it just that I was more willing to let the demon take the wheel and drive sometimes? This latest redhead wasn't even an actress. Couldn't blame that one on the business. But nothing really happened, then, did it? I made my flight. I went home.
It would take me more than another twenty years before I could ever really say that I wrestled that demon to a draw. But by then, of course, I was well into my fifties. It might just have been that he was getting a little tired.

Chapter Forty-Two

"You're killing me, Howie! You're killing me!" Marty the literary agent said. "Every woman in the world hates you right now and none of the guys give a shit. They're all watching ESPN."

Chapter Forty-Three
Polly Just Around the Corner

Back in Berkeley, we were repairing the damage done by the fire to the front house and we were also building a new children's wing for our cottage. The race was on. We were trying to get all this work done before the second bun came out of the oven. Baby Polly was due in January.
We were doing all this building in the rainy season. It was blue collar and it was messy. Did you ever try to shovel mud? The dirt was twice as heavy because of all the water. And when you went to throw it somewhere, it didn't go anywhere. It stayed right there on your shovel. You had to remove each shovelful of muck by hand. And you had to scrape it

all off before you could take your next shovelful. It took forever. It wore you out, even when you were working on your own house.

Carly had that late pregnancy waddle going and was having an awful lot of the Braxton Hicks contractions. They reminded me of labor trying to start itself the way drivers and pilots used to have to hand-crank those old engines of yore. I thought, *Just one more of those cranks would surely do the trick and labor could begin itself in earnest! Polly appeared to have all of her bags packed and was in the final approach for launch down the birth canal. Baby Traffic Control was monitoring her flight.*

The electrician made his first appearance since breaking our toilet some ten days ago. He was busy doing wiring in the kids' new bedroom. Most of the indoor construction had already been completed and we were left only with the odds and ends like installing some shelves.

Outside, there was still much to do, but who cared! After three months, it appeared we would meet our deadline of getting the cottage ready before Polly's birth.

Uh-oh, the electrician just broke the toilet again! What is it with this guy?

Chapter Forty-Four
Showtime

Carly woke me just after two o'clock in the morning.

These were still the days before TVs had remotes and the cable control box was on my side of the bed. Carly had been having trouble sleeping in the late stages of the pregnancy and was watching a lot of all-night television. To get at the controls, we had to switch sides of the bed. I thought that's what we were doing again, but she kept on shaking me.

"I'm in labor," she said.

We did it differently this time. I was not going to be the labor coach. During the birth of our first child, Carly had completely bonded with a hospital nurse named Marian. She was both gentle and firm as a rock. Helping women to deliver babies was her profession. Marian just seemed to have come out of nowhere to be exactly what Carly needed to get through that difficult first birth. When it was time to get on that rollercoaster again, Carly definitely wanted to ride with Marian.

I was grateful and relieved. To begin with, it completely freed me from the preposterous notion that I should somehow be monitoring the doctor's medical decisions in order to keep to some kind of hippy-dippy, delusional fantasy of natural childbirth. It freed me from having to pretend that I knew what I was doing. With Marian there, I could feel safe and secure because Carly was in the hands of a skilled, birthing angel.

Marian, I loved you then and I love you now. Thank you. Juliana, Polly, say thank you to the nice lady. *Bobby, you'll be getting your turn in a couple of years too.*

Labor, which took over thirty hours with the first-born, took about twenty minutes with the second. The hard part this time was pushing the baby out.

She didn't want to go. It took two or three hours to convince her.

Carly was spectacular. As I watched her in the throes of giving birth, I saw a galloping horse, the breath pushing and pulsing from her nostrils, her mane flowing in the wind, in the moonlight. She was strong, pulsating, and gorgeous.

Polly was born at 6:27 a.m. She weighed nine pounds, ten point two ounces. She looked like an Eskimo with dimples. Everyone breathed a sigh of relief.

There was joy in the land.

– *Gordon Archive*

POLLY!

Chapter Forty-Five
From My Diary,

Homecoming 1984. Whatever time there was, there's less of it now. A newborn and a toddler have us spinning.

– *La Belle Dame Sans Merci* – John William Waterhouse

Mommy and Daddy.

Carly and Polly came home today. I picked them up around 2:00 p.m. at the hospital. Polly is a bit jaundiced and must be watched. We take her in early tomorrow morning for some shots or something.

Juliana and I have severe colds. She gets away with being cranky, I don't. Such is the transition in life from child to adult.

Other than sickness and exhaustion, things are terrific.

Chapter Forty-Six

At the San Francisco Zoo's Birds of Prey Show, we met a great horned owl named King Richard who they told us was mentally unbalanced because he'd only been fed baloney for the first two years of his life. Kind of like the people who watch *Fox News*.

Chapter Forty-Seven

– Gordon Archive

I've got daughters!

Chapter Forty-Eight

I was delighted to win the first two acting awards that the Adult Video News ever gave out:

A Monthly Newsletter For Today's Sophisticated X-Rated Viewer

Vol. 1 No. 12 | February/March 1984 | $2.00

1st AVNA Awards Announced:
"Scoundrels," Howard, Pacheco, Mitchell Score Big

Best Picture - **SCOUNDRELS** *(Command Video)*
(Other nominees: All American Girls, Irresistible, Night Hunger and Nothing to Hide)

Best Director - **CECIL HOWARD** for Scoundrels *(Command Video)*
(Other nominees: Gerard Damiano for Night Hunger, Warren Evans for Hot Dreams, Henri Pachard for Devil in Miss Jones II and Anthony Spinelli for Nothing to Hide)

Best Actor - **RICHARD PACHECO** for Irresistible *(Essex Video)*
(Other nominees: Jerry Butler for In Love, Eric Edwards for Sexcapades, Ron Jeremy for Scoundrels and John Leslie for Nothing to Hide.)

Best Actress - **SHARON MITCHELL** for Sexcapades *(VCA)*
(Other nominees: Lisa Be for Scoundrels, Chelsea Manchester for Scoundrels, Kelly Nichols for Puss 'N Boots and Kay Parker for Intimate Lessons)

Best Supporting Actor - **RICHARD PACHECO** for Nothing to Hide *(Cal Vista)*
(Other nominees: Misha Garr for Irresistible, Jamie Gillis for Naughty Girls, Andrew Nichols for Cafe Flesh and Steven Tyler for Body Talk)

Best Supporting Actress - **TIFFANY CLARK** for Hot Dreams *(Caballero Home Video)*
(Other nominees: Lisa DeLeeuw for Up 'N Coming, Samantha Fox for Babe, Linda Shaw for Sorority Sweethearts and Honey Wilder for Taboo II)

– Adult Video News

These two awards given to me by AVN in 1984 might very well have been the mountaintop of my career.

You know what my Dad would have said about me putting something like that in here? He would have said, *"Self praise stinks!"* But then again, my Dad never tried to make it in show business.

Publisher Paul Fishbein and his AVN crew were just a small newsletter coming out of Philadelphia at this point, but they were the future and they were coming on strong. I felt seen by them and I felt appreciated. I thank you, gentlemen, then and now.

The awards season continued in 1984, with those of the Adult

Film Association of America. These guys were the old guard. By 1986, they would be out of business. Film would essentially be over by then as a source of adult product. The video revolution would have been completed and the Adult Video News (AVN) would become the new standard bearer for the entire industry.

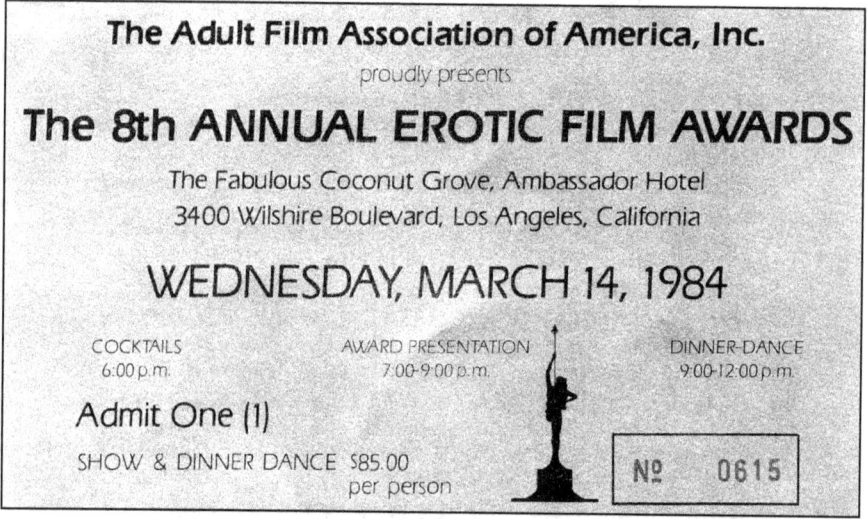

– *Adult Film Association of America/Gordon Archive*

This year, it looked like the Awards Show would belong to Colleen.

– *Vincent Fronczek*

Colleen was named Shauna Grant now.

– *Vincent Fronczek*

Shauna Grant the X-rated movie star!

By now, she had fucked John Leslie and Jamie Gillis. She had fucked Joey Silvera too. She fucked Paul Thomas, Jerry Butler, Ron Jeremy, and about twenty-seven other guys as well, but who's counting. This was the game we were all in.

They dressed her up. They undressed her. They posed her and they hosed her. She wasn't the first and she wouldn't be the last. They made her *Suzie Superstar!* And they made her *Virginia*.

– *Vincent Fronczek/Caballero.*

They took her picture and put her in the magazines and in the movies. They made her Shauna Grant, the porn star.

It was who she thought she wanted to be.

– Gordon Archive

But this is who she was without the war paint.

Her escort for the Awards that night was Francis Ford Coppola, the acclaimed director of *The Godfather*. Yes, that was extraordinary. Hollywood royalty did not generally show up for an X-rated awards show. It made you think that something extra special was happening for this young woman.

Shauna Grant was nominated four times in three different categories. Even for an X-rated actress, where the term "star" was bandied about loosely, Colleen's rise had been astonishingly meteoric. She'd made a bunch of movies since we'd worked together. Two of them were now nominated for Best Picture, and Shauna Grant was nominated for Best Actress in each of them.

I saw Colleen at the Awards rehearsal early that afternoon. All the freshness was gone. The baby pudge had melted away from her cheeks. She was now a sleek, young, LA greyhound.

She told me that she had quit the business. Wow! She said she'd been out of it now for about six months. She had a boyfriend, she said, but he was in jail. She was working in his store and trying to get him out.

Colleen invited me to come to her room after the rehearsal to have a drink. She said she wanted to introduce me to her new friend, Francis Coppola. I was impressed, but I declined the invitation. I didn't figure he was hanging around Colleen because he wanted to meet me. We got on with the rehearsal.

When I got back to my hotel room, I discovered corsages that Colleen had sent over for Carly and my daughters.

– Gordon Archive

They were very nice. It was a sweet gesture. When I called to thank her, she again invited me to her room for a drink. She said she was alone. So was I. Carly was out somewhere with the kids.

We had champagne. I thanked her for the flowers. She started talking about her boyfriend in jail. She said that she was trying to get rid of him. She said that she had landed in the middle of a bunch of cocaine heavies and that she was trying to get out. She told me, and I quote her verbatim here, "If some people knew that I know what I know, I'd be in a lot of trouble."

Okay. I told her that sounded like a good scene to get out of. I asked her if she was still using cocaine. Her reputation for the stuff had become an industry joke. She said that she was off of the drug. We toasted to that.

It was awkward then. The conversation seemed to have exhausted itself. We drank our champagne and very self-consciously did not touch each other. Carly was probably waiting for me with the kids by now. I knew she would not be too crazy about me being in Colleen's room anyway. When another friend showed up at Colleen's door, I took it as my cue to leave.

I wished her well in the evening's awards. We gave it a kiss and a hug with no hint of past feelings. I told her to call me anytime if I could ever help her. Then I heard what I had just said. It made me laugh. I amended it by saying, "Call me anytime you want before eleven at night." She laughed. We said good-bye.

With Coppola and his entourage at her table that night, Colleen was the belle of the ball. But it wasn't to be her night after all.

In fact, for a while there, it looked like it wasn't going to be anybody's night. Early in the show, some crazy had set off a smoke bomb in the orchestra pit and the whole room had to be cleared. The glitterati of the entire X-rated industry went spilling out into the LA streets in their ball gowns and tuxedos.

In time, order was restored and the smoke cleared away. Many people thought it had all been intended as part of the show.

Actress Lee Carol and I presented the award for Best Supporting Actor. It went to Ron Jeremy for *Suzie Superstar*. I think it may have been Ron's first major award. I was happy for him. Nobody in the business worked harder at it than Ron Jeremy.

Shauna Grant was shut out. The Best Actress went to Kelly Nichols for *In Love*, and Kay Parker won Best Supporting for *Sweet Young Foxes*. Paul Thomas, who was Colleen's leading man in *Virginia*, got the Best Actor for it, and *Virginia* won Best Picture as well. Shauna Grant didn't win anything.

The night belonged to my old mentor, John Seeman. He had both produced and directed *Virginia*. It was probably the most successful movie of his career. It won a ton of awards that year. And my personal highlight was getting to watch dear friend Vincent Fronczek mount the podium and accept an award for his brilliant photography. That was sweet. Vincent was usually the worker who was hidden in the workshop. It was nice to see him get some recognition.

I ran into Colleen late at night in the hotel lobby. She was sniffing.

At first, I thought she had been crying. Then, I realized it was cocaine. She was embarrassed that I knew, and that I knew, that she knew, that I knew. She shrugged it off. Said it was a special night. We chatted a moment or two as we waited for the elevator. I kissed her goodnight. I didn't know it was a kiss good-bye.

Chapter Forty-Nine

Late night on March 22, just eight days later, I got a call from John Seeman. He said he wanted to talk to me about Colleen.

"Sure," I said, "what about her? What's she gotten into this time?"

"You haven't heard then," he said.

"Heard what? I haven't spoken with her since the Awards."

"She shot herself in the head," John told me.

"WHAT?!?" My shock was so big that Carly came running in from the next room to see what happened.

"She's being kept alive by life support systems," John said. "There's no brain activity."

I didn't want to believe it. The X-rated world was filled with drama queens and kings. This was all just another rumor, a terrible, terrible, unfunny rumor.

I called Laurie Smith. Laurie was Colleen's drinking buddy, her snorting buddy, her fuckfilm buddy, and her best friend. Laurie was crying over the phone.

She had just gotten home from the hospital where she'd been with Colleen all day. She left when Colleen's mother had arrived from somewhere in the Midwest. Laurie confirmed all the worst news.

Within several days, the family pulled the plug. Colleen was gone. And then Colleen was gone gone. They took her back to Minnesota for burial.

Shauna Grant became another Hollywood story.

"If some people knew that I know what I know, I'd be in a lot of trouble," she had said to me, and now, a week later, she was dead. How was I supposed to believe that her death was a suicide? And not just that but that she had shot herself in the head with a rifle! For God's sake, how the Hell do you even do that?

If I were a Russell Crowe or a Sylvester Stallone character, I'd have bought myself a big gun, hired myself some great writers, and then flown down to Palm Springs to flush out and chase down the bad guys.

And "if a frog could fly, he wouldn't bump his ass so much." This was real life. It wasn't the movies.

The police, the family, all of Colleen's friends, they were all pretty much content to call it a suicide. Who was I to argue? In time, it didn't make a whole lot of difference. No matter what which way, Colleen was gone and she was gonna stay gone.

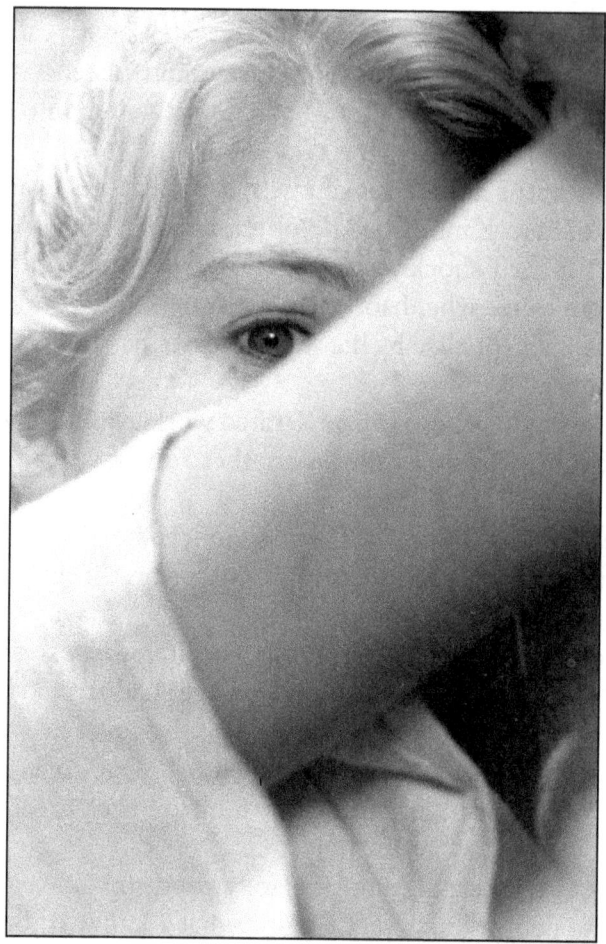

– Gordon Archive

Colleen was dead.

The mainstream media was all over this, from the tabloids to the networks. I stayed in the shadows. I didn't want any part of that circus.

I'll always remember that Jamie Gillis wanted to make a movie about a young woman like Colleen. She'd be new in town, a countrified lusciousness come to Hollywood straight from the farm. She'd be all set to make her first sex film with a big star like Jamie. But instead of taking her to the set, he'd drive her back to the train station, kiss her good-bye, and send her home.

– *Gordon Archive*

Colleen, I wish we had. Would you have gone?

Chapter Fifty

How do you go on after something like that? Did the business kill Colleen? How could I not ask? Or was it the cocaine? Was it rooted in the conflict with her family back home? Was it even a suicide? Or was it really a very clever killing done by bad guys connected to her boyfriend's drug dealing? Was somebody here getting away with murder?

There were questions. Lots of 'em. There were responsibilities to sort out. There was blame to cast. There were scapegoats to hang. There was coping to be done.

If she did take her own life, Colleen would not be the first suicide to come out of pornography. It seemed like there was almost one a year. Sometimes, it was a man and sometimes a woman. Megan Leigh, Savannah, Marcy from *Reel People*, Jon Dough, and Alex Jordan were some of the ones I remember. Inevitably, family disputes, drugs, financial debts, and loves gone wrong were almost always part of the story.

The big difference for me was that I didn't get particularly close to any of those other people as I had done with Colleen. It changed things. It changed the way I did my career. I began steering way away from all the young ones. I wanted to work with only the seasoned pros now, the ones who knew what they were doing, the ones who had demonstrated that they could handle it. Whenever it was possible, there would be no more rookie partners for me.

Chapter Fifty-One

Video was upon us. Anthony Spinelli came to town in April to shoot *Spectators*, his first video.

Spinelli hated video. He loved the movies. He loved the magic of the big, silver screen in the darkened theater. He had lived and breathed movies all his life. The producers just weren't making that many X-rated films anymore. And the few films that were being made no longer had the budgets that could afford an Anthony Spinelli directing.

The video revolution was making its impact. The message was clear: embrace the new technology or get out of the business. And the first results seemed to be sending the X-rated industry heading straight backwards. Everything was being made cheaper and crummier. With a project like *Spectators*, Spinelli was just trying to pay the rent.

Spectators was a feature-length movie shot entirely in video. It took all of two days to make. Spinelli had originally cast Jerry Butler and Kay Parker as his leading players. After a last-minute cancellation by Butler, I was rushed in as his replacement.

The good news was that I helped my friend Sam overcome all kinds of obstacles and make a feature-length movie in just two days. The bad news was the movie that we made.

Spectators was brutal. It was brutal both in story content and in the pace that we had to work at to get the job done. It was dark, the kind of movie that Spinelli made when he was depressed. Unlike most of our earlier movies, there was no rehearsal. There was no rewriting. There was no arguing with Spinelli about what was erotic. There was no time. There was just plugging me into my lines and then plugging me into the women.

"Action!"

Spectators was the story of a couple on some kind of games-playing sexual retreat. The man had the woman as his toy. He used and abused her through five sex scenes until she discovered the good sense to pack up and leave him. It was mean, nasty, and stupid.

– *Gourmet Video*

Pacheco and Kay Parker.

Following, as it did, on the heels of Colleen's death, it was the last kind of character that I ever wanted to play. Kay Parker, however, was not Colleen. She was an experienced woman and a veteran X-rated actress who probably knew the game even better than me. As individuals, the script disappointed both of us. As actors, we played pretend and did our best to just get through it. It was not our cup of tea.

Shooting ended that first day when Kay quietly excused herself from the set and went offstage to have herself a good cry. This was after working for hours on what had been her second sex scene of the day. It had just gotten to be too much. Kay just popped. She was embarrassed by the whole thing. She later told me it was the first time anything like that had ever happened in her whole career.

It had been important to me to help Spinelli in his transition from film to video. Sam had done so much for me. His films had been the backbone of my career. Still, after watching this movie, I wished that I would have been out of town when he called. It was the worst thing that Sam and I ever did together. I was not right for the part. The feelings I got when I saw myself playing such a role were not worth the money or the tsouris.

Kay was all wrong for her part too. There were people out there in the business who would have enjoyed playing in that kind of thing. It wasn't us. We both loved Spinelli and endured the exercise, but it was a burden to the spirit. If I'm not mistaken, that may have been Kay's last video. I think by then she realized that she just might have had enough of sex in front of the camera.

Within all that, Kay and I remained grateful for being able to be there for each other. She signed this Polaroid for me from that last day on the set of *Spectators*. She wrote:

– Gordon Archive/Gourmet Video

Chapter Fifty-Two

Marriage is a career and acting is a career and you can't mix two careers. An actor's marriage isn't like other marriages. We don't think about marriage as something going on and on, with children from generation to generation. It's often just a passing whim.

– Mae West, Hollywood star

I don't know what it was about Kelly Nichols, but Carly smelled it right away and she was right. It was just chemicals or something. I was a goner.

I actually had more sex off screen with Kelly than on. That was a pretty good clue right there. We only "worked" together once. Kelly and I had some history going in. We'd been on a few sets together, smelled each other pretty good, but never had the chance to touch each other. There was a hunger there. It had been building. She was no misguided dove who was wandering around in the wrong world. She was a red-hot flamethrower coming into the top of her game. We wanted to know each other.

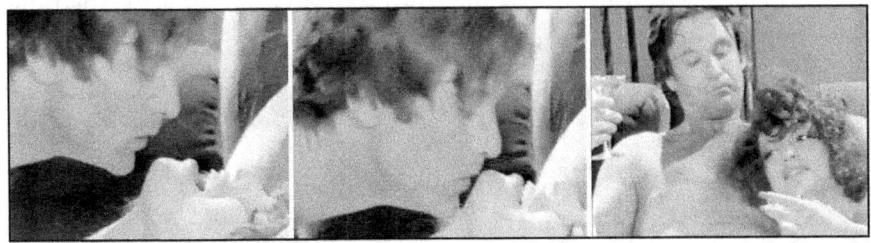

– Gordon Archive/Kelly Nichols

Pacheco and Kelly Nichols.

The show was *Electric Blue* for *The Playboy Channel*. We were there to do a straight sex scene. We went at it with a delight, but every time I got hard and inside of Kelly, the director cut the tape. He said it was going to be an R-rated scene and he didn't want any real sex going on.

What?

It made no sense. The camera couldn't see what we were doing, but it made the "simulation" we *were doing*, look real. There were no other sex scenes scheduled for me to do afterward, so I wasn't saving it for anything. I had it to give. No director in his right mind would ever have stopped rolling on that. But every time I got myself hard and inside of Kelly, which was not any kind of a chore at all that day, the schmendrick director would cut the tape. This was a first.

Well, he was the director. I protested. He ruled. We had to finish the scene his way. Later, on our own time, we finished it our way. That was also when Kelly decided to share that our director was an old boyfriend of hers who just might have been having himself a few jealousy issues on the set that day.

Oh.

When that video was wrapped, I found myself alone in LA with Kelly. She had these two Australian money guys that were wining and dining her in limos. They were trying to get her to commit to doing some dancing and making movies for them in Australia.

Kelly said that she didn't entirely trust being alone with them and wanted me to hang around and be her "date." It was fun. Them limousines in LA that somebody else is paying for are a lot of fun. And there's hardly a man alive who wouldn't be thrilled having Kelly Nichols on his arm. I think this is the kind of stuff that they call "the fast lane." Riding around Berkeley in a VW bus doesn't exactly prepare you for it. Along the way, Kelly asked me to think about coming to Australia with her.

– Kelly Nichols

Then, like an alarm clock interrupting a dream, the phone rang. It was Carly. "Come home," she said.

Oh, yeah, I thought. I did.

At home, Carly was truly upset. While I thought of the musical beds of LA as just part of my movie life, Carly was clutching her gut and feeling abandoned.

Many years later, she told me that this episode was one of the worst times for her of our marriage. She had to invite our friends Bob and Kim to come stay with her just to help her get through it.

When I came home, I saw even more clearly that Carly's willingness or ability to tolerate me being with another woman, and therefore me having my X-rated career, was evaporating. With the kids continuing to alter the balance of power I could see the writing on the wall.

If I wanted Carly as my wife, and if I wanted to be a father who got to live with his kids … then the as-yet unspoken choice was coming down to Casanova or Daddy.

Who you want to be, gringo?

On the surface, the arguing was all about Kelly Nichols, but beneath the waves, it was about the lifestyle conflict, monogamy or not.

I was not ready to let go of my career. This was the battle of the sexes. I fought back. I was sticking up for my own rights. I had labored hard to get from the bottom of the industry to a position near the top. I was angry. I felt betrayed. I had never signed on for monogamy … ever. I had never misrepresented myself. I liked having sex with lots of women. And now, it had become the business I was in.

Yeah … yeah … yeah.…

She said that she could live with the stuff when the cameras were rolling, but that the offstage stuff was now making her crazy. Yeah, I could see that. But sometimes, the offstage stuff was what made the onstage stuff possible. It was also a source of alliances and future work. It was the business I was in, but I had to admit that it was hard to draw a line between the personal and the professional. We had different ideas about where that line should be drawn. I loved Carly. I didn't want to hurt her, but her suffering felt like a betrayal of us, of me, and I didn't want to hurt me either.

Yeah ... yeah ... yeah....
Why did I get the feeling this was General Lee trying to avoid the decision to meet with General Grant at Appomattox?

I was offering whatever I could to allay her fears. It wasn't much. I didn't want to quit. I felt like my career was just hitting high gear. I was telling her to back off. Times had changed. People changed. We had changed. It pissed me off.

We were at odds. We bumbled on.

Chapter Fifty-Three

Alex de Renzy. Like Leonardo da Vinci, Michelangelo Buonarotti, Joe DiMaggio, Frank Sinatra, Arthur Fonzirelli, and Gerry Damiano, Alex de Renzy was yet another in the long line of the great Italian Masters.

– Gordon Archive

de Renzy and crew.

He was a legend of the adult industry and I was happy to finally get the chance to work for him. Alex operated as an independent producer and director and seemed to work completely outside of all the conventional porn procedures that most of the others had to follow. He made his own movies and he sold his own movies. His films were consistently celebrated as some of the best of the business. Unlike many of the other filmmakers, if a sex scene didn't turn out hot, he just didn't use it. Alex had only to please himself, and by so doing, had won himself a large and loyal following.

It was June of 1984. de Renzy had hired me for just one day. His production manager called a few days in advance to get my sizes for a costume. When I asked her about the script, she told me that Alex wanted it to be a surprise. All I had to do was to show up at his house at 8:00 a.m.

My work would include a sex scene with a new girl named Angel. Not too crazy about working with a new girl, but okay. This was de Renzy. In the meantime, his call hadn't given me much notice. I thought I was perhaps sitting on the wrong side of pudgy, but there would be no time for the gym to make much of a difference. Fuck it. I was just going to show up. If it was okay with him, it would be okay with me. I was both grateful and flattered when he offered to pay my full daily rate without any haggling at all. Apart from my dealings with Spinelli, that was a pretty rare occurrence.

de Renzy's house in rural Marin County turned out to be the actual set that day. We shot some outdoor scenes in his gardens and did the sex scene in one of his bedrooms. Upstairs in his home, he had a complete editing facility for doing all of his own postproduction work. de Renzy had a production crew of four people including his current wife and an ex-wife. In short, he seemed to have a very nice little cottage industry going there.

de Renzy, himself, was tall, sure of himself, and very low-key, not a lot of bullshit to the man. With me, he was simple and direct and very easy to get along with.

There was nothing porny or sleazy about him. It was all pleasant enough and strictly business. We worked at a nice leisurely pace. The man knew what he was doing.

And then there was Angel. Good Lord!

Angel looked like a Miss Texas or something. She was a tall, leggy piece of fresh apple pie, the kind of young woman who never would have had anything to do with me were it not for the wonderful world of porn.

It was like God said, "Here, Howie, have one on me. Just don't be an asshole if you can avoid it."

– Gordon Archive/Las Vegas Video

You don't need me to tell you she was young and beautiful.

Angel was clear-headed, bright, and cheerful. Still, in the early going, there was no way I could not be gun-shy around her. Like Colleen, she was young and a great beauty. Like Colleen, she was brand new. And like Colleen, she was about to get on that meteor ride straight to the top of the industry.

Angel was the beginning of the story all over again. "I don't know, Howie," the words of fellow actor Eric Edwards came back to me again, "every year I get a year older and every year, they're still eighteen." I did not want to be stuck in a repeating *Groundhog Day* version of pornographic tragedy.

But Angel wasn't Colleen. She just wasn't. It wasn't three weeks alone in LA either, and there was no cocaine involved. This was just a bright sunny day in Marin playing romantic make-believe with a bright sunny young woman named Angel. It was one of the good days.

We made a mini-movie, a vignette like a loop with sound from the old days. It was a fairy tale. A young maiden had captured a frog in her garden. We had a real frog too. He was a big one. She took it to her bedroom and gave him a kiss. Wouldn't you just know it! He turned into a charming Prince in black tights with an English accent!

– Gordon Archive/Las Vegas Video

Angel and the Prince.

We stumbled awkwardly through the preliminaries, but then got it going. It was like high school sex, all white cotton panties and wonderful. Surprisingly, we turned out to be a good match. When Angel's genuine arousal became involved, it took us both to a whole other level. Yes, sir, amazing how all that stuff works. "Acting" took a backseat. Alex de Renzy got exactly the kind of scene he wanted. It was our pleasure, thank you. A wonderful time was had by all. And when it was all over, I turned back into a frog.

> Dear Howie,
>   It's been a real pleasure working with you. You're a fine actor & a good person. I hope I can work with you again! Good luck with your family & I wish you the best of everything! I hope we can become great friends.
>   Call if your ever in L.A.
>   Love + Lust
>   Angel
>
> "I think that you're going to be the next John Leslie!"
>   — Angel

– Gordon Archive

Chapter Fifty-Four

I can't believe a man of my refined sensibilities could ever be in a movie called *The Maltese Dildo*, but there I was.

Who could say, "No," to producer Dave Friedman, the carny Godfather?

He was even acting in it himself. It was an X-rated parody of the classic *The Maltese*

– Vincent Fronczek/Hustler Video/ LFP Video Group, LLC.

We called him "Glutman."

Falcon. He played the Sydney Greenstreet role.

Just being around Dave Friedman, you could hear the calliope playing, smell the popcorn, and feel the midway. Stories, he had a million of 'em. He played his character like an old Kentucky colonel of the deep South. He was pretty good.

– *Vincent Fronczek/Hustler Video/
LFP Vidseo Group, LLC.*

I was in the Elisha Cook part as
"Wilmer the gunsel."

Not surprisingly, John Leslie played the lead Humphrey Bogart role. Seka, Angel, and Gina Carrera provided the heavy female artillery, but I didn't get anywhere near them.

I was booked for three days in this one. Dave Friedman asking me was some incentive, but it really was a job that I took for the money. We needed some. Dem babies was 'spensive. And with cheap video production rising, there were fewer and fewer higher paying film roles coming my way. Compromise was the order of the day. I worked below my rate and took what I could get. Even at that, roles for me were becoming sporadic.

Day One

I felt like an old-timer out there today in *The Over-the-Hill Gang Rides Again*. I was a fastball pitcher who had lost his zing and was getting hammered. I don't know how many more of these fiascos I have left in me.

My sex scene was today. It'd been two months since I'd last been on camera and naturally, I had to start out with a sex scene. Well, okay. I lost my weight. I had exercised and starved off twelve pounds in ten days. I got over a lingering summer cold, and I hadn't had an orgasm in three days. That was my usual prep. I thought I was ready for anything.

I was told that I'd be doing a sex scene with two women. A couple of names that I had never heard of had been mentioned at first, but I figured what the hell, no big deal.

When I got on the set, there was Laurie Smith. She told me that I'd be working with her. Oi. If I'd have seen that one coming, I would have ducked.

– Gordon Archive

I'd be working with Laurie Smith.

I didn't want to have sex with her. At best for me, Laurie was like a kid sister who talked too much. At worst, she was Colleen's best friend.

Somewhere in my Hollywood convoluted universe, my real life aside, this was like being asked to have sex with my dead girlfriend's sister. I did not want to do a scene with Laurie Smith.

That's when Laurie told me about Tina Ross. Tina played with us in the Colleen movie too. She was the lead actress opposite Jamie Gillis in what eventually was released as *Bad Girls IV*.

– Gordon Archive

Tina Ross.

Laurie told me that Tina Ross had *also* committed suicide.
And that, my dear friends, was foreplay!

(For the Record: I learned many years later that Tina Ross, aka Lauren Wilde, did not commit suicide in 1984. According to the Internet Movie Database (IMDb), she did die that year, but it was from being in a car accident.)

Our threesome was rounded out by a woman named Jill. This would be her first film. I was already in my makeup and costume when we met.

When Jill found out that I was to be the guy in the sex scene with her, she made a face one usually reserves for discovering a fart in the elevator. Wow, that was distressing.

Admittedly, with my hair slicked down and all dressed up as the village idiot, I may not have been at my ravishing best, but still, Jill, a fellow has feelings. No doubt about it, Jill was less than thrilled. She squirmed noticeably. It was just shaping up to be one of those days.

– Vincent Fronczek/Hustler Video/LFP Video Group, LLC.

Don't I look dashing?

Maria, the makeup lady, tried to tell Jill that underneath my character, was a very cute and a very nice man. I don't think Jill was buying it, but she didn't walk off the set. And when the sex scene got underway, she was still there.

It started with Laurie Smith sucking me to erection. Okay, that was really weird, but, okay, it was working. They shot a little footage and then they cut. I looked around to see what was happening. They were having a nice little meeting about the lights. My penis shriveled as we waited.

When we began again, "Action!" Laurie sucked me to another

erection. Okay, I'm workin' here! I'm workin' here, but they soon cut again. What the fuck! They're having another little meeting. My erection again retreats. My penis asks the obvious question,

"Okay, what the hell's going on here?"

Uh-oh, by now you should know, that when my penis starts to get chatty, bad things can happen.

I sought out the director and told him that this has to stop. I explain that I am not an up-and-down machine that can function at his whim. I suggest that when they want me to get hard, they better be ready to shoot this thing and stop messing around. He said he understood my dilemma and asked for my patience. Fine. Harumph!

When we went back to work, I asked Jill to do the sucking this time. I wanted to give Laurie a break and get Jill involved.

Jill flat out said, "NO!"

I looked at Laurie and she looked at me and we both started laughing. My penis began looking at travel brochures. I didn't want one partner and the other one didn't want me. Okay, this *was* a weird day!

We spent about half an hour trying to get me that next erection. Laurie was working overtime, but it just wasn't happening. The director was telling me all about four different insertion shots that he wanted to shoot and my dick was on the phone trying to book a flight to Rio. We took a break. The director sent me off to take a cold shower. It actually turned out to be a very good idea. It calmed me down and helped me to reinhabit my body. I was only in a mild panic at this point. It was like visiting with an old friend again.

Back on the set, Laurie worked really hard to get me going, but I had Colleen on the brain. I don't know what it was, but it certainly wasn't erotic. In the meantime, our partner Jill was trying hard to disappear.

At one point, the director directed me to suck Jill's pussy. I did. I licked and chewed for all I was worth, but it didn't seem to be having any effect. None at all.

In the meantime, Laurie Smith was doing whatever she could to compensate. And while I appreciated her efforts, my dick was still looking for the car keys.

Finally, realizing that Jill was the answer to everyone's problems, the director took her aside and told her that she had to get with the program.

I don't know exactly what he said to her, but I feel fairly confident that it may have had something to do with her getting paid.

When Jill got back in bed, the director had her give me head. Well, Jill was now diligently sucking and I could be the forgiving sort. My whole body began to ease out of panic. Once again, the blood started flowing in the right direction.

Earlier in the day, I had overheard Jill tell the director that she wasn't into any girl-girl stuff. The director had said, "Fine." Unfortunately, Laurie Smith never got that memo. While Jill was sucking me back to life, Laurie put an intimate hand on Jill's body. Jill flew off the bed like a snake had just bit her ass.

"Taxi?" my penis called out. "Taxi?"

When we got this latest episode quieted down, I shoved my limp dick back into Jill's mouth, closed my eyes, and hoped for the best. I crawled through all the old used-up fantasies until I found one that still worked.

I pumped. Jill sucked. When I was up to full erection, the director told me to insert myself into her vagina. I tried. I couldn't get it in. Jill was clenched so tight and dry that you couldn't get an idea in there.

My penis looked at me and started to weep. I stroked him tenderly and told him that it would all be over soon. All we needed was a little bit of baby oil. I gently lubricated Jill so that when I got hard again—now there's an optimist for you—I'd be able to get myself in there.

Once more, Jill deigned to suck. I got it up and then I got it in her. I pumped. It was like fucking a large salmon on Valium. Jill received my plunging as if she were doing her nails. I mean, the phone was ringing, but there was nobody picking it up, not even an answering machine. Still, she was earning her money, I suppose, but taking the absolute minimalist approach to this entire adventure.

Hard to imagine there was ever anybody who watched this scene and tried to jerk himself off. Poor bastard.

And while I pursued the money shot waiting at the finish line, Jill was whispering in my ear, "How much longer are you gonna be? What should I do? Is this the last shot? Are you close? Can I go home after this?"

It was so odd, but the plumbing worked anyway. As per instructions, I eventually pulled out of the young wench and deposited 173 very confused sperms on her belly. They looked like cockroaches when somebody suddenly turns the lights on in a darkened New York City kitchen. We were wrapped.

Loveless, lustless, mechanical, and haunted, it was one of the four craziest fucks of my entire life and I've repressed all memories of the other three.

Day Two

I worked a lot with John Leslie.

As the story went, I was a petty gangster following him around in his role as the hero detective. He spotted me, roughed me up, and sent me back with a message for my boss, Morris Glutman, The Fat Man. That was it. That was gonna be the whole day's work.

In the course of filming, John smashed my knee, hit me in the Adam's apple, choked me, and drew my blood when he scraped my hand over something sharp on the prop phone booth. In addition to which, he spent the better part of an hour twisting my arm behind my back while he had to force my character to give up some vital information.

When I told him that I wasn't too crazy about my role in this one, he had the nerve to ask me why.

One time, he hit himself in his own balls with my hand by accident. He hurt himself. I laughed and looked skyward to thank God. John asked me how I could do such a thing.

Later in the day, John was telling me all about this wonderful new diet that his lady Kathleen had just put him on. He wanted to bet me a hundred dollars that his shit didn't stink. He also told me that his farts didn't stink and that his dog Louie's farts didn't stink either.

These were the highlights of my day.

Day Three

I hung around all day as a background player in everybody else's shot. Afterwards, they paid me. Whatever it was, it wasn't enough.

Chapter Fifty-Five

I liked Nina Hartley. I did. She was different. She was special. But coming along well into my married life and late into my career when she did, I had learned to be well-guarded.

> *"An' here I sit so patiently*
> *Waiting to find out what price*
> *You have to pay to get out of*
> *Going through all these things twice."*
>
> – Bob Dylan
> "Stuck Inside of Mobile With the Memphis Blues Again" (1965)

When I picked up the phone and spoke to her that first time, she said, "Hi, you don't know me, but my name is Nina Hartley and we're scheduled to do an anal intercourse scene next week and I've never done that before on camera. I was just wondering if you wouldn't mind getting together with me to rehearse."

Full circle. It had come full circle. Now, a nervous newbie was calling me up, to ask for my help, just as I had called upon Nancy Hoffman before The *Candy Stripers* and Candida Royalle before *Pizza Girls*. They both had been kind enough to try and help me. How could I refuse this young maiden?

I didn't.

The movie was *Little Anal Annie and the Willing Husbands*. Charles de Santos, my old friend from *Madame Lau* days, would be directing. It was going to be another one of those new feature-length videos that would be entirely shot in two days.

Nina Hartley was cast in the title *Anal Annie* role as a hands-on sex therapist who goes around saving troubled marriages by letting the husbands fuck her in the ass and then teaching their wives how to do it for themselves. I was cast as one of the husbands. There wasn't any script. Charles was going to let the actors improvise the dialogue.

As feature films go, you could pretty well anticipate that this movie would stink. Whether the sex would be any good or not, well, that was always a roll of the dice come game time.

The odd thought occurred to me that the rehearsal I was arranging with Nina would probably make a better movie than the movie, itself.

The more I thought about it, the more enamored I became with the idea of shooting the rehearsal. Backstage in porn always seemed far more interesting than so many of the foolish movies we were putting up there on the screen. Now, with the shrinking budgets of the video revolution, it seemed truer than ever.

If we shot this rehearsal, we would have the two fully developed characters of Nina Hartley and Richard Pacheco trying to get themselves ready to shoot an anal intercourse scene in a porn farce. We could make a strength out of our weakness by tackling it head on! A movie about the movie could be real. It could be charming. It could be as funny or as factual as we wanted to make it. And the sex could just be the sex, free to be whatever it really was.

This could be a way to make a cheap movie about porn instead of just another cheap porn movie. Now, wouldn't that be interesting?

And even if our little rehearsal shoot didn't work out, so what? If we only shot video, we could always just reuse the tape. The only expense would be our time. Yeah, I was all for it. Shoot the rehearsal. We could come out of this with a whole second movie and we could all agree to split the profits. That's the way I pitched it to both Charles and Nina.

Nina was all for it, but Charles needed some convincing. He thought it would be a waste of time. Eventually, though, he agreed to shoot it, but I think it fell under the category of humoring the talent. Besides, it wasn't like a "rehearsal" was going to hurt his movie any.

On the day before the rehearsal, I pulled a hamstring muscle while playing softball. It was a painful injury. I ended up using crutches and wearing an ace bandage to the rehearsal. No matter, we were after reality. We just had a little more reality to work with, that's all.

Nina Hartley turned out to be bright, clear blue-eyed intelligent, and pretty.

Nina Hartley was different. For one thing, she was from Berkeley. Not many Berkeley women were getting involved with pornography back then. She was twenty-five years old and calling herself a pro-sex feminist in an era when angry, anti-porn lesbians had largely hijacked the feminist movement.

In the face of activist "anti" radicals like Andrea Dworkin and

– Gordon Archive

Nina Hartley's Anal Rehearsal.

Catherine MacKinnon, sex-positive young women like Nina Hartley and writers Susie Bright and Carol Queen, among others, were standing up to be counted. They were a breath of fresh air.

Nina was a nursing student and the daughter of leftwing politicos who had become Zen priests. Nina Hartley was trying to relive the Berkeley of the 1960s, in the 1980s. Good luck with that. She was even part of a three-way marriage with both a husband and a wife. I liked Nina. I was attracted to her. She was a mindful wild child, who in finding pornography, was exactly where she wanted to be.

The great X-rated performer Juliet Anderson, Aunt Peg herself, had introduced Nina to the business. At this point, Nina was serving as her apprentice.

Shoot the Rehearsal

We were breaking new ground. No one was sure exactly what we were doing, but we were doing it. I imagined the camera(s) as a backstage presence that would capture the intimacy of that situation in a real and candid way. *We would just get used to the cameras being there and behave in our "normal" ways, I thought. It would reveal us as we were offstage, between takes, when we were not performing, when we were being ourselves.* That was my fantasy, anyway, but our shooting the rehearsal didn't turn out that way at all.

Charles was the director and from the get-go and he just took over directing the rehearsal. We went along with it while he tried to make things happen. He began by sitting Nina and me on a couch and as an off-camera voice, asked us a whole battery of questions about our characters and their development throughout the movie.

It treated *Anal Annie and the Willing Husbands* like it was some kind of off Broadway show that we were preparing to open instead of just being what it was, a half-baked porno script.

It wasn't "backstage" at all. It was onstage. It was an interview, a performance. It was stiff and formal and not very intimate or candid at all. Nina and I got stuck on that couch "acting" like actors. It was like being interviewed for a television show. It was the stilted staged imagining of what a rehearsal would be like if we ever had rehearsals with "the grownups" watching. In the end, there had been a few interesting moments, but, basically, things were pretty dull on that couch. Fortunately, things got better when we moved to the bedroom.

In order to lend some credence to the concept of sex therapy, I had

– Gordon Archive

Maybe one of these days we'll actually figure out how to market it.

asked Carly how we might go about preparing a woman for anal intercourse. She suggested the same treatment that was used for vaginismus (painful intercourse). It was the insertion of a series of gradually enlarged dilators ranging from a pencil thickness to one of a full-sized erect penis. By allowing the body sufficient time to adjust to each size, eventually the male insertion could be achieved without undo pain.

And that's what we did with Nina's tushy, improvising a running commentary along the way. It was real and it was loving. It amounted to being an entertaining primer on how to do anal intercourse. And once my penis was actually inserted, well, school was out. We captured a real, live sexual experience that had some wit, charm, and some genuine heat to it. That was worth the price of admission right there.

My favorite moment in shooting the sex scene came when the phone rang. We were in a private home and there was no answering machine. When the phone rang, I was in the middle of performing oral sex on Nina. As Fate would have it, the phone was right next to the bed and I was the closest person to it. No one off stage was in any position to pick it up without cutting the cameras and it was just ringing.

So, I reached over, picked it up, and talked to the caller while I continued to lick, suck, and nibble the young Nina. This was fun. Multi-tasking, I repeated the caller's phone number so that someone off-camera could jot down the information for the homeowner.

Then, when finished, I simply hung up the phone and returned to concentrating on my orals.

Our session ended on a high note. Pleased with our efforts, we all agreed to be of help with the editing and to share whatever profits there were to be.

Chapter Fifty-Six

Shooting the real *Anal Annie* movie followed in a couple of days. It was entirely anticlimactic. We worked at that same feverish pace I had experienced with Spinelli in making *Spectators*. Like in the days of loops, it was all get the actors on the set, get them fucking, and get them off. Next.

As expected, *Anal Annie* was completely asinine.

Charles had talked about doing a whole series with the *Little Anal Annie* character. The irony here was that Nina Hartley didn't particularly like anal sex. She had worked it out with me so that she could handle it well enough, but desire and pleasure were another story. I suggested that she might want to reconsider building her reputation in the business as this *Anal Annie* character. She was immediately able to grasp the implications. She did not really want to become, how would *Screw* magazine have put it, "the Queen of the Hershey Highway."

On the first day, we reprised our rehearsal scene with all the dilators, but it was nowhere near as charming when done in our movie characters, as it was when we played ourselves. At the end of the day, Nina wrote in my diary:

> Howie — 3/19/84
> I don't know just what to say on such short notice so I'll have to settle for truthful instead of witty or urbane. I haven't been in the business long, but before I got into it, Dave & I talked about what type of people we hoped to find in it. You turned out to be one of them. I found you to be sensitive, witty, knowledgeable about female anatomy/response (refreshing!), entertaining & certainly someone whom I would ask to work with over others — you're the most compatable male I've found so far, & someone I believe I can learn a lot from — about acting & the business, among other things. I look forward to getting to know you better, & maybe having you over for coffee & talk. I also invite you to come see me at the O'Farrell some night. Well, I better quit — see you around & hope to work with you again. We could make some beautiful erotica/porno together.
>
> Nina Hartley

— *Gordon Archive*

The next day, I had another anal sex scene with a young actress who played my wife. I had completely forgotten this scene until I read about it in my diary. That surprised me. It wasn't like me to forget a woman I had sex with, but I had very good reason to forget this one.

We were supposed to shoot our sex scene first thing in the morning. I showed up bright and early, on time, all scrubbed and douched and ready to go to work. She showed up late, over an hour late, and said that she was sick. She said she needed to get some sleep and offered to play the sex scene later. Director Charles sent her upstairs to a back bedroom and then changed his shooting schedule to work around her. He asked me to be the good soldier and to just hang out until she was ready to work.

I was pissed. I'm going to do this actress the favor here of not saying her name because I personally diagnosed her illness as suffering from an all-night cocaine binge. We used to call that being unprofessional.

I spent all day watching the Summer Olympics. Normally, that might not have been so bad, but I caught the one particular day when all they showed were hours and hours of *synchronized swimming!*

It was a cruel and unusual punishment!

In the evening, Miss Snow White arose from her coma. She was miraculously cured and ready to go to work. We did. Though we were able to successfully do our scene, I apparently still needed to pay her the ultimate disrespect by having forgotten for years that we had ever touched.

Chapter Fifty-Seven
Ten Little Maidens

– Gordon Archive and M Joseph Shaller PhD.

(L-R) Vincent Fronczek, Mark Focus, & Paul Johnson.

This is my "Homage to the Photographer" chapter. It is a dedicated thank you to Vincent Fronczek, Mark Focus, and Paul Johnson, three of the best still photographers it was my pleasure to work with during my career.

In this chapter, I'll display a whole series of photographs I took backstage with my own camera.

I was on a wee bit of a roll there throughout the summer of 1984. I picked up a couple of days here and there in a few movies. They were all pretty schlocky, but they were helping us pay the bills. And things were nice and quiet at home. We were still working out the new rhythms with the kids and all, but for the moment, Carly seemed all right with me continuing to work in the business. I was keeping most of my extracurricular activities confined to the set and nothing else particularly scary was happening—yet.

My old mentor John Seeman got me an audition for a big, new film getting ready to shoot called *Ten Little Maidens*. I was to call up director Ken Collins and arrange for a meeting.

"Hello, I'd like to speak with Ken Collins," I said.

"This is Ken Collins," a woman replied.

"Oh," I said, "I thought Ken Collins was a man."

"I am a man!" replied an indignant Ken Collins. Ooops, I thought, *kiss this job good-bye*. But no, Ken recovered pretty quickly while I removed my feet from my mouth. He said that he was used to it. He just had a high voice. Later in the day, I met him and his wife. They were nice people and they hired me to be in their movie.

Ten Little Maidens was an Agatha Christies murder-mystery adapted as a farce for the X-rated screen. I was hired for one day to participate in a huge banquet scene. At the end of a sumptuous meal, I would have a sex scene that would have something to do with a chicken leg and Lisa De Leeuw's vagina. Following that, I would be killed by poison. Sounded like a good day's work to me!

By the time we got on the set in Los Angeles, John Seeman had been called in to co-direct this big banquet scene with Ken. Arthur King, the writer and producer from Excalibur Films, was also on the set. He was calling some shots too. Three directors on the set was a recipe for chaos, but for my one day's work, I wasn't all that concerned.

In this new era of low-budget video and cheaper films, King was definitely putting some bigger bucks into this feature. *Ten Little Maid-*

ens was *huge!* When compared to most of the video movies being churned out at that point, it was a Hollywood extravaganza. I was glad to see it happening. King was new on the scene as a producer. I hoped he knew what he was doing. He was making a big film when they just weren't making big films anymore.

– Excalibur Entertainment, Inc.

Our banquet was an All-Star parade of X-rated talent.

– Gordon Archive

(L-R) Eric Edwards, Harry Reems, Paul Thomas, Richard Pacheco, and Jamie Gillis.

You could have made two or three complete video features for just one day's worth of what they were paying the guys alone. The sign I'm holding was a shout out to John Leslie, who was working on another movie or else he would have been there with us. It says, "Nuzzo (his real last name), wish you were here."

– Gordon Archive

Among the women, newcomer Ginger Lynn had top billing ...

– Gordon Archive

... with Lisa De Leeuw ...

– *Gordon Archive*

... Amber Lynn ...

– *Gordon Archive*

... Janey Robbins ...

– Gordon Archive

… and Nina Hartley.

They were a spectacular bunch. When the camera wasn't on me, I took a lot of pictures that day with my own. If I was in the shot, I passed my camera to whoever was nearby and asked them to shoot some for me.

– Gordon Archive

Harry and Jamie, a pair of Kings!

The first half of the day was spent getting everybody into costume and makeup. Just hanging around the set was a lot like being backstage at the X-rated awards. There was good gossip and grab-ass, and a lot of singing. We were having a terrific time.

The banquet scene took place early in the movie. Our story was that a very wealthy eccentric had invited us all to his lavish estate with promises of orgiastic splendor. Our host did not attend the banquet in the great hall of his mansion, but he received us with a prerecorded message.

Earlier in the day, I had won the Alfred Hitchcock soundalike contest and was chosen to do the voiceovers for the host.

Our plot then turned on the fact that our host grievously disapproved of our libertine sexuality and wanton ways and set about to murdering us one by one. At banquet's end, I would be the first to die.

While everybody was getting ready, I asked Lisa De Leeuw if she'd heard anything about a chicken leg and her vagina. She told me that she had not heard anything about a chicken leg and her vagina and that she did not want to hear anything about a chicken leg and her vagina either.

When John Seeman found me wandering around in the gang, he quietly asked if I had a preference for any of the women.

- Gordon Archive

"Janey Robbins," I told him. There was no hesitation.

I had gotten close to Janey during an episode of *Playboy's Electric Blue*. We shot a scene where I pretended to get my penis stuck in my zipper. Janey had been on her knees in front of me for an hour pretending to help me to get it unstuck. We never touched. It had been an inelegant torture to be so close and yet so far away from all of the obvious.

She had the classic hourglass shape of big hips, large breasts, and a narrow waist. She was like the 1940s film star Jane Russell without the sneer. Janey Robbins was shy and sweet with a tattoo, which was still fairly rare on a woman in those days. She was a very interesting collection of contradictions. I very much wanted to spend a little time visiting in her cage.

– Gordon Archive

"Janey Robbins," I told John. "I want to work with Janey Robbins."

– Excalibur Entertainment, Inc.

Off-stage playing for the camera.

– Excalibur Entertainment, Inc.

John said it would be fine if Janey and I worked together. He was right!

They began filming us eating and improvising small talk about our very mysterious host. We were all wearing odd, torn pieces of costume with various organs exposed.

– *Gordon Archive*

Dinner guests Paul Thomas and Amber Lynn.

– *Gordon Archive*

Acting as host, Jamie Gillis sat at the head of the table.

Along with Nina Hartley as his wife, both Jamie and Nina cooked and served us the meal.

In the kitchen before dinner, there is a scene of Jamie feverishly fucking a raw chicken as he kisses and tongues Ms. Hartley's legendary bottom.

Later, after the meal has begun, Ginger Lynn requests "creamy Italian" dressing on the salad order she places with Jamie. Out of sight of the guests, we see Jamie in the kitchen masturbating and spraying his orgasm all over her salad. "Let's see if the bitch likes 'creamy Polish,'" he grumbles to himself.

Both Ginger Lynn and Harry Reems positively adore their salads, declaring the dressing to be "delicious!"

'Ere long, as the meal progressed, we had the gradual transformation of the appetites.

– Gordon Archive

If only she knew.

Eating became "eating."

– Gordon Archive

– *Gordon Archive.*

The hunger for food became the snarl for sex.

Eric Edwards ended up with Lisa De Leeuw. No chicken leg was involved.

– *Gordon Archive*

All around the table, couples were fondling each other amidst the splendor of the great meal.

On the other side of the table, I lay down in my chair and placed my head in Janey's lap.

Janey had her voluptuous breasts dangling free and fed them one at a time to my waiting mouth. I closed my eyes and delighted in the tender mercy.

I soon felt a tongue and then a mouth upon my cock. I looked down and saw the cute, little Ginger Lynn smiling back at me with her mouth full. I had just met Ginger that day. How nice! She was just saying hello. I waved to her.

- Gordon Archive

Hello, Ginger.

As the sex all around the table heated up, Jamie Gillis, the Mad Satyr himself, was about to hijack this whole scene and take it into another galaxy. It was about to become a classic for the Ages.

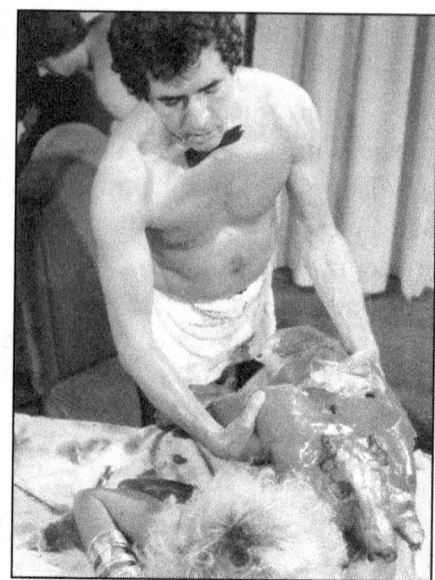

Uh-oh, there goes Jamie ...

– *Gordon Archive*

It began when Jamie brought in an entire roast suckling pig, complete with the apple in its mouth. He soon bent Amber Lynn over the banquet table and placed the entire roast suckling pig upon her back.

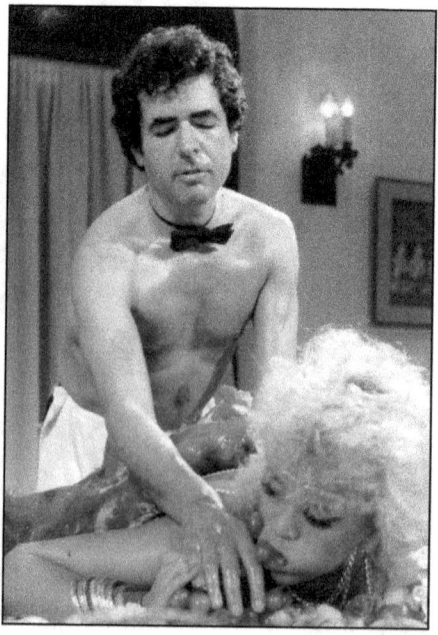

– *Gordon Archive*

– Gordon Archive

Then, he began alternately fucking Amber and the pig. Jamie. Jamie-Jamie-Jamie. There wasn't another actor of this generation who could have lit such a fire. There was only one Jamie Gillis and he was just getting started.

As he warmed to the task, he tore off huge chunks of pig meat and greasy fat and began smearing it all over Amber's body.

He was fucking the pig, Amber and stuffing food in her mouth.

We sat around the table in awe. The cameras were rolling. All three directors were silent. Jamie was making it up as he went along. He was on his own.

When he smeared the pig in Amber's face and hair, there were audible moans and groans at the table. Surely a line had been crossed. Ginger Lynn looked white as a ghost. You had to wonder if they could even use a scene like this in their movie, but nobody was stopping Jamie. He was a runaway locomotive and Amber Lynn was looking like the train wreck.

– Gordon Archive

It was hard to tell who Amber was in all of this. She could have easily stopped the scene at any time and just walked away, but she hung in there. I didn't know what to think. She had been presented as Jamie's current girlfriend. Who knows, maybe they did this kind of stuff at home.

I think it was Eric Edwards who took a mouthful of fruit and pretended to barf it all over Jamie's cock, Amber's ass, and some part of the pig.

By now, I had Janey bent over the table and we were going at it doggy-style. In this crowd, that may have qualified us as conservative Republicans.

Harry Reems had the starring role in this film. This was supposed to be his big comeback movie after some time away from the lens. After a while, it seemed like he just got tired of Jamie stealing the scene. He vaulted up on to the center of the table and joined in the pig smearing. He offered his cock to Amber fore and aft and if memory serves, she took him in both ways.

As I recall, Harry pulled out of Amber and jerked his cock furiously until drops of sperm came raining down upon all of us around the table. After extracting the last drop, Harry then plunged his dick into a cherry pie.

– *Excalibur Entertainment, Inc.*

Chaos!

There was a film run-out. The camera(s) were quiet. It was still on the set for a moment as all involved just surveyed the wreckage. It quickly dissolved into an eruption of laughter and activity. Surprisingly, no grown-ups came in and yelled at us. I just stayed close to Janey.

When we got back to work, we went in for close-ups on one couple at a time and did the sex until each male orgasm. As you might expect, simple fucking could be decidedly anticlimactic after such pyrotechnics, but, not really, if you were personally involved. The show carried on and I enjoyed the time I got to play with Janey Robbins.

And after the sex, I got to die! I jumped up choking and gagging from the table! *Ach du lieber*, I had been poisoned! With this royal assemblage of porn stars watching, I reeled from the dinner table and stumbled into an expensive vase sending it crashing into the floor. After that, I chewed whatever other scenery I could find, and then collapsed and died. I was good too. I was ten years old playing Cowboys and Indians.

When they cut film, my honored colleagues gave me applause. How gratifying! I felt like Bette Davis! It was perfectly silly.

There was more dialogue amongst the surviving guests. They had to examine my body to see what had killed me. (It was the writers!)

I was wrapped. Whatever happened in the rest of the film was none of my business.

I had been in the most disgusting sex scene I had ever seen. I wondered how much of it could possibly be in the movie. We had either just done the greatest food sex scene since Albert Finney's *Tom Jones* of the 1960s or else we had just made a very expensive contribution to Producer Arthur King's outtake reel.

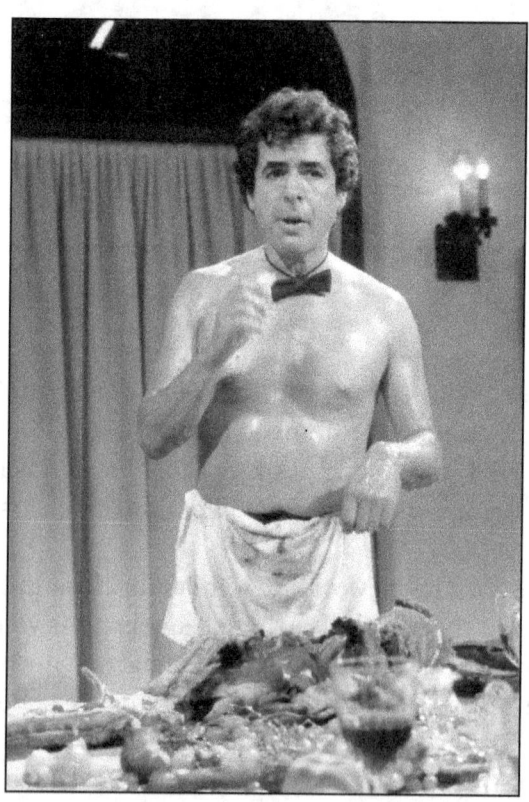

– *Gordon Archive*

"Could you please pass the salt?"

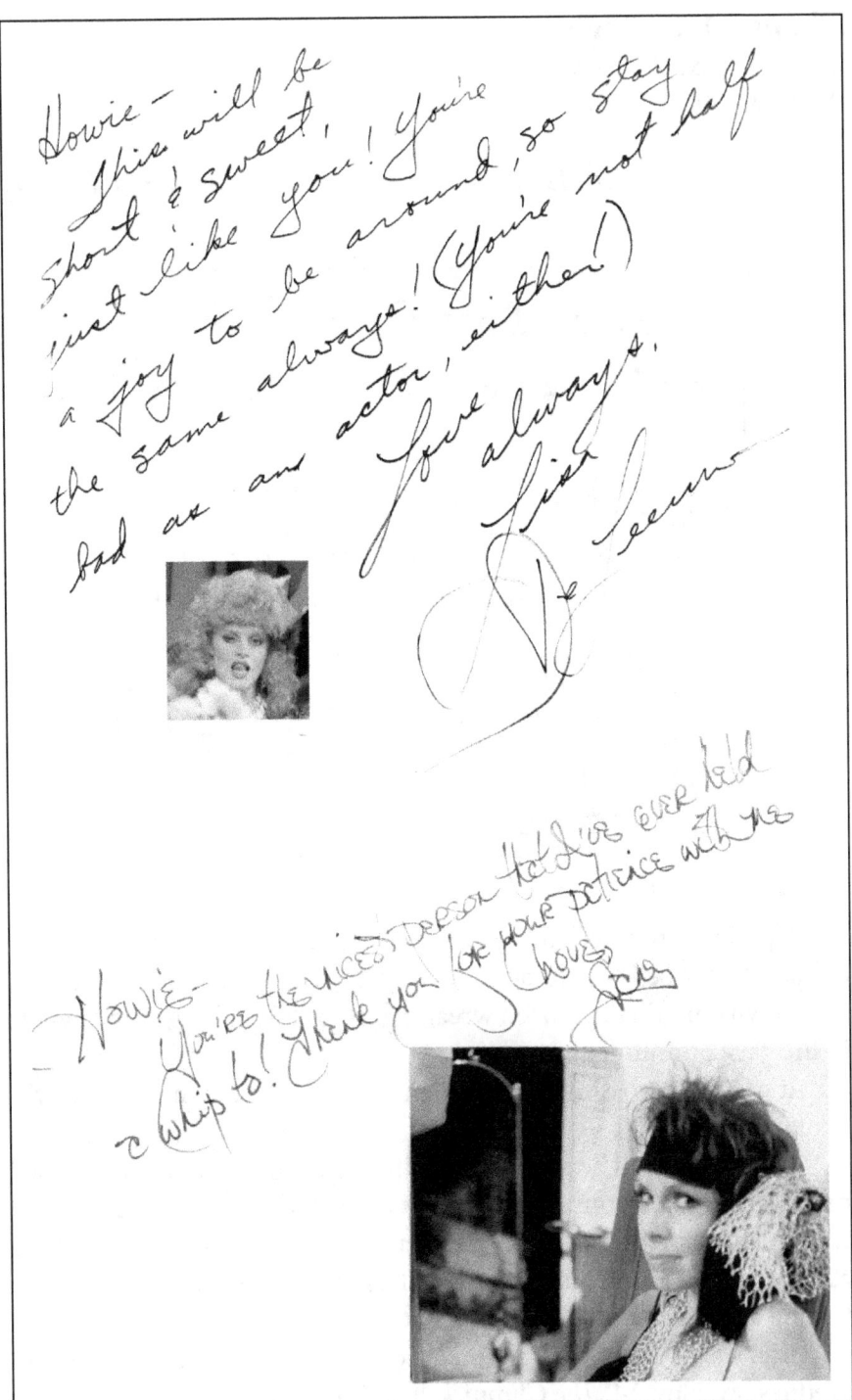

– Gordon Archive

Chapter Fifty-Eight
THE SKY IS FALLING!
THE SKY IS FALLING!

On November 10, 1984, The San Francisco Chronicle ran this story on the front page:

> **Two Men Get AIDS After Sex With Women**
>
> By Randy Shilts
>
> The first known San Francisco cases of women transmitting AIDS to men — apparently through sexual contact — were reported yesterday by the Department of Public Health.
>
> Two heterosexual men appear to have developed the lethal disease after sexual contact with two women who were intravenous drug users and may have shared contaminated needles with other addicts.
>
> People who inject drugs have long been among those at high risk for contracting the acquired immune deficiency syndrome.
>
> They make up a large percentage of New York City's AIDS caseload, and there have been a few reported cases of male drug users giving AIDS to female sexual partners in that city.
>
> In San Francisco, where 98 percent of AIDS cases are among gay men, seven heterosexuals have contracted AIDS since last year, four of them in the past six months, said Dr. Dean Echenberg, director of the health department's Bureau of
>
> Back Page Col. 1

– *San Francisco Chronicle*

Up to that moment in history, AIDS had been thought to be a gay disease. It was believed to be a sexually transmitted lethal disease with no known cure that had been wreaking havoc and killing many people in the gay community.

It was now crossing the sexual orientation border into the heterosexual population.

In the realm of sexually transmitted diseases, herpes had caused me great personal concern four years earlier when we had first begun trying to get pregnant. With AIDS now, we were no longer talking about a pimple on the mouth or genitals that came and went, we were talking about *dead!*

Every day, there was another front-page story about AIDS. On Wednesday, Nov. 14, *The Chronicle* headline was:

"New AIDS Warning Aimed at Straights"

The high-risk group for potentially transmitting the disease was identified as gay or bi-sexual men, Haitians, and intravenous drug users.

The X-rated industry had two out of the three there.

> *"Any sexual activities that involve the exchange of any bodily fluids—whether heterosexual or homosexual—should be considered to have risk now."*
>
> – Dr. Harold Jaffe, Center for Disease Control
> *The San Francisco Chronicle*

Amidst the flurry of AIDS headlines that week, our friend Michael Rossman came over to pay us a visit. Among other things, Michael was a mathematician. He told Carly and me that he'd done some projections on the spread of the AIDS virus based on the numbers that had been reported in *The Chronicle's* news stories.

"Howie," he said, "you're in the wrong business at the wrong time. You need to retire."

I didn't consider Michael to be an alarmist and it was not what I wanted to hear. It was not what I wanted to believe.

I'd worked my way up from the bottom of the pile to become a performer of some standing in Adult films. I thought I was just coming into my own. There was no way I wanted to quit.

Carly was all over it. She wanted me to retire too, but I didn't entirely trust her motives. I thought she was just using it to her advantage in the continuing monogamy wars that had long been raging between us.

I didn't want monogamy and I didn't want to lose my job. I wanted to believe that the newsmakers were just selling newspapers and that this whole AIDS thing would soon blow over like a bad hurricane. We would clean up from the mess and move on.

In the meantime, I had three movies lined up for early December. They would provide us with some much-needed cash for the holidays. Over both Carly's and Michael's objections, I decided to do them.

Then again, I may be dumb but I ain't stupid. I put a call in to my old friend David Sobel. We had grown up together in Pittsburgh. We both had moved to California. He was a doctor now. I asked him to look into this AIDS thing for me to see if he could think of any way it could be safe for me to continue working in the X-rated business.

Chapter Fifty-Nine
White and Wong

It began with Director Charles De Santos parading me in front of Linda Wong. She would be auditioning me as a potential partner for her planned return to the Adult Cinema.

In films like *Oriental Babysitter* and *Jade Pussycat*, in which she costarred with Georgina Spelvin and John Holmes, Linda Wong had been a major star of the early seventies. Her last film had been released in 1977, round the time I was just getting started in the business.

When I met her, she was an aging *China Doll*. The *Doll* had become a mature woman. She had rounded edges.

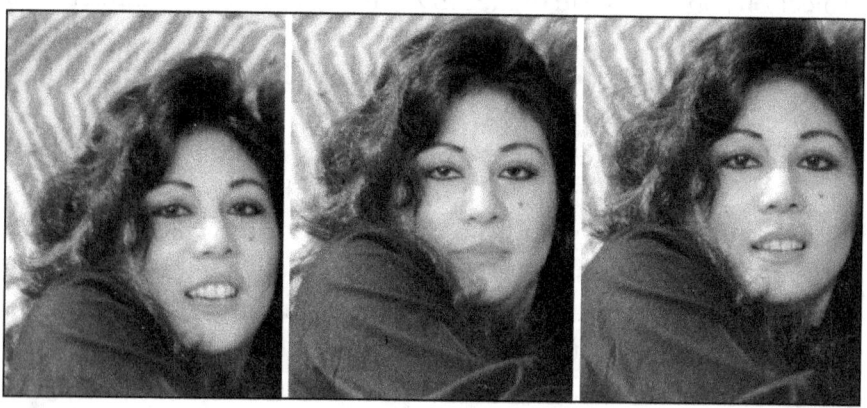

– Gordon Archive

Linda Wong.

We awkwardly hello'ed. My first impression was that she was not very interested. She later explained that she told Charles she wanted an eighteen-year-old guy in the part. Charles delivered her me. I was thirty-six. If I did the gym religiously for a month, I could play twenty-five, but I was clearly beyond eighteen.

Charles cued up a scene of mine from *Anal Annie* on the VCR and then left us to watch it and get acquainted while he dealt with some other business.

Linda quizzed me. She hadn't followed the business at all since she had dropped out, and she had never heard of me. She emphasized that she was looking for men who could act. She was fairly intimidating. I did my best to let her know that I felt that I knew my way around a set. After a while, our conversation became friendlier. The ice had broken when we both agreed that this *Anal Annie* movie was really stupid! It cracked us both up. We turned it off.

Linda expressed her desire to make a real quality sex film. She acted as if she were slumming as an actress to get involved with porno again. She thought of herself as beyond it. She carried a copy of Shakespeare's *Romeo and Juliet* in her bag. I was impressed, but then again, I was easily impressed, especially by women who I would later have to have sex with on camera.

Linda made a big deal about how her movie was going to be head and shoulders above all the rest. I told her that was fine with me. We did no rehearsing, took off no clothes, and did not touch during our encounter. Eventually indicating that the audition was over, she told me that I had the part. She said she and Charles would change the scene so that I would be more appropriate for the role. She told me that I'd get a script.

It was all strictly business and it seemed like good foreplay.

Couple days later, Charles called with the dates for shooting the scene with Linda. She got on the phone and told me not to have sex with any Oriental women for three days prior to the scene. I promised her that I wouldn't if she likewise stayed away from any Jewish guys during that same time. She didn't laugh. That was not a good sign. And I never did get a script. That wasn't a good sign either.

Linda's high-quality movie, better than all the rest, turned out to be an ad-libbed feature-length video shot in two days. Uh-oh.

When I first got to the set, Linda was already in costume, made-up, and ready to go. Charles was on the set shooting a sex scene with three other actors. Linda told me that she was trying to get herself "in the mode" for work. She paced nervously. She didn't like my hair. Our makeup man didn't do hair. I was sent out to Supercuts.

When I got back with my new haircut, Linda was still trying to get herself "in the mode." I asked if there was anything I could do to help.

"No," she told me. She said that she had to do it for herself. She told me that once she got it started, I wouldn't be able to stop her. I didn't know what that meant, but I took it all quite seriously for a while, until she started to repeat herself. Eventually, the light bulb just came on and I realized that something wasn't quite right here.

–Vista Video

"The Legend" did return, but we had a hard time getting her out of the makeup room.

I spent a long time with her trying to make contact. A lot of words were spoken, but they weren't doing anybody any good. We weren't getting anywhere. For whatever reasons, Linda wasn't coming out of that makeup room. I had no answers. This was a job for the director. Besides that, Charles was also her friend. I passed him the baton.

There was a lot more waiting. A lot more.

Eventually, Charles applied about a half a bottle of brandy therapy with Lord only knows what else on the side. It worked. Linda eventually made her way out of the makeup room and onto the set. She was in the mode.

– Gordon Archive

I was playing a nerd again.

This time I was a vanilla banker from Nebraska with spectacles. Linda was to play a cross between a guru and a high-class courtesan. She was going to heal my pain and expand my sexual consciousness with a mystical Oriental experience.

– Gordon Archive

Do we look like a happy couple?

It was *The Seven Seductions of Madame Lau* all over again, the first picture I'd made with Charles De Santos. Instead of Annette Haven, we had a real Chinese Madame Lau this time.

The long delay had forced Charles into his hurry-up offense. The lack of a script had us improvising a dialogue to set up the sex scene. We were going at it rush-rush-rush, just trying to get the scene done.

Looking at the movie now, we were just jabbering. It took all the air out of the scene. Less would have been so much more. In fact, it all would have been so much better if we had just said nothing at all and let our touching tell the tale.

Instead it was yakety-yakety-yakety-yak and fuck. That was too bad too, because by the time we finally got it going there, the sex was pretty good. The orgasm was great! But, alas, it may have been too little, too late to recover from all the damage done by our insipid yammering beforehand.

I watch the movie now, and I see that it was a good orgasm, but it wasn't worth getting AIDS over. And don't think that that dreadful thought hadn't crossed my mind a time or twenty when we were shooting that scene.

My career as a sexual performer really ended on November 10, 1984, when I had first read of the heterosexual transmission of AIDS in the San Francisco Chronicle. I just didn't know it yet.

Chapter Sixty
Sex Wars

This was supposed to be the X-rated answer to *Star Wars*.

Erotic Star Warriors was our working title, but by the time we were finished, *It Came From Uranus* would have been much more apt. It stunk. This little film never had much of a chance. It died before it even got started.

That was too bad because it was being produced by Arthur King again, the same guy that did *Ten Little Maidens*. I liked him. He was a cool guy and he seemed intent on trying to produce better quality sex films. In this movie, King had actually put money into the budget for the construction of miniature spacecraft and special effects. Who was this guy? As the videos were getting cheaper and cheaper to make, Arthur King was still putting his money into the far more expensive world of film. He rented Bob Vosse's soundstage in San Francisco, which was all well and good, but he also hired Vosse to be his director, which turned out to be a colossal mistake.

Harry Reems was to be the star. I would play his sidekick. Annette Haven was cast as the female lead. On paper, we looked great. A week before production, we were all given big, fat scripts to learn. We were scheduled to begin shooting the day after Thanksgiving.

My parents were in town. They were staying at our house. I was going to wake up one morning, say good-bye to my wife and kids, my mom and my dad, and then go off to make a dirty movie. Life was full of surprises. I needed the job and my parents just happened to be visiting. I supposed that we could all handle it somehow.

Two days before the shoot, Harry Reems quit the job, saying that he had developed a contagious rash and couldn't work. At the urging of Annette Haven, Paul Thomas was his replacement. Paul Thomas— or PT as he would later be known in the business—was an excellent actor. There wasn't any drop-off there. It would be a big push for him to learn so much script so fast but PT could handle it. We'd been through this exact same kind of thing before together in *Pizza Girls*. We made it work then, we'd make it work now.

On Thanksgiving Day, Annette Haven called Vosse to arrange transportation for herself to and from the set. Annette lived way out in the boonies and didn't drive. Bob Vosse refused to accommodate her in any way. And they managed to get on each other's nerves in a hurry.

In the course of several phone calls throughout the holiday, Annette offered to stay in San Francisco and pay her own hotel bills if Vosse would provide a driver or pick up her cab fares. Bob Vosse's diplomatic response was to fire her. Less than twenty-four hours before shooting was to commence, he had to recast the female lead. He gave it to one of the bit players that had been hired named Robin.

It was good-bye Annette. And it was good-bye movie.

Robin was a thin, leggy, young woman with very large breasts. She was now our female lead.

- Gordon Archive

Robin Cannes was her stage name.

When I met her backstage that first morning, she was mortified. She was afraid of delivering her lines and freaked out about having sex on camera. That made her two for two and this was all before coffee. The poor girl had never even been in a high school play. She had gone straight from being a model doing some nude stills to being cast as the lead actress in this feature film.

It wasn't her fault. I went looking for Paul Thomas, and we gathered in a dressing room to rehearse.

Within a few moments, it was clear to Paul and me that we were going to be in for a rough day. Robin was clueless. It wasn't about good or bad, it was about total inexperience. Large breasts notwithstanding, Mr. Rogers would have made a better female lead.

I found Vosse and told him we had a real problem. First of all, he just categorically rejected the idea of calling up Annette Haven and getting her back on the project.

Okay, that being the case, I thought I had an absolutely brilliant backup idea for a Plan B. This being science fiction and all, we could just make Robin's character an alien who communicated telepathically. All of her lines could be delivered by an off-camera voice and it would be as if we were hearing her thoughts. Robin wouldn't have to remember pages and pages of lines nor have to fret at all about how to deliver any of them. We could just zip through this script and get on to the sex scenes.

I thought it was pure genius, but Bob Vosse did not. He wanted her to speak. PT and I were sent back to the dressing room to work with her.

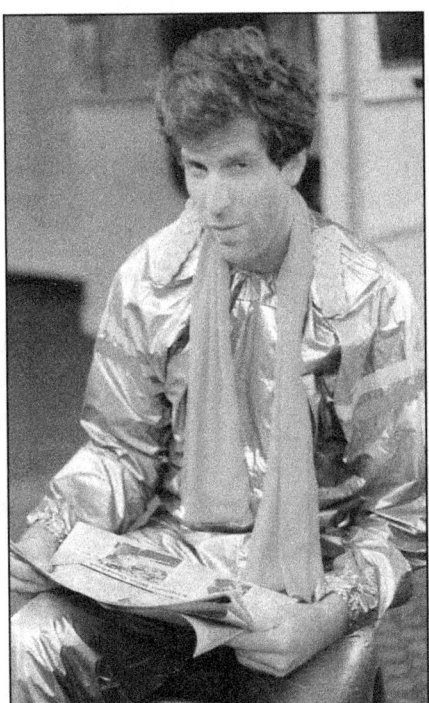

– Gordon Archive

Paul Thomas was Brinker Duo and I was Mark Starkiller.

- Gordon Archive

Robin Cannes as Princess Layme.

Things were going slowly backstage. The situation sucked, but we were stuck in it. We did our best to help Robin. She was just a victim of circumstance here. If Vosse hadn't copped such an attitude with Annette Haven, we wouldn't have been in all this shit. Hell, if I would have had any idea how green Robin was, *I would have offered to pay Annette Haven's cab fares myself!* At this point, we had to live with it. We prepared as best we could.

Once we got out there on the set, Robin was lost. She was still at the stage where she was trying to stop looking directly at the camera. It wasn't fair to ask her to take this big a step. As the hours passed, they ripped pages and pages out of the script in order to cope with the situation. I thought of all that time spent learning my lines.

What? And give up show business?

Director Bob Vosse was of so little help. At one point he said, "You're the actors, go act! What are you bothering me for?" He stayed busy with his lights and lenses and seemed to be involved only with the technical aspects of each scene. When he didn't like our performances as actors, he just yelled at us. He remained like that throughout the whole movie. He was a horseshit director. Sadly, we were the horseshit he directed.

Turned out, Harry Reems and Annette Haven were the lucky ones.

But the guy I really felt sorry for was producer Arthur King. I thought he must've sunk a lot of money into this movie. He'd even written the script that we were now eviscerating. One had to wonder how he could just let Vosse seem to run rampant over the whole thing. I discovered later that Vosse was also one of the producers of this film. I don't know who had the power.

– Excalibur Entertainment, Inc.

At the end of that first day, PT and I had a
three-way sex scene with Robin.

Paul got hard first and I got out of his way. I watched as he fucked Robin. It was like a tag-team wrestling match. When he finished, I jumped right into the saddle.

I was weak, just getting over a cold. The sex felt good for about thirty seconds and then degenerated into a contest to see if I could maintain an erection. I lost it a few times and I got it back. Robin was real nervous. I was real weak. Vosse displayed the sensitivity of a yak. The sex became desperate. Robin managed to do what I asked and co-operation and imagination pulled us through.

I managed a wimpy orgasm for the cameras and we cut.

- Gordon Archive

And then it was my turn.

Back in the dressing room afterward, Robin cried. I held her. Few words were said, but if I had to guess what she was going through, I'd say this:

She was going through that stage-one door where the performer has just been exposed to the world of difference between personal and movie sex. She was feeling the shock and emptiness of having just had a wildly impersonal sexual experience. It was devoid of love, romance and desire.

It was "de void."

It had been filled with performance anxiety. There had been harsh lights, unblinking cameras, leering witnesses, and, ultimately, shame.

Paul had fucked her and I had fucked her. She had been fucked. She had allowed herself to be fucked. It's unlikely that she got anywhere near orgasm. Her own personal desire had been teased, ignored, locked-up, submerged, and buried somewhere. It was not part of the job. Robin had been as helpful to us as she could be. Our orgasms had been the job. It had been difficult.

I just held her while she cried.

Of course, she hated Vosse. He had scared her. His direction in the sex had been coarse. The sad part was that he was treating her with kid gloves. He was probably being as gentle as he could be. After all, he was stuck with Robin. He needed her to make it.

It occurred to me that we were actually lucky that Annette Haven hadn't been in that scene. If Vosse had given some of that barking dog direction to Annette, well, she was very likely to have returned the favor—and then some. Annette Haven did not tolerate any disrespect. The whole set would have exploded.

With Robin, we got the whimper, instead of the bang.

Y'know, I'd made a lot of films in Vosse's Studio. It was high up on the third floor of a huge warehouse in the industrial section of San

Francisco. I'd spent hours and hours in that space. I knew Bob as the Studio owner, a host, and a provider of props. He was a real collector and the studio was filled with all kinds of interesting stuff. In that capacity, Bob was often a delightful, old, Texas-like curmudgeon with lot of stories and a long memory about life in the adult film business, but I'd never worked for him before.

While I was grateful for the money coming in from this job, I knew that I would never work for him again. It was a waste of caring. He was strictly factory porn at the brutal level. He was hard on his actors and murderous on his crew. I had been around long enough to be able to handle it, but, seeing it fresh, through Robin's eyes, it was just sad.

When things calmed down, I tore off my costume, jumped into my street clothes, and was out of that studio in five minutes flat. I wanted to make it home before my eldest daughter's bedtime at nine. I hadn't even taken off my makeup or washed the blonde out of my hair. I flew to my car and raced across the Bay Bridge in the rain.

I made it home by nine too, where Carly met me at the front door. She reminded me that the baby had been going to bed at eight-thirty now for almost two months. Oh, I totally forgot. It had been that kind of day.

I worked two-and-a-half more days in this film. Paul and I got used to working with Vosse and Robin, and we began to enjoy ourselves a bit. We always used to sing on the set together. Paul was a truly great singer, and he would often carry me through a version of Don & Juan's big hit, "What's Your Name?" We sang it a bunch of times. He'd do all the harmonies and I'd try to hang with him and not choke. I always enjoyed working with him.

Laurie Smith was there on Day Two. She was the last-minute replacement for Rachel Ashley who had flaked on showing up for the second female lead part of Princess Orgasma. I was happy to see Laurie this time. Compared to Robin, she was Meryl Streep. Laurie brought some confidence and fresh energy at a time when we all really needed it. That was the good news.

The bad news was that Laurie had a tumor on one of her ribs. She was going in for surgery upon completion of the film. We weren't scheduled to be partners in this movie, but we somehow came face-to-face right in the middle of the orgy scene. We kissed. It was surprisingly tender, and intense. In some crazy way, I had come to love her.

The kiss was filled with all the anguish we shared over Colleen's death. And it was also filled with all the hope and healing I could pass on to her in such a moment. It had nothing to do with lust. It had nothing to do with the movie. But that's where we met. Right there in the middle of an orgy, we said what we had to say in the silence of that one surprising kiss.

And once said, it ended there and we moved on to do our jobs.

I started out with Robin and was once again having troubles keeping my penis involved. Along came Morgan Lee, I think that was her stage name. Just when I was beginning to feel like the only gear I had left for film sex was desperation, Morgan Lee had a zest for the sex that lit up all the lights on the Christmas tree. She was an amazing Amazon. Well over six feet tall, she looked like a cross between Liv Ullman and Sally Kellerman.

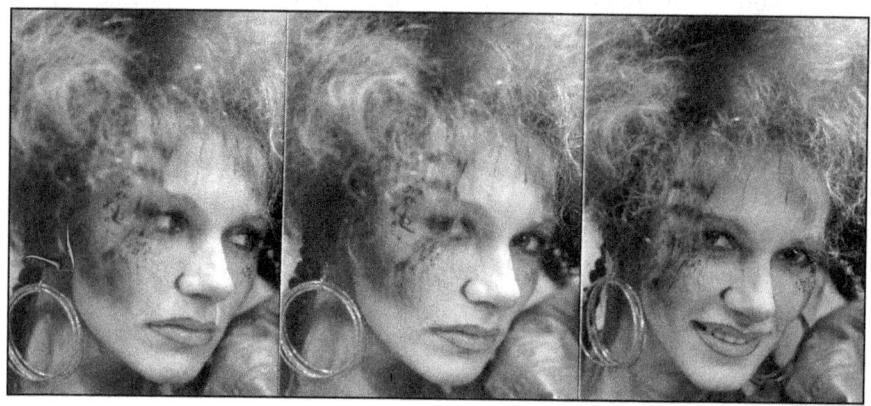

– Gordon Archive

Morgan Lee.

She spent most of the movie in gold paint playing an alien who was in love with a robot. She played a second character in the orgy and happily found her way over to me. Usually, when a woman is taller than me, I turn into an asexual little brother, but this was something different. She was so much bigger than me, it was like an inter-species dating. It was a fairy tale. It was Rabelaisian. I was making out with a giant. I was the mortal man and she was the Goddess Athena. The sparks flew. It was juicy and exciting. It was such a relief to once again discover how easy the movie sex can be when both parties are getting turned on.

It was so good and I was so revved up, that when I was redirected to finish the scene and have my orgasm with Robin, I had no trouble at all.

Speaking of trouble, just before the orgy had commenced, I found myself locked out of my own dressing room. I knocked indignantly and was let in by two of the other orgy actors who were busily snorting up lines of cocaine. They offered me some, and I passed it by. The last thing I needed before movie sex was cocaine. They'd have to peel me off the ceiling and use a splint to keep my dick straight. Different people just used different things to be able to do the job. With me, lust begat lust and cocaine begat a breathless frenzy. No, thank you, I closed the door and left them to their party.

- Gordon Archive

My old friend Howard Darkley was in this film.
He played the villain Lord Balthazar.

Howard Darkley was the wildly talented writer, actor, and director John O'Keefe, a dean amongst the Bay Area *avant garde*. He was my friend, my former acting teacher, and he used to love occasionally slumming in porn, but always playing in a non-sex role so as to not compromise his "legitimate" career. It was fun for him and the paycheck didn't hurt either. The porn producers I'd introduced him to were very happy to have him in their films. For this one, he had agreed to play the part of the half-human, half-robot villain for $300. When he was wrapped, they paid him $400. That was cool.

– Gordon Archive

Setting up the box cover shot: (L-R) Writer-Producer Arthur King, Laurie Smith, Paul Thomas, and Robin Cannes (along with a garbage can doing an R2-D2 imitation).

– Excalibur Entertainment, Inc.

Adding me to the mix.

And here it is:

– Excalibur Entertainment, Inc.

Chapter Sixty-One

When it was all over, I came home.

– Gordon Archive

There was my mom playing with my baby Polly.

– Gordon Archive

And there was my dad at my desk reading an earlier version of this book.

I sat around the kitchen table with my wife and my parents and recounted some tales of the day's adventures. They laughed at the funny parts and worried at the stuff they figured was weird. I felt unbelievably relieved and pleased that I could share as much as I dared share with them about my most unconventional and strange career in the world of adult films.

Their love made me feel as if all the burdens of the world had been lifted from my shoulders. As I sat there with my wife and my parents and we watched the kids play, I knew that I was a very lucky man.

Chapter Sixty-Two
For Love and Lust

I had one day off from *Sex Wars* and then went right to work on Sam's next video.

– *Gourmet Video*

For *Love and Lust* was the third in the trilogy of movies that I had set out to complete before the Christmas holiday season set in.

Spinelli was doing two videos back-to-back. While I finished with *Sex Wars*, Spinelli starred John Leslie in the first of his two-day shoots. Now, it was my turn. This was a different Spinelli. I didn't know about John's, but for mine, there was no script!

As Day One commenced, I took the pieces of the puzzle that Sam and his wife Roz laid out before me. There were the number of characters the budget could afford, the constraints of the location, and the number of sex scenes that they wanted. I percolated on these facts and worked them up a cute, little story that I finished writing on our way to the set that morning.

It didn't win any awards, but it did provide the framework for the five or six sex scenes that helped them bring in their second video on time and on budget.

Opposite Nina Hartley, I also starred in this movie, did three sex scenes in two days, and recruited most of the cast. By this point, my working for Sam Weston was a family affair. We seemed to get even closer after Carly and I started making babies. I tried to help Sam out wherever, whenever, and however I could.

- *Gourmet Video* – *Gordon Archive*

I worked the first with Nina Hartley and the second with Lili Marlene.

Sam insisted on paying me my full rate. I wanted him to cut it in half so that we'd have more money to spend on the production. Thank God he wouldn't hear of it. He was trying to maintain the salary structure of the earlier film days when we were all riding high. Video had rendered that obsolete. Most performers were doing videos for a lot less than their earlier film rates. Most producers insisted on paying the reduced salaries. It was a Don Quixote-like gesture for Spinelli to still pay John Leslie and me the top dollar. Sam was trying to maintain some kind of standard against the advance of cheap crap, but the cheap crap had him completely surrounded.

– Gourmet Video

And Morgan Lee was dessert.

Still, I was grateful for his effort. And Roz even slipped me an extra $250 for "finders' fees," she said, for helping with the casting.

My sex scenes were all great!

There was strong heat and real, live, man-woman connection going on in all three of those scenes, *but*, if it is ever your misfortune to have to sit through this movie, you will discover that all three sex scenes have been completely destroyed by the insertion of up-tempo, Hollywood game show muzak that was insanely cut into the sexual action like a series of inescapably bad farts.

Sam! How could you let that happen?

Ladies and gentlemen, the threat of AIDS was about to end my career. This was not the way I wanted to go out!

Chapter Sixty-Three

The kids had gone to bed. My parents had gone to bed. Carly and I were finally alone. She hadn't wanted me to make those last three movies. I had made them anyway. I was home now. The work was finished. The money was in the bank. I couldn't remember the last time we'd had sex. I reached for her.

"Do you really think we should?" she asked.
"What?" I thought it preposterous that she would even ask.
She said, "Don't you think it would be prudent if one of us remained alive to raise the kids?"

It was the brick wall. I crashed right into it. When I woke up, I was retired and monogamous.

– Gordon Archive

Part Six

THE AFTER PROM

*"The greatest thing you'll ever learn ...
is not to be making love and getting yourself
stuck trying to hold in a fart.*
   *You can't be letting go and holding on
at the same time. It just doesn't work.*

   *Actually, it may not be 'the greatest
thing that you'll ever learn,' but it's way, way
up there!"*

- Richard Pacheco

Chapter One

C'mon, now, you didn't really think my career was like "over" over. Did you? C'mon!

Oh, there was no doubt that Carly had just knocked me out. I was retired and monogamous. Clearly, Carly had won that fight—but I figured there had to be a rematch. I mean, people liked to fuck, right? This disease wasn't going to hold the whole world hostage from having sex for very long, was it? Or should I say reduce it to one where only monogamous couples would fuck. Somebody would soon be figuring something out!

Yeah, well, that may be so, but it wasn't going to be my old high school buddy, Dr. David Sobel. On January 7, he called to discuss who was going to whose house to watch the Super Bowl that year. It was a tug of war that we could not resolve. We decided to let our wives work it out. Then, I could hear David's voice completely change as he slipped into his doctor identity.

"Remember when you asked me last month if there was any safe way for you to continue to work in the sex films?" he asked.

"Yeah, I remember."

"Well, there isn't," he said. "It's time for you to retire. Not only that," he said, "but it looks like it's a great time to be monogamous too." We both laughed hard. When the laughter stopped, there was an awkward silence.

"Boy," I said, "that sure puts a dent in the plans I'd made for the rest of my life!" And then, we both laughed again.

That was it. The good doctor had merely confirmed what I already knew. I was retired and monogamous. Still, I was stunned. Again.

Was this good-bye, Richard Pacheco, or what? It seemed unnaturally premature to think of myself as retired from the business. I felt like I was just coming into my own. It wasn't fair!

Wasn't fair? Who was I kidding? I was still alive! A lot of people were already dead from AIDS and a lot more people were busy dying!

Yeah, but they were all gay! Or needle users! Or Haitians! Haitians? What the fuck was that all about? God was so weird.

And now AIDS was crossing over the sexual orientation border into the heterosexual world. Performers in the X-rated business, with all their multiple partners and all their wild-child behaviors, seemed like an inevitable and unavoidable target for this disease.

I couldn't keep my head buried in the sand on this one, not when I was endangering Carly's life too, and the future lives of our kids. No. I didn't have any more jobs lined up and I wasn't going to schedule any more until this whole AIDS thing got itself sorted out.

AMA President Calls for Fidelity To Fight AIDS

Detroit

The spread of AIDS poses the greatest health threat in the United States, said the president of the American Medical Association, and he proposed fidelity to combat its spread.

– San Francisco Chronicle

This was not Jerry Falwell or some other nutcase from the religious right preaching on the virtues of their self-serving, often hypocritical, fairy tale moralities. This was the President of the American Medical Association saying that there was a real honest-to-God shitstorm going on out there and people were dying. These were the scientists. These were the experts. These were the men and women that we were counting on to know.

Alright, I thought, maybe this could be like a vacation. Yeah, I could take like a paternity leave! It could be six months, maybe a year, and by then everything would have settled down. Who knows? Maybe it would all just go away. Things could be right back to the way they were. It will all have blown over and I'll be picking up my career right where I left off.

Yeah, it'll all work out, I told myself. I was cool.

Chapter Two

My cool lasted about twenty minutes. I stopped working out and I stopped going to the gym. I gained ten, fifteen pounds fast. I didn't give a shit. I had no need to stay skinny. My vanity had been all about attracting women. It appeared to me that that game was over. At least for now, that ship had sailed. I shaved and showered about once a week and smoked a ton of pot. Groovy. My wife tells me that I wasn't so much fun to be around.

Chapter Three

Of all the other actors and actresses I talked to at any length, only Annette Haven seemed to echo my concerns about AIDS. She was planning on getting married and retiring from the business soon anyway. The AIDS plague had just moved up her retirement date.

Oddly enough, Nina Hartley, who had actually been trained as a nurse, looked over the medical facts and didn't really believe there was much of a threat from being an actress in the business. I was surprised by this, but put it down to her newness and her huge desire to become a player in the game. I told her that I thought she was nuts. She told me that I was being overly cautious, but thought it understandable, given that I was a man with a wife and three young kids at home. She said that she was going to miss me.

Paul Thomas waxed philosophical. "When it's your time to go," he said, "it's your time to go."

Anthony Spinelli just took me at my word. He respected what I was doing and what I needed to do to take care of my family. It was always understood between us that family came first. He said he'd do what he could to offer me some paying work behind the camera.

It was John Leslie who got downright pissy with me on the subject. I was taken by surprise. We were talking on the phone. I told him that I was only going to do non-sex roles for right now. I wasn't going to do any more sex scenes until they came out with some kind of reliable test or vaccine for this new disease. He got angry and yelled at me over the phone. The gist of what he said was this:

"Why don't you just quit? You've always hated the business anyway! You never belonged in this business!! You should just quit and forget about it!"

It made me furious. It was an old argument that John and I hadn't had in years. He had always rejected my criticism of the business for being so overwhelmed with the theme of male dominance. As well he should have since it had been by playing that kind of sexuality that John had become a star. I was always after something else. I wanted a more egalitarian view of the sex. I wanted men and women to share the power. John shit all over that.

It was the wrong time and the wrong place to be having this conversation—again. It turned out, as far as the business went, that we were both right. It wasn't an either/or situation. There was enough box office for both of us. And when you put us together, we both won awards and the pictures made a lot of money. He was a centerfielder and I was a catcher. We weren't really rivals at all. We were teammates. We had long ago proven that to each other.

This AIDS thing had gotten us all on edge.

"In stress, we regress."

So, John and I had this shouting match over the telephone. We were two little boys screaming at each other. Not a whole lot of listening was going on, either way.

We knew each other well enough to hurt each other. And we did. We were all over each other's raw nerves.

Our conversation ended with him saying. "Well, I'm not gonna get AIDS! Can you dig it?" He was going to out-tough the disease.

"Well, I hope you don't!" I answered, but was angry enough to not give a shit if he did. If you were going to fight with John, you had to get your blood boiling.

When I got off the phone, I was shaken. Carly gave me some needed perspective. She said that it would be a lot easier for John to dismiss my retirement because I didn't like the business than it would be for him to accept that there really was a clear and present danger from AIDS out there.

It was a good point. I calmed down. John could be a real hog fart sometimes, but so could I. I really didn't wish him AIDS. I didn't wish anybody AIDS. I just wanted the whole thing to go away.

It didn't.

Chapter Four

Hey! I thought I had a great idea! I thought it was a career saver! I would pick out one actress to be my sex partner and we'd agree to only work exclusively with each other. It would be like a business marriage. We'd also agree to live monogamously in our private lives where our mates would agree to live monogamously too. In this way, the actress and I could continue our careers and yet still remain insulated against any other outside threat of a sexual transmission of AIDS.

Some trust would have to be involved. I wouldn't be able to work as much as I once did, but it would still be better than not having any career at all. And hopefully, it would suffice until doctors and researchers could come up with a cure or a vaccine to fight this new plague. It was a plan.

For me, it came down to a choice between Annette Haven and Nina Hartley. I leaned toward Nina at first. I thought Annette was going to be retiring soon, and besides that, she was very expensive. I figured that I'd probably get more work partnering with Nina. Carly said an emphatic, "No."

At the time, Nina lived in a three-way marriage that practiced a swinging lifestyle. Except for a couple of films a year, Annette, as far as we knew, lived monogamously with her soon-to-be husband. Based simply on the potential number of sexual encounters, Carly chose Annette. I didn't put up any fuss. Annette was fine with me. I was just happy that Carly went for any of my idea at all.

When I proposed my plan to Annette, she was very encouraging. She even had a few projects lined up in the not-too-distant future and said that she'd love to work in them with me.

Annette and I both shared the anxiety that we'd already been exposed to the AIDS virus. At that time, there was no test available to the general public, but some kind of testing was not far off. State medical officials were getting ready to offer one that couldn't exactly tell you if you had the AIDS virus, but it could tell you if you had been "around" it. If that test came up negative, the odds were that you did not have the disease. This was the mid-eighties. Our knowledge about AIDS was next to nothing. The latest research had theorized that AIDS could incubate anywhere from three to fifteen years before becoming active.

Annette and I planned to take the test as soon as it became available. If we both showed negative, then we would work with each other. The newspapers said it was now only a matter of days before the test came out publicly.

In the meantime, I got a call to work on a film for Essex being directed by Henri Pachard (Ron Sullivan). Ron told me he had a juicy part for me in a classy film. He said that he'd wanted to work with me for years. That was cool! Ron Sullivan/Henri Pachard was one of the best. He said paying my daily rate would not be any problem. Outstanding!

I explained my concerns about AIDS. He said they were understandable. He said that I'd only have to do one sex scene and that we'd be able to work it out so that I felt safe. I suggested Annette Haven for my partner. Ron Sullivan said that Annette Haven would be great.

Porn again. I shaved and showered and hit the gym hard to melt the fat. In three weeks, I was looking good and ready to go back to work.

The problems started when Ron told me that Annette was unacceptable to the Essex producers. Annette had predicted as much. They'd had a previous falling out over something and Essex wasn't about to hire her for anything. Annette's feelings were mutual.

Pachard proposed me working with Joanna Storm. I had never heard of her. After some bewilderment in trying to keep the project alive, I told him that the only way I could do it would be if the sex scene was conducted within "the safe sex" guidelines as defined by the AIDS Foundation. It was the first time I had ever heard the term "safe sex." It meant "no exchange of bodily fluids and use of a latex condom."

Pachard said, "Fine." Then he said, "the hell with it. We'll shoot the whole scene simulated!" He really wanted me to play the part. And after reading the script, I really wanted to play it too! The role was outstanding! I would be a piano player in a nightclub who would age from being a young man in the roaring twenties, all the way up to being an old man in contemporary times.

It was delicious. I had only to wait for them to negotiate a deal with Carly before I would start learning my lines.

Annette wasn't happy about me taking that job. Even a kiss, she argued, would put me at risk. She didn't want to pay for my sins and I couldn't blame her. The AIDS related virus test wasn't even available. She told me that I was a fool to put myself and my family in jeopardy.

I was willing to take a calculated risk. There was widespread disagreement among the AIDS specialists as to whether or not the disease could even be spread through saliva, through a kiss.[1] Besides that, Pachard had promised me that the sex scene could be simulated.

Annette said that our plan was off. She decided to work only with her boyfriend, her husband-to-be, in any future sex scenes. Given her frame of mind, I completely agreed that it was the best course of action for her to take.

When the Essex people called to cut a deal with Carly, their offer was about one-third of what Ron had said it would be. I was disappointed and relieved.

We turned them down. When I called Ron to see what had happened, I never got past his assistant. She explained that the project had transformed from a big-budget special into what insiders called "a savage dog shoot." All the budgets had been cut to the bone.

They made their movie without me.

Chapter Five

Alex De Renzy called with an offer for me to work with a hot newcomer named Traci Lords. He was perfectly willing to pay my full rate, but he was not willing to make any concessions to the AIDS threat at

---

1. We now know that kissing does not transmit HIV, the virus that causes AIDS. Saliva does not transmit HIV, only blood, semen, pre-cum, vaginal fluid and breast milk. – Current AIDS information supplied by Robert Gordon, Director of Special Projects for the UCLA Art & Global Health Centers.

all. There'd be no tests, no condoms, no nothing. Sexually speaking, it would be business as usual. "Take it or leave it, Howie."

I left it. When I argued that the business was putting its talent into life threatening situations, Alex said he understood. He also said that he hoped I wouldn't make too much of a public fuss about it because "it could hurt the business." I told him that the business should be put on hold until we figured out a way to make it safe for all of us to work. It made absolutely no impression at all—on Alex—nor hardly on anybody else who continued to work in the adult industry.

Chapter Six

It was at this point that I worked in *Tragedy in New York*, the Italian gangster film with "Willie Cicci" (Joe Spinell).

I was hired to work as an extra in this movie, but they soon gave me a couple of lines in a scene and liked what I had to offer. I was given more scenes and more dialogue. I was being discovered again.

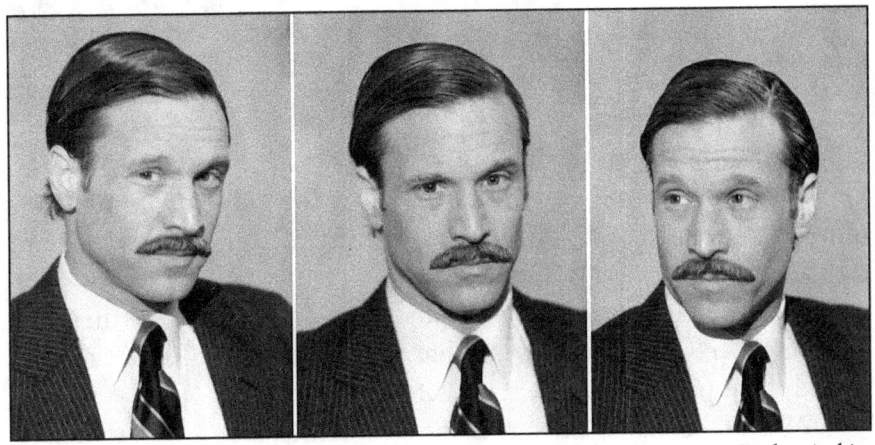

- Gordon Archive

Pacheco joins the mafia.

My last scene was shot in the middle of the night. We were in yet another of those cold San Francisco warehouses. I was lying in a puddle of actors' bodies. Maybe six of us had just been machine-gunned to death in the climactic scene. It was exciting. We'd had exploding special effects and blood capsules. I recall being on the floor with the fake blood and the irony dripping down my face and thinking.

"Oh, boy! I've finally been in a movie that I can take my kids to see!"

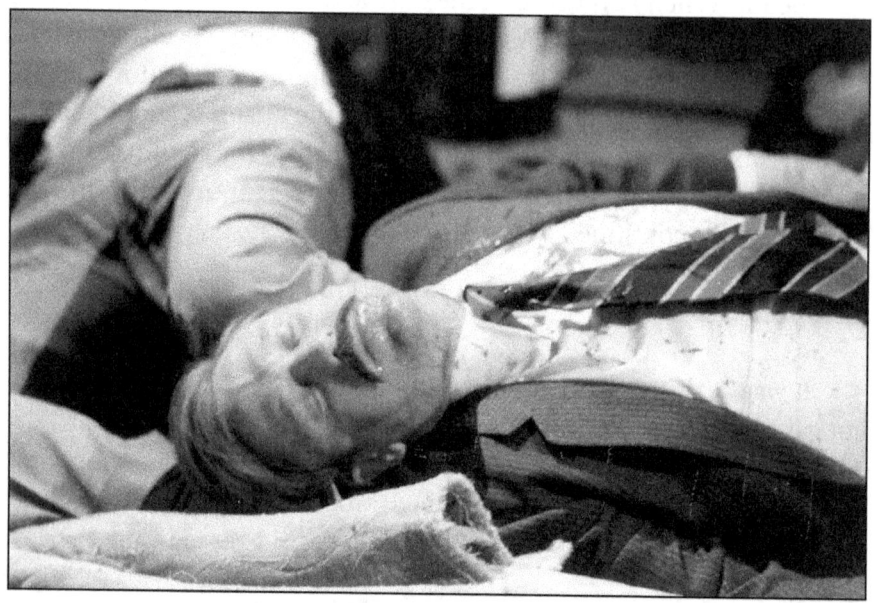

– *Gordon Archive*

Bloody Howie!

Yeah, I was going straight. But I soon ran afoul of my own agent. There was talk of me continuing on with the company when they moved to the next location in New York City, BUT, I would have to sign a new contract.

The problem was that they wanted to go on paying me as an extra. "Willie Cicci," himself, told me that was complete bullshit. He suggested that I have them take it up with my agent.

When I did, my agent surprisingly took their side. This was a non-union shoot and my agent apparently had made some kind of side deal just to deliver them bodies for a flat fee, period. My own agent tried to bully me into working for a lot less than what the part called for. I'm afraid I lost my cool.

I didn't sign the contract. I didn't go to New York. And I no longer had an agent. So much for going straight.

Chapter Seven

Joan Rivers had me on her late afternoon talk show. They flew Carly and me to New York City and put us up at The Plaza. That was pretty cool. We even rode around Central Park in a horse and carriage. If I hadn't been sick with the flu for the whole trip, it might actually have been some fun.

They were having me on the show as Richard Pacheco, the porn star who was refusing to go to work because of the threat of AIDS.

Beyond the serious moments created by the topic, I was pretty funny talking to Joan that day, especially about the great difficulties I'd had in getting erections for the camera.

On a break during the taping, Joan Rivers generously said to me, "You're very funny. You should be doing stand-up!" It was exactly the kind of thing that I was hoping would happen by my coming to New York. I was being "discovered" again.

– Joan Rivers Show

The Joan Rivers Show.

So, I said to Joan, "Fine, what do I do?" She pointed to a guy off stage and said,

"When we're done up here, you go over and talk to him. He'll get you started."

"You are funny," he said. He was an agent, he was a this and a that, and I'm not sure what else he was, but he told me he owned a string of comedy clubs across Canada and said that he'd love to put

– Joan Rivers Show

me to work right now. He'd start me out on the East Coast and then over a couple months, I'd work my way West across Canada and end up in LA.

I was excited. But when I told Carly all about it, she was considerably less than thrilled. Did I tell you that we were pregnant again? Bobby was on the way. Our third was going to be a boy.

"Oh," Carly said, "is this the part where you leave me home alone with the kids while you run off to become a movie star? I don't think so, asshole."

"Well, when you put it that way," I said. But it made sense to me and I appreciated it. It made me feel the "*us*" in us.

"My love," she said, softening—

But I was already hooked; she had me at "asshole." I didn't really want to work in nightclubs, though it was fun to think that I could! It was certainly flattering, but, nah, I didn't want to be alone, on the road, working in smoke-filled, drunk-filled rooms until the middle of the night, and then sleeping all day. I knew me. I'd be out chasing women and just confusing myself. I wanted to be married and have kids—like I already was.

"My love," Carly said, "we have to find something for you to do that can keep you at home with us."

– Gordon Archive

Anybody need a writer?

Chapter Eight

Actually, the first job I took after AIDS drove me away from porn was clerking for my friend Andy at his Captain Video store. The job wasn't bad, but I really didn't fit into that scene very well. After a couple of weeks, it was best for me just to move on.

Next up, I enrolled in a training program to become an AIDS Information Specialist. Daily we met in San Francisco where doctors, community leaders, and various people with AIDS held seminars about the disease and what they'd all learned about living with it.

Some of those AIDS patients who lectured to us the first week were dead by the second. It was a pretty terrifying experience. Many of the AIDS patients were covered with the purple blotches of Kaposi's Sarcoma. It certainly got your attention. In those early days, we didn't really know if shaking hands, hugging somebody, or even being breathed on had the potential to infect you with the HIV virus.

All over San Francisco, lots of people were dying. We knew so little about the disease. I felt like I had a scared fever the whole time I was in those rooms receiving the training. Then, I'd go home to my wife and babies and wonder what I might be bringing into the house.

It was too crazy making. I lasted about two weeks and then I had to let it go.

Chapter Nine

I wrote a screenplay for Seka. She titled it, *Careful, He May Be Watching* and chose to both produce and star in the film.

Wow! How cool was that! I would be directing my first film! Oh, I'd helped out Spinelli by directing a scene here and there, but this time, I was gonna be the Big Cheese. Seka was taking a considerable risk. She was a major queen of the industry at this point, a big-time player. As a producer, she was betting a lot of her own money on this one and she was offering me the reins.

It would be my first time officially directing anything.

Yeah, Seka was taking a risk, but she also was no dummy and this wasn't her first rodeo. She hired Alex de Renzy to be my cameraman.

What?

Yeah, she hired Alex de Renzy to be my cameraman.

– *Suze Randall/Video-X-Pix/Caballero*

Seka also asked me to direct it.

Y'know, the story was that God once tried to hire Alex de Renzy to shoot some love scenes in the Garden of Eden with Adam and Eve; de Renzy turned Him down. Said he couldn't stand the idea of working for somebody else. Alex de Renzy was a fiercely independent filmmaker and a legendary master in the X-rated domain. One would think Seka wise for having him at the ready just in case I faltered. I know I would. I heard Alex only took the job because he just happened to need some extra money when Seka called with the offer.

It was presented to me as a fait accompli. It was a done deal. Alex de Renzy was going to be my cameraman! He had never before worked as anybody's cameraman, ever. He had always been the director and shot his own films.

Well, this would all, no doubt, prove to be very interesting.

Regarding AIDS, it gave me some pause to consider the moral dilemma of how I could ask performers to do things sexually that I was no longer willing to risk myself.

Well, there were all kinds of ways I could try to rationalize it, but the bottom line was that nobody would be forcing anybody to do anything that they didn't want to do.

My withdrawal from performing sex was a distinctly minority

- Vincent Fronczek/Gordon Archive/Seka

On the set with Seka & Richard Pacheco.

point of view amongst my fellow actors and actresses. Indeed, the business pretty well had its head in the sand on the AIDS issue and most wanted it kept that way. Nobody really wanted the goose to stop laying those golden eggs.

For the time being, I was content to let every other actor and actress make their own decision. For my part, I would write the script and direct the picture.

I put together my own little production team to get started. I hired the multitalented porn veteran John Seeman to be my Production Manager (PM). John had experience producing, directing, acting, writing, and knew every part of the adult business inside and out. Besides that, he was my friend. I trusted him. He would have my back.

I also hired filmmaker Billy Rubin to be my Assistant Director (AD). Billy made industrial films for a living and was very familiar with all the technical aspects of directing, which I was not. He would be my go-between with Alex in the technical discussions of lenses and lighting and the like. Billy was also my friend. We'd been racquetball partners for several years. He was a tenacious bulldog. I trusted him to have my back too.

As director, like my mentor Spinelli, I saw that my primary job would be to get quality performances out of my actors. And I did think of them as *my actors*. That part didn't take long at all. I had Seka, Mike Horner, Kay Parker, and Shanna McCullough in the leads. That was a good bunch right there.

About a week before production was scheduled to begin, I tried to arrange a meeting with Alex and my team.

Alex declared there would be no such meeting. He said everything would be much better, much fresher, if we worked out all of the little details on the set. Said he wouldn't even read the script until we were on the set. It was not open for discussion.

When I told Alex that I wanted Billy to work with him on technical matters, Alex simply said, "No." He said the only person he would be talking to on the set at all would be the director.

Oh.

On the first day of shooting, one of the main actresses in the first scene was two hours late arriving on the set. We were already behind before we even got started.

When we were finally all together, on the set, and ready to launch that first shot of the first day, Alex de Renzy completely ignored me and called, "Action!"

I felt like I'd been slapped across the face.

I don't even know if he understood what he had done. This was Alex, after all, he wasn't used to answering to anybody, but himself. We'd made a couple of movies together before. We'd been on the set together before. I was Howie, the actor. He was Alex, the director. It was just another movie. It was just another day on the set.

But it wasn't.

And when Alex first started telling one of my actresses about how to play her scene, I could have run and hidden under a rock.

But I didn't.

I wanted to fire him. Of course, I did. So far, he'd been making my job harder at almost every turn. I told him I wanted to use a zoom lens on one particular shot. He told me he didn't have any zoom lenses. Said he didn't believe in them. If we'd have had that goddamned production meeting a week before we started when I wanted it, I wouldn't be finding that out now on the goddamned set and having to rewrite the whole goddamned scene.

And another thing! The film in the magazines that he was using kept breaking in the camera. Something about being taped in the front and in the back of the magazines.

What did I know? We just kept falling farther and farther behind.

My first day as a director lasted twenty-three hours and fifteen minutes.

When Alex had called that first "Action," ignoring me, I could just feel the blood rushing to my face with the insult and the humiliation. That was hard to swallow, but I did—because I had to.

In taking that job, my first allegiance was to Seka and making her movie. I was supposed to have her back! Even if I could have had Alex fired, the bottom line was there we would all be, Day One on the set, without a camera or a cameraman. It would be Seka's movie that would end up getting fucked.

You "don't insult the alligator until you're on the other side of the river." At that point, we needed Alex de Renzy more than we needed me.

Eventually, we made it to lunch. I found Alex and invited him to have a private word with me in a back room. It was just him and me.

"Alex, I can't compete with you out there, but I am the director. You've got to let me direct this thing."

"Oh," he said matter of factly. "Okay, then, you direct!" And after that little conversation, Alex de Renzy really was my cameraman. He never stepped on my toes again.

In fact, in one scene, after I had struggled with an actor through a whole bunch of takes to finally get him to give us what we needed, Alex de Renzy took me aside and said to me, "Hey, you really improved that scene!"

It may have been the highlight of my entire directing career.

– Vincent Fronczek/Gordon Archive

Alex de Renzy & Richard Pacheco on the set of *Careful, He May Be Watching*.

Chapter Ten

My son Bobby was born on January 8, 1986. He was a month early. He was in a hurry. He's still in a hurry.

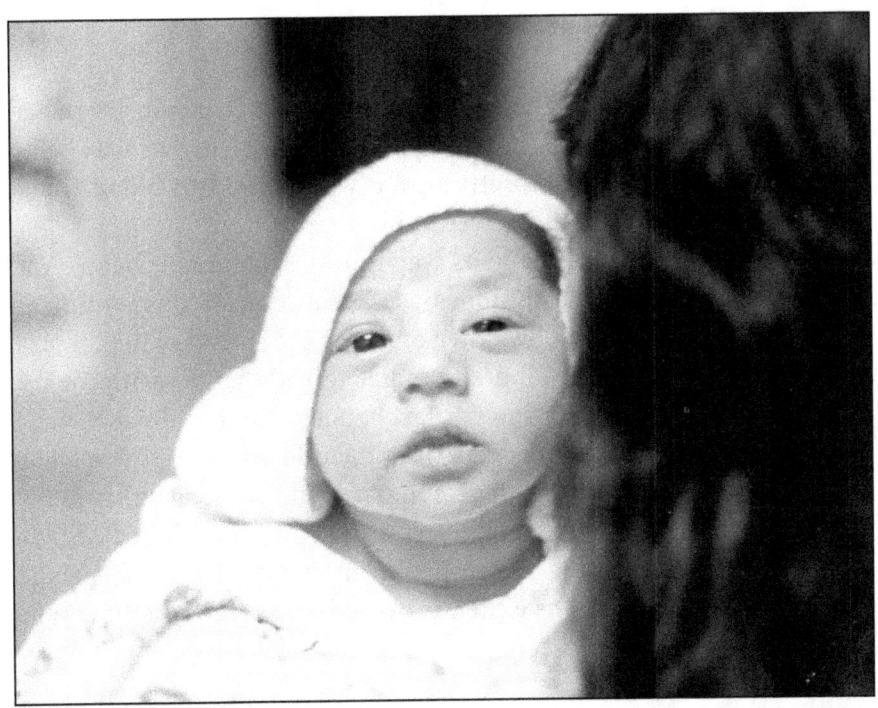

– Gordon Archive

This here's Baby Bobby!

– Gordon Archive

Juliana and Polly say hi to their baby brother.

Chapter Eleven

By February of 1986, the AIDS landscape had changed. There had been some progress made in understanding how the virus was being spread sexually. They were pretty sure it was a blood-to-blood transmission, but other body fluids were still suspect.

The term "Safe Sex" made its way into the national lexicon. And the practice of safe-sex techniques was gaining great momentum in the medical campaign to slow down and stop the spread of the disease.

By now, experts were all pretty much agreed that sex with the use of a latex condom and having "no exchange of bodily fluids" would pose little risk to spreading or receiving the infection.

Hey, I could do a sex scene like that! I could work again!

And when Anthony Spinelli came to town to shoot *The Red Garter*, he agreed and invited me to begin my comeback. At this stage, Carly offered no objections either, provided we agreed to follow safe-sex practices in all of my scenes.

- Gordon Archive

Sam said he had no problem with that.

I was back in the business!

- Gordon Archive/Hustler Video/LFP Video Group, LLC.

And I'd be working with Hyapatia Lee!

- Gordon Archive/Hustler Video/LFP Video Group, LLC.

– Gordon Archive/Hustler Video/LFP Video Group, LLC.

– Gordon Archive/Hustler Video/LFP Video Group, LLC.

Hyapatia played the owner of a strip club. I was her attorney. In the foreplay to our lone sex scene, I sat at a table in her club. I was an audience of one. Hyapatia came out and did a strip tease for me.

I was pretty nervous getting back into the ballgame after such a long lay-off. I had a lot of false bravado. When it came time for the touching, Hyapatia gave me what we called "the AIDS blow job." She licked the sides of the shaft, but did not take the head of the penis into her mouth.

"*No exchange of bodily fluids.*"

For a while, it all worked perfectly. There was the usual starting and stopping for the cameras. I'd be hard. They'd shoot. They'd cut the take and I'd get soft. Then, here we go, up again and then, down again, several times. Soon, it was time to put on the rubber and get down to it.

That's when the first flicker of the panic wafted through. She was stroking and licking the shaft, just as she had done all those times before, but it stopped working. I wasn't getting hard this time. Uh-oh, my stomach began to clench. I knew this Hell very well and I did not want to go there—but by the time you noticed it, you were already there.

Hyapatia Lee was completely tuned into me. She felt my terror. On her own, she took my whole penis into her mouth and gently began sucking—like AIDS, and fear, and chaos didn't even exist. It was a bold move and a brilliant rescue.

I hardened in her mouth and the sun came out. I could breathe again. It began a lovemaking of calm and delicious gratitude. It celebrated a trust and a friendship that the world was safe and uncruel.

It was also stupid, and wrong, and dangerous, but for the moment, we gladly ignored all of that.[1] In no particular hurry now, we made the transition into the condom and then I mounted her. Eye to eye and pleasure to pleasure, we soon began in earnest. When lust came, it came free and easy, and unencumbered by doubt. We were both pretty happy there at the end. There were times when this job was both a gift and a blessing. And right there, in the middle of all those scary other things, this was one of them.

---

1. *We now know that the risk of transmitting HIV through unprotected oral sex is significantly less than that of unprotected vaginal sex or anal sex. In terms of 'relative risk' the riskiest sexual activity is unprotected anal sex, followed by unprotected vaginal sex, and then unprotected oral sex. – Current AIDS information supplied by Robert Gordon, Director of Special Projects for the UCLA Art & Global Health Centers.*

> Feb. 8, 1986   "The Red Garter"
>
> To Howie,
>   It was a very nice change of pace working with you. You're the most sensitive man I've ever made love to on screen, besides Bud, of course. It's so different to actually "make love", and enjoy it so much. You are truely a real person and I hope Bud + I will always be good friends of you and your beautiful family.
>   With love + best wishes,
>   Hyapatia L

– Gordon Archive/Hyapatia Lee.

Chapter Twelve

What did it say that we lost control and broke our own rules? We turned out lucky that neither Hyapatia nor I had the virus at that point, but we had risked everything before finding that out. Not unlike playing Russian roulette, this was not a comforting notion.

What would happen the next time I had trouble maintaining an erection? Would the condom come off? In the heat of the moment, I saw how easy it had been to toss out the rules. In a blink! Should I trust myself to take that risk again? Should Carly allow me to take that risk on her behalf? There were three kids now depending on the two of us to go on living.

Maybe if there hadn't been such a long time between jobs I could have gotten myself back into a rhythm and gained some confidence. But it's not like there was any great demand for an actor who insisted on "safe sex."

The bottom line, according to the producers back then, was that films with condoms in them made a lot less money than those without. And that pretty much put an end to the whole discussion. As far as most of the industry was concerned: there was no AIDS. It was all business as usual, and nobody was particularly pleased with me for even bringing up the subject.

The "safe sex" jobs came weeks and months apart. In-between, I became a Mr. Mom. We lived off of Carly's paycheck as a therapist, and I was the stay-at-home dad with the kids, doing the shopping, and the cooking, and the cleaning, and driving the kids to and from school and everywhere else. Oh, and in my spare time, I was trying to get the first version of this book published and find myself another line of work.

– *Gordon Archive*

Job Hunting.

On the one hand, the loss of my X-rated star identity was like having Shredded Ego for breakfast every morning, but on the other, we were keeping our little family together and finding ways to make it work. When I wasn't pissed off, I was actually pretty happy.

Chapter Thirteen

When Candida Royalle called to offer me a part in *Sensual Escape*, I leapt at the chance. Finally, New York! Not only was it another lead role coming at the time like some manna from Heaven but it was also a chance to be part of a budding new direction in porn. Through Candida's Femme Productions, I would be working with a group of experienced and talented industry women who were all intent and capable of bringing about some real change to Pornoland. I thought it an honor to be asked to work with them. In many ways, it was a dream job for me.

I loved everything about the idea of going to New York to do this job, right up to the moment that Carly asked me not to go.

Carly liked that I was "retired." In the weeks and months of my inactivity, waiting for the infrequent safe-sex jobs, she got used to me being home. She got used to living without the tension of my going off to "connect" with some other woman at "work." It had been monogamy by default. She lived with the illusion that I wanted things this way.

I didn't. I wanted my career back. I wanted my family and I wanted my career too. It was not an either/or thing. I wanted them both! It was the same argument that we'd been having for several years now, only the births of our children and the onset of the AIDS plague had completely changed everything.

In prioritizing things, I did what I had to do to make my family safe and to protect my marriage. But a part of me always resented it. Yes, I wanted my marriage, but no, I didn't want a lifetime of monogamy. Even though I would later spend years actually behaving monogamously, I could never agree to make her that promise, that commitment. It brought out the claws in me. I was deeply conflicted over this issue and so were we. It lived with us for many years like a quiet elephant in the house. To our credit, protecting the marriage always came first. But every now and then, the elephant would blow his trumpet and we'd all have to dance. Truth is, those moments became rare.

But at this particular time, I wanted to go to New York and I wanted to make this movie.

It wasn't a knockdown, drag-out fight. There was no broken glass. There were no ultimatums and it wasn't a deal breaker. But I wanted my career back. And I wanted this job. It would only be a few days of work and all of the AIDS precautions would be in place. Though Carly would certainly have preferred it otherwise, she gave in. She let me have it. I was grateful.

– Elizabeth Schwegler

Off I went, alone to New York.

– Elizabeth Schwegler

Carly stayed home with the kids.

Chapter Fourteen

"Club 99" was the closest thing to a union I ever came across during my time in the business. I don't think they ever were an official anything. From the outside, they looked to be a group of industry women who morphed from being just friends and colleagues into being a support group.

It was centered on the New York side of things and it was made up of well-known players Gloria Leonard, Candida Royalle, Veronica Hart, Annie Sprinkle, Kelly Nichols, Sue, Nero, Veronica Vera, and probably Samantha Fox and Vanessa Del Rio too. It inspired West coasters Nina Hartley, Porsche Lynn Angel Kelly, and Jeanna Fine to start up their own group called The Pink Ladies for a short time in LA. All of these women were heavy-hitting, award-winning All-Stars. They were actresses, directors, editors, photographers, producers, writers, and production managers, who were all not inclined to want to take too many more come shots to the face.

When Candida started up Femme, her own production company, and declared its mission to make hot, entertaining couples movies from a woman's perspective, it seemed that the women had gained a much-needed, new voice in the adult industry.

Brava!

– Annie Sprinkle/Candida Royalle

Sensual Escape was actually the umbrella title for two "mini" movies that were being marketed together, *Fortune Smiles* and *The Tunnel*. Candida and her then-husband Per Sjostedt produced both. Candida also wrote and directed *The Tunnel*, which starred Siobhan Hunter and Steve Lockwood.

- Annie Sprinkle/Candida Royalle's Sensual Escape
Gloria Leonard, Nina Hartley, and Candida Royalle.

Gloria Leonard wrote and directed *Fortune Smiles*, which starred Nina Hartley and me. Gloria Leonard was a delight. I wished we had crossed paths earlier in my career. She was way taller than me, and while that generally cooled any romantic ideas on my part, it did not preclude a meeting of the minds. Gloria Leonard was smart and tough. She was seasoned and seemed to operate in the world with a very effective bullshit meter. I was most impressed with her. We bonded quickly and decided we were old friends.

> Darling, dearest Howard,
>
> I resent the vast distance geographically separating us and though we've only recently become friends, I sense we've really known each other a very long time — you are a rare and lovely human being and I only wish for you the things I want for me — and mine. And I like to think that now, you're my friend. I am proud to be with you — you are a prestigious peer. Many blessings on you, Jeremy and your kiddies too. Stay in touch! Glo xxx

— *Gordon Archive*

And I met Annie Sprinkle for the first time on this shoot too. She was the still photographer. Annie was another gem. Luckily, we've gotten to know each other in the years since we've both retired from being actors in the movies.

Annie Sprinkle was and is a force of nature.

Fortune Smiles—here's what the box cover had to say about this movie:

> Media Superstar Gloria Leonard takes us on a touchingly funny walk through the minds of two people who have been dating and are about to take the leap into bed. What is your lover really thinking about before the big plunge?
>
> … And what happens when the (movie's) stars are allowed to choose their own costar? Watch the sparks fly with the debut return to films by award-winning actor Richard Pacheco in a hot pairing off with the beautiful Nina Hartley.

Part Six ◯ 601

– *San Francisco Chronicle*

Old friends.

– *Annie Sprinkle/Candida Royalle's Sensual Escape*

Ready …

— *Annie Sprinkle/Candida Royalle's Sensual Escape*

Get set ...

— *Annie Sprinkle/Candida Royalle's Sensual Escape*

Go!

If I ever wanted to hit a home run, this was it. But I didn't get there. Oh, it's not a clunker by any means, but I was all set for a monster smash hit, and I didn't get there. You might not even notice something was amiss from watching the movie, but I know. I know that I got lost. I got strangely lost.

The story was clever. The script was clever. It was one of those scenes where we got to hear the inner thoughts of the characters as they met for a date at a restaurant en route to what they both hoped would be their first time making love. That part went well.

From Gloria's directing on down, we all did a fine job of playing out our little scenario and setting up the sex scene. There was even some very titillating foreplay going on under the table at the restaurant. That was a good scene.

It went kerflooey afterwards, at the apartment, when we got naked, when we got into the sex scene.

It started off just fine. It was me and Nina, old friends. I was comfortable, at ease. This was the way I liked it. I had a willing and able partner, a lover I could trust. We'd been around the block before. Several times. Sure, I had my pre-sex jitters. It had once again been a long time since my last sex scene, but otherwise, it was all set up the way I liked it.

It began well and the pleasure mounted. They did their movie-making stopping and starting, but no matter. We'd both been through this ritual more than a hundred times each.

We'd done about half the sex scene when it happened. I'd gotten hard and had put on the condom. Nina opened for me and there had been an insertion. Some hardcore footage had been shot. Somewhere, like in the middle of a kiss, there was a complete power outage. My body just turned off. For no apparent reason, arousal simply vanished.

Fear showed up. There was shame too. Y'know, the usual suspects, but I was still surprised to see 'em showing up again this late in my career. Nina Hartley shifted into another gear. She was gonna save me. She went at it like a trooper. She went at it like my friend. She went at it like she was trying to pull me back from the abyss.

The cameras stopped running. They were in standby now. Nina continued with her rescue effort. We were like an episode of *Grey's Anatomy*. Sometimes, the patient died. This was one of them. They waited for as long as they comfortably could and then they pulled the plug.

There was no stunt cock for use as a Plan B, so they had us simulate the orgasm. I think. I don't know. These aren't really the kind of moments that I want to remember.

When we were done, everybody put a happy face on it, but I was embarrassed—and puzzled. To our credit, we did not violate our commitment to maintain the safe-sex boundaries. The rubber had stayed on and the captain went down with the ship. So be it. R.I.P.

Okay, I just made myself go back and watch that whole scene again. Wow! It's quite good! None of that shit I just fretted about showed up on the screen at all. The editors saved that scene! They used a montage of quick cuts to make up for the missing second part of the sex scene. They used some of the same hardcore footage twice, but you might have to be me to even notice. It was all very well done. It really worked! By the way, we did simulate those orgasms. And surprisingly, we did a helluva good job acting them.

That said, I still was embarrassed by my sexual collapse, and puzzled by it too. This was strike one in my latest comeback.

P.S.

Years later, when I reminisced about this scene with Candida, she had no memory of me having had any difficulties in the sex scene. In fact, she told me the scene had won AVN's award for 'Hottest Sex Scene' of that year!

I never knew that! It's not likely that I would have forgotten an award. I just don't think I ever even knew about it. In any case, I told Candida that I hoped she gave that trophy to her film editor!

Chapter Fifteen

The homecoming was awkward. While Carly didn't hire a marching band to greet me at the airport, she didn't have the locks changed on the house either. My key still worked, but there was a murky distance between us.

It didn't help that we were being audited by the IRS. Our accountant said that an unreported savings account had automatically triggered the audit. It was our daughter Juliana's account. It had like $3.46 in it. We spent the morning of my homecoming preparing our taxes with the accountant who would be representing us. You might just guess how this all contributed to the general merriment.

After he left, we went a few more rounds on money and on our recent separation. We were both feeling pretty beat up, but, I was home.

The New York adventure hadn't exactly turned out to be the stuff of my dreams. I had fought for it, fought hard, and here I was paying some serious dues for having had that less than thrilling experience. Didn't quite seem fair. There used be this expression amongst the young and hip in the 1960s: "The hassle was not worth the copping." It was too true. The gods were having their fun with me, but I was home.

Within a couple of days, we found each other again. Carly left me this note:

My love my heart my pancreas
my nail clippers
my tax audit my heart
my love

You my you

I have tasted you
in all the little back rooms
of my soul
    and said

Yes

Love,

Carly

I know, I'm a lucky man. After all, whatever other madness was going on, she was never not the love of my life. I was a lucky man then. And I'm a lucky man now.

Chapter Sixteen

We had a little financial meeting. Carly would continue her work as a therapist. We'd hire childcare to help with the kids. My job was to come up with $2,000 a month and to stay close to home doing it.

Okay. I had resumed my X-rated career, but the $1000-a-day jobs were all over. Everything was cheaper nowadays. Salaries had plummeted with the video revolution. As an actor, I was still offering to do a safe-sex scene, but there weren't many takers. Mostly, I did non-sex roles for about $200 or $300 a day, whatever I could get. And there weren't a lot of those coming my way either.

Both Anthony Spinelli and John Leslie used me as their assistant director. I'd make about $200 a day working for them. I didn't do much of anything in either job, but they both liked having me around.

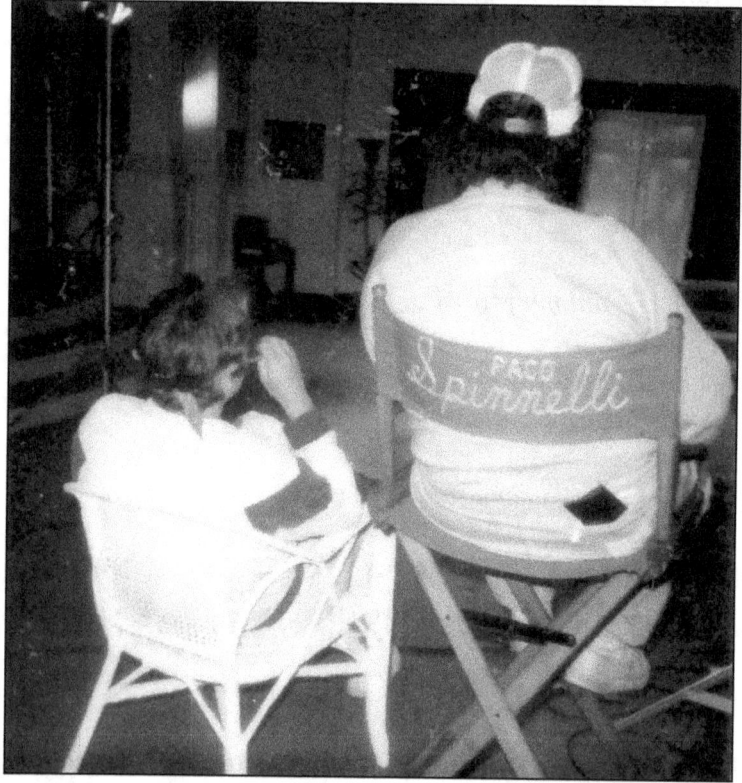

– Gordon Archive

Sitting at the Maestro's side.

With Sam, I think my primary job was just to remind him of better days. He was tossing me a bone because I'd always been loyal, and, like him years before me, I had three babies at home. I'd run lines with his actors, play a bit part here and there, do whatever I could to help him make his videos. I felt like the used-up fighter who still hangs out at the gym. Hey, money was money. Dem Huggies didn't pay for demselves.

It was different with John. Basically, he just wanted me to hold on to his money. John trusted me. That was an honor. I paid his actors, doled out the petty cash whenever he said so, and kept accurate records of where every dollar went.

Turns out, without having sex, I didn't much like hanging around an X-rated set. I'd get aroused by ten o'clock in the morning and then have a stomach ache all day until I could get home to do something about it. I don't know how the X-rated crews put up with that. Made me crazy. I hated being around the sex if I wasn't going to be having any. Not my cup 'o tea at all!

At home, I was turning my attention to writing. I wanted to harvest my stories about the X-rated industry and turn them into money. It was my get-rich-quick scheme, and thirty years later, I'm about ready to cash in on it.

Chapter Seventeen

The Huntress was an attempt by the people at Intropics Video to make a socially responsible movie. In their advertising for this film, Intropics stated that:

- Virus testing has been made available to participants in this production.
- "Safe Sex" practices are demonstrated within story context.
- A portion of the revenue from this feature will go towards AIDS research.

Well, let's hear it for the good guys. At this point, they were one of the few companies trying to do the right thing. They certainly had my applause. I just wish I could have done a better job for them.

I was paired, once again, with Annette Haven for this one. The back of the box cover proclaimed "Featuring the sensational return of Annette Haven and Richard Pacheco."

We once had burned white-hot together back in the days of *Madame Lau*. That was ten years earlier. She was the ruling queen then, it was her world. I was a rising prince, just grateful to be at her feet. Our lovemaking was a gift, a peak experience. It was a rite of passage. It told me that I belonged. It was another galaxy.

This time around, well, I can't speak for her, but I was tired, tired like a married man with three kids trying to pretend like he still could cut it in a world called yesterday—a world that was no longer there.

– *Intropics Video.*

Of course, I didn't know any of that then, but that's the beauty of hindsight. It all seems so obvious these many years later.

I watched the scene again last night. Annette and I started out like a house afire. We did have passion between us, and mostly we kept it under such restraint. The movies gave us a permission that real life did not. And when we began touching in this movie, it just like bubbled up all over us. The moans were a delight. The touch was real. The relief was tangible. I seemed to fumble and savor the gift.

– Caballero

Howie & Annette Revisited.

It roared right on through the placing of the condom and the joining of our bodies. They were running their cameras, but we were running something else. A forbidden love? Time travel? Who knows what to call it?

I landed on my back and Annette rode me. I watched her. She seemed happy. And then. Goddamn it, out of nowhere, there was that turning off of the engine again. It was the power outage. I was stunned. My erection was fading. It had been very hot and heavy just prior, so, in the moment of panic that followed, I just continued like I was still in her and Annette wisely followed my cue. We acted the orgasm. We acted the orgasm so well that the cameraman thought it was all for real.

When she rolled off I said, "Okay, now, let's see if we can't give them a real one." It was false bravado. I was gone. The condom mocked my softness.

Annette seemed as confused as I was. Where did it go? What happened? We were pros. We retreated into scene saving techniques. This shouldn't have happened. I was ashamed to make Annette struggle to rekindle my desire. I was ashamed. Such work should not be for her. She was Annette Haven! I let us both down. I didn't mean to do it.

Annette was lovely about it all. She worked hard to revive me, but it did not happen. I went into my sexual fantasy closet and dragged out all the old pictures, but they did not work either. The director waited a while and then gave up. They had to move on. He had us simulate a few more orgasms so that they would have some options from which to choose.

Unlike Candida and Femme, the editors of this failed scene were not able to save it in the post-production. In fact, they made an even bigger mess of it. It's way too long. It just goes on and on. They repeat footage and it's obvious that they're doing it. And worst of all, they didn't choose just one from all the simulated orgasms, they put them all in there! It looks like we both come four or five times in this one scene. It's phony baloney and very confusing. I'm pretty sure this scene didn't win any awards.

In fact, this was Strike Two!

Chapter Eighteen

For years after I stopped doing sex scenes in the business, I always remembered that scene with Annette Haven as my last one, but it wasn't.

In 1987, I did the one with Nina in March, the one with Annette in April, and then my diaries tell me that there was one more with Shanna McCullough in August. I didn't even write down the name of the movie. It's given short shrift there in my diaries and you'll soon see why.

We were working for Ona Zee and her husband Frank.

– *Gordon Archive/Ona Zee*

Ona Zee.

Ona Zee was a fiery, spectacular actress in the early days of video. At this point, she was trying to graduate to being a producer and a director. I had never played a scene with her and it was my loss. I adored her. She was always full of life and bursting with energy.

Ona and Frank had partnered me to work with Shanna McCullough in their movie.

I had already been on many sets with Shanna McCullough, mostly where she served as an actress and I had been the assistant director for either John Leslie or Sam. They both had used her often. She was vivacious and young, one of the rising stars of the industry. She could play a part well, handle the sex, and would show up on time and sober.

I had been in her home, met her boyfriend, and even interviewed her for some porn magazines—as I now profiled the stars to help get my writing career off the ground.

I felt like her uncle.

– Shanna McCullough

Shanna McCullough.

So, what happened in our sex scene?

Nothing. Absolutely nothing.

It was an unsuccessful mating. It felt like a mismatch from the start, and I don't recall if there were even any erections at all before the lights went out. I don't think they ever came on. If I had to come up with a reason, I would give you two words: incest taboo. It wasn't erotic to me at all.

Mercifully, I have driven all memory of that last colossal failure out of my brain. Couldn't tell you the name of movie, the characters we played, whether we simulated some atrocity, or if they just scrapped the whole scene from the movie. Didn't write much about it in my diary either. It just says:

"My dick inside the rubber kept screaming, 'I'm suffocating!'"

This was Strike Three! Never even got the bat off of my shoulder.

Chapter Nineteen
Oh, by the way....

Over the years, I've struggled to explain this simpering, whimpering, embarrassing end of my career as Casanova. Recently, this article appeared in *The San Francisco Chronicle*, reprinted from *The New York Times*:

Study Says Kids Sap their Dad's Testosterone Level
By Pam Belluck, The New York Times
Updated: 09/12/2011

This is probably not the news most new fathers want to hear.

Testosterone, that most male of hormones, takes a dive after a man becomes a parent. And the more he gets involved in caring for his children - changing diapers, jiggling the kid on his knee, reading "Goodnight Moon" for the umpteenth time - the lower his testosterone drops.

So says the first large study measuring testosterone in men when they were single and childless and several years after they had children. Experts say the research has implications for understanding the biology of fatherhood, hormone roles in men, and even health issues like prostate cancer.

"The real take-home message," said Peter Ellison, a professor of human evolutionary biology at Harvard, is that "male parental care is important. It's important enough that it's actually shaped the physiology of men."

Testosterone was measured when the men were 21 and single, and again nearly five years later. Although testosterone naturally decreases with age ... men who became fathers showed much greater declines, more than double the childless men.

And men who spent more than three hours a day caring for children - playing, feeding, bathing, toileting, reading or dressing them - had the lowest testosterone."

Oh.

Chapter Twenty
Stale Kimonos

Well, I didn't know about any of that stuff back then. What I did know was that I had just had my thirty-ninth birthday, and I began thinking that this whole sex star business might just be a younger man's game.

I had just had four difficult sex scenes in a row. I was one for four in orgasms, but I was on a three-scene losing streak, and those failures really do take it out of you. Twenty, thirty, forty people are watching you. It was one thing to struggle with all that pressure on my way up the mountain, on my way to learning how. It was quite another to fail as a star, to plummet into the embarrassment, to be an aged Willie Mays stumbling in the New York Mets outfield after he had previously known life as a GIANT.

And in this whole last "comeback year" of safe sex, I must say that I never could really get comfortable with the idea that on the other side of this condom, might just be death. It all wasn't much of a turn on. It was a different world.

At home, there was no AIDS, there was no condom, and there was no fear of death. There was Carly, waiting, both patiently and un, for me to have done with all this madness of my youth. And, of course, there were three little kids who needed Daddy to just be Daddy.

It was time. It was like baseball to me. It had always been like baseball to me. I just couldn't get around on the fastball anymore. It was time to hang 'em up. Spikes, by the way, the shoes with the metal cleats, that's what you're hanging up when you quit baseball. You're hanging up your spikes.

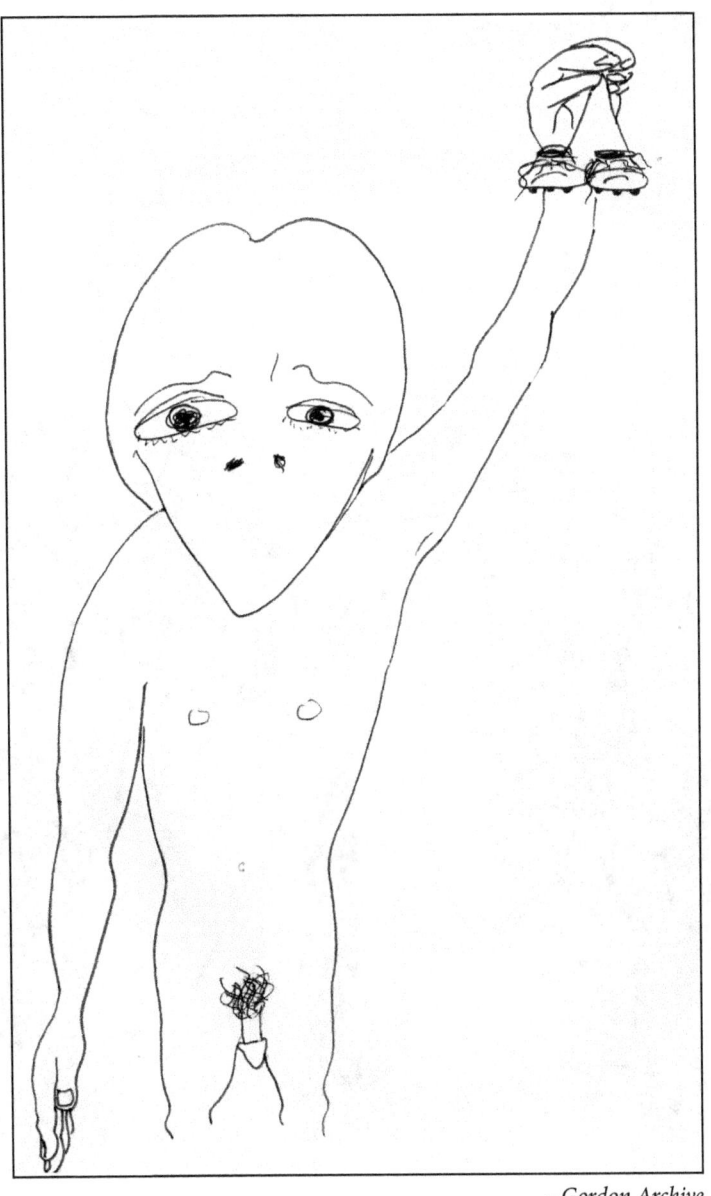

– *Gordon Archive*

Yeah, it was time for me to hang 'em up.

Part Seven

THE TIPPY-TIPPY END

– Gordon Archive

Believe it or not, that's Marlon Brando and my wife Carly in 1957. She wasn't my wife then, she was twelve years old. Their families knew each other.

Chapter One
Many years later ...

A Mid-Summer's Night Scream
or ...
My Wife as in France

> "As men get older, the spirit is often embarrassed by what they have to go through to put the will in their willies."

"Who said that?"
"I think you did."
"Oh. Okay, but don't quote me."

My wife was in France.

Did you know that the noted philosopher, the vastly worldly Marlon Brando once said, "I don't think it's the nature of any man to be monogamous. Men are propelled by genetically ordained impulses over which they have no control to distribute their seed."

And while one could easily argue the point about a man's actual ability to control that urge, I, like many another married men, have certainly had the occasion to resent the need for such an exercise.

But, like I said, my wife was in France.

Albert Einstein, a mere sliver of a man when compared to the great Brando, may very well have been the most oft-quoted scientific genius of the twentieth century, but his views on marriage were largely given short shrift. The father of the atomic revolution failed at marriage, y'know—twice.

– Public domain

Albert Einstein.

Einstein regarded falling in love as "an incident." He proposed that the idea of two people remaining happily married and together for the rest of their lives based upon "an incident" was a virtual mathematic impossibility.

In any case, as I told you, my wife was in France. Carly had gone on a ten-day excursion to an artists' retreat. I had amicably declined the offer to accompany her, and now there was a big ocean between us. Not surprisingly, I was looking to mess around. Please, after all we've been through, spare me your shock.

But, before we get any deeper into this story, I must say that it would be naively unsophisticated on your part to assume that these are the ravings of a man who no longer wishes to remain married. I assure you, it's quite the contrary. I love my wife. I love the kids. I love our house and all of our things. I even love the goldfish too, though it is a major pain in the ass to clean the fish tank. We could certainly use a little more cash flow around here, but then again, who couldn't?

The point is, as sure as there is rain, there comes a time, or two, or five, in every marriage, when the husband looks around one day and feels like "the ass is definitely greener on the other side." No doubt, Brando and Einstein, amongst others, perhaps even you, would concur.

The whys and wherefores of such a moment may or may not be significant to a lasting marriage, but the problem remains. What is the husband to do about it? Or the wife, for that matter, this being an era of feminist revolution, but my experience has shown that it is the male of the species who is most vulnerable to that call of the wild. And we men, the valiant keepers of the precious prongs, seem far more capable of the delusion that sex and love can be compartmentalized. Despite centuries of experience and mountains of evidence to the contrary, we are still able to believe that there really are women out there who will enjoy flaming-hot, extra-marital sex with us—without it having to wreak havoc in our marriages.

"The seven-year itch," it's been called and "the mid-life crisis." Call it what you will, but when this moment arises for a couple in their mating, there are as many attempts at solution as there are marriages.

My wife, who was in France, and I have been together for almost thirty years now. As I told you many pages ago, in the early days, we both slept around. Plenty. And Chaos had ensued. The green-eyed monster of jealousy proved formidable. As I've said, we found it difficult to practice Free Love and try to be Romeo and Juliet at the same time.

If Carly had been a mere lover, this relationship would have ended years ago. But alas, from the very outset, I knew that she was destined to be the great love of my life, the beans in my burrito, the one I was intended to marry, and the mother-to-be of my children. The deceptions and shenanigans that had worked well enough for so many years with previous lovers no longer applied. Carly and I had to make up our own new rules. And we did that, endlessly talking about our relationship.

Yes, we agreed upon telling the truth. Fidelity was not determined by who stuck their what where, but by the willingness to engage in the telling of the truth. While this necessitated hours, days, and months of slow, agonizing torture—which might have perhaps been easily avoided had we the strength of character to successfully lie—in the end, it at least afforded us the opportunity to actually know what we were dealing with at any given time.

For both of us, this amounted to a significant improvement upon previous relationships. We lived and we learned.

Of course, the truth, while sounding so noble, high gloss, and universally praiseworthy, does not always play well in black and white. It is colorful, vulnerable, and subject to any number of accents and shadings. Like the infinity point of mathematics, it can be approached, but never really attained.

In truth, there was little room to maneuver with a "Did you fuck her or did you not?" A simple "yes," or "no," pretty much covered all the options. But with issues like: "Do you want to fuck her?" "Are you going to fuck him?" "When are you going to fuck her?" "Where are you going to fuck him?" and the like, the game was afoot.

But somehow, our marriage survived all of that. In time, Carly settled down to a monogamous approach, even though I remained loath to accept such a fate. In fact, my entire career in the sex industry developed as a means to insure the flow of extra cookies into my sex life.

After I retired, we tried everything from the occasional carefully orchestrated and negotiated extra-marital indulgence for me, to my agreeing to abstain from such a thing.

Indeed, one of the great pay-offs for my willingness to forgo some extra-marital fling and stay at home had been the mutual revelation and exploration of those deeper and darker, secret, sexual desires between us. They were the kind that didn't even emerge until we'd been married for maybe ten or fifteen years. They were the kind that had me sniffing around outside of the house to begin with, because I never thought I'd be able to satisfy them at home. Those treasures have greatly served to enrich the marriage, but still, time, repetition, and familiarity, eventually, take their toll. Sooner or later, the eyes begin to wander again. And in this case …

My wife was in France. And there was a big ocean between us.

Unfortunately, she did not take our three children with her. One of the main reasons she so easily acquiesced to my not going along with her was that it would clearly be beneficial—and cheaper—if one of us stayed at home to take care of the kids. Yea, Daddy!

Well, the net result was that far from being given ten days off, free to exorcise recent years of repressed lust for other females, I was more like a single-parent with double the usual amount of child care!

BUT, there was a weekend sandwiched in the middle of those ten days that my wife would be away in France—and it was over that weekend, my weekend, that I was determined to make my stand. I would arrange babysitting, sleepovers, or do whatever I had to do so that both Friday and Saturday night would be mine to prowl and howl in an attempt to sate my wanderlust.

Uh-huh. It should be noted here for future fools that the married man loses all touch with reality when fantasizing about the actual availability of loose, free, interesting, uncomplicated, and undiseased women on hand at any given moment to suit the needs of his own schedule of desire. I had no secret admirers waiting in the wings, none that I knew of anyway. The fact that I had once been Richard Pacheco, the Pre-Columbian Panty Sniffer of Porn, no longer meant a thing. In fact, by now, the whole industry had actually moved away from the Bay Area down South to LA. My "little black book" had been rendered useless. I truly had become a civilian again, just another bozo with a boner.

I suppose many men would seek the services of the professional ladies of the night under such circumstances, but between the threat of incurable disease and the perpetual funding crisis, this offered me no solution.

I did, however, still have one lady friend who owned and managed a dungeon in San Francisco. Yes, I said a dungeon, where SM play parties were still held every Friday night. By invitation only, you paid twenty bucks at the door and stepped into a kinky fantasyland. Most people came in couples. If you came alone, you had to take your chances of attracting a partner. At a minimum, you got to watch SM sex players "playing" all around you. At a maximum, well, maybe you got the opportunity to connect with someone of like mind and possibly "distribute a little seed."

Having chosen that course of action, it was amazing how the days preceding the event rapidly passed without incident. I was the perfect father, patient, loving, and kind, and spent my time cooking, cleaning, and driving as the week came to its close.

The daylight hours of Friday could not go by fast enough, and when some child-care complications extended on into the night, I ended up being over an hour-and-a-half late to the party. But arrive I did. And when I descended the steps into the dungeon, the party was in full swing.

There was a big man, a truly large man, a truly large, big, and naked man, who was chained by his wrists and harnessed from the ceiling. A smaller man—at least I think it was a man, he had facial hair, but he also had beautiful breasts—was slowly and forcefully spanking the big fellow with what looked to be a kitchen cutting board. A small crowd, which I was now joining, watched in complete silence with rapt attention.

"Ugh!" the big man grunted in answer to a smack from the paddle.

I noticed that there was a second harness secured between the big man's balls and his body. From this second harness hung three heavy chains.

"Ugh!"

At the end of those three heavy chains was a bowling ball, a big, solid black bowling ball, the kind that weighed sixteen pounds. I swear to you that this man had a sixteen-pound bowling ball dangling from his stretched and severely taxed scrotum.

"Ugh!"

While spanking the big man's ass bright red, the smaller man with the facial hair and the beautiful breasts would occasionally give the bowling ball a little shove so that it swayed back and forth in a further pendulum of pain.

You're laughing. This was my big night out, and you're laughing.

There was a second scene going on in the dungeon. I slunk my way over to join that little clutch of revelers. There was a woman. She was a hard-looking woman. She looked like the kind of woman who would sprinkle roofing nails on her breakfast cereal. She was dressed in black with silver chains about her body. This paragon of femininity had a naked man tethered on his back to a table. There was a shoe-box-sized lid of some kind placed over the man's genitals, which were protruding through a hole. The man's penis was erect. It was tied back to the lid with some kind of twine. His scrotum was splayed wide against the bottom of the lid like an animal skin drying on the side of a barn. When I had happened upon this little scene of erotic bliss, the woman had just finished securing the scrotum with some kind of staple or tack.

I retreated to the foyer.

It was a small party, maybe twenty people or so, and most of them were there in couples. The few unpartnered women on hand could have all played on the offensive line of the San Francisco 49ers. In all, I lasted about an hour at the party that night. Mostly, I tried hard to eat $20 worth of hors d'oeuvres, and then I went home early.

My idea of some SM activity was a little spanking. You spanked me or I'd spank you, and then we could get down to some serious sucking and fucking. It was like a patty cake of foreplay to the main event of orgasmic activity. I didn't know what those people were doing. Somewhere along life's line, their wires of arousal appeared to have been recircuited in such a way that heavy pain was reinterpreted as ecstatic pleasure.

Well, they might as well have been breathing salt water or speaking Urdu. It wasn't me, and it wasn't my night.

Wasn't my night? My wife was in France! I had childcare! "I coulda been a contender!"

Have another cheese puff, Herman, I says to meself, *and get yerself on home. Live to fight another day.*

Saturday. Saturday came and who can remember if it was baseball or soccer practice, but I was driving my son to it. I let the obligations of family steer me out of the immobility of depression.

I had nothing planned for Saturday night lust-wise, and I rejected all acts of desperation as available options. The years have taught me that desperate fucks aren't worth having. No one is breathing, shoulders can't relax, and assholes are tightly clenched. A desperation orgasm is less satisfying than Kraft's Macaroni and Cheese.

I needed to recover from Friday night. It had been a tough first-round knockout. The bar scene, perhaps my best remaining opportunity, was out of the question. All my giddy-up-and-go had gotten-up-and-went. I needed something safer. As it happens, I was invited to another party.

This one was a circle of old college friends. It was not likely to get me laid, but it would still be nice to get away from the kids and enjoy some adult company.

The party was at Susan's house. Susan lived in a house on a cliff that overlooked the Pacific Ocean.

"Where's your wife?" she said upon my arrival.

"My wife is in France."

"Ohhh," she said disappointedly, "I was really looking forward to getting to know her better. I think she's terrific," and on and on she went. The gist of which was that she really wanted to become closer friends with Carly. Well, that was nice, and I moved on to another old familiar face and then another. The sun was beautiful, the beach was spectacular, and it was shaping up to be a pleasant and peaceful day. Libations and intoxications made their rounds and lubricated the tales of old friends and college days long gone by.

As the dinner hour approached, Susan reappeared on my screen, all harried and bedeviled with hosting the meal preparations. I offered my help and fell into step at her side. We gabbed as we cut the vegetables. We laughed as we pulled down the plates. We danced to the music in the kitchen as we prepared the chicken. It was busy and it was constant, washing, cooking, cleaning, and preparing. When the meal was finally placed upon the table and the guests all dug in, we served the drinks and kept refilling the platters. When all had quieted down some, we took our own meal together, quietly, away from the throng.

Susan and I had never really looked at each other in college. Back then, she had a lover, I had a lover, and we were both just part of a larger circle of friends. This pattern had lasted for thirty years.

At this point, her mate had been gone a week camping and wasn't due back for a few more days. And my wife, my wife was in France.

I think we were both surprised just to be looking at each other after all these years. And then it was time for the cleanup. What a mess! Susan and I spearheaded that campaign too. Others joined in. By the time the last dish was dried, Susan and I were joined at the hip.

The darkness came and the party moved down to the beach to make a bonfire. Susan and I were almost holding hands. The stars, the night, the beach, you know what's coming. The fire blazed. After a while, we drifted down the beach, away from our friends, and into the darkness.

In one brief, magical moment, we gave vent to the magnets, which for hours had been straining at keeping propriety. We came together like the cover of a romance novel. As we melted in torrid embrace, fire and sand, surf and stars all swirled about us to the sound of crashing waves. I feasted on her neck while she pulled me to her body. Our hands moved as blurs with the hunger. Blessed connection. The days of her missing lover and mine were screaming to be done. Solitude was broken. Our longing was strong, mutual, and well met. We were there for each other. Right now was calling.

My hand reached down into the back of her jeans and clenched a naked buttock. I squeezed her hot wetness toward me. My maleness calcified into a bone of contention that mightily sought to rend the fabric of my clothing and hers, that demanded entrance to her body, that craved completion of the circle. The sand we stood upon threatened to become a molten glass from the heat.

And then—

"Ding!" came that tiny sound, like the gentle strike of a spoon upon crystal.

"Ding," like an air bubble risen from the deep, still pond of conscience. Susan's first words of the day came back to me, the words that had declared how much she said she wanted to be my wife's friend.

I was compelled. I withdrew to arm's length and said, "Susan, if we do this, my wife will never be your friend." There was a beat.

Susan had taken in my words and then added, "Yeah, and I don't think my lover could handle this either." There was a timeless pause.

"I know," I said to her, "Let's pretend that we just fucked and that it was spectacular. Because we did, and it was. You know it and I know it, and then we can trade this one night of passion for a lifetime of friendship."

It had been a moment. It was a moment like after the last burst of a fireworks display. The explosion had filled the sky with bright light and then fell downward, dimming and plummeting to a final dark quiet.

I was so caught up in the drama of my own conscience that I remember being struck odd that Susan would have had a say in the matter too, that her own commitments would rise up to douse the fire as well. In the stillness, our heartbeats normalized. The sand had become cold to the touch of our bare feet. It was over. I knew it was over. She knew it was over. Only broken sleazeballs that neither one of us wanted to be would have persevered.

Uh-huh, I was hoping that she'd talk me out of it.

But no, Susan was a strong woman, a woman of substance and character. I don't think we had revealed ourselves to be any lost soul mates. More's the point that we were both just lonely. We played stand-in for each other's lover and we had played the parts quite well, but when the true moment of truth arrived, it just didn't happen.

Amid warm smiles, it was quickly agreed. We sealed the bond with a hug that had already alchemized into something safely tucked far away from the fire of erotic passion. And when it was done, feeling all grown up with ourselves, feeling pleased with having done the right thing, we rejoined our friends round the bonfire.

Fuck!

And even on that sour note, if my story had ended there, I would still count myself among the luckiest of men. Little could I imagine what sport the gods were about to make of me.

When it came time to leave that night, Susan asked me for my phone number. I was standing by the back of my car. I'm not likely to ever forget it. I took out my wallet because I had some blank cards in it, upon which, to write my phone number. I withdrew one of the cards and put my wallet on the roof of the car. Don't ever put your wallet on the roof of your car. I wrote the phone number on the card and gave the card to Susan. We shared a chaste kiss, the kind that Lancelot might have given Guinevere after she had entered the convent. And off I went into the night.

Down her driveway I drove, along the short stretch of road to Highway One, and then off toward the bridge for the long drive back across the bay.

When I got home, I gathered with my teenagers around the kitchen table. We talked about our day's activities and I casually began emptying my keys and such on the table. That's when I realized that my wallet was missing.

Panic. Shivers of fear ran up and down my spine. Everything was in my wallet—money, credit cards, access to all the bank accounts—

My wife was in France! You knew that. I called Susan's house and got her answering machine. It was twelve-thirty at night. I grabbed a flashlight. I had to go back and find my wallet.

I flew from Berkeley to Marin County as fast as any automobile has ever made that journey. Susan had gotten my message while I was en route. She joined me with a flashlight for a while. My wallet did not turn up. By two in the morning, she looked exhausted and beaten up, she had to call it quits. Though I resisted that notion, it didn't look like I was going to find anything in the darkness. She offered me an office floor to sleep on. The house was already full with overnight guests. What had transpired between us earlier was gone, long gone, ancient history, and not even a factor.

I declined the office floor, told her that I had to get back to the kids, and we said our goodnights. I went back to square one and started looking all over again with the flashlight. Still nothing. Damn. I got back to Berkeley around three-thirty in the morning.

I suppose you could call it sleep, what I did in my bed the rest of that night, but I'm not sure. At the first ray of dawn, I was back in the car and rushing off to Marin. I figured I had one chance to find the wallet that I had left on the roof of my car—and this was it. I had to get there before the day's crowd started showing up on the beach.

It was still very early when I pulled into Susan's driveway. I was the defective detective in search of the wallet that the Fates were hiding. On foot, I began retracing my car's path of late last night, from Susan's house toward the highway. I thoroughly investigated the bushes on both sides of the road. Nothing turned up. When I came across a Park Ranger unlocking the gate to the beach, I explained what had happened and gave him my home phone number. He said he would call if someone turned it in. Oh, yeah, I thought to myself, fat chance. I had little faith in my fellow man.

As I walked that dirt road to Highway One, I reasoned that I hadn't actually been going fast enough for the wallet to fall off until I turned onto the highway. Yeah, that was it, I decided. I would find it on the highway.

By my calculation, I had walked about half-a-mile on that highway, when looking ahead, I saw that the road took a sharp, upward swing to the left. In my best Sherlock Holmesian deduction, that's where I decided I should concentrate my efforts. If I were a wallet, that's where I'd have flown off.

And sure enough, when I got there, right under the guardrail, against a roadside shrub, I spotted a bright, little orange envelope. I was jubilant. I had made that very envelope myself in order to house my winning Monopoly stickers from the last McDonald's Contest. It obviously had spilled out when my wallet had hit the highway. I was so smart.

When I opened the orange envelope, there was my little sticker for a free cheeseburger and two more for free ice cream cones. Though not immediately visible, I knew that my wallet could not be far off. I began digging in the brush.

An hour later, my wallet still had not turned up. The brush was thick and dense. The wallet was brown and would be well camouflaged by its own earth tones. I had to dig deeper, really get down in there and pay closer attention. The search continued, still, no wallet. On my belly now, rooting like a pig for truffles, raising branches, carefully exploring in months, maybe years of composting foliage. Still, no wallet. I was in a sleeveless T-shirt and wearing thin cotton pants. My arms were getting scratched. My butt was getting poked. My wallet had to be there. I searched and searched. Cars whizzed by on the highway. The late morning sun rose in the sky.

I was on my ass, leaning backwards and holding up a branch under a pine-like shrub, when I spied a smallish rattlesnake winding its way away from me to disappear into deeper, denser brush. I looked around where I was sitting. There were several shed snakeskins within reach of my butt.

Sherlock! I said to myself, *how important is this wallet to you?* This was a whole new ballgame. I extracted myself from the brambles as rapidly and as carefully as I possibly could.

Defeated. Dirty and sweaty, I walked the roadway defeated. I held onto my little orange envelope and wondered how the gods could tease me so. As I approached the house, Susan was in a terrycloth bathrobe having just emerged from the hot tub. She could have been naked with a two-headed dildo stuck in her and it wouldn't have made any difference. She had seen my car and wondered where I was. It was of no consequence. I mumbled pleasantries, she offered sympathies, and I got in my car and drove off.

As I approached the Richmond Bridge, I dialed home on the cell phone.

"Dad," my eldest daughter said on the phone, "your wallet's in San Francisco."

"What?"

"This guy called. He's a fireman that works in San Francisco. He lives in Bolinas. He was driving to work this morning and found your wallet sitting there on Highway One." It was music to my ears. "He's at the fire station near Candlestick Park. You want the phone number?"

"You bet I do!"

It was Fireman Jerry Dunn. Jerry, you did a great thing! Aren't firemen just the best?! He didn't even want to take any money. I had to force him to take half of what I had in there. Lord knows, he could've had it all. My spirits soared. What a goddamned rollercoaster ride! Sunday had all of a sudden become a very wonderful day!

The hours passed in a fog of relief. I was gently bumping into walls and sleepily doing all the things that I had to do. With my faith in my fellow man feeling newly secured, I went to bed early that night.

I was awakened out of a dead sleep in the middle of the night. Scratching and tearing at flesh, it felt like my balls, my arms, and my ass were on fire.

"Late at night when you're sleepin' poison ivy comes a-creepin' around...."

Poison oak, in this case, and so bad, so intense—that calamine lotion couldn't even begin to touch the fires. Into the bathtub of ice I went. I called my dermatologist the next day. I was beyond over-the-counter remedies. I knew it. I needed professional help. She was all booked up. There were no openings. "How about next week?"

"NO!" I pleaded my case. She agreed to see me after closing at eight o'clock that night.

"Alright," she said, tired from her long day at the office, "let's see what you got that couldn't wait." She examined my arms first. "Hmmm, let's see the rest of it...."

I dropped my shorts and my underpants and she bent me over a table. She and her nurse looked at me and just started laughing. They both agreed that it was a pretty horrible case of poison oak.

As I was, with little to hide, I ended up telling my whole tale of weekend misadventure to both doctor and nurse. I'm very funny when I'm miserable and I actually took great pleasure in shocking and flirting with my bungled tale of male madness. When the merriment died down, I was given a shot in each cheek and a prescription for the latest and greatest in scientific ointment.

As I was leaving her office, the good doctor suggested that perhaps it would not be such a good idea for me to tell my wife about my recent escapades.

"Oh, no," I explained. "My wife and I tell each other these things. It's our way." The good doctor confided that she couldn't even begin to imagine playing out such scenarios in her marriage.

That very day, Carly ended her e-mail from France to me with, "I miss the feel of your skin." I answered,

"The feel of my skin has itchy bumps all over it at the moment. Poison Oak! It's a long story, but in a soulful way, it's just God stepping in to save me from myself." I signed it, "Itchy Lust."

"Dear Itchy Lust," she returned. "I am empathizing and giggling with you, ol' boy, whose God would do such a thing to you. I cannot in good faith take any actual delight in this. It would be too unkind. However, perhaps a tiny smile would not be out of line?"

P.S. Here's further inescapable proof that Carly is actually a bruja with truly Castanadian powers:

My beloved departed again for yet another artists' retreat. This one would be for six days up North somewhere along the picturesque California coast. It is our first separation since France and the poison oak episode, from which, as a man, I quite naturally learned absolutely nothing. For indeed, as her recent departure approached, I once again began entertaining fantasies of what willing females were out there and how I could go about getting me one of those safe, yet exotic "temps" to satisfy my middle-aged cravings for just one more lap around the fast lane.

On the morning she left, literally within minutes of her car pulling out of the driveway, I was conducting my bathroom ablutions when I discovered a hemorrhoid forming where hemorrhoids usually form. In almost fifty-two years of life on this planet, I had never before experienced the joys of such an event. Hemorrhoids, hmmm, you can just imagine my exaltation.

Within hours, it was bigger than Rhode Island and is now roughly the size of Delaware. Surveyors suggest that if this trend continues, it will soon be large enough to qualify for U.N. aid as a third world country.

Needless to say, all thoughts of dusting off my old, white, John Travolta Disco suit and going dancing tonight have vanished. What's your bet that this hemorrhoid from Hell won't be gone until long after Carly comes back home? The only saving grace to this whole story of my man-eating hemorrhoid is that its screenplay may soon become another chilling Johnny Depp movie that will premiere next summer in Cannes.

Considering that I appear to be seriously overmatched in this battle between the sexes, my doctor, therapist, clergyman, insurance agent, personal trainer, and guru have all advised that it might be better for my health if I attended that event — with Carly!

Chapter Two

Some porn star I turned out to be, I spent the night sleeping alone in my car.

I did! There I was, a featured player at the World Pornography Conference, virtually surrounded by world-class perverts of every ilk, and I ended up all alone in the middle of the night trying to fall asleep in the back of my station wagon.

Well, maybe that's why I'm an ex-porn star.

– *Gordon Archive*

Beginning with Annie Sprinkle's invitation to come down to LA and contribute to an opening-night round of performances—I was the token heterosexual male—the World Conference On Pornography had been an absolute gas for me. It was magical time-travel. It was a resurrection. I was once again, Richard Pacheco, the porn star.

Since my retirement from the business, there haven't exactly been too many job applications where I've been able to put that on the résumé. But here at this conference, it was once again a badge of honor! They were proudly showing some of my old films and calling them classics! I ran into a whole bunch of my old friends and colleagues. And the best part was, if I didn't look too closely in any of the passing mirrors, it was all just like yesterday in *Brigadoon!* Time had stood still.

Oblivious to the gray in my hair, the deeper lines in my face, and a certain thickening around the middle, I felt a bounce to my step that I hadn't felt in a long time. For four days, with the possible exception of those weird hours spent trying to sleep in the car, I was back in the game.

I turned fifty years of age in May of that year. The only thing that I was sure of in facing that monumental milestone was that I didn't want to do it fat. Beginning in January, I fought back the tide of middle-aged spread with a tennis racquet. My birthday in May came and went. I stayed with the program. By conference time in August, I was tanned, lean and mean, and almost too pretty for Carly to let me out of the house.

This little drama of vanity and self-esteem reached its zenith as I stood naked on the stage that opening night of the conference. I did my little performance bit and was well-enough received, but the real story was, that after a long absence, filled with colossally mixed emotions over my retirement, my self-imposed exile, my increased family responsibilities, and the sheer weight of all that time, I had once again successfully grabbed at the brass ring of sex star!

While the audience applauded, I stood there holding it and feeling it, like some glorious Achilles fresh out of a timeless rehab from his heel injury. I was ready and eager to do the battle once again. I was Ponce de Leon with my finger firmly planted on life's rewind button.

What did it all mean?
I don't know.
What did it all mean?

The moment came and the moment went. In the afterglow, I found myself at a hotel party in Jeffrey Douglas's room. He was a bright, young attorney for the Free Speech Coalition. I was looking for a place to sleep, an uncrazy woman to fuck, and something to eat.

The food came first. In order to get my body ready for that big performance, I hadn't eaten much for an entire week. I was starved. And while I was grazing at the food table, a fresh batch of rowdy revelers entered the party. An odd looking guy made his way over to me and said, "Hey, you don't look too happy to see us!" Fact is, I wasn't, but I mumbled something welcoming, non-threatening, and tried gently not to strike up too much of a conversation with this way-over-the-top lad.

A truth I've learned about the porn world over the years is that sometimes the fans scare me more than the enemies.

This guy looked like a Hollywood street person to me. He was a bum, some mother's lost child, another in a long series of twisted, attention-seeking oddballs who had somehow found their way onto the bus. If they weren't naked in the streets, shouting and breaking glass in the middle of the night, with their eyeballs chemically enlarged to the size of silver dollars, you were lucky. This guy had augmented his beard with black magic marker and was playing with a latex penis, stretching it from his ragged groin to comical lengths like a yo-yo. He was followed in by Betty Dodson—yes, that Betty Dodson—and she came right up to me and promptly sat down in my lap.

Now, understand, despite the fact that Betty Dodson and I had never met before, her gesture did not seem all that extraordinary to me at the time. For one thing, they say, "the rich are different." And I always figured that you just might as well throw "the famous" in there too. Maybe this was just the way that she did things. Hell, if she behaved like everybody else, she wouldn't even be Betty Dodson, then, would she? Besides that, you had to factor in some major chutzpah because she lived and worked in New York City.

But none of that even occurred to me at the time. It may have been Jeffrey's room and Betty's chutzpah, but it was my return to backstage, backstage in Pornoland, and backstage was mine! I had paid the dues. Hell, I'd done some of my best work backstage. If you belonged there, it was a wonderful place. It was different. The conventional rules of intimacy did not apply. Clothing was optional. Titties fluttered. Grab-ass abounded. Friends were friendlier there and strangers who were about to go out and get naked together on a bright, hot set, did not remain strangers there for very long.

Backstage was one of my very favorite places on earth. Sure, Betty Dodson had just sat down in my lap. Big deal! Hadn't she just seen me naked on the stage?

And aside from all of that, this night was my triumphant return from exile, I was still Achilles, wasn't I? Still bathing in the afterglow of my little performance, what did it matter if Barbara Streisand, Whoopi Goldberg, and Betty Dodson all sat in my lap? What the hell did I care? As long as it wasn't that street bozo with the elastic penis, it was just fine with me.

I certainly knew who Betty Dodson was. I had admired her greatly for years thinking her to be one of the planet's good guys. She was a sexual pioneer, one of the heroes of Eros. My own wife had once plied the masturbation trade herself. In the early seventies, Carly led workshops training mental health professionals on how to treat "pre-orgasmic" women. Unlike Betty's direct approach where the women would essentially circle jerk under her supervision, Carly's used the less confrontational Masters & Johnson's model where the women were sent away to do "homework" assignments and they'd later report back to the group. Either way, it was the work of "the flower," and it was work that we both valued highly. I was nothing but honored that Betty Dodson had landed in my lap!

And once there, Betty and I found an instant and easy comfort with each other. We were like old friends. In fact, many old friends had reconnected that night. It was like a high school reunion where the elixir was powerful and the heart was buoyed by easy laughter and warm memories.

The party got loud, as good parties tend to do, and the hour became late. Neighbors, trying to sleep, registered their complaints with the front desk. When the hotel security folks came knocking at the door, our host announced that the party was over.

I had already found a bed and a relatively uncrazy woman who had volunteered to share it with me. No, it wasn't Betty.

Betty, as a matter of fact, left the party that night on the arm of the oddball with the magic marker beard and the elastic penis. Jesus Christ, this woman was just full of surprises. I thought maybe the guy was her son?

Where did I sleep that night? Who was the woman? What are you, my wife? Get out of here! It's none of your business. You're a troublemaker!

"None of my business? Who are you arguing with?

Myself! Isn't it clear?

"Well, you've told us about a hundred different sex scenes with a hundred different women and all of a sudden, you're getting coy. Did you fall in love with this woman or something?"

Hell no! I just didn't want to sleep in my car again.

"Did Carly believe that?"

Not for a minute.

"Well, what then?"

This one was just different.

"Well, what was so different about it?"

It ended 13 years of monogamy, that's what!

"Oh."

But I never had agreed I'd be monogamous! I never promised anything. It just happened that way. Until it didn't.

"Wow, you really were time-traveling, weren't you?"

Yes, I was. And I liked it too, until I got back home and had to fight with Carly about it all over again. All that same old crap just came right back from where we had left it. I never wanted to be monogamous. I just didn't want to fight with Carly anymore about it.

"I know. I know. But shouldn't we tell them about how you and Carly finally worked all that out?"

Oh, I will, in the last chapter. I see now that it's the only real ending that this book ever could've had. Who knew? But I'm getting ahead of myself. First things first: Let me get back to finishing the story about the World Pornography Conference.

- Patti Thomas

Me and Betty Dodson had become pals.

It was the next morning. I was walking through the hotel lobby and I saw Betty Dodson as she was getting off the elevator. She came up to me rather sheepishly and said, "Remember when I sat in your lap last night like I knew you?"

"Yeah," I responded.

"Well, I thought I did!" she said exploding in laughter. "I thought you were somebody else! The whole thing was a mistake! But I'm really glad I made it because I really like you and I feel like I've known you forever!" I let Betty know that the feeling was definitely mutual. "Good," she said, "Now, the only thing is that I wish I could remember who it is I thought you were from New York???"

And when I asked who was that guy she was with when she left the party, Betty howled with laughter.

It was her cross-dressing girlfriend Kim Airs, who ran a sex shop in Boston called GRAND OPENING. Betty couldn't believe that I had

- Femme Productions

There was hanging out at a cocktail party with
Vanessa Del Rio and Candida Royalle.

mistaken Kim's male persona of "Leo DeGennaro" as a true penis-bearing man, let alone her son! She couldn't wait to tell Kim.

The next two days of the conference raced by like life at a fanciful, adult, summer camp. There was the pool and the hot sun. There were the movies and the meals.

But best of all, were the over sixty workshops happening that completely cross-pollinated the porn stars with the mental health professionals and the First Amendment attorneys. There was a lot of fascinating stuff.

The net result was that we won each other's respect. We discovered that we were all players on the same team. And now, with the conference nearing its end, we all felt that we had just been part of something very, very special.

The last session of the conference was to be a general assembly that would bring everybody together for one last time. It would be held in the Sheraton's main ballroom and would feature An All-Star Porn Panel, subtitled: Everything You Ever Wanted To Know About the Actors and Actresses in Erotic Films and Videos From The People Who Know.

Will Jarvis would be the moderator and I would be one of the many speakers that day including Nina Hartley, Ron Jeremy, Gloria Leonard, Vanessa del Rio, Miss Sharon Mitchell, Dave Cummings, Bill Margold, Serenity, Christi Lake, Annie Sprinkle, Juli Ashton, Randi Storm, Chris Cannon, Fiero, Meridian, Tracy Love, Shane, Johnnie Black, Anita Cannibal, Mike Horner, R. Bolla, and anybody else in attendance who had ever done a sex scene.

Show Time

I took a seat next to Nina Hartley on the dais. I had been one of her mentors when she was first starting out years ago in the business. By this point, Nina had taken on the Georgina Spelvin role as one of the grand old dames of the industry. *Playboy Magazine* had just declared her "the smartest woman in porn," a distinction clearly open to a variety of interpretations. We were joined by a statuesque, young starlet named Meridian who took the seat on my other side. Meridian handed me a sleek business card that showed her naked with a long snake draped about her.

– Meridian

Since the snake was not present at the time,
I didn't mind her being there.

Meridian and Nina fell into an animated conversation about a recent shoot in LA as the main ballroom of the Sheraton Hotel rapidly filled with people.

That's when I took off my pants.
"You what?"
I took off my pants.
"What were you thinking?"

I was thinking of baggy-pants comics. I was thinking of burlesque. I was thinking of Mel Brooks. I remembered reading that he once said, "Nobody ever snuck into show business. Don't be afraid to do something bold. Don't be afraid to make them sit up and take notice." That's what I was thinking when I decided to take off my pants.

There were a lot of us up there who were going to speak and it looked to be a long session. The tables where we sat were draped in front so that the audience could only see us from about the chest on up. I thought, *Wouldn't it be funny to look out at them in all their Sheraton Universal Grand Ballroom finery — with my pants off?*

It was kind of a reverse, anti-nervous, performance gesture of imagining the audience in their underwear. The more I thought about it, the more it seemed like the thing to do.

As the first speaker spoke, I quietly took off my shoes, slipped off my pants, and put my shoes back on. Nina and Meridian watched in amusement as I folded my pants neatly and tucked them under my chair. No one else knew.

– David Steinberg

Nina Hartley, Richard Pacheco, & Meridian.

As I sat back in my underwear, a hand from each side reached down to caress a thigh and beyond. This was an unexpected bonus. I sat there surveying crowd and grinning to myself. So, there was a God, after all. Nina and Meridian were fondling me like we were backstage at a shoot. It was fun. Lord knows, I did nothing to discourage them.

The speakers came and went and no one else was aware of me sitting up there in my jacket, shirt, tie—and underpants—until it became my turn to speak. Even then, as I stood and walked to the podium, the audience still could not see me below the waist.

– David Steinberg

This is pretty much all the audience could see. But if you were on stage or behind me when I took the podium, it looked like this:

– David Steinberg

And there was a good deal of laughter onstage when my fellow actors and actresses saw me standing there in my underwear.

– David Steinberg

You can see it even better in close up.

I looked around at them saying, "What? What?" with a deadpan face. Bill Margold motioned to a set of risers behind the podium as if I should mount them to let the audience in on the joke, but I declined. Somehow, this gesture was for me and the other actors, not for the crowd. I began my speech.

It was a rare performance moment for me when fear just took a hike. The conference was about to end and this wondrous bubble of living again in my youthful yesterday was about to burst. I knew that within twenty-four hours I would be driving to soccer practice, clipping coupons, doing dishes, and assuring my wife that I wasn't moving to LA to resume my career. I would be sitting alone again at my desk again wondering what to write about next that might pay a few bills.

When I retired from the porn business, there were no ceremonies and there were no gold watches. My decision to quit, based upon the threat of AIDS, had not won me any friends from those continuing on with the business. At first, I thought that the epidemic would be over in six months and I'd be back at work. Somehow, six months had become thirteen years and the threat of AIDS was still no less imposing. Hell, it may even have been worse.

– David Steinberg

The bottom line was, that over the years, I had moved on from a hugely significant part of my life without any real closure. I never wanted to, and I never did get to say any good-byes. And while former colleagues I viewed as absolute mediocrities were being honored and inducted into porn's Halls of Fame, I was being ignored, reduced to being a quiet footnote of the now bygone Golden Age of Porn. Well, that sucked! My heart was full as I took the microphone.

"How'd you like the conference?" I asked the audience. "Wasn't it great? Don't you just hate that it's going to be over? I don't want it to end."

I told them the story of how I had met Betty Dodson, of how wonderful it had been that night, and of how it had all been a mistake. Betty was sitting right in the middle of the audience at this final session when I said, "Lady, did you ever pick the right lap to sit on because I think you are one of the most provocative women of the twentieth century!"

The audience roared its approval. I had the good sense to just stand there and shut up as the audience poured out their love for her. She rose to her feet to acknowledge the adulation.

– David Steinberg

Betty enjoying a well-deserved ovation.

And while this seemed to go on a long time, I had another one of those crazy thoughts. Who knows why these things happen, I think I was possessed. I reached down and pulled off my underpants. The audience couldn't see what I was doing, but I think they came to understand the gesture. It became very apparent when I rolled them into a ball, held them up over my head, and then threw them out into the crowd. The joint was absolutely jumping.

"Would somebody please see that those get to Betty?" I spoke into the microphone. And hand-to-hand, my underpants traveled row-to-row to where she was standing. Betty took them, drew them to her face, inhaled them deeply, and then thrust her arms into the sky like a triumphant Sylvester Stallone in *Rocky*. The audience howled.

I wouldn't trade that moment for a bigger dick.

When the tumult died down, I began reading to the crowd from a piece I'd done called *Richard Pacheco Is Dead*.

It was funny and poignant and I knew I had the audience with me. I knew it. I could feel it. And though I had never performed this piece before, I read the hell out of it.

> *Back then, they didn't have an AIDS test that was worth anything and it was to be a whole year before they even started talking about "safe sex."*
>
> *It was over. The common sense of the family dictated that Richard Pacheco retire. He did. In effect, he died, but it would be six more years of mortal combat before his spirit would let his body rest.*
>
> *All that was left him were the occasional performances on the TV talk shows like "Hour Magazine" and "Joan Rivers." During their ratings sweeps, the talk shows were always hungry for porn stars—even ones that made sense. Soon, however, the phone just stopped ringing altogether for Richard Pacheco.*
>
> *In his last years, Pacheco was attacked by a kind of creeping respectability. He became engulfed by its bloblike nature and was excreted like any other parent at a private school who couldn't really afford to be sending his kids there. His ticket to the land of Suck-This-Uniqueness had been revoked. He trembled as he saw himself becoming ordinary.*
>
> *It all served to drive him quite mad. His mind became a war zone between the past and the present. His once proud centerfold's body went to pot as he tried to eat his way through the chaos. He became addicted to Diet Coke and peanut butter. It was painful to watch. The utter tyranny of normal life was suffocating him.*
>
> *When he caught himself in bed watching daytime soap operas on TV, he ran out of the house screaming like Richard Pryor on fire.*
>
> *Soon after that, I visited Pacheco in a mental hospital where the doctors had him on enough Valium to make an elephant slur. He was so low he had to look up to see the caterpillars.*
>
> *I tried to cheer him up. "It's over," I told him. "You're fin-*

ished. You're old news, stale popcorn, flat soda, dead meat, washed-up, finito, the end, sayonara, goodnight, sweet dreams, over and out, roger and wilco, 10-4, good buddy, turn off the lights, adios, and hit the road. The fat lady sang six years ago! Your wife and kids don't need this. Richard Pacheco, you're dead."

"I know," he said. "I went into an Adult Video store last week and no one recognized me. The last time I was in there, the owner gave me my tapes for free and told me his wife wanted to fuck me. This time, some guy charged me eleven dollars and twenty-nine cents and told me I'd be fined if I didn't rewind." I stroked his head compassionately. He looked up at me with clear knowing eyes. "I'm going, aren't I?"

"Yes, you are," I told him. It broke my heart. He was like Peter Pan. He just wasn't meant to grow any older.

"When I started in the business," he said, "it wasn't like it is today."

"I know," I told him.

"We spoke a language of sexual liberation and human potential. You remember Esalen?"

"Yes, I remember."

"People were all uptight about sex, but there was no reason to be! We were like noble rogues in some divinely human struggle to make life in a body easier. It was important work! We shook the world! My generation tried to make lust respectable!"

"Yes, Richard, I remember."

"Ah, but the Fates would not have it be so," he waxed poetically. He was a man trying to understand the significance of his own existence. "God has a terrible sense of humor," he said.

"Yes, terrible." I agreed.

"The AIDS curse destroyed the X-rated business," he said. "Only the fools and the desperate remain. There's no respect left. Society has down-graded the occupation of porn star to one right in-between child molester and village idiot."

Just then, the nurse entered the room. She turned to me and asked, "Do you want me to sit on his face? Sometimes, that helps them."

"No! no!" shouted Pacheco sitting up angrily in bed.

"Alright," said the nurse. "I'm going. I'm going. I just thought you might like to know that I'm not wearing any panties."

"Really?" said Pacheco. The nurse smiled back at him and nodded. "Turn around, slowly," he said. "and pull up your skirt."

The nurse turned her back to Pacheco and bent over slightly so that her buttocks would be protruded. She slowly raised the hem of her white dress while her bottom cheeks seemed to be dancing with each other. She paused when the dress reached the top of her thighs. "Are you ready?" she asked with a smile. He nodded eagerly. She pulled up the dress and revealed her naked bottom.

An involuntary, "Ohhh," escaped from the lips of Richard Pacheco, along with a thin line of drool that landed on his hospital gown. "Reminds me of Nina Hartley," he said turning to me.

"Yeah, kind of," I agreed. My cock stirred in my pants.

"Thank you, nurse," he said. "That'll be all." With a pout, the nurse lowered her skirt. I caught a fleeting glimpse of her brown bush. She straightened her uniform and then left us to each other.

Pacheco lay back on the bed with his eyes closed. "You know," he said, "in sex, sometimes you see more with your eyes closed." I didn't know what to say to that. Then, he turned to me, and with the saddest eyes I ever saw, he said, "I've done my last come shot."

"One day," he continued, "there will be a cure or a vaccine to fight AIDS. It'll be too late for me. I know that, but it will benefit the children. Let me see a picture of the kids."

I took out my wallet and gave him a picture.

"Yeah," he said, "they're beautiful. Growing-up did me in. Richard Pacheco's lust was one thing, but Daddy's lust is quite another. It's a whole different banana factory."

"I know," I told him. I understood.

"Take care of those babies, pal," he said to me.

– Gordon Archive

"I will," I assured him. *He closed his eyes again as if he was going way inside.*

When he spoke again, he said, "All that stuff I told you about helping humanity and important work? You know making sex acceptable and all?"
"Yeah?"
"Well, it's true and all that, but it didn't really matter. I was just trying to get all the pussy I could get." *A hundred pound weight seemed to dissolve from his shoulders.*
"I know that," *I told him.*
"Sometimes, it wasn't worth it," *he chuckled to himself, recalling a hundred different incidents.* "But sometimes, it was great!" *he said contentedly, recalling a hundred more. He was a man making his final peace with himself.*
"You know," *he said,* "I looked at the box cover of the last movie I was in..."
"Yeah?"

"My name wasn't even listed in the credits!"

"How quickly they forget," I said to him, but I can't forget Richard Pacheco. I'll never forget Richard Pacheco and that's when I reached over and pulled the plug.

Pacheco became agitated. He grabbed his dick and gurgled something about not being able to find a literary agent. I held him closely to my bosom and rapped, "Lisa's Got a Big Ol' Butt," softly in his ear. Pacheco stopped struggling. He smiled up at me, sighed deeply, and then left this world for a better place.

And when I was finished, when I was done, they gave me a standing ovation. The group of performers on the stage and maybe a thousand people in the audience all stood up and applauded me.

I wasn't prepared for that.

It scared the hell out of me.

It was like the time in golf, I shot a hole in one.

It was like opening the wrong door and stumbling upon God getting dressed. Emotions welled up in my chest and I hurriedly took my seat while making what were not immodest gestures for the applause to stop.

In some fracture of time, the program continued. Nina Hartley was taking her turn at the podium. When my body ceased it's trembling, I decided I should probably put on my pants. I leaned back in my chair to quietly pull the jeans up over my buttocks and promptly flipped myself over backwards. The unexpected commotion stopped Nina in mid-sentence. All eyes were once again on me.

Ooops! I had nothing further to offer save my embarrassment. I righted myself as quickly as possible and sat back down to appear as an appropriately attentive audience member. Nina graciously continued. I marveled at how I'd gone from Demosthenes to Jerry Lewis in a matter of moments.

Afterwards, all the performers posed for one big group shot.

– David Steinberg

If you look closely in the lower left-hand corner of the photo above, you will see that I am just about to lift up Hall of Fame actress Sharon Mitchell and put her over my shoulder.

And as you study the close-up, intimate portrait of Miss Mitchell to the right, you will discover that I was not the only performer without any underpants on that day.

– David Steinberg

"… is worth a thousand words!"

Shortly after that final session, I got in my car alone and headed North on Highway 5. There was no point in my hanging around LA any longer; I knew it couldn't possibly get any better. This had been my missing good-bye. And this memory would be my Cooperstown. "Top of the world, Ma, top of the world!"

As the miles passed, I wept with the gentle, fragile joy of having felt God's sweet breath.

Chapter Three

– Adult Video News

In 1999, Annie Sprinkle and Richard Pacheco were both inducted into the Adult Video News Hall of Fame and both were given Lifetime Achievement Awards by the Free Speech Coalition.

Chapter Four
Sam

Sam died in the year 2000. And who could believe that I had drifted so far out of the X-rated world that I only learned of Anthony Spinelli's death while leafing through the pages of the Adult Video News (July, 2000).

I read the piece by Gene Ross and spent the rest of the day walking into walls trying to make my peace with it. I called his son Mitchell and his wife Roz. I called John Leslie. Nobody was home anywhere. It was probably better off that they weren't, I mean, what was there to say to them? My conversation was with Sam, a conversation I had sorely missed since first departing the industry in the 1980s. After that, we lost Sam to the effects of what we thought were stroke activity and later Alzheimer's. Those who knew and loved him had to live with Sam really being gone long before his body finally gave out.

"You hit the peaks with Anthony Spinelli!" he once told me and that we did. Tears in one scene and laughter in the next.

I used to call him every year on his birthday, Feb. 21. When I called back in 1996, his wife Roz had to ask him if he still remembered me.

- Gordon Archive

This man, who was my mentor and friend in the skin trade, had often roared with life. When he spoke to me that year, his voice was halting and trembling with confusion. He was fighting a losing battle to remember his own life. His self was melting. It was heartbreaking.

This man had often paid me more money than I had asked for. We rode through some battles together, both taking the hits and sharing the glory. We had built a bond of trust in a sea of harshness, greed, and human corruption. Now, his wife had to ask if he still remembered me.

Life is funny that way. Odd, where we find love. Odd, where we share truth. Odd, how we give our loyalty. And most odd, how things fade away.

"Happy Birthday, Sam," I told him. "I love you."

I never called him again after that.

Chapter Five
John

John Leslie died in 2010. It was completely unexpected. His wife Kathleen told me that the doctor said it was a massive stroke. He said that by the time John would have realized that something was wrong, he was already gone.

John Leslie - Extra Crispy

Just returned from the crematorium where I stood next to John's wife, his best friend Joey, and his dog Holmes, as we all held each other up, said good-bye and then watched as they loaded his shell into a very big oven. It kinda looked like an industrial, working-class, MRI machine. Never saw one of those ovens before. Don't really care if I never see another one again.

On the way back across the Bay, I listen to the John Leslie Blues Band on a CD. It's very comforting to hear John's voice again. I will have to get used to the idea that there will be no more new conversations.

At home, back in my kitchen, I go looking for the obituary that ran in yesterday's Chronicle. I can't seem to find it. I search the recycled papers twice. It finally turns up in the garbage can with a noodle on it. I rescue it—the obituary, not the noodle. I will fold it up and save it somewhere. It will no doubt be thrown out one day when one of my own kids is going through my old papers after I'm gone. Who knows, maybe it will have another noodle on it again one of these days.

It takes two-and-a-half hours to cremate a human body. Then they sweep out the oven. They still have to crush some bones and pulverize the teeth I guess. It's a very good thing to be dead when they do this otherwise it could all be very painful. They package whatever is left in an urn. I knew a man once who wanted to have his ashes taken after he died and put into a plastic mold where they make bicycle seats. He then wanted the seat to be given to Raquel Welch.

– *John Leslie*

To Howie, Time goes by. John Leslie.

The Memorial at the Sportsmen's Lodge in L.A

John Leslie didn't like funerals, and if he were alive, he never would have attended, but he would have missed out on two, sometimes three generations of people who came here to celebrate his life, his work, and to tell his spirit how much they really loved and appreciated him.

It was a send-off for a King. The words were all spoken. The feelings were all felt. We all saw each other with gray hair and wondered, "How the hell did this happen?"

John's assistant, Kevin Moore, in conjunction with Kathleen, John's wife; Joey Silvera, his Sancho Panza; Jules Jordan, his Evil Angel colleague and friend; and Chris Mann, an organizer of this event, put together and showed us a video titled, *In His Own Words*.

In it, we revisited John Leslie the young actor, the water colorist, the lover, the filmmaker, and saw a bring-down-the-house rendition of John as the incredible blues musician that he also was. The only thing missing was that John wasn't around to cater the affair.

For a long time, the room was even quiet for the speeches, a rather incredible accomplishment for a porn crowd unused to honoring the simple civilities of the social contract. John Leslie was loved. He was respected. And he was admired. There was no doubt in anyone's mind why we were all drawn to be there this night and why we all paid our respects to this passing master.

Bill Margold made the comment that this was probably our generation's last hurrah. With John Holmes and Jamie Gillis already being gone, and now John Leslie too, nobody else had the power to bring us all together again.

It was back at the end of *Talk Dirty To Me* or *Nothing To Hide*. John and I were together in the hotel room after the shoot, just the two of us. I found myself being astonished that I had really come to care about the man.

"Y'know, John, I really love you!"

"What?" he said.

"I really love you!" I repeated.

"You want to fuck me?" he asked.

"No," I said.

"Then calm the fuck down," he told me.

John Leslie was the Benvenuto Cellini of the weenie, a Frank Sinatra from Pittsburgh, and the living intersection of Jackie Gleason, Babe

Ruth, and Curly Howard, three of the heroes of his younger life.

Amongst the players of porn's Golden Age, we'd all have to say that John Leslie was the best of us.

– Vincent Fronczek/Gordon Archive

Supporting John Leslie.

Chapter Six
Me

I haven't died yet. I'm still here. And in order to finish this book, I want to tell you about *forty-four years of foreplay*.

The hottest sex I ever had was in the ninth grade. Sally was the first girl I ever made out with.

Sally, my sweet Sally! Had I only known that my first hands-on sexual experiences were going to be carved and burned into my erotic psyche for the rest of my sperm-bearing years, I would have done things differently.

I wasn't kidding. I have spent much of my sexual life revisiting those torrid make-out scenes of our youth. It was in her game room, in Pittsburgh. The Kingston Trio was on the record player. It was the hottest sex I ever had. And it was all just petting. We never did get to go all the way.

But oh how I wanted to! I wanted to when I was fourteen and I still wanted to when I was twenty-four. How many times have I masturbated and finished that sex act in the magic of my own imagination? Hundreds? Easily. A thousand, two thousand? Perhaps.

It never went away. I still wanted to have her when I was thirty-four and when I was forty-four too, but there were always reasons why we couldn't and why we didn't.

Out of sight was not out of mind, as I often saw her while in the arms of all the other women who came after her, including my wife. Now is not the time to play pretend. My memories of Sally had inserted themselves like some sort of stepping stone in the very DNA of my sexual arousal process.

Every time—well, not every time, but enough to be allowed to exaggerate and say, "every time" —every time I got aroused, I'd see her again. It was like a French postcard of a century ago that might have been being remembered by our grandfathers.

In mind's eye, I would see myself pulling down Sally's panties, again, just as I had done that first time. And I would be aflame. The years did not pass in that game room. We remained young and fresh. We remained eager and reluctant lovers, both conflicted and mesmerized. We were driven beyond fear by all that brand new desire.

I lived with it. Obsession? Fixation? Arrested development? I don't know where it fit in the textbooks. Mostly, I just moved on after we broke up. After all, I had the tenth grade to deal with. There were never any walls covered with her pictures in my house. There were no secret shrines built to her in hidden alcoves. It never stopped me from falling in love with other women and enjoying them sexually too, and it didn't stop me from marrying the love of my life.

But it was in my mind. I lived with it. I never sought the cure. I never thought it was that big a deal. I thought everybody felt that way about their first sexual experiences. I lived with it. The price I paid was sexual. I brought a ghost into bed with me. What do other people think about when they fuck?

We were a sex act frozen in amber. I wanted to melt that amber and finish what we started.

I never wanted to run away from home and go live with Sally. I didn't want to break up her marriage, neither did I want her to break up mine. Over time, it all became very specific:

I just wanted us to finish what we had started.

Sally shared none of these visions with me. She went from being angry and frightened, when I had first approached her on the subject, to being somewhat amused, then later intrigued, and eventually grateful for my continued attention.

It happened in Pittsburgh during one of my trips back there alone to help care for my aging dad. On one occasion, Sally was in town to visit with what remained of her own Pittsburgh family. By now, she had been divorced for a number of years and was single once again.

It was finally the right time and the right place and she said, "Yes."

The foreplay had lasted for forty-four years. I think we were ready.

The sex we had that night was perfect.
Life gave us a pass. We were the fourteen-year-old kids again. Only, this time, we were not afraid of sexual pleasure. We had the benefit of knowledge and appreciation. There was no fear and there was no shame. There was consummation. There was completion.
And when we were done, we were done. We could put on our clothes and go back to our adult lives.

What a gift she had given me!

Chapter Seven

When I came home, I told Carly about what had happened. She got very still and quiet, and said,

"Well, are you ready to be monogamous now?"

She seemed pragmatic and matter of fact. It had skipped all the drama that we could have had about me having had a sexual encounter, and for that, I was grateful.

But it was still a question I hated. It was a question that I had hated for years. It always drew an angry response from me. It was physical. My hands would curl like claws were going to extend from my fingers in some kind of full-moon, wolfman transformation. It was like a fight or flight response.

And just for the sake of perspective, let me say again that I pretty much already was living monogamously. In the time between my last sex scene in the movies and when I connected with Sally, I could count the number of other women on one hand. To my way of thinking, five other women in the space of nineteen years hardly qualified as promiscuity. Carly, however, had arrived in the land of—one other woman was one too many.

"Well, are you ready to be monogamous now?" she had asked.

I waited for my claws to come out. They did not come. They were gone. I waited for my anger. It was not there. It was gone. The great epiphany that remained was quiet. It was both obvious and stunning. It had gotten to the point where I had just been holding out against monogamy because of Sally. I just wanted to finish what I'd started with Sally.

That made sense, I thought to myself, *because everything else I'd already done twice. I didn't feel like I'd missed out on much of anything. All I could do now, would be to just do it all some more. I loved my wife. I loved my family. But I had been holding out for Sally. There was no way, if I could help it at all, that I was going to go to my grave without Sally and I having finished what we'd started.*

And now we had.

"Well, are you ready to be monogamous now?" Carly asked. And for the first time in my life I answered that question,

"Yes."

There came a great melting of Carly after that. It was a tearful release of all the years spent clutching her stomach, waiting for me to get involved with some other woman again. I thought she was afraid that I would fall in love, run off, and leave her.

"No, no" Carly said. *"My fear was that you would fall in love with another woman and that you wouldn't run off and leave me!* You'd keep adding these women that you loved to our marriage and I would have to deal with them, and you, and your love. My fear was that I would have to leave *you!"*

In one way or another, she was saying that fear had always been with her. She was hoping maybe I could finally understand that she had lived with it all along. In that moment, I did. And in a wave of recognition, I figured if she could give me all those years living with it, I could give her whatever time we had left, without it.

She says now that she saw my offer of monogamy as my way of saying that I wouldn't put her through that anymore. I would agree to control my appetites. And I would try to do it without resentment.

And, yes, that's what it was.

Carly was skeptical. "Let's try it for a year," she remembers having suggested, "and then we'll see where we are after that."

Well, it's been more than a few years since then, and they've all been pretty good.

"Are you still monogamous?" she asked me tonight.

"Yes, I am."

Part Eight

THE LAST P.S.

Chapter One
Some Words from Carly

Howie has asked me to weigh in on his book rather than to argue with him about the things I would just as soon he hadn't said. Finally, after much resistance, this makes sense to me.

My least favorite thing to do in life, hands down, is to argue with Howie.

Oral surgery sounds to me like an attractive alternative.

In my mind, we are each other's advocate and champion and protector from harm, so when we become adversaries in any serious way it is a kind of lonely, piercing hell. Maybe that bespeaks the big, fat inescapable love and/or the deep dependency we have on one another. Or maybe I'm just a mess, and I come unglued too easily.

I am not, in this circumstance at least, an artist, memoirist, performer, or a person much in the mood to make public the details of my emotional life. Still, I am married to a magnificent man, who has been writing memoirs from the day I met him nearly forty years ago. He is a writer to the marrow of his bones and to the end of his fingertips, and he tells his own story with a kind of candor and honesty and humor that cannot be underestimated, let alone argued with. So, I will weigh in.

I must say I like this book very much, but I admit some of it is difficult for me. I am proud of Howie as a writer, an actor, and a person of excruciating integrity. I am proud of the work we have both done to live this life together, to raise three wonderful children, and to get to where we are today.

I have said before that after accumulating the war wounds of free love (to which I gave myself with equal abandon) I began to experience jealousy and hurt feelings that became harder to talk myself out of as time went by. I did not take other lovers after our marriage, because I believed I could eliminate half our misery right there. (He's no fan of feeling hurt and jealousy any more than the next guy.) To me, it wasn't worth it. For him, remaining sexually available in the world seemed to be an inescapable need. A birthright. A necessity. Honestly, I feel fortunate that I did not have the sexual urgency or interest in sampling the world that seems to be the clarion call to so many people, particularly men.

The playground/workplace of the X-rated film world, oddly, provided an interesting compromise. He was an actor, learning the world of film, making a living, and getting his "extra cookies" in a way that had structure and limits that I could accept. It seemed contained, somehow.

So the stories of the movies don't make me crazy.

They are more than "just tolerable." They are tender, funny, and engaging. I must say I do love this book. It tells the story of my favorite person in the world, written in his own unmistakable voice.

Howie's work in adult films did not make me nearly as uncomfortable as his hooking-up off screen with other women, be they friends, strangers, new crushes, etc. That continued to be very unsettling to me, and we made our best effort at compromises in that regard. In some instances we did better than others. I'm certain the times he stayed back at my request are as faded in my mind as the times he had a "moment" with someone else and I made the best of it. Such is the nature of memory.

After the children were born, my ability to be cheerful and flexible about it began to diminish even more. As I've said before, I used to be a good sport about it; I'm not a good sport any more.

As the story gets closer to the present, the tales get harder for me. The stories about his sexual forays while I was out of the country years and years ago are surprisingly not embarrassing to me because they are funny and long ago, and I can almost read them as if they were written by someone else's husband.

But in all the years that followed, Howie would never promise monogamy, and at some deep level I remained poised for a "next time." Then, many years of de facto monogamy would pass, and I would relax too much and be not quite expecting it, so when there was an occasional event, I would feel my knees buckle with the embarrassment of my possessiveness and of the insecurity I had been trying for years to talk myself out of. Then I would quietly vow not to relax in that way ever again. It wasn't fair to him or to me to get knocked off my pins like that.

By the time of his climactic reunion with Sally, I had relaxed far too deeply into my denial. I was tucked nicely in with our whole family, keeping the home fires burning while he was off caring for aged parents. I confess I was completely, totally blindsided. The bottom fell out for me, hard, and I knew for certain I could not continue to live this way. I just didn't have the chops any more. We had used me up.

This was one of the most horrid moments in my life, and boy-oh-boy do I not like remembering it, or knowing the story is being told. Not just told but retold in juicy prose.

For me, not enough years have passed for this to be held at a distance. It still shakes me to overlook the ledge I stood on. I don't want to ever be there again.

When Howie offered monogamy, I was afraid to trust it. I said, "Well, why don't you try it for a year, and see how it feels? Let's talk again in a year." I wanted to see how much anger or resentment or trapped-animal was going to surface after the warm glow of his decision. It turned out that the anger was there, but in manageable measure, and we're able to dispatch it with good talking and good empathy in both directions.

So the last Chapter of the book makes me shaky. I dread being questioned or interviewed about it, because there are still tears there. I am fond of my dignity.

Should I have married someone who adored and protected my tender feelings all day every day? Should Howie have mar-

ried someone who truly didn't care who else he loved or who else he had sex with?

Probably if we shoulda, we woulda, but we chose each other. We still choose each other. We are not the victim of one another. If it had gotten impossible, someone would have left.

I aspired to be the all-loving, all-accepting, unjealous woman. He wanted to never give in to the confinement of monogamy.

So maybe we both failed.

I still want with all my heart to spend the rest of my days beside him.

So, go figure.

And Chapter The Last

We once got a fortune cookie that said:

– Photo by Carly

The End

Love,

Donna

Acknowledgements

Mi famiglia. Carly, Juliana, Polly, Bobby, Gammy, Dan, Marina, Victor, Siona, Xena, Rajah, Kuno, and all the in-laws.

My *Hindsight* Team of Big Who, Lloyd "Bugsy" Segal, Myzz Lyzz Schwegler, Lou Cove, P. Wally McWiggles, and Matt Stenberg.

Ben Ohmart and Jill C. Nelson, Michelle Morgan, Ann Grant, Wendy Finn, and John Teehan.

John Leslie and Jamie Gillis. John Holmes. Marlon Brando and James Dean.

Cynthia Moore-Miller, Whoopi Goldberg, Bob Ernst, John O'Keefe, and David Schein of the Blake St. Hawkeyes and beyond.

Michael Rossman and Karen McLellan, Danny and Hilary Goldstine, all of BTI, and all of Dragon's Eye, plus Kimmy Hahn, Kimmy Hahn, Kimmy Hahn-Hahn-Hahn.

Rabbi Dan and Yael, David Miller, Andy and Max Brier, Mary Ann, Amy, Steve Ciannella, Matt & Iggy, Bill Fox, Etta James, Jed Handler, Peter the Great and Ruby Barcelona.

Sam Singer, the Master of Disaster, Sharon Singer, Tim White, Kevin Berndt, Yancy Derringer, and Paladin. Kirk Douglas and Burt Lancaster. Doc Holiday and Wyatt Earp. Val Kilmer and Kurt Russell. Victor Mature and Henry Fonda. Eleanor Roosevelt and Doris Day. Helen of Troy.

Pat Morrow, Jeff Freilich, Carlos and Caroline Hill, Mike Fuller, Gary Horvitz and Jennifer, David Piloti, Kai and Kamani. Cheeseboard pizza and my mother's goulash. Watermelon agua frescas.

Marcia Perlstein and Nyla Dartt, Devora and Jared Rossman, Dr. Andy Ross, Dr. Neil Stollman, Dr. Neil Malamuth, Dr. Susan Block, Dr.

Cornelia Pessoa, and four different Bay Area knee surgeons.

Mark Kernes, Jared Rutter, and Paul Fishbein of the Adult Video News. Christian Mann, Kathleen Nuzzo, Edward Lewine and Richard Freeman of *Batteries Not Included*. Bingo Long and the Traveling All-Stars. Scott Small of *Buttman*, Dries Vermeulen, Dian Hanson, Joy and Valerie Gobos, and Juliana Piccillo. Rudolph Valentino and Florenz Ziegfeld. Ethel Merman and Vivian Vance. Johnny Yuma, the rebel and Temujin, son of Yesugai.

All the Ancestors.
All the MARQUIS.
All the defenders of the Alamo.
All the adult film crew people.

The Greenfield Cubs, Pittsburgh Pirates, and Pittsburgh Steelers. Roosevelt & John Minadeo Elementary, Taylor Allderdice H.S., Northwestern University, and Antioch College. John DeFebo, Lenore Mussoff, Arlene Sinkus Lewis, Faye Rattner, Bruce Forry, Horace Mann, Arthur E. Morgan, Judson Jerome, and Michael Kraus.

Every woman who ever said, "Yes." And especially any of the women who added on an "I love you."

Alexander the Great, Nikos Kazantzakis, Georgina Spelvin, and Barry Gifford. Elmer Bernstein, Cecil B. DeMille, Phyllis Cove, and Jimmy Durante. Sam and Roz Weston, Mitchell, Michael, Jody, and the new Sam. Annette Haven, Barry Manilow, and Trini Lopez. Muhammed Ali, Seka, Bob Dylan, Mona DeLeonardis, and Nina Hartley.

The Marquis de Lafayette and the Marquis de Sade. Tony Curtis, Laurence Olivier, and Elliot and Sharon Rosenblatt. Sandy Koufax.

Gary Graham, Joe Prosky, Gar Heard, and Steve Young. Joe Louis. Frank Sinatra and Joe Frazier. Sidney Poitier and Tyra Banks.

Warren Beatty, Jack Nicholson, Betty Page, and Emile Zola. Secretariat and Willy Mays. Bartholomew Cubbins and Gerry Damiano.

Peter Cove, Steve Freedman, Peter Sherin, and Adonis Torres. Adlai Stevenson. Desiderius Erasmus, Richard Pryor, and Skippy Peanut Butter. Malcolm X, Franklin Roosevelt, Abba Eban, Brigitte Bardot, and O.K. Freddy. William S. Hart and Lash LaRue. Kevin Costner and

Lawrence Durrell.

Irma the Body, Julie Christie, and Johnson's Baby Oil. Jerry Butler and Herschel Savage. Pete Seeger, Jackie Robinson, and Haystacks Calhoun. Harold Harris, El Cid, Leonard Cohen, and Yakima Canutt. Cal Ripken. The Beatles, Paul Thomas, Kay Parker, and Winston Churchill. Billy Dee, Bill Margold, Mike Horner, Milton Ingley, John Dirlam, and Marilyn Chambers. Sharon Kane, Jesie St.James, Lloyd, Jeff, and Beau Bridges. Barbra Streisand and Barbara Edelstein and Barbara Maitland. Uncle Izzy, Emma Johnson, Julie Andrews, and Bud.

Joey Silvera, Randy West, Harry Reems, Kelly Nichols, Cas Paley, and Wesley Emerson. The Cisco Kid and Pancho. Hope and Crosby. Bob Chinn. Phaedra Grant. Liza the Moaner. Chet Huntley and David Brinkley. Stu Segal. Jon Martin, Carol Queen, Robert Lawrence, and Annie Sprinkle. Lou Rawls. Candida Royalle, Al Jolson, Robert Altman, and Gary Cooper. R. Bolla and Robert Mitchum.

Vincent Fronczek, John Seeman, Yevgeni Yevtushenko, and Louis Prima. Paul Johnson and Paul Johnson, Larry Bird, Eliot Ness, Neville Brand (fabulous Al Capone), and Keisha. Shana Grant and Anton Cermak. Pope Celestine V. Phil Ochs.

Tony Montana, Janey Robbins, Eric Edwards, Anwar Sadat and Menachem Begin. Hyapatia Lee, Lisa DeLeeuw, Christy Canyon, Ginger, Amber, and Porsche Lynn, The Lone Ranger, Tonto, and Laurie Smith. Daniel Ellsberg. Bruno Sammartino. Paul Robeson, Mai Lin, Helen Reddy and Ethelred the Unready, Roy Campanella, Nancy Wilson, and Peter Baum.

Netta Gilboa, Louisa Trotter, Davy Crockett, and Margaret Singer. Mike Ranger, Mike Tyson, and Michaelangelo. Loni Sanders, Carol Connors, Angel, Alex de Renzy, Dave Friedman, Eva Cassidy, and Israel Kamakawiwo'ole.

Legs McNeil, Legs Diamond, and Crazy Legs Hirsch. Roy Karch, Larry Ravene, Tallulah Bankhead, Hank Greenberg, Mark Twain, Ted Kluszewski, Pee Wee Reese, and Herb Gardner.

Thomas Becket and Henry II of England. Aunt Kitty and Uncle Manny. Bogie and Bacall. Randy Spears, Steve McQueen, and Christa Speck. Robert J. Stoller, John Candalaria, Tom "the Bomb" Tracy, Chelsea Handler, Tamarlane, Jonas Salk, and Jason Robards Jr.

Robert Rimmer, John Cleland, Kurt Vonnegut Jr., Joseph Heller, Elmore Leonard, Malcolm X, and Anne Rice. Judy Garland, Mighty

Mouse and the man who shot Liberty Valence. Abbie Hoffman and Thomas Paine. Aaron Sorkin and Nicolo Macchiavelli.

Barbara Shore, Julia Child, Marilyn Monroe, and Eleanor of Acquitaine. Harry Truman, Hare Krishna, and Harry Houdini. Knute Rockne. Sammy Davis Jr. and William Pitt. Brad Pitt, Leonard Pitt, Debby PeachPit, and Pickadilly. Jack Shore, Erotica Boing-Boing, Slinky, and Benita Mae.

JoAnn Weinstein, Chuck Stepkin, Anna Lechner and Pi, Frankie Avalon, Fabian Forte, and Richard Boone. Natalie Wood and Natalie Wouldn't. Paul Lynde.

Jiminy Crickett, Sam Cooke, Dean Martin, and Jerry Lewis. Gayle Palmer. Betty Dodson, Joan Baez, Jane Fonda, and Cathy Tavel. Matt Damon. Perry White and Perry Como. Red Skeleton. Michael Rosen. Brooke West. C.J. Laing.

Catherine the Great, Susie Bright, Gloria Leonard, Ramona Pudding and Marcy Wheeler. Jim McDonald, David Steinberg, Cousin Charlie and Myra. Charles de Santos, Dorothy Kilgallen, Aunt Boomie, Uncle Walt, Caryn and Bruce, and Bruce Lee. James Donahoe, Leland Carroway, Lawrence James, and Clyde Johnson. Veronica Hart, Ricky Frazier, Thomas Eikrem, Darklady, and Juliet Anderson.

Walter Cronkite, William Bradford Huie, and Huey Newton. Mallard Plumbing, Walsh Brothers, Bob Kelso, Megan and Logan, Gwen Downer and Daniel Bruce.

Marianna Beck, Jack Hafferkamp, Chris Hall, and Michaela Goldhaber. Simone Corday, Connor Habib, Sam Benjamin, Harold Adler. Dorothy Le May & Flip. Sugar Ray Leonard. Jerry Mahoney and Knucklehead Smith. Elvis and Don Fernando. Peter, Paul, and Mary. Jack Benny. Alan Shepherd.

Al Goldstein, Ron Jeremy, Hugh Hefner, Larry Flynt, and Golda Meir. Jeff Zittrain, Fred Gwynne, Vanessa Del Rio, Bob Hoskins, and Diane Lane, Maurice and Gregory Heinz, Richard Gere, Nicolas Cage, James Remar (the best Dutch Schultz ever!), and Sir Francis Coppola, Ray Charles and Willie Nelson.

Rod Serling, Lili Marlene, Samantha Fox, Eddie Gaedel, Phary Burd, Simon Bolivar, Sharon Mitchell, Tigr, Radio Richard Harris, Tito Bobby Frank, Umbrella Ronnie Kaufman, Wayne Richard Sablowsky, Sean Michaels, Gayle Sterling, Pat Manning, and The Great Gildersleeve. Liberace.

Aaron Stuart, Jessie Adams, David Morris, Blair Harris, Tina Ross, Monique Gabriel, James Sullivan, Danielle, John Wayne, William Holden, and Stan Musial. Chris Cassidy, Holly McCall, Lynn LeMay, Megan Leigh, Irv Carsten, Dave Cummings, Bullwinkle, and Banana Cream Pie.

Peter North, Anna Turner, Joao, Tom Byron, Ecclesiastes, Gilda Radner and Gene Wilder. Kat Sunlove, Layne Winklebleck, Steve, George, and Martha Reeves. Richard Burton, Joani Blank, Anthony Quinn, Ichabod Mudd—with two D's, Rin Tin Tin, Corporal Rusty, Fury, and Redd Foxx.

Hernando Cortes, Patroclus, Mel Brooks and Anne Bancroft, Lou Gehrig, Paul Bunyon, Peter O'Toole, Dorothy Provine, Louis Armstrong, and Dorothy Malone.

George Brett, Oliver Wendell Holmes, and Bennett Cerf. Eddie Murphy and Carol Lombard. Shanna McCullough, Robert Bullock, Anissa Malady, Nadine Jolson, Ira Levine, Kenji, Roger Carr, Denise La France, Ellen Rosenberg Woods, Roy Rogers, Steve and Bonnie Landes, Kathryn Reed, Butch Cassidy, The Sundance Kid, Jim Babb, Ashley and April Spicer, Diana Wiley, Rebecca Giardina, Wiley Coyote, and Ona Zee.

Oh, let's not forget Picante, Everett & Jones, and Salerno's in Berkeley. Weinstein's, Mineo's, Polonsky's and Sodini's in Pittsburgh and the S & W Diner on Washington Blvd. in Culver City. Hi, Michelle!

... and everybody else.

Endorsements

"As his college roommate, I take partial credit for derailing his goal of becoming a rabbi. My collection of erotic paperbacks (each borrowed several times; some returned with pages stuck together) ignited his passion and inspired him to venture down the path of adult entertainment. His journey is fascinating. I plan to read it at night, under the covers, with a flashlight."

> Jeff Freilich,
> Writer/Producer for film and television

"What can one say about Richard Pacheco ... WONDERFULLY WITTY, DEEPLY THOUGHTFUL and CARING, one of the "BEST MEN" I have ever had the pleasure to have known in my entire life. It has always been my pleasure to have and call Mr. Pacheco my friend but more than that it is such an honor to KNOW that he is my friend. Mr. Pacheco is one of those kind of ... YOU DON'T WANT TO MISS A MINUTE OF THIS ... kind of people. We are very, very lucky to have him with us."

> SEKA,
> Hall of Fame Adult Actress
> Author, *Inside SEKA*

"How can I ever forget this senior class president who charmed and challenged teachers and students alike? It's been 45 years since I was Howie's English teacher and his wit, personality and talent still shine brightly in my memory. His ability to write from a fresh perspective and his creative phrasings and mastery of language serve him well in all his writing. A reader who seizes upon Howie's writing is in for a memorable ride. Buckle your seat belts, readers. Howie will take you to places you've never been before!"

> Lenore Mussoff,
> Teacher

"Despite his keen insights into the world of adult entertainment, Richard Pacheco remains a stylish writer and a terrific dad."

> Scott Small,
> Managing Editor,
> John Stagliano's *Buttman* magazine

"Enlightening! One of adult entertainment's true survivors, after a particularly rough last couple of years which saw too many lustful luminaries snatched from our collective bosom : John Leslie, Jamie Gillis, Marilyn Chambers, Gerard Damiano, etcetera, all of whom you will learn plenty about within these packed pages.

Howie Gordon a/k/a Richard Pacheco has seen it all, done most of it and is now telling all anyone, with even a passing interest in the halcyon days of theatrical hardcore, needs to know. A vital backstage chronicle of an era in American filmmaking the likes of which we will never see again."

You can quote me on that !

> Dries Vermeulen a/k/a
> Dirtymoviedevotee (www.distribpix.com)

"A gifted raconteur whose extensive career as an adult film star has been enriched by his intelligence, sense-of-self, education and acting chops, Richard Pacheco has written an important memoir. A balance for his film career has been his successful marriage of long-standing, and fatherhood. While still in the business he brought heart, and the view that sex (in life and in film) could show sensitivity, and be beneficial. Memoirs by male porn stars have been very rare. Who better to share a male star's insightful view of the adult industry than the talented Richard Pacheco!

> Simone Corday,
> Author of *9 1/2 Years Behind the Green Door,
> A Memoir: A Mitchell Brothers Stripper Remembers
> Her Lover Artie Mitchell, Hunter S. Thompson, and
> The Killing that Rocked San Francisco.*

"I too often felt about the x rated community that I wouldn't want to belong to any club that would have me as a member. Howie, aka Richard, was one of the few with whom I always thought I could have been friends. His intelligence and sensibilities, his bright character and demeanor begged the question...'what's a nice boy like you doing in a place like this?' And yet when the time came he always 'rose to the occasion.' The business was much better for having Richard in it."

"Let the side show begin!"

> Paul Thomas.
> Hall of Fame Adult Actor, Writer,
> Producer and Director

"Richard Pacheco, the first talent to render double duty during the dawn of what we now consider The Golden Age of Porn. He not only dandled and pierced the big screen with his 'thrusty' rapier but he was also the first acknowledged real actor in the biz. No part of us did he not arouse. Now he amusingly takes his fine talents and memories to pen."

   Robert Altman (Photographer) *The Sixties*
   Santa Monica Press

"The final word on the jizz biz from one of its greatest actors. On film and video, Pacheco turned the "sexy nerd" into an art form with his vulnerable, memorable characters. *Hindsight* puts his wit, witticisms, insight and unique experiences—husband/father/adult film star—into an unforgettable package."

   Ariel Hart/Cathy Tavel,
   Writer, Co-Author, *Raw Talent*
   Catherine Gigante Brown
   Author, *The El*

"Howie Gordon is one of those exuberant souls that change your worldview before you even knew you had one. He is more alive than most of us will ever dream of being, and he is unafraid to experience the wilds, both inner and outer.

In *Hindsight*, he shares his adventures through the torrid jungles of the sex industry: a narrative which is often comical and sometimes profound, it cracks the door to reveal a poignant glimpse of a forbidden world. Here's to Howie—his courage and his candor will shock and tickle you."

   Cynthia Moore,
   Author of *Spencer's Pond*

"I'll never forget the time Howie acknowledged me on stage at the porn awards. He dropped his pants behind the podium, slipped out of his skivvies and asked the folks in the audience to pass them back to me.

What a tribute! And I love the way he writes! His huge humor keeps me laughing at the truth sprinkled with pathos. Let's exchange our X-rated memoirs. I'll show you mine if you show me yours!"

    Betty Dodson,
    Author of *My Romantic Love Wars: A Sexual Memoir.*
    available from www.dodsonandross.com

"I have been waiting to read this book for years and years, ever since Richard returned to our alma mater to tell the new students that he was no longer ashamed to die, because he had won some victory for humanity. I'm sure that Horace Mann would have considered Richard's book, not to mention his performances in Seven Seductions of Madame Lau, to be a considerable victory for suffering humanity, as well as for poor sex-starved Antioch College. Who else among his fellow alumni can say that they'd been there and done that?"

    Richard Freeman,
    Antioch College, *Batteries Not Included*

"Howie 'Richard Pacheco' Gordon is one of the funniest, most socially/culturally insightful guys I've ever met whose job used to be dipping his wick in stunningly beautiful women on camera."

    Mark Kernes,
    Sr. Ed., *Adult Video News*

"The advantage that Pacheco has over other porn celebrity memoirs is that the man can actually write. I know, that's an under-appreciated talent today, but for those of us who like a good read along with our salacious revelations, it's a major plus."

    Dian Hanson,
    Taschen Books

"The world had better read and pay attention to this book. For male or female, puritan or hedonist, there are lessons here … if one can stop laughing long enough to recognize them. The writing ranks with the heavies, Yeah, I mean like Vonnegut and Vidal. Having spent most of the last twenty years reading books, I know what I'm talking about. The post script penned by Mrs. Gordon is a matchless little maraschino atop a delightfully decadent repast.

I once asked Howie if it was hard being a guy in porno films. "It better be," he replied.

I laughed, not realizing how deadly serious he was.

Thanks for the preview, Howie/Richard. I just can't hardly wait for your first signing party."

>Georgina Spelvin,
>Hall of Fame Actress,
>Author of *The Devil Made Me Do It*

"Mark Twain meets Don Juan - a delectable fusion of brains and balls!"

>Dr. Marianna Beck, Ph.D.,
>*The Material Culture of Sex*

"Be ready with hankie in hand for tears of uncontrollable laughter as well as for being deeply moved by the heartfelt, self-revealing, in-your-face honesty with which "Richard" weaves his stories of an exceptional male dancing between his conscience and libido, at all costs remaining in his heart. As a contemporary of Pacheco's during the Golden Age of Adult Entertainment, I witnessed his artistry—yes artistry—and creativity first hand. Thank God he was there, in an industry which to a large degree and unwittingly so often promoted heart-less sex.

I have personally waited with great anticipation for the completion of *Hindsight*. Yippee!!!"

>Kay Parker,
>Hall of Fame Actress
>www.kaytaylorparker.com

"Richard Pacheco wasn't your typical 'porn stud' and thank Goddess for that. He became a much beloved and sought out performer during the golden age of porn thanks to his timeless good looks, his wit, his great personality, and an ability to deliver a great performance under the hot lights and scrutiny of an unforgiving crew. His legend will live on in the hearts and minds of both the women who worked with him and those who watched."

> Candida Royalle,
> author, entrepreneur and erotic film pioneer

"I understand that The Nobel Committee for Literature are with great anticipation waiting for *Hindsight* to come out! It is rumored to be the best thing since Hemingway's 'The Dirty Old Man & the Sea'..."

> Thomas Eikrem,
> *FILMRAGE* Magazine

"Dear Howie, Having the pleasure to meet you, and get a taste of some of your stories, I want to hear them all! Cheers to you."

> Valerie Gobos,
> Gobos Film & Entertainment

"Mr. Pacheco has written a most wonderfully enjoyable account of the x-rated industry—stories that amaze, amuse and astound ... a must read..."

> loves ya long time sailor boy.
> famed director Wesley Emerson

"Actually, parts of it are quite good!! And other parts make me want to pull my hair out! Still other parts find me saying 'wow, I didn't know that about him.'

The theme of misogyny in the porn business contrasted with his appreciation for the intimacy he shared with 'extraordinary women' is what really fascinates me as a reader.

Overall, the good news is that it's a 'page turner,' which in the end is all that really matters."

      Lloyd Segal,
      Tycoon and Marquis buddy

"I have the greatest respect for your writing ability and for you as a person.

I love you … and I'll leave it right there."

      John Seeman,
      Hall of Fame Actor. Writer, Producer & Director

"His voice is a unique chemistry. It combines a pure, almost naive idealism and an old-world, wise-man wisdom. It is seasoned with a dash of Henny Youngman, Mel Brooks, and Joan Rivers thrown in there for good measure. Like good method acting, it's believable and true to life. His prose makes me laugh, makes me cry, and, occasionally, gives me a hard-on."

      Bob Ernst,
      Actor, Writer, Director, teacher, and
      Founding member of THE BLAKE ST. HAWKEYES

"It's easy to categorize Howie Gordon's *Hindsight* as a porn actor's memoir but for the fact that the setting, i.e. the American adult film industry of the 1970s, serves to propel the story without being THE story. Howie Gordon's tale is about one man's journey at the historical watershed moment when the forces of suppression and expression competed in a societal tug-of-war that strengthened both sides for the cultural battles that followed. One cannot have a complete discussion about this era, the Woodstock generation, Viet Nam, Watergate, the Beatles, the Kennedys, Playboy, women's liberation, gay rights — the so-called counter culture, without including sexual liberation and its commercialization.

Any movement that takes root creates a market. The by-product of the morality conflict was a visible vice that gave rise to the concept of prurience as a product, the business component of sex, drugs and rock n' roll.

No one is better qualified to set a personal memoir against this backdrop than Howie Gordon. An articulate man with a passion for self-expression, Gordon used his skill-set to launch a career in pornography before the home video revolution replaced adult film actors with sex performers more akin to acrobats than thespians.

Decades later, having dropped out of the commercial sex industry, Gordon harnesses this same talent for fearless self-exposure that served him in front of the camera to deliver a no-judgment point of view about his career choice as a vehicle not only for easy income, but also as a raison d'être, a conscious trade-off that closed doors to more respectable career opportunities that might have been, while exposing him to life experiences, good and bad, that ultimately informed Gordon's psyche, turning him into a mature, unapologetic, revealing, self-fulfilled and highly interesting raconteur ... perfect qualities to write a memoir worth reading."

                Christian S. Mann,
                Over 3 decades in the business side of "The Business"

"Howie Gordon writes about life as a porn star with more honesty, integrity and humor than any other porn star, ever! You will laugh, cry, and fall in love. I hope his book gets made into a movie, because it will be a one-of-a-kind blockbuster."

                Annie Sprinkle, Ph.D.
                Internationally Acclaimed Performance Artist,
                Author of *Post Porn Modernist*

"Howie Gordon inhabits his voice and history as the ghost of Richard Pacheco with clear-eyed analysis of the adult business and wry, engaging humor. He takes us into the mind and body of his porn-star alter ego (one of the best actors ever to hit the studio naked) and gives us a glimpse of the waning days of the Golden Age of Porn, when some of the best explicit work ever was put on film."

    Carol Queen, PhD,
    Founding Director of the Center for Sex & Culture
    (San Francisco) *Author of Exhibitionism for the Shy.*

"Mr. Gordon's story will make you laugh, cry, gasp with surprise and move your soul. He holds back nothing in sharing his extraordinary journey from Fat Boy, Athlete, Hippie, Swinger, Actor, Model, Porn Star, Devoted Husband, Doting Dad and all-around Mensch. We should all be so lucky to count him as a friend or neighbor. Buy this book!"

    Nina Hartley,
    Author of *Nina Hartley's Guide to Total Sex*

"Howie Gordon is one of the most insightful and humorous storytellers of our generation and *Hindsight* is an extraordinary look into the pornography industry from a very personal point of view. If you really want to Get Yer Ya-Yas Out, see the sex industry and learn firsthand what it was like to be a porn star in the go-go 70s & the early 80s, this is the book for you."

    Sam Singer,
    Master of Disaster

"I had a chance to taste a small morsel of Richard Pacheco's new book, *Hindsight*, read by the author, and this little snack was a far more honest understanding of the adult industry and a man's relationship to it than any entire books I've heard or read so far from adult talent. More a discovery of ourselves in sexuality and its portrayal in the media and porn, than a menu of celebrity stories, or an ego trip overcooked as more, Pacheco's writing genuinely recognizes that the real meal in porn, sex and life is in the hidden ingredients that produce insight rather than more fast food writing. This is a book that offers the possibility of meaningful truth, not a common commodity, but rather cuisine for the soul."

> Mike Horner,
> Adult talent for 35 years, and over 2000 movies

"Richard Pacheco has managed to synthesize the perfect blend of humor, wit and gravity in this refreshingly authentic personal account, magnifying his scintillating and also touching experiences as a leading male star during the classic golden age of pornographic filmmaking. Readers who fondly recall the vestiges of liberation and rebellion that punctuated the '60s and '70s decades will thoroughly enjoy Pacheco's intimate recollections of one who helped cultivate the heritage of the erotic movie industry, along with several beautiful and sensuous first generation ladies.

Hindsight is one of the finest and engaging memoirs in recent years to aptly and honestly chronicle behind the lens of the X-rated film industry."

> Jill C. Nelson,
> Co-author of *John Holmes: A Life Measured in Inches*
> & author of *Golden Goddesses: 25 Legendary Women of Classic Erotic Cinema (1968-1985)*

"Howie has his own sad & happy stories to tell."

> Barry Gifford,
> Author of *Sad Stories of the Death of Kings*

"It was eye opening! I felt like I was reading my own dissertation on my own checkered past."

>Kelly Nichols,
>Hall of Fame Adult Actress

"Howie,
Glad to find you well and up to your usual tricks, horrifying the staid and fucking 25-year-old girls in the ass, if only in the recesses of your memory. The writing sample you sent me is great, in your style and the reason why I too would bet on you if you were a horse. The best thing about it is that it sounds a lot like the opening of a memoir of your early days in the Bay area and leading up to and including your days in Porn. As I said to you all those years ago, you have an amazing and I think important book in you on this topic. Here's why: you were there, legitimately there, and you are a great writer and you aren't freakin nuts. A lot of people were there. Many are dead, nuts or disappeared; none who remain can write well much less with style and energy. That means, if the world wants/needs a great book on what it was all about at that time, there's really only one guy to tell us ... HG aka RP. When it gets published, you owe me a steak."

>e
>Edward Lewine interviewed me for *Stuff* magazine,
>"*Easy Come, Easy Go*" (Feb. 2003).
>Author of *Death and the Sun*

"Insightful Title. Superb Introduction. Enticing Photographs. I WANT MORE! It is written with an amazing and beautiful understanding of a world I remember so fondly. There is an honest enthusiasm for a subject so often victimized by lies, scurrilous attacks, and unprecedented abuse from and by those who oppose the portrayal of sex on film for entertainment purposes. I applaud your efforts.

>Anna Turner,
>Adult Film Actress

"*Hindsight*, yes, it's a book about porn, but it transcends the genre. It's an honest book about men, sex, relationships, and seeing the world through the eyes of a Baby Boomer.

Hindsight is a generation in the making and is a tale written with humor, insight, and skill. Highly recommended."

>Dr. Neil Malamuth,
>Professor of Psychology and Communication
>at UCLA, World leader in scientific research on porn

Howie Gordon is a model citizen, loving father, devoted husband, trusted neighbor, thoughtful friend and a very funny guy who just happens to have once earned a living with his penis. Then again, maybe it was Gordon's brief but intense career as "Golden Age" porn star Richard Pacheco that prepared him to be the ultimate Family Guy. Written with passion, warmth and wonderful self-deprecating wit, *Hindsight* is a rear view mirror of the soulful side of pornography from a very special time, the late 70s-early 80s, that could well be considered the climax of the Sexual Revolution.

>Dr. Susan Block,
>Author, Entertainer, and Sex Educator

My favorite paragraph: "That out of this gallery of the broken, the curious, the rogues and the desperate may be born defenders of freedom and sexual pioneers is truly the unfathomable sense of humor of our Creator at work. But on occasion, lust, chaos, and greed have alchemically mingled to produce both beauty and nobility, in addition to all the stereotypical and wretched excesses that one would also expect."

The quality of thought, the voice, both humble "a chronicle of underachievement" (I would say, rather, you led a very brave life) and passionate—make for a really compelling intro. I can't wait to read the book.

>Juliana Piccillo,
>Writer and Filmmaker

"Editing your book has certainly brightened my days. And for the record, I definitely think that it would be interesting to those outside of your typical niche—of course you have to get them to pick up the book in the first place, but I think once they do, anyone would be hooked.

The thing I like about it is the brutal honesty, and that you give us a great insight into not just the adult film industry but also into your life too. I read a lot of bios, and my favorite ones are those that really give you an idea of what that person is actually about. There are a lot of interesting ones that tell you their little stories about when they worked with X or dated Y, but you don't really get to know them. With your book, you really get to know about you too, whether it's good, bad, or ugly (not that I'm saying you're bad or ugly, you get the point). But I think that's what an autobiography should be because it's just like life, and that's really the idea."

>Wendy Finn
>Writer and Book Editor

Mr. Howie Gordon, it is an honor. Steven Morowitz here, and I am not really anyone you would know. But, I grew up watching your films and without a doubt, you are one of the best. It is an honor to friend you.

>Steven Morowitz,
>aka Distribpix Man

www.ingramcontent.com/pod-product-compliance
Lightning Source LLC
Chambersburg PA
CBHW060905300426
44112CB00011B/1355